BOLLINGEN SERIES XCIX

DREAM ANALYSIS

NOTES OF THE SEMINAR

GIVEN IN 1928-1930 BY

C. G. JUNG

EDITED BY WILLIAM McGUIRE

89.

BOLLINGEN SERIES XCIX

PRINCETON UNIVERSITY PRESS

THIS EDITION OF THE NOTES OF JUNG'S SEMI-
NARS IS BEING PUBLISHED IN THE UNITED STATES
OF AMERICA BY PRINCETON UNIVERSITY PRESS,
AND IN ENGLAND BY ROUTLEDGE & KEGAN PAUL,
LTD. IN THE AMERICAN EDITION, THE VOLUMES
OF SEMINAR NOTES CONSTITUTE NUMBER XCIX
IN BOLLINGEN SERIES, SPONSORED BY BOLLIN-
GEN FOUNDATION

The text here edited is that of the 2nd edition, 1938, privately issued in multigraphed
form by the Psychological Club, Zurich; the
same text, unaltered, was privately issued in
printed form, 1958 and 1972

LIBRARY OF CONGRESS CATALOGUE CARD NUMBER: 82-42787
ISBN 0-691-09896-4

PRINTED IN THE UNITED STATES OF AMERICA
BY PRINCETON UNIVERSITY PRESS, PRINCETON, NEW JERSEY

TABLE OF CONTENTS

INTRODUCTION

Jung's seminars, in which he expounded his psychological ideas and his analytical methods as well as his views on society, the individual, religion, history, and much more, have been known to only a few even among Jung's followers. The classes of auditors were limited, and the multigraphed transcripts, prepared by devoted seminar members, were not published but were circulated privately to a restricted list of subscribers. The volumes of Seminar Notes (as they are properly called) in special Jungian libraries have customarily been withheld from any reader not having an analyst's approval.[1] Jungian publications contain occasional references to the Notes but seldom quotations. Although the policy of restriction had Jung's consent, he eventually agreed to the inclusion of the Seminar Notes among his published works.

The earliest "seminar" recorded in the General Bibliography of Jung's Writings (CW 19) was held in 1923, but there is evidence that Jung was using the seminar method as early as 1912. In that year he accepted as an analysand an American woman, Fanny Bowditch, who had been referred to him by James Jackson Putnam, M.D., professor of neurology at Harvard and the first president of the American Psychoanalytic Association (1911). Jung had met Putnam when, with Freud and Ferenczi, he came to the United States in 1909 to lecture at Clark University. Putnam invited the three visitors to the camp in the Adirondacks that belonged to the Putnam and Bowditch families,[2] and there Jung could have met Fanny Bowditch (1874-1967).

During 1911, Fanny Bowditch fell ill with a nervous disorder of some kind, and Dr. Putnam, acting both as family friend and as physician, advised her to go to Jung, whom he still recognized as a fellow psychoanalyst. Having arrived in Zurich in early 1912, Fanny Bowditch began psychoanalysis with Jung, presumably at his house in Küsnacht. In May, she began to make entries in a

---

[1] Based usually on the completion of a certain number of hours of Jungian analysis.

[2] *The Freud/Jung Letters*, pp. 245-6. (For complete citations, see the Abbreviations.)

notebook,[3] reporting on weekly lectures by Jung that she was attending at the University. The content of the course, which carried the title "Einführung in die Psychoanalyse" in the University program, included the general principles of psychology, psychoanalysis (with citations of Freud's writings), the association experiment, cases in Jung's analytic practice, and mythological and religious material. The notes, in English, go on through summer 1912 and resume in summer 1913, in German (which Fanny had learned from her German-born mother). The title "Seminar" appears in the notebook for the 1913 lectures. During summer 1913, Fanny also made notes on lectures in the history of religion by Professor Jakob Hausheer—apparently a course given in conjunction with Jung's. It is not surprising that Fanny Bowditch, a well-educated woman, was able to enroll in a summer course at the University; that her teacher was also her analyst may seem an unconventional psychoanalytic procedure, but Jung had already distanced himself from Freudian orthodoxy. At that stage of his career, he was using the seminar format, admitting a student who was in analysis (and was not an M.D. candidate), and co-opting a professor of religion.

In April 1914 Jung resigned his post as privatdocent at the University, after nine years of lecturing;[4] he was not to have another formal teaching appointment until 1933. In October 1916, however, Fanny (now married to Johann Rudolf Katz, a Dutch psychiatrist of Jungian orientation[5]) devoted a notebook to still another seminar conducted by Jung. During the war years, while Jung was a medical officer in the Swiss army, in charge of a camp for interned British officers in Canton Vaud, he evidently carried on his private teaching when on furlough in Zurich.

After the war ended, Jung traveled again—to London for lectures to professional societies in 1919 and again in late 1920; to Algeria and Tunis in the spring of 1920; and, during the summer of 1920, to England, out to the tip of Cornwall, for his first seminar

[3] The Fanny Bowditch Katz Collection, Francis A. Countway Library of Medicine, Boston, contains this notebook and the other documents that are mentioned. The material was consulted through the courtesy of Dr. Richard J. Wolfe, librarian for manuscripts and rare books at the Countway. I am grateful also to Mr. Franz Jung for information on his father's University teaching.

[4] *The Freud/Jung Letters*, p. 551, n. 2.

[5] See Jung's letters to Fanny Bowditch (Katz), 22 Oct. 1916 and 30 July 1918, in *C. G. Jung: Letters*, vol. 1.

abroad. There is no record, but this seminar at Sennen Cove, near Land's End, was kept in memory by several of the dozen who attended. It was arranged by Constance Long, and its members included M. Esther Harding and H. Godwin Baynes—the three of them British physicians and early adherents of analytical psychology. Jung's subject was a book called *Authentic Dreams of Peter Blobbs and of Certain of His Relatives.* The first *recorded* seminar convened also in Cornwall, at Polzeath, during July 1923. Baynes and Harding organized it; twenty-nine attended, including Emma Jung and Toni Wolff.[6] Longhand notes, set down by Dr. Harding and the American physician Kristine Mann, carry the title "Human Relationships in Relation to the Process of Individuation."[7] Two years later the British Jungians organized still another seminar, at Swanage, Dorset, and about one hundred were there—"far more than Jung liked," Barbara Hannah tells us, and surely far too many for a seminar. Again, Dr. Harding's longhand notes survive, under the title "Dreams and Symbolism," in twelve lectures, from 25 July to 7 August, after which Jung visited the British Empire Exposition at Wembley and resolved to undertake his well-known journey to British East Africa.[8]

Earlier in 1925, however, from 23 March to 6 July, Jung gave the first of the series of Zurich seminars in English that were to go on for fourteen years. Entitled simply "Analytical Psychology," the seminar, in sixteen lectures, was recorded by Cary F. de Angulo, who soon afterward was to marry H. G. Baynes. Jung reviewed the transcript, which was issued as a multigraphed typescript of 227 pages. The contents were devoted to an account of the development of analytical psychology, beginning with the year 1896, when Jung was a university student, and dwelling at length on his relationship with Freud. Several passages were incorporated by Aniela Jaffé in *Memories, Dreams, Reflections.*[9] The 1925 Seminar contains some of Jung's most trenchant observations on his psychology.

---

[6] Barbara Hannah, *Jung: His Life and Work* (New York, 1976), pp. 141, 149-53. The *Blobbs* book (xvi + 42 pp.) was written by Arthur John Hubbard (1856-19??), M.D., "assisted by Mrs. Hubbard," and published by Longmans, Green, 1916. Jung owned a copy.

[7] Unpublished typescript, 38 pp., in the Kristine Mann Library, Analytical Psychology Club of New York.

[8] Hannah, pp. 164-5. The Harding notes: unpublished typescript, 101 pp., in the Kristine Mann Library.

[9] Introduction (by Aniela Jaffé), p. vii/11.

✓   In early November 1928, Jung embarked on the seminar on Dream Analysis, to which the present volume is devoted. In weekly meetings, broken by seasonal recesses of a month or more, the seminar met until late June 1930. The members convened on Wednesday mornings in the rooms of the Zurich Psychological Club, in an ivy-covered, turreted mansion in the Gemeindestrasse that Edith Rockefeller McCormick had purchased for the Club's use. Few administrative records of either the seminar or the Club survive. According to the recollections of surviving members, no tuition fee was paid; there was only a small assessment for tea. Jung's permission to attend was a requisite, and the members were, or had been, all in the course of analysis with Jung or one of the few other analysts in Zurich. Though no membership rolls exist, the seminar transcript yields the names of some fifty persons who contributed to discussion. Certainly there were other members who remained silent, such as Mary Foote.

To Mary Foote is due the principal credit for the recording of Jung's seminars from 1928 until 1939. Born in New England in 1872, Mary Foote became a portrait painter of some reputation, living variously in New York, Paris, and Peking.[10] Her friends numbered Isadora Duncan, Henry James, Mabel Dodge (later Luhan), Gertrude Stein, and the stage designer Robert Edmond Jones, of New York, who, after his own analysis with Jung and Toni Wolff, persuaded Mary to go to Zurich. She arrived in January 1928 and remained for the next quarter-century. Her analytical work with Jung must have commenced soon after she took up residence at the Hotel Sonne in Küsnacht, and she probably attended the Dream Analysis seminar from its first meeting, in November.

Quite a few people were involved in producing the notes of the seminar. In the absence of Cary de Angulo, who had gone off with her husband H. G. Baynes to live in Carmel, California, the notes of the autumn 1928 session were taken down by Anne Chapin, a teacher at Mount Holyoke College, in Massachusetts, and were transcribed, multigraphed, and circulated to the members. The meetings during the first half of 1929 were recorded by another American woman, Charlotte H. Deady. Mary Foote became involved with recording the session that began in October 1929, and

---

[10] Edward Foote, "Who Was Mary Foote," *Spring* 1974, pp. 256ff.

letters from Jung to her in December[11] show that she was editing the transcript (compiled from various members' notes) and sending sections of it to Jung for review. She carried on this role to the end of the seminar the following June. The entire "first edition," multigraphed from typescript, was issued in five volumes of quarto dimensions. In 1938, Mary Foote brought out a "new edition," in which the Chapin notes were augmented by "fuller shorthand notes taken by Miss Ethel Taylor"; the Deady notes were re-edited by Carol Baumann; the October-December 1929 notes in longhand were the work of Mary Foote and others, with "much help" from Cary Baynes and Mary Howells; the January-March 1930 notes were taken, also in longhand, by Mrs. Baynes, Mrs. Deady, Barbara Hannah, Joseph Henderson, and Miss Foote; and the May-June 1930 section was, Mary Foote wrote, "edited from shorthand notes taken by Mrs. Köppel and my own longhand notes." The drawings throughout were the work of Mrs. Deady. Emily Köppel, an Englishwoman married to a Swiss, became Mary Foote's secretary in 1930 and continued to take down the transcripts, type the stencils, arrange for the multigraphing, and conduct all the administrative detail until the war brought an end to the seminar series.

At first Mary Foote financed the work from subscriptions, supplemented from her own resources. Later in the 1930s, funds were contributed by Alice Lewisohn Crowley and by Mary and Paul Mellon. Jung was not expected to contribute, and he received free copies of the Seminar Notes.

Throughout the war years Mary Foote remained in Zurich, and it was only in the 1950s that she returned to New England. She died, among friends in rural Connecticut, on January 28, 1968, in her ninety-sixth year.[12] Her papers, including successive drafts of the Seminar Notes, are now in Yale University Library.

In October 1930, a few months after the end of the Dream Analysis seminar, Jung opened another English seminar, entitled "Interpretation of Visions," based on paintings by an American woman patient depicting images she had experienced through the process of "active imagination." This seminar, which is considered a useful exposition of Jung's techniques of "active imagination" and of am-

[11] Ibid., p. 262, and *C. G. Jung: Letters*, vol. 2, p. xxxiii.
[12] Edward Foote, loc. cit.

xi

plification, continued until March 1934. The transcript was edited by Mary Foote in eleven volumes, plus one volume containing twenty-nine plates. A new edition, supported by a donation from the Mellons, appeared in 1939-41. During a recess in October 1932, Jung joined with J. W. Hauer, professor of Indology at the University of Tübingen, to give a seminar in six sessions on "The Kundalini Yoga," subsequently issued by Mary Foote in a 216-page illustrated version, followed a year later by a German version.

Two months after ending the Visions seminar, on 2 May 1934, Jung began an English seminar with the title "Psychological Analysis of Nietzsche's Zarathustra." It went on until 15 February 1939, with several long interruptions while Jung made lecture trips to the United States in 1936 and 1937, traveled in India in winter 1937-38, and returned ill with dysentery. Again, Mary Foote edited the transcript, in ten multigraphed volumes.[13]

Jung's lectures in German at the Eidgenössische Technische Hochschule (Federal Technical Institute) in Zurich are usually classified with his seminars, but they follow the lecture style and were addressed to a general public in a large academic auditorium. For Jung it was a return to his situation as a lecturer in the University more than twenty years earlier. The ETH lectures, on Friday afternoons, began on 20 October 1934 with the general theme "Modern Psychology" and continued, with the usual academic breaks, until July 1935. They were taken down in shorthand by Jung's secretary, Marie-Jeanne Schmid, and subsequently issued in English translation by Elizabeth Welsh and Barbara Hannah, in the same format as the seminars. Jung continued to lecture sporadically at the ETH until July 1941; his subjects included "Eastern Texts," "Exercitia Spiritualia of St. Ignatius of Loyola," "Children's Dreams," "Old

---

[13] With Jung's permission, excerpts of the "Interpretation of Visions" seminar, prepared by Jane A. Pratt, were published in ten installments in *Spring* (the annual journal of the Analytical Psychology Club of New York), 1960-1969. These, with three concluding installments prepared by Patricia Berry and a postscript by Henry A. Murray, were published as *The Visions Seminars* (Zurich: Spring Publications, 1976; 2 vols.). / The four lectures comprising Jung's "Psychological Commentary on the Kundalini Yoga," from the 1932 seminar, were published in *Spring*, 1975 and 1976. (During 1970-1977, *Spring*, still an organ of the Analytical Psychology Club of New York, was published in Zurich; thereafter, under other auspices, it has been published by Spring Publications, Inc., in Dallas, Texas.) / An excerpt from the "Psychological Analysis of Nietzsche's Zarathustra" was published in *Spring* 1972.

Literature on Dream Interpretation," and "Alchemy." Most of the lectures were issued in translation by Barbara Hannah.[14]

Each volume of seminars and ETH Lectures carried a caveat to the effect that "they are strictly for private use and no part can be copied or quoted for publication without Professor Jung's written permission." When the "Dream Analysis" seminar and the "Modern Psychology" lectures were issued in new editions, under the joint auspices of the Psychological Club and the C. G. Jung Institute, the same warning was printed as a preface, in the name of the Club and the Institute. The sale of the volumes was strictly limited to those qualified by analysis and professional approval. Nevertheless, copies found their way into general libraries and into the hands of bookdealers.

When stock was exhausted and new editions were planned in 1954, the Institute proposed that the texts be revised by a professional writer in order to smooth out what were thought to be flaws of style and expression. On the urgent advice of R.F.C. Hull and others, Jung wrote to the Curatorium of the Institute: "I would like to inform you that after mature consideration and the solicitation of authoritative opinions, I have decided to let my Seminars be published unaltered as before. I have been asked in particular to let nothing be altered in their style." He suggested that each publication be prefaced with this notice: "I am fully aware of the fact that the text of these seminars contains a certain number of errors and other inadequacies which are in need of correction. Unfortunately it has never been possible for me to undertake this work myself. I would therefore request the reader to read these reports with the necessary criticism and to use them with circumspection. They give in general, thanks to Mary Foote's descriptive skill, a lively and faithful picture of the actual proceedings as they were at the time." The notice was not printed, after all, in the new editions, but Jung's concern about errors in the transcripts was evident. The idea of publishing the seminars for a general public was now in the wind. Michael Fordham, one of the editors of the *Collected Works*, strongly urged publication. On 24 May 1956, Jung wrote to Gerhard Adler, also an editor of the *Collected Works*: "I should like to refer to our talk of the 14th of May. I am in complete

[14] Excerpts from the lectures on "Exercitia Spiritualia of St. Ignatius of Loyola" were published in *Spring*, 1977 and 1978. / All the seminars and ETH lectures are listed chronologically in CW 19: *General Bibliography*, pp. 209-15.

agreement with the publication of my 'Seminar Notes' as an appendix to the *Collected Works*, and I should like you and Dr. Fordham to make the necessary cuts or corrections of actual mistakes. The shorthand report has not always been quite accurate. As far as the style is concerned it should, if at all possible, not be altered." Jung had become aware, one may infer, of the futility of restricting his seminar texts; and he was obviously conscious of their value to analysts in training and the larger body of serious students. In a letter of 19 August 1957 to the Bollingen Foundation, he formally stated: "I hereby confirm my agreement to the inclusion of the writings designated in your letter (i.e., Seminar Notes and correspondence) in the *Collected Works*."

There the matter rested until after Jung's death, in June 1961. Meanwhile, the original plan to bring out the Seminar Notes as well as the Letters as part of the *Collected Works* was modified. The editing of the correspondence had been delegated, with Jung's approval (1957), to Dr. Adler as chief editor, together with Marianne Niehus-Jung and Aniela Jaffé.[15] As Jung had accepted the translator of the *Collected Works*, R.F.C. Hull, as editor of the seminars, the project was postponed until Hull's time would be free— that is, until the completion of the *Collected Works* was in view. During the mid-1960s, the Bollingen Foundation had Hull draw up a provisional plan of publication, in consultation with Herbert Read, the Jung family, Adler, Fordham, Cary Baynes, Jessie Fraser, Joseph Henderson, Aniela Jaffé, Henry A. Murray, and Jane A. Pratt. The project, in five or six volumes, would include the 1925 Seminar, "Dream Analysis," "Interpretation of Visions," "Kundalini Yoga," "Analysis of Nietzsche's Zarathustra," and provisionally a selection of the ETH Lectures. The Jung heirs agreed in principle. Hull was able to begin editorial work only in the summer of 1972, when he moved to New York City. He was still concerned with residual details of translating Jung's part of *The Freud/Jung Letters*, the selected letters written in German (about half), and CW 18: *The Symbolic Life*. Nevertheless, in spite of a gradual decline in his health and energy, Hull was able to edit and annotate nearly half of the Dream Analysis seminar in a tentative fashion, relying on research assistance from Lisa Ress and advice on matters of sub-

[15] Mrs. Niehus-Jung died in 1965. Jaffé subsequently edited the German/Swiss edition "in Zusammenarbeit mit Gerhard Adler"; it appeared in three volumes, 1972-1973. Adler edited the American/English edition "in collaboration with Aniela Jaffé"; it appeared in two volumes, 1973-1975.

stance from Edward F. Edinger, M.D. In spring 1973, Hull returned to his home in Mallorca, in a state of deteriorating health that prevented professional work of any kind; he died in England in December 1974. His working papers had been preserved by his widow and were eventually sent to Princeton. In taking over the editorial responsibility for the Dream Analysis seminar in 1980, however, I made a fresh beginning.

My editorial principles have departed somewhat from Hull's. I have deleted and altered text as seldom as possible, giving editorial notice of any significant change. Deletions are, for the most part, confined to passages Jung repeated for the information of new members of the seminar. Silent textual alterations chiefly concern punctuation, spelling, grammar, and clarity. The insertion of a good many full stops and semicolons in the transcribers' rather loose-jointed sentence structure does no violence to Jung's style. Much of the annotation drafted by Hull and Lisa Ress has been preserved and has been considerably augmented. Interpretive notes by Hull carry his initials. A principal departure from Hull's policy is the retention of the names of the seminar members who made comments. Many of them are persons of interest, even of distinction, in the Jungian world and beyond, and most of them are deceased. Of the four I know to be living in 1982—Miss Hannah, Dr. Henderson, Dr. Kirsch, and Mrs. Gaskell—all have given permission for their names to be used. It is possible that, in the case of about ten persons I could not locate or even identify, some may be living; if so, I beg their indulgence. Surely no remarks were made that would cause anyone regret fifty years later. It should be remarked, also, that no case material was given in the seminar that could be identified with an actual person.

I have made every effort to preserve "a lively and faithful picture of the actual proceedings as they were at the time," which Jung had hoped for in 1954, and have reproduced the diagrams and illustrations directly from the earlier editions of the seminars.

The Seminar Notes have a substantive importance in the Jungian canon: that is evident, and they possess several other aspects of significance. The character of Jung's speaking style—indeed, his conversational style—is conveyed faithfully: such is the consensus of those who knew him well, and especially those who sat in any of the seminar meetings. "The notes have the reality of a transcript from tape, in a time when tape was undreamed of," one seminar member observed. The recording skill of those who took the notes is responsible—and that skill was all the more remarkable in the early days, when notes were written in longhand and patched together. Mary Foote's editorial work concentrated on fidelity of record, in style as well as in content.

Jung's mastery of the English language, demonstrated in these transcripts, need not be occasion for surprise. He had studied English in school and, during the early 1900s, had spent a summer in London.[16] At the Burghölzli Clinic, when Jung was Bleuler's assistant, American and British doctors came to train and observe: Ricksher, Peterson, Macfie Campbell, Gibson, Burrow, among others.[17] And English-speaking patients—arrestingly, Harold F. McCormick and his wife, Edith Rockefeller McCormick, of Chicago—became Jung's responsibility quite early. From 1909 onward, there were frequent visits to England and America, marked by lectures, conferences, and analytical appointments conducted in English. By the 1920s, the circle of students and analysands around Jung in Zurich was as much English- as German-speaking. (French was in a minority.) Jung wrote and spoke in English almost as often as in German or in Schweizer-Deutsch, his language at home.[18]

Finally, Jung's seminar colloquies are rich in material that is not to be found, or is only hinted at, in the published writings. For Jung they were germinative: he was often evolving ideas as he talked. The seminar published in this volume gives the fullest account of Jung's method of amplification in the analysis of a patient's dreams and the most detailed record of the treatment of a male patient by Jung himself.[19] Altogether, the seminars give us a Jung who was self-confidently relaxed, uncautious and undiplomatic, disrespectful of institutions and exalted personages, often humorous, even ribald, extravagantly learned in reference and allusion, attuned always to the most subtle resonances of the case in hand, and true always to himself and his vocation.

WILLIAM McGUIRE

[16] Information from Mr. Franz Jung.
[17] See *The Freud/Jung Letters*, index, for reference to details of these psychiatrists.
[18] See *C. G. Jung: Word and Image*, pp. 142-4.
[19] The case dealt with in *Psychology and Alchemy* (CW 12), involving serial dreams in which mandala symbolism has prominence, was that of a man analysed by one of Jung's colleagues.

ACKNOWLEDGMENTS

I have expressed my indebtedness to R.F.C. Hull, Lisa Ress, and Edward F. Edinger, for their work at an earlier stage of the editing. I am particularly grateful to three members of the seminar in 1928-1930 who responded warmly with their recollections of "the actual proceedings" and with answers to queries, especially about the identity of other seminar members: Barbara Hannah, Joseph Henderson, and James Kirsch. And I am grateful to all the following persons who answered my questions, either with the required information or with advice on sources to consult: Gerhard Adler; Doris Albrecht; John Alden; Nora Bangs; John T. Bonner; C. Marston Case; Margaret H. Case; Gerald Chapple; Margot Cutter; Ivan R. Dihoff; K. R. Eissler; Jay Fellows; Marie-Louise von Franz; Patrick Gardiner; Felix Gilbert; Rosamond Gilder; Beat Glaus; Leon Gordenker; Norbert Guterman; John Hannon; Martyn Hitchcock; Aniela Jaffé; James Jarrett; Lilly Jung; Violet de Laszlo; Phyllis W. Lehmann; Michael S. Mahoney; Mary Manheim; Bruce M. Metzger; Paul Meyvaert; Joseph P. O'Neill; Emmy Poggensee; Edith Porada; Frank H. T. Rhodes; Richard Rorty; Angela Richards; Merle Greene Robertson; Beata Sauerlander; Gershom Scholem; Marjorie Sherwood; Elisabeth Rüf; Richard Taylor; Pamela Teske; S. G. Thatcher; Elizabeth Thomas; Fr. Chrysogonus Waddell; Charles F. Westoff; Hellmut Wilhelm; John F. Wilson; James E. G. Zetzel; and Herbert S. Zim.

For quotations from the Louis MacNeice translation of Goethe's *Faust* (1951), acknowledgment is gratefully made for permission from the publishers, Oxford University Press, New York, and Faber and Faber, London.

W. M.

MEMBERS OF THE SEMINAR

The following list accounts for persons whose names appear in the transcript; others undoubtedly attended whose names were not recorded. No register of Seminar members has come to light. Only surnames are given in the transcript, and the given names, country of residence, etc., have been supplied in so far as possible. An asterisk indicates a member who, according to present knowledge, was or later became an analytical psychologist. The column at right gives the date of the first seminar meeting at which a member's name turns up. Also see the index of this volume.

Bacon, Mr. Leonard (U.S.)	4 Dec. 1929
Barrett, Dr. William G. (U.S.)	6 Nov. 1929
Baumann, Mr. Hans H. (Switzerland)	11 June 1930
*Baynes, Dr. Helton Godwin (U.K.)	29 Jan. 1930
Baynes, Mrs. Cary F. (U.S.)	6 Nov. 1929
*Bertine, Dr. Eleanor (U.S.)	22 May 1929
*Bianchi, Miss Ida (Switzerland)	13 Mar. 1929
Binger, Dr. Carl (U.S.)	6 Feb. 1929
Binger, Mrs. Carl (U.S.)	28 Feb. 1929
Chapin, Miss Anne (U.S.)	28 Feb. 1929
Crowley, Mr. Bertram (U.K.)	21 May 1930
Crowley, Mrs. Alice Lewisohn (U.S.)	22 May 1929
Deady, Dr. Henderson (U.S.)	5 Dec. 1928
Deady, Mrs. Charlotte H. (U.S.)	6 Mar. 1929
Dell, Mr. W. Stanley (U.S.)	22 May 1929
Draper, Dr. George (U.S.)	23 Oct. 1929
Eaton, Prof. Ralph M. (U.S.)	18 June 1930
*Fierz, Mrs. Linda (Fierz-David) (Switzerland)	5 Mar. 1928
Flenniken, Miss Margaret Ansley (U.S.)	19 Mar. 1930
Gibb, Mr. Andrew (U.S., orig. U.K.)	30 Jan. 1929
Gibb, Mrs. Helen Freeland (U.S.)	30 Jan. 1929
Gilman, Dr.	26 June 1929
*Hannah, Miss Barbara (U.K.)	13 Feb. 1929
*Harding, Dr. M. Esther (U.S., orig. U.K.)	9 Oct. 1929

*Henderson, Mr. Joseph L. (U.S.)	16 Oct. 1929
*Henley, Mrs. Eugene H. (Helen) (U.S.)	12 Feb. 1930
Holdsworth, Mr.	26 Feb. 1930
Hooke, Prof. Samuel Henry (U.K.)	21 May 1930
Howells, Miss Naomi (U.S.)	26 June 1929
*Howells, Dr. Mary (U.S.)	9 Oct. 1929
*Jaeger, Mrs. Manuela (Germany)	25 June 1930
*Kirsch, Dr. James (Guatemala, later Germany, Palestine, U.S.)	5 June 1929
Kirsch, Mrs. Eva (Germany, later Mrs. Gaskell, (U.K.)	5 June 1929
*König, Miss: Olga, Baroness von König Fachsenfeld (Germany)	20 Nov. 1929
Leavitt, Dr.	15 May 1929
Muller, Mrs.	20 Feb. 1929
*Nordfeldt, Mrs. Margaret D. (U.S.)	14 May 1930
Ordway, Miss Katherine (U.S.)	12 Feb. 1930
Pollitzer, Miss	26 Feb. 1930
Richmond, Mr.	11 June 1930
Rogers, Mr.	13 Feb. 1929
Roper, Mr.	30 Jan. 1929
Sawyer, Mrs. Carol Fisher (later Mrs. Hans Baumann) (U.S.)	6 Nov. 1929
Schevill, Mrs. Margaret E. (Schevill-Link) (U.S.)	30 Jan. 1929
Schlegel, Dr. jur. Eugen (Switzerland)	6 Feb. 1929
Schlegel, Mrs. Erika (Switzerland)	20 Feb. 1929
*Schmaltz, Prof. Gustav (Germany)	29 May 1929
Schmitz, Dr. Oskar A. H. (Germany)	15 May 1929
Sergeant, Miss Elizabeth Shepley (U.S.)	21 May 1930
*Shaw, Dr. Helen (U.K./Australia)	21 Nov. 1928
Sigg, Mrs. Martha Böddinghaus (Switzerland)	6 Feb. 1929
Taylor, Miss Ethel	8 Dec. 1928
*Wolff, Miss Toni (Switzerland)	30 Oct. 1929
Zinno, Mrs. Henri Fink (U.S.)	6 Mar. 1929

CHRONOLOGICAL ORDER OF DREAMS

* These dreams are out of sequence.

* These dreams are out of sequence.

LIST OF ABBREVIATIONS

B.S. = Bollingen Series.

C. G. Jung: Letters. Ed. Gerhard Adler in collaboration with Aniela Jaffé. Translations from the German by R.F.C. Hull. Princeton (B.S. XCV) and London, 1973, 1975. 2 vols.

C. G. Jung: Word and Image. Ed. Aniela Jaffé; tr. Krishna Winston. Princeton (B.S. XCVII:2), 1979.

C. G. Jung Speaking: Interviews and Encounters. Ed. William McGuire and R.F.C. Hull. Princeton (B.S. XCVII) and London, 1977.

CW = *The Collected Works of C. G. Jung*. Edited by Gerhard Adler, Michael Fordham, and Herbert Read; William McGuire, Executive Editor; tr. R.F.C. Hull. New York and Princeton (B.S. XX) and London, 1953-1979. 20 vols.

ETH = Eidgenössische Technische Hochschule (Federal Technical Institute), Zurich.

The Freud/Jung Letters. Ed. William McGuire; tr. Ralph Manheim and R.F.C. Hull. Princeton (B.S. XCIV) and London, 1974.

Golden Flower = *The Secret of the Golden Flower*, tr. from the Chinese by Richard Wilhelm, with commentary by C. G. Jung; tr. into English by Cary F. Baynes. New York and London, 1931; revised and augmented, 1962.

I Ching = *The I Ching, or Book of Changes*. The Richard Wilhelm translation rendered into English by Cary F. Baynes. 3rd edn., Princeton (B.S. XIX) and London, 1967.

LCL = Loeb Classical Library.

Letters = *C. G. Jung: Letters*, q.v.

MDR = *Memories, Dreams, Reflections by C. G. Jung*. Recorded and edited by Aniela Jaffé; tr. Richard and Clara Winston. New York and London, 1963. (As the edns. are differently paginated, double page citations are given.)

R.F.C.H. = R.F.C. Hull.

Sems. = previous edns. of the present seminar. A superscript number indicates a particular edn.

Spring: An Annual of Archetypal Psychology and Jungian Thought. New York, 1941-1969; Zurich, 1970-1977; Dallas, 1978-

Symbols of Transformation, 1912 edn. = *Psychology of the Unconscious; a Study of the Transformations and Symbolisms of the Libido.* Tr. Beatrice M. Hinkle. New York and London, 1916. Translated from *Wandlungen und Symbole der Libido.* Leipzig and Vienna, 1912.

The Zofingia Lectures. Ed. William McGuire; tr. Jan van Heurck. (CW, supplementary vol. A.) Princeton (B.S. XX:A) and London, 1983.

WINTER TERM

First Part: November / December 1928

LECTURE I

7 November 1928

Dr. Jung:

Ladies and Gentlemen: Dream analysis is the central problem of the analytical treatment, because it is the most important technical means of opening up an avenue to the unconscious. The main object in this treatment, as you know, is to get at the message of the unconscious. The patient comes to the analyst usually because he finds himself in an impasse or *cul-de-sac*, where there seems to be no way out, and he assumes that the doctor will know a way. If the doctor is honest, he recognizes that he also does not know the way. But doctors sometimes are not: only one hundred and fifty years ago, doctors were those quacks who went to fairs and pulled out teeth, performed marvellous cures, etc., and this attitude still prevails to a certain extent in the medical profession at the present day—human beings are everywhere bad! In analysis we must be very careful not to assume that we know all about the patient or that we know the way out of his difficulties. If the doctor tells him what he thinks the trouble may be, he follows the doctor's suggestions and does not experience himself. Suggestions may work for a time, but when he is away the patient collapses because he has no contact with himself and is living not his own way but the doctor's way. Then he has to return to the doctor for new suggestions, and after a while this becomes disgusting to both. It is important that the doctor admits he does not know; then both are ready to accept the impartial facts of nature, scientific realities. Personal opinions are more or less arbitrary judgments and may be all wrong; we are never sure of being right. Therefore we should seek the facts provided by dreams. Dreams are objective facts. They do not answer our expectations, and we have not invented them; if one intends to dream of certain things, one finds it impossible.

We dream of our questions, our difficulties. There is a saying

3

that the bridegroom never dreams of the bride. That is because he has her in reality; only later, when there is trouble, does he dream of her—and then she is generally the wife. We are quite unable to influence our dreams, and the actual surroundings do not necessarily furnish the dream material. Even when something really important or fascinating happens there is often not a trace of it in our dreams. I was very much disappointed, when I was in Africa,[1] that in the whole series of my dreams there was not a trace of Africa in spite of most impressive experiences; not a single dream of African scenery or of Negroes—save once, at the end of three months, and then the Negro turned out to be a barber who, I remembered later, had cut my hair in Chattanooga (in America).[2]

Our dreams are most peculiarly independent of our consciousness and exceedingly valuable because they cannot cheat. They are as difficult to read as the facts of physiology have always been difficult to read. Just as a serious technique is required to make a diagnosis of heart, liver, kidneys, etc., so have we had to work out a serious technique in order to read the impartial facts of dreams. There is no doubt as to the impartiality of the facts but much as to the reading of the facts; therefore there are a number of points of view—the Freudian, for example. I cannot discuss the different methods here, but submit the material. We shall try to work out the reading together, and you can do the guessing. The dreams chosen for discussion are the ordinary dreams of a patient of mine, because one learns more from ordinary dreams. The more interesting dreams are very thrilling, but they are easier to understand than the minor ones.

Primitives believe in two different kinds of dreams: *ota*, the great vision, big, meaningful, and of collective importance; and *vudota*,[3] the ordinary small dream. They usually deny having the ordinary

[1] Jung led an expedition to East Africa, fall 1925 to spring 1926, through Kenya and Uganda and down the Nile to Egypt. See *MDR*, ch. IX, part iii.

[2] There is no record of Jung's being in Chattanooga, Tennessee, though possibly he stopped there on a railway trip he made from New Orleans to Washington, D.C., in January 1925. See W. McGuire, "Jung in America, 1924-1925," *Spring*, 1978, pp. 44-45.

[3] The accuracy of these Swahili terms is debatable, and there may have been mistakes in transcription (or Jung may have heard a dialect). According to advice from the Yale University Program in African Language, *ota* is a verb form meaning "to dream"; the form *vudota* is not recorded and may be a transcribing error for the noun *ndoto*, simply "dream."

dream, or if, after long efforts on your part, they admit such an occurrence, they say: "That's nothing, every one has that!" Great and important dreams are very rare, and only a really big man has big dreams—chiefs, medicine men, people with mana. They said I also would have a big *vision* because I was a great lord, and one hundred years old because I had white hair and was able to read the great book, the Koran. Our usual prejudice against dreams— that they mean nothing—is probably just the old primitive tradition that the ordinary dreams are not worth noticing. Explorers say that when a chief or anyone with mana had a big dream, he always called the village together, and they all sat and listened and waited and considered, and often followed the advice given.

Perhaps the last traces of dreams of such public importance are to be found in Roman times. The daughter of a senator dreamt that a goddess appeared to her and reproached her for the fact that her temple was decaying through neglect, and asked that it should be rebuilt. So she went to the Senate and reported her dream, and the senators decided to rebuild the temple.[4]

Another instance occurred in Athens, when a famous poet dreamt that a certain man had stolen a precious golden vessel from the temple of Hermes and had hidden it in a certain place. He did not believe in dreams, and the first time it happened he rejected it. But when it came a second and a third time, he thought that the gods were insisting and it might be true. So he went to the Areopagus, the equivalent of the Roman Senate, and announced his dream. Then a search was made, the thief was found, and the vessel restored.[5]

African primitives now depend on the English to guide them, no longer on the medicine man's dream. The general opinion is that the medicine man or chief has no such dreams since the English have been in the country. They said the Commissioner knew everything now—the war boundaries, the boundaries of the fields, who has killed the sheep, etc. This shows that the dream had formerly a social and political function, the leader getting his thoughts straight from heaven, guiding his people directly from his unconscious.

Rasmussen obtained from an Eskimo (the son of an Eskimo woman

[4] See "The Tavistock Lectures" (1935), CW 18, par. 250. The goddess is Minerva.
[5] See ibid. The poet is Sophocles, the temple that of Herakles, and the dream is documented in "Life of Sophocles," sec. 12, in *Sophoclis Fabulae*, ed. A. C. Pearson (Oxford, 1924), p. xix.

and a Dane, who had lived with him in Greenland) a marvellous story about an old medicine man who, guided by a dream, led his tribe from Greenland across Baffin's Bay to North America. The tribe was increasing rapidly and there was great scarcity of food, and he dreamt about a further country with an abundance of seals, whales, walruses, etc., a land of plenty. The whole tribe believed him and they started out over the ice. Halfway over, certain old men began to doubt, as is always the case: is the vision right or wrong? So half the tribe turned back, only to perish, while he went on with the other half and reached the North American shore.[6]

Our small dreams have no such importance, no collective or universal solutions, though they are valid in a particular case, but one can see in any ordinary dream such as those I am choosing, the same guiding function and attempt at a solution of the problem.

The dreamer is a business man of forty-five, a good intellect, cultivated, prosperous, very polite and social, married, with three or four children; not very neurotic but "touchy"; his main trouble is that he is irritable and particularly anxious to avoid situations where some one might reproach him or hurt him. He had a pain in his stomach and felt nauseated once when the police held him up for speeding. This shows that something is not quite right. He tries to be terribly righteous, and only those who have the ability or tendency to be very wrong try to be so very right, to attain perfection; when people try to be abnormally good, something is trying to go absolutely wrong. He has a very correct surface—manners, speech, clothing, he is very careful in every possible way; doesn't smoke much or drink, and has reasonable views about how one should live. But behind that virtuous surface there is some trouble in his sexuality; he has grown more or less apart from his wife, who is no longer particularly interested in him and is therefore frigid. So he began to be attracted by new things, chiefly by what we call women; he occasionally goes to high-class prostitutes, and then, to compensate, he tries to be more and more correct. He won't face his trouble, he explains it as an "occasional mistake," repents, and says each time it "will not happen again," like masturbation—until the day after tomorrow.

This is an immoral way of behaving towards the problem, for so it is never solved but keeps the person feeling chronically morally

[6] Knud Rasmussen, *Across Arctic America* (New York, 1927), ch. III: "A Wizard and His Household." Cf. "The Symbolic Life" (1939), CW 18, par. 674.

inferior. A state of morbid inferiority which has to be compensated by an excess of correctness is not nice for himself or his family or for others. It has a very bad influence on his wife; she is chilled by his awful correctness, for then she must not be improper in any way, so she cannot become conscious of herself and punishes him with frigidity. Such correctness has a terribly chilling effect, it makes one feel awfully inferior. If I meet any one so very virtuous, I feel meant for hell, I don't feel well with very virtuous people! That problem swamps him. He has read a good deal of psychology and books about sex, but still has this unsolved problem which should be dealt with; therefore he came to me. Although he was not particularly neurotic, things would slowly grow worse and worse, and he thought I could tell him what to do about it. I said I had no idea. He was upset: "I thought you would know." Then I said: "I don't know the solution of your problem, but there are dreams, impartial facts, which might give information; let us see what they say." So we began his dream analysis. The first dream contains his whole problem and a hint as to its solution.

Dream [1]

"I hear that a child of my youngest sister is ill, and my brother-in-law comes and asks me to go with him to the theatre and dine afterwards. I have eaten already, yet I think I can go with him.

"We arrive in a large room, with a long dining-table in the centre already spread; and on the four sides of the big room are rows of benches or seats like an amphitheatre, but with their backs to the table—the reverse way. We sit down, and I ask my brother-in-law why his wife has not come. Then I think it is probably because the child is ill, and ask how she is. He says she is much better, only a little fever now.

"Then I am at the home of my brother-in-law, and I see the child, a little girl one or two years old. (He adds: There is no such girl in reality, but there was a boy of two.) The child looks rather ill, and some one informs me that she would not pronounce the name of my wife, Maria. I pronounce that name and ask the child to repeat it, to say 'Aunt Maria,' but I really say 'Aunt Mari—,' and instead of merely leaving out the 'a,' I say 'Mari —ah—ah,' like yawning, despite the protests of the people around me against that way of pronouncing my wife's name."

7

Dr. Jung: This ordinary dream introduces us into the home atmosphere of the patient. All the particulars here given are about his family, therefore we can draw an important conclusion. What is that?

Suggestion: That the dreamer's interest was very much centred in his family and individuals particularly close?

Dr. Jung: Yes, and that is in accordance with the proverbial idea of dreams. We express ourselves through the language which is easily accessible to us; we see that in the dreams of peasants, soldiers, etc., who dream of familiar things the language differs according to the profession. I must also emphasize the fact that this man has lived very much abroad; he is a man of the world, a great traveller. Then why does he not dream of that side of his existence, scenery, etc.? Later dreams have nothing to do with his home, so there is special reason for paying attention to the fact that he dreams first in family terms.

Suggestion: Is it because that is where his problem lies?

Dr. Jung: He is obviously caught in the terminology of his family, so perhaps his unconscious tends to emphasize the fact that his problem is there. Now to detail.

Child of his youngest sister: Two years ago her first child died, a beautiful boy of two. He said: "We very much participated in the sorrow of the parents during the illness and at his death from dysentery—he was my god-child." The sister is connected with the dreamer chiefly through that loss, and there is a similar situation in the dream: the illness of the little girl recalls the time when the boy was ill and died. It is very important to know that he is connected with the sister through an emotional memory of loss; and here he is again emotionally disturbed through the *image* of a child of his sister that is again ill. He is threatened now with a similar loss but this one is psychological, a symbolic *façon de parler*, represented by a girl-child. Therefore the situation is somewhat similar, but in reality there is nothing of the kind, no illness in the family. If a child of his sister were really ill we could say the dream coincided with reality. But it is not, this is only a memory-image called back to construct the image of the girl. Such an *imaginary case always refers to the dreamer*; the memory-image must be taken as a metaphor.

His youngest sister was always his particular pet. She is eleven years younger, and he loves her dearly, although he teased her a great deal when they were children. That sister is important because she is the link with the ill child, and the child belongs to his own psychology and is therefore between himself and his youngest sister, close to his heart. So the sister is symbolic; she lives abroad in a far-off country and he has no actual correspondence with her.

One must be very careful in dealing with such figures in a dream. If the person is very close to the dreamer and has important dealings with him, he must be taken as tangible reality. If a wife dreams of her husband as he really is, she must not assume he is merely symbolic. But a dream of an unknown person, or one known far in the past, becomes largely symbolic.

The little sister has grown rather indifferent to him actually and plays no role in the dreamer's present life. Freudian theory would explain the sister as a substitute for the wife, but is there anything in the dream which would allow us to think that?

Suggestion: Is the sister a substitute for the wife because his affection in both cases has weakened?

Dr. Jung: That element might come into it. But she is in every way different from the wife, and the dream gives no clue to her identity. The main aspect of the sister does not allow the assumption that she is a substitute for the wife, and she is not the real sister because she plays no actual role. Therefore she represents an unknown woman, or a feminine factor of unknown nature in himself, that has an imaginary child who is ill, a psychological, personal mythology concluding in blue air as much as if we were in ignorance of the whole dream. So we may assume that this is subjective symbolism, a peculiar condition in his psychology. My method throughout has been to make no assumptions but to accept facts. In arbitrary interpretations anything can be a substitute for anything; beware of prejudices in favour of substitution. There is no proof at all that the sister represents the wife, the facts are even against it.

Illness of child: His sister's first child had suffered from intestinal trouble and died of it. It is very important that after the death of this child, his sister became quite anxious lest the second boy might fall ill, but he did not. She became rather serious and went in for Christian Science, and it was as if the boy were really made better; the man does not know whether that was coincidence or a consequence of the fact that the sister was quieter and treated the child with more self-assurance. If a mother is tortured by fears, the child

9

will probably go wrong to fulfil the expectations of the mother. That the death of the first child had the effect of making his sister take to Christian Science is a fact belonging to the sister, but he mentions it here. The connotation of Christian Science has also to do with that female character in his own psychology; it is decidedly a hint. The female factor underwent a certain conversion, and that man within the last two or three years has begun to be interested in philosophy, occultism, theosophy, and all sorts of funny things; he was too level-headed to be much affected by them, though he had a mystical streak.

Question: Did he have this dream after he started work with you?

Dr. Jung: Yes, after his decision to work with dreams. When his sister became interested in Christian Science, he went in for spiritualism, etc., so the female element in himself led him to this interest. There was a change in him. He was a business man, and all his "pep" was associated with business matters, but these other interests filtered into him; he was slowly imbued with philosophical ideas. He didn't read as a student, he was not actively making for a goal; he read around the subject, this or that, something would catch his attention and he allowed it to influence him, to sink into him—the feminine way of giving an object the chance to have an influence over him. He shows an entirely female character in his mystical and philosophical interests. So we know that the child is a child of that female factor in him.

His *brother-in-law* is the second figure in the dream. They had been friendly for a long time, he knew him before his marriage with his sister; they had been in the same business and went to the opera together, his brother-in-law being very musical. He said: "I got all my music—not much—from my brother-in-law, as he came through me into my business firm; he has now a position as director; I was rather disappointed that he took so long to get *au fait* with the new business, yet he has more facility in dealing with people than I have." I asked if he was still in connection with his brother-in-law and he said no, he had withdrawn from the business altogether and left the country. So actually the brother-in-law also lives far away, there are very few letters, and he plays no part worth mentioning in his life. It is as difficult to make out any reality in the brother-in-law as it is in the youngest sister. I got the impression of very little present reality about him, though he was on better terms with his wife than in his own case. The patient is not artistic at all; therefore we are led to believe that the brother-in-law, through his musical and less businesslike qualities, symbolizes another side of the dreamer; he is not as efficient as the patient but has a plus on the artistic side. Music is symbolic of a more rounded outlook for the dreamer; it is the art of feeling *par excellence.*

Socrates was a terrible rationalist, insupportable, so his daemon said to him: "Socrates, thou shouldst make more music."[7] And dear old Socrates bought a flute and played horrible things! Of course the daemon meant: "Do practise more feeling, don't be so damned rational all day long." This could be applied to the patient very suitably. He is very intellectual and dry, and tries to force everything into a rationalistic scheme, tries to regulate life along straight lines, and does not allow for anything like feeling except an occasional concert, because respectable and right people sometimes go to concerts or the opera. He went, not because he believed in it, but because correct people went; no love led him there. So I think the brother-in-law symbolizes this man's less efficient side, the dreamy, emotional figure which he is on the other side. As he is a human being he naturally has every tendency in him, as we all have. He cherishes the purposeful illusion that he is an efficient mechanism, and, because he can go on rails in a straight line, he has had considerable success as a business man; he has that advantage over his brother-in-law who is deterred by his emotions. Our patient thought he could get rid of them, but that is an illusion. No one can switch off human feeling without bad consequences. Evidently he tucks away his own feelings, but then they accumulate, and this will cause damage; either the weight of whatever accumulates will fall down on him, or it will blow up from the cellar below. Since we are human, we have all functions, and each function has its specific energy which should be applied or it will apply itself.

Brother-in-law, according to his nature, *asks him to go to the theatre and to dine afterwards:* The patient says: "I cannot remember having been to the theatre with my brother-in-law since his wedding; if so, then together with our wives; or that I have ever dined with him except in his own house." Again this is not a reminiscence of an actual situation; it never happened in reality, and is therefore

[7] Cf. *Phaedo*, 60e; M.-L. von Franz, "The Dream of Socrates," *Spring*, 1954; Foreword to the *I Ching* (1950), CW 11, par. 995.

11

a symbolic invention. The theatre is the place of unreal life, it is life in the form of images, a psychotherapeutic institute where complexes are staged; one can see there how these things work. The movies are far more efficient than the theatre; they are less restricted, they are able to produce amazing symbols to show the collective unconscious, since their methods of presentation are so unlimited. Dreams express certain processes in our unconscious, and while the theatre is relatively poor and restricted, dreams are not restricted at all. So in inviting him to the theatre, his brother-in-law invites him to the staging of his complexes—where all the images are the symbolic or unconscious representations of his own complexes.

And to dine afterwards: To eat the complexes. Communion means eating a complex, originally a sacrificial animal, the totem animal, the representation of the basic instincts of that particular clan. You eat your unconscious or ancestors and so add strength to yourself. Eating the totem animal, the instincts, eating the images, means to assimilate, to integrate them. What you first see on the screen interests you, you watch it, and it enters your being, you are it. It is a process of psychological assimilation. Looking at the scene, the spectator says to the actor: "Hodie tibi, cras mihi!"[8] That Latin proverb is the essence of acting. Look at the unconscious images and after a while you assimilate them, they catch you and become part of you—a sort of meaningful moment.

St. Augustine, in his *Confessions,* tells of his friend Alypius, a Christian convert, who felt that the worst of paganism was not the cult of the gods but the terrible cruelty and bloodshed of the arena, and so he vowed he would never go again. But passing one day, he saw all the folk streaming in and got the fever and went in. He shut his eyes and swore he would not open them, but when the gladiator fell and he heard the people shouting, he opened his eyes, and from then on was shouting for blood with the crowd—"in that moment his soul was wounded by a more terrible wound than that of the gladiator."[9]

It is not quite indifferent what images hold one; one cannot see

[8] "Today for you, tomorrow for me." A reversal of Ecclesiasticus 38:22, read either as "hodie mihi, cras tibi" or as "Mihi heri, et tibi hodie" (Yesterday for me, today for thee).

[9] *The Confessions of St. Augustine,* VI, 7-8 (tr. F. J. Sheed, 1943, pp. 88-91). For the story of Alypius in more detail see *Symbols of Transformation* (1952), CW 5, par. 102 (not in the 1912 edition). (*Sems.:* "Aloysius" for "Alypius.")

just anything, the ugly for instance, without being punished; the aspect of ugliness builds something ugly in the soul, especially if the germ is there already. At first we don't recognize it as ourselves. St. Augustine wrote: "I thank Thee, Lord, that Thou didst not make me responsible for my dreams." A saint would have terrible dreams! We are human, anything can reach us, for we reach from the gods down into hell. Then only, when we are horrified and upset and chaotic, do we cry out for a Saviour; as in the time of Christ, what was staged every day in the arena showed the need of a saviour. It is an interesting fact that in several Gnostic systems, the definition of saviour is "the maker of boundary lines,"[10] the one that gives us a clear idea of where we begin and where we end. Most people don't know, they are either too small or too big, particularly when they begin to assimilate the images of the unconscious. It is like the story of old Schopenhauer: Deep in thought, in the state garden of Frankfurt, he walked into the middle of a flower-bed, and a gardener called out to him: "Hey! What are you doing in the flower-bed?—Who are you?" "Ah, exactly, if I only knew!" said Schopenhauer. That is why people prefer a safe persona:[11] "this is myself"; otherwise they don't know who they really are. The main fear of the unconscious is that we forget who we are.

Theatre and dining are an anticipation of the process of analysis. In the first dream people often get the gist of the whole process ahead; I saw this patient for a long time off and on, and it took him eighteen months to realize what the private theatre meant. The feeling side of his personality, that side of himself which was not in business, was shut away from life, it was not even in his marriage. The brother-in-law is like a second unconscious personality, who invites him in the dream to dine alone with him, without the women. Here we come to the symbolic meaning of wives: they are the emotions, for that is the way man usually becomes acquainted with woman. He must leave at home the emotional factor

[10] In the Valentinian gnosis, the power that prevents Sophia, in her search for the Father, from being dissolved in the sweetness of the Abyss and consolidates her and brings her back to herself, is called Limit (*horos*). [R.F.C.H.] Cf. Hans Jonas, *The Gnostic Religion* (Boston, 1958), p. 182, and *Aion* (1951), CW 9 ii, par. 118, n. 86.

[11] Lat. *persona*: in classical drama, the mask worn by an actor to indicate the role he played. In Jungian terminology it is the official, professional, or social face we present to the world. See *Two Essays on Analytical Psychology*, CW 7, pars. 243ff.; *Psychological Types*, CW 6, pars. 800ff.; and below, p. 74.

13

or there will be no objectivity; he cannot look at the pictures or think about himself when emotional. This is all pretty metaphorical. This man was so correct, so sincerely right, that if anyone showed him what was really going on in himself he would be horrified and have no objectivity. He must first do away with emotions and look at the images in a very calm objective way. I always kept him away from emotion to let him see the facts.

Question: What about a woman?

Dr. Jung: It is quite different with women; women must have emotions or they can't see anything. A woman weeps because she is bored, tired, angry, joyous, *anything*—but not because she is sad. Her emotions are always for a certain purpose, she can work with her emotions; whether she admits it or not is another matter. A man never has emotions for a purpose; he cannot be analysed through his emotions; work with his emotions and he is stupid; it is destructive. While a woman can only be analysed through her emotions; she gets emotional in such a fruitful way; if one can't get at the emotions of a woman one arrives at nothing, one can only talk to her so-called mind as if to a library, perfectly dry. Her real being is Eros.

A voice: Don't make us feel inferior because we really feel superior!

Dr. Jung: That's right, get emotional about it! It is difficult to deal with tears in analysis; a man finds it exceedingly difficult to find out how these weapons are to be used; and a woman has the same trouble in finding out how to take his intellect. A woman cannot take pure Logos from a man, or a man pure Eros from a woman.

Question: Are a man's emotions ever valuable?

Dr. Jung: Yes, as raw material, like unpolished diamonds. The emotion of man is a natural product, there is nothing purposive in it; but it is genuine and valuable if one can make use of it. Like a dream, it happens. It is only useful when, through tremendous self-control, he can play his emotion when it is cold; then with that purposive element, he can play and perform. But they are not really emotions at all! A woman works through her emotions, with every gift, as a man works with his mind—there is always purpose. While a woman's mind has the innocence and purposelessness of a natural product. That is the reason why there are so many power devils among women, like Mme de Maintenon or Mme de Pompadour. When a *femme inspiratrice* works with her mind she produces in man the "seed Logos." The man fears in a woman "le formidable secret de ses hanches," her form of creative power. And woman fears in a man "le formidable secret de son cerveau"; the creative womb of man is in his head. A woman has the same terror of what she sees in a man's mind that a man has of the child produced. A man finds it mysterious, dangerous, terrifying, that she brings forth a child: he follows love and something grows. This takes a comical form in Erskine's *Adam and Eve*,[12] in Adam's terrible anxiety about a cow that has brought forth a calf. Why not something entirely different? And he wonders why a woman should always bring forth a child. Why just a human being?—Why not perhaps a calf? What comes out could be anything, one is not sure a bit! It is the characteristic fear of man for an indefinite sort of effect.

Now the next thing in the dream is that *he thinks he has already dined*, and it is therefore superfluous to dine again. He has no associations so we are free to guess. Perhaps he thinks that he has already assimilated himself, feels that he is complete, a perfectly normal, up-to-date individual, with no need to come to me nor to assimilate anything more—some resistance against analysis. Nevertheless he agrees and goes with his brother-in-law. "It is not a habit of mine to go out in the evening, I prefer to remain at home. It must be a particular condition that would induce me to go out, for instance, a play in which my wife would be interested, when, if I don't go, she would go to bed early." He accepts the fact that he could see more of himself and go through analysis: yet he emphasizes the fact that he does not like to go out, and would only go to something especially interesting or something that would interest his wife. This is his correctness; a man out of his home is suspect, a husband should only be interested in public affairs or in things his wife likes, and never go to out-of-the-way plays or places. His last remark—that she goes to bed early—opens up a vista. His wife would rather sleep than bore herself to death with him. Most exciting evening! Therefore yawning with internal resistance: Mari— and yawn! Obviously this is the situation at home: that association with "ah" at the end of "Mari."

[12] John Erskine's novel *Adam and Eve: Though He Knew Better* (Indianapolis, 1927).

LECTURE II

14 November 1928

Dr. Jung:

We have here a question: "How is it that we create symbols in dreams? How can we be sure that the interpretation is correct, especially when there are no associations?" That is, of course, a very practical and fundamental question. I had not taken it up here because I took it for granted that you understood the theory of dream analysis. We are by no means sure that dreams have symbolic meaning, and we don't know that the interpretation is correct, but we make the hypothesis that a dream means something. Suppose one has a case that presents a difficult problem and one has come to an impasse in the analysis, there are neurotic symptoms, one has tried hypnosis and other methods, but nothing works. Then where is the key to unlock that door? The patient doesn't know. It is most difficult to give a demonstration of dream analysis; one cannot give full particulars of a case to make it plain, because it involves the whole life history of the patient. But here is a simple case.

A Swiss lieutenant,[1] an infantry officer, a very simple-minded man of no great intelligence, quite devoid of any mental complexes, came limping into my room, walking in a very gingerly fashion and complaining of pains in his feet, especially in the heels, and also in his heart "as if stabbed." (We always have pain where it does most harm and is most disturbing, in the feet for an infantry officer; a tenor would have it in the throat.) These symptoms began two months before he came to me; he had been treated by several doctors and had tried hypnosis, electricity, baths, etc. but got no help. I asked where the trouble began but his face was absolutely blank; it was evident that he had no idea, and it seemed impossible

[1] For a more detailed account of this case and its connection with the Egyptian legend mentioned in the next paragraph, see "The Structure of the Psyche" (1927), CW 8, pars. 303ff., and "The Tavistock Lectures" (1935), par. 230.

for him to give me any material. All questions were in vain. I felt almost hopeless—the man was a Swiss and perfectly innocent of any psychological complications—but thought as a last resort that there might be dreams from which to catch something. Dreams "leak out," they are not under control; no matter how innocent and simple a person is, there are dreams from which to get something if one can only catch any little tail that may be sticking out. I was sure the trouble must be due to some emotional conflict or he would not have had such symptoms all at once. So I said to him: "I don't know what is the reason for your symptoms, but you might tell me your dreams." By doing so I ran the risk of being taken for a sorcerer with such a simple-minded man, to ask about dreams is almost obscene, so I had to explain very carefully why I did so. He had great difficulty in remembering his dreams but produced some scraps and finally brought one that struck him as very peculiar and had evidently made an impression on him: "I was walking in the open somewhere and stepped on a snake that bit me on the heel, and I felt poisoned. I woke up frightened." I asked him if he thought of anything in particular concerning the snake, and he said: "A dangerous one—that snake could kill a man—very painful to be bitten by a snake." He has never actually been bitten by a snake, but snake bites might cause pain such as his. You remember the Biblical saying in Genesis: "The serpent shall bruise thy heel while thou art treading upon its head."[2] I suggested a metaphorical snake and he said: "Oh, you mean a woman?" and showed emotion. "Is there perhaps something of that kind?" At first he denied it, then finally admitted that about three months before he had been almost engaged, but when he came back from service, another man had her. "Were you sad?" "Oh, if she doesn't want me, I take another." I pointed out that sometimes very strong men were greatly distressed. He maintained an attitude of indifference, tried to bluff it off, but presently he was weeping. The case was perfectly plain. He had repressed his feeling about her and his emotion at being jilted. He cursed her, said that all women were the same, and tried to take another, and couldn't see why he didn't succeed. When he realized his real feeling, he was profoundly moved and the pains in his heels and feet were gone, they were merely repressed pain. The pains in the heart continued, but they referred to something

[2] Cf. Genesis 3:15.

else; I won't stop over that—I took the pains in the heel as a useful example. This dream led directly to the heart of the matter.

A snake for a man is eternally a woman. The snake of Paradise in old pictures is represented with a woman's head. This man probably did not know the Biblical saying about the snake bruising the heel of man, but the image was there in his unconscious. One thinks of Ra, in the Egyptian hymn, bitten by the snake formed out of the earth, and put in his path by Isis, his beloved wife; she poisoned him that she might be able to cure him again. This is the psychology of women poisoners. In the time of Louis XIV, there was a famous case of a woman who poisoned her faithful manservant in order to have the pleasure of nursing him, which she did with extraordinary self-sacrifice for four years until his death; everyone called her a saint. Then she poisoned her old uncle in the same way and nursed him, but this time she was discovered and torn into four pieces by four horses, a fitting punishment which she richly deserved.

The case of the officer shows how a dream can give the key. Something leaks out even in people who are well defended; one can eventually procure the necessary help without which the analyst cannot unlock a patient's psychology. This is why we consult dreams. But one can never say of any particular dream that it has a meaning; it is always a hypothesis, one is never sure; one experiments and finds out if the dream is correctly interpreted by the effect on the patient. Most people after a certain amount of dream analysis know when the interpretation "clicks"; when there is the feeling that it absolutely hits the fact, one knows one is on the right track. One explains dreams on a certain theory, and if the interpretation is absolutely wrong, the effect on the patient will show it, the unconscious will react in the next dream, and so the interpretation can be corrected. If one gives a patient arsenic instead of sodium chloride, the organism will react and throw out the poison, and it is the same in psychology, one cannot feed a person on psychical poison any more than on physical poison and expect it to be assimilated.

The dream we are dealing with now is far more complicated than the one I have just given you. Our dreamer is not really neurotic; he is an educated and very intelligent man, and his dreams reflect this. The dreams of peasants, young or simple people, or primitives are as a rule astoundingly simple. But the dreams of young children are sometimes very clear and sometimes very difficult; the more unconscious children are, the more they are under the influence of the collective unconscious, or they may absorb the unconscious problems of their parents. I had great difficulty with a man patient who never dreamed, but one day he mentioned the dreams of his nine-year-old boy. I asked for them at once. The boy dreamt the problems of his father, and I analysed the father by the boy's dreams; the boy was unusually intuitive. After four weeks the father began to have his own dreams and the boy's dreams ceased to deal with his father's problems. These connections between children and parents are most amazing; the dreams of children belong to the most interesting phenomena of analytical psychology.

The *big room* in which our patient and his brother-in-law were to eat was like a village hall in an inn, like those where the Vereins [clubs] meet in Switzerland. One often finds, especially in villages, a hall for concerts, etc. where numerous meetings are held, with or without ladies, with or without beer, etc. On two official occasions the patient remembers he has participated in such meetings in a room like this.

The *long dining-table* in the middle of the room was spread as though for a great number of people. Then he discovers the peculiar arrangement of the seats, rising on the four sides like an amphitheatre, but with their backs turned to the table. But before we go into this point we ought to have a certain idea about the big room. How can we link up the big room with a theatre?

Suggestion: It was his private theatre, where he would see his own inner drama staged.

Dr. Jung: Yes, and then comes dinner—he thinks he has already eaten, yet goes again to dinner. Last time we made the supposition that eating meant the assimilation of complexes. For about twenty-five years I have analysed about two thousand dreams or more every year, and from that experience, I would say that most probably eating, in connection with the theatre, means the assimilation of the images seen in the private theatre, that is, the fantasy material or other material revealed through introspection, This is a most important activity and is the purpose of analytical treatment. It is also just what nature does in the physical body. If you have a foreign body in you, nature sends a host of special cells to assimilate it; if they don't succeed in absorbing it, then there is suppuration to bring about expulsion. And the laws are the same in the unconscious mind.

Probably in absolute reality there is no such thing as body and mind, but body and mind or soul are the same, the same life, subject to the same laws, and what the body does is happening in the mind. The contents of the neurotic unconscious are strange bodies, not assimilated, artificially split-off, and they must be integrated in order to become normal. Suppose a very disagreeable thing has happened to me and I don't admit it, perhaps an awful lie. I have to admit it. The lie is there objectively, either in the conscious or in the unconscious. If I don't admit it, if I have not assimilated it, it becomes a strange body and will form an abscess in the unconscious, and the same process of suppuration begins, psychologically, as goes on in the physical body. I shall have dreams, or, if introspective, a fantasy of seeing myself as a criminal. What am I going to do with these dreams or fantasies? One can reject them, like the Pharisee, and say "Thank heaven, I am not like that." There is such a Pharisee in each one of us who doesn't want to see what he is. But if I repress my fantasies about this, they will form a new focus of infection, just as a foreign substance may cause an abscess in my body. When it is reasonable I have to admit the lie, to swallow it. If I accept it, I assimilate that fact, add it to my mental and psychological constitution; I normalize my unconscious constitution by assimilating facts. The dream is an attempt to make us assimilate things not yet digested. It is an attempt at healing.

Primitives say they rarely dream. When I was in Africa, I was very anxious to get some dreams from the tribesmen, and I offered them high prices, two packets of cigarettes, salt, etc., for every dream they would bring me, but they were so honest that no one brought a dream though many came daily to watch me. One day an old chief came, very proud and excited, waving his hat two hundred metres away and making signs from far off that he was bringing a dream, a treasure: "I dreamed that the black cow had a calf down at the river, at a place I do not know." For a primitive to have such a dream means that he has been blest by heaven. This was *Ota*, the big vision, and the man must be a great chief to be appreciated by heaven to such an extent. The dreamer was quite a rich old man, and slaves looked after his cattle so he did not know what was going on. They are a cattle-loving people, cows are their totem animal, and, like the Swiss, they are identified with their cattle; they have the same thing in their eyes as the Swiss. He knew he had a beautiful black cow but did not know it was with calf, but after the dream he went down to the river in the morning and there was the cow with her calf. Was it a bit of telepathy? Had he seen the cow once when pregnant and become aware of its condition? He denied ever noticing it. In this tribe there was no castration, no oxen, the bulls were always with the herd; very nice bulls, lovely beasts, mild, timid, almost cowards, not like our bulls; so there was no season for calves, no control, a cow might become pregnant at any time, and it was quite reasonable that he should not have known it. But the dream informed him. Why should he assimilate such a thing? To cattlemen the birth of a calf is more important than the birth of a child. I have lived in the country, and when a peasant had a calf everyone congratulated him, but not when he had a child. Hence this very important event, being in his unconscious, was revealed to him through a dream, and his adaptation was put right, for he should have kept himself more informed about his cattle. The medicine man used to dream about where the cattle had gone, when the enemy was coming, etc., and if we lived under primitive conditions, it would be so with us. As it is, we are informed by our dreams about all the things which are going wrong in our psychology, in our subjective world, the things which we ought to know about ourselves.

I am going into detail for the interpretation of our patient's dream because it is exceedingly important to develop it from step to step, to go from fact to fact: because he went to the theatre, because he ate, so and so happened. Thus the irrational sequence is to be understood as a *causal* sequence. We have seen the connection between the big room and eating and the theatre: we have the amphitheatre seats in the big room as in the theatre; both are public places, the table is spread; and we have been told that he went to the theatre and to a certain place to dine, so we may be perfectly sure that this part of the dream belongs to the same theme.

Now we come to those *seats* which are turned away from the table. He said: "We had to climb a stair beginning at the door as if going up to a sort of tribunal, and from the stair we had access to rows of benches turned to the walls of the room. I saw how people were sitting down on those seats and noticed no one near the table in the middle of the room; dinner was not to begin yet, apparently." He remembered having seen a room like that in an

Algerian town, where they were playing *jeu de paume*, a kind of *pelota basque*, like the old English tennis. That room also suggested an amphitheatre, but the seats were arranged along only two sides of the room, coming almost to the middle, but leaving an open space for the game. In this game a ball is beaten against a wall with tremendous force so that the arm gets swollen up to the shoulder. It is somewhat like the English "fives," the forerunner of the English tennis. He also had an association with a clinic, where there were amphitheatre seats in the lecture-hall. He had seen a picture of such a room, and also been in one in reality where a professor demonstrated on a blackboard an operation which was to be done on his wife.

Remember that a dining-room is a place where things ought to be assimilated; but eating has not begun, and it seems to be meant that it should not yet begin. I would emphasize that that dining-room is a public place. Why does the dream emphasize the collectivity in which the assimilation of the images ought to take place? The dream says: "Assume that you are in a public place where there are other people, as at a concert, theatre, or ball-game, and you have to do 'like so many other people,' a collective job, by no means an individual one; here are the phantoms of your dreams, and it is very difficult to have to swallow that you are a coward, a lazy dog, etc." This seems to the patient to be an almost impossible job. He takes it with so much hesitation, so little appetite, because he assumes that he is the only individual from the beginning of the world who has had to do it. It is true that analysis is an individual thing; the collective part is confession, as in the Roman Catholic Church confession is collective; and the analytical confession is a particularly disagreeable kind. Catholics have told me in analysis that they don't tell everything to the priest. I once said to such a patient: "Just go and tell the priest that!" "Won't he be upset?" "I hope he will; just go and do it." These patients become much better Catholics after analysis; I have often taught Catholic patients how to confess. Once a priest, a high authority in the Catholic Church, asked a patient of mine: "But where did you learn to confess like that?"—and was a little shocked when informed.

So the dream says to the man: "This thing you are doing is a collective job; you think you are doing it privately in the doctor's room but many other people are doing the same thing." Analysis is analogous to confession, and confession has always been collective and ought to be collective; it is not done for oneself alone but for the sake of collectivity, for a social purpose. One's social conscience is in trouble and forces one to confess; through sin and secrecy one is excluded, and when one confesses one is included again. Thus human society will be built anew, after the seclusion of the Protestant age, on the idea of universally recognized truth. The idea of confession being a collective duty is an attempt on the part of the unconscious to create the basis of a new collectivity. It doesn't exist now.

That, you may say, is a very far-reaching conclusion, but for this man it hits the nail on the head. He is very conscientious and he realizes painfully how much people today are separated from each other; he is separated from his wife, he can't talk with her, and also from his friends because he can't discuss his real concerns. This is perfectly foolish, an irrational conglomeration of nonsense! In primitive circumstances one can discuss anything, everything can be told to everyone. When a man says his wife has slept with another man, it is nothing—every wife has done that. Or if a woman says her man has run off with a girl from another village, it is nothing—everyone knows that every man has done that. These people do not exclude each other by secrecy, they know each other and so they know themselves, they are living in a collective current. What strikes one most in living with a primitive tribe is that feeling of being in the current of collective life; if a man is clever, he dissociates himself from himself even, in order not to be separated from the tribe; the whole tribe is really a unit. One feels that our towns are a mere conglomerate of groups, every man has his own set, and doesn't venture to betray himself even to them, he tries to hide even from himself. And it is all a matter of illusion. So-called most intimate friends don't know the most important things about each other. A homosexual patient told me how many friends he had. "You are very fortunate to have so many intimate friends!" He corrected himself: "I have about five intimate friends." "I suppose you are homosexual with your intimate friends?" He was shocked at the idea, he hides it from them. This hiding away from friends destroys society; secrecy is anti-social, destructive, a cancer in our society. The patient suffers particularly from the fact that he cannot tell the truth, and the dream says this is a collective task.

Now why this ball-game? A table would be the place where eating takes place, and the seats would serve the people who are attending that collective eating—really a psychological communion table. The psychological root of communion, and the necessary preliminary, is always confession; we must confess before we are worthy to receive communion. The apostolic command: "Confess your faults, one to another"[3] was given to the early Church in order to establish brotherhood. So why are these seats turned with their backs to the table? This obviously means something very abnormal, it is very strongly put; any absurd fact which is much emphasized in a dream refers to something almost pathological. To interpret it, we must put ourselves into the position given by the dream. Suppose you entered that room where communion should take place and found the seats with their backs to the central thing in the room, what would this mean? That you are refusing to enter into the communion, of course. If everyone turns his back on his fellow-beings the game cannot be played, no communion is possible, there is no concentric interest in the thing going on, it is a sort of excommunication; everyone looks at the wall away from other people, and so everybody is excommunicated, everybody is isolated. This is a very personal dream, which social considerations enter; there is nothing mythological in it, it is not a dream from the collective unconscious. The dream says: "What you are doing in your secrecy is what everyone else is doing, everybody is turning his back on his fellow-beings."

The centre of a social group is always a religious symbol. With the primitive, it is the totem; later it is a sacrificial symbol, like the Mithraic killing of the bull; and in higher forms of religion it is a sacrament. The centre of social activity under very primitive conditions is dancing or magic ceremonial in a circle in the midst of the huts. Probably those ancient stone circles still found in Cornwall were such community places. And it was understood that when people came together, the ancestral souls were there too, watching them; not only their conscious was in communion, but their ancestors, the collective unconscious. The ceremonial was a symbolic game. The bull-fights in the cult of Mithras were not as they are now in Spain; the bulls had a belt around the chest in different colours, and the toreador had to jump on the bull's back and stab him from above in the shoulder—not with a long sword. Mithras was supposed to be such a toreador, like a Jesus of the boxing-ring

---

[3] James 5:16.

or the football match. These games were communions, the people turned their faces to one another. Bull-fights are still the symbol in Spain of behaving decently through sheer violence against oneself; the Spanish temperament would not allow decent behaviour if they did not have bull-fights, they must have the toreador attitude: passions must be controlled by living them as the toreador controls the bull.

Mithraism was the cult of the Roman legions because of its discipline. In Rome, they met in caves; there was a place for meeting and dining, a sort of triclinium, with two parallel rows of benches, and at the end of the room a symbolic picture of Mithras killing the bull; the picture was made to revolve and show, on the other side, the new life sprouting from the dead bull, cattle from the genitals, wine from the blood, etc., all the fertility of the earth.[4] People reclined on the couches where the picture could be seen, and the middle space was open. It was a sort of theatre and dining-room where they communed with the god through the sacred meal: "As the god Is killing the bull, so I am killing my own passions." Water was drunk and little loaves of bread with a cross marked on them were eaten. The bells used in the Roman Catholic mass came from the cult of Mithras; also the date, December 25th, was taken over by Christianity. The bull-killer is a fit hero for the soldier, Jesuits are soldiers of the Church in this sense, and the Salvation Army uses this form; for a soldier, to have discipline, must kill his own selfish passions. Many other things from the Mithraic cult went into the Catholic Church. The original Christian love feasts were sometimes of a rather doubtful nature, they often ended in revels. St. Paul was not quite happy about it and took over a good deal from the cult of Mithras for purposes of discipline because nothing else was available. Hence the first ritual form was the sacrifice of the "lamb,"—no longer the bull-fight—the sacred feast which became the Catholic mass.

The idea of a ritual game survived until about the thirteenth century. They really used to play ball in churches, the *jeu de paume*, and this gave rise to the rumour that Christians killed a child by tossing it to one another like a ball till it died. The Gnostics accused the Christians of this, and the Christians in turn accused the Jews. There was a rumour in Bohemia only thirty years ago that the Jews

[4] Cf. *Symbols of Transformation*, CW 5, par. 354 (as in 1912 edn.).

had killed a child, a ritual murder. That *jeu de paume* had a ritual meaning just as carnival had. In the monasteries during the spring carnival, they used to reverse the position of the abbot and the young lay brothers, the youngest lay brother became the abbot, and vice versa. There was also a feast at which they changed places, the abbot and elder monks serving the young lay brothers; and a mock mass was celebrated, the youngest lay brother officiating, at which the songs and jokes were obscene, and they all drank the wine, not only the celebrant; then drunken orgies took place, and they all streamed out of the church into the street and upset the whole place. These feasts and the *jeu de paume* were stopped by the Pope in the thirteenth century because they went to such extremes.[5] Historical publications are exceedingly important, but in ecclesiastical publications a lot is hidden; there has been much cheating about religious matters, many lies and many omissions. The old phallic cult, for instance, taken over from paganism by the early Christian church, is never mentioned; a remnant of it appears in one of the forms of the cross, but people avert their eyes.[6] One would seek such a fact in vain from ecclesiastical publications.

The central symbolic game, then, is historically true. This dream hardly touches the collective unconscious, except that here perhaps is a slight allusion to what was once historical fact. Mead had a paper on ecclesiastical games in an early volume of *The Quest*. He also published a paper called "The Sacred Dance of Jesus,"[7] a perfectly impossible idea from the Christian point of view, but it belongs to the first centuries; and a little book called *The Hymn of Jesus*, a dance- and passion-play from a Gnostic document of the second century.

Turning the back on the dining-table means the anti-social attitude of our time and society, like the splitting-up of our Protestant world. The church that was once universal is now cut up into more

[5] Jung described some of these revels in "The Psychology of the Trickster Figure" (1954), CW 9 i, pars. 458ff.

[6] For an example, see below, 6 Nov. 1929, fig. 12.

[7] G.R.S. Mead, "Ceremonial Game-playing and Dancing in Mediaeval Churches," *The Quest* (London), IV (1912-13), 91-123; "The Sacred Dance of Jesus," ibid., II (1910-11), 45-67; *The Hymn of Jesus* (Echoes from the Gnosis, London and Benares, IV; 1907). Cf. also the "Round Dance" in the Acts of John (2nd cent.), in *The Apocryphal New Testament* (1924), tr. M. R. James, pp. 253f.; and Max Pulver, "Jesus' Round Dance and Crucifixion according to the Acts of John" (1942), *The Mysteries* (Papers from the Eranos Yearbooks, 2; 1955), pp. 179-180.

than four hundred sects, dissociations *ad infinitum*. And that has reached society so completely that we all belong to the "people that turn their backs on one another." So the symbolism in the dream leads back to the problem by which the patient is troubled. For society as an abstract thing I don't care a hang, but I am connected with society through the representatives of society, those nearest to me, beginning with my own wife, children, relatives, and friends, the bridges that connect me with society. And I am disconnected from society when I am disconnected from those I love. This cannot be indifferent to me. Such is the case with this man: he is partially separated from his wife, they have no communion, no *jeu de paume* takes place between them.

Now the dream leads back to that very personal problem. *"We sit down and I ask my brother-in-law why his wife has not come.* While I ask I remember at the same time the reason of her being absent; I did not wait for an answer because I wanted to show my brother-in-law that I had not forgotten that the child was ill." As to the illness, he says: "My wife is never social, never goes out for pleasure if one of the children is not perfectly well, or if she thinks the children would be insufficiently controlled while she is away." As they had lived so much in tropical countries where much care is required with young children, bringing them up had been more difficult than if they had lived in Switzerland. In Africa I saw the difficulty myself of guarding children from the dangerous heat of the sun. The *sick child* is now much better, only a little fever. In his associations with this fact he referred to the boy of his brother-in-law: "Before the boy died I had repeatedly asked my brother-in-law how the child was." All this discussion about his brother-in-law's wife of course refers to his own personal problem, to the fact that his wife does not come with him, that they have no communion. He said: "When a child is ill, my wife is always terribly troubled, out of proportion." The illness of the child is the most obvious reason why he and his wife turn their backs on each other; but the illness of a real child would not create an obstacle between a man and his wife. We know already that that absence of communion is a general social problem which becomes evident in almost every marriage. Just as in fact a wife is called elsewhere by the sickness of a child, just so psychologically she does not join him because of the illness of the child in the dream. Now, since the illness of the child goes all through the dream, we must assume that it means more than the mere opportunity for the wife not to be in the game. And it is important that the ill child is a girl.

Suggestion: We saw before that the girl-child was some aspect of himself.

Dr. Jung: The real child who died was a boy and has no actual importance here. Therefore if he dreamt of a boy, it would express something in himself. I have observed in dreams and in clinical experiences a certain tendency in man to personify his ages. There was the case of a country doctor, early in the nineteenth century, a man living a very strenuous life, who was coming home late at night from a bad case, walking along very tired, when he became aware of a shadow figure parallel with him in the middle of the road. He recognized the figure as himself about ten years younger. Then the vision disappeared but appeared again as himself about twenty years younger, and so on down to a boy of eight or ten. It was a personification of himself: "The boy or man that I was then, I see him still as he was." So the allusion to the dead boy is an allusion to the patient's own dead youth. He has arrived in the second part of life, where one's psychology changes: youth is dead, the second part is beginning. But this is only an allusion; our interest now is in the sickness of the girl-child.

LECTURE III

21 November 1928

Dr. Jung:

There are two questions today. The first one is: "Is it a characteristic of images in dreams which should be taken on the subjective
level that they bring up few associations?"

No, one cannot decide by the number of associations whether a
dream is to be taken on the subjective level. The criterion is quite
different. That is the subject of the second question also: "Could
you discuss further the factors which make you choose between a
subjective and objective interpretation?"

There are certain definite principles which decide whether I
should prefer the objective or the so-called subjective interpretation. You are aware perhaps that there are subtle differences in
the ways of using the words *subjective* and *objective*. I must make it
quite clear that the subjective interpretation does not mean what
one ordinarily designates as subjective—that a subjective opinion
is not very substantial for instance, that it is personal, just what *you*
think about it, but by no means sure to be an objective truth. I
don't use the word *subjective* in that sense. When I say that a dream
is correctly interpreted on the subjective level, I mean that the
image in the dream primarily or exclusively refers to the subject
himself; and in an interpretation on the objective level, the image
refers to an object, another person than himself. It is exceedingly
important to know when to apply a subjective and when an objective
interpretation. The general criterion is: when a person in a dream
is known to you intimately, playing a role in your life at the present
moment, one may consider an interpretation on the objective level,
because the object is then important. But be very careful not to
make mistakes here. According to the Freudian point of view, the
person of whom you dream is a disguise for another person—one
person is substituted for another.

29

For example, if a patient dreams of Dr. Jones, who has been the family physician, she may assume that Dr. Jones would be a disguise for me. That is the way Freud would take it in order to make it fit his theory. But it is by no means certain that the unconscious does mean me even though the patient makes the connection. Of course it is understandable that the patient prefers that interpretation— I am here, while Dr. Jones is far away. But the unconscious is perfectly free to take my image if it wishes to do so, there is no obstacle to dreaming of me, so we must explain why the unconscious chose Dr. Jones. In this case Freud would say that the reason the patient dreamed of Dr. Jones was on account of certain fantasies connected with me which were difficult for her to mention; better to dream of Dr. Jones, who is a long way off. That is Freudian theory, but since I believe more in real facts than in theory, I say that is perhaps so, but I am not sure. I must see if that theory explains every case. And I find that in many cases such an explanation is unnatural and does not succeed. If we are forced to take the idea seriously—that I am expressed by Dr. Jones—why does the unconscious take that trouble? The unconscious uses the figure of Dr. Jones because it means Dr. Jones and not me. There is no reason to believe that the unconscious does not say what it means; in sharpest contradiction to Freud. I say that the unconscious says what it means. Nature is never diplomatic. If nature produces a tree, it is a tree and not a mistake for a dog. And so the unconscious does not make disguises, that is what we do. It is disagreeable to have albumen in the urine, but albumen should not be taken as a disguise for sugar. Freud's theory was made by his patients. The analyst is too much under the influence of his women patients, they fill his mind with their thinking. These dynamic wishes of women are a source of error to the doctor; one has to work all the time against such suggestions. The absolute truth is that the unconscious spoke of Dr. Jones and said no word of Dr. Jung.

Now in cases where you dream of a remote relative, or someone whom you have not seen for ages, or someone who is perhaps known to your family but plays no actual role in your own life and is in no way important, in such cases there is no point in assuming that the person is, say, an autonomous factor in your psychology. Since he doesn't enter your sphere with the onslaught of a real person, since he doesn't arouse a psychic vortex in your mental atmosphere, he is more probably merely an image which has to do with yourself alone. Someone with whom you are immediately connected may cause great disturbance in your mental atmosphere, and therefore you are perfectly safe in assuming that the remote person is only an image in the dream referring entirely to yourself.

Even where the objective interpretation is advisable, it is well to consider also a subjective possibility. Probably the reason that certain persons come particularly close to you is that they are carriers of a symbolic truth, for whoever gets at your psychology can do so only on the basis of *participation mystique*.[1] Otherwise the other person would not have a handle on your soul. Therefore from the theoretical point of view, and also for practical purposes, it is exceedingly valuable and wise to see how far the object that is to be taken objectively is also a subjective factor in yourself. But this is a philosophical postulate, and it is a great mistake to substitute that for reality. If you should always interpret the object as subjective, it would make your life relative and illusory; you would be completely isolated because you would have burned the bridges which connected you with reality. I must insist on the objective value of such objective images.

I would not, however, lay stress on the object but on the *image*. If you dream that a certain remote person with whom you have no dealings of any kind lies to you, to say that this person, whom you haven't seen for ages, is a liar conveys nothing at all, that is subjective. But if you dream that a person actually in your atmosphere lies, then you must look at him under that aspect because there might be something in it; it becomes important to decide whether the lie is in you, or in the other, or if there is deception between. There may be a certain quality of your own in a state of non-recognition. Many people think they are very good and that the black substance is almost non-existent in them, yet they have a fair amount of it, being human! If they dream of a black sheep, the black sheep is not very important, but to call themselves black

[1] Jung took the term and concept *participation mystique* from the French philosopher Lucien Lévy-Bruhl (1857-1939), who introduced it in *Les Fonctions mentales dans les sociétés inférieures* (Paris, 1912), tr. L. A. Clare, *How Natives Think* (London, 1926). Jung first used the term in *Psychological Types* (1921), CW 6: see especially par. 781, definition: "psychological connection [in which] the subject cannot clearly distinguish himself from the object but is bound to it by a direct relationship which amounts to partial identity." See also *Mysterium Coniunctionis* (1956), CW 14, par. 336, n. 662, and par. 695, n. 106.

sheep is exceedingly important—much better that they take it all to themselves. So if you dream that your best friend is a black sheep, it means that either you are a black sheep, or the friend is, or there is dirt between you,

I should like now to come back to the *jeu de paume*, that *pelota basque*. I told you that our patient's associations about the arrangement of the hall point to a communion ceremonial or ritual; and that there also seems to be an allusion to a sort of pelota game because he remembers a hall where it was played, and to the hall of a Swiss Verein where the members come to play and to eat—a communion. From mediaeval manuscripts we learn that the old ritual *jeu de paume* was played up to the twelfth century, and in certain remote places, at Auxerre in France for instance, up to the sixteenth century. I have been doing some special research concerning these games. I dug up Latin texts from mediaeval manuscripts that describe this pelota, and I want to read you the translation. Unfortunately, since it was very familiar in those days, and everybody knew about it, the description is perfunctory and the texts are a bit vague, but you will get something from them anyhow. You remember the hall in the dream has a dining-table spread for dinner and dinner ought to take place, but instead, his associations pointed to a ball-game going on, *pelota bosque.*

Fragments from Mediaeval MSS.[2]

"When the ball, called *pelota*, had been accepted from the newly-elected canon by the dean—his head being covered with an amice or hood—the rest of the canons began to intone antiphonally: "Praise to the Paschal Victim." Then the dean, supporting the ball with his left hand, danced, and the rest joined hands and, chanting, executed a choral dance round the labyrinth; meanwhile the *pilota* was thrown by the dean alternately to the dancers, one by one. After the dance, the choir hurried off to the repast (the dean and canons and more distinguished citizens sat on benches with high backs, in the orchestra or choir) and all without exception were served with the repast, and with white and red wine in moderation (cups filled

[2] The various examples described by Jung are paraphrased from Mead, "Ceremonial Game-playing and Dancing in Mediaeval Churches," specifically in pp. 97-111. (See above, 14 Nov. 1928, n. 7.)

two or three times) while a reader intoned a homily from the pulpit. Then a large bell rang, and the canon most recently elected stood ready holding the ball before his chest, and in the nave of St. Stephen at about 2 o'clock, he presented it to the dean, who turned back his amice from his head that he might manipulate the ball."

Here is another game that was played at Narbonne, an Easter Monday ritual, also from a Latin manuscript of the thirteenth century: "While the bells are ringing for vespers, the whole chapter assembles in the archbishop's house, and his servants serve certain dishes and wine to all. Then the archbishop is to throw the ball. And the prefect, or political governor of the town, is to provide the ball and to throw it in the archbishop's absence."

And here is a nice fragment from Naples (Bishop of Naples, 508-536) in a ninth-century codex: "In memory of this event were celebrated every year certain games of ball for the comfort and refreshment of the soul." These took place before a great populace in the Santa Maria Maggiore at the feast of St. Januarius, on the third Sunday in the month of May. It is interesting that these games were played "for the consolation and recreation of the soul."

Then from the twelfth century, there is a manuscript in which Jean Beleth, a theologian of the Faculty of Paris, writes: "There are some churches where even the bishops and archbishops play with their subordinates, stooping even to play ball—although it seems more praiseworthy not to do so." This was obviously written at the time when the game was becoming unpopular.

There are other very interesting facts in connection with this exceedingly peculiar custom. Possibly there is a connection with the ceremony of the "bride-ball" which was thrown between bride and groom. And in other games in the churches the ball was kicked or torn to pieces as the god of the past year. There was once a trial, a *cause célèbre*, on account of the ball-play in the church, at the time when it became unpopular; the text speaks of the "ball of the past year" which had to be kept by the old canon and handed over to the canon of the new year, an old Easter custom. That is like the god of the past year that had to be dismembered in order that everybody should participate. Compare also the Christian communion where the god is dismembered and eaten. This is all connected with the sacrificial ceremonies in the springtime, like the anthropophagous custom of the king being dismembered and eaten at the spring festival to strengthen the tribe and for the fertility of the fields in the coming year. So it is quite probable that this ball symbolizes the sun.

It is also linked up with another strange custom, "the burial of Alleluia." In the middle ages Alleluia was believed to be a woman—because "a" is a feminine ending—an unknown woman who was buried at Eastertide, so she would be a sort of queen of the past year. In the archives of a church at Toul, in Lorraine, is a manuscript, written in 1497 by one Nicolas, canon of the Cathedral, in which is registered, 15th article: "Alleluia is buried." The Latin text which refers to it prescribes what to do at the burial. "On the Saturday preceding Septuagesima Sunday, at nones, the choir boys are to assemble in festal attire and arrange for the burying of Alleluia; and after the last benediction they are to go in procession with torches, holy water, and incense, carrying a clod of earth on a bier, through the cloister, wailing, to the place where Alleluia is to be buried; there to sprinkle water and grain on the clod of earth, to swing the incense, and to return the same way." This custom is very old. The clod of earth is the ball, and the ball is the sun, which is renewed at Eastertide, as well as the earth. The original meaning is very simple: the sun would not rise again if not supported—renewed through sacrifice at Easter time. Alleluia was simply Mother Earth, a feminine potency made to suffer death, burial, and resurrection, and supposed to be responsible for the new sun. The American Pueblo Indians assume that they support the sun by their ritual, and this is the same thing, death, burial, and resurrection. My Indian friend Mountain Lake in a letter to me said: "If the white man keeps on interfering with our religion, in ten years they will see something!"—the sun would not rise again.[3]

When we first discussed the *jeu de paume* I did not remember all these details, that it was really also called *pelota*, etc., and it was probably unknown to you; nor had the dreamer the faintest idea of these connections; so his dream is curious—the dining, the seats, the *pelota*, all that material comes together in the dream and his associations.

And there is another contribution. You remember that we were talking in our last seminar of the community idea, which the dream

[3] Mountain Lake (Ochwiay Biano) or Antonio Mirabal (c. 1890-1975), of the Taos Pueblo, whom Jung met when he visited Taos in January 1925. Cf. *MDR*, ch. IX, part ii, and Jung's letter to Mirabal, 21 Oct. 1932, in *Letters*, ed. Adler, vol. 1. There is a photograph of Mirabal in *C. G. Jung: Word and Image*, p. 155.

alludes to in the statement that "everyone is turning his back to it." While we are listening to our conscious transactions, we forget that our unconscious is reacting at the same time: when we speak of a disturbance of the community idea, we constellate directly a disturbance of community in ourselves; the patient's psychology is also our own, and the rapport is not so good. We think this is just a dream, and forget that the unconscious is reacting in its particular way. The fact that *we* turn our backs upon communion is constellated in us and has certain effects. Therefore after the last seminar certain people complained of a disturbed atmosphere, and some gave the rationalized explanation that it was because we stopped and took tea and that broke up the continuity of the meeting. Evidently they did not feel the communion of eating together. If they were aware of the upset community idea, to take tea together was really the thing to do; it should have been an expression of community. I was accused of not taking a cup of tea, but at least I smoked the pipe of peace! Now when people have been disturbed by a reaction from the unconscious, there is always a medicine man who has a dream concerning the matter. A community is an organism, a symbiosis, and we form a sort of organism here while thinking together; and if anything disturbing happens within this organism, some mind receives the disturbance and says "look out!" In a primitive community, it would be the mind of the chief or medicine man. For the time being we form something like a primitive tribe, and the medicine man will say: "In the night while sleeping I saw a vision and a spirit spoke." Dr. Shaw has had the dream of the medicine man and she will tell it to us.

Dr. Shaw: I dreamed that I went to Spain, and there a bull-fight was going on in a big arena; a man and a bull were fighting and a great crowd was shrieking that the bull must be killed. I did not want it to be killed and I fought for the bull all night. Then Dr. Jung at the lecture next day told of the killing of the Mithraic bull.

Dr. Jung: Now link up this dream with the problem in question. You remember that we discussed the Mithraic bull-killing and the question whether killing the bull has still the same symbolic meaning; in a bull-fight people turned their faces to each other and therefore it symbolized community; and we spoke of the importance of that symbol as self-discipline when the cult of Mithras was the religion of the Roman legions. Only men were admitted to the

35

Mithraic ritual, the women all went to the Earth Mother. Now, in Dr. Shaw's dream the bull is not to be killed, she fought against it. What does this dream mean to you? Any one of us might have dreamt it.

Suggestion: It might be the struggle against making a sacrifice—we all object to making a sacrifice.

Suggestion: Is there not something good in this bull that we should not kill?

Suggestion: Killing the bull might signify an old-fashioned way of making a sacrifice. Perhaps a new way can be found.

Dr. Jung: There is a connection between the last two suggestions. Killing the bull as a symbol of community is very old-fashioned, to us that does not express community. Not long ago I had a letter from a patient [in Mexico], a lady who had just been to a bull-fight, and she hated those blood-thirsty people, she said it made her so angry that she was quite ready to kill everyone there with a revolver! So a bull-fight does not now promote a feeling of community. The whole performance is most despicable, our feeling is entirely against it. One should not behave like a bull in a china-shop, one should not be uncontrolled. We can understand the symbolic meaning, self-discipline, but we don't get that inspiration from watching a bull-fight; an actual bull-fight would give the opposite effect. We have outgrown that symbolism, just as we have outgrown the idea of redemption by eating the flesh and drinking the blood of the victim; few people today feel the mediaeval emotion when eating the body and drinking the blood in communion.

There is still a lot of very buried and archaic earth mysticism in Switzerland, however. A Swiss woman who came to me recently for treatment confessed after long resistances that she had a secret means to help her to sleep, or to help against indigestion, etc.: "An old man told me that secret. I drink the blood of Jesus. In the night, when I can't sleep, I repeat to myself: 'I am drinking the blood, drinking the blood of Jesus, the blood, the blood,' and then I feel myself drinking it and can sleep. If I wake, I do it again—sometimes a dozen times in a night." One day she went into the cellar—she was a very good housewife—and in standing on a chair to reach some apples on a shelf, she slipped and crashed down. She said: "I quickly drank the blood and was not hurt." She got a tremendous mystical association from drinking the blood; such things are still realities.

So the bull-fight as a mystical symbol is antiquated, like much of our Christian symbolism; our common emotion can no longer be aroused by these symbols. If anyone should dream of killing a bull in our day, we should put an entirely different interpretation on it. Therefore we need a common interest which would allow us to build a community feeling again. That Dr. Shaw dreams she is fighting against killing the bull means that the bull should not be killed. The bull is *natural* force, the uncontrolled animal, which is not necessarily destructive. We have the Christian prejudice against the animal in man, but an animal is not evil, just as it is not good. We are evil, man is necessarily evil, because he is so good. Only domesticated animals misbehave; a wild animal never misbehaves, it follows its own natural law; there is no such thing as a good tiger that eats only apples and carrots! A wild animal is a pious, law-abiding being who fulfils the will of God in the most perfect way. The bull is a fairly wild animal, and if we kill the animal in ourselves we kill the really good things in ourselves too, not the apparently good things. Therefore for us to kill the bull would be blasphemous, a sin, it would mean killing the natural thing in us, the thing that naturally serves God. That is our only hope—to get back to a condition where we are right with nature. We must fulfil our destiny according to nature's laws or we cannot become true servants of God. So we understand what the message of the medicine man would be. Dr. Shaw was most righteously wrestling against killing the bull: "Don't make the mistake of killing the bull, because this is the only thing which can connect us; we must come back to the natural and eternal laws; then we shall be in the blest state of the animals, and that will bring together again all which has been separate before." The advice of the medicine man is valuable.

Now I also appear in the dream—Dr. Shaw and I know each other pretty well, and when we meet in dreamland we don't take each other too seriously—in her associations I say that the toreador has killed the bull; the bull that should not have been killed has been killed. Why do I confirm that? Well, just because our bull is killed, Mithras killed the bull for us. Don't forget that Christ completely absorbed Mithras; that old Mithraic idea has been continued in Christianity through the middle ages up to recent times; bulls and even little lambs have been killed, everything that was animal has been killed throughout the ages. And I confirm that the bull has been killed, the toreador has done his work. Of course, it is a

37

figurative kind of speech to say the bull is dead; it is alive again and again and has to be killed again and again. Now since it is an individual and not a collective problem, what can we do to bring the bull back to life? We should seek to re-establish connection with him, or he might become alive in a part of our psychology where our conscious cannot reach. How can we get at that? The bull must be alive, otherwise community would be impossible. I emphasized that dream to show the interaction of the conscious and unconscious, but now we will go back to our patient.

We were discussing why the brother-in-law's wife had not come with them—that it was probably on account of the *illness of the child*. That is the subject of the next part of the dream. The dreamer is now at *the house of his brother-in-law*, where he sees the child, a little girl, one or two years old. Change of locality means a shifting of the psychological scenic background, and that means a different kind of problem, a change from a collective to a familial basis— for example, from a public place to a private house. The main statement of the middle part of the dream was that there was no community, no coming together, the reason being that the woman has not joined in; as in the nature cult of Mithras, the women did not join in; and *jeu de paume* was also a man's game. If the woman does not come in, man is in it only with his intellect, not with his feeling. This is the reason why some men dislike to have women on committees, etc.—they have no proper connection with the feminine part of their own psychology. This woman has not joined in because the child is ill; and the child is not in a public place, but in the house. The scene has shifted to a private place inside the individual.

He said about the house of his brother-in-law: "My father lived several years in that house, and my sister inherited it; it is only about a hundred paces away from my own house, so we often see each other. The house and shutters are all monotonously painted grey, and it gives a dreary, monotonous aspect. I wish they would paint the shutters at least a different colour to animate it a bit."

The description of the locality is very important; the place where the dream is staged, whether hotel, station, street, wood, under water, etc. makes a tremendous difference in the interpretation. We have already discussed the fact that the brother-in-law must be considered as a very subjective image, he is really a part of the dreamer himself, a part which isn't properly connected, and therefore he projects it into his brother-in-law. But we get the important information from his association that his house is not far away, which means that it is not very far from consciousness. He could easily become aware how far he is the brother-in-law, and how far the child of his brother-in-law is his own child; the house of his brother-in-law would be, of course the unconscious aspect of his own house, the place where the drama is going on. The house recurs very often as a symbol in dreams, and it generally means the habitual or inherited attitude, the habitual way of living, or something acquired like a house, or perhaps the way one lives with the whole family. His habitual attitude is uninteresting and grey as the house of his brother-in-law, and he longs for more colour in it. We must see how this is connected with the other events in the dream; it might be connected with the sickness of the two-year-old-girl.

The child: In reality it was a boy of two who was ill and died, and the dreamer's two other sisters have each a little girl in her seventh year whom he likes. He says: "I like little girls much better than little boys, they are much nicer and more expressive. I like my own little daughter better than the boys." There are no other associations, so I call his attention to the age of the child. I told him he should have some association with two years—a certain length of time: "What about two years ago?" "Two years ago I came back from abroad and settled in Switzerland. I began then the study of occult literature, spiritism, theosophy, all sorts of things; only lately I gave it up more or less, because I was not quite satisfied, not just lack of interest, but some odium around such study. When my little nephew died two years ago, I was just reading a book by Dennis Bradley, *Towards the Stars* (evidently a religious book).[4] I liked it particularly and gave it to my sister after the death of the boy."

He had also read German occult literature: "I read a famous German book: *The Visionary of Prevorst*, written by Dr. Justinus Kerner, 1829,[5] the first history of a case of somnambulism psychologically observed, and most interesting." He told me he knew

[4] Herbert Dennis Bradley, *Towards the Stars* (London, 1924).

[5] *Die Seherin von Prevorst* (1829), 2 vols.; English tr. by Catherine Crowe, *The Seeress of Prevorst* (New York, 1859). Jung himself had known the work since at least 1897, when he cited it in a lecture to his student fraternity: see *The Zofingia Lectures*, pars. 93-94. Also see CW 1, index s.v.

a certain doctor who was acquainted with analytical psychology but not expert at it, and he thought of suggesting that he should write an analytical study of the visionary, on the condition that he should not rationalize Kerner, make a fake of him. "I desisted because I saw the doctor was himself a bit neurotic and such a study might injure him." I know that doctor and he is not a psychological light; if he had attempted to write this analytical study, it would have been poor stuff—a good thing he desisted!

We have now an enormous mass of material connected with that child. I will repeat certain facts:

(1) It is a non-existent child, a mere creation of his unconscious imagination.

(2) The patient prefers girls to boys.

(3) Two years ago he took up the study of occult things, also pathological psychology, etc., and is particularly connected with his sister through such an occult book, *Towards the Stars.*

(4) He was especially interested in *The Visionary of Prevorst*, and wanted a certain doctor to write a study of her but did not do so, fearing that the man would be injured by it.

The little girl is the child of his anima,[6] and has to do with creative energy, and coming from the occult side is spiritual. He says there are positive values in that book, it is a sort of spiritual creation, a poetic intention, but he is afraid the doctor might be badly affected by it, and he gave up the study himself because it had a bad influence on him. He thought occult studies made people very unreal; there was so much doubtful matter, so speculative and yet so impressive, that it filled people's heads with all sorts of vaporous ideas; there was a poisonous unreality in those things very often, just as certain works of fiction make one feel poisoned. So one side of himself is concerned with a decided spiritually creative factor that is two years old, and the doctor represents his rational side which he is using in studying this poetical element expressed by the child.

---

[6] *Anima*: Jung's term for the feminine component of a man's psychology, representing his function of relationship (Eros) with the opposite sex and also with his unconscious. The anima appears personified in dreams as the unknown woman or "dream girl" and is invariably projected onto a real woman or series of women. The *animus* personified the masculine (Logos) component of a woman's psychology. These two archetypes often express themselves in the irrationalities of a man's feeling (anima moods) and a woman's thinking (animus opinions). For full accounts of both, see *Two Essays*, CW 7, pars. 296ff., and *Aion*, CW 9 ii, ch. III.

40

In the last two years a new thing has been growing in this man, not only this interest in occult matters which kept his mind busy, but also a creative interest and intention, which would be the expression not of thoughts but of feeling, and which would give colour to his house.

Now, the colour of this child's face is bad, and her features are distorted exactly like the boy who died. And he adds without apparent connection: "I am reading very little about occultism now." The occult stuff transcended his digestive powers, he suffered from mental indigestion. Then because the girl is linked up with the boy who died, we must assume she suffers from intestinal trouble too; she has been fed with occult literature, and that is not the proper kind of food for the little poetic soul developing in him.

"Someone informs me that the child would not pronounce the name of my wife," and on account of that he pronounces the name of his wife to the child and tries to make her repeat it. He says: "My wife is most beloved by all her nephews and nieces: usually the first name that the children succeed in pronouncing is hers." And he mentions that not long ago he received a letter from one of his other sisters in which she told him that her little boy had composed a melody to which he sang: "Aunt Maria is a dear boy." In contradistinction with reality this dream-child will not or cannot pronounce the name of his wife, she is evidently in opposition to her. We know that the relation between the dreamer and his wife is rather monotonous, and within two years a development has begun in him which produces a living being that deviates from his wife. This child of his anima is linked up with occult interests and a possible sort of scientific or artistic activity. He is puzzled by this, and tries to teach the child to pronounce the name properly, rather shocked that something should develop in him that is not in accordance with his wife, that does not fit into marriage. "I often made the effort to teach my own or my sisters' children to pronounce words in the right way which they pronounced wrongly." He stands for proper form; there should be nothing in his mind or in his heart that is not correct. So, that something in him does not want to pronounce the name of his wife is a fact which should not be; when the theme of his wife appears, every part of him should shout in unison. A very instructive detail concerning his attitude.

His wife's name is Maria and he mentions: "An old aunt of my wife is also called Aunt Maria, but she is quite remote, we have nothing to do with her." Then he goes on: "While I was teaching the child to pronounce the word 'Maria' properly, I was amused that I only said 'Mari'—and instead of pronouncing the 'a' was yawning, adding a yawn to the name instead of the last vowel; in the dream I found myself extremely witty in doing so, but cannot see the joke in waking life. All *the family protests* against his so-called joke, and he says: "Yes, they are quite right, one should not show the children such bad manners, because they cannot, like adults, make a distinction between reality and a joke." Again the correct attitude. This part of the dream was anticipated in the house with shutters painted grey. The house is grey and he is bored, and his unconscious expresses this by that funny allusion—that he yawns in pronouncing the name of his wife. But consciously he won't admit it, he won't see that life is now developing on another line.

In a later dream he was travelling in a cabin on an ocean liner with his wife and the liner came to a standstill; he looked out of the porthole and saw that they were near the coast and quite close to a ruin on a hill. Then he was on deck and saw that he was not on an ocean liner but on a flat-bottomed steamer on a river; and then not even on a river but on a duck-pond in a village, where the ship couldn't move at all, it was completely blocked, and people from the village came on board. It ceased to be a ship and he wonders: why the devil are we living on a ship after all?

LECTURE IV

28 November 1928

Dr. Jung:

Before continuing our dream, I must tell you about certain things which have happened in the meantime. Those of you who are intuitive probably observed that the mood in our second meeting was somewhat upset. We had the bull dream with its community aspect, and so we lived through a little scene which we might have watched in ancient Athens—I mentioned the fact that important men used to tell their dreams, and illustrated it by the dream of the senator's daughter and the dream of the Greek poet. Or we might have watched such a scene in the market-place of some primitive village, where a man gets up and says: "In the night I saw a vision, a spirit spoke," and then everybody gathers round and is dreadfully impressed. All this has brought interesting co-incidences to light.

You remember that on the 21st of November we spoke of the bull and the meaning of the bull-fight. The dreamer is a man whom I occasionally still see—that means analysis has not killed him yet! Now from the 20th to the 24th he spent four days making a picture which he could not understand, and which astonished him so much that he came to me to ask for an explanation. He had to draw a bull's head, and it must be a very sacred bull because he holds the disc of the sun between the horns. Unfortunately I cannot show you the picture because the man thinks we have already been very indiscreet in discussing his dreams here in the seminar. I get my examples from my patients—from you too! I told him that we were talking of the bull in connection with his dream, and that his drawing synchronizes with that, and then I explained to him the meaning of his drawing.

Then after our last meeting, after Dr. Shaw's dream, when I commented on the antique meaning of the bull-fight, I got another

43

letter from Mexico, from the friend who had just actually been to a bull-fight. This letter came two days after the last seminar, it would have been about two weeks on the way, so she must have written it just about the day when we first spoke of the bull in the seminar. She does not describe the fighting. I will quote what she says: "The one point of supreme art in the whole thing is the moment when the bull stops still, confused, and faces the matador, and the matador standing in front of him makes the gesture of scorn to show his complete mastery." "The matador is the point of perfect conscious control in that weltering mass of unconsciousness, in that black background of barbarism."And it seemed to me that that was the meaning of the symbol: one must have perfect conscious control, perfect style and consummate grace and daring, to live in the bosom of barbarism; if one weakens anywhere one is done for. That is why the bull-fight was the symbol of the divine. And the toreador is the hero because he is the only shining light in that dark mass of passion and rage, that lack of control and discipline. He personifies the perfect discipline. My friend is a quite independent observer, but she got the gist of it and in that moment found it necessary to convey it to me.

This is what we call just a coincidence. I mention it to show how the dream is a living thing, by no means a dead thing that rustles like dry paper. It is a living situation, it is like an animal with feelers, or with many umbilical cords. We don't realize that while we are talking of it, it is producing. This is why primitives talk of their dreams, and why I talk of dreams. We are moved by the dreams, they express us and we express them, and there are coincidences connected with them. We decline to take coincidences seriously because we cannot consider them as causal. True, we would make a mistake to consider them as causal; events don't come about *because* of dreams, that would be absurd, we can never demonstrate that; they just happen. But it is wise to consider the fact that they do happen. We would not notice them if they were not of a peculiar regularity, not like that of laboratory experiments, it is only a sort of irrational regularity. The East bases much of its science on this irregularity and considers coincidences as the reliable basis of the world rather than causality. Synchronism[1] is the prejudice of the

---

[1] Apparently Jung's first use of this term in the sense of "synchronicity," or mean-

East; causality is the modern prejudice of the West. The more we busy ourselves with dreams, the more we shall see such coincidences—chances. Remember that the oldest Chinese scientific book is about the possible chances of life.[2]

Now we will continue our dream. We are practically through with the associations, and we ought to try our hand on the interpretation. We should sum up all the associations, in this case a pretty strenuous business because there are so many of them if we take in all the connotations mentioned. The *jeu de paume* and the bull-fight are not in the dream itself, but we must consider the whole context because the mind of the dreamer has been moulded upon that model. Our minds have been made by the history of mankind; what men have thought has influenced the structure of our own minds. Therefore when we go into a careful, painstaking analysis of our mental processes, we must get back into what others have thought in the past. To explain certain thinking processes in a modern man, one cannot get along today without the past. One can explain the personal to a certain extent, for example, that this man wants to buy a new car; but to buy a new car, a modern thought, is only the cause that excites a certain kind of thinking which he has not made; for the most important part of his logical deduction, the whole past is responsible. Only in the middle ages did we learn to think logically—and then through religious teachers. The primitives did not possess logical thinking, simply because they could not produce the same kind of abstract reasoning which we can produce. There must have been a long period of time before our minds were trained to produce an abstract condition of mind over and against the temptations of the senses or emotions.

In technical matters the ancients never could hold an abstract thought for any length of time, they were always interrupted by the playful instinct. We see this in old engines or machines as late

---

ingful coincidence, as an explanatory principle of parallel physical and psychic events, equal in importance and complementary to the principle of causality. Also see below, 27 Nov. 1929, n. 6, and 4 Dec. 1929, p. 417. Jung first published the term "synchronicity" in 1930, in his memorial address for Richard Wilhelm (CW 15, par. 81). The concept is fully developed in the monograph "Synchronicity: An Acausal Connecting Principle" (1952; CW 8).

[2] *The I Ching, or Book of Changes*, tr. Cary F. Baynes (1950) from the German tr. of Richard Wilhelm (1924). Jung wrote a foreword especially for the English tr.; it is also in CW 11, pars. 964ff. Cf. below, 6 Feb. 1929, n. 8.

as 1820; in an old pump, for example, the axles were placed upon two Doric columns; and certain machines were built in the rococo style—perfectly ridiculous. That is playing; and the more they played, of course, the less chance there was of the machine being efficient. They stopped at the curiosity which pleased their senses so never got to any serious kind of thinking. Sailing against the wind, tacking, was not known in antiquity; it was invented by the Normans in the twelfth century. Before that time sailors always had to wait till the wind was favourable or take to the oars; and they had no deep keels or even heavy keels, only flat bottoms. Yet they had boats up to 1500 tons, and the Egyptian vessels which brought wheat to Rome were about 1800 tons. We began to build ships again of that tonnage only in the nineteenth century, about 1840.

These are the historical ways in which our mind has developed and they need to be taken into account; we need to consider the historical connotations in trying to explain dreams; we cannot understand them on the personal basis only. In practical analysis however, one cannot go so far into the historical pathways. As far as it is feasible, I try to be short, practical, and personal. In this first dream that I analysed with the patient, I did not draw his attention to the cult of Mithras, the *jeu de paume*, etc., there was no reason to do so, I was quite satisfied to give him some superficial idea of its meaning. But here in the seminar we must go into detail to see what the dream is made of, perhaps more so than in the dreams I have analysed with you personally. This man would be astonished to hear us talking of his dream, he would not recognize it.

Now let us go back to the dream once more and try to make a general interpretation. Very often the end of a dream can teach one something; at the end something has usually happened to the figures that appeared on the stage, so that the situation at the beginning and the events between are quite explicable. In this case we could easily begin at the end, where we strike the very important fact which the whole dream leads up to, that the dreamer is obviously bored by that name, Maria, and yawns in pronouncing it; and the protests of members of the family show that he himself protests against it from the family standpoint. He is a family man and the family is an almost sacred thing, it is rather awful to yawn over the name of one's wife. So we are introduced to his personal conflict right away; he is bored against his will, it is not his intention

46

and he dislikes it. In such a case we can draw a conclusion as to the economy of his mental state. What would you conclude?

Suggestion: He is unconscious of being bored?

Dr. Jung: Yes, quite right: he would not need to dream of it if he were aware of it; his non-admission goes so far that he has to dream of it. The dream has to tell him: "My dear fellow, you are just bored!" We are always assuming that we know even the unconscious, which of course is perfect nonsense; the unconscious is what we don't know. You would assume that you would realize it if you were bored, but there are situations in which you would not dare to realize it, you would rather think you were ill. There are situations in which we cannot afford to admit the truth, it may go too much against our own interests; we cannot admit the true nature of our emotions, they are too shocking. He is a very nice man, a family man, a father and all that, so of course he is duly interested in his wife, and the dream has to tell him: "You are just bored, that's the truth!" Now when a man is forced to realize that he is bored, what happens to his life force, his libido?

Suggestion: I should think it would begin to occupy itself with what he could do about it.

Dr. Jung: What would be his preoccupations?—that is the right word, the things that come before occupations. Haven't women been bored by husbands? What could they do?

Suggestion: That is too much in the psychology of a man.

Dr. Jung: I am not so certain! But here the dreamer is a man so let us keep to his role. What will he do?

Suggestion: He would begin to look out of the window.[3]

Dr. Jung: In this dream nothing of the sort is mentioned. Your conclusion is not proven in this case.

Suggestion: I think he must have looked out of the window before he had that dream.

Dr. Jung: Quite right, he has often looked out of the window and is beyond the state where this would come in a dream. He is now in a situation where he is seeking more; he is still bored with his wife, looking out of the window has not helped that, and he has come to the conclusion that that won't do. Certain hints in the dream might help him out, such little things, but he could not accept them; they would seem ridiculous to him, they represent no

[3] German colloquialism for casting a roving eye around for another woman.

47

answer, he needs another answer; so he arrives at a standstill. We assume that the dream contains an answer to his very big problem, so we must read it as a message coming from the unconscious, we must take it very seriously, and all the more because the situation of this man is similar to that of many other men, and there are innumerable women who are bored to death with their husbands. Plenty of people between forty and seventy have been or might be in a similar situation. Therefore the dream is of general importance. Going into it with the associations should give us an idea of what one should do in such a situation.

The dream speaks first of the child of his youngest sister and of the invitation of his brother-in-law to go to the theatre and to dine afterwards. Obviously he is put in rapport with that part of his family. You remember that this youngest sister was his particular pet, eleven years younger, and he still feels her to be a little child and is very fond of her; he was almost as grieved when she lost her child as he would have been had it been his own, so there is a particularly close relation between himself and this sister; and he is also on good terms with her husband. These people, with whom he is at present not actually concerned, would be taken on the objective level if they were near or of any actual importance. But since they are far away, we are safe in assuming that they represent subjective contents in the dream, parts of the dreamer himself, stage figures in his private theatre. So we can only arrive at the real meaning of this part of the dream when we see what these people represent in him. The child, as you know, is an unreal, imaginary child; the real child is dead. We will leave that imaginary child for the time being.

First, the *brother-in-law:* The dreamer has been in an important position, a director of a business company, and his brother-in-law, being a younger man, has succeeded him; so he followed him, he is the representative of the one that follows us, the shadow. The shadow is always the follower.

Suggestion: The shadow often goes before.

Dr. Jung: Yes, when the sun is behind. But the old idea of the *synopados*[4] is the one that follows and comes with us; it is the idea of a personal daemon:

---

[4] "he who follows behind" (Greek). See "Basic Postulates of Analytical Psychology" (1931), CW 8, par. 665.

scit Genius, natale comes qui temperat astrum,
naturae deus humanae, mortalis in unum
quodque caput, voltu mutabilis, albus et ater.[5]

—a god of changeful face, white and black, that is in everybody, a daemon of contradictory aspects. Now why should we translate such a figure in such a way? Why should we call his brother-in-law his shadow?

Answer: The dreamer has been so much in business that parts of him have been neglected which are represented by the brother-in-law.

Dr. Jung: Well, the more one turns to the light, the greater is the shadow behind one's back. Or, the more one turns one's eyes to the light of consciousness, the more one feels the shadow at one's back. That term is in complete harmony with ancient ideas. There is an excellent book called *The Man without a Shadow*[6], from which a very good film has been made, *The Student of Prague*, a sort of second *Faust*. It is the story of a student, pressed for money, making a contract with the devil. The devil offers him 900,000 gold sovereigns heaped up on the table before him, and he cannot resist. He says: "Of course I can't expect you to give me all that gold without something in return?" "Oh, nothing of importance", says the devil, "just something you have in this room." The student laughs—there isn't much in the room, old sword, bed, books, etc., very poor. "You are welcome to anything you please, you see there isn't much of value here!" Then the devil says: "Stand here and look into the mirror." The great asset of the movies is the amazing effects they can produce. One sees the man and his reflection in the mirror, and the devil stands behind and beckons to the reflection of the student in the glass, and the reflection comes out in a quite extraordinary way and follows the devil. The student stares

[5] "Why so, the Genius alone knows—that companion who rules our star of birth, the god of human nature, though mortal for each single life, and changing in countenance, white or black."—Horace, *Epistles*, 2.2.187ff. (tr. H. R. Fairclough, LCL).

[6] Adelbert von Chamisso, *Peter Schlemihls wundersame Geschichte* (1814); the title is usually translated *The Wonderful History of Peter Schlemihl* (e.g., trs. of 1844, 1923). The film *Der Student von Prag* (1926), directed by Henrik Galeen and starring Conrad Veidt, was not credited to the Chamisso original though its story was similar. "It seemed to make the Germans realize their own duality."—S. Kracauer, *From Caligari to Hitler* (1947), p. 153.

into the mirror and can no longer see himself, he is a man without a shadow. And the devil walks away. Then the film goes on picturing all the embarrassing situations the student finds himself in because he has lost his shadow. For instance, the barber hands him a mirror after he has shaved him, and he looks in and says, "Yes, that is all right," but he sees nothing, no reflection, he has to pretend he does. Another time he is going to a ball with a lady, and in a mirror at the head of the stairs he sees the lady with an arm as if through his, but he is not there. It is the situation of a man who has split off all consciousness of his shadow, who has lost it.

Our patient is more or less like that, and his shadow is here represented by the one who follows him, his brother-in-law. There is no scientific proof that this is so, we assume it as a working hypothesis. And if the brother-in-law represents the shadow, it follows that the wife of the shadow is a very definite figure; and must have the characteristics of that figure, the wife is the anima. To elucidate such obscure and complicated concepts, as shadow, anima, etc. a diagram is useful to show what is or is not logical.[7] We must start from archetypal ideas, we must begin by the idea of totality; and we express the totality of personality, male and female, by a circle. There would necessarily be a centre to it, but one cannot assign the central place to consciousness because our consciousness is always one-sided. If one looks at what is before one's eyes one is unaware of what is behind one's back; one cannot be conscious of everything in a given moment. To be conscious one must be concentrated; one is always conscious of something specific. The total personality could be described as consciousness plus the unconscious. There is the area of the habitually unconscious, and the area of the relatively unconscious. And so there is an area which is only relatively conscious; there are times when one is conscious of this and times when one is conscious of something else. Consciousness is like a searchlight wandering over the field; only those points which are illuminated are conscious.

---

[7] The diagram is reproduced here from *Sems.*[2] (1938), where it is explained in a footnote that Jung's original diagram had been lost and had been reproduced from memory by Ethel Taylor. Reference was made to a similar diagram in Joan Corrie, *ABC of Jung's Psychology* (1927), p. 21. *Sems.*[3,4] give the same version of the diagram; it is not in *Sem.*[1]

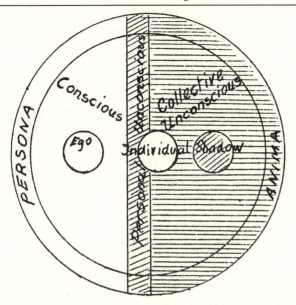

The unconscious or dark side, the part that is habitually unconscious, is the sphere of the shadow, and that has no particular centre
because we don't know where it would be. The shadow is of course
a sort of centre, a certain personality different from the conscious
one, in this dream the brother-in-law.

Our consciousness is turned to what we call the world. In order
to move in the world we have need of a certain attitude or persona,
the mask we turn toward the world. People with a very strong
persona have very mask-like faces. I remember a woman patient
who had such a face. She was an anima figure to men, mysterious
and fascinating just because of her mask—mystery behind, a mystery woman. I get sick when I hear of it, but not everyone does.
The "mystery woman" of the movies is an anima figure. This woman
was said to have a very peaceful harmonious nature, but inside she
was just the opposite, terribly torn and full of amazing contradictions of character. Without her mask she would be just pulp, no
countenance whatever. Persona is a sort of paste one wears over
the face.

What we see of the world is far from the totality, it is merely the surface; we don't see into the substance of the world, into what Kant called "the thing in itself." That would be the unconscious of things, and inasmuch as they are unconscious they are unknown to us. So we need the other half of the world, the world of the shadow, the inside of things. The split between the conscious and the unconscious goes right through the world. Now, if I have a skin of adaptation for the conscious world, I must have one for the unconscious world too. The anima is the completion of the man's whole adaptation to unknown or partly known things. It was only very lately that I arrived at the conclusion that the anima is the counterpart of the persona, and always appears as a woman of a certain quality because she is in connection with the man's specific shadow.

In the case of our dreamer we have a very typical demonstration of the anima. She is connected with the brother-in-law, the shadow, as his wife; with the little sister, his female pet, the innermost female that he loves the most; and with the child for whom he has very tender feelings, as something close to his own soul. Therefore it is a figure that one can designate as a soul symbol. I have chosen to use the word *anima* to avoid all trouble with the meaning of "soul." That sister of his in the dream is the figure that is married to the shadow, and the further statement of the dream is that this female has an imaginary child. An imaginary fact is not a non-existent fact, but one of a different order. A fantasy, for instance, is a very dynamic fact. Remember that one can be killed by a fantasy, and to be killed by a shot fired in war or by a lunatic here is all the same—one is dead! When the dream speaks of a child, that is a definite entity, as his sister and brother-in-law, the dream-mother and the dream-father, are definite entities. They have a psychological existence, they are facts that work and they constitute a world that works.

There is not one thing in our civilization that has not first been in the imagination, in fantasy; even houses and chairs have first existed in the imagination of the architect or designer. The World War came about through mere opinions that war should be declared on Serbia, opinions based on fantasy, imagination. Fantasies are most dangerous; we would be wise to make up our minds that an imaginary child or woman is a dangerous reality, and all the more so because not visible. I would much rather deal with a real woman than with an imaginary woman. An anima can bring about the most amazing results: she can send a man practically anywhere in the world; what a real woman could not do the anima can do. If the anima says so, one must go. If a wife talks boring nonsense, one curses her, but when the anima talks boring nonsense—

Question: Why has the anima such power?

Dr. Jung: Because we undervalue the importance of imagination. The anima and animus have tremendous influence because we leave the shadow to them. By not being aware of having a shadow, you declare a part of your personality to be non-existent. Then it enters the kingdom of the non-existent, which swells up and takes on enormous proportions. When you don't acknowledge that you have such qualities, you are simply feeding the devils. In medical language, each quality in the psyche represents a certain energic value, and if you declare an energic value to be non-existent, a devil appears instead. If you declare that the river which flows by your house is non-existent, it may swell up and fill your garden with pebbles and sand and undermine your house. If you give such a limitless possibility to nature to work by itself, nature can do what she pleases. If you see a herd of cattle or pigs and say they are non-existent, they are immediately all over the place, the cows will eat up the rose-garden and the pigs will climb into your bed and sleep there! In this way the non-existent grows fat. Meyrink's *Die Fledermäuse*[8] (otherwise very bad) describes very vividly a world in which are living some extremely poor specimens of people, pale, sad, unhealthy, and getting worse and worse; and then the discovery is made that as they decrease, certain corpses in the graveyard are growing proportionately fat. The thing you have buried grows fat while you grow thin. If you get rid of qualities you don't like by denying them, you become more and more unaware of what you are, you declare yourself more and more non-existent, and your devils will grow fatter and fatter.

As the shadow is a definite entity, so the anima is a definite entity, and so is this child a definite entity, and all the more dangerous because it is an imaginary child. She is dangerous because she might reflect back on the patient himself. This is again empirical, a mere working hypothesis, but we are forced to make them. The main point is that she is about two years old, that she is pale and ill, and that she is the product of the union of the shadow and the anima—

---

[8] Gustav Meyrink, *Fledermäuse. Sieben Geschichten* (1916).

they come together somehow. It is very mysterious, very difficult to explain it at all. We know the product is two years old and that the patient began his occult studies which led him into analysis two years ago; that is the significant fact. If such a definite time is stated in a dream, it is a hint that it is necessary to pay attention to the time element in the history of the case. To dream of a child of seven years means that seven years ago something started.

Another patient of mine dreamt she had a child just five years old who gave her terrible trouble and might have a bad effect on her mind. I asked: "In the same month just five years ago, what happened?" The woman could not think at first and then she became very much embarrassed: she had fallen in love with a man and had declared her feeling non-existent. She had had a hell of a life in her marriage to another man, and was now devil-haunted for fear she would go crazy. Women who have kept that fact secret have really gone crazy! Because she was of a simple family, and he of a more aristocratic one, she felt her love was hopeless, never assuming that he could love her; so she married another man and had two children. Then three years ago she met a friend of the first man who told her that he had loved her and had therefore never married. "Your marriage stabbed him to the heart." Soon after this, while bathing her older child, a little girl of three or four, with the eyes of her first lover—she liked to think of her as the child of her lover—she noticed the little girl drinking the water from the bathtub, very infectious, unfiltered water. She knew this but let it happen, and even let her boy drink the same water. Both children were taken ill with typhoid, and the older child died. The woman went into a deep depression, like dementia praecox, and was sent to a lunatic asylum where I treated her. I soon found out the whole story and felt that the only hope for her was to tell her the brutal truth: "You have killed your child in order to kill your marriage." Of course she didn't know what she was doing; because she denied her former love, declared it non-existent, she fed her devils and they suggested killing the daughter of her husband. In this case the awful thing in her dream was born of the bogie of three years ago at the moment when she heard that her first lover was deeply grieved that she had married another man. She had "fed her devils," the animus, and they had killed her child. The woman recovered.[9]

[9] For a more detailed report of this case, see "The Tavistock Lectures" (1935), CW 18, pars. 107f.

Question: Do you think there is really a connection between the marriage of the shadow and the anima, and the fact that the patient was led to occult studies?

Dr. Jung: I assume that the occult science he was trying to study would represent symbolically the dark and unknown side of things; since that interest was born out of the union of the shadow and anima it would naturally be expressed by something occult. The union of the shadow and anima has the character of something exceedingly mysterious. That it eventually led our patient to occult studies is an important hint as to the kind of experience. It feels like something strange and amazing like an event that could only take place in a non-existent imaginary world; one can't express it properly, it is too odd, too unheard of, one gets only a repercussion from it. I asked this man what had brought him into such studies and he could not tell me; he just felt that the world had another side. He had got out of it all that outward success could give, but had the idea that this was not all; so he drifted toward the occult, he began to read about Atlantis, etc., in order to find where "that thing" was hidden. Whatever that union between the shadow and anima may be, it has that effect.

Now the unconscious says it is an unsound kind of occupation and therefore the child is ill. This is a piece of important information to him and to me. Otherwise I would have no right to be critical. Neither I nor anybody else could assume that his occult studies were necessarily morbid; the dream gave us the hint that it was pathological, that these studies were wrong. Then he is invited to go to the theatre and to dine, but Mrs. Anima is not there, she is staying away, concerned with the ill child. The shadow invites the dreamer to the theatre so that he may see all that the shadow sees, the scenery of the unconscious. What is the secret purpose of the brother-in-law? What is he driving at? He is trying to arrive at some kind of communion; by going with the shadow the dreamer goes with the part of himself which he has declared to be non-existent. When I say I am going to dinner with someone I give reality to that person. The fact that he goes to dinner with the shadow means that he accepts the existence of the shadow as he accepts his brother-in-law; he admits the reality of his shadow side— that he is so terribly bored, that he has fantasies, etc. He will go and see those images, and by assimilating them the ultimate goal of the dream, that the child shall be cured, will be furthered. The child is ill because he has begun his studies in the wrong way, he

ought to begin by the shadow. Just recently a representative theosophist told me that he thought they ought to introduce analysis
into their theosophy. They begin to realize that unless they begin
at the right end, with the shadow, their occult pursuits are morbid.
The right beginning is within. Learn of one's own dark side, then
one can tackle theosophy. Theosophy means the "wisdom of God."
Can we have that? Heavens, no! Be wise about yourself, then you
know something.

Next week I should like you to give me your own interpretations
of the dream, either your individual interpretations, or form groups
and discuss it, with one member as the spokesman. The teacher
hasn't to do all the work!

LECTURE V

5 December 1928

Dr. Jung:
Today I want to hear your interpretations of the dream.

Dr. Deady (First interpretation):   The problem of the dream is an anima one. He went into the occult under the influence of his sister, not as a man should but in a mood which always means anima. His sister was his anima, so it was not as an intellectual, conscious job.

Dr. Jung: One can't quite say that of this man. He is very widely read, and has a very thorough mind; he did it in quite a conscientious way. One must be careful in speaking of the anima as the promoter of an interest. Moods are only one symptom of the anima—there are other most conspicuous symptoms. The anima can give one very strange ideas: she can, for instance, give that peculiar quality which makes a man lead his life as a sort of adventure or quest, making the task the goal of his whole life. Napoleon is an example, whose dream it was to be like Alexander the Great; his life became a quest, a romantic adventure; that shows the influence of the anima.

Our Swiss dreamer is thoroughly romantic, he went at the occult studies in the way of a quest, set out like a knight seeking adventures, and that is the doing of the anima. The anima doesn't busy herself with nonsense alone, she is also the *femme inspiratrice*: she gives a man very great ideas and generous impulses, she can make a man's life grand and noble, not merely a bundle of moods. It is true that when the anima is behind a man there is also some trap, as if the incentive were somehow wrong, or as if it were done with only half his brains, as if it were not the whole man, his complete personality. This man is a merchant, and when he goes into the occult, he is living only half of himself, not the sum total of his personality. He is like a person with a hobby. His later dreams constellated the fact that he is a merchant and that he has a practical

57

mind; he would be dreaming of very mythological situations and then in would come the practical merchant. Once he dreamed he was in the presence of a peculiar evil deity, a yellow ball, and he was doing some magic with it, so one would expect something tremendous; but in making a picture of it, what should have been a yellow god came out like a piece of money, a gold coin. He wanted to burn up that yellow ball but someone had cut the wires. Then he was irritated, he wanted to kill people, and the only weapon he could find was a horseshoe—not sufficient to kill his enemies, so he got into a funk and rushed, like a boy, sliding down the banisters to escape, thinking that he wasn't up to that problem. It was as if he himself had cut the wires so that the yellow god couldn't be burned. The dream showed how near the pairs of opposites had approached each other, it was a close fight. But then he was still far away from the problem of what the yellow god means and what the occult studies mean. He was primarily a business man and then he switched off to occult studies. That is what the anima can do alone, when she works unaided by the man; she can switch him off to an entirely different sphere where he forgets his ordinary life. But she remains apart, as in *She*.

Dr. Deady: Therefore that study, the birth of a new interest, is the birth of a child; so the child is his interest in the occult. But his interest in the occult is an anima interest, not a masculine logos interest; consequently the child is sick. It is his shadow and his anima that have this interest, and they are both in his unconscious, so he is led into something over which he has no control. He has to know his unconscious, to be related to his shadow, if he is to go into theosophy, etc., consciously. The dream represents the situation and is dynamic: he goes to the theatre and dines, that is, he takes steps towards a new attitude, towards consciousness.

Dr. Jung: You should mention that his brother-in-law, his shadow, invited him to go to the theatre, he does not think of it himself. The message came from his unconscious, as if a low voice had spoken: "Go to the theatre." Just so the voice said to Socrates, "Make more music." And another time, "Take the street to the left," and by listening to the voice of his daemon, Socrates avoided a great herd of pigs that were rushing down the street he had been on. I was consulted recently by a woman who hears such a voice; she is just nicely mad, sort of home-like. She has a voice that speaks from down below, in her belly, and gives excellent advice; she comes to be cured of her voice yet wants to keep it. It is the voice of the shadow, of course. For instance, she was accustomed to write individual notes to all her people at Christmas, but then her voice suggested that she should send the same note to everyone. Since our man is not mad, he hears the voice in sleep, not in consciousness. The voice is peculiarly banal and also great. One may make a mistake, as Socrates did when he took his voice literally and went out and bought a flute. And that woman is bewildered, she doesn't know whether it is the voice of God or the devil. One ought to be afraid and yet it should not be taken entirely seriously. A Negro woman who was a bit mad once told me: "Yes, the Lord is working in me like a clock, funny and serious." That is exactly what dreams are—funny and serious. So it is important for our patient to notice where the message comes from, that it comes from the unconscious. For his conscious thinks he has already dined, has already made some occult studies. But you have not got to the main point of the dream.

Miss Taylor (Second interpretation): The message of the dream is conversion, a change of attitude. When the old way of living begins to lose interest, any time between forty and seventy, the moment has come for a change, not of outward conditions but one within: for a union between the ego and the shadow, by looking at and assimilating the images of the unconscious to obtain the mana stored up in them to create anew: "his brother-in-law asks him to go to the theatre with him and to dine afterwards."

The problem of the dreamer is (1) his ultra-correctness—he gave up the study of the occult not through lack of interest but because there was "some odium" around that study; (2) consequent boredom—grey shutters, etc.; and (3) his unconscious primitive feeling—he asks a sick child to pronounce correctly and yawns in saying his wife's name. He is bored by his wife but his correctness prevents him from realizing it until his dream tells him, and hints that the blame lies in himself—"people protest."

"Girl two years old": Two years before on the death of his sister's boy his feeling was constellated and a girl-child was born, the Eros principle in himself. He began to question: he had had an active, successful life, yet he was bored, and a new interest was awakened in him, an interest in the other world. Also two years before, his sister, on whom he had projected his anima, went away. As he had no real relation with an actual woman, his libido fell to his anima, who drove him to occult studies—he did "not know exactly why" he studied the occult. So the child was the creative expression of his own unconscious, and "was sick" because it was fed on occult studies; libido had gone from the child to feed his anima. The food for the child would be free expansion and the study of his unconscious images, not occultism, since it is the child of his anima and therefore within, not without.

"My brother-in-law asks me to go to the theatre and to dine": His irrational side suggested that he should look at dreams, the images of his unconscious, and then assimilate these unconscious parts of himself. "Alone": Without the women, that is, without emotion. "I think I have eaten already, yet can go with him": He thinks he knows all about himself, yet he will see what the analyst has to say; this is some resistance to analysis. "Big room, dining-table, seats reversed, etc.": An intuitive conception of analysis as a forerunner of a new kind of collectivity; first confession, the unburdening of secrets that make a real communion for everybody impossible; he is separated from his wife, friends, etc. The player, the ball and the wall, that is, the ego, the self and the analyst. Then the meal, the real communion. "I ask why his wife has not come, and think because the child is ill": As if he realized that there could not be feeling or the right communion when his interest was fed on occult studies. "Child is better, only a little fever now": He had given up the occult studies, analysis is the right line. "At the home of his brother-in-law": The scene shifts to his personal problem which lies in his own psychology.

Dr. Jung: There is an element of legend, of fantasy, in this. In reality the sister is the man's anima in his dream only, not in actuality. He had no positive anima projection into a living woman, he had only moods. Until this time his anima has been almost entirely negative. But we must have the end of the dream.

Mrs. Fierz (Third interpretation): The little nephew's poem and song, "Aunt Maria is a dear boy," and the old Aunt Maria the man gave as an association seem important. His wife is to him something like a distant aunt, and the old aunt seems boring, as his wife does. The song might show him he could really *do something* with his own wife; that is what children often mean when they call a person dear. Not so much sentiment as expressing a desire to play with, do something with, the person who is "dear." Perhaps this man could, with his wife, do something for their children, help in their education, etc. He admits he doesn't care so much for the boys, likes the girls better; here is something to work on. He says of himself only that he corrects the children's language, a stupid part of their education. So perhaps the dream means he could show a change of attitude towards his wife and children; for his attitude towards his children is evidently like his attitude towards his wife.

Dr. Jung: In that family Aunt Maria means the old aunt. She is boring and she refers to his wife yet his wife is declared to be a "dear boy."

Mrs. Fierz: The child who wrote that song is a boy, and he makes his aunt his companion. Children's comradeships are active.

Dr. Jung: He thinks of her as on his own level?—that is right. One of the symptoms of the sick child is that she doesn't want to pronounce the name Maria, and that is associated with the other fact that all the children of the family do just this.[1] His wife has an attraction for children, she is child-like, she is the playmate of all the children in the family, a fact which is exceedingly important for his own problem, for it means that his wife is not a good play-mate for a man. The anima type of woman can always play with a man and therefore is important for his mental and spiritual development. His association explains that his wife is a good playmate for children and implies that she is *not* a good playmate for him. The child will not pronounce that name because she doesn't like the wife; that little girl-child in him, occult studies, leads him away from his wife to secrecy. And he does not want secrecy, or that any part of him would not like the name of his wife, so he tries to teach the child to pronounce the name, and cannot do so without yawning himself. That gives him away, he can no longer deny that he is bored. Men may go to cocottes and yet insist that they remain correct; and women may fly away with devils and yet say they are loyal wives. We must settle down to the fact that the world is very serious and very funny. The dream forces this fact upon the dreamer in a very obvious manner. He told me frankly that he hates the idea that he is not the correct husband, it is disgusting to him to have to acknowledge this fact. A man usually treats the children as he treats the women and as he treats his own feeling self.

The dream is rather bewildering on account of not having one main thought. It contains two entirely different sets of things—

[1] See above, 21 Nov. 1928, p. 41.

exceedingly personal material on the one hand and very impersonal material on the other. The beginning and end of the dream are very personal; and you have heard how that material in the middle came in and what it has to do with the dream.

[Here a discussion was started on the relationship of man and wife, whether individual or collective.]

Question: Is whatever relation a man has with his wife collective?

Dr. Jung: A man may find his relationship to his wife to be nothing but collective, and that won't do. He ought to have an individual relation; if that is lacking, there is no individual adjustment. He is just the ordinary perfectly respectable husband, and his wife is the woman with whom he finds himself in the institution of marriage, and he tries to fulfil his duty as a husband as he tries to be a good director in a company. But his wife is a particular woman with whom he should have a particular relationship.

To understand marriage, we must think of it as an institution and go back historically to know what it means. Since times immemorial, marriage has been arranged as a system of matches, and there were very few love matches; it was chiefly barter, women bought and sold; and in the royal families, it is still almost a sort of cattle deal, and has much the same character in very rich families. That is quite certainly true with peasants for powerful economic reasons. So it is often "the bacon to the sausage," as we say, two fat things together. Marriage is a collective institution, and relationship in marriage is a collective relationship. Then when the times become more sophisticated and there is a certain culture, the individual gets spoilt; one has more desires and claims, one psychologizes and wants to understand, and then one finds one is not really adjusted and hasn't really a relationship. After a great catastrophe one seeks a water-tight room where one can be safe, any room will do provided the roof doesn't leak; but one has no relationship to this room, it is just any hole which is covered and relatively safe. So in former times and under more barbarous conditions, and among primitive tribes, any woman would do more or less. That explains incest among peasants. There are extraordinary cases in Switzerland. Here is a case I have just heard of: A peasant boy wanted to marry; he and his mother had a good place so the mother said: "why marry?—it only makes more mouths to feed; I should have to go, and you would have to support me; if you want a woman, take me." That is the peasant, and that was for economic reasons. It has been stated by the courts in certain districts that incest for economic reasons is so frequent that the cases are not dealt with at all, they don't bother about it. Everywhere one discovers these things. In some of the British islands, in the Hebrides, etc., the condition of the people is exceedingly collective, just instinctive, not at all psychological. So the general condition of marriage has always been exceedingly collective; the personal element is the attainment of a cultural age; and only very recently has marriage become a problem one can discuss without being accused of immorality. Morality is the only thing that can't be improved upon, we say. It is the one thing that can't!

We have a great problem today because that collective marital relation is not what people expect of it—an individual relationship, and it is exceedingly difficult to create one in marriage. Marriage in itself constitutes a resistance. This is simply a truth. For the strongest thing in man is *participation mystique,* just "you and your dog in the dark"; that is stronger than the need for individuality. You live with an object and after a while you assimilate each other and grow alike. Everything that lives together is influenced one by the other, there is a *participation mystique;* the mana of one assimilates the mana of the other. This identity, this clinging together, is a great hindrance to individual relationship. If identical, no relationship is possible; relationship is only possible when there is separateness. Since *participation mystique* is the usual condition in marriage, especially when people marry young, an individual relation is impossible. Perhaps the two hide their secrets from each other; if they admitted them they might be able to establish a relationship. Or perhaps they have no secrets to share; then there is nothing to protect one against *participation mystique,* one sinks into that bottomless pit of identity and after a while discovers that nothing happens at all any longer.

Now, in this state of affairs our patient obviously realizes that something is wrong, that he is dissatisfied. His sexual relation with his wife doesn't work at all: she keeps him away as much as possible, and at forty-seven to always do uphill work is terribly uninteresting, and he more or less chucked the whole thing. So it is an unpleasant situation. His attempt at occult studies is rather like Freud's sublimation idea—intercourse with angels. Theosophy provides one with all sorts of things in that respect! If I could hear the vibrations of Atlantis, listen in to old Egypt, and all that, I would forget all about my wife and all about my dear patients too! Theosophy is a tremendous lure to such a man, and sublimation is a good word, it sounds like anything; but, peculiarly enough, in reality sexuality cannot be entirely sublimated. Suddenly one day, in Paris perhaps, the man makes a mistake, the sublimation hasn't worked that day. Once in a fortnight it does not work perhaps, but the theory is very good! Out of that mood of dissatisfaction came this dream. The shadow appears and says: "Now come, let us look at the true pictures of the unconscious, the real, impartial pictures of things as they are; and let us eat them and assimilate them afterwards without the women—without emotion, objectively, impersonally, just looking at things as they are."

Since the theatre is a public place it means: you are like all the others, you are in the same boat, doing what everybody ought to do or has done. He associates the amphitheatre seats with a room where the game of pelota was played, yet the setting of the room has nothing to do with pelota, it is rather like a table d'hôte in a hotel; but the benches are facing the wall so they cannot sit at the table. Here, you remember, we got into a tangle of historical associations. It is obvious that we are getting into something collective here; the dream, in emphasizing it as being a public place, intentionally puts forward the importance of its being collective. At this point in the problem the collective must come in. In contradistinction to his intensely personal feeling about his problem, the unconscious says it is a collective problem—not in just that form perhaps, but happening everywhere in the world. Only people who haven't lived can have any illusions on this subject; it is all over the world.

As soon as a problem is collective it has to do with the history of that particular society, and there must be collective symbolism. No collective problems have arisen just today, our conditions are thoroughly historical. Take the question of marriage in general: it has tremendous historical connections, the laws about marriage have considerable age, and all our marriage customs and our whole moral system in dealing with sex are very old. People say: "These are old-fashioned ideas—to hell with them!" But if a problem is collective, it is historical, and we can't explain it without explaining history; unavoidably we get into historical discussions. It is not just you who are a fool to be married like that, we are all married like that, according to ancient laws, sacred ideas, taboos, etc. Marriage

64

is a sacrament with unbreakable laws; you must criticize the customs, not the individual people.

Back of everything we do is a general philosophy; a living one is a religion. Christianity is our philosophy. That was already blossoming in the time of Augustus and is at the back of innumerable taboos, laws, etc. So you see we cannot avoid going back into history—it is not out of the way. We must acknowledge that the dreamer in his literal associations did not bring this in; only later he became conscious of the need of it. Naturally, we see nothing historical in what we do when we are unconscious. Our language is full of the most extraordinary things of which we are not aware, we use them without stopping to consider. For example, when you say, "I am under the treatment of Dr. So-and-So," you are using the Latin word *trahere*, to pull; the doctor is pulling you through the hole of rebirth, and when he makes you whole and sound, you say, "The doctor pulled me through." There was a prehistoric clinic in Cornwall, the Menanthole,[2] a huge slab of stone with a hole through which the fathers pulled their children, and sick people were supposed to be cured in that way. I myself went through the hole. And in Germany, in the nineteenth century, they had the custom of making a hole in the wall behind the sick man's bed and pulling him through and out into the garden for rebirth.

Now the dreamer speaks of a room where many people come together, not everyone for himself but together, like playing a game or dining together, where all sit at the same table facing each other and doing the same thing. So we are united with him as in a theatre or restaurant, we are all looking at the pictures together. The shadow admonishes him to come and do something with many other people, in order to feel community in that particular problem of his. You will realize what that means for a man who thinks he is the only one who suffers from his particular ailment and feels responsible for it. When he hears that it is a general problem, he is comforted, at once it puts him back into the lap of humanity; he knows that many people are having the same experience, and he can talk to them and is not isolated. Before, he didn't dare speak about it; now he knows that everyone understands. The particular prescrip-

[2] Near Penzance, and not far from Polzeath, where Jung gave a seminar in July 1923. The stone is also called Menetol; see Jaquetta Hawkes, *A Guide to the Prehistoric and Roman Monuments in England and Wales* (1951), p. 169, cited in S. Giedion, *The Beginnings of Art* (1962), pp. 159-61, with illustrations of the stone.

tion in the New Testament—"Confess your faults one to another," and "Bear ye one another's burdens"[3]—shows the same psychology that we have here in the dream. We should have communion and fellowship in the trouble which is our particular burden, that is the admonition of the dream.

First of all there was the association of the *jeu de paume* and *pelota basque*. They were not quite the same. The *jeu de paume* was played in the middle ages, not with a racquet, but with the palm of the hand; and the same idea was in the *pelota basque*, but the ball was played against the wall; then a third version was the *jeu de paume* as it was played in the church, the clerics throwing the ball to one another. I don't know what kind of figures they made but all were playing the same game. And we play it too, the *ball* game has become almost a figure of speech with us; we often use the similes "throw the ball," "play the game," "I catch it," etc. It simply means playing together; we all play together and since we react, we are all in it responsible and alive—that is the idea.

Then there is a particular version here, a mere association, so we must not press it too hard: in the case of the pelota played against the wall where the ball is caught not by other people but by oneself, there may be an element of self-isolation or autoeroticism. In playing the ball like that, not with a partner but against the wall, there is a particular connotation. But we must not force this point; we must handle dreams with nuance, like a work of art, not logically or rationally, as one may make a statement, but with a small restriction somewhere. It is the creative art of nature which makes the dream, so we must be up to it when we try to interpret them. That there is here a nuance which might point to an autoerotic game, played alone, not together, would easily come from the fact that the man will play it alone first. Some people speak "against the wall" and not to their fellow-beings: such speakers are more or less autoerotic, they talk to themselves even though they speak in community.

If the dreamer follows the intimation of the shadow, he will see his problem as a collective one which ought to be brought into general connection with the spirit of his own time, and not hidden away, assuming that it is the mistake of a single individual and that normal happy families are not like that. His problem should not

---

[3] James 5:16; Gal. 6:2.

be discussed just in the pretty terms of general prejudice, assuming that the world is all nice families in nice little houses, with five o'clock teas, and prams, and sweet little babies! There are the most terrible things underneath all that stuff, and I have to bother with it. People play to the gallery as if nothing was the matter at all! All that part of the dream prepares him for the fact that he is entering on a collective problem and the solution will be something equally impersonal: something like a communion, an initiation, a mystery play in church, a sort of ritual play like the central symbolism of the cult of Mithras. You will remember that when we spoke of that cult the unconscious began to react all over the place, and we got a whole crop of bull dreams, which proves that the thing is practically active even here and is a general problem for people right here.

Now, after this general statement, which prepares him for an entirely different attitude to his particular problem, the dream returns again to the personal aspect of things, the pathological condition of the child. Its condition is morbid because occult studies lead nowhere; they are just an attempt at sublimation, a sublimation which never answers the real, urgent problem of the times. What must be done now with the child? It is all very well to say that this is a collective problem, *mais il faut cultiver son jardin*,[4] come back to your own problem, your own child, come and admit you are bored with your dear wife at home. Psychologically that means he must *acknowledge his shadow*, the inferior man who does not live up to rational conditions, a sort of primitive more aware of the needs of nature, who forces him to admit his boredom. He would then gain a knowledge of his shadow, he would admit his natural being and shake hands with him, and no longer deny the truth about his own psychology. Since he cannot escape his shadow he will become conscious of the less elegant side of himself. Then the shadow will be detached from his anima, because as he becomes conscious of his shadow, it is released from his unconscious. Then between the shadow and anima a real relation can take place, with the outcome that the child will be normal.

And when the shadow and anima have a proper relationship, there is a chance that his relation to his wife will become better, that he can have an individual relationship with her. For he can

4 Voltaire, *Candide* (1759), closing lines.

only establish a real relationship when he is aware of his shadow. We allow ourselves the most amazing illusions about ourselves and think other people take us seriously. It is as if I should have the illusion that I am only five feet tall—just mad! This is no more absurd than people who want to make us believe that they are very moral and respectable. It isn't true, and how can you establish a real relation unless people are real, as they really are? We know that people, instead of being respectable or moral, are just hopelessly blind. How can you establish an individual relationship with such a creature? One gets seasick, it is nauseating. I would far rather have an individual relationship to a dog, who doesn't assume he is a respectable dog, a sacred dog, a taboo dog, or any other kind of a dog—nothing but a dog! There are people who have the illusion they are better than other men, assume that they are different, as if they had another kind of blood. This is all illusion; therefore no individual relation is possible with such people.

First of all, our man must give up his illusions, admit he is not respectable and that he is bored; and he must *tell his wife* he is bored to death and at the same time that "sometimes my sublimation fails to work." If he only knew his wife this would be easier. She will be outraged at his infidelity but she herself in the night will be going away with the animus devils—only he doesn't know it. If he asks her to be interested in what he is reading, very likely she says, "Oh, I can't read such difficult books," and he thinks she is too good and sweet! If only he were aware of her as she really is, he could find it easier to tell about his sublimation not working as it should.

Now to get all this into practice, that is something else!

LECTURE VI

12 December 1928

Dr. Jung:
We come now to an important part of the interpretation of this dream, namely, to your critique and the question of the historical character of the associations. I have exposed my views about this dream quite freely and given you an opportunity to see how one may understand it. I have given you much of the patient's personal material and the whole atmosphere of the dream, by which I understand the historical disposition which underlies our actual mind. The latter is often misunderstood. People say, "Why bring in the historical parallel at all? It is irrelevant and mere fantasy." But the historical parallel is not irrelevant, it is exceedingly important, particularly because we white people don't realize to what extent we are the descendants, the children, of a long series of ancestors. We like to behave as if we were just recently made, fresh from the hand of God, with no historical prejudice at all, our mind a *tabula rasa* at birth. This is a peculiar projection of our minds, this wanting to be free, not held down by any background: it is a sort of illusion of our consciousness in order to have the feeling of complete freedom, as if the historical past was fettering and would not allow free movement—a prejudice which again has psychological reasons.

Our actual mind is the result of the work of thousands or perhaps a million years. There is a long history in every sentence, every word we speak has a tremendous history, every metaphor is full of historical symbolism; they would not carry at all if that were not true. Our words carry the totality of that history which was once so alive and still exists in every human being. With every word we touch upon a historical fibre, as it were, in our fellow-beings; and therefore every word we speak strikes that chord in every other living being whenever we speak the same language. Certain sounds count all over the earth: sounds of fear and terror, for instance,

69

are international. Animals understand utterances of fear of entirely different species because they have the same underlying fibre.

So we can't possibly understand a dream if we don't understand the atmosphere, the history of the underlying images. There are personal problems in dreams which one may think only important for that particular case, but if one goes deeply into the structure, the speech symbolism, one enters historical layers and discovers that what seemed to be merely a personal problem goes much deeper, it reaches the analyst himself and everybody who hears it. One can't help bringing in the way in which our ancestors tried to express the same problem, and that leads one to historical matter.

When you are asleep in your own quiet bedroom dreaming your own private dream, what connection is there between your particular dream and the pyramids?—the two seem incommensurable. Yet you might find a close parallel to your dream in an Egyptian text containing the same symbols. Or you may see in a very learned book by E. A. Wallis Budge a translation of certain hieroglyphs and you think: that is Egypt and this is my dream and it is foolish to compare the two, there is nothing in common. But the scribe who produced that text was a human being, in most respects exactly like yourself—hair, two eyes, a nose, two ears and hands, the same natural functions, he was happy, sad, loved, was born and died, and these are the main features. Even our diseases are practically the same; a few diseases are extinct and a few are new, but on the whole there are no differences. The main features of human life have remained the same for five or six thousand years or more, for an interminably long period. Primitive tribes are moved by the same emotions as we are. A peasant's horizon is different but the main features are the same, the fundamental conceptions of life and the world are the same; and our unconscious speaks a language which is most international. I analysed dreams of Somali Negroes as if they were people of Zurich, with the exception of certain differences of languages and images. Where the primitives dream of crocodiles, pythons, buffaloes, and rhinoceroses, we dream of being run over by trains and automobiles. Both have the same voice, really; our modern cities sound like a primeval forest. What we express by the banker the Somali expresses by the python. The surface language is different yet the underlying facts are just the same. That is the reason why we can make historical parallels; it is not far-fetched, these things are far more alive than you would think or assume.

There is an ancient parchment written in the old Germanic language which contains an invocation to Wotan (Odin) and Baldur; it is exceedingly rare and precious, yellow with age, and it is kept under glass in a museum in Zurich. When one reads it, one might say: "Oh, how far away; it could just as well come from the moon!" One thinks all this has died out. But there is a village in the Canton of Zurich where the peasants are still living by the same book, only now instead of Wotan and Baldur it is Jesus Christ and his disciples.[1] There is a bit of mediaeval psychology in it, but it is still the same old thing *au fond*. Now, if a boy or girl from one of those families comes to the analyst and dreams of any old thing out of that book, and the analyst relates the two, people would say it was far-fetched. But they just don't know, and don't want to know; they hate to think of old superstitions as still going on.

Take a gathering of fifty normal people and ask them if they are superstitious and they will swear they are not, but they would not live in house No. 13! They are sure they are not afraid of demons, ghosts, bogies, but knock on the wall of their study and they jump, they believe in ghosts. And they develop ideas and fantasies which are to be found only in old literature. Or perhaps in Babylon, Mesopotamia, China, India, one finds the same material. It all comes out of the same unconscious mind, the irrational and eternal stock, the pre-functioning collective unconscious, which repeats itself throughout the centuries, a sort of eternal, imperishable language. Insane Negroes, very black Negroes whom I have analysed in the United States, had Greek myths in their dreams—Ixion on the wheel, for instance.[2] It is only illusion when you think they are far apart; the Negro has the same kind of unconscious as the one that produced those symbols in Greece or anywhere else. Scientists like to think that symbols have migrated. This is not true; they are

[1] For a discussion of survivals of medieval magic in Switzerland, see "Flying Saucers" (1958), CW 10, pars. 700f.

[2] In Fall 1912, while in the United States for his lectures at Fordham University, Jung "analysed" some Negro patients at the Government mental hospital, St. Elizabeths, Washington, D.C.; see *The Freud/Jung Letters*, 11 Nov. 1912. He never wrote up the material but referred to it in *Psychological Types* (1921), CW 6, par. 747; "The Tavistock Lectures" (1935), CW 18, pars. 81ff.; and *Symbols of Transformation* (1952; added to this edn.), CW 5, par. 154. *Sems.*: "Sisyphus," error for "Ixion," the mythological figure mentioned by Jung in the last two citations.

quite autochthonous. An old Babylonian symbol may be produced by a Zurich servant girl. Those old peoples were exactly the same as we are, not even anatomically different; you can see a Neanderthal man in the street-cars of Zurich today. We must go back fifty to sixty thousand years to find real anatomical differences in human beings. I wanted to make all this clear because I felt that some of you did not understand why I was talking so much about the *jeu de paume* and the bull-fights. This is the reason for the historical parallels.

Question: I think you said—in the Zurich seminar, 1925—that when the anima has a child, she dies.

Dr. Jung: That is only metaphorical. It is as if a personification of the unconscious received life through certain contents, and when the personification is depleted of those contents then that particular personification collapses. Like giving a ghost its right name—it collapses.

Question: At the Sonne[3] we discussed the illness of the child. Was it chronic or acute?

Dr. Jung: The dream gives the answer. You remember that the association with that child's disease was that the sister of the dreamer had lost a child who had dysentery. According to this association we can assume that the dream-child is ill as the sister's actual child was ill. There is always a parallel; the dreamer usually couches his unconscious idea in the terms of actual life or experience, as the dog dreams of bones, and the fish of fishes. So when you analyse a man whose profession you don't know, if he dreams of meat, joints, etc., you can assume that he is a butcher, or a surgeon, or a professor of anatomy. Since that child is closely associated, we must assume that it was infected and not born ill necessarily. The child is a symbolic expression of his new interest in occult studies, which is not necessarily wrong. It all depends upon the attitude. If one studies the occult with the wrong attitude one can get infected, for this whole field is full of metaphysical traps through which one can fall, disappear as into an oubliette, and became the astrologer, the theosophist, or the black magician. This man was in danger of becoming a theosophist. Nothing is said directly in the dream about the duration of the illness, but we can conclude

[3] Small hotel in Küsnacht, near Jung's house and frequented by his patients and pupils.

from the parallel that it must have been pretty quick, that the occult studies did not trouble the child for long. It is probably an acute disease which came from indigestion. He told me he felt "peculiarly empty" after a time and threw away the books: "I became sick of it."

Question: There is something not quite clear to me about the animus and anima. Isn't the animus the mediator between the individual and the shadow world? Doesn't the ego get its raw material through the animus? Is not Faust an animus?

Dr. Jung: If we take Goethe as a human being, then one part is Faust, and the other part is the devil, the typical shadow. Faust would be the grand, heroic, idealized personification of the conscious aspiration of Goethe, and Mephistopheles the personification of all his drawbacks and shortcomings, the negativity of his intellect, the dark part, the shadow. That has nothing to do with animus or anima, however. But if you dream of Goethe, then he functions as an animus figure, the personification of the unconscious Dr. Goethe in you. You might express the situation in a picture of a woman on a mountain between two seas, light on one side and dark on the other, and out of the dark a great figure looms up, Goethe. This is the way it looks to your imagination. But let us go back to our diagram (page 51). The individual would be the centre of the personality. And we would represent Goethe by the small circle on the dark unconscious side. What is that man doing down there in the shadow world? He is a psychological function bringing some message from the unconscious, or carrying some intention down into the unconscious. You can ask him, and he can inform you, or you can tell him something. He is a sort of human figure to be your mediator and messenger, a function of the personality.

On the other half of the circle appears another figure. That is your persona or mask, how you like to appear to the world or how the world makes you appear. The persona also gives you information. This morning before coming here I put on my professional cloak, Dr. Jung, for the seminar. In this I appear before you and can be more or less satisfactory to you, as I please: I am partly doing what you want or expect me to do and partly what you don't want or like—that is my choice.

The personal unconscious is a layer of contents that could be conscious just as well; it is perfectly superfluous to have a personal unconscious, a sort of negligence. People should not be unaware

73

of natural facts: there is just no sense in not being aware of hunger, trouble with sex, certain relations to certain people, etc. All these things should be conscious. Nobody should imagine they are different from others, or that they are perfectly moral or aesthetic or any other illusion. Such people are incapable of realizing the impersonal unconscious, quite naturally, because they are always in the dark and therefore never aware of it until the personal unconscious disappears, that is, as long as they have wrong theories, expectations, illusions, about themselves or about the world. No one approaches the Kingdom of Heaven without having passed through the flame and been burnt through and through. The collective unconscious is the unknown in objects.

People who have no psychological criterion assume they are always the same, but this is too big a role. What we see of the individual is the persona. We are all shells here, only surfaces, and we have very dim ideas of what is inside. In doing all their small tasks, most people believe that they are their masks, and thus they become neurotic. If I should believe I was exactly what I am doing, it would be a terrible mistake, I would not fit that fellow. As soon as I say that I am only playing a role for the time being to please you, I am all right. I must know that for the time being I am playing Caesar; then later I am quite small, a mere nothing, unimportant. So this personal crust is a ready-made function from which you can withdraw, or into which you can step at will. In the morning I can say "Je suis roi," and at night "Oh, damn it all, it is all nonsense!" If people are identical with the crust, they can do nothing but live their biography, and there is nothing immortal about them; they become neurotic and the devil gets at them. Wagner was the great artist, the great creator; he was nailed to that cross. When he invited friends, they had to bring the bottles; and he had to write letters to a lady in Vienna about pink silk dressing-gowns! This persona may be a very attractive thing; if anyone chances to possess an attractive persona, he is sure to identify with it and believe he is it, and then he becomes the victim of it. Dreams often personify the persona as a most unattractive object. If I imagine I am what I appear to be, I would have a dream of a miserable scarecrow that symbolizes my persona. For we are living not only in this figure and in our relations, but also in all sorts of ordinary ways, while we eat, sleep, dress, bathe, etc. Wagner was not the great composer day and night: when occupied with his natural functions, he performed them in the general human way, in no way extraordinarily; if otherwise, it was a perversion and entirely wrong. So people who are identified with their persona are forced to do amazing things behind the screen as a compensation, to pay tribute to the lower gods.

The opposite of the persona is the anima and animus. It is exceedingly difficult to see that we have a dark side. Of course, this is merely a diagram, it is all metaphor and figurative; it is to express the fact that when you turn to the conscious world to perform any kind of activity, you will do it through the mask or persona, through that system of adaptation you have painfully built up through a lifetime. And then when you step out of this world, you withdraw and think you are alone with yourself, but the East says: "You forget the old man that is dwelling in your heart and sees everything." Then, alone, you come to the critical point, to your personal unconscious. Extraverts, and all people who are identified with their persona, hate to be alone because they begin to see themselves. Our own society is always the worst: when we are alone with ourselves things get very disagreeable. When there is much personal unconscious the collective is overburdened; the things which we should be aware of seem to press down on the collective unconscious and enhance its uncanny qualities. There is a sort of fear, a panic, which is typical of the collective unconscious: like the bush fear, a particular kind of fear which seizes you when you are alone in the bush. It is that peculiar feeling of going astray in the bush—the most terrible thing you can imagine, people go mad in no time— or you may develop the symptom of feeling yourself looked at on all sides, of eyes everywhere looking at you, eyes that you do not see. Once, in the bush in Africa, I kept turning around in a small circle for half an hour so that my back would not be turned to the eyes which I felt were watching me—and they were there, doubtless, the eyes of a leopard perhaps. When you come to that loneliness with yourself—when you are eternally alone—you are forced in upon yourself and are bound to become aware of your background. And the more there is of the personal unconscious, the more the collective unconscious forces itself upon you. If the personal unconscious is cleared up, there is no particular pressure, and you will not be terrorized; you stay alone, read, walk, smoke, and nothing happens, all is "just so," you are right with the world.

But there may still be some independent activity in the collective unconscious caused through some wrong attitude in the conscious. You are aware of your personal shortcomings, aesthetic and moral, but your conscious attitude may be somehow wrong. For example, you may know that you are not quite trustworthy and you think: "I should not be untrustworthy, I must deny it, I must leap into a redeemed condition: from today on I must be trustworthy, I shall never do that again, I am now redeemed." But it does not work and the next day you are doing the same old things. It is the typical Christian formula: From today on I shall never do this again.

An old Father of the Church was terribly bothered because certain holy men had sinned even after receiving baptism and being redeemed. He concluded the baptism hadn't been right, that something must be wrong with the ritual, and therefore people who sin again must be baptized once more, morally sterilized a second time. But again there were certain devils who sinned. So he gave them up as hopeless and decided that those were lost souls, making for hell! This is the Christian idea of jumping into the kingdom of heaven in one big leap. That is *not* true; this idea of sudden reform is wrong. You cannot jump out of your sin and cast all your burdens aside. To think like that is wrong.

The whole meaning of sin is that you carry it. What is the use of a sin if you can throw it away? If you are thoroughly aware of your sin, you must carry it, live with it, it is yourself. Otherwise you deny your brother, your shadow, the imperfect being in you that follows after and does everything which you are loath to do, all the things you are too cowardly or too decent to do. He commits the sin, and if that fellow is denied, he is pressed towards the collective unconscious and causes disturbances there. For it is against nature, you should be in contact with your shadow, you should say: "Yes, you are my brother, I must accept you." You must be nice to yourself, not say to your brother, "Raca, I have nothing to do with you!"[4] It is a mistake to deny the shadow. If you do, a reaction from the collective unconscious will loom up from the dark in the form of some personification. The pious man says to himself, "No, not that!" and pushes the shadow away and is quite satisfied. Then suddenly peculiar pictures, sexual fantasies, begin to come up into his mind from the abyss; the more pious he is the more evil are the things that befall him. He is a sort of St. Anthony, and such a

4 Cf. Matthew 5:22.

pious man would have terrible visions. Perhaps a woman comes into his mind; that is the anima coming up, usually as a nude woman, terribly natural. This is nature striking down a taboo, the revenge of the collective unconscious. The collective unconscious is real, so when an anima or animus comes up, that is real. And anyone can be the collective unconscious to anyone else; people will behave as demons would behave if they could come up out the abyss—"homo homini lupus,"[5] man is a wolf to man, the werewolf idea.

Even when you think you are alone and can do what you please, if you deny your shadow there will be a reaction from the mind that always is, from the man a million years old within you.[6] You are never alone because the eyes of the centuries watch you; you feel at once that you are in the presence of the Old Man, and you feel your historical responsibility to the centuries. As soon as you do something which is against the age-long plan, you sin against eternal laws, against average truth, and it will not fit. It is just as if you had eaten something that did not fit your digestive organs. So you cannot do what you please, think what you please, because it might hurt that awareness which has the age of a million years; in a sudden way it will react. It has many ways of reacting, and perhaps you don't feel the immediate impact, but the more you are aware of the unconscious, the more you develop your intuitive sense of law-abiding, the more you feel when you touch the line over which you should not go. If you trespass, you will get a reaction either immediately or indirectly; if you have done the wrong thing, a very powerful reaction may reach you through yourself, or you may just stumble or bang your head. You think that is merely accidental, without remembering what you have done wrong or when you have had the wrong thought.

That is simple, but there is a far more complicated way; a reaction may reach you through your fellow-beings, through waves in your surroundings. The reaction is not only in you, it is in your whole group. You may not react, but someone next to you or in your immediate surroundings, someone near and dear to you, your children perhaps, will react; but they will have done justice to you because you have trespassed. Or baffling circumstances may take

[5] Cf. Plautus, *Asinaria*, 495.
[6] Cf. "The 2,000,000-Year-Old Man" (1936), an interview in *C. G. Jung Speaking*, pp. 88ff.

over the revenge. For the collective unconscious is not a psycho-logical function in your head, it is the shadow side of the object itself. As our conscious personality is a part of the visible world, so our shadow side is a body in the collective unconscious, it is the unknown in things. So everything that possibly can gets at you through the shadow. Not all reactions reach you in the form of psychological effects but as the apparent actions of other people or circumstances.

How far these circumstances hang together is hypothesis, but the superstition of all times has claimed this hypothesis—someone has done wrong or a thing like that wouldn't happen. If there is evil circumstance, you are perfectly safe in assuming that there is a wrong somewhere. In a storm at sea, for instance, one assumes that there is a wicked man on board—the general mind blames some wicked man. It is just as if I said, "This chemical medicine won't work, but drink this draught, and you will be well," and it works. It sounds like the most old-fashioned superstition, to seek the evil-doer if the boat is sinking, but it is wise to assume that if things are going wrong someone has been trespassing; for that suits the un-conscious and makes for the smooth running of our psychology and our digestion. We can't say why, it is just a fact that it is wise to think in a way that suits the Old Man; to do otherwise might suit you or your rationalism, but it takes something out of the world.

There is a Jewish legend, beautiful and shameful, of the Evil Demon of Passion.[7] A very pious and wise old man, whom God loved because he was so good, and who had meditated much about life, understood that all the evils of mankind come from the demon of passion. So he prostrated himself before the Lord and begged him to remove the evil spirit of passion from the world, and since he was such a very pious old man, the Lord complied. And as always when he had accomplished some great deed, the pious man was very happy, and that evening as usual he went into his beautiful rose garden to enjoy the smell of the roses. The garden looked as it always had, but something was wrong, the perfume was not quite

---

[7] According to Gershom Scholem, the idea on which this legend is based is found in the Talmudic treatise *Yoma* 69 b, where it is told that at a certain time Israel succeeded in doing away with the "evil urge" (sexual drive), but after three days no fresh egg was to be found in the whole land of Israel. Scholem speculates that the source for Jung's enlargement of the idea might be a Jewish-Arab folktale in some collection unknown to him. (Personal communication.)

the same, something was missing, some substance was lacking, like a bread with no salt. He thought he might be tired, so he took his golden cup and filled it with some wonderful old wine which he had in his cellar and which had never failed before. But this time the taste was flat. Then this wise man had in his harem a very beautiful young wife, and his last test was that when he kissed her she was like the wine and the perfume, flat! So up to the roof he went again and told the Lord how sad he was, and that he was afraid he had made a mistake in asking to have the spirit of passion taken away, and he begged him: "Couldn't you send back the Evil Spirit of Passion?" And as he was a very pious man God did what he asked. Then he tested it all again, and marvellously enough, it was not flat at all—the roses had a wonderful perfume, the wine was delicious, and his wife's kiss was sweeter than it had ever been!

That story should tell you that you take something out of the world when you trespass against the eternal laws of the Old Man, whether reasonable or not. The world and our existence is absolutely irrational, and you never can prove that it ought to be rational. You are perfectly safe in assuming there are certain rational considerations which we ought to reckon with; the Alps are in the centre of Europe and we must reckon with this fact—since they hinder traffic we must tunnel them. And so our psychology is subject to certain laws which are *irrational*, the Alps in the centre of our psychological continent, and we have to settle down to that fact. Otherwise the evil spirit world disappears. It is wise, it is vital that we are convinced of certain irrational facts. The criterion for psychological truth in general is that we submit what we think to the very Old Man; if he agrees we are probably on the right road and not very far from truth. But if the Old Man should disagree, we know we are on an errand of our own and we run big risks. We can experiment, there is no objection to trying it; if you prefer to walk on your hands, then do it!

Question: What happens when the anima returns to the unconscious?

Dr. Jung: The anima acts as a filter: she gives certain effects, as she can receive certain effects. Through the persona we get certain effects and we also produce certain effects on other people, and we must assume it is the same with the anima. There are reasons, merely empirical, for this statement. The anima knows many things

79

which most people are unaware of. In Rider Haggard's *She*[8] you
see how the anima from the collective unconscious knows all the
secrets which She transmits to Leo and Holly, the man and his
shadow. In the first part of the book, we see how She can work
upon her secret world; in the second part Isis is always looming
up behind. By having the ear of Isis as her priestess, She may have
influence upon Isis and receive also an influence from her. It is a
psychological fact that the anima is able to influence us in our
psychology—just as we pray to Mary or ask the intercession of the
saints with the deity. Saints are helpful anima figures on the way
to the deity, helpers in a state of need against special disturbances
or evils of mankind. And they have their special districts. The anima
is a sort of intercessor between Isis and the man in *She*.

You see something similar in your psychology when you understand the anima as a peculiar feeling reaction inside. Suppose you
get disgusted on the world side and fix yourself into this scheme,
you draw near and approach the other side: then you get a peculiar
feeling reaction within, and that is the anima. An old Chinese text
says that when a man wakes up in the morning heavy and in a bad
mood, that is his feminine soul, his anima—a peculiar mood which
has an influence on him, and on his dark side, the unconscious, as
well. This is proved by the results of that mood. This morning, say,
I have been down in the collective unconscious, and then I crept
up 365 steps and arrived on the threshold and stepped into my
house, into the conscious, where I find my mask, Dr. Jung, all ready,
just as in Mme Tussaud's.[9] If I got something very disagreeable in
the collective unconscious, I curse and bring with me a very bad
mood. Then I affect you with a bad mood, and you affect me, and
I am disgusted and go back and affect the collective unconscious
with my mood. And it will react with a series of peculiar images,
which you will surely get if you allow your creative fantasy to play
on it. It may create a nocturnal scene, a wild, vast, stormy sea, such
as a poet would create. These images may become very specific and
go much further if you put yourself in the scene: now where am
I, in what condition? You may see yourself in a boat tossed about

[8] Jung often cited the eponymous figure of H. Rider Haggard's novel *She* (1887)
as an example of the anima. The earliest citation appears to have been in the original
version of "Mind and Earth" (1927), CW 10, par. 75.
[9] The famous wax museum in London.

by the waves in the midst of that sea, and then you get the impact of the unconscious and realize all the other pictures.

From these fantasies you can see what your mood has produced in the collective unconscious; they tell you much about the nature of the collective unconscious and how this whole thing functions. You study the influence of your mood on the background of your conscious mind by the effects that come back to you, as you can study the influence of your persona on the outside world from the reaction of the crowd. There are many who only learn about themselves from the reactions of others, by somebody knocking them between the eyes. A man comes to me and complains bitterly, "He said so and so"—while as a matter of fact the man himself has said something which brought about this answer, as one finds out by asking what he did to produce that effect. People must see the effects to know what their persona really is. And if you want to know what the anima is, that is the way: get at the contents of a mood, see the pictures that come back from the unconscious. Some moods are real and necessary. But if they are unaccountable and too strong and irrational (the Scotch say, "A shadow fell on me out of a blue sky"), it means that certain unconscious contents have been constellated; and if you go into that mood with fantasy, the collective unconscious will produce a series of peculiar pictures or images which explain the state you are in. Some Eastern religions try to organize in religious ritual a substitute for the living thing—for that process in the collective unconscious.

WINTER TERM

Second Part: January / March 1929

LECTURE I

23 January 1929

Dr. Jung:

We are going to continue the series of dreams we began in our last seminar, for you will get a better impression of how dreams are analysed if we follow a series of dreams of the same patient.

I have noticed that there are certain prejudices in regard to analysis which I should like to speak about before we go on. One of the most important things to consider is the age of the individual; that should make a tremendous difference in our attitude when we analyse. Everything that is important in the latter part of life may be utterly negligible in the early part of life. The next consideration should be whether the individual has accomplished an adaptation to life, whether he is above or below the standard level of life and whether he has fulfilled the reasonable expectations. At forty, one should have roots, a position, family, etc. and not be psychologically adrift. People who have no objective at forty, who have not married, who are not established in life, have the psychology of the nomad, in no man's land. Such people have a different goal from those firmly established in homes and families, for that task is still to be accomplished. The question to be asked is, is the individual normally adapted or not? The young are unadapted because they are too young, others for various reasons; because they have met obstacles, resistances, or through lack of opportunity. Things must change in the one case which must not change in the other. Certain forms of fantasy may be the worst poison for the person who is not reasonably adapted. But when you find germs of imagination in a man who is firmly rooted, perhaps imprisoned, in his environment, they should be treated as the most valuable material, as jewels or germs of liberation, for out of this material he can win his freedom. All young people have fantasies, but they must be interpreted differently. They are often beautiful, but for the most part of a negative importance, and unless young people are very carefully handled they get stuck in their fantasies. If you open the door of symbolism to them they may live it instead of real life.

A young girl who came to see me a few days ago is engaged to be married, is in love with the man as the man is with her. She has been analysing for four years, five days a week, and has had only three weeks of vacation in the year. I asked her why the devil she didn't marry. She answered me that she must finish her analysis, that it was an obligation which she must discharge first. I said to her, "Who told you that you had an obligation to analysis? Your obligation is to life!" That girl is a victim of analysis. Her doctor is also stuck. This is a case where the girl is living in her fantasies, while life is waiting for her. The girl is caught by her animus. Even should she do something foolish, it would nevertheless push her into life. As it is, the result is confusion, air, nothing. Her analyst follows a theory, and the girl makes a job of analysis instead of life. If she were a woman in the second half of life the treatment should be altogether different, that of building up the individual. I do not question that doctor's motives, but by contrast I am a brute in the way I treat my patients. I see them only two or three times a week and I have five months of vacation during the year!

I will briefly go over the case we are following. The dreamer is forty-seven, not neurotic, is a big merchant, very conventional and correct, a highly intellectual and cultured man. He is married and has children. His trouble is that he is too much adapted, he is entirely chained by his environment, by obligation to his world. He has lost his freedom. So in his case if there is any trace of imagination it must be cherished. He has sacrificed all creative imagination in order to be "real," so fantasies in his case are extremely valuable. Now his problem is very subtle. Consciously he could not see what it was. He has had some erotic adventures with women, not satisfactory; then he slowly discovered that he felt there must be something more to life. He began to read theosophy, and he had read some psychoanalysis, and then he came to me to see if I could help him, I have seen him for two years off and on. From the analysis of his first dream he discovered that he was terribly bored with life in general and with his wife in particular. The second dream was four days later and dreamed on the basis of his knowledge of the first dream.

Here is the dream [2]: "My wife asks me to come with her to pay a call on a poor young woman, a tailoress. She lives and works in an unhealthy hole, she is suffering from T.B. I go there and say to the girl that she should not work inside, she should work in the open. I tell her that she could work in my garden—but she says she has no machine. I tell her that she can have my wife's machine."

The dreamer has the impression of having forgotten important parts of the dream. In his associations he says "in spite of the fact that there is nothing erotic in the dream I felt that it had that atmosphere. When my wife asked me to pay the visit I felt that something might happen." You can see that same look of expectation on the faces of men sitting in the lobby of a hotel, the look of a dog who might have a sausage dropped on his nose. So the dreamer had the expectation that something might happen. "My wife played a completely passive role but I apparently acted as though I were quite alone. She [the tailoress] was dressed in dark colours, and I remembered that someone had told me that people who had T.B. were often erotic. When people have unused libido the erotic comes up. The sewing-machine belongs to my wife, and I had the feeling that she should say the first word."

He associates his own imprisoned life with the girl's life. He cannot allow his feelings to work in the open—the only thing to do is to have the girl work in his own garden with his wife's sewing-machine. The feelings of a respectable man cannot work in the open, hence "in his own garden" means pressing his feelings back into his marriage. One of his motives for respectability is the fear that his health might be affected by venereal disease. The result of the analysis of the first dream is that he can admit his boredom in his marriage. It is very difficult for a rational man to admit what his Eros really is. A woman has no special difficulty in realizing her Eros principle of relatedness, but it is exceedingly difficult for a man for whom Logos is the principle. Woman has difficulty in realizing what her mind is. The Eros in man is inferior, as is the Logos in woman. A man must have a fair amount of the feminine in him to realize his relatedness. Eros is the job of the woman. You can fight with a man half a year before he will admit his feelings, and the same with a woman and her mind. It is so contradictory. My mother had a split mind, and from her I learned the natural mind of woman. I was an awful boy and I hated all the nicely behaved boys whom my mother liked, with nice clean clothes, clean hands, etc. Whenever I got a chance I used to beat those boys up and play tricks on them; to me they were disgusting. "Such nice children," my mother would say, "and so well brought up." A family in the neighbourhood had such children and my mother was always holding them up to me as examples. One day when 1 had done something particularly outrageous to these nice children my mother scolded me and said that I would spoil her life if I went on like that. I was deeply depressed and went off and sat down by myself in the corner of the room. My mother forgot that I was there and began talking to herself; I heard her say, "Of course one should not have kept that litter," and I was instantly reconciled to my mother.[1]

Woman has two minds, the traditional, conventional mind, and Nature's ruthless and sensible mind which says the truth. She can think on both sides. This is illustrated very beautifully in *Penguin Island*, by Anatole France. When baptism was administered to the penguins the dispute arose whether it was not a blasphemous thing to do, because the penguins have no souls. They are only birds, and birds could not have immortal souls because souls belong only to human beings. The dispute waxed so hot that finally a Council of the Fathers of the Church and the Wise Men was called in Heaven. Unable to settle the question, they called upon St. Catherine. She paid compliments to both sides and said, "It is true that penguins, being animals, cannot have immortal souls; but it is equally true that through baptism one attains immortality, therefore," she said to God, "Donnez leur une âme mais une petite."[2]

Woman, to a certain extent, is Nature and Nature is terrible, inconsistent and logical at the same time. Naturally when a man looks at his Eros side he finds it hard to reconcile with what he has been taught. His Eros has opposite ideas, conflicting tendencies. Yet there is his relation with Nature and it bewilders him. He *feels* the awful thing which woman *thinks*.

It was a great achievement that the dreamer was able to admit his boredom. He is lonely with his problem. All people feel that taboo of the natural mind. Of course the dreamer keeps all this from his wife. The dream soothes him, we might conclude, but

[1] Jung describes this episode in *MDR*, pp. 49/58f. His mother was alluding to the "nice children."

[2] *Penguin Island*, tr. E. W. Evans (1948), p. 30. Cf. *Mysterium Coniunctionis*, CW 14, par. 227.

that is not true. It is not a benevolent thing saying something consoling, for kindness is not natural. Kindness and cruelty are human categories, but not nature's way. When the dream says, "My wife asked me to go to see the girl," it mitigates the man's trouble. If the man can feel that his wife is not against him, it begins to make him feel less lonely. We must assume that this dream has constellated an attitude as there is no satisfactory way of reaching the real truth about it.

What is the wife in the dream? The girl represents his feelings which go abroad, the wife the feeling at home, the respectable feeling. The interpretation is "my feelings, which are with my wife, have an interest in trying to deal with those other feelings." Actually his wife has no interest in those feelings towards other women, but the dream says it will make his feeling towards his wife more individual, more real if he deals with these. He has perhaps been thinking of his wife in a rigid and inflexible way because he has done a similar injustice to his feelings. If he can learn to deal with his feelings that go abroad, which are creative feelings, his relation towards his wife becomes living, because doubtful. Doubt is the crown of life because truth and error come together. Doubt is living, truth is sometimes death and stagnation. When you are in doubt you have the greatest chance to unite the dark and light sides of life. As soon as he begins to deal with feelings abroad, relationship with his wife becomes doubtful and experimental and alive. The dream has not the intention of helping him, but it does call his attention to the fact that his relation to his wife will be benefited by a new feeling relationship on his part.

When a woman is brought up to think only certain things, she cannot think at all. You cannot bring anyone up to function only in certain ways. If you hinder anyone's feeling or thinking, he will not function properly any more. If you are bound to believe a certain dogma you cannot think about it. Feeling, just as any other function, must have space. The dreamer's relation to his wife will suffer from the fact that he is not allowed to feel. If he can deal with his feelings which go out, he can have a relation with his wife. "Don't doubt" is a great mistake. We have arrived now at the understanding of the fact that dealing with his unconventional feelings will help him with his relation to his wife.

When he pays attention to his feelings, he finds them associated with a girl who is infected with a serious illness. Feelings and thoughts can grow sick and die.

A few days ago a woman came to me for a consultation. She had been a patient of mine fifteen years ago. She was a difficult case because she would not see certain things, she would not play the game, she wanted to remain a child. Certain people cannot take life seriously, as if they were born to be eternal children. If a case comes to me with diabetes and the patient will not pay attention to his symptoms or take my advice, there is nothing I can do. A few days ago I saw my old patient again. She looked awful and I was shocked. She saw it and said, "Yes, it's very bad, but I have no problem any more." She wanted me to tell her husband that she was no longer hysterical, and it was true she had no problems, no troubles; she had sucked them in, converted them into her body. In such cases the heart races for psychological reasons, and the result is a neurosis comparable to a shell-shock. One jumps at everything and has no control of action. When problems are converted into body, outer problems go, but the body rots. If the neurosis has gone deeply into the psychological[3] processes a tremendous scourge is necessary, perhaps a risk of life itself. Generally a trap-door shuts down for ever. Heraclitus, the Dark One, the most intelligent of the old philosophers, said, "It is death to the soul to become water."[4] It is death to the soul to become unconscious. People die before there is death of the body, because there is death in the soul. They are mask-like leeches, walking about like spectres, dead but sucking. It is a sort of death. I have seen a man who has converted his mind into a pulp. You can succeed in going away from your problems, you need only to look away from them long enough. You may escape, but it is the death of the soul. If our dreamer does not pay attention to his feeling problem, he loses his soul. Go into the lobby of a hotel—there you will see faces with masks. These dead people are often travelling on the wing, to escape problems; they look hunted and wear a complete mask of fear. Some time ago I met a woman who was on her third trip around the world. When I asked her what she was doing it for,

---

[3] Transcript error for "physiological"?

[4] Frag. 68 in John Burnet, *Early Greek Philosophy* (4th edn., 1930), p. 138: "For souls it is death to become water, for water death to become earth. But from earth comes water, and from water, soul." (Cited in *Psychological Types*, CW 6, par. 708, def. of "Enantiodromia.")

she seemed surprised at my question and answered, "Why, I am going to finish my trip. What else should I do?" Another woman I saw in Africa in a Ford car. She was fleeing from herself with flickering eyes full of fear. She wanted to confess to me, to tell me how she had given up her life. She had only the memory of herself as she used to be. She was hunting what she had lost. When you see that a certain spark of life has gone from the eye, the physical functioning of the body somewhere has gone wrong.

The girl in the dream is a tailoress, meaning a maker of clothes; the maker of new attitudes. The birth of a new attitude has a long historical background. There is a Negro myth which tells of a time when all were immortal and everyone could take his skin off. One day they were all bathing and an old woman lost her skin; she died, and that is how death came into the world. By analogy, people must behave like snakes, casting the old garments aside. In Catholic confirmation, the young girls wear white clothes. In Africa I have seen the boys who have been circumcised in the initiation cere- monies wearing a bamboo hut, entirely covering their bodies. This is the new spiritual skin, a spiritual clothing. The Polynesians put on a mask to denote the spring renewal. During Carnival one puts on the garment of the new year. You are reborn in the new year. — It is most flattering to the analyst to be called a tailor. When he is dreamed of as the tailor he is the maker of the new body, the new skin; he is the initiator of a new immortality. — The unconscious feelings of the patient which have been going abroad and which have been repudiated contain the possibility of new birth. That unconventional feeling, the tailor girl, is the maker of a new skin, the creator of immortality. If he goes the way of that new feeling, new life will be given him.

Everything you do and repeat often enough becomes dead, worn out. Women beyond the age of forty begin to realize their mas- culinity, and men their femininity, because it is new and untried. There is an Indian myth of a chief having Manitou appear to him and bidding him eat with the women, sit with the women, and dress like the women—a curious psychological intuition. In some places, in Spain for instance, the old women have strong black beards of which they are very proud. Women's voices sometimes get deeper. We often see here, among the peasants as they grow older, that the man loses his grip on things and the woman gets on the job. She will open a small shop and earn the living. Man becomes woman and woman becomes man. The thing that has not been considered, the thing that has been despised—that will be the birthplace of the Saviour. Therefore the feeling, which is the most awkward to him, contains the making of a new attitude.

There are two machines, two methods. One the girl's, the other the wife's. The machine is a psychological factor, a mental machine which one can learn to use and by which you produce results. The machine is method. With a method you follow a certain way, a definite way. Now we can see deeper into the dream. The girl says "I have my own way." He offers the method of his wife. How is the new method produced? Sewing is fastening things together. The method must aim to fasten together, to join that which has been separated. That which should be joined together in the man, psychologically, is the conscious and the unconscious. Analysis fastens them together—and that is integration.

LECTURE II

30 January 1929

Dr. Jung:

You remember that we left off last time with the sewing-machine.

Mr. Gibb's question: "Last week you interpreted the symbol "sew-ing-machine" as "method." May we not go farther and particularize the method from this symbol? Cinderella got a ball-dress including slippers, and the method was a movement of the wand of a fairy. For the purposes of a dream, a charm, a cheque-book, a thread and needle and scissors, or a fairy with a wand could all have symbolized a method of producing a new suit of clothes, just as effectively as the sewing-machine, but would there not have been a significant difference in the principle involved in each case?

My point is, are we not justified in assuming that dream material has a sort of logic of its own, provided we accept completely the premises its symbols suggest and refrain from projecting into it our own obsession in favour of some particular premise or prin-ciple? In the dream in question, the symbol *sewing-machine* suggests to me that we should accept a rather mechanical cause and effect atmosphere, so far as the element of it is concerned."

Dr. Jung: The very nature of the machine suggests a very particular kind of method. This is where I differ from Freud. You cannot say the symbol in a dream is merely a façade behind which you can hide and then say what the dream is. The symbol is a fact, as in this dream it is a sewing-machine, and we can only go on with the dream by understanding what the sewing-machine means. We cannot merely say that the sewing-machine means a method of getting new clothes, for you can get new clothes in a number of ways: in a mystical way, a magical way, etc. The point of the sewing-machine method would mean a mechanical way, purely of cause and effect, a soulless way. You get the idea of what this mechanical way can be by studying the patient's associations. A symbol in a

93

dream is meant to be what it is. When a doctor analyses urine and finds sugar he cannot say it is only a façade, so we must follow the way Mr. Gibb has pointed out.

We have not exhausted the meaning of the sewing-machine. I would particularly point out that the sewing-machine is a mechanical thing. In his associations the dreamer says, "Could it be that the girl, who is infected with T.B., represents my sick feelings, that they must live in a dark hole? I had the feeling that the sewing-machine really belonged to my wife and that she should say the first word." With this association what does the sewing-machine mean?

Answer: An anatomical relation, sexual only.

Dr. Jung: He understands the method as purely mechanical, and that is the way he looks at sex. This is the source of the eternal misconception between man and woman. For most men the idea of sexuality is purely mechanical and unpsychological, while with women it is associated with feeling.

Mr. Gibb: What prompted that question was that you so often speak of dream material as irrational and now you say it is rational.

Dr. Jung: There are certain irrational things which must be accepted as facts, as for instance that water reaches its greatest density at $4°C$. That is irrational, but it is a fact.

The dreamer asked me how he should take this material and I told him to accept these things as facts; that this is the way things are. And I said, "I don't know whether your devil or your good angel has suggested this; we must just wait and see how it works out. I admit that it would be very awkward for you to fall in love with this girl and upset your marriage, but you are immensely attracted to the idea of getting your feelings out into the open. You must be patient and wait and see." The role of saviour to this poor thing shut up in a dark hole appeals to him immensely. Few men could resist this role.

Freud's idea is that the dream is rational. I say that it is irrational, that it just happens. A dream walks in like an animal. I may be sitting in the woods and a deer appears. It is Freud's idea that dreams are prearranged, which I do not agree with.

The general meaning of this dream is a continuation of what we have been working on. The patient's feelings do not permit him to come out into the open. As the sewing-machine belongs to his wife, the sex mechanism belongs to his wife. He got a tremendous

94

kick out of this dream, although he is confronted with the fact that it would be awkward for him to be in love with the girl.

Mrs. Schevill: Three ladies would like to know more about the natural mind of women.

Dr. Jung: I gave you an example last time, about my mother— without sparing myself. You can ask yourselves this question. I am sure that you have something behind this question in your black souls. Natural mind is a thing you never see on the surface, for every woman is afraid of that kind of mind, just as a man is afraid to admit his feelings.

Mrs. Gibb: What can you do about it, can you educate it?

Dr. Jung: No, you must just accept that it is there and have no illusions about it. If you try to educate it you fall into it. It cannot be touched, it is a live wire.

A man will admit every kind of sinful thinking but not feeling, and a woman cannot admit thoughts. You get a very good example of this in Wells' *Christina Alberta's Father.*[1] There the girl is doing all sorts of nonsensical things during the day, and in the evening she holds a court of conscience which tells her just what she has been doing during the day. This is inexorable thinking, she cannot get away from it. You must accept the fact that there is such a dissociation in your minds. The only thing you can do with the natural mind is to accept it. We all want to have one God, we all want to have one soul, etc., we all want to escape the duality of life, the contrast, the dissociation in our nature, but we cannot. On one side you are what you appear to be, perfectly innocent, on the other side there is the natural thinking. Young people are quite right to jump away from it; but for older people, it is very important that they should know that they themselves, the world, etc., are ambiguous. It is the beginning of wisdom to doubt. It is important that they begin to doubt the value of existence, so that they can disentangle themselves from the world. Young people cannot live in doubt. If one has profound doubts of life one cannot get into the world, but a mature man should have more detachment from the world. This is perfectly normal when one has passed the middle

[1] According to E. A. Bennet (*What Jung Really Said*, London, 1966, p. 93), this novel of H. G. Wells (1925) originated in a conversation between Jung and Wells. Jung discussed it at length in *Two Essays*, CW 7, pars. 270ff. (i.e., the 2nd edn., 1935, of "The Relations between the Ego and the Unconscious").

of life. If a man loses his grasp earlier in life he goes to pieces, and if he does not attain a new attitude later he becomes a nuisance.

Dr. Shaw: Is the natural mind type of thinking animus thinking?

Dr. Jung: A woman gets that type of thinking through the animus, but if she accepts it, she is herself and so depotentiates the animus. The animus of a woman is always powerful at the expense of the extension of her mind. As her mind expands the animus grows less powerful, so that as a woman gets conscious she should no longer see that kind of thinking with a doubt, for she is thinking in a perfectly normal way. As soon as she has depotentiated these things they lose their power, they belong to the veil of Maya.

If you could put yourselves back into the primitive world there would be so much outside of yourselves and so little inside that anything could happen, all the world would begin to act in a queer way, trees to talk, animals to do strange things, ghosts to appear. Now, increase your consciousness and these phenomena will all vanish, they were only expressing to you what you yourself thought. The trees will no longer talk, and no ghosts will walk.

This is the progress of man, that he depotentiates the outside world; the last remnant is the idea of an absolute God, or such figures as the anima and animus. The more you increase your consciousness the less these things exist. This is what the East says. They came to it from a continuity of the experience of living, I came to it through psychology. People often reproach me with materialism. This is not materialism at all, it simply advances the importance of what we call the psyche. We have not the faintest idea what the psyche is, we have not the faintest idea what we are, We do not know, and it is childish to say that we do.

Mrs. Schevill: But you have not given us more examples of the natural mind. We all admit that we have examples we might give but they are too personal to talk about.

Dr. Jung: That's just it. You never can get a woman to express her real thoughts, just as you can never get a man to tell his real feelings. To give examples of these things is always going to the core. I have a great many but they are very personal. They would concern you or someone whom you know and that would never do. The natural mind is a very immediate thing and goes right to the core. Often the son gets his first idea of the natural mind from his mother. I could give you another aspect of the natural mind;

96

if the boy is strong and full of the devil he can resist it, but if not then he may be crushed by it—poisoned.

Mothers are capable of injuring their sons by letting loose their natural minds. When I was a little boy my father was a clergyman in a city which is famous for its narrow-mindedness. If I had lived on in that set I should have been completely suffocated. People were living in the actual rooms where their ancestors had lived for hundreds of years, with portraits of them hanging on the walls, by Dürer and Holbein. One of my best friends had a library which dated from 1680 to 1790, a library that simply remained as it was, nothing new was ever added to it. The whole atmosphere of this life was tremendously captivating. The natural mind says that a boy can never get out of it. Of course I had to create my whole life anew, I had to work it out.

At a very critical moment in my life, when I was working very hard, my mother came to see me. My mother loved me very much and tried to help me, but she could undermine me with her natural mind. I had been working very hard on my association tests and my walls were covered with charts, when my mother came unexpectedly to visit me. She looked all around my walls and said, "Do those things really mean anything?" What she said was thin as air but it fell on me heavier than tons of lead. I did not touch a pen for three days. If I had been a weak boy I would have been crushed and said, "Of course, it is no good," and given up. My mother would have said that she loved me and meant nothing by it, but man is a civilized being and his greatest danger is nature. Many men remain nice spectres painted on the wall, the devils in them are all killed; the mother has eaten them with her natural mind. A good mother would not use her natural mind on her son, as a good father would not use his natural feeling on his daughter. Well, I had a terrific fit of anger and then I could work again.

The next dream [3] follows. The patient says: "It is as if I were seeing a sort of steamroller from a point above. The machine is going and is apparently making a road, forming a particular pattern like a labyrinth." And in the dream he thinks, "That is my analysis"; and then he is in the picture which he has looked at from above. He is standing at the bifurcation of the road in a wood, and he does not know which way to go. At first he did not pay much attention to the arabesque the machine was making.

The patient's association with his *position above* is that one can see things more in their true relation, less personally, while when one is closer the machine dominates.

About the *road machine* he says: "I have read in a technical paper that with these machines one can make a macadam road in a relatively short time."

The *arabesque* association is: "There is no sense in building roads that lead nowhere." (I reply that the particular design these roads make may lead somewhere.) He says, "This design looks like a puzzle. Perhaps if one has the necessary patience one can find the goal, perhaps it means I must have patience if I want to get anywhere with my analysis. The bifurcation of the road might come from the conversation about the preceding dream. The doctor said to me there is no compulsion to go through analysis if the problem seems too difficult." Apparently I had told him that he should think about whether he felt a resistance and whether he wished to go on.

He associates *in a wood* with Dante's *Divine Comedy*.[2] This is a well-known symbol of the Middle Ages, and it means the descent into the unconscious. Dante loses his way then finds the descent into

---

[2] The *Divine Comedy* opens: "Nel mezzo del cammin di nostra vita / mi ritrovai per una selva oscura, / che la diritta via era smarrita." ("Midway in the journey of our life I found myself in a dark wood, for the straight way was lost."—Tr. C. S. Singleton, 1970).

the unconscious. The patient thinks also of another old story, dating about 1450, of the monk who lost his way in the Black Forest and a wolf becomes his guide to the Lower World.

One thing is quite conspicuous, the motive of the "machine" is on his mind. When a subsequent dream takes up the problem of a previous dream it means that the analysis of the previous dream has not been exhaustive. His problem is a sex one. When a man comes to something urgent it is always expressed by sex. The unconscious says, "What about sexuality now?" so the problem is not finished. A man has to deal with his active urgent type of sexuality. In a woman it is not so; it only becomes so in the second half of life; in the beginning it is not so. With a man sexuality becomes the symbol for the urge of what has to be.

The fact that he is placed high above the machine means he could be less personal, less difficult. He could see himself and his problem more impersonally as Mr. and Mrs. Ant who are having some dispute about ant sexuality and Mr. Ant's interest in another ant, and then he can look at it easily. Even a steamroller looks smaller when you look down from an airplane; everything is Lilliputian. When you are high up you are no longer under the power of the steamroller, you see the road, the way in; when you are near you see the power of the machine, the dirt and the noise and the fuss, but you cannot see what the roller is doing. But from above you see a symmetrical pattern. In a dream a pattern always makes sense of a sort. He says, "It is very interesting to see that the apparently meaningless pattern is a labyrinth." That is what he must get into his mind—once in there is no way out. That is why he is avoiding it. Of course, no one wants to get into a place where there is no way out, but that is just what he must see. If he is going to go into analysis he must see that he must go through that way. There is no escape from himself. He is getting into something from which there is no escape. He thinks, "That is analysis." In the next part of the dream he is at the parting of the roads. Shall he go on? He notices that he is in a wood, like the *Divine Comedy*. That is the divine comedy of Man.

In the drawing of the pattern the road may begin anywhere, and he noticed at the end that he was no longer on the road made by the steamroller, but on a spiral foot-path. The whole plan is symmetrical: outside are very bewildering roads, but presenting an unmistakable pattern, and inside is a spiral made by his own feet.

The pattern is nearly square and consists of symbols, yonic and phallic symbols meaning the productive, generative power of nature, the Yang and Yin power, male and female. There is also a peculiar rhythm in the design, in and out, approaching the centre and leaving it again, such a pattern as people would make in dancing, if you marked it out on the floor. Do you remember the pattern of throwing the ball back and forth, associated with a previous dream? We get some valuable contributions to the idea of patterns, the unconscious source of them, and what the machine is meant for. One of the fundamental laws of natural development is that it moves in a spiral, and the true law of nature is always reached after the labyrinth has been travelled. The man who discovered the mathematics of the spiral lived in my town. On his tombstone is engraved: "Always changing in the same way, yet I arise."[3]

Psychologically you develop in a spiral, you always come over the same point where you have been before, but it is never exactly the same, it is either above or below. A patient will say, "I am just at the place where I was three years ago," but I say, "At least you have travelled three years." What we are concerned with is the pattern. The idea that it suggests is that the road made by the steamroller has a goal in itself—it leads to the spiral. Some day the spiral will branch off and reach its own goal. The "way" the steamroller makes is in and out, suggesting the function of the male and female, but I think we are perfectly justified in letting the sex go and thinking of this as the rhythm of life, as active and passive phases, heights and depths.

In the Gilgamesh myth,[4] the idea of the Perfect Man, the Complete Man, is that two-thirds of man is divine and one-third human.

[3] Jung grew up in a suburb of Basel and was a student at Basel University. The discoverer of the mathematics of the spiral was Jacob Bernoulli (1654-1705), of a famous Basel family, who requested that the spiral be engraved on his tombstone with the words "Eadem mutata resurgo" (translated above). Bernoulli's wishes were followed, on his grave slab in Basel cathedral. (*Die Kunstdenkmäler des Kantons Basel-Stadt*, III [1941], pp. 261f.) Cf. *Psychology and Alchemy*, CW 12, par. 325 (as in 1936 version).

[4] The Babylonian epic of the hero Gilgamesh was found on tablets at Nineveh, in modern Iraq, and has been dated to the second millennium B.C. Jung made frequent reference to the Gilgamesh epic in the 1912 version of *Symbols of Transformation*; see CW 5, index, s.v., and summary in "The Tavistock Lectures" (1935), CW 18, pars. 235ff. The epic was translated into verse by Herbert Mason (1970), among others.

He is the man of woe and joy, the one who makes the two movements, high above and deep below. Gilgamesh is shown in greatest joy and deepest despair, rising to the greatest heights and descending to the lowest depths. The idea of the complete life is the enormous swing from high to low, from low to high; from extraversion to introversion and vice versa. If life does not contain the pairs of opposites, it is just a straight line. It is just as if you did not breathe, it is just as though you did not live. When life is lived as rhythm, diastole and systole, then it is a whole, it is approaching completion. So when the dreamer looks at himself in a three-dimensional (temporal) way, it is in and out, but if he sees himself *sub specie aeternitatis*, then he is suspended in the water of life, breathing back and forth as a cell.

When the steamroller, the rhythmic quality of life, has fulfilled its duty, this particular movement of in and out can branch off and become a spiral. In that inner sphere the man can give up moving back and forth and the rhythm is then like the life of a plant. This pattern suggests something exceedingly meaningful, and it is surely most significant that the dream says, "Here you are in the mythological situation of the hero, like Hercules. You are in the wood of the *Divine Comedy*." Remember how Dante swung from heaven to hell, from hell to heaven.

Dreams are very marvellous. They stop just where a great artist would leave the drama. The great question of fate has been put to this man—are you a hero? Which way are you going to take? We must wait for the man's answer.

Mr. Gibb: Isn't he already lost in the wood?

Dr. Jung: Well, he could run away. Do you think he will run away?

Mr. Roper: The roads in the outer designs intermingle continuously—and never cross.

Dr. Jung: Well, we have not exhausted all the possibilities. There are at least two melodies. A second line is weaving through which has far less swing; the one is larger, the other smaller. I do not know exactly what that hints at. If I am right in the assumption that it means the rhythm of life, there is a wave-length of different amplitude. We have two amplitudes. — Man can live in an active or a passive way, in a masculine or feminine way. A man may be knocked by fate in some way, and be completely changed and become female, for he has a female wave-length as well. The mas-

culine amplitude is more excessive. In a woman it is less excessive. — A woman less often flies off the handle, or loses herself in
the world. When she does she loses herself altogether, but she rarely
does. A man must be able to get out into the world with its greater
risks in order to adapt. Women often get the shock of their lives
when they see how their husbands act in their business lives.

6 February 1929

Dr. Jung:

I want to call your attention again to the patient's drawing, because it is very important in his analysis. It is the first intimation of the whole course and purpose of analysis. While I cannot go into every detail of the design I can give you some general ideas about it. There are two interwoven courses. At a place where they meet another line starts, forming a spiral, which ends in the centre of the design. The patient calls this a labyrinth and thinks the irrational path of the steamroller is like the course of analysis. He has a sense of relief because he feels less confused about all the material which comes up in dreams. The first dreams often do this. He had had an idea about analysis [a wrong one]—that it was trying to get down to some root complex and then you could pull up that root. His idea didn't fit in with the analysis, so he was confused, and his feeling of confusion in the dream was expressed in the drawing. This pattern of lines which makes a labyrinth leads to no goal. It is just a criss-cross of irrational lines interwoven with no end. I called his attention to the symmetry of the design, but he had no idea to what it referred. If I had shown that design to an Eastern philosopher, he would have said, "Oh yes, we know all about that, it is a mandala." We in the West have no conception of such figures. We might call it a magic circle. There are a few examples in Western Europe. There is one specimen in the British Museum from an English collection, and Prof. Wilhelm has shown me one recently from a Taoist monastery.[1] When you analyse this

---

[1] The word *mandala*, Sanskrit for "magic circle," has been widely applied in Jungian terminology to circular figures of whatever provenience. Cf. 13 Feb. 1929, at n. 8. / Richard Wilhelm (1873-1930), German theologian, formerly a missionary in China, translated several Chinese classics, most importantly the *I Ching* (see below, n. 8). At this time Wilhelm was director of the China Institute, in Frankfurt a. M.

figure you see that it consists of four divisions; often the centre is a square with a circle inside and the four divisions may be subdivided making eight or more. An Eastern mandala is used for meditation. What we understand by meditation is a very different thing. For instance, there are Loyola's exercises in the Catholic Church.[2] People meditate on certain prescribed subjects, and a dogmatic image helps the mind to concentrate towards a certain goal.

Mandalas are not unknown in the West. A frequent form is the mandala with Christ in the centre and the evangelists in the four corners—the angel, eagle, ox, and lion, arranged like the four sons of Horus.[3] The myth of Horus has played an extraordinary role, and has not yet been fully explained. In the myth Horus gave his eye to his father who had become blind from having seen the evil one. Horus gave his eye to restore the light of day, to restore his father's sight; so he plays the rôle of a saviour.[4] The eye is also a mandala.

In Norman art there are manuscripts with mandalas; there is one in the treasury of the cathedral of Cologne dated about 1150. There is a Mexican mandala, the famous Calendar Stone,[5] which has a face in the centre with four tower-like forms grouped about it. The whole is surrounded by a circle and the calendar reckonings are in the intersections of the circle.

The design of the dreamer indicates the way in which his analysis will continue, and at the same time it is a means to concentrate him. When a Taoist priest meditates on a mandala and gradually

---

In late 1929, he published *Das Geheimnis der goldenen Blüte* (tr. Cary F. Baynes: *The Secret of the Golden Flower*, 1931; rev. edn., 1962), with a commentary by Jung and illustrations of mandalas (commentary and illustrations in CW 13). The "mandala from a Taoist monastery" Jung mentions is probably the one reproduced as fig. 2 with "Concerning Mandala Symbolism" (1950), in CW 9 i. It has four divisions and is related to the *I Ching*; see ibid., pars. 640ff. See also below, the lectures of 12 and 19 Feb. 1930.

[2] Cf. Jung's lectures, *Exercitia Spiritualia of St. Ignatius of Loyola*, at the Eidgenössische Technische Hochschule, Zurich, 1939-1940, the notes of which were privately issued (in English translation) in the seminar format as vol. 4 of *Modern Psychology*. Reprinted in *Spring*, 1977 and 1978.

[3] For instances of a mandala with the four Evangelists, see *Psychology and Alchemy*, CW 12, figs. 62, 101. There are numerous references to the Egyptian deity Horus and his four sons throughout the CW; see *General Index*, CW 20, s.v., but especially CW 12, fig. 102 and par. 314.

[4] See below, lecture of 26 June 1929.

[5] See CW 12, fig. 41.

concentrates his libido on the centre, what is the meaning of the centre? The centre of consciousness is the ego, but the centre represented in the mandala is not identical with the ego. It is outside of consciousness, it is another centre. The naïve man projects it into space, he would say it is outside somewhere in the world. The aim of the exercise is to shift the guiding factor away from the ego to a non-ego centre in the unconscious, and this is also the general aim of analytical procedure. I did not invent it but found it to be so. Ten years ago if I had seen that picture I would not have known what it meant. Up to a certain point the conscious ego should be the centre, the guiding factor, but if we are in the second half of life, there seems to be a necessity for another centre. The ego is only that field which is in my consciousness, but the psychic system is much vaster, it is the whole unconscious too, and we don't know how far that reaches. We can as little assume that the earth is in the centre of the solar system as that our ego is in the centre of the psyche. If we create a centre outside of ego-consciousness it may be an even more real centre than our ego. But we get into deep water if we go into this.

The Pueblo Indians make mandalas, sand-paintings,[6] in the same fashion as the eastern mandalas. Perhaps they are remnants of the Eastern origin of the Pueblos.

The *next dream* [4] of *the next night*. The patient says: "I possess a sort of cage on a wagon, a cage which might be for lions or tigers. The cage consists of different compartments. In one of them I have four small chickens. I must watch them carefully because they are always trying to escape, but in spite of my frantic efforts they do escape near the hind wheel. I catch them in my hand and put them in another compartment of the cage, the one I believe to be the safest. It has a window but it is secured by a fly-screen. The lower end of the screen is not properly fastened, so I make up my mind to get some stones and put them on the lower edge of the screen to keep the animals from escaping. Then I put the chickens in a basin with smooth, high sides, assuming that they will find it difficult to get out. They are down at the bottom of the basin, and I see that one does not move and I think that it is because I have pressed it too hard. I think that if the chicken is dead it cannot be eaten.

[6] Jung does not reproduce a Pueblo sand-painting, but he discusses such representations in "The Tavistock Lectures" (1935), par. 271. For a Navaho sand- or pollen-painting, see CW 12, fig. 110, and *C. G. Jung: Word and Image*, fig. 74.

While I watch it, it begins to move, and I smell an aroma of roast chicken."

His associations are very few. *Cage*: "Wild animals of a circus are kept in such cages. We human beings are the keepers of our thoughts, and we ought to be careful that our thoughts do not run away, because if they do it would be very difficult to catch them again." He asks himself, are the birds thoughts or feelings, psychological factors which try to liberate themselves and which he tries to hold back even at the risk of pressing them too hard so that they die and are no longer eatable? But the fact that they are animals seems to point to something instinctive.

Hind wheel: In an automobile this is a very important part because it is the motive part and indispensable to the car.

Dr. Jung: What occurs to you as especially important?

Dr. Binger: The number four. Had you discussed the mandala with him?

Dr. Jung: No, not particularly. The number four plays a very important part in the philosophy of Pythagoras.[7] It is the mystic four, the essence of all existing things, the basic number. Most mandalas are based on four.

What is the next thing? Why do these little animals always try to run away and make it very difficult for him to hold them together? This would be especially strange if they represent the mandala.

Dr. Schlegel: They obviously represent the dissociation of his personality.

Dr. Jung: Individuality, not personality. There is something in him that fights against concentration. He is obviously sick of constraint, he has so much in his present life. This is the reason for his dissociation, he thinks he has had enough of concentration, and he would hate to hold himself together still more. His unconscious is showing him in the actual process of holding these animals together, so the unconscious obviously wishes him to hold his individuality together. His resistance is in the way of a false analogy. We might conclude that this holding together is like his life, but there is nothing in the dream to show it. He needs to concentrate on the centre of individuality. I do not feel quite justified in saying that it is just like the constraint in his ordinary life, that would mean

---

[7] Concerning the tetraktys, see "Psychology and Religion" (1937), CW 11, par. 61.

the ego centre. The centre of individuality is not necessarily in the same place as the ego centre. We should rather associate personality with persona, but we need another word for the actual individuality. Individuality is the quality of the whole being which we call man, so the individual centre is the centre of the self, and these four chickens obviously belong to that centre; and the patient's interference and his greatest care are needed or else the centre is always disintegrating and separating. I am inclined to separate the problem of his conscious constraint and resistance from the problem of the constraint of the self; that is, the integration of the centre outside of the field of consciousness. It might be that the patient has a resistance against the very word *constraint* or *self-control* because he has had enough of the problem of his conscious restraint. The thing which is meant in the dream has nothing to do with the problem of his consciousness. It has to do with the centre outside of consciousness. It has to do with four chickens to be assembled in a basin, and also the idea of roast chickens. It is a funny way of representing this centre.

In the *I Ching* there is a hexagram, No. 50, which is called "The Cauldron."[8] According to Prof. Wilhelm, a cooking-pot with three legs signifies in yoga the technique for producing the new man. There is something very good in the pot, it is the meal for the king, the fat of pheasants is in it. There you have the chicken. This part of the dream suggests that the non-ego centre does not really exist by itself, it has to be produced by the patient himself and with great care.

Part of the text of "The Cauldron" reads: "Fire over wood. / The image of the Cauldron. / Thus the superior man consolidates his fate / By making his position correct." . . . "A *ting* with legs upturned." (Everything is thrown out, then it is ready to be used.) "There is food in the *ting*. / My comrades are envious, / But they

---

[8] At the time of this seminar, Richard Wilhelm's translation of the *I Ching* (*I Ging: Das Buch der Wandlungen*, Jena, 1924) was in use by Jung, who translated quotations from it orally. The only English version available was that of James Legge: *The Yi King* (Sacred Books of the East, 16; Oxford 1882; 2nd edn., 1899), which Jung had used before 1924. Cary F. Baynes, a member of the seminar, began work in 1929, at Jung's request, on a translation of the Wilhelm version, which was completed twenty years later and published in 1950: *The I Ching, or Book of Changes*, with a foreword by Jung; 3rd edition, 1967, which also has a preface by Hellmut Wilhelm. Quotations from and references to the *I Ching* in the present work are conformed to the 1967 edn. (Baynes often uses the Chinese word *ting* for "cauldron.")

cannot harm me." . . . "The handle of the *ting* is altered. / One is impeded in his way of life. / The fat of the pheasant is not eaten. / Once rain falls, remorse is spent." . . . "The legs of the *ting* are broken. / The prince's meal is spilled." . . . "The *ting* has yellow handles, golden carrying rings." . . . "The *ting* has rings of jade." (This means great good luck.) "Nothing would not act to further." This idea of the pot comes from a sort of sacrificial vessel used in the Taoist ancestor-cult. It is a symbol of the spiritual womb in which the new being is formed. It is the same as the *krater* of the early Christians, or the retort of the alchemists, in which the new being is made. Fragments of things are thrown together which do not ordinarily mix, but they unite in the fire and produce the gold, the new man. So the pot gets ears of gold and even of jade, the most valuable, the *lapis lapidum*, stone of stones. Here we have the same idea as in mediaeval alchemy, the *lapis lapidum* is the philosophers' stone. The idea that pheasants are cooked in the pot as a meal for the prince is used because that whole cooking procedure refers to the fifth line of the hexagram, the place of the Ruler. The fifth line is the gold, the prince to be made, the new man. But first one has to get the pheasant, it has to be shot. There is much hunting symbolism in the *I Ching*. It all means that the bundle of instincts of man, his chaotic ensemble of instincts, is not integrated at all. Instincts are most contradictory, and man is torn by them. They are like animals in a zoo, they do not love each other at all, they bite each other and try to run away. So if you want to do anything for that bundle of instincts which you are, you must hunt down your instincts, get them together and transform them. It suggests that you must collect rare things from all over the world, cook them together in the pot, and something may appear, perhaps the gold. That is the idea in the dream. There are four animals which try to escape, and they must be hunted and put into the pot. It seems to the patient that one of them is all ready to eat. The meal is ready for the perfect man. Instincts are the food to be held and transformed over the fire. This is the preparation of the prince's food. After such a process one is no longer torn by the pairs of opposites, but is at one with himself—the old desideratum. Nothing is said of all this in the former dream. The design suggests that the dreamer shall go about everywhere, according to the pattern, into all four corners of the world, not only once but twice. He must make the great voyage of error in the world of illusion in order to experience everything. Everything that happens to him is himself. This voyage is the hunting, and when that is accomplished, the cooking process takes place and the making of the being who is one. Important parts of ourselves are waiting for us in the world and we must meet a particular fate in order to experience that quality. If we experience it, it is caged, we taste that chicken. Fate is to be lived in this sense in order that we may experience other aspects of ourselves and then be integrated.

The patient had almost no associations with "chicken" except for eating. Chickens are animals for which we can have no great respect. They are usually panicky, blind, dumb creatures which run into the road just as an automobile comes along. They are an excellent simile for fragmentary tendencies repressed or never come across by us, living autonomous lives quite apart from our knowledge. These bits of fragmentary soul, like the chickens, are working up terrible nonsense, all the foolish things wise people do, or like the spendthrift who saves his matches. You know any number of examples of people who have something absolutely inconsistent with their characters. All the things which escape our control and observation are "chickens."

Mr. Roper: Why does he feel that the chicken he pressed is the one roasted?

Dr. Jung: He had no associations with that. Sometimes people have no associations because of resistances but sometimes because they are quite baffled. Had the patient's attitude towards dreams been different he would have had associations. Sometimes I have no associations because a thing seems such nonsense that it makes me angry, so my emotions prevent associations. So this man is angry with the silly chicken dream after the beautiful previous dream and has no associations. Why is he pressing the chicken so violently that it seems dead? This chicken is obviously one of his functions which tried to escape, so we may assume that it is his inferior function, the one most out of control. He is an intellectual type and his inferior function is feeling. He has squeezed his feeling too much; he has been squeezing it to please his wife, but the apparent gain is not worth it. We are pretty safe in assuming that he caught his feeling, squeezed it, nearly killed it, and then he looked at it. Now comes in a piece of old magic. Through looking at a thing, concentrating or meditating on it, you make it grow or hatch it out. He is in the act of brooding over himself. When the gods want to bring something about they brood over it, make *tapas*,[9] contemplate it. So in this case when the patient begins to look at the chicken which he thinks is dead, it comes to life again. Feeling will come to life however hard it has been squeezed if you meditate over it.

Dr. Schlegel: We understood that it was a question of principle, that it was a good thing to get the chickens together and roast them?

Dr. Jung: I must repeat that the unconscious has no moral intention; it is just Nature, it says what is happening, as an objective event. The dream never says what ought to be or what ought not to be. We have to draw our own conclusions. We cannot say the unconscious wants us to do things or not; we say, "Some things are happening like that—we had better look out" or "It is nice they are happening like that." The dream is merely a statement of things which are actually going on. We may assume that it is good or bad that this chicken escapes or that one is roasted. Everything is possible. We speak of the "chickens" as fragmentary souls or tendencies without brains which are outside in the world, in other people. All the fragmentary things in us, inasmuch as they are unconscious, are to be met with in other people outside. This man has not completed the sum of his errors. He is forty-seven, but there is still much time for errors. One never knows, perhaps this chicken is a fragmentary soul which should escape; I cannot say. Some may escape, some may not escape; because they are not strong enough. There are certain people who are just too weak to be bad, they have no particular gift for it; for it is a gift to be bad. Some people have it and their goal is the jail, just as the Royal Academy is the goal for others. Some time ago I heard of a man, a pillar of the church, a most respectable citizen. He grew more and more dissatisfied with his life, until once he woke up in the middle of the night and said, "Now I know what kind of a man I am. I belong to the devil," and after that he was converted to Evil.

So the chicken may be just a fragmentary soul which might run away and escape. I could only say, "Well, it has succeeded in escaping, what can you do about it?" I once met a chance acquaintance, who had a dream in which he was in the police department and had been given control of a house in a sort of convict settlement.

9 *Tapas*, Sanskrit, means self-incubation through meditation. See *Symbols of Transformation*, CW 5, pars. 588f. (as in 1912 edn.).

There were no really bad criminals in this house, just tramps, and swindlers, etc. He thought he had locked the door, but while he was away all the "birds" got out. He told me the dream and thought it was very funny that they all got out. I thought, "That is queer, something is wrong with that man," and my idea was right. About a year later he went to the bad. He had a bankruptcy and collapsed completely. That was no chicken. That was serious, his unconscious had said to him, "Now look out—your unconscious is full of vagabonds and they will get out." This man had a peculiar interest in tramps and queer people. He would talk to them and enjoyed being with them. It was odd to me, for his life did not seem to fit in with it, but his unconscious was full of vagabondage and irresponsibility. This is like the clergyman who took a similar interest in prostitutes. He even travelled to Paris and went into all sorts of brothels to rescue them. There seemed something odd about that, and the upshot of it was that the man got syphilis and was very ill. So with these chickens, it is a question whether they ought to run away or should be rescued. Here comes the whole art of the doctor. Suppose I have some swans or even eagles in a cage. I could say, "Of course they must be allowed to get loose, eagles should fly," but it is absurd to talk in the same terms of chickens. It is good for an eagle to be free, but it is ridiculous for the chickens to escape and run all over the place. This is a wonderful opportunity for an analyst who is not sure of himself. If the analyst felt that the patient was a man full of worries, it might be better that the chickens should get away. One could say he makes himself ridiculous in the dream trying to keep them in. Better he should kill an ordinary little hen and eat it, it is only a chicken. But I am not yet sure of this man. He has a very complex nature and I am not sure that he is not a chicken. He has no neurosis, but great intellectual interest. If he had lions or tigers behind the bars they would roar. We have heard no roars and I have known him for two years. The man is a very quiet soul and I don't know where he got the fleas that irritate him. It may be that these chickens are like fleas and they should "come off." His feeling in the dream was that they should not escape, so that makes me doubtful. I am rather inclined to assume that there is no voice in that man for liberation. Sometimes with some of you I don't know whether it is a lion or a chicken. These are the qualms of an analyst. This man is absolutely respectable. When he dies the parson will say that he lived a blameless life and was a model husband, yet he has picked some fleas on the way, the high-class cocotte (100 Frs. so that he does not get an infection). Slowly he becomes aware that this does not work. He has some feeling for such a girl. Perhaps he has a vision of how she may look when she is old, when she is fifty, like those terrible old cocottes one sees in Paris. Such things may begin to come up in him and cause very disagreeable feelings. He has been blind like a boy, and the running away of the chickens may mean the blind escapades of his life.

Dr. Binger: Do you see anything of a compensatory nature in this?

Dr. Jung: It depends on how he takes it. If that man, for instance were an innocent boy living in paradise with his sweet little girl wife it might be necessary that his chickens should run away so that he could realize what the world really is. But this man is not naïve, he is a hard-boiled business man, yet he is something of an idealist. He has a human streak, so he continues with his analysis.

Mrs. Sigg: Who is the "I" in his dream? Isn't he the domesticated man?

Dr. Jung: The chicken-catcher is not the conventional man. It is the conventional man who chases prostitutes. His conventional outside has gone with prostitutes, this is convention. The chickens are fragmentary unconscious souls which organize escapades. This man has a philosophy and is well read; he does not provide for escapades but—given a bottle of wine, etc., there is no longer philosophy. This is convention and many people do not mind as long as it is not found out. Many women even say they do not mind if their husbands go with cocottes, or if they are homosexual and entice boys and do all sorts of ugly things. They only mind if the husband falls in love with a decent woman. This man thought that prostitutes were all right; except occasionally a mist arose, a question. Once a very conventional man said to me "Don't you think I can divorce my wife? We have been married twenty-two years and I like her well enough but I have seen a younger woman and I would like to marry her. I was legally married to my wife and I see no reason why I cannot be legally divorced." That man was quite logical but he had no feeling at all.

My idea in summing up this dream is that it gives the ingredients for the making of the new man. Therefore we have the parallel to the *I Ching*. Whether he lets the chickens run or whether he kills them and roasts them is practically the same thing. If the chickens run away he will have a series of chicken adventures out in the open and he will return from the play and have to integrate them. Or if it is not worth while to have such adventures then he must integrate these tendencies. For example, suppose I am walking along the Bahnhofstrasse and I see a particularly beautiful cane and I think, that is just what I want, and then I think, why do I wish for that? It is not like me, I have too great an accumulation of objects already and I would just throw it away. I think it is foolish, but I buy it and pay a hundred frs. for it and then I throw it away. Then I think, well, I bought it and threw it away, there is an experience. I can book that in my favour, or I can say what a fool I am to do that, how inconsistent of me to wish for that cane; but I can book that realization also in my favour. So with this man, if he has some experiences with prostitutes it may make things more clear to him; or he may say, "It is all just an illusion," so he cages the chickens and roasts them; it has the same result. The main thing is that he should see himself and learn to hold himself together for he is quite scattered. I am not sure, he may be quite charming in his family and with his relatives and friends, but possibly in his business he may be capable of playing a dirty trick. I don't know, but I have an impression that he may be a bit of a scattered character. He must learn to see himself, no matter by what technique and hold himself together. Some people become acquainted with themselves by spreading out all over the world, others by locking themselves in. It all depends on temperament. There are many reasons for this, extraversion, introversion, tradition in the family, etc.

LECTURE IV

13 February 1929

Dr. Jung:

We have quite a number of questions to deal with, most of them about the *I Ching*. This seems to have aroused general interest. Mr. Gibb's question goes to the root of the whole thing: "This question refers to the design in the previous dream and to the subject of such designs and patterns in general. Are we justified in assuming that such dreams and fantasies support the truth of a particular form of philosophy, for example one based on the idea of four functions? Or should we just take them as an expression of an unconscious desire or need for a philosophy of some kind; that is, for some way of making a complete integration or synthesis of experience? I feel that at most they indicate that there is a need for a philosophy based on psychic experience instead of on the collected abstractions of physical science. But are we justified in saying any more than that?

"An example of what I mean is the Mogul emperor Akbar's Divan-i-Khas (hall of private audience) at Fatehpur Sikri.[1] This building is constructed so as to form just such a design as we are discussing, and Akbar used to sit in a sort of saucer in the middle of it, while learned men from all parts of the world told him about all sorts of religions and philosophies and discussed them with him. There he tried to make an integration for himself.

"The red sandstone saucer is supported on a pillar with a jet-black stem, in the middle of the square hall. Four gangways lead

[1] Akbar (1542-1605) built his capital first at Fatehpur Sikri (near Agra, in north central India); the royal city, though abandoned by Akbar, is well preserved. Gibb, who had lived for some years in India, evidently had visited it. (So did Jung, ten years later. See "The Dreamlike World of India" [1929], CW 10, par. 983.) Akbar embraced an eclectic faith compounded of Moslem, Hindu, Zoroastrian, and Christian elements.

114

to the saucer from the four corners where they meet a gallery that goes round all four sides of the hall. When one looks up at the saucer the black stem of the pillar is practically invisible so that the whole thing seems to be suspended in mid-air."

Dr. Jung: I admit that what we said about the mandala and its possible meaning sounds like philosophy, but it is not philosophy. It is akin to Pythagoras and his four. It has to do with principles, yet in itself it is not philosophy. It is merely an expression of *unconscious* facts.

I would not even say that it expresses an unconscious need for a philosophy, as many people would prefer a religion to a philosophy. These figures are naïvely produced by the unconscious and therefore you can find them all over the world. The earliest one I know has just been found at Chichén Itzá, in the Mayan Temple of the Warrior. An American explorer[2] has broken through the outer wall of the pyramid and discovered it was not the original temple; a much older, smaller one was inside it. The space between the two was filled with rubbish, and when he cleared this out he came to the walls of the older temple. Because he knew that it had been the custom to bury ritual treasure under the floor as a sort of a charm, he dug up the floor of the terrace and found a cylindrical limestone jar about a foot high. When he lifted the lid he found inside a wooden plate on which was fixed a mosaic design. It was a mandala based on the principle of eight, a circle inside of green and turquoise-blue fields. These fields were filled with reptile heads, lizard claws, etc., One of my patients has made a similar mandala with the same sort of divisions but filled in with plant designs, not animals. These are expressions apparently so natural that they are to be found all over the world. Mr. Gibb gives us a beautiful example. It is a naïve expression of the same idea: the Mogul Emperor, Akbar the Great, in his hall of private audience. The pattern of the building quite clearly forms a mandala, the Mogul sits in a sort of saucer of red sandstone supported by a slender pillar, so that the saucer appears almost to be suspended from heaven. It is a fine idea for the old man to sit in that manner

[2] Jung evidently had read of this Mayan discovery at Chichén Itzá, Yucatán, in the *Illustrated London News* of 26 Jan. 1929 (p. 127), as his description closely follows the account published there, with illustrations of the temple, jar, and mosaic mandala. The discovery was made by Earl Morris, head of an expedition of the Carnegie Institution of Washington, D.C.

in the middle of his mandala, so that wisdom should come to him from all four corners of the world.

In Chinese philosophy the mandala is the "Square Inch Field of the Square Foot House."³—It is said that the house means the Imperishable Body and the building up of that mandala means the building up of the Imperishable Body. Mead wrote a very interesting study on the theory that man possesses a subtle body besides his physical material body.⁴ Geley has a complete theory of it, a new physiology called "système psychodynamique,"⁵ a new word for an old thing—as are most of our scientific terms. The subtle body is the definite abode for what old philosophy would have called *entelechia*, the thing which tries to realize itself in existence. Now, the Chinese idea is that the mandala is the symbol of the subtle body. According to the Eastern theory, by meditation on the mandala all the constituents of the subtle body are withdrawn from the outside and are concentrated in the innermost man, where they build up the imperishable body. The new man of St. Paul's early Christian teaching is exactly the same thing as the subtle body. It is an archetypal idea, exceedingly profound, which belongs to the sphere of the immortal archetypes. There may be something in it, it may be true, I do not know; I am not God himself who knows everything; I must keep to my psychological world.

At all events, the Eastern theory and its symbols agree, in the most astonishing way, with our work. A Chinese text explains the art of prolonging life by building up the subtle body.⁶ It contains

³ See "Commentary on 'The Secret of the Golden Flower,' " CW 13, pars. 33, 76.
⁴ G.R.S. Mead, *The Doctrine of the Subtle Body in Western Tradition* (1919).
⁵ In his "Commentary on 'The Secret of the Golden Flower,' " par. 76, n. 2, Jung cited the "paraphysiological theory" of Gustave Geley, M.D. (1868-1924), director of the Institut Métapsychique International, in Paris. See also Jung's comment in *Letters*, vol. 1, 30 Sept. 1933. His library contained three works by Geley: *From the Unconscious to the Conscious*, tr. S. de Brath (London, 1920), *L'être subconscient* (Paris, 1926), and *Clairvoyance and Materialization: A Record of Experiments*, tr. S. de Brath (London, 1927). The first of these works discusses (in Book II, parts 1 and 2) Geley's "système psychodynamique" under the English term "dynamopsychism." (James Kirsch recalls, from an interview on 30 June 1929, that Jung was writing the commentary on the "Golden Flower" that summer.)
⁶ Jung and Wilhelm published "Tschang Scheng Schu: Die Kunst des menschliche Leben zu verlängern" (= "Ch'ang Sheng Shu: The Art of Prolonging Human Life"), *Europäische Revue*, V:8 (Nov. 1929), 530-556, half of which was Jung's introduction. According to Hellmut Wilhelm (private communication), it was expanded into *Das Geheimnis der goldenen Blüte*, published near the end of the same year. The two are essentially the same work, with variant titles.

a lot of symbolism which I have seen with my patients, and while all this symbolism is well-known to me I do not dare to make bold interpretations such as the East is making. The East dares to use such terms as the "transmigration of souls."

To the early Christians it was nothing to call a man a "Son of God," it was a commonplace, it was their daily bread. For thousands of years the King of Egypt was the Son of Ra, so that when Christ was called the Son of God there was no difficulty in believing. But to us it sounds rather incredible because our belief in God is an abstraction, we have become philosophical. So with our archetypes of immortality, the more we come to talk of immortality the more impossible it seems, even to hard-boiled spiritualists. What about the teeming population of all the ages, what about the animals and insects, the dogs and fleas, etc.? It soon becomes absurd, and we could hardly imagine heavens and hells enough for all. In metaphysical matters you can never decide the truth, the only criterion is if it "clicks." If it does, then I can feel that I think properly, and thinking like that I function properly. We have no other proof. All so-called spiritualistic experiences can easily be criticized. You never can prove a ghost. There are a thousand loopholes for self-deception.

Dr. Shaw's question: "How do you account for such things as are found in Chinese philosophy being so applicable to our psychology today? I conclude you draw our attention especially to the 50th hexagram of the *I Ching* because it symbolizes the way of analysis as well as of Yoga."

Dr. Jung: Dr. Shaw points out the analogy between analysis and Yoga. The chapter of the *I Ching* dealing with pot is one of those chapters which contain Yoga procedure, and our analytical procedure produces Western forms of what in the East is Yoga. The terminology is different, but the symbolism is the same, the purpose the same. The Chinese form of Yoga is quite like the symbolism we get in dreams and from the unconscious in general.

To speak of Yoga is to speak of a certain form of analytical method. These things are little known and arouse resistances. Resistances are usually founded on ignorance. Very few people in Europe know anything about Yoga. We are filled with the most amazing megalomania, we assume that people in the East are ignorant and that we in the West have discovered a great truth. Many people assume, for instance, that astrology is all nonsense. It is true that astrology has nothing to do with the stars. The horoscope may say that you were born in Taurus, but the constellations today have moved and horoscopes no longer correspond to the actual position of the stars. Since 100 B.C. our time-measuring system has been kept at a standstill quite arbitrarily. Our spring point is now at about 29° of Pisces and is no longer in Aries, although horoscopes are made on that basis. The spring point is about to enter Aquarius. But people criticize astrology as though it had something to do with the stars.

If one mentions Yoga, people at once think of fakirs, people standing on their heads for seven years, and all that nonsense. A real knowledge of Yoga practices is very rare in the West. I felt quite small when I became acquainted with these things. Here is a reproduction of a picture in the temple of the "White Clouds" in Peking.[7] It belongs to the Chinese Tao system. It is just as though I should write a treatise on how to proceed along the road of analytical psychology. This picture has not been published, but if it were no one would know what it meant. The mandala and the idea of the cooking-pot are in it. A tremendous experience of unconscious symbolism would be necessary to understand all these details. The form of this picture shows the human spine—head, eyes, the region of the heart, and below there are other centres or zones. Instead of the vertebral column there are rocks standing on the bank of a river which flows up hill from the water-zone. The Taoist Yoga has many parallels with analysis. Just recently a text one thousand years old has been found by a Chinese and deciphered by the Chinese Institute at Frankfurt.[8] Wilhelm tells me it contains material similar to our results here. It is a sort of psychological bridge between the East and the West. There is no reason why we should have any sort of megalomania in connection with Eastern things. We cannot assume that the Chinese is an idiot, and

[7] The picture is discussed at length in Erwin Rousselle, "Spiritual Guidance in Contemporary Taoism," in *Spiritual Disciplines* (Papers from the Eranos Yearbooks, 4; 1960), pp. 75-84; originally a lecture at the first Eranos Conference, 1933. Rousselle reproduced the picture from a rubbing of a stone tablet in the Monastery of the White Clouds (formerly in the collection of Richard Wilhelm).

[8] Hellmut Wilhelm believes that here Jung was referring to the Chinese text of *The Secret of the Golden Flower*, which could be traced back to the 17th century and in oral tradition to the 8th century. An edition of 1920, in Peking, was the basis of the translation (rather than "decipherment") by Richard Wilhelm at the Chinese Institute. See *The Secret of the Golden Flower* (new edn., New York, 1962), R. Wilhelm's discussion of the text, pp. 3ff.

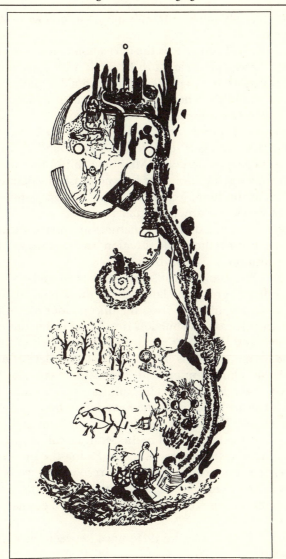

that we are terribly intelligent. It is always a mistake to underrate an opponent.

Dr. Binger: Will you give us the derivation of the word *mandala?*

Dr. Jung: *Mandala* means orb or circle with a connotation of magic. You can draw a mandala, you can build a mandala, or you can dance a mandala. The "Mandala Nritya" is a dance in which the figures describe a mandala.

Here is another question that has to do with the famous chicken which runs away and gets squeezed and was found in the pot in a more or less eatable condition. Mrs. Sigg thinks that the chicken which ran away was intuition. But I see no possibility of interpreting that chicken as intuition. I cannot see that we can assume that the patient has developed any particular function.

Mrs. Sigg: The first dream was naturalistic, then comes the mandala which expresses the whole situation, and now we see the whole process by intuition; it is synthetic.

Dr. Jung: The man was confused and bewildered, so something had to happen to give him clarity about the whole situation. The mandala was a sort of letter from the unconscious meant to clarify his mind. In this case its function is to bring order out of a state of confusion, and this order seems to be established in this particular mandala pattern. It is like an amulet. Amulets often have a mandala form. Quite a number of prehistoric mandalas from the Bronze Age have been excavated and are in the Swiss National Museum. They are called sun-wheels and have four spokes like old Christian crosses. This is also the design on the Host in the Catholic Church and on the bread used in the Mithraic cult, a sort of "mandala bread" as shown on a monument. Eating the bread is eating the god, eating the saviour. This is the reconciling symbol. Eating the totem animal symbolizes the strengthening of the social unity of the whole clan. This is the original idea repeated eternally through the ages.

Mrs. Sigg: I don't see the difference between an inner vision and intuition.

Dr. Jung: When you dream, you can't say that you use this or that function, yet something can get into your head. You do not need your eyes to get it. Intuition can mean a conscious effort. If I need it in a situation I must look for it in order to get it. It is quite possible that this man has made the effort before, but the thing in the dream is just a vision of a fact. It is no function of the mind.

Mrs. Sigg: It is difficult in a dream to exclude the effort which he has made consciously.

Dr. Jung: We do not need to comfort ourselves and the patient by saying that he has made an effort and now as a reward there is the good dream. Sure enough, this thing is the result of his thinking, but it is not intuition. We have said so much about this dream already that we might assume it has been sufficiently dealt with. Are there any points not clear to you? Do you see the whole meaning of the dream in connection?

Mr. Rogers: How do you know when to include consciousness and when to leave it out? In some explanations where there were three figures, as in *Macbeth* and in *Faust,* you added consciousness to make four. But if you added it in others there would be five. In *Macbeth* the three human beings with consciousness would be four; here with the four chickens it is not. How do you know when to exclude?

Dr. Jung: The difference is that in our dream there are four animals, four chickens. That points to the fact that the self, as represented by the mandala, is unconscious (animal!). There is no consciousness to add.

Mr. Rogers: How about the four sons of Horus, how would that work out?

Dr. Jung: Horus is in the centre and his sons are his four attributes. With Horus as with the four Evangelists, the central figure is human and the four are merely attributes. The Horus as well as the Christ (*Rex gloriae*) group symbolizes the self with three unconscious functions and one that has reached consciousness. Thus the sons of Horus are often depicted as three with animal heads and one with a human head. The same is true of the Christian mandala. It would be difficult if we encountered a group of four such things alone, but we never find them without Horus. So with the Evangelists, you never see them alone but always grouped around the Saviour.

You have to be careful in speculating about numbers and geometrical designs. I am giving you mere conjectures in explaining our mandala motif by mythological parallels and in interpreting the mythological figures by our psychological observations. It looks as if four animals without a centre would represent the unconsciousness of all four functions, whereas three animals and one human-headed figure would represent the fact that three functions are unconscious and one only is conscious. A fifth figure in the centre would represent the sum total of man: his four functions [conscious and unconscious] under the control of a God or "non-ego centre."

Is there anything else about our dream to be considered?

Miss Hannah: What about the hind wheel? You have not told us about it yet.

Dr. Jung: What does the hind wheel represent?

Dr. Binger: The dreamer himself interpreted it as the driving force.

Dr. Jung: What is that psychologically?

Dr. Binger: It means libido, the chicken is escaping with the man's libido.

Dr. Jung: One of those functions is escaping where the motivating libido is. Why?

Mr. Roper: Is it going with that woman?

Dr. Jung: That woman was fantasy. There is no indication in the dream that it goes to a woman. The dream says one function escapes where the motivating or creative libido is. If you assume that he is motivated by the fantasy of a woman, then this may be where the chicken escapes.

Mr. Roper: Could it be the occult studies?

Dr. Jung: How are these connected with the libido?

Mr. Roper: They are one of his two strong lines.

Dr. Jung: Yes, one doesn't know with this man whether the stronger motivation is his fantasy about women or his occult studies. If he has devoted more time to his occult studies than to his experiences with women then you can be sure he is more interested in them. I always try to get at the exact amounts of time and money one has expended on a thing, then I know how important it has been for the patient. A woman counts not by the intensity of feeling but by the time you spend with her. Better four hours with less insistence on beauty of feeling than fifteen minutes with only marvelous words. Women are merciless, but this is a very efficient means. I learned it from women. Three-fourths of analyses are made by women, and I learn from them.

In this case we have no way of knowing whether or not the motivating libido, "the hind wheel," is more concerned with the occult studies than with sex fantasy, but we at least may assume that it is concerned with the leaking-out by the hind wheel. The leakage in analysis is very important. There are many people who when they are being analysed try to establish a sort of stronghold, an island, a place where nothing moves, where nothing happens, where nothing is displaced. It is the construction of a counterpole which I would not destroy, and the idea of such an island is a happy and important symbol, but many people make a wrong use of it by reserving their judgments, or witholding something. Out of politeness, these reservations are always rationalized or pretexts are made. By such subterfuges they create a safe place where they can sneak out. A certain lady comes to me for analysis and falls in love with another man at once. One wonders why. He is not particularly the sort one would expect to attract her. It is simply a safety valve for her, she is protecting herself against the transference. The other man becomes the place of leakage. The patient will not quite admit her falling in love, she says, "Oh just a little fantasy"; but there her libido is leaking away. Nothing happens at all in analysis because it is all leaking out. Then the analyst has to work on a sort of background of wet cloth. You get no reaction, everything is postponed by leakage into this safe place. When you have to deal with such people you can do just nothing. Whenever you try to catch something it recedes. You do a sort of provisional analysis. It may be the same in life where the son remains in the father as a safe deposit. You may discover that these people have a counterpole or safe deposit where the leakage is. The influence of the analyst is counteracted by a steadfast autonomous something until he discovers the counterpole.

So this man at that stage of analysis was inclined to make a *restriction mentale*, a curious kind of trick. For example, there is a story about a monastery of the eighteenth century, which wanted to get the estate of a peasant. They had no right to it but they did everything they could to get it. Then the abbot learned from a wise man that he could apply *restriction mentale* for certain things that would be decided by oath. So the abbot got some earth from his own garden and put it in his shoes, then he stood on the peasant's land and swore "I am standing on my own earth."

Passe-partout par l'Eglise Romaine[9] is a book on such restrictions.

[9] An anti-papist tract by Antonio Gavin (fl. 1726), a Catholic priest of Saragossa,

They are terrible things, but they do happen. The *restriction mentale* in this case would be that the patient might say, "Yes, I am doing analysis. Oh yes, it is very interesting but it can be explained in a different way, as for instance, that Dr. Jung is a sort of medium. The things he says which are good are inspired by Mahatmas in a monastery in Tibet, and the other things that he says are nothing." With such an assumption, I could do nothing. He had no such reservations really, but some tendency to it. This is happening in analysis all the time, the animus and anima are busy at such things. Once I had a case which really made me mad. I was trying to explain something to a woman patient and I used a good deal of vitality to make it emphatic, but she got more and more dull and soon I saw that she was not listening. I found that she thought I was in love with her and was sexually excited, because I was so interested and lively and she saw no importance in what I was saying. That was a *restriction mentale* where something was leaking, and I could do nothing. So with this man, my idea is that the occult studies are the leak in the motivating libido.

later an Anglican priest in Ireland. Originally published in Dublin 1724 as *A Master-key to Popery*, it was sometimes entitled *The Great Red Dragon*. Throughout the 19th century it was widely reprinted in German and French translations.

LECTURE V

20 February 1929

Dr. Jung:

Today we are going to continue with our dreams, no more chickens! The next dream came two days later.

Dream [5]

"I am coming to a place where a saint is worshipped; a saint who is said to cure diseases when one mentions his name. I am there because I suffer from sciatica. I think there are many other people with whom I continue my way, and someone tells me that already one patient has been cured. I think that I need to do something more than to call on the saint, that I should take a bath in the sea. I come to the shore and notice some powerful boulders on the shore towards the land. Between the boulders and the rocky hills is a valley, a sort of bay. The ocean penetrates it in quiet and powerful waves and loses itself slowly towards the recess of the bay, which penetrates the land to a considerable distance. For a while I watch the majestic surf and high swell passing in. I climb the high rocky hill. Then I am with my youngest son. We are just about to climb higher up when I see a spray of water rising above the hill we are climbing, from the other side, and then I am afraid that the surf would be so powerful on the other side that it might wash the hill away, which was not made of bed-rock but heaped-up gravel and boulders. The hill might collapse and a big swell might wash it away. On account of this I take my boy away."

The picture of the dream is very clear, well visualized. There is a flat shore, yet towards the land are heaped-up boulders. He comes to a hill of gravel and loose stones which could be washed away.

Associations: Saint: "I can't remember the name of the saint but think it was something like Papatheanon or Papastheanon. I can't explain this Greek or Romanian name." There is much Greek in Romania, because of the mixture of Greek in the lingua rustica,

125

the language of the peasants throughout the Roman Empire. It still remains as the Romansch in Switzerland. *The magical cure:* "This is like the cure at Lourdes or at the tombs of saints all over the Mohammedan world, in North Africa, Egypt, etc. I can only explain these cures, whose reality I certainly cannot deny, through belief in the effect, through auto-suggestion, which is always enhanced by cures. The atmosphere of Lourdes where people see magic cures has a tremendously suggestive effect, crowd suggestion." He talks of how one gets under the suggestion of the belief of the crowd, the effect upon the whole crowd.

Then he comes to the fact that he thinks even in the dream it is doubtful that such a cure could come about: "I am doubtful if I could be cured by a miracle or blind belief despite the fact that others are so cured, and I think it would help to bathe in the sea, and contemplate the powerful movement of the surf during the day."

Associations: The sea: Here he uses a German term meaning the primordial medium of life. Evolution began in the ocean and the first germ of life appeared there. One could call the sea the womb of nature. The *majestic rollers that come in from the sea:* "One could say that our unconscious is like that. The unconscious sends powerful waves with almost certain regularity into our conscious, which is like the valley that contains the bay." He uses a simile that I have often noticed my patients expressing, that the conscious is like a bay, or lacuna in the unconscious, connected with the sea but separated by a dam or peninsula. He continues, "It is tranquillizing and at the same time most interesting to watch those waves. Speaking in that way our conscious is moved by the up and down movement of the unconscious." He means that the unconscious movement is a sort of rhythmic respiration of nature, like Goethe's idea of "diastole and systole." This is the first kind of movement, as in the protozoa. The movement of extraversion and introversion is what he is aiming at.

The dreamer continues: "But it can also be quite dangerous to approach the ocean on a stormy day. The violence of the sea can wreck its own walls, the shores and dunes built by the sea itself; and many could not rescue themselves from the powerful waves."

He says about the *boy*: "He is probably my pet. He is my youngest boy, and he identifies himself with me and wants to become what his father is. He is very jealous of the other children and he always watches to see that he has no less than his brothers." After the dreamer has contemplated for some time the majestic play of the ocean, he wants to climb higher up on the hill. He sees the spray dashing up on the other side and is afraid the hill might be destroyed. His association with this is: "On the other side there is apparently such strong tension that it might cause a catastrophe, so one must be careful that one does not reach the top of the hill and have it give way so that one falls into the water." He expresses himself here ambiguously. He speaks partly in the metaphor of the dream and partly psychologically, meaning "Tension on the other side is dangerous."

When you translate the German language into English you cannot give the whole meaning. It loses something for it is still in a primitive ambivalent condition, so it is particularly well-suited to express psychological meanings with shades and nuances. When it comes to definite formulations of scientific artificial [not natural] facts, the German language is not very good, it has too many connotations, too many side lines. (This is not the case in English or French. As a legal or philosophical language French is ideal.) As Mark Twain said, the word *Zug* has twenty-seven different meanings: A German uses *Zug* to express the meaning he wants it to convey and never thinks of its other possible meanings. This is like primitive language, where sometimes the same word is used for black and for white. The primitive uses it and means white, but to another it might as well mean black. In German a draught is a *Zug*, a train is a *Zug*, tendency is a *Zug*, and one of those elastic ribbons which you put somewhere in your dresses is a *Zug* too. That is primitive. In English you have the words *good, better, best,* and *best* comes from *bad*.[1] In Anglo-Saxon it was *bat*, "bad." The French word *sacré* has a double meaning also, *Sacré coeur, Sacré nom de chien.*

I want to hear your impressions of the dream. First the saint; you remember the dream before? In the interpretation of dreams it is always our first duty to link the dream up to the dream before. Can you see any possible connection between the chickens (in the last dream) and the saint? It is very far fetched. I myself could not tell if I had not analysed many such dreams; and from knowing the motif of the dream before and of this dream. The motif of the dream before was the archetypal motif of assembling in the pot

[1] The Oxford English Dictionary does not give this etymology.

the sacrificial food, the alchemical procedure for the reconstruction of the new man. This is the old idea of the transformation of the individual, of the man who is in need of salvation, redemption, cure. He is like an old broken-down machine, he consists of rags and bones. He is burdened with the sins of the "Old Adam," and with the sins of his ancestors too. He is a whole heap of inconsistent misery. He is thrown into the pot or krater, boiled or melted in that pot, and comes out new! This is just faintly alluded to in the chicken dream. The cooking of the ingredients is a sort of cure. In German *heilig* is connected with *heil*, or "being whole"; *geheilt* means cured. Healing is making whole, and the condition into which one gets is a whole or complete condition, while before it was only fragments held together. So collecting and roasting the chickens means curing or making new.

Here the idea of medicine comes in. The Saviour is always the medicine man who gives *pharmakon athanasias*, the medicine of immortality· which makes the new man. When you take the *tinctura magna* of the alchemist you are cured for ever, you never can fall ill again. These are the mythological connotations of the alchemical procedure, or the melting pot of transformation, so it is no wonder that in the next dream he starts in with a saint. Why just a saint? It could have been a medicine man or a magician. Why did he pick out a saint? It is a nice piece of patient's psychology. The saint is the doctor. He calls me up on the telephone. "Are you Dr. Jung? Can you cure me? How long will it take?" He invokes Dr. Jung as a saint. The patient of course does not think of me as a saint. But his unconscious says, "You are invoking the name of a saint." The unconscious conveys it as that same old truth repeated again, that a man has called upon his Saviour, an Indian has called upon his medicine man, the Arab upon his Marabout. The Catholic rubs the tomb of St. Anthony in order to get healing power from it. Why does the unconscious speak like that, what would be the use of that?

Mrs. Schlegel: It would help belief.

Dr. Jung: Yes, belief need not mean anything but a willingness to believe, a sort of expectation: "My belief and hope are in the Lord." The dream says that the patient is in the same old archetypal situation. One of the effects of an archetypal situation is that when you get into it there is a great deal of feeling, and the more the unconscious is stirred the more expectation there will be that things will get into the right way. What happens in our psychology when we touch upon an archetype?

Dr. Binger: There is a welling up of a racial or tribal image from the collective unconscious.

Dr. Jung: An archetype belongs to the structure of the collective unconscious, but as the collective unconscious is in ourselves, it is also a structure of ourselves. It is part of the basic structure of our instinctual nature. Anything brought back into that instinctive pattern is supposed to be cured. This structure of man is supposed to be a wholly adapted animal, a remarkable thing able to live perfectly. Most of our psychogenic ills consist in the fact that we have deviated from the instinctive pattern of man. We suddenly find ourselves in the air, our tree no longer receives the nourishing substance from the earth. So you see, when you get back into an archetypal situation you are in your right instinctive attitude in which you must be when you want to live on the earth's surface; in your right atmosphere with your right food, etc. The archetype is the instinctive natural man, as he always has been. The old priests and medicine men understood this, not by knowledge, but by intuition. They tried to get a sick man back into an archetypal situation. If a man had a snake-bite we would give him serum, but the old Egyptian priest would go to his library and get down the book with the story of Isis,[2] take it to the patient and read to him of the Sun God Ra, how while he was walking over Egypt his wife Isis made a terrible worm, a sand-viper with only its snout showing out of the sand. She put it in his path so that it would bite him. He stepped on the venerable worm and he was badly bitten and poisoned, his jaws and all his limbs were trembling. The gods picked him up and thought he must die. They called in Mother Isis, for she could cure him; then the hymn was read over him, but her magic could not cure him entirely and he had to withdraw on the back of the Heavenly Cow and give place to the younger god. Now, how could reading this hymn over Ra cure him of the snake bite? What is the use of such foolishness? I assume that these people were by no means idiots. They knew very well what they did, they were as intelligent as we are, they had good results with these methods, so they used them, it was "good medicine."

[2] For a fuller account and analysis of the story, see *Symbols of Transformation*, CW 5, pars. 451-455 (as in the 1912 edn.).

When you study the pharmacopoeia of old Galen you get sick, a most amazing dung-heap, yet he was an excellent doctor. They had a pharmacology that was absolutely ridiculous according to our ideas, but we do it from the outside in, in a rational way, while they did it from the inside out. We never see the curative things that come from within; Christian Science recognizes them, but clinical medicine even in our day is living and working by the outer facts. What that old Egyptian priest tried to do was to convey to that man that his suffering was not only man's fate but God's fate. It had to be so, and Mother Isis, who made the poison, can also cure its effect (not entirely but nearly so). By bringing the patient to the eternal truth of the archetypal image of the snake-bite brought about by the Mother, his instinctive powers are aroused, and that is exceedingly helpful.

Now with our patient, if the archetypal powers could be brought out he would be helped. But with us it is not so easy, we are much too far away from such an image.

Someone is in despair or very sad, and the parson comes along and says, "See here, think of our Lord on the Cross, how he suffered, how he bore the burdens for us all." We can understand this kind of technique, and for people to whom the archetypal image of Christ still has meaning it has a definite effect, but to those who have deviated from the archetype it is just air. All such technique naturally started from the unconscious. Those old doctors like Galen asked their patients for their dreams. Dreams played a large part in medical cures. One of the old physicians tells of a man who dreamed that his leg had turned to stone, and two days later he had paralysis of one leg from apoplexy. Certain dreams are very important for the diagnosis of a case. The ordinary technique of the dream is that it gets the patient into the archetypal situation in order to cure him, the situation of the suffering God-man or the situation of human tragedy. This was the effect of Greek tragedy.

Now this dream suddenly gets the patient into a pilgrim role, travelling to a shrine, as to the tomb of St. Anthony at Padua or to Lourdes. He is put into the situation of the ordinary man of all times, and through that he is brought nearer to the fundamental nature of man. The nearer he gets to it the nearer he gets right, and we can assume that with some people it works. Instinctive powers are released, partly psychological, partly physiological, and through that release the whole disposition of the body can be changed.

One of my students made some experiments on the viscosity of the blood, following the viscosity through different stages of analysis. The viscosity was much less when the patient was muddled, resistant, or in a bad frame of mind. People in such a state of mind are in a condition for infections and physical disturbances. You know how close the connection is between the stomach and mental states. If a bad psychic state is habitual, you spoil your stomach, and it may be very serious.

Mr. Rogers: May I ask a question, a little apart from the discussion. When the same word signifies opposite things, what is it in the primitive mind which brings the opposites so close?

Dr. Jung: It is the baffling symbolism of things that are still in the unconscious where things are existent and nonexistent. That is a thing you will often find in dreams and in the unconscious. It is as though you have a hundred-dollar bill in your pocket, you know you have it, you have a bill to pay with it, but you can't find it. So with the unconscious contents, things are yea and nay, good and bad, black and white. Perhaps there is a possibility in your unconscious which you cannot get at. There are high qualities and low qualities. It cannot be both, but it may be either. So good people have a certain likeness to bad people in that they both have a moral problem. Primitivity and accomplishments, as in an artist, may go together. All Negroes are marvellous artists in what they might produce. All artists have a very primitive side in their characters and way of living. In their unconscious there is an ambiguous condition. This is not really a new discovery. The Gnostics had that idea and expressed it as Pleroma, a state of fullness where the pairs of opposites, yea and nay, day and night, are together, then when they "become," it is either day or night. In the state of "promise" before they become, they are nonexistent, there is neither white nor black, good nor bad. Often it is so symbolized in dreams, as two indistinct animals, or an animal which eats another. It is a symptom of unconscious contents. In northern Lombardy one sees friezes of animals which eat each other, and in early manuscripts of the twelfth and thirteenth centuries there are many interlaced designs of animals eating each other. Since the human mind in the beginning was unconscious, and the origin of languages betrays the way in which things were, you can still in a way feel it. In the dimly lit mind you see something black which almost gives you the feeling of white. With some primitives it is the same word. You can see an ambiguous reaction every day, when something upsets you and produces conflicting emotions. Suppose your servant smashes a valuable statue, you get very angry and you swear "Oh Hell!" or "The Devil!" or you might say "Oh God!" What does "God" mean when used in such a way? You use it when you marvel, when you are astonished, angry or in despair, just as a primitive says "Mulungu"[3] in all sorts of states. When he hears a gramophone he says "Mulungu." The ambiguous concept "Mana" is used in Swahili to mean importance or significance, so "God" to us not only contains pairs of opposites but it is absolutely undifferentiated in that kind of use; it is ambiguous, it is like "Mulungu," the concept of something extraordinarily efficient or powerful. When we think of the unconscious we must think paradoxically, often in terms of yea and nay. We must learn to think of something good which may be bad, or of something bad which may be good. When you think of good you must think in terms of relativity. That is a very important principle in the interpretation of dreams. It all depends upon the standpoint of your consciousness whether it is good or bad. Good in psychological terms must be related to bad. Originally that feeling of good and bad signified favourable or unfavourable. For example, once a chief was asked the difference between good and bad. He said "When I take my enemy's woman, that is good. But when another chief takes my woman that is bad." It is not a difference between something moral or immoral, but of favourable and unfavourable. The superstitious attitude always asks "Is it favourable?" The mind is terribly alert to these things. The moral concept comes up very late. There are plenty of things which we call good and beautiful in the Primitive, but he does not think of them in that way, but only as favourable and unfavourable. "Have I behaved in such a way that this thing will not hurt me?"

In Hubert and Mauss, *Mélanges d'histoire des religions*,[4] the basic concepts of the mythological mind are recognized categories of creative fantasy, what Kant calls "categories of pure reason." Categories of reasoning are only intellectual applications of the archetypes. The archetypes are the primordial vessels in which you

---

[3] Jung cited this term as of central African occurrence, in "On Psychic Energy" (1928), CW 8, par. 117; of Polynesian, in *Two Essays*, CW 7, par. 108; and of Melanesian, in "On the Nature of the Psyche" (1946), CW 8, par. 411.

[4] The work (1909) is cited variously by Jung. Cf. CW 8, par. 52, n. 44.

express anything mental or psychological. There is no getting away from that.

Well now, in the progress of the cure idea the dreamer comes to the spiritual guide or saviour. Such a process is never gone through without a teacher, medicine man, guide, or guru, a man who watches the initiation process, as in the old puberty rites. The interesting fact that the saint in the dream is called Papatheanon suggests the father, since of old "Father" is a symbol for a guide, but why not just Papa? Why this peculiar Papatheanon? Miss Bianchi suggests that the patient might have been influenced by the opera *The Magic Flute*, which is a story of initiation. The word Papagei, meaning a parrot, occurs in the opera.[5] Papagei is Italian. It is a Polynesian word of exotic origin. It might be that the patient has some association with this opera, or it might be that he did not associate anything of the kind. He emphasizes the Greek and the Romanian.

Mrs. Sigg: Perhaps he means more than the father. Also the fathers of antiquity?

Dr. Jung: Yes the father is not enough, he wants to add a particular, symbolic form. The patient speaks Italian and he also knows Greek and Latin, so the word *papa* or *papas* suggests to him the Pope, the absolute Father. The cult of Attis had a temple on the site of St. Peter's in Rome, and the high priest was called "Papas" so there was already a "Papas" several hundred years before there was a Pope in the Vatican. The patient has also some associations, which I cannot give here, which would connect with the Greek form. So it is more or less certain that the Greek form contains the idea of a patriarch, or pope. The Romanian connotation I could not make out, but I am sure that I could if I had gone into it with unlimited time. The patient speaks Romanian so it must mean something to him, but we have enough material in connection with the saint to make it perfectly clear that the saint means the guru, the leader, guide, and spiritual adviser; so the patient is put into an archetypal situation.

His next association is that he is in a sacred place like Lourdes. A sort of archaic cure is suggested by the invocation of the name of the saint. When I was travelling on the upper Nile in a steamer

[5] In Mozart's *The Magic Flute*, the character Papageno is dressed as a bird. The transcriber of the *Sems.* evidently misheard the name. The Italian word for "parrot" is *pappagallo*, from Greek and Italian roots.

which drew very little water we had barges alongside to stabilize it. An Arab lying on one of the barges was suffering from malaria, and all through the night I heard him call "Allah!" and then after an interval "Allah!" That was an invocation of the name of his God for his cure. In an old Greek papyrus attributed to the cult of Mithras there is a prescription of initiation, an admonition to the pupil, where the initiate is instructed to hold his sides and shout as loud as he can the name of Mithras. This is a very important part of the ritual.

This patient has travelled in the East, and no doubt his unconscious has assimilated these things. He brings up the fact that he suffers from sciatica and that he would need more than a mere invocation to cure him. He is a layman, not a doctor, and he thinks of a pain in his leg as having nothing to do with a nervous disease, because it has nothing to do with his head or his brain. The layman thinks of sciatica as a physical disease and to cure it something physical must be done for it, as for instance the bathing in the sea.

Mrs. Muller: Sciatica could retard movement, couldn't it?

Dr. Jung: Yes, the patient's idea is that sciatica is a physical disease; it suggests that the machine would not go, he could not go forward, certain developments cannot take place. Any disease or wound of the legs suggests this, and such symbolism is often used in dreams. With the patient then, the suggestion is that things are at a standstill, also that there is not only mental but physical trouble. What physical trouble is there?

Mrs. Muller: His relation to the outside world might be the physical trouble.

Dr. Jung: What would that be?

Mrs. Sigg: He is not related to his wife.

Dr. Jung: The lack of sexuality, a physiological trouble. He has no physical relation to his wife; call it a gland trouble if you wish, a complicated condition, something physical which leads him to the idea of bathing in the sea. On the way home someone tells him that already one of the pilgrims has been cured.

He gives an association to this, the suggestive atmosphere of the crowd. If anyone is cured among them it is encouraging, so the dream tells him that something has already happened in his analysis. The dream makes the statement that he is already under the spell. Why should his unconscious hint at this?

Mr. Gibb: Something in him is already cured.

Dr. Jung: Yes, he is already under the spell, one suggestive effect has already happened. The unconscious gives him this hint for his orientation. It is exceedingly valuable for him to know that he is getting under the spell of a person or situation. If one does not realize it, one might be secretly moved by that person. In analysis if a patient does not know this he gets away from himself. Primitives are afraid of the evil eye. If you look at them a bit sharply they mistrust you. The primitive mind is always looking out for getting under a spell or a charm. In Greece if you point a finger at a man he points two, that makes three and breaks the spell. It often happens with us that we get under a spell and are unconscious of it. I have seen so many people get under the influence of other people. A young girl who consulted me got into the most amazing condition in which she was working out the fantasies of someone else. You can even live the fantasies of other people quite against your own interests. One asks, "Did you want to do this?"—"Well, I thought I had to."

The primitives know this but we do not. When one is under such a spell one cannot help it or see it, but when you get out of the atmosphere you cannot understand how you ever got like that, how you ever thought or felt like that. How often do I see tranferences which are perfectly obvious to everyone else, but the patient himself has no idea of it. He may be on fire and out of the chimney without being in the least conscious of it. You can get under the spell of very evil people. That is why so many dreams hint at the situation so that we may know where we are. They may seem ridiculous, but they are highly important. It is important to this patient to know that he is under a spell or he will discover it afterwards and then think there is something evil in it and try to get away from it. He would be likely to develop terrific resistances unless he has understood.

When we analyse our dreams and fantasies we have to analyse not only our own material but sometimes that of our neighbours also. I think l have told you about a patient who did not dream and whom I analysed from the dreams of his son. This lasted for several weeks until the father himself began to dream. You sleep in a room and something creeps into it from the next room. We are such gregarious animals that we divine the slightest psychic change in the atmosphere, like fish which swim in a school, one turns a little and they all turn. Here it is the suggestive atmosphere the patient gets into. He enters into this group of people under analysis and he gets under the spell, he must know it or he will develop resistances later. Sometimes this happens in a grotesque way. A highly educated, very respectable, reasonable young girl came to me for analysis. She could not go on with her analysis and went home. Some time later she said to an old patient of mine: "I could not continue my analysis with Dr. Jung because he became sexually involved with me." My patient asked her how it was and she replied, "Why, I had quite sexual dreams about him." She could not assume that *she* could have sex fantasies, so I had to have them.

28 February 1929

Dr. Jung:

Mr. Gibb's question is important and simple. It goes back to leakage and chickens; they must be magic.

Mr. Gibb's question: "Referring to what you said about 'leakage' two weeks ago, would not the contradiction inherent in the duplicity of attitude always come out in dreams? Take for example, a man who has come for analysis, but who retains a secret fondness for Christian Science, Behaviourism, or Theosophy. He is consciously treating his experiences from an analytical point of view with one part of his mind, and also giving himself a different account of it in terms of his pet theory with another part of his mind. If this contradiction is not dealt with consciously, will it not inevitably produce unconscious conflict and therefore dreams?—in which case the matter would be dealt with in the course of analysis in the ordinary way.

"Would there be any difference in this respect due to the psychological type of the man? For example, the kind of conflict suggested above might be more disturbing in the case of a thinking type than in a more intuitive person.

"Or does the trouble really arise from such a person's unwillingness to give the associations of his dream material which might lead to the discovery of the contradiction?"

Dr. Jung: Such a conflict disturbs a thinking type more than an intuitive or feeling type; a thinking type is bound to be playing the game fully and to the best of his ability. In the beginning of his analysis you can dismiss feeling; it will come later. A feeling type must get his feeling clear first; he cannot bear to have dualistic feeling. An intellectual type might have a whole magazine of contradictory feelings about you and it would make little difference. You have to approach every type in his own way.

137

A contradictory point of view, a *restriction mentale*, is often retained as a sort of counterpole, a safeguard against a possible transference. Then there is an unwillingness to give associations which might lead to the conflict, exactly like ladies who, when they are under the impression that an impending transference might be discovered, develop a great love for some other man and so construct a counterpole against a possible submission. In Logos, also, one builds up a stronghold against possible submission. In the Catholic Church, for example, there is no such thing. They have submitted entirely to authority, but the Protestant has lost all this. He is running wild, yet his secret desire is to find a place where he can submit, but he doesn't dare to admit it.

Let us go on with the dream of last time. We had come as far as the bath in the sea and the contemplation of the surf.

The picture is a bay, a sort of recess, into which the ocean is coming, in powerful and majestic waves breaking upon the farther shore. The dreamer stands upon the shore and watches this spectacle. He associates that the unconscious is sending its waves into the conscious, as the ocean is sending waves into the little bay. From a theoretical point of view this is an interesting description. Try to paint it in your mind, what would it suggest?

Mr. Gibb: All the activity is coming from the ocean.

Dr. Schlegel: The amazing difference in size between the conscious and the unconscious.

Dr. Jung: Yes, the amazing difference in size. We like to think of the unconscious as something below the conscious, a little dirt left in the corner. The dream itself brings an entirely different picture. The little boy of the conscious is nothing beside the immensity of the ocean. That is how the unconscious depicts itself. Walking up the hill is an approach to the unconscious in his associations. What are the great waves coming in from the unconscious?

Dr. Binger: Powerful waves sweeping into consciousness.

Dr. Jung: How does he feel it?

Dr. Binger: As a dream.

Mrs. Sigg: As emotions.

Dr. Jung: What emotions? Is there evidence of emotion?

Dr. Binger: Fear.

Dr. Jung: Yes it might be fear, anything else?

Mrs. Sigg: It might be that he has an enormous transference on his doctor. He had not a good relation with his wife, he has much feeling in the background, and in analysis this sometimes happens to men.

Dr. Jung: To try to ascertain that would be fatal; it would frighten the patient. Whether those waves are an emotion of love connected with the transference is too delicate a thing to find out. The patient rather denies feeling, he cannot admit it. We need more evidence. For the time being, it is decidedly fear. That would mean that the ocean is sending in waves of fear, but if that is so how can he admire it?

Mrs. Sigg: There might be some religious feeling. Admiration is sometimes mixed with fear in religion.

Mrs. Schevill: The rhythm is impressive regularity.

Dr. Jung: Yes that is impressive, but what does it remind you of?

Dr. Shaw: His sexuality.

Dr. Jung: Yes it is his sexuality that he fears. But to what did he compare the sea? You must all have mother complexes!

Mrs. Schevill: To the eternal mother.

Dr. Jung: Yes. It is very important to remember that in his association with the sea he called it "the primordial cause of life, the eternal mother, the womb of nature."

Dr. Binger: You could call it a regressive symbol, longing for the mother.

Mrs. Sigg: It is like the ocean against which Faust had to build a dam.

Dr. Jung: Yes, but the dam is not mentioned here. It is a sand dune, a natural dam. How would you value his associations with the sea?

Mrs. Muller: He associates it with the source of creative energy.

Dr. Jung: What is the quality of that association? Aesthetic, scientific, religious, sentimental, regressive?

Mrs. Muller: Biological.

Dr. Jung: No, decidedly *not* biological.

Miss Chapin: It is philosophical.

Dr. Jung: Of course. You can read those very morals in the old philosophy; "the womb of nature," "the evolution of the first germ." This is not biology, but old-fashioned, rather romantic, archetypal philosophy. So when he contemplates the movement of the sea, it is as he has qualified it. It obviously arouses philosophical ideas in him. He looks at the sea with a kind of philosophical emotion.

Mrs. Sigg: He has been forced to change his mind about sexuality, and therefore he is obliged to change his philosophy about it.

Dr. Jung: Yes, in the first part of his analysis he thought of sexuality as an uncomfortable thing in the corner, a personal difficulty which he did not feel up to at all. The unconscious is slowly trying to open his eyes to a wider vision or conception of sex. The pitiful symbol of the sewing-machine is now increased to almost cosmic size. The rhythm of the sewing-machine is now the systole and diastole of life, which shows itself in sex, too, so he should look at sex as though it were the rhythm of the sea; the rhythm of the primordial mother, the rhythmical contraction of the womb of nature. This gives him another aspect of sexuality. It is no longer his miserable personal affair, something he has to put into the corner, but a great problem of life. It is not a dirty intrigue, but it becomes a big thing, a generally human universal situation. So he will mobilize quite different troops to deal with his sexuality than when he treated it as though it were a case for the police court.

Now he sees his problem as the great rhythm of life, a problem of nature, which he looks upon philosophically, and now he can allow its creative functioning in himself. First it was the sewing-machine which did not function, then the steamroller which made the mysterious path creating the mandala, and now it is the ocean itself which has become a universal symbol. This gives him a philosophical attitude and he has a greater chance to deal with his problem. To have a personal attitude toward it would not do at all. A young person would have to deal with such a problem personally, but a man of his age cannot deal with it personally; he must deal with it as gaining something for his spiritual development, and not for the propagation of his particular blessed family.

In the next part of the dream, he tries to climb that hill of gravel with his youngest boy, and then he observes that the spray is dashing up on the rocks. He thinks it is dangerous, the hill might be washed away and he retires. This is an attempt to approach the unconscious in motion, exposing himself to the powerful waves. Psychologically, this means he is going to deal with his problem, he is going to do something about it. What about his youngest boy who is with him?

Mrs. Sigg: That means progress. Before, the child was ill, dead, now it is alive, in health.

Dr. Jung: He is a substitute for the father (the patient). He says this child is especially identified with him. According to the primitive idea the child is truly the prolongation of the father, the replica of the father; bodily and spiritually he is the father. There is the story of an old Negro who shouted at his grown son, and when he paid no heed the father said, "There he goes with my body, and he does not even obey me!" So the patient says he is now, with his new attempt (the boy), hopeful, progressive, beginning. He says let us approach the sea, then he is afraid. What is the fear in the dream?

Dr. Binger: The fear of the unconscious and of the forces which might be let loose by it.

Dr. Jung: Yes, he has obviously undervalued the tremendous power of nature, but now he sees it could wash away the ground beneath his feet, his established situation. That means that this force could wash away his natural, social, physical, philosophized position. He is standing, interestingly enough, between the conscious and the unconscious. These forces might wash away the hill on which he is standing, for it is all loose gravel and stones, it has no cohesion. It had been heaped up by the sea, made by the power of nature. This is the way we are, just loose gravel, stuff washed up by the power of nature with no cohesion. It is not *our* merit. We have not yet found cement to get this stuff together. This is the task of the dream.

When I explained the mandala I spoke of this loose stuff, the grains of different materials which must be brought together by a sort of alchemical procedure, so that this action of the sea cannot destroy it again. Our patient is still in fragments, all is loose, so he is quite right in not trusting the hill, for it could easily be washed away. That means he has no individuality yet, nothing is cemented in him, so he can be dissolved by the power of the unconscious. He had better go back.

Dr. Shaw: Does the child show him how to approach his problem in a trustful attitude?

Dr. Jung: Yes, the patient was trying to build up a philosophy of an old virgin about his sexuality. He tried to be one of the eleven thousand virgins just initiated, not taking nature into account. He is more or less identified with the child, and the child with him.

141

He approaches his problem in a sort of childish enthusiasm, and jumps at it. Patients often jump and break a leg.

Mrs. Sigg: Female patients often build a philosophy without sex. Why must he be cleansed by sea-baths and by fire?

Dr. Jung: The fire was very lightly referred to. The bath is purification. Whenever we touch nature we get clean. Savages are not dirty—only we are dirty. Domesticated animals are dirty, but never wild animals. Matter in the wrong place is dirt. People who have got dirty through too much civilization take a walk in the woods, or a bath in the sea. They may rationalize it in this or that way, but they shake off the fetters and allow nature to touch them. It can be done within or without. Walking in the woods, lying on the grass, taking a bath in the sea, are from the outside; entering the unconcious, entering yourself through dreams, is touching nature from the inside and this is the same thing, things are put right again. All these things have been used in initiations in past ages. They are all in the old mysteries, the loneliness of nature, the contemplation of the stars, the incubation sleep in the temple. In Malta an underground temple of the Neolithic Age has been found, which has dormitories for the initiates, and there are small statuettes showing prehistoric women in the sleep of incubation. They suggest the Venus of Brassempouy, an ivory carving found in France, a palaeolithic statuette in which all the secondary sex characteristics, the hind parts, the breasts, etc., are greatly exaggerated.[1] In the incubation dormitories at Malta the initiates were plunged into the unconscious for rebirth. Curiously enough there was a corridor leading from the incubation niches to a square hole, six feet deep, dug in the floor and filled with water. The temple itself was quite dark, so that when the initiate walked along the corridor he must have fallen into the cold water, and so he had his cold bath and incubation sleep all together.

After this last dream there followed a very peculiar reaction. The patient wrote me several notes about his family. He has three children and he writes certain observations about them. "For several days I have observed that there is something wrong with my wife. When I asked her what was wrong she said, with some hesitation, that she was afraid that the children were not quite happy with

[1] For the Maltese statuettes, see Erich Neumann, *The Great Mother* (1955), pl. 3. For the Venus of Brassempouy, see S. Giedion, *The Beginnings of Art* (1926), p. 438 and fig. 287.

their parents. She said that the daughter had behaved queerly, she had suddenly gone out of the room weeping and couldn't say why."

Dr. Jung: That doesn't mean that there was a reason, she might have been weeping just because she thought it was nice to weep. Had she been a boy it would have been different!] "Then she is afraid that the boy might be tubercular because he coughed. The youngest boy is not psychologically what he should be, egoistical and a bit neurotic; he also has been weeping, but his mother assumed that he thought he might get something by it." The dreamer writes this the day after his last analysis. Here is a good example of practical psychology. How do you explain all this reaction? The patient was obviously quite frightened by all this badness, his wife was in a bad mood, etc.

Miss Chapin: He feels some connection between his family and his psychological condition, so he writes the notes.

Dr. Jung: Yes, but what is the connection? Why does he have this feeling just after the last dream?

Dr. Binger: The gravel is being washed away.

Dr. Jung: Mind you, it is his *wife* who comes out with these things.

Dr. Shaw: Her unconscious is infected by his problem.

Dr. Jung: You are coming to it now. He has been working on this problem for some time. The sewing-machine, the steamroller, the mandala, the sea. He has observed his wife getting worse for several days. After the last dream when he asked her what was the matter she comes out with all her fears about the children. She is infected with his problems. He has never discussed them with her, she is at a stage where everything psychological is taboo.

Mr. Gibb: Isn't he projecting it all?

Dr. Jung: No, this is real, he is a very objective person. He comes out with the fears and complaints of his wife, obviously repeating what she says.

Mrs. Binger: As soon as his problem takes on less personal terms then he can approach it, but for the wife it becomes dangerous.

Dr. Jung: Yes, as long as she can keep the whole thing down, so that it cannot be approached in a personal way, she can hold it, but as soon as it takes on an important aspect she smells a rat. Not that he has ever mentioned it, but at that very moment, as it were, when he envisages the problem philosophically, feels the fresh air of dawn, and is no more arrested, no more split, she becomes affected. It reaches her through the atmosphere somehow. There are a good many marriages in which this happens. He might have looked a bit more enterprising that day, he went up a few degrees, and she went down. She couldn't see that there was anything the matter with him, so she put it on the children. This is the way with mothers, it is either husband or children. In this case it is too obviously not the husband, therefore it must be the children. Why the children?

Mrs. Sigg: Children are the symbols of a new thing coming. His children are such a symbol.

Dr. Jung: In this case the children are the mother's symbols. This is the mother's psychology. The children are symbols of the undeveloped things in her. She is going the wrong way, she develops resistances against analysis, the thing that might be good for him; and she projects her fear into the children, and poisons them thereby. It is always thus with mothers. The real mother is never wrong. Why should she be wrong? She is a mother and has three children and she is married. If anything is wrong it must be with her husband or the children. The children are not bad, therefore they must be sick. Mothers can get their children sick in no time, they can project sickness into them. The devil will make tuberculosis or what not. You project tuberculosis into a child and it comes. Often you have to take children away from certain families to relieve them from the terrific pressure of wrong assumptions. The point is that things are wrong with the wife. So the patient is alarmed. He is a very nice family man. His wife understands how to work it, she makes a sort of psychological noise to disturb him. She gets his attention away from his analysis by talking of the children's sickness. In this way the bogey can be handled by the wife, so he wastes at least half an hour with me over these non-existent diseases. I told him to get a doctor for them and to stop worrying. He was wasting his time, and it was not his business. Thus progress can be hampered by a wife who refuses to be interested in what her husband is doing. She has terrible power, she can raise hell all over the place, she can kill the children even. She is always perfectly right, but she is killing her children. I have treated a woman who actually murdered her pet child. It does happen.

Not in vain are little children afraid of their own mothers in the night. Primitive mothers can kill their children. It is absolutely incompatible with the daytime, for then they are most devoted mothers. But in the night they take away the mask and become witches; they upset children psychically, even kill them. The more they are devoted to them in the wrong way the worse it is.

I told the patient that he should talk with his wife, to try to make her realize what analysis really is, otherwise the children would be really ill and the wife, realizing later that it was her fault, would be a wreck. You can do something to stop it, when you know that situation in the very beginning. I was quite certain that she could stop everything, infect the children, and take him from his analysis without solving his problem. It sounds superstitious, but I know such things do happen, like the mother who let her child drink infected water and even gave it to the younger child with the secret hope that the children would die. I had a patient who succeeded, after trying three times, in killing his wife in a beautifully indirect way. Then he went into a bad neurosis. I found out the whole story and told him that he had murdered his wife, then his whole psychosis cleared up and he was cured. Since then I am amply convinced that when a woman begins like this, one must be careful and stop it.

Four days later the patient had the following dream [6]: "My brother-in-law tells me that something has happened in the business. [The brother-in-law took the patient's place in the firm.] Some stock that had been sold was not sent away when it should have been, long ago. It is now June, and it should have been sent in May. It was forgotten then and a second time in June. I got quite angry and said to my brother-in-law that if the buyer should claim damages one would be forced to meet his claim."

Associations: "My brother-in-law, who entered our firm as a partner, wrote me yesterday that he had been on a business trip, and he wanted to ask me certain things about affairs connected with the business. But he did not tell me what they were, and in the dream I wondered what it was he wanted to discuss with me. There is something wrong or he would have told me in the letter."

About *selling* and *forgetting:* "I was always very careful to live up to any obligations. I took the business very seriously, and when I left I was a bit afraid that my brother-in-law would not give the business this particular kind of attention. If now, according to the dream, things are forgotten like that in the short time since I am away from my post, things are wrong with the business, which would cause no end of damage. My brother-in-law is something

145

like my shadow, he is younger than I am, entering the firm after me and holding the position I held formerly." It is as though his brother-in-law, being his shadow, informs him that there is disorder in the business, that is, disorder in his life (in his unconscious), so that he does not live up to obligations that are fully recognized. Such forgetfulness could only be made good by allowing for the damages. That is a clear dream, now how do you explain it?

Mrs. Sigg: He thinks perhaps that it is his own fault that his wife is upset.

Dr. Jung: Yes, he feels it is his own fault, but how do you explain the dream?

Miss Chapin: Has he talked to his wife?

Dr. Jung: Yes a little, but it was not much good. It has nothing to do with this.

Mrs. Sigg: It is an obligation to that part of his being that is not continued, something to do with his soul.

Dr. Jung: Yes, the thing developed in a sort of childish enthusiasm. In the previous dream he was trying to throw himself into the fulness of life. He tries to throw himself into the fulness of nature, into the waves of the ocean of love. Then he sees that his situation is a bit dangerous, and he withdraws, lest the loose gravel and stones be washed away from the hill where he is standing.

This is as it should be. Then his wife smells a rat and threatens to kill his children. This is her revenge. It is as though she said "Oh, if you dare to change I will kill the children." Naturally that gets him going and it takes him away from his task. He is concerned with the children, so he desists. He might have gone further in this task of cementing the ground together. He was interested, but his wife threatens and he stops. Then up comes the dream and says, "That is the disorder in your business. You left it to your shadow and he forgot his obligations. Your business is with the sea, you must deal with it. Fortify your island, establish yourself. Your business is not with the little illnesses, like an old nurse." He should know that his wife is jealous, but that is all. The dream is holding him to his job.

Dr. Binger: It seems to me that it might be just a guilty conscience dream. He might feel that he had been neglecting his wife.

Dr. Jung: But as a matter of fact he has done all he could do. He is trying to do the right thing all along the way. He has tried to talk with his wife. He is going into analysis, trying to solve his problem. That would be in favour of his children too. It is better for the children to have a well father. His fault is that he was going at it a bit rashly perhaps, acting on boyish enthusiasm. The waves were pretty high. His wife's reaction began with his withdrawal. He is just, reliable, and clear in his mind, so I really assume that he has been led away too much. That is often so in analysis, external circumstances make it impossible to go ahead, he is not quite ready to take the next step, or he still has resistances.

The next dream [7] *one day later:* He sees a peculiar machine, which is a new device for rooting up weeds. It was so peculiar-looking that he could not describe it. He only knew, in the dream, that he should apply it.

Associations: "I have read recently in the paper a sort of sentimental article about an old roadmaker, who watches a new machine cleaning the streets. This machine works one hundred times more efficiently than he did. Therefore the meaning of the dream is quite clear to me. I should apply the machine to my case."

Mrs. Sigg: It seems to me that he has not dealt sufficiently with all the material in the first dream, so the machine has to come again.

Dr. Jung: Yes, he has to take up the machine again. The former dream said, "In case the buyer puts in a claim, one must pay damages." So much time may have been lost, and now the machine is for pulling up weeds, and it is one hundred times more efficient than when one works alone. This dream shows where the damage lies. The regression he made was concerned with his wife; he got infected with his wife, and he got the idea that he could pull up his own weeds and then he would not have any trouble in his family. The dream shows him that instead of giving up analysis, he should apply this machine for pulling up the weeds which have sprung up.

Always remember the Hymn of Ra: Isis, his lovely wife, was making the worm.

The next dream [8] *one day later:* "I am touring in my car near the Riviera. Some one tells me the *route d'en haut et route d'en bas* can be used from now on only by those who stay for two months in the country, that all cars have to go one way on the lower road, and the other way on the upper. These regulations change every day. Monday it is so, while on Tuesday it goes the other way, so that one could enjoy the beautiful view from every direction. Someone shows me a map with a plan of the two roads; green and white circles indicate the days of the week and the direction to be observed by the visitors, east-west and west-east.

"The visitors who were there for only a short time need not observe the regulations, and I thought it rather illogical that they could go just as they pleased. I also heard that other visitors were protesting against these regulations, because one had to pay for permission to travel on these roads for not less than six years. We all thought that terribly exaggerated."

Associations: "I have never been on the Riviera but I have a beautiful fantasy of this country, as of eternal spring, like in the Island of the Blessed. I thought I would go down in my car, because travelling there would be such a wonderful excursion. I am not certain whether there are really two roads. I suppose travelling on these roads symbolizes life, if one lives it systematically without changing too often. The fact that those staying two months have to submit to the regulations, but those who are only there for a few days can do as they please, would not fit my life, but it could fit my travelling into the unconscious. Perhaps it is just as interesting and beautiful as travelling on the Riviera. If one wants to stay two months or longer, one must submit to the regulations even if they do not appear to be very logical and even if the people who are there for only a short time do not have to observe the rules. Under the right conditions, one can travel up above on the mountains or down below in the valley; there one can see things right and left. *White* and *green* show a free course—only *red* means stop."

Permission to travel for six years: The patient thought that I had told him that a complete renewal of attitude would take him six years. But I could not remember telling him anything of this sort. I might have told him of a case which took six years. There can be nothing arbitrary about the length of time for an analysis. What is a complete renewal anyway? Certainly I did not say what he had made of it. Now what do you make of this? Remember we are beginning again, and again there is a machine.

Dr. Binger: It seems to me that it is a commentary on his analysis. If he stays only a short time there is not much progress, but if two months or more he must keep to the regulations. There is resistance to regulation and the time element, also to the two roads, high and low.

Dr. Jung: Sure enough, the whole thing has to do with his analysis, and you meet the same kind of resistance as in the mandala dream with the roads. Here he is travelling on roads, the machine is the car. He is again afloat. The weed-pulling machine is a sedentary thing, slow like the steamroller, and you could not travel with it. But with a car you can go fast and far. When you use the road you want to get somewhere. The goal is "The Island of the Blessed," "Atlantis," where Immortals live. But it is a bit awkward because in that country they have certain regulations. It is as though these regulations were forced upon him by the country. It is the unconscious where he wants to go, and it is the nature of that country that he must go in this peculiar way. In the mandala the way was all wound up. In this it goes first one way, then another, there is one impulse, then the contrary one! This is a fine, accurate description of the unconscious. Often it is a sort of weaving impulse, or a pump going up and down. This is typical of the unconscious; not only are there pairs of opposites, but contrasting impulses going right and left. When he follows first one road and then the other he has ample time to see the country from all points of view. It is optimistically expressed.

You must put yourself in the position of the patient. He is a man of the world, a good business man, he is used to doing things accurately, to directing his affairs with no waste of time. Suddenly he finds himself in the unconscious, where everything is up and down, to and fro, with the most contradictory impulses and opinions. We talk of this and that, and he cannot understand what the devil it is all about. He is lost, he loathes it, and he cannot understand that this peculiar experience is the main thing. He cannot mature until he has exposed himself to such a process of obstacles. They are the tests of the initiate in the old initiations, like the twelve labours of Hercules. Sometimes they seem useless things, like cleaning the Augean Stables, or strangling the hydra headed-serpent. The business man would say, it is none of my affair to clean the stables, or to kill the lion that lives somewhere. But in the unconscious he must submit to the slow progress of to and fro; to a sort of balancing deliberation, a sort of torture. One day you think you have come to a clear decision, next day it is gone. You feel like a fool and curse it until you learn that this thing is pairs of opposites, and you are not the opposite. If you learn that, you have got your lesson. This man has not learned it.

LECTURE VII

6 March 1929

Dr. Jung:

The last dream was about the two roads, the one above and the one below, in the Riviera. Now, what is the actual situation in our patient's problem? A series of dreams is like the development in a play. We don't know what the actual goal is; we can only watch the development of the drama. I wish you would always make up your minds before the seminar, as to the actual situation which has been reached in the analysis.

There was the dream about the sewing-machine and the tailoress, a girl ill and working in a humid hole; after that the steamroller making a pattern, then later he had a dream of a new machine for pulling up weeds, and now we have the dream of the Riviera. How do you see the situation of the dreamer's problem? What does the last dream demonstrate?

Mrs. Deady: He has made a regression because of his wife's reaction, and the fuss she made about the children. The symbolism of the upper and lower roads shows him where he is in his analysis.

Dr. Jung: What is the dream emphasizing?

Mr. Gibb: Was he not originally more or less identified with his respectable side? The dream showed that things are in a disordered condition with him. Must he not deal with his opposing impulses as well?

Dr. Jung: Yes, he took up that problem before, and then he ran into his wife's reaction, and that showed what the possible effects might be, so he was frightened and held back; then came the dream showing the disorder in him which needs a machine for pulling up the weeds.

Mrs. Sigg: Isn't the unconscious forcing him to take the irrational road?

Dr. Jung: Yes, in a situation where he should accept it.

Dr. Binger: He must go through the horrid thing though it is difficult and long.

Dr. Jung: Yes, his mistake was to take the whole thing too simply. He thought he could just turn a switch then things would be all right, so he went at it quite enthusiastically. Analysis is like a chemical laboratory where people take steps experimentally, but they see all the consequences which would arise if they took the steps in reality. As in cannon practice, one uses a low charge of gunpowder two hundred grams instead of two kilos. It shows how the thing works without the risks. So he took the steps and ran into difficulties, which were hints of what might happen if he should make the move in reality. His eyes were opened and he withdrew. Now again he goes forward and finds himself going to the Blessed Island, the Riviera, and there he learns that the whole enterprise is not so easy as he thought it would be. He finds an awkward situation, all those peculiar traffic regulations which one has to observe when one is there for two months, but one who stays for a few days only need not observe them, and at the last he is told that he must pledge himself for six years. The unconscious means by six years a *long* time.

In Nigeria there was once a story that a thousand Germans had marched through British territory, so a company of soldiers was sent out to inquire about it, and they came back and reported that just six soldiers of a patrol which had gone astray had gone through. The explanation was that six in the language of the natives meant many. They could only count to five, so six meant anything beyond five, therefore 1000 or 10,000. I worked with an old medicine man who said he could count to 100. He did it with sticks, and when he got to 70 he said "70 and that is 100"; he could not count beyond 70. In the course of civilization all numbers between 1 and 9 have become sacred: in religious language, for instance, the three of the Trinity and the seven-armed candelabra, the seven times seven, etc. But two and one are also sacred, and in Indian religion it is four, in Egypt eight and nine. Three times four = twelve, also a sacred number. The fact that all root numbers are sacred simply means that they have retained a certain taboo, a mystical value. Originally they were not merely numbers but qualities and not abstract quantities. When our unconscious says three, it is less a quantity than a quality. [Dr. Jung demonstrated this by placing three matches together in one place and two in another.] If a primitive is asked how many matches there are here, he says, "Three matches," and in this place he says, "Two matches." Now, if one is taken from the group of three and put in the group of two, he will say, "Here are the two three matches and there are the two two matches and one three match." The *quality* of twoness and threeness is involved. The primitive counts from the figures things make. He makes an aesthetic distinction because he counts without counting. For example, an old chief knew whether all his six hundred head of cattle were in the kraal, although he could not count more than six. He knew them all individually by name, so that he could tell if "little Fritz" hadn't come in yet. The count is made by the extent of the ground covered by the cattle, and the way the ground is checkered by them; it is a vision of the ensemble. The number has a quality value, a visual, aesthetic form value. You could say a man is three, not three people, but meaning taboo or holy three. It all depends on the value people give to the number.

Geometric figures have high psychological values and therefore magical qualities. Numbers take on the qualities of degrees, as $3 \times 3 = Holy$—the Holiest of Holy. The figure seven is one of the most sacred numbers which can be imagined, therefore a figure which has seven points, seven angles, or seven units is particularly powerful.

So when the dream says "six" it has all those connotations in it. It seems to the dreamer that quite a number of car-drivers are protesting against paying for a license for six years, when they may only mean to stay for a little while. He is thinking of a pleasure trip to the Riviera and associates it with a trip in the unconscious. He will have a few pleasant dreams and then return, but he finds it is otherwise.

His unconscious says, "You just wait! You must pay for six years, pledge yourself for a long time and with great intensity." When the unconscious forces such an understanding on him it disturbs him, he doesn't quite like it. He wants to have the thing simple and reasonable, so he is rather doubtful about this dream business.

In the next dream [9] he is in a somewhat intimate situation with his wife. He wishes to show her some tenderness, but she is pretty negative. He begins to talk with her very seriously and asks her to be reasonable. He tells her that he thinks she should allow him to have intercourse with her at least once a month. While he is talking to her all of the children come into the room, or perhaps not all, but only the eldest boy who is fourteen or fifteen, so he cannot continue the talk with his wife.

Associations: "I make an attempt to talk to my wife occasionally, but when I feel the slightest resistance on her part I give it up, for I know from her remarks what resistance she has against sexuality. This is particularly evident since she was sterilized by x-ray treatment for a tumor. Since then she has developed quite a serious resistance against sexuality. When the children came in, they seemed to make further discussion impossible."

The oldest boy: "He has always been a particular pet of his mother, and has caused her much sorrow. When he was eight months old he almost died of enteritis. Since his third year he has suffered from asthma. There is something queer about that boy. I get quite irritable with him when he is a little naughty, in a way that is quite unreasonable on my part. I am sure that if the other children should do the same things they would not irritate me so much; my wife has called my attention to this fact."

Dr. Jung: Now what is your idea about this dream? What connection has it with the former dream?

Dr. Binger: The impasse in the former dream is like the impasse with his wife.

Dr. Jung: What would you conclude about the former dream? Has he accepted it? You can always tell. He sees that analysis is a very serious business. Has he accepted it?

Dr. Binger: He has seen the situation with his wife and that drives him to realize what analysis might mean.

Dr. Jung: First comes the dream which makes him realize that analysis is a very serious business. He is trying again to bring about some reasonable solution of the problem with his wife, so we can think that he has accepted the Riviera dream, but is this attempt to solve the problem with his wife reasonable?

Dr. Binger: It is compensatory, but it is unreasonable in the sense that it is ineffective.

Dr. Shaw: It is reasonable, but after all he is up against a woman and she has something to say.

Dr. Binger: He is butting against a stone wall.

Dr. Shaw: But his wife is not a stone wall!

Dr. Binger: His technique is not reasonable, arguing is no good. He should win her love first.

Dr. Jung: Yes, he should win her love first. It is terribly stupid

of him to treat his problem in that way. Rational treatment never
has appealed to a woman's heart. You can talk to a motor and
convince it that it should go, you might convince a sewing-machine,
but never a woman in such a way! The dream shows him how
stupid he is, but of course he has not done this in reality. We don't
know what would happen if he tried in a right way. I have never
seen the wife but she seems to be something of an ass, as she is
afraid of me. After a while the devils will take care of her. She is
the X in the whole situation. There is something wrong there, and
I don't know at all how this case will end. The dream points out
to him that the way he has taken is wrong. Why should the children
interrupt, why do they come in?

Dr. Binger: The children represent his feeling side.

Dr. Jung: Have we any evidence of that?

Dr. Binger: Yes, the way he took the suggestion of the children's
illness.

Dr. Jung: Yes, that is a good point. What about the oldest boy?

Dr. Binger: He is a symbol of the parents' first love.

Dr. Jung: Yes, and he suffers. He is the symbol of conflict between
the parents. The child evidently has a neurosis and is labouring
under the weight of the wrong relations of his parents. The child
has been ill since he was three years old with asthma, what does
that prove?

Dr. Binger: That something has been wrong between the parents since the child was three years old.

Dr. Jung: Yes, when a woman refuses herself like that to a man
there must be a serious thing in between them. You can be absolutely sure that something has been wrong since the child was three
years old. The constant oppression of that black pall of suppression,
the cloud of fear hanging over him at night, causes the difficulty
in breathing. Asthma is a suffocation phobia, and the more the
fear increases, the more actual the suffocation, darkness, and unconsciousness. In the daytime everything seems reasonable and all
right, but in the night all that heaped-up sexuality makes an archaic
fear! When you come into certain houses where there is such a
situation you feel it in the air. You get it from the atmosphere,
inhibitions, fears, taboos, ghosts, so a little child gets it. Asthma at
that age is either organic or it comes from the parents. Children
of three have no such psychic problems of their own. They are not
dissociated. They can be terribly nice and amiable one minute and

154

the next minute horrid, without being split by it. They have no moral values at that age, because they are not conscious enough. While such a child has no psychological conflict, it is not beyond the reach of parental problems. The father as well as the mother is full of vibrations and the child gets the full impact of the atmosphere. If you had to live there you would jump out of the window and run away, but the child cannot escape it. He has to breathe the poisoned air. The child is *memento mori*, the very symbol of the things which are wrong. That child is the silencer. When he comes into the room, the silencer works. "Shut up, this thing is deeper than your rational arguments."

Next dream [10], *the night after:* The problem is going on, and we shall see for ourselves in how far it has to do with the problem of love. The patient says: "Someone brings me a sort of mechanism. I see there is something wrong with it. It does not function as it should. I take it apart and try to see what is wrong with it. The piece of mechanism has the form of a double heart, the back and front are connected by a steel spring. In the dream I think there must be something wrong with the spring, it doesn't function because of unequal tension, as if twelve on one side and four on the other."

Association: "As a rule the spring is something like the soul of a mechanism. The fact that this object has the form of a heart is perhaps a sign of human mechanism. I should identify, for instance, thinking with the head, intuition with the sympathetic nervous system, feeling with the heart, sensation with the limbs. In this dream I naturally think of my marriage. The mistake must be in the different tensions of the feeling. Probably I should begin there, in order to bring up feeling to a conscious level; to try to induce my wife to think about delicate subjects without getting emotional."

Dr. Jung: How about this dream?

Miss Chapin: It is less purely mechanical than the former dream. He goes over into something human.

Dr. Jung: Yes, he says in the dream before that the rational way did not work. Now he sees that he is not dealing with a rational mechanism, but with a human heart. What about this double heart with a spring as the soul of the mechanism, like the spring in a watch? The heart as the spring of the mechanism is an excellent simile. We speak of the heart as the seat of life, and it has always been the symbol for emotions. The Pueblo Indians say they think with their hearts, which of course means an identification of thinking with feeling. They think that the white man is crazy because he thinks with his head. Often Negroes say that they think in the stomach, sensation and intuition are mixed, all the functions are drawn together. They talk of dreams as reality; you cannot tell in which world they really live. So thoughts are localized in the stomach. With the more civilized man the thinking is in the head. Now what about the symbol of the double heart connected with the same spring?

Dr. Binger: The heart of himself and of his wife with a difference of tension between them of twelve to four.

Dr. Jung: Yes, he assumes this is the symbol of the feeling of himself and his wife and his tension is twelve, hers four.

Dr. Binger: Mechanically that is a good spring.

Dr. Jung: Yes, but he must get away from that cramp of thinking. He has had a hard business life in which he had to fight for himself and for success. He has reduced everything to rational thinking, and he knows what he can do with his intellect. He is identified with it, so that now he is in a sort of spasm of intellectuality which allows him no free movement. He is one-sided, and it will take him a long while before he can get rid of that and get back to the human heart. He thinks that he is full of feeling, but it is all sentimentality; he has no feeling because he is only mind.

Only men are sentimental; a woman as a rule is not sentimental if she is on good terms with her animus. Sentimentality is a weakness, an indulgence, always a sign of inferior feeling. Some people believe that they have wonderful feelings because tears flow. We go to the movies and weep! Aren't we full of feeling? Marvellous! I am not quite satisfied with this idea that the other half of the double heart is the heart of his wife. It does not quite fit in with reality. One bed, one dish, one cup, one spoon, etc. is his sentimentality. His idea of a perfect marriage is one heart, one mind, one soul, etc. I should much prefer the idea that the unequal tension is in himself.

Dr. Binger: This man has a double heart.

Mrs. Zinno: Number twelve is in his business and number four is in his feeling and the spring is made of steel.

Dr. Jung: Yes, his heart is still a mechanism made of steel! A mighty good substance, steel! The vibrations of the steel, he thinks, are his feelings. In reality it is his tension, icy cold and hard. So he has two hearts, but in reality it is one with an unequal tension between the two halves. The greater tension is business, money, power, and the smaller one is the marriage. It is the idea that every respectable man holds, that the wife goes by herself, that the marriage will work itself out. The only thing that does not go by itself is business. With the wife the only thing that does not go by itself is marriage, for that is her business. Some difference in the point of view!

Are there any questions about the dream? I think the interpretation is perfectly clear and to my idea satisfactory. I feel a sort of satisfaction when the interpretation seems to fit the dream. The mechanistic idea is a prejudice of our rational mind. Nature hates this petrification. The dream seems to be driving home the idea that the unconscious is going to root up this mechanistic idea, that is the meaning of the machine for pulling up the weeds. A man stops living when he lives by rational ideas alone.

Dream [11] *one night later:* "I am in a bathing place on the seashore, diving through high waves which are coming up on the shore. I see there the son of a certain prince." (In his business he has to deal with this prince; let us call him Prince Omar. He knew the prince himself, but he does not know the son.) "Then comes my father but as a terribly fat, unshapely, formless man. He says that he almost fell down the stairs, and that they had to carry him down into the water. He talks with the General Manager of the estate of the prince, a man with a thick black beard." (This man has no such beard in reality.) "Then comes Prince Omar himself and invites us to have lunch with him after bathing. We are sitting at a table with many others, and my father talks to the General Manager, speaking Swiss." (Of course the man would not understand Swiss. I must explain about the business. Much cotton was raised on this estate, and the dreamer was in a business connection with the General Manager.) "My father says that our firm could compete with any other firm when it came to buying the cotton crop, but the price is so high that our firm would prefer to leave the buying to other firms. He assumes that the estate make better terms to other firms than to ours. It has often happened that we were asked higher prices than other firms were, but it was never so bad as this. Then he blamed the General Manager directly for being paid by someone to raise the price to our firm and so making a profit for himself, as such things were often happening in that particular trade. The

157

prince himself did not know of the deal. My father tells me that I should explain the whole situation to the prince. I am of the same conviction, but it is clear to me that I should lose any further business, even the cotton seed trade with this firm, if I explain as directly as my father wished me to do. I was quite hesitant, and afraid that I could not explain so that the business manager would not be offended. But I tried, speaking French." (In reality this business manager used to buy cotton seed from the dreamer's firm because they used the best seed, but as a rule he did not sell his cotton to their firm.) "I said that we could buy their cotton at a higher price than that given to other firms, if an allowance could be made for it in the handling of the shipping by his own people." (When you buy from a plantation, the selling is done by one set of men, and the shipping by another set, just as when you buy wine in the vineyard you have still to pay for collecting, for barrels for transportation, for storage, etc.) "I am convinced that the shipping is handled better for the people who have bought hitherto. This is understandable because other firms were known to the people on the estate, while our firm is unknown to them, since we have never bought from them before. Shipping conditions are always far more reasonable on other estates than on that of the prince. The prince saw the point and agreed to look into the matter, to remedy the situation."

Associations: Bathing in the sea: "I have often thought of the sea as my unconscious and the waves that come up against the shore as that part of the unconscious which comes up into the conscious." *Diving through the waves:* "When one is swimming in the waves one can be easily carried away by the breakers, but one can get along quite easily if one dives, then you are not carried away. It seems as though I could deal with those waves coming up from the unconscious when I have learned to dive through them." *Father:* (The father had not been in business but was a clergyman and is long since dead.) "My father is deformed in the dream. Fat and formless people are, as a rule, somewhat slow physically and mentally—and are inferior. Obviously the dream disfigures my father in every respect. He was not at all like that in reality. It represents him as quite inferior and also the future development of the dream shows how tactless he is in the way he discusses the business about the General Manager. This could do no end of damage to our firm. It obviously shows that I put myself far above my father in the unconscious, for I would not handle a matter where there might be a question of such foolish corruption. In my conscious I could never have such feelings of superiority over my father."

Black beard: "The General Manager had no such beard, but my father had in my youth, later it grew grey." *Prince Omar:* "He is the type of a very distinguished aristocrat, a beautiful tall man with a truly royal demeanour. He also plays a great role in politics, although he has no official position; he is an obviously powerful figure."

The long business discussion: This is rather tricky, and the patient is confused, because he realizes that he has mixed up his father with the General Manager and himself with the prince. He asks: "Is the whole dream a conflict of my father with himself? My father and the General Manager disagree, and this could end in a fight, therefore is my father in conflict with himself as the general manager of the estate and have I to step in, to solve that conflict by explaining the situation to the prince, thus taking the whole matter out of my father's hands?"

Dr. Jung: Obviously the father and the General Manager are getting into a disagreement, and the prince must step in and do something about it. As yet there is no sign that the patient and the prince are one, but as his father has the black beard of the General Manager, the patient feels that they are somehow identical and draws the conclusion also that the prince is identical with himself. But he is not convinced that he is right. He says that from his eighth to his tenth year his parents were living in a house right opposite to the palace of Prince Omar, on the other side of the street, so he can identify himself with the prince.

Detail of the business transaction: This is a reality. The General Manager has always quoted higher prices to the patient's firm than to others, so he thought it might be a question of corruption on the part of the General Manager. But the General Manager always bought cotton seed from his firm, as they had the best seed on the market. Now what do you make of this?

Dr. Binger: The disfigurement of the father in the dream is a compensation for the admiration and the infantile overvaluation of the father.

Dr. Jung: Yes, that is right. The father was a highly educated clergyman. The dreamer, as the oldest son, admired him very much. The father was learned, the son went into business, so the father

159

remained on a pedestal, the wise unalterable one! So he stayed his whole life there. In the dream a negative image of his father comes up. The dreamer despises the General Manager from the bottom of his heart but he identifies him with his father, so he puts his father into the category of such feelings, he also disfigures his father's physical beauty, which in reality was great. So the father in him is lowered considerably. How would you think of the father in the dream?

Dr. Binger: The father image is disfigured.

Dr. Jung: Yes, but that is figurative speech. What does that mean psychologically? The father has been dead for a long time. If he were still living near him in the next street or was associated with him in the business we could say that the unconscious was showing him his depreciation of the father, and that he might be open to corruption like the General Manager. But the father is dead and one does not depreciate the dead, so it must be something left over from the father, a beautiful memory of him perhaps. When he thinks of the father as the dream presents him, what does it mean?

Dr. Binger: If the father is a fine man, he is able to shift his responsibility into him and be infantile himself.

Dr. Jung: That would be the psychology of a son whose father is still living. Then the son might live a provisional life. He feels father will somehow always come across with an open pocket-book.

Dr. Binger: Can that attitude not survive the death of the father?

Dr. Jung: Yes, somewhat, but not in such a definite form. I have seen two cases of sons who collapsed when their fathers died. They had been living the provisional life and believed it to be reality, so when the father was taken away they collapsed. This reminds me of a story by Alphonse Daudet, *Tartarin de Tarascon*.[1] Tartarin was the greatest bluffer and swindler in all Provence. He belongs to the Alpine Club, but he has never done any mountains in Switzerland, so he decides to go there and climb the Rigi. He arrives with a sun helmet and all the paraphernalia of the expert mountain climber. He finds a railway going up to the top and there are lots of uninteresting English tourists. He gets drunk and rages against such stupidity, then he hears that the Rigi is by no means the highest mountain, he should try the Jungfrau. So he goes up with two

---

[1] Novel, 1872, first of a trilogy, including *Tartarin sur les Alpes* (1885). cf. below, 12 Feb. 1930, at n. 9.

guides. There is not the slightest possibility of danger, it is all arranged for tourists by the Compagnie Anglo-Suisse. He laughs, it is all so easy, then he goes home and tells the most outrageous lies about his exploits. One of his friends doubts the truth of these stories, and challenges him to climb Mont Blanc without guides. So the two set out and very soon Tartarin discovers that this is real, that it is a duel between life and death. They lose their way in the *mer de glace*, clouds of mist come up, all is dark and fearful! If we fall we die. By God, this is real! They rope themselves together and try to walk on the glacier. Suddenly there is a jerk on the rope, and Tartarin whips out his pocket-knife and cuts the rope behind him and there he stands with his little tail. After hairbreadth escapes he manages to creep back to Chamonix. At home in Tarascon he tells his friends of his bravery and courage and how his companion died in his arms. Then after several days the other man turned up and said, "But you are not dead!" The mystery was solved when the guides found the rope cut at either end. This is an example of the provisional life. Tartarin had believed in the Compagnie Anglo-Suisse, his father, then nothing was real. So it is quite possible for a man to keep the attitude he had when his father was alive, and go on living in a provisional way. We all have done the same. Ask yourselves whether this has not been true of you. It is the greatest temptation to make the assumption that "something will arrange it" and live in that way. That is a father complex, a positive one. If a man has a negative father complex he believes that nothing in life is prepared for him.

LECTURE VIII

13 March 1929

Dr. Jung:

Let us see now what we can get out of this rather long and complicated dream. The first symbolism is that of the great waves through which the dreamer is swimming. He identifies his unconscious with the waves coming up out of the ocean into consciousness. Are you satisfied with that? This association is the sort of interpretation which thinking types make. In sensation and intuitive types[1] the associations are not of an explanatory character but are coincidents or coexistences, things which are in the same picture. For example, if it is a question of the wall, the sensation or intuitive type might associate that chair with it, which is just coexistent. This is an irrational type of association. With the rational type we get explanatory associations. If the rational type tries to have irrational associations they are always false, they do not fit, so I ask them just to tell me what they think about it. Are you satisfied with the dreamer's interpretation? Where has he spoken of the same symbolism before?

Mrs. Deady: It occurred in the dream before, where he associated the little boy with his conscious, and the waves of the great ocean of the unconscious sweeping into it.[2]

Dr. Jung: Yes, and he was afraid that the waves would wash away the ground under his feet. What was he afraid of really?

Mr. Gibb: Of his unconscious emotions.

Dr. Jung: Yes, the connotation of the waves is that they are emotional, dynamic. The rational type does not like the irrational

---

[1] In his theory of psychological types Jung distinguished four functions of consciousness, two of which are termed rational, *thinking* and *feeling*, and two are termed irrational, *sensation* and *intuition*. The term "thinking type" designates a person in whom thinking is the superior function. See *Psychological Types*, CW 6, ch. X.

[2] See the beginning of Lecture V, 20 Feb. 1929.

quality of things. There is no safety in it, so he leaves out the irrational or emotional element. Even in his associations he does not pay attention to the fact that these waves coming up from the unconscious are emotional. He is shown dealing with the situation in a perfectly competent way. He is diving through the waves, and in his associations he says that one can do this and not be washed away. This dream cheering him up. The former dream said that the waves might wash away the place where he is standing, but this dream says, "You can deal with the situation, it is not so dangerous."

It is all positive, and up to him, then comes the *but*. He sees the son of the prince (whom he does not know personally). The prince himself is a very important man, an aristocrat, playing a very important rôle in his own country. When such a figure appears in a dream, you can be sure it means a very important, an almost ideal figure. Now the son of that man appears here, but the dreamer has no associations with him. When a patient has no associations it is difficult. Look for the next thing in the dream, perhaps it is a *contre-coup*. The next figure that comes into the dream is that of his father, therefore the son of the prince must have some connection with the dreamer's father. What is it?

Mrs. Zinno: Isn't the son the dreamer's brother-in-law, who is in business with him? As his father and the manager are associated, then his brother-in-law and himself could be.

Dr. Jung: But it is doubtful whether these figures in the dream are psychologically real persons for the dreamer. He is now no longer in actual business relations with the General Manager, so he (the business manager) is a symbol. Thus the son of the prince cannot be a psychologically real person.

Dr. Binger: Isn't it the dreamer himself?

Dr. Jung: Yes, as his father follows immediately after the prince's son in the dream, it probably means his father's son. Hence we get the fact that the father is the prince, in contradistinction to what the dreamer says later on in his associations that he himself is the prince. Can it be possible that he expresses his father by such an ideal figure?

Dr. Binger: Yes, through his father complex.

Dr. Jung: Yes, he expresses his father by the figure of the prince. He has a positive father complex but he goes on saying in the dream that his father is a fat formless man, who almost fell on the stairs and had to be carried down into the water. This looks very negative.

He says in his associations that such fat and formless people are often inferior, also in the further development of the dream, his father is blundering and tactless with the General Manager, so that much damage might be done in the firm. Hence the dream represents his father as an inferior person in every way. He is really reviling his father. Why is that?

Mr. Gibb: It is showing a negative view of his father.

Dr. Jung: But why?

Dr. Shaw: An unconscious compensation for his positive father complex.

Dr. Jung: Yes, his father complex is too positive. A positive father or mother complex can be just as injurious as a negative one. It fastens one down. The unconscious cares little for love or hate. You are held down by either. Whether it is love or hate matters only to the conscious, to the ego. Hate can be just as passionate a force as love. We speak of people clinging together out of pure hatred, so the dream is attacking the positive father complex. Why?

Mrs. Sigg: If these positive qualities are invested in the father then he hasn't got them himself.

Dr. Jung: Either a father or mother complex projects a sum of energy in an impersonal or ultra-personal form. It is just as if I were ascribing certain qualities of my own to some one else, as if they belonged to the other person and not to me. Why do we do it? Is there any gain?—any loss?

Mrs. Sigg: When good qualities are projected, they do not have to be lived.

Dr. Jung: Yes, then you have the advantage of being able to live the provisional life. If I had inherited a fortune, which happily I did not, and could give it away, I would lose the fortune, but at the same time I would not have the responsibility of it. So if you can project your qualities into the father you are freed of the responsibility for them, and you can lead the provisional life. You can live undisturbed because you have given over to the father all the qualities for which you alone are responsible. The dreamer's father was a clergyman. What was he likely to project into him? The object of your projections must offer a little hook. You cannot project genius into an ass. Suppose you want to project lies into someone, when it is really you who are the liar. You can only make such a projection into someone who has a suitable hook. [Laughter.] I know this well and am ready to meet the occasion. It can happen to any of you that someone may project into you, so you are in the same position as I am. We all have hooks, you have to look for the hook in yourself as I do. Projection is a terrific force. You are moved by it and you do not know why. The impact of the projection comes at you like a billiard ball. Through projection terrible things can be brought about. If you do not know of the hook in yourself or of the open door, then the devil creeps in (the projection) and has a tremendous effect. You cannot be indifferent to a projection. It is just as important whether I am projecting into someone else or someone is projecting into me. It functions in both cases with almost mechanical effect. From projections there can arise the most amazing and inexplicable things. In the story *The Evil Vineyard*[3] a man is led to commit murder through a woman's unconscious projection. It is the story of an animus projection.

The Arnstein case in Germany may be a similar one.[4] A man in one night killed eight people, and absolutely no motive, no reason for it, could be discovered. Why should a man who is not mad commit such murders? Up to the time of the murders he could not sleep, he felt burdened, but did not know why. After the murder, in prison, he slept like an old rat. He ate well and gained eight pounds and seemed perfectly satisfied. He had killed eight innocent people, his wife, his mother-in-law, all the family, the gardeners and even his dog, which was much worse. When I inquired into the case I found that his wife belonged to a sort of praying sect. There is always a reason why people do that, put a question mark after *her*. My idea is that this woman was a sort of devil and projected the whole thing, and he got it all out of the atmosphere like a medium. He was weak and harmless. His own brother could not understand it at all. He may have committed those murders under a projection, just as was the case in *The Evil Vineyard*. This man was also weak while his wife was strong, and it is possible that the wife's unconscious (the wife who goes to a prayer sect could have such an unconscious) insinuated what it was that he ought to do. He may have been labouring for years making an hypothesis in his unconscious. He always had the feeling that there was another person in him with whom he ought to deal. He had written a diary, and a diary is a sign of an unconscious that is alive and has the

[3] Novel by Marie Hay (London and New York, 1923), discussed by Jung in "Mind and Earth" (orig. 1927), CW 10, pars. 89ff.
[4] The case is also discussed in "Crime and the Soul" (1932), CW 18, pars. 817f.

need to converse with someone, so he had the feeling that he should write the story of his other life. A few weeks before the crime there appeared several entries in the diary about a long knife, a suggestion of the unconscious. It might mean, "Get ready, this is what you are expected to do." So it might be that his wife's unconscious was projected into him and he was ready, as was the husband in *The Evil Vineyard*. But of course there was a hook.

In the case of our dreamer we cannot speak of the effect on the father, but parents who receive projections can be forced into the role of a God-Almighty-likeness. Many analysts are made into the Saviour, and it gives them such a push out of reality that they go wrong. This is the typical disease of the analyst, because he offers a hook for projections by bothering about the souls of people. The doctor must expose himself to infection, so the analyst must expose himself to projections but he must be careful not to get washed away. What is the value of the projections which the patient makes into his father?

Mr. Gibb: Moral and intellectual ones.

Dr. Jung: The whole thing began when he took up the occult studies, substituting them for moral and intellectual values. So it looks now as though the unconscious was criticizing his father, the stronghold of moral and intellectual values, in order to destroy these projections. Then what could happen?

Mr. Gibb: All these responsibilities would fall back on himself.

Dr. Jung: Yes, he can like the provisional life no longer, hereafter he must depend on his own decisions of right and wrong, no longer on his father. Anyone who leads the provisional life can depend on values and decisions made for them. This is the advantage of the Catholic Church. Eternal laws have been decided beforehand, so one is freed from deciding these matters for oneself. Now the patient becomes his own father. But we are still in the process of undermining the father image. When I project my moral values into someone else, my responsibility is projected into him. I am not burdened with responsibility or with self-criticism, so I can blunder along without any blame or consideration of the consequences. I say, "I am very sorry, but I did not know. Excuse me, what can I do about it? I will pay damages for the blunder," but I go right on the same way. There are people, you all know them, who blunder about like this. They fall into a hole and have to be pulled out. Then away they go and fall into the same hole again, as if it had never happened to them before. It gets to be almost a system with them, they go on committing the same nonsense again and again and never see it. These are the people who live the provisional life, not conscious of their responsibility. When the father complex is undermined then the dreamer inherits the responsibility and self-criticism. Now the father talks to the General Manager of the great estate, who has the black beard that the actual father used to have. Obviously this man is identified with his father. The fatness was just to make him disagreeable, he was not like that. Now he is mixed up with a man who is definitely corrupt. What would that mean psychologically?

Dr. Binger: A split in the dreamer, here represented by the father's two sides, the father as a prince and as a fat imbecile.

Dr. Jung: Yes, but do not forget that this is not the father himself but projections of the various elements of the dreamer onto the father. Things appear in the image of the father that really belong to the dreamer; values as well as vices. Hence on one side he is the prince and on the other the corrupt manager. On one side he idealizes his father as the superior man, *the Prince,* on the other side he depreciates him as the General Manager, who is corrupt. Both of these are parts of the dreamer himself projected into the father. He makes himself a more successful and intelligent man than his father, but he is also more corrupt. This he does not see. If he projects his moral values he does not have to recognize his corresponding vices. There is nothing high that is not built on low. Nietzsche said, "The tree whose branches reach to Heaven has its roots in Hell."

The prince has now invited the dreamer, the General Manager, and the father to stay for lunch to talk business. What about that rôle of the prince? We say that the prince is an overvaluation of the father. Now this superior person invites them to talk business and obviously highly psychological business.

Mrs. Sigg: The word *business* has in it something very definite, very positive. It is a good thing psychologically to be business-like, positive.

Dr. Jung: Sure enough, the business aspect can be a very positive aspect because of its reliability and justice. If I understand you rightly you mean that the prince, being the positive father, suggests fair dealing, a business-like procedure.

Mrs. Sigg: Ruskin[5] said, "First justice, then love."

Dr. Binger: Isn't this a sort of Board of Arbitration?

Dr. Jung: Yes, there is so much injustice, such a confusion in these projections, that it is as if the unconscious said, "Now, let us sit down and discuss the whole situation." The rest of the dream is an important clearing up of things which need an explanation. The first point is that the father does not behave like a business man at all. He even tells the General Manager that he suspects him of dishonest dealings. This would be an impossible beginning and shows how unfitted his father is as a business man. The dreamer makes the remark, "The father is dismissed as a business man so the responsibility falls to me." Yet the General Manager is the dreamer, in the last analysis, the one who is doing underhand things. Occasionally his left hand does not know what his right hand is doing, so it is relatively easy to have a good conscience. The point is that one cannot do honest and successful business because the General Manager is corruptible and does not offer decent conditions. This is what the dreamer must explain to the prince, that there is no dealing with the General Manager, who is bought by the other firms. What do you make of this?

Dr. Shaw: The prince is the best side of his individuality.

Dr. Jung: Yes, the prince, the positive father image is a sort of superior man with high moral values, which are now drawn out from the father and come back to the dreamer, to the superior man in himself, his superior self. This sounds very clumsy, but in reality it is quite simple. For instance, when two men who are on good terms quarrel and it comes to a fight, and one of them says, "We are not fools, why should we fight like two dogs? Let us be reasonable and look at things calmly," that is the superior side coming to the fore. This would be the prince and the dreamer, coming together to exclude the corrupt methods of the General Manager, really the interference with effective psychological activity. You see, the General Manager would be the mean inferior man in the dreamer, his own lower self who tries cheap or corrupt means for momentary advantages or profits, having no horizon. In the long run a big business is only thriving when it is honest, it cannot

---

[5] John Ruskin (1819-1900), English critic of art and society. Cf., in his *The Crown of Wild Olive*, "Do justice to your brother (you can do that whether you love him or not), and you will come to love him" (*Works*, ed. E. T. Cook and A. Wedderburn [1903-12], XVIII, pp. 420f.).

thrive on corruption because corruption eats itself. The dream is trying to put that man right in his psychology, because the problem, the onslaught of these unconscious waves, which he has again encountered, can only be dealt with by honesty, not through sly corrupt means. His problem can only be dealt with by making an appeal to his higher self, but that appeal would be worthless so long as the man is not his own higher self, so long as his higher values are projected into the father, and he is living the provisional life. Those who lead provisional lives are in metal cases, there is no access to them. Therefore the unconscious has to call back all the projected vices and virtues, and then, when the man is fully conscious of himself, he can be appealed to for honest dealing, This refers to analysis! Some people think of it as a technique which you can buy in order to make everything smooth and simple. "Doctor, could you analyse me? I am suffering from a father complex. Could you get that stuff out of my system?" That is using corrupt and cheap means. That is like removing an organ from the body, as though one could remove an arm in a minute, or pull out the heart and throw it away. It can't be done. You cannot just remove a complex and the case is cured. There are numerous publications representing the technique of analysis in that way. It is mere corruption, and yet well-meaning people have published such stuff, as though it were all as simple as that. Are there any questions in connection with this dream? It is fairly simple when the main idea is clear.

Dr. Binger: How much of his projection is due to the fact of the split in his own private life?

Dr. Jung: That is difficult to say. I assume that his father complex has always existed. Whenever a thing is projected it is always split. He undervalues and overvalues his father at the same time. It is a yea and nay; plus and minus; positive and negative. We have to learn that kind of paradoxical thinking when we want to understand psychological facts. It is the same with all pairs of opposites—inferiority feelings mean megalomania, sadism means masochism, etc. So I assume that this man was always split, only lately when his development became urgent did he destroy the provisional life. He has to see that he is the maker of his own life. There are no rails, the track is not trodden. I would not explain his complex as due to the difficulties in his marriage, rather the other way round. Because of the father complex he did not take enough responsibility in his relation with his wife. Father would take care of all that. Thus people dismiss the Eros problem. People with a father complex are exactly like people in the Catholic Church. A good Catholic might say, "Why worry over philosophy and psychological questions? All this was settled two thousand years ago by wise men at a conclave in Rome." Such people can do amazing things, without having any qualms.

Mr. Gibb: Must not the active business discussion have to be taken into account, as a cotton business that might be of great value? Has he not in mind some new value of life?

Dr. Jung: Obviously his life is his business. Unsettled business deals are grave obstacles. His business cannot advance because his firm cannot deal with those big estates. The unconscious is trying to get over to him the idea that he should establish a different rule for his life, that this business cannot be dealt with in little cheap ways, but only with his highest values.

Mr. Gibb: You don't think it is something more specific?

Dr. Jung: Not consciously. I am quite positive about that, he must deal with the prince himself, with his own higher values. People want the doctor to juggle away their difficulties, but it cannot be done.

Next dream [12], *the same night:* There is an extraordinary difference between the next dream and the last, with a most remarkable compensation. "I am in a bedroom with my wife, and I see a door which leads into another room slowly open. I immediately go to the door, push it open, and in the other room I find a little boy completely naked. I carry him into the bedroom and I am convinced in the dream that he is not a natural boy. In order to prevent his getting away (he is struggling in my arms) I press him against me, and he gives me the most remarkable feeling (not at all a sexual feeling) of satisfaction as if this true thing were satisfactory to the longings of my feelings. Then my wife brings in a variety of food for the child. I see black bread and white bread. The child does not want to eat the black bread but eats the white. Then suddenly he flies out of the window and beckons to us from the air."

Associations: Door slowly opening: An allusion to a passage in the second part of *Faust* when Faust is getting old and has been trying to live a rational life. There is a monologue about the fact that he likes to think along the rational lines of the day and be scientific; then night comes and all is different, the door opens and no one comes in! We cannot do without magic. In the man's dream the door opens and no one comes in.[6] That means something super- natural. He has studied occultism, and he uses the word exterior- ization, the theory of what formerly was attributed to spirits, table- tipping, rapping, noises in the wall. His theory is that it is not done by a ghost but by something in ourselves, the exteriorizing of psy- chological contents, and the dreamer is convinced of the reality of such facts. In the dream he has the feeling that the door is opening in a queer way. So he goes to see and finds the little naked boy in the other room.

The boy: The only association he had is the traditional represen- tation of Eros, the naked baby boy. It gives a peculiar satisfaction to his feelings when he presses the boy against him.

Bread: The black bread is more nourishing than the white because it contains a protein in the silver skin of the grain. "The little amourette has not been fed in the right way by my wife, therefore he flies away and is beckoning from afar." Here you get a precious piece of masculine psychology. I am giving the whole sex away! That dream needs some mending. It is a good dream, an intimate, personal dream. How do you explain it after such an objective dream?

Dr. Binger: The contents are much the same. He sees himself as a child, Eros his infantile self. In the other dream he projected himself into his father, so he himself was a child.

Dr. Jung: Well, that needs discussion. I think we had better begin with the text to be sure that we are going right. The dreamer is in the bedroom with his wife, therefore it means in an intimate situation with his wife. That statement in the dream before, that he has to deal with his highest values and not with his lowest, leads

[6] *Faust*, Part II, Act V, in the tr. of Louis MacNeice (*Goethe's Faust*, London, 1951), p. 281:

> "But now such spectredom so throngs the air
> That none knows how to dodge it, none knows where.
> Though one day greet us with a rational gleam,
> The night entangles us in webs of dream.
> We come back happy from the fields of spring—
> And a bird croaks. Croaks what? Some evil thing.
> Enmeshed in superstition night and morn,
> It forms and shows itself and comes to warn.
> And we, so scared, stand without friend or kin,
> And the door creaks—and nobody comes in."

him to his intimate problem with his wife. Something in the business does not work, something in his relation to his wife does not work. The man who leads a provisional life does not deal with Eros. His father knows all about that, so he does not have to bother about it. He can close his eyes to the whole Eros side, and he is not adapted to his wife at all. You cannot deal with a woman with mere objectivity, so it is quite natural that in this dream the obstacle appears. The dream leads him right into the bedroom, for it is also a sexual trouble, sex being the strongest and clearest expression of relatedness. In this situation, certain contents of the unconscious seem to be exteriorized. As far as my knowledge reaches, those contents of the unconscious that are so near, so close that they are almost conscious, have a tendency to get exteriorized. They are almost ready to burst into consciousness, but certain obstacles are in the way and they are exteriorized. Here we have a little miracle. I have no prejudice against these little miracles. Such peculiar things take place occasionally, but how they are connected with our psychology God knows, I don't. Only fools think that everything can be explained. The true substance of the world is inexplicable. In this case it should dawn upon the dreamer that the thing lacking in his relation to his wife is Eros. It is almost a miracle that he has not seen it. It is Eros that ought to come in. He opens the door but no one comes in, then he finds the little boy in the other room and he holds him in his arms for a minute, feeling a peculiar satisfaction when he presses the child against him, and he thinks it is odd that it is not a sexual feeling. That is one of the foolish ideas which men have. They think that Eros is sex, but not at all, Eros is relatedness. Woman has something to say to that! He likes to think that it is a sexual problem, but it is not, it is an Eros problem.

Bread: Black bread would be more nourishing, yet the child refuses it and eats the white bread.

Dr. Shaw: Does the black bread stand for his thinking, his superior function?

Dr. Jung: There is no sign of that.

Miss Bianchi: He stresses the difference between the white and the black, the contrast. Can one assume that it has something to do with the nature of the two people?

Dr. Jung: I am not so sure of that. I would say that bread suggests food. Our mind, heart, body, every function must have its specific food, to continue living, so Eros cannot live without being fed. The food given to Eros is here called bread. Black and white is the ordinary symbolism for moral values. White is innocence, purity; black is earth dirt, night, Hell. The very black bread (pumpernickel) is very heavy and not easy to digest. They have a very primitive way of grinding the grain, so that all the husks are left in. It makes moist and heavy bread, but it is very nourishing. The boy refuses the black bread and accepts the white. What does that mean?

Mr. Gibb: He accepts the more idealistic.

Dr. Jung: The dreamer is much concerned with the kind of food he eats himself. He has a complex about food, and if you study such complexes you always find something interesting behind them. White bread is made from the very heart of the grain and the husks are thrown away, or given to the swine, so white bread gives the idea of luxury, nobility, or soul. It is made from the "soul" of the grain. The people who eat only white bread are noble, fine people, and those who eat black bread are coarse, vulgar, plebeian, earthy. Now, the question is whether the child is fed with heavy substantial food of the earth. To our Christian conscience that means food of devils and Hell. What is of the earth, earthy? Sexuality! But the general assumption that Eros is fed on sexuality is wrong. Curiously enough, he is fed only on white bread, on the very heart of the grain, by something hidden within sexuality, that is the *feeling,* the *relatedness.* If I should say to the patient, "Having sexual intercourse with your wife does not prove that you are related to her," he would not understand, for he thinks it would. You have relatedness by your feeling, by your rapport, and that is what feeds Eros. One expects that after sexual intercourse the soul should not be sad, but often the worst fights and misunderstandings in marriage happen after sexual intercourse, because sexuality does not feed Eros. This is often the direct cause of quarrels and separations.

The dream so far is a very important realization. Eros comes in a miraculous way and disappears in a miraculous way. He flies out of the window. What does that mean?

Dr. Binger: The man is not ready for a feeling relation.

Dr. Jung: We don't know what Eros would do if he stayed long enough. He might feed on the black bread too after a while, but he does not stay long enough. He just says, "Nothing doing; goodbye!" It is a good joke and a terrible truth. It is the promised land, but only for a moment is the fleeting vision clear; then he flies away before he can feed on the black bread. This is often the way in analysis. Just for a moment you see the way ahead quite clearly, then the vision vanishes, the mist gathers, and again you are in confusion. It is a sudden vision of the truth that appears and vanishes again without concretization. Eating the bread in his house is an archaic symbol for hospitality. But Eros does not eat all the bread, only the white, then he disappears, beckoning from afar, "Au revoir, nice to have seen you, perhaps I will see you again, it's not quite certain."

Mrs. Sigg: I have some doubt about the boy being only Eros. In *Faust,* the boy had something to do with poetry and imagination. He was something else.

Dr. Jung: True, he may not be Eros alone. I have my doubts too. But I kept to Eros as the dreamer was unaware of the general quality of his dream. One could say that the fact that he associated with Faust in the beginning points to the charioteer, Homunculus, and Euphorion,[7] the three forms of that element which I technically term the Puer Aeternus symbol in dreams. To my mind it refers to this symbolism. After the father complex, the infantile complex necessarily appears, where he is the son. First he turned his eyes to the father, now he is the son, still in the psychology of a boy of eight or ten years, so the Eros figure would be the infantile side of the dreamer. But if you say that, then the infantile side is to come into relation with his wife, and he isn't quite up to that situation yet. You could say that his natural unsophisticated feeling had better come into relation with his wife. It is quite true that the child is the infantile side of the dreamer, but it is also the promising thing in him. The things which one has developed are finished, but the undeveloped things are still a promise for the future. So the boy represents what may be developed, the self-renewing thing in man, and a good term to give to this figure is the Puer Aeternus. The old idea was that the Puer Aeternus was a Divine Child who eternally appeared and disappeared in a miraculous way. The Etruscan boy Tages,[8] a little naked boy, appears in the furrow

[7] *Faust,* Part II, Act II. A summary of the fates of these three figures is given at the beginning of the lecture of 27 March 1929, below.

[8] For Tages, the legendary founder of Etruscan augural lore, and Oannes, mentioned a few lines further, see CW 5, pars. 291-2. Adonis was a Phoenician vegetation god and Tammuz his Babylonian equivalent.

where the peasant is ploughing, and he teaches the people laws, arts, and culture. Adonis was such a boy. Tammuz appears to the women every spring. The Babylonian fish-god Oannes comes out of the water as a fish, appears at sunrise, and teaches the people agriculture, laws, etc., during the day, disappearing at night into the sea again. Meister Eckhart had a vision of a little naked boy who visited him.[9] Then there are some English fairy stories of the radiant boy, in which the vision of the boy is always unlucky, sometimes absolutely fatal. There must be some reason for this, I do not know what it may be. The Puer Aeternus[10] is simply the personification of the infantile side of our character, repressed because it is infantile. If the dreamer allows that element to come in, it is as though he himself had disappeared and come back as a little naked boy. Then if his wife could accept him as such, everything would be all right. The little boy ought to be brought up, educated, perhaps spanked. If the inferior element can enter life, then there is a promise of future life, things can develop, there can be progress. In mythology, the figure of this little naked boy has an almost divine creative character. As the Puer Aeternus he appears in a miraculous way and then disappears in the same way. In *Faust* he has three forms: Boy Charioteer, Homunculus, Euphorion. They were all destroyed by fire, which meant in Goethe's case that the Pueri Aeterni all disappeared in a passionate outbreak. Fire puts an end to everything, even an end to the world. Fire that is the sap of culture can burst forth and destroy everything. This happens from time to time, as for instance in the Bolshevist Revolution, when the cultural form could not hold the tension of energy any more, and the fire broke forth and destroyed the Russian civilization.

[9] For further details see below, p. 188.
[10] Jung was to develop this theme later in "The Psychology of the Child Archetype" (1941), CW 9 i.

LECTURE IX

20 March 1929

Dr. Jung:
We haven't finished the collective symbolism of the last dream. But first are there any questions from the last seminar?

Mr. Gibb: What about the fact that the dreamer's wife brings in the bread, and not he himself?

Dr. Jung: Yes that is important, it belongs to the personal part of the dream.

Mr. Gibb: His wife in reality is rather apathetic, why does she bring in the food in the dream?

Dr. Jung: In the patient's associations he explains this by saying that his wife brought the wrong food, so Eros goes away.

Mr. Gibb: The wife seems to have brought a considerable variety of food.

Dr. Jung: Yes, the statement of the dream is against this fact. You remember I brought out that point in the last seminar. The wife brought the white bread too, which the child ate, so the husband's statement is not quite just. We had better go through the dream again. This is a difficult dream because there are two very different elements in it, first, the personal concrete situation of the dreamer, the lack of sex, of Eros in his marriage. But secondly there is something else introduced: the supernatural intervention which complicates the personal concrete aspect of the situation. On the personal level it is apparently an insoluble problem. Often people who suffer from certain symptoms that appear to be personal are not able to solve their problems on that level, because their importance is due to a collective fact. A personal situation can be upset by the general conviction that the things which cause the particular problem ought to be so and so. So long as people suffer from the idea that certain situations are due to their own personal mistakes they cannot be corrected.

It is as though they would build a house lightly and there comes a very cold winter so that the house cannot be heated properly; they think it was their fault, in the way they built the house, while the real difficulty is that the winter was unusually cold. It is not their fault. The same thing is true of opinions. General convictions can be the cause of individual trouble. People in India have queer religious ideas that are not at all hygienic, so their individual troubles are due to the general mistake. If you ask the people why they share such ideas, you ask them why they are moral and religious, because these ideas are their religion. They injure themselves by a sort of idealistic attitude. The good which must be considered as a virtue may be the cause of the worst consequences. The very thing that makes it a virtue produces the unhappy consequences. In the interpretation of his dream, if we do not consider the collective character of the Eros symbolism we cannot understand it. We will try to get as far as we can with the personal interpretation. You remember that the dreamer is in an intimate situation in the bedroom with his wife. Then the supernatural comes in. The door opens and no one enters. But when the man goes into the next room there is the little naked boy. He brings the boy into the bedroom, and thus far one could say surely love is lacking; but that is not so, for in a way he loves his wife, and his wife loves him. It is sex that does not work. Ordinarily people make little difference between sex and love and the two words are interchangeable. "Faire l'amour" in France means having sexual intercourse. So one could say that the Eros figure in the dream is sex, because that is obviously what is lacking in the marriage. Yet when the man embraces the boy he notices that his feeling is not sexual, he feels the satisfaction of a different kind of love. The dream points this out, therefore the boy cannot be sex. Then comes the statement in the dream that the wife is bringing something for the child to eat, mostly white and black bread, and he refuses the black bread, but eats the white. Then the dreamer assumes that the child goes away because his wife has not given him the right kind of food. In his assumption that the boy means sex, he can say that, as his wife is rather negative in that respect, she does not give the right kind of food to Eros and so he goes away. Obviously his personal interpretation gets him nowhere, so we must go into the dream more deeply. First of all you remember that I have told you that this patient is a thinking type, therefore he makes interpretative associations. It is the only way for his type to associate. Some analysts refuse such interpretations and say to their patients, "You must give simple facts, not explanations." If a thinking type tries to give this kind of associations he will get way off and not connect the right facts at all, and this will falsify his associations. So you must accept his explanatory way, his associations may not fit, but that is true of the irrational type as well; they may give facts and feelings that lead the analyst astray, he must take all this into account. The dreamer does however associate the little naked boy with an antique figure, which we can call Eros; but that is a Greek idea that is capable of many interpretations, it cannot be taken as sex alone. The man's feeling in the dream is a feeling of love. He says in his associations, "There was no sex in it at all," so even in his dream he expected something sexual. That is to be expected in the unnatural relation with his wife, his nonsexual relation. The man really loves his wife as he understands love, and his wife loves him; you cannot expect of people anything beyond their understanding. The man does as much as he can do with the exception of sex. The dream says that the wife is doing what she can to feed the child, so his explanation that his wife does not give the child the proper food does not apply at all. We could rather conclude from the dream that his wife is doing as well as he is. He and his wife are together in their room at night, and a miraculous situation develops, the door opens and no one comes in. This would make even the most hardboiled intellectual shiver, but the man courageously goes into that room and finds the boy and brings him over into the bedroom, then his wife does her share and brings the child food. This shows hospitality in the true primitive form, but it does not work either, and the child disappears out of the window. It is as though he said to them, "You are both doing what you can, but sex doesn't work." So this boy is something else. What is he? He is not sex because the facts of the dream contradict it. He may be love, he surely is not sex alone. We have another hint in the dream which helps: the boy is naked, why should he be? The dreamer says that it is the traditional way in which Eros is represented, hence his association points to the idea of a deity. Do not be alarmed when I speak of a deity. People think that with a metaphysical hook I am getting something down from Olympus. Thinking a thing does not mean that it is true, nor that it exists. We can think an hypothesis. We are here concerned with an idea, an inherited psychical fact. The tendency of the mind is to function as it always has functioned, and it is far more probable that it will continue to function as it did five or ten thousand years ago, rather than in a way it never has functioned. Those ideas that have been alive through the centuries are most likely to return and to be operative. They are archetypes, the historical way of functioning, and so the general way.

Meteorologists infer weather prognoses according to what the last few days have brought; when there is a series of bad days your most probable prognosis for the next day will be that it will be bad again. Continuity is natural from inertia, and so it is with our mentality. When the mind of man has functioned in the same way for centuries it is most probable that it will continue to function in the same way. When the dream introduces a deity to the dreamer's consciousness, it means nothing to him except a sort of figure of speech. I can say of a wine, "Isn't it divine," as a sort of speech metaphor, an exaggerated way of praising the wine; it doesn't mean that the god dwells in it. And so Eros is here introduced in a metaphorical way, as a poetic personification of the thing called love. Yet to the unconscious the concept of the coming in of a deity is a divine fact with all the paraphernalia of the deity. When the idea of deity appears in the functioning of the mind, what the Greeks called the *deisidaimonia* (fear of the demonic) is present. The door opens and no one comes in. Now look out for ghosts, devils, etc.! The deity is always preceded by terror, fear, or a feeling of a divine presence, a special atmosphere, a sort of emotional fringe comes up with it. This is shown quite plainly in the dream, so we are safe in assuming that it is in line with the old idea of the appearance of the god. The old Romans and Greeks understood the deity. They did not say that a man fell in love, but "The arrow of Eros has hit him." It was the personification of the emotion of love, an active autonomous principle working in man. They projected it, of course, into sacred trees, groves, caves, rivers, mountains and into Olympus. We do not understand that kind of psychology now, but primitive man (and the Greek was primitive man) was so connected in a *participation mystique* with the object that these gods were part of his life. So if he said, "The god of this table spoke to me in the night," he would mean about the same as if one of us said "I dreamed that a certain complex appeared in the form of that table." For example, a woman who had lost her father dreamed that she met him and he told her that after his death he had

179

reincarnated as a clerk and was a very poor young man (he had been rich). She said to him, "How did you get out?" for she knew that he had been in her hot-water can. He answered, "Oh, you know, Jung lifted the lid and I escaped." This is a most amazing idea, but if you know something of primitive psychology you can understand it. There the ancestors are living in pots and jars. That is why the Indians in Central America make their water-jugs like human faces, they paint legs and arms, eyes and ears on their cooking vessels, for they are the spirits, the lares and penates, gods of the hearth sitting near the fire. When I told my patient this she was much enlightened and made a father transference to me, which meant that her mind was liberated and she could get to work. She associated her father's reincarnation with her own rebirth and renewal. That is the archetypal idea in dreams.

In the present dream of our patient we have a similar case. A deity is a personification of an autonomous factor. What would it be when you boil it down to a psychological fact?

Dr. Binger: I think it is the man's own soul, a sort of anima. He takes it in his arms. It is some part of his completeness.

Dr. Jung: But it is not a woman.

Dr. Binger: It may be his renewed self.

Dr. Jung: It is surely some part of his psychology, but introduced as a god, a boy.

Dr. Schlegel: Something that belongs to his future. It is younger than the dreamer, a younger self.

Dr. Jung: Yes, some future part of himself as a boy, but that would not explain the idea of the deity. It is something not within his personal reach. I have told you before that there are such historical parallels. Tages, the Etruscan boy-god who springs from the furrow as the peasant ploughs, teaches laws and crafts to the people and disappears again. Then there is Meister Eckhart's vision in the fourteenth century. Once Meister Eckhart was visited by a beautiful naked boy. He asked him where he came from. "I come from God." "Where hast thou left him?" "In virtuous hearts." "Whither goest thou?" "To God." "Where wilt thou find him?" "When I leave all created things" (appearances, veil of Maya). "Who art thou?" "A king." "And where is thy kingdom?" "In my own heart." "Mind no one shares it with thee." "So I do." He took him to his cell and said, "Take any garment thou likest." "Then I should be no king," said he, and vanished. It was God himself whom he had had with him a little while. Then there is the report of Meister Eckhart regarding a dream of Brother Eustachius, in Paris. He saw that many brethren of the monastery stood in a circle in the refectory, but he could not see what was going on, something new that was pleasurable and most enjoyable. He wondered what it could be, and went closer and saw amidst the brethren a most beautiful little child, our Lord Jesus Christ the Son of the Maid, our dear Lady, and he was so beautiful that no man however sad or serious he was, but had to laugh at his extraordinary beauty. The little child demanded bread to eat and Brother Eustachius went to the store-room; but he could not find any bread good enough; only a little piece of white bread. He went on seeking until he found a whole loaf, but it was not entirely white, so he would not give it to the child. He got quite anxious, then Brother Ruopreht, who had charge of baking the bread, came and asked him what he was seeking so assiduously. "I am seeking quite beautiful white bread, that I may give it to our Lord." Brother Ruopreht said, "Don't worry, I shall find you such bread." He found it and Brother Eustachius took it to the child. The child said, "There are many great priests but they do not want to bring me anything so pure and perfect, and simple. They have things that are pure and things that are perfect, but nothing that is pure and perfect and simple. But there are a few, often not learned men, who bring me something that is pure and perfect and simple." Then Eustachius realized that the humble brother who found the bread was such a man and from that time on he did great honour to Brother Ruopreht and loved him with the whole force of his heart, because he was the man who was able to bring something that was pure and perfect and simple.[1]

You can see what kind of a deity this is, a new thought, a new spirit. All the old gods were psychological facts which later on became ideas. The old gods represented by the planets Saturn, Jupiter, Mars, are the old personal gods living on Olympus. They became later on psychological constituents of human character. We speak of a saturnine expression, a mercurial temperament, a martial bearing, jovial behaviour, etc., and we forget that we thus liken man to the great rulers of Olympus. A god may appear to you if

---

[1] *Texte aus der deutschen Mystik des 14. und 15. Jahrhunderts*, ed. Adolf Spamer (Jena, 1912), pp. 143, 150. (Note in *Sems.*)

it pleases him to do so, and if you integrate or entertain him, as it were, that means a new spirit, a new attitude in you. Christ is a personal ideal, then he dies and is a spirit. At Pentecost he descends from Heaven in the form of fiery tongues. The disciples were filled with a certain spirit, a new agency began to work in them, a new idea. Suppose I get active with a new idea. Before I had it, when it was still in my unconscious it was a deity, a daemon, something divine; then it becomes my new attitude, my new spirit. Hence all the different meanings of the word *spirit*.[2] "In the spirit of my dead father" can mean "I don't want to displease his ghost" or it may mean "in harmony with his convictions" and that means an attitude merely. Now we come to the question of what the deity really is. Meister Eckhart says that little naked child is God or Jesus. The child himself says he comes from God, that he is a King, his Kingdom is within the virtuous heart. So you could say the equivocal quality of the child in this vision is not just a God but a King of the Kingdom of Heaven that is within, within ourselves, not the God without. That "God within" is almost a technical term demonstrated in the figure of a child. This would mean that God has the qualities of a child. From this psychic fact you can understand the words of Jesus, "If ye do not become as a little child."[3] This God, this divinity, has the appearance of a child. If you do not become as a little child you cannot enter the Kingdom of Heaven, you cannot make true the God within.

The difficult thing is that when the God within makes himself visible you can only trace his way by the things we call infantile, childish, too youthful in ourselves, but these very things promise future development. Whatever is already developed in you has no future, it has reached its culmination. The continuation of life always originates in those things which are undeveloped. That is the ever-creative basis from which new developments are born, and when things are contained in an autonomous form, things that are not subject to our choice are gods and daemons. Everything that is resisting us in our psychology is a god or daemon because it does not conform to our wishes. It is as though we were possessed by fears, emotions, undertones outside of ourselves. All new contents are at first autonomous contents; and where there is such a content

---

[2] For various connotations of "spirit," see "The Phenomenology of the Spirit in Fairytales" (1945), CW 9 i.

[3] Matthew 18:3.

we may be sure that in its development it will possess the individual either with or without his consent and it will bring a great change into his life. Later on it will be a spirit in which things are done or said. So in this dream a new spirit has come in. While the man is still intent on the problem of sex, his unconscious says, "That is not it at all, it is God," a thing that is there and not there, not at your command. If you have the spirit or attitude which gives the best welcome to a deity, then he might appear, he might bestow his blessing upon you. The dreamer does not understand this at all. As we have seen from his association, he regards his problem as a mechanical one, a sexual one, but his unconscious says that the solution of his problem depends on the god entering the scene. The god is still an autonomous complex, not yet an attitude, or a ruling principle. The collective parallels show this child as always connected with the existing ideas of the time. In the Middle Ages it is Christian, the Bambino, Jesus. They did not dream of calling it Tammuz or Dionysos. Perhaps they did not even know that the ancients worshipped Dionysos in the form of a little boy. They called it the Christ Child. They represented it in the form that meant something to them, something impressive, therefore they called it the Son of God. God was then an external fact. We could not call that little deity Tammuz or Dionysos, because we are no longer living in that age. In our actual modern mind we cannot explain it like that any more; we understand it more psychologically than ever before. We explain the little naked boy as a psychological fact. A thousand years hence they may have an entirely new name but it will be merely a new form of expression for the same old fact. The planets will never protest at the names you give them. Jupiter is quite indifferent as to whether you call him Jupiter or some other name. You must interpret these facts psychologically, but you must interpret them according to the best theories at your disposal. The original Christian teaching was the best in its day. An old Greek Father who lived in A.D. 190 spoke of Christianity as "our philosophy that flourished in the time of Augustus." The Christianity of those days was interpreted like a philosophy, it was one of the Gnostic systems, a sort of theory of how best to live. We see such a possibility in a psychological adjustment to life. We no longer believe in an authoritative revelation. We no longer think along those absolute lines. To the people of two thousand years ago it meant something to say, "The Son of God has appeared."

In the old days everybody had revelations. The principle that worked for two thousand years was that someone had the truth and could reveal it. The backbone of the Catholic Church is the claim to the possession of the eternal truth. It is invested in the Pope and you must simply accept it. But for us this does not settle it. No one would say now that the truth has been revealed to him, we cannot build on revelation. We believe in the honest attempt to understand psychological facts. If you take these things seriously enough, in the spirit of scientific devotion, they will have the same effect that was formerly reached by authoritative revelation. Are you satisfied with this interpretation of collective symbolism?

Dr. Binger: In the terms of modern symbolism what name would you give the Boy?

Dr. Jung: I always use metaphors in order to designate these things. If I should name it such and such a thing, I would catch it and I would kill it. People would cling to the *word*, but if I say Puer Aeternus, using a metaphor, we all understand what is meant.

Dr. Binger: Is there any modern symbolism?

Dr. Jung: No, there is no such thing. I definitely prefer not to invent a cage in which I suggest that I have caught the Puer Aeternus.

Dr. Binger: I mean that "Christ" was used before. Is there anything for a symbol of this?

Dr. Jung: These things that originated in earlier times have come down to us through use. The Puer Aeternus is a shepherd boy. In Christian philosophy there are many forms of the shepherd figure. "The Shepherd of men" is also a title for Christ, "The Mystery God," "Teacher of mysteries." In *The Shepherd of Hermas,*[4] the shepherd is Christ, but the name of Christ is not mentioned in the whole book. Hermas was said to be the brother of the second pope,[5] a Christian, but at the time when Christianity was a mystery cult, and as the gods could not be named, he was simply called the Shepherd. There was a time when Christ was represented as Orpheus, or as the good shepherd, with a lamb over his shoulder. The custom then was to call this guiding principle the "Shepherd that was herding the flocks," "The leader of men," "The Fisher of

[4] Hermas flourished about A.D. 140. *The Shepherd* is in *The Apostolic Fathers*, tr. Kirsopp Lake (LCL, 1917), vol. 2, pp. 6-305. Jung gives long extracts, with comment, in *Psychological Types*, CW 6, pars. 381ff.

[5] Pius I, died ca. 154.

men," so Christ was identified with Orpheus and also with Bacchus. The fish symbolism of the early Christian church was frequently represented in pagan mystery cults. There is an old mosaic floor in a temple of the Bacchus cult, where the fish symbolism is used as in the Christian cult. The Etruscans called Tages the "unearthed boy," the "ploughed up boy." Where the name of Tages originated I don't know but obviously it was the custom to give that boy a name. Those of my patients who have had an experience with Puer Aeternus call it just "The Boy." When I hear them talking of "The Boy," "The Star," "The Sea Hawk," or "The Fire Spark" it sounds just like an antique text, just as in Egypt one spoke of "The Eye of Horus." You cannot see why "The Eye of Horus." It is just an abbreviation for a very subtle kind of experience that creates obvious values, a sort of mystery atmosphere. Nobody knows what "The Boy" could possibly be. Those people who talk of "The Boy" are in a way taboo, naturally they are thought to be a little mad. I am quite certain that in antiquity when they talked of the "Poimen," "The Fisher of men," "The Hanged God," people considered them mad. In the Palatine in Rome there has just been discovered on the walls of a room supposed to have been a sort of military academy for cadets, a mock crucifix, a childish design of a man with an ass's head,[6] with the Greek inscription "Thus Alexandros worships his God." It relates to the old Jewish tale of Jehovah worshipped as an ass. There are representations of Set, the Egyptian devil, with a head like an ass (probably not an ass but an okapi,[7] a sort of antelope with long ears found in upper Egypt), crucified by having three knives stuck through him. The effect of such a cult on the people of that time, who didn't know what it was about, was peculiar. The great writers of those days didn't know on what it was based and did not know the language of the new cult. It was a sort of Jewish mystery cult, but the people only knew that its members would not sacrifice to the Caesars.

Question: What is the significance of the crucified God?

Dr. Jung: That would take us too far from the subject of the dream. The shepherd is a symbol of the "Guide for the flock," a

---

[6] See *Symbols of Transformation*, CW 5, pars. 421, 622, and pl. XLIII.

[7] *Sems.*: "ogapi." Presumably the okapi is meant, but that giraffe-like animal has its habitat in the Congo (modern Zaire). A. Gardiner (*Egyptian Grammar*, 3rd edn., 1957, p. 460) says that the animal associated with the god Set is "perhaps a kind of pig." Cf. below, 26 June 1929, p. 285.

figure that brings them together. The shepherd is just what we have here in the dream, the one who holds them together in the flock. Here he is the unifier between the man and woman. These two people are both concerned with the boy. The man brings in the boy while the wife brings in the food. The boy is *tertium comparationis*. When there are two things that are opposites, they must be united by a third thing, that is, a new unity, not just by a compromise between the two. The process must be triangular. Unless something new comes into the relationship it cannot work. In this case it is sexuality that does not work, because the thing from above is lacking. If the thing from above is not there or if the thing from below is not there, it does not work, They would both be quite capable of realizing the importance of the thing from below, but not of the thing from above. We seek from the tangible and concrete world and we would hesitate to assume that the fact that we have no living religion could matter. In the Roman Catholic Church two people are not married as we are. They are married *in Christo*, Christ holds them together. Two people not married *in Christo* are not married at all, it is not real. The authority of the Church is supreme for either marriage or separation. The idea is that human beings cannot be connected except through God. I have seen a Roman vase of the second century, probably made by a Christian, since it has a Christian marriage scene on it. It has several scenes showing different aspects of the relation between men and women. There is a couple united through a trident—through *Neptune!* A man is using a mandrake root to charm a woman—*seduction, witchcraft*. Then a couple with hands united through a fish. The fish stands for Christ. That is the idea of the Catholic Church, that the two are united in and through that spiritual fact. With us the fish stands for a content of the unconscious. So this "Boy" as a new personification represents a revelation from the unconscious, the birth from the unconscious. The idea in the dream is that the boy should intervene to establish the connection. He appears, then he says good-bye! He cannot stay because these people do not understand what he means.

LECTURE X

27 March 1929

Dr. Jung:
You will probably wonder that I pay so much attention to the symbol of "The Boy," but one can hardly overestimate the importance of that symbol. It worried me a great deal, so I went into its history as far as possible. I have already given you some glimpses of historic examples of this "Boy," and today I want to give you more recent examples along the same line. In the second part of *Faust* the "Boy" appears. Very few people are acquainted with the second part of *Faust*. When I was a young man I could not understand it at all, and only later it came to me. Certain things in it are beautiful and marvelous, but without knowledge of the collective unconscious you can hardly understand what Goethe means. Commentators have no real idea of what he is concerned with. The first part of *Faust* was written when Goethe was a young man, the second part when he was quite old, so there was the experience of a long life in between. It was his last work, and it contains a great deal of unconscious material. It was Goethe's way of expressing his experiences of the collective unconscious. As he was a genius he was in touch with this. When the collective unconscious is really experienced it is the fateful experience of one's life, a tremendous experience. You can compare it with nothing but the real experience of this visible world, with all its beauties and risks. In *Faust* Goethe says to Wagner,[1] "You are only conscious of one side of life, be glad you know nothing of the other side." This means that human life is enough for ordinary people, they cannot even deal with that. Yet certain people have to experience the other side of the world, the collective unconscious, the world within. So we can-

---

[1] *Faust*, Part I, "Outside the City Gate." Cf. the MacNeice version, p. 40: "You are only conscious of one impulse. Never seek an acquaintance with the other."

not be astonished when we find the Puer Aeternus in Faust. The symbol appears there in three forms. Faust goes through many different situations of external life. Goethe was much impressed by the tremendous social revolution in France, and also by the invention of bank notes. So Faust first appears as great social and economic reformer at court, an adviser of the king. He was also a sort of sorcerer, a clever juggler, a financial genius, a Mussolini. That would be a diagnosis of Faust's character. The last labour of Faust was engineering, which was just coming into prominence when Goethe wrote, and it was an actual fact going on in Switzerland at the time.

Konrad Escher, a Swiss engineer, carried out the great project of draining off large malarial swamps at the foot of the mountains.[2] He did his work in the spirit of great personal devotion, and Goethe has used this devotion as a symbol in the second part of *Faust*. In Holland, in the seventeenth century, the great storms of the sea had broken the dykes and there were plans for building a great dam and winning back the land from the sea. So in *Faust* they are building dams and winning back the fertile lands for cultivation. "The Boy" appears for the first time under the name of "Knabe-Lenker," the Boy Guide or Charioteer, when Faust is at the court of the king. In reading the text we cannot see why this boy appears, and Goethe himself was almost embarrassed at his appearance and how to explain him. The boy speaks: "I am generosity, poetry. I am the poet who perfects himself by wasting his own goods. I am also infinitely rich, and I think of myself as Plutus. I even animate and decorate his dancing and his meals. I am spending what he is lacking"[3] (outdoing Plutus, rich beyond all imagination). He increases in intensity, as if he were getting more and more on fire. He speaks to the crowd at a great festival: "The greatest gifts of my hands I send about, and there behold on this or that head there is a little flame which I have put on. Now it jumps from head to head. Here it flares up for a short time, then it escapes. Rarely it stays, and in many, before they are aware, it dies down sadly exhausted." Then the final fate of the Boy Charioteer. The whole festival ends with fireworks, and suddenly everything bursts into

[2] Johann Konrad Escher von der Linth (1767-1823), builder of the Linth Canal, which corrected flooding of the Lake of Zurich.

[3] For poetic renderings of the quotations in this paragraph, see *Faust*, Part II, tr. Philip Wayne (Penguin Classics), pp. 55, 57, 148, 155, and 203-8.

flames and he disappears into the fire, only ashes are left. That figure is finished. In the next appearance of Faust he is still moving on in the world doing wonderful things. He returns and finds Wagner, the rationalist, installed in his former laboratory, where he is doing a marvelous thing, producing a little man in a retort, a homunculus. It was the dream of the Middle Ages to make such a little man, and Faust marvels. Then in the night Homunculus escapes in his glass bulb through the air and comes to the Elysian fields. Mephistopheles played a tremendous rôle in the Middle Ages, but here he appears in a bewildered condition, for he feels rather like an ass among these figures of Greek mythology, in the antique world where there is no evil and no good. Homunculus appears in this world of gods and goddesses and consults with them as to how he can manage to get out of his glass bulb into the real world. Only the old god Proteus, who is always taking on new forms, can give advice: "When thou wilt become, begin first in the smallest things," very wise. Homunculus is glad to receive such good advice and begins to jump about in his bottle, and then a wonderful thing happens. Galatea comes over the seas on her throne. You remember Pygmalion, who made a beautiful statue of Galatea, and then prayed to the gods to make her real. His wish was granted and she came to life as a real woman. Now Homunculus sees her coming, is delighted, and rushes to meet her; he hurls himself against the throne, his bulb bursts and he disappears in flames. So we have the third form of the "Boy." Faust, dissatisfied as ever, descends to the Mothers. There he finds the magic tripod, and out of the flames of the tripod he produces the perfect couple, Paris and Helen. Faust falls in love with Helen (who is really hidden behind Marguerite), the most beautiful and perfect woman. He lives with her and the fruit of their union is Euphorion (the happy one), of a fiery nature, air and flame, and soon it begins to be evident that he is after the girls, leaping after them like a flame. He continues a short existence until he burns up in the flames of love and is gone. The typical thing in all this symbolism is the short flame-like existence, which comes to an end each time in fire. In the first case it is power that puts an end to the "Boy"'s life (he burns up at the height of his power). In the other two cases it is the emotion of love in which he burns himself up.

There is another apparition of the Puer Aeternus in a book by an author quite unknown.[4] He is probably a crank and the book is cranky, but the idea is extraordinary. The story is of a small highly respectable cathedral town in Germany. There is a Lutheran parson and the ordinary society, the doctor, the burgomaster, and the high officials of the town; everybody is small and respectable. There is a rumor that several peculiar boys have appeared, and these boys wear brown leather caps. (This is a regular dementia praecox vision. This author may have a hole in his brain.) There seems to be something uncanny, inexplicable, about the evil rumours connected with these boys, because no one can protect himself against them. There is an evening party, where a strange man turns up. He is very interesting, he has travelled and is full of stories. He produces a peculiar little phial, with a tiny flame in it. He tells the company that this is a very rare thing, and whoever looks into it will see the truth. The ladies and gentlemen all put their heads together and look into the bottle, where two small human beings appear, the hostess and a man who is not her husband. They are naked and are in a violent embrace. Everybody is scandalized but continues to look. Then the party breaks up, all the guests ashamed and outraged. The stranger had disappeared, and was never seen again. A few months later all the respectable people gathered at the great event of the season, the official ball. The little girls came in white and the old ladies in black, everybody was sitting stiffly around the walls, they talked a little bit, and danced a little bit, things were terribly respectable and boring. No one noticed that through the back door a little boy with a brown leather cap came in, and went up onto the balcony and hid. Instantly the atmosphere changed, the band played with more pep, the girls laughed loudly, and the burgomaster made queer jokes to his lady. Things grew worse and worse, more and more wild, until there was a real orgy, a tremendous primitive thing, and no one was conscious of it. Then the boy disappeared, laughing slyly. Instantly they all came to their senses, and found themselves in the most extraordinary attitudes with strange partners. They were much ashamed, bewildered, and scandalized. They shut themselves up in their homes for weeks and no one dared look into his neighbour's eyes. Then news came from the outside world that these boys had

[4] Bruno Goetz, *Das Reich ohne Raum* (1919), which Jung often cites. In "Wotan" (1936), CW 10, par. 384, Jung interpreted the novel as an adumbration of Nazi Germany.

worked terrible things abroad, so the people began to think that the strange goings on at the ball were accounted for; one of the boys must have been there and it was he who was responsible and they were reconciled. But the parson, who had not been present at the ball, was not reconciled at all. The people had not dared to go to the church before, but now they felt that they could go again. The parson had waited for them, and he began to curse them up and down for their hellish orgy, he did not believe in "Boys" at all. The people wilted under his wrath. But the parson had not noticed a little boy with a brown leather cap stealing in the door and who was climbing up a column near the pulpit. He looked at the parson and instantly the parson smiled and brightened up, he went on preaching but he found himself using words that he didn't mean to say at all. He became more and more involved, still cursing but in different terms, using obscene language and making evil jokes and working the congregation up to a fierce orgy. This was worse than the ball, right in the church! Then the boy disappeared, and they all came to their senses again. There was the parson with the wife of the burgomaster, etc. This was too much, it could never be lived down. — This is exactly the psychology of the character of the child in the second part of *Faust*, ending in flame that soon burns itself out, leaving only ashes behind.

The third example is in a philosophical and theological form. In the book of Wells, *God the Invisible King*,[5] God is a sort of ignorant youth who tries to improve the world and who has need of our support. Wells' description of God is that of an adolescent boy who tries to do his level best with great enthusiasm. Wells has been severely reproached for writing that book but I have seen a young boy in this country, a gifted boy of sixteen, who had a religious revelation and who gave me his idea of God, which was just like this one of Wells; it was his dearest revelation. The symbol of the "Boy" seems to be an archetypal image, still very much alive in our time. You can include Goethe as a modern, for *Faust* is by no means worn out, it is still very true.

For instance, if I should have such a fantasy and if my analyst should interpret it, he would say, "You are no longer a young man, but you have the idea of the boy in you. Feeling perhaps the inevitability of old age, the boy is your compensation. Why is this?

[5] H. G. Wells, *God the Invisible King* (1917).

You are too old in your attitudes, conduct, and beliefs. You are older than you need be, so the unconscious compensates for your oldness by the figure of the "Boy." Goethe is, of course, the megaphone of modern times. Every great poet expresses the ideas and feelings common to all, or he would have no audience. He would not be understood nor appreciated at all. I have experienced the effect of Nietzsche's ideas when no one else was capable of understanding him. He lived in my own town. His style and thought were peculiar. No one dared to admit that they saw something in Nietzsche, because that would put them outside of the flock. They would have felt outside of their world. But Nietzsche foreshadows our time, as does Goethe in the second part of *Faust*. We can speak of general symbols, common to many people and expressed in many different ways, and we can apply the individual interpretation to the social phenomena of our time. How would you apply it?

Dr. Binger: Just as you would in the individual. We are old.

Dr. Jung: Yes, we are oldish, and the general collective unconscious feels the need of bringing up the symbol of youth as a compensation. In what way are we too old?

Dr. Binger: We are like the burgers.

Dr. Jung: Our attitudes, our ideals are too old-fashioned. Why? Ask our parsons, they won't admit it.

Dr. Binger: We are afraid of the little boys, I guess.

Dr. Jung: The point is that there are no little boys in leather caps. People do not realize that our general ideas, our general theories, are based on principles that are no longer alive; they are not modern ideas. Many people are beginning to fight our institutions because they can no longer believe in the principles they uphold, so everywhere there is a state of unrest. Our morality is still based on medieval assumptions. We would no longer admit that we believe in Hell-fire, but as a matter of fact, we have no other basis for our morality except the Hell-fire idea. This idea works in certain minds with horrible results. Lamprecht, a German philosopher, no longer living, wrote a little book called *The History of Civilization*[6] in which he said, "Obviously mankind has been very immoral, because it has had to pass through an age of incest. The first human beings were brothers and sisters." This is based on the

[6] Karl Lamprecht (1856-1915), German historian; none of his works appears to correspond to the title given here. Jung later cited Lamprecht, in a similar vein, in "Answer to Job" (1952), CW 11, par. 576.

assumption that the first parents were Adam and Eve. That man has never thought. These archetypal ideas work in that way. The author had accepted the story of Adam and Eve, so naturally for him man has had to pass through an age of incest. If man was to propagate there was no other way than through the sister. He published this as a scientific work!

A professor in Bern in the fire of enthusiasm said: "Humanity is reaching from the icy regions of the North Pole to the eternal and fiery flames of the South Pole." He got away with it for a time, then it was too much and he had to resign, but Lamprecht got away with his swindle, nobody caught him up on his tale. The acceptance of these archetypal ideas influences us in the way we think and act, but these things are never discussed. Just recently an American has written a marvelous article, "The Death of an Ideal," the ideal of love. It is generally believed that love is the highest ideal. This is never discussed but it should be. Our age is going to demonstrate that love is not the highest ideal—Life is! This author has not been influenced by me, for I have never said publicly that love was not the highest ideal.

After all the things I have been telling you about the Puer Aeternus we can come back to the dream once more and the white bread that he prefers; the white bread, as you have already seen, signifies purity. The "Boy" wants pure white bread, as in the story of Brother Eustachius. There is a particular connection between this dream and the complicated business dream. How would you link it up?

Dr. Binger: There is a contrast between the corrupt Business Manager and the prince.

Dr. Jung: Sure enough, the Business Manager couldn't provide white bread. This is a sort of moral stain. It is dangerous to use that word *moral*. It is not a good word, for it has no definite meaning. It is moral to sacrifice children, to torture, to buy and sell slaves in certain societies. The word *moral* comes from the Latin *mores*—habits, customs. We connect it with the idea of good and evil, but we must always keep in mind that the word has a relative meaning. The idea of good and evil is not the same in different centuries or in different countries. Here a person who tells a lie is immoral, but in Italy it may be a gracious custom, it may be a kind-hearted thing to do. Only Germans are offended by it when they come to Italy, and possibly the English. Once while I was travelling on a bicycle in Italy, I was caught on a pretty bad road, I got a nail in my tire, and an Italian peasant helped me very kindly. He was much pleased when I invited him to have a glass of wine with me in the osteria and was evidently proud to be seen drinking with me there, and he would take no tip. I thought certainly this man will not lie to me, so I asked him about the road further on. He hesitated just a moment and then said, "Bellissimo, marvellous! It is the very best road in the world, everybody travels on that road." I took it and for about ten minutes it was fine, then it turned out to be a hell of a road. The ruts were so deep that riding was impossible and for two hours I walked in the dark. I was very mad at first, then I realized that the Italian had made me happy for ten minutes at least. A Swiss would have told me the truth at once and damned the road, so I should have been unhappy ten minutes sooner! That was moral for Italy. It would have been uncivil to tell such an evil thing as the truth. Luther said, "If your wife is unwilling take the maid," and he was a religious reformer. That would now be considered very immoral. If you will read his talks at meals you will find many savory passages, now of course not mentioned. So the moral advice in this dream is to be understood as custom, the best thing according to your best knowledge, different in different centuries, but always the best for that particular thing and time. The dream says it must be your best attempt. According to the best of your abilities you must provide that child with the best food. In the dream before, he must mend the warp of the corrupt Business Manager. Now here he must make his best attempt to provide the child with the best food. What is your probable prognosis? What would be the next dream, perhaps? He is not so far along yet that he can link up his conscious life with his dream world. His life is on the safe rails and his unconscious is all being lived in my office.

Dr. Binger: He might easily have a dream that he had an erotic experience with his wife.

Dr. Jung: That is one guess. Another?

Mrs. Sigg: A dream might give him advice as to what he could do next.

Dr. Jung: What would that advice be?

Mrs. Sigg: I don't know.

Dr. Jung: But it is important to know. Do you mean advice as to how to put the relations right with his wife?

Dr. Shaw: That he should try to put his relation with his wife right in a wiser way, not by sexuality.

Mr. Gibb: You said that he was not yet able to put into practice what his dreams were telling him, so why may not the dream be something of an opposite kind, of a contrasting nature?

Dr. Jung: We have two clearly defined points of view. What do you vote for?

Dr. Binger: I can see that I am wrong. I am willing to withdraw.

Dr. Shaw: I think he should stick to it.

Dr. Jung: That would be the conscious way, but we said that the patient could not link all this up with his conscious. The question concerns the next dream, not his conscious reaction.

Dr. Shaw: What sort of a contrast does Mr. Gibb mean? He might say a little more.

Mr. Gibb: Not indicating a hopeful thing, something in the nature of a regression.

Dr. Shaw: To what sort of thing?

Dr. Schlegel: The real problem of the dreamer is less his actual relationship to his wife than his relationship to his own soul. So you would rather expect the dreamer to go down into the unconscious depths behind reality.

Mr. Gibb: I think I agree with that.

Dr. Jung: Any other idea?

Mrs. Sigg: I think the coming of "The Boy" has something to do with the analyst.

Dr. Jung: I definitely refuse to be identified with the Puer Aeternus! One can say that in a way I am responsible for that dream. He wouldn't have had such a dream save for his relationship with me, but that is the whole working basis for dream interpretation.

The next dream [13]: "My wife and I are going with some people whom we apparently know (I am not at all sure who they are) to a feast or celebration. There are a number of big decorated halls representing the bottom of the ocean. It is as though one were seeing through into a marine scene, electrically lighted, where you could see all sorts of swimming and crawling marine animals, as if one were a diver standing on the bottom of the sea. There were many tables, and we began to sit down. These tables were not as elegant as they would be in such a place, but rather rough-looking, like the tables at our popular shooting-matches in Switzerland. (It was only after the dream that I began to remember these tables.

195

It did not occur to me in the dream.) Now I am alone, going up a long flight of stairs. An oldish woman receives me and conducts me into a large room, a sort of salon beautifully decorated. In the centre of the room is a sort of fountain, along the walls are a number of doors that evidently open into other rooms; these doors are partially open and I see there are prostitutes in the rooms. The lady does the honours, and after having passed the whole length of the room without my expressing a wish to enter into relations with one of these girls, the hostess said that several of the girls had not come yet, among them the sisters X (Kaiser, he thinks, was the name). Then I am under the impression that I am reading a French book. I turn the page and come to the beginning of a new chapter.

"There is a vignette and the words, 'The night has been very satisfactory.' The picture represented an orgiastic scene, peculiarly shown. In the upper part of the page, in a hemicycle form, there are gentlemen in evening dress and ladies in very light toilettes, sitting and lying on carpets and cushions. Among them, hung up like marionettes on threads, are policemen and soldiers on horseback. The threads form a sort of borderline between the groups. In the first group, on the left, I recognize myself and another man whom I know (I cannot tell who he is). After that I go downstairs with my wife, but I cannot find my hat. I search everywhere in vain. Eventually I decide to take another hat which does not belong to me. My wife thinks we should wait for our friends with whom we came (cannot remember who they are) but we continue on our way, and as we go out I look into the mirror to see how the hat fits me and I discover that I am wearing a dark brown cap."

You see, our prognosis fits the dream. In practical analysis I can usually see what the next dream will be. I could not pledge myself, of course, but in a dream like the one before this, where we have extraordinary intuition leading far away above the man's mental situation and a figure (Eros) appears beckoning from afar, we can be sure that the dreamer has overdone himself and has got a glimpse of something that he is not up to at all. There is nothing so disappointing as such a far-reaching vision; it leaves you high and dry, fully convinced that it is far beyond you. You go deeper down than ever when you cannot attain to it. In the interpretation of that dream (which was not as full as that given here) I had to take him to a spiritual atmosphere that he was not used to at all. The air was too thin, too spiritual, so it simply tickled all his devils. When

196

people go too far in spiritualizing sex they are led into a sexual orgy, the eternal serpent of the abyss will react and bite, so this man was led into a regression. That is the reason why in this dream he is led down into the sea, but it is not a real regression, he is not really drowned. The truth is that in reality it is a brothel, just the truth artificially dressed up.

Associations: Bottom of the sea: "The bottom of the sea reminds me of an advertisement I saw of the Lido. There were quite a number of pictures of a ballroom, apparently at the bottom of the sea. The marine scene with the fishes, etc., reminds me of an aquarium. I have repeatedly compared the unconscious to the bottom of the sea. I remember that when I went upstairs alone I admired the beautiful marine scenery." *The rough tables:* "I associate with our Shooting-matches, where they have such tables and benches and where all is forced gaiety with too much drinking." He says he hates that sort of thing, for it is too artificial, he emphasizes the fact of its artificiality. *The room above:* "reminds me of a certain big hall in a German watering-place, where there is also an artificial pond with a fountain. People like to compare that big hall with the Thermae of Caracalla in Rome." (An ambitious comparison.) *The sisters who have not come and the name Kaiser* mean nothing to him, though the word *Kaiser* stands for a very important personage. Then comes an explanatory association that sums up the dream: "After one has looked at the images of the unconscious (the marine scene) wherein are connected some uncomfortable situations (the hard benches in these rooms) then one can go to these orgiastic adventures without any particular excitement; the orgy of the vignette in the book, and the prostitutes." *The pictures in the book* remind him of pictures that he has seen of Roman orgies, the baths of Caracalla.

Then he philosophizes: "A man who understands himself should be able to participate in such an orgy and to see himself as if in a book" (he saw himself in these scenes in the dream). With the *officers and soldiers* he associates public authority and control. He says: "In the dream these police officers are represented as marionettes, and it is true that public authority is such a marionette. This has to do with my fear of public opinion, public control." *Hat:* In spite of the fact that the strange hat suits me, I discover, when I see myself in the mirror, that I cut a funny figure. It is not just the cap of a fool but it is a queer cap."

Now you have a picture of the dream, the downfall after the

previous dream, and again this critique. With these associations you can see that the idea of the dream is getting down into a collective situation, a festal scene where thousands and thousands of people come, a popular collective situation. "The bottom of the sea" is a metaphor for the collective unconscious, the great collectivity at the bottom for the sea. There is nothing human about it, only fishes and other crawling swimming beasts. Then, coming up from that level, he at least reaches a level of relation, metaphorically participating in an orgy in a house of prostitution, and leaving with the wrong hat, the funny brown cap.

SUMMER TERM

May / June 1929

LECTURE I

15 May 1929

[Dr. Jung repeated the dream of the last seminar with the patient's associations for the benefit of those who had not heard the earlier seminars. He also added some further suggestions to the patient's associations, and spoke of the decorations of the rooms at the bottom of the sea as similar to those of the Tonhalle here—at carnival time. The dreamer says these scenes remind him of the aquarium at Naples, but there were many more compartments here than in that aquarium. The peculiar rough tables and hard benches remind him of public festivals and pageants, which he dislikes. It is disagreeable sitting on hard benches, and the gaiety seems to him forced. The next part of the dream seems to him just a brothel, with scenes of his own reminiscences describing the quality of the place. The two prostitutes whose name was Kaiser convey nothing to him, but he has a feeling that those two sisters are particularly important people, though they are evidently prostitutes. The word Kaiser implies importance and it may also be a play on words. He says that after having experienced the unconscious images one should be able to experience orgiastic scenes without particular excitement. Dr. Jung asked him why he thought so, and he said, "When you look at pictures from the unconscious, you see so many difficult and disagreeable things that these scenes in the dream would convey very little in the way of excitement. A man who knows himself would even be able to share such orgies, to watch them as though he were reading about them in a book." He says that the figures of policemen and officers hanging by strings are mere marionettes, and associates them with his fear of authority.][1]

Dr. Jung: As soon as something goes beyond his experience, he is exceedingly afraid, and wants some authority to lean on, so it is

---

[1] Note by one of the original editors of the Seminar.

not improbable that his guess about the marionettes has something to do with the authorities, but I am not clear what his association really means.

About the scene with the hat, the dreamer says, "It is as if I were pretending, decorating myself with the hat or feathers of someone else. It seems to suit me, but when I look in the mirror I discover that I am ridiculous. It is the cap of a fool, yet not quite, but it looks rather foolish, a cap of two colours."

The beginning of the dream is rather obvious, I should say, but I should like to establish the connection with the dream before. I want to convey the importance of that dream with the symbol of the Puer Aeternus. Its symbolism is almost too remote to describe fully its particular value. Whenever a dream takes such a long shot a regression is likely to follow. Going too high means going too low. In the last seminar you yourselves came to the conclusion that the patient's next dream would be in the nature of a regression, and sure enough this dream begins with the bottom of the sea, the lowest place on earth. The subsequent scenes in the dream are not at all spiritual but as carnal as they can be, a brothel really. The dream goes from the unconscious to the brothel, decidedly from bad to worse. In the very beginning of the dream there is the fact of his taking his wife to such a show, a sort of Lido festival, a rather doubtful place. What would you say to that? Have you any idea about it?

Miss Chapin: His problem in the other dreams was his relation with his wife, and now he is taking her along with him into this situation.

Dr. Jung: But she was with him in the dream before. Isn't it odd that he took her to such a place as this?

Dr. Binger: He takes her for decency's sake.

Dr. Jung: That is very good. That might be an explanation. This man likes protection and he takes his wife and respectable friends with him as a sort of bodyguard. This is true but it is all negative. You must be careful with an introvert, as this man is. If I should suggest to him that he is a moral coward and that he is afraid to go alone and therefore takes his wife and friends with him, he would accept it as true, as I am authority to him, and fall down under it. I should pull the bottom out from under his feet, so we must not be too negative and lay stress on this bodyguard as a shield against the evil thing. We have to look at this part of the dream in a more positive way.

As Miss Chapin has just said, his wife is a problem—but his relatives and friends are also problems. His trouble with his wife is his own attitude. He shows only a very respectable side to his wife, so that attitude stands in between them; he is not a real man to his wife, he is always in respectable company even when he is alone with her. So we can see that he is doing something rather unusual in the dream. He has had any number of experiences with prostitutes where he did not take his wife along with him. He did not want a bodyguard there, although of course morally he did, but he would be shocked out of his senses at the very thought of taking these respectable people to such a place. But here in the dream he is carrying along his whole respectable social atmosphere down into Hell with him. This is something that he could not do in reality. So when he is doing such a thing in the dream, it is a deed of extraordinary courage, or perhaps a fatal mistake. It says you are going down into a brothel where you watch a very orgiastic scene with all your relatives, which means that he would be making them acquainted with the other side of himself. That is of course just what he is not doing, he would never dare to tell his experiences or fantasies to his wife. So the dream puts the finger on the sore spot as usual. What is the bridge in his relationship to his wife? In the dream before, the bridge consists in the truth. In came the Puer Aeternus, and he tried to understand it as relationship, but what he needs is to tell the truth! From what he says I would assume that he could not do that, for she would blow up, she is a baby. Still you cannot tell.

Not long ago I had a consultation with a man who told me his story of an affair with another woman. It had produced a negative feeling in him for his wife. I insinuated that he might be frank with his wife, but he said that he could not possibly tell her. After a while I saw the wife, who gave me a story of a whole string of affairs, six men in succession. She had contracted gonorrhoea and then told her husband that he was to blame. He had had gonorrhoea before his marriage, and her doctor had told her that it might not have been entirely cured, and in that case it could light up again enough to have infected her. The man felt so inferior that he didn't even tell me this. Such a situation is exactly like the problem of parents who hesitate to tell their children anything that will enlighten them about sex. The children say, "How stupid mother is, she seems to know nothing about these things." So the dream presents an impartial truth. It shows the situation which by law of nature *is*. It does not say you ought to do this or that, nor does it say what is good or bad. It simply shows the dreamer in a situation. Man *is* so underneath. This is the truth. He is going with his whole set into such a place. What conclusion do you draw from all this? Perhaps it is left for the doctor to advise him. I can only say, "Your wife is now old enough not to be shocked, she cannot be such a baby that she does not smell a rat." Perhaps she is filled with fantasies, perhaps she is such a moral coward that she cannot see the truth. He should get her analysed and let things come out. She may be shocked, or she may only pretend to be. The whole thing is perfectly ridiculous. Any woman with common sense must know that a man in his situation would not be quite reliable on the sexual side. Many people, both men and women, are not. It is a universal fact, and it has always been so. Why should she be torn to pieces by such a fact? But in reality perhaps she would be. I could do nothing with that man; he is so afraid of his wife that he does not dare tell her. The dream, however, tells the truth as it is. The reasonable thing would be to say to him, "Now go ahead, have a sensible talk with her, say this is the world, this is the truth." But what I really told the patient was that I thought there were certain reasons why he should not have a serious talk with his wife. Before he had this dream I thought that he seemed to be a bit of a moral coward, and that I should give him a good kick to make him have it out, but then I got something from this dream, and other things came up in later ones, so I began to hesitate and I have hesitated ever since. Now, the situation in this dream is down at the bottom of the sea; that is a pretty dangerous thing, and unless you are a diver equipped with a helmet you may be a corpse. It is certainly going into the real unconscious. Now why do you suppose the dream represents the unconscious as an aquarium? A marine aquarium is a good representation of the unconscious, but anyone can go into an aquarium. Remember that I said this man is a bit of a moral coward.

Mrs. Schlegel: It is an artificial bottom of the sea.

Dr. Schlegel: It is arranged in compartments.

Dr. Jung: For him it must be so, the artificiality and the compartments. The same thing comes in later, the factor of unreality.

He is not really experiencing it. It is only a play, as though he were reading it in a book. This is what the dream says. We would say, "Oh, go ahead; have that talk with your wife, get into the hot soup," but the unconscious in the dream speaks a different language. It points a warning finger and shows the situation as artificial, a play, an aquarium, a book. When we have such a dream, what does it mean? What would it compensate? The dream might have put him in a situation of blood and thunder so real that he would sweat and scream as in a nightmare. That would be a compensation for a flippant and perfunctory attitude of the conscious.

Mr. Gibb: The conscious takes it too seriously.

Dr. Jung: Yes, now the dream has a flippant setting to compensate for the man's too serious view of it in the conscious. Remember this man is an introvert and afraid, so the dream says, "Oh, it is only a fantasy, only an aquarium, you are reading about it in a book." It is like Mother's voice, "Only a bear at the zoo."

Dr. Binger: Isn't that an unusual way for the unconscious to present itself? It usually makes things more horrible.

Dr. Jung: It is true that the unconscious usually makes things horrible, but nowadays people do not take things seriously enough. Therefore you must give them a good hump. But this man is rather serious and just a bit afraid of the unconscious. At first I did not see it at all, then I discovered that he was too much afraid of the unconscious. When you have to do with the unconscious you must not be afraid. If you are too flippant in your conscious attitude your dream will enhance the situation so that you will sweat and have a nightmare. If you have the right appreciation of the unconscious you will not be afraid. If you are afraid you are gone, the game is already lost. For then the unconscious disappears. As long as it is visible you can catch it and integrate it into consciousness, but when it disappears it will work in the dark, and then it is dangerous. An invisible foe is the worst. When the unconscious is invisible, it can assail you from every side. This man is afraid of his unconscious, therefore he must be careful or he will get into a panic, and if he talks to his wife in that state, he will himself shoot his wife to pieces. People in a state of panic are the most dangerous, the next thing will be an explosion. When I have borderline cases I have to keep myself very quiet in order not to let an explosion happen. If my patient keeps his head, he may be able to handle the situation. His wife naturally is in a state of tension, she must be terribly stored up, like a mine ready to go off. So if the husband is in the least afraid he would most likely handle the situation awkwardly, he would infect her with panic and cause the powder to explode. Such women sometimes use a revolver, or commit suicide. I have the impression that it is a vital matter. Such things should never be forced. So he must be cautious, and not moralistic. It is better to be wise than good. In the next part of the dream, after the aquarium scene, he discovers that the seats are rough wooden benches, such as one sees at a peasant festival; they do not seem to suit the occasion at all. You would expect rather elaborate seats, but in the dream the benches are very uncomfortable. What do you make of it? Remember they are in the aquarium.

Mrs. Deady: He says it reminds him of the festivals given here, and they always seem to him very artificial.

Dr. Jung: But it would not be artificial for the natives. He does not like such affairs, he is not a good mixer anyway, so it would be very artificial for him. The whole thing refers to his analytical hours with me. The sitting is the analytical "sitting." It is rather uncomfortable, and these hours have too a forced gaiety for him. Of course he enjoys all the beautiful vistas analysis opens up to him, but he pays for them by hours of uncomfortable sitting on rough benches. I shouldn't wonder if he wouldn't put that down to my rough Swiss ways. I have told him things that have made him squirm. In the dream he moves further up, upstairs, into a brothel! Isn't that rather astonishing? You would expect that he would go down, open a trapdoor and go even lower, as low as he is in a brothel. But he goes up. Why?

Dr. Binger: He is going up to his conscious mind where these things are.

Dr. Jung: Yes, but that is not it.

Dr. Leavitt: It means he has been pretty low.

Dr. Jung: He has been pretty low in my office. Is it higher in a brothel?

Dr. Leavitt: He would feel better there.

Dr. Jung: You assume he would feel better there! The dream says, "Yes, analysis, but on a higher level you rise to a brothel." Now what would that mean?

Mrs. Deady: It is a more human relation.

Dr. Jung: Probably he minds the inhuman relations of analysis.

Better that we should have some orgiastic scenes together! But I have not discovered any homosexuality in him yet.

Dr. Leavitt: But that would be getting out of his repression, wouldn't it?

Dr. Jung: But he does not repress his sexuality, he represses his feeling for his wife.

Dr. Deady: The dream says it is higher than analysis, up to a higher level, franker.

Dr. Jung: You can take any lady to an aquarium, it is perfectly proper and decent, there is no implication in going to an aquarium. But if you take your wife to a brothel it would be much more dangerous. So the dream says "up" to it. It is a greater moral effort than analysis. In the unconscious he is now confronting his wife with the reality of things, with the real facts which he has learned about himself through his analysis.

Mrs. Sigg: It seems to be a very important problem with modern women. They do not hide their knowledge of the brothel any longer, but discuss the subject very frankly.

Dr. Jung: Prostitution is a function of marriage. According to statistics the real supporters of brothels are the married men, not the bachelors.

Mrs. Sigg: The man represses his soul by doing this.

Dr. Jung: Now, don't go too far. The dream says that he takes his friends to confront the fact of the brothel. Then the whole thing becomes unreal, as though he were reading about it in a book. The unconscious has been made into a museum, unreal because it is too real in the conscious.

Mr. Gibb: It has become an obsession.

Dr. Jung: Yes, too real means obsessed by it. When a thing becomes too real, I walk right into it, as a bird walks into the mouth of a snake. His miserable sexuality has become so real, so overvalued, that he cannot dream of talking about it. It is too real, it is absolute. Therefore the unconscious says, "Oh, it is only something you read about in a book, a story, not even an official report, probably something quite incredible. It is so far away that it need not touch you. Even in reality you could go through with it. There is nothing to get excited about." So the dream is just soothing him, for he is so afraid at the thought of telling this to his wife that he gets in a blue funk about it.

Dr. Leavitt: Is that a wish-fulfilment?

Dr. Jung: There is no wish-fulfilment in the dream. He is too frightened to wish to take his wife; he might wish it could never happen.

Dr. Leavitt: Then it just says what he ought to do?

Dr. Jung: A dream never says what one ought to do. Nature never suggests. You must know the details of the conscious condition in order to interpret a dream, for the dream is made up of all we don't live or become conscious of. In my conscious I might go too far to the right. When you lean too far over on one side, there will be a compensation in the unconscious. The unconscious is like a compass, it doesn't tell you what to do. Unless you can read the compass it cannot help you.

Dr. Leavitt: Then after the interpretation the dream is a guide?

Dr. Jung: Yes, as the compass is a guide—if you know how to read it, it points, but it is no good unless you understand it. It is like the Delphic oracle, it never tells you what to do. It is a mystic situation, and you yourself must make head and tail out of it. Now as soon as the dream is explained and the situation is sensed as unreal, the man is free to paint the worst, an orgiastic scene; and that is something he might show to his wife. He could say, "See here what I have found in this old book." *He* is not responsible for it, it was done by some artist long ago. Do you notice the peculiar thing in the picture of the marine scene?

Dr. Binger: The aquarium is divided into compartments.

Dr. Jung: Yes, that is it, it is divided into compartments. But first I want to point out that there is something quite suggestive about the undulating movements of the primal creatures in an aquarium. They show you quite openly in their squirming and wriggling the sort of movements you do not see on the surface. They are like the movements of the body, of the intestines and of the sympathetic nervous system. There is a peculiar analogy that I have often seen in patients' dreams and fantasies: intestinal movements with a sexual analogy. So the pictures that are down in the aquarium which develop into orgiastic scenes upstairs in the brothel are practically the same. They end in sexuality. Now we are almost forced to speak of these compartments. Why should they be divided into compartments?

Dr. Binger: That was what the dreamer had done in his actual life.

Mr. Gibb: Things can be better controlled in compartments.

Dr. Jung: The very idea of a compartment means control. You separate the different compartments by water-tight walls and you can say that this belongs here and that belongs there. Things are more manageable when one can separate them and there is no danger of getting them mixed. They stay where they belong and an avalanche can be avoided. This is what man has done with the dark side of the world, separated it from the other side by water-tight compartments. But why should the fish in the tanks be separated from the other marine scenes? They are much the same thing; we are rather at a loss to understand why they should be divided into compartments. To be sure, it is tidy, more manageable, and gives one a sense of security, but I am not satisfied with that. There is still more to it.

Mrs. Sigg: It is a very strange thing that in the old forms of literature they wrote in a very detailed and pedantic way. There must be some analogy there.

Dr. Jung: You are quite right about that particular form of pedantry in early writings. Everything is described with the most amazing detail, so that in these descriptions everything is given the same importance.

Dr. Schmitz: There is a similar pedantic arrangement of scenes in Italian and Indian pictures, the same analogy.

Dr. Jung: That points to the thing I mean. That peculiar pedantry can only come about by extraordinary concentration of libido on each particular event, hence there is superfluous detail. There is increased subjective value, therefore each event must be shown by itself, depicted in amazing detail, surrounded by a frame, decorated by statues, etc. This shows that every event has an enormous value attached to it. Every fact stands by itself, there is no attempt at synthesis in the picture. I am quite certain that if these orgiastic scenes had not been so blurred in the dream, my patient would have been able to tell me each particular situation through which he had gone, and which is still standing out separately, not synthesized at all, and here we come back to the idea of security. Suppose that you have once committed a murder, once stolen something, and have a long series of awful things each in its own compartment. But you are only in the present compartment now, just concerned with a little swindle. This is the way of the criminal, and explains his feeling of "goodness." He has his life all divided off into compartments, until the police come with their records.

A man once came to me and said, "The thing that is the matter with me is that I have never had any experiences with women." I said, "Why, how is that? You are married." "Ah yes, but no other." "You told me you were engaged before." "Yes, but that was long ago." After I had pressed him to tell me about his life, he came out with one love story after another, until I had counted thirty-two of them. But that man said he had never had any experiences with a woman, and it was true. After analysis he slipped once again and then he was conscious, and said, "Never again." The compartments were gone.

I had another case, a very charming man who had relations with five women, including his wife, at the same time. I had not said much about this, but once, in explaining a dream, I said something of the polygamous nature of man. "But," he said, "I would not be polygamous, I know nothing of that." I said, "What about Mrs. X." "Ah that, well, you see she is musical and we sometimes play together, and of course after the music—." "But Mrs. G." "Oh, we play golf and after that—" "But Miss—" "Why, she is just my secretary, I take her out sometimes, but that is not polygamous." You see, that man had his girls in different compartments, music, golf, office, wife, so he felt respectable, his whole life was in compartments. I said to him, "I call that polygamous—you have sex relations with five women at the same time." "Why, doctor, I believe you are right! It is awful!" "Oh, not awful, but hardly wise, better change things a bit." Do you know what happened to that man? He became completely impotent. I can hardly believe it, but it is true.

I had an aunt[2] who was a bad woman, bad with her tongue, and my uncle was an inventor who had a phonograph and made records. One day she gave him an awful sermon, and without her knowing it he made a record. Next day when she was reasonable, he said he had something to play to her, and put the record on. She said, "I never said that, it is not true!" I often advise people to keep a diary and read the old entries, or hear other people describe their lives for them, then they may break through the compartments. Hearing someone else give a vista of one's life is very illuminating. The things we do are in compartments which keep us singularly unconscious. The dreamer has never summed up his life until now, and I am quite sure that if the unconscious

[2] Evidently on the Preiswerk side.

had been more clear in the dream he would have had the shock of his life. An introvert often keeps the events of his life in different compartments, he has a sort of wall between so they cannot blend. When they do come together there is a conflagration. This man is protected against a conflagration.

LECTURE II

22 May 1929

Dr. Jung:

Today we are going to continue our dream. We got stuck somewhere near the end. There is only one part to which I want to call your attention. You remember the memories of the dreamer's life are kept in compartments, and in the dream they are divided by strings from which hang marionettes of policemen and soldiers, and these mark the divisions between the compartments. The dreamer has an idea which is a sort of interpretation, but he has no associations. What do you think is the meaning of that particular symbol? The fact that his compartment psychology is divided by policemen and soldiers who obviously guard the compartment walls?

Dr. Schlegel: The guardians of morality. Policemen are the symbols of conventional morality.

Dr. Jung: Yes, and at this point I'll make a "joke," like the old German professor. It is the story of a Zurich father who, when his son came of age, said to him, "Now you are entering life and you have got to know something. Stupid people believe that the Bible will tell you what is right and what is wrong, but for the more intelligent people there is the penal code, and that is all there is to it." That boy went into life convinced that policemen and soldiers stood for morality. Formerly the police were enough to enforce it, but now people don't believe in authority, so we have more soldiers and machine-guns. The penal code is surely the idea in the dream; this man has the conventional notion of morality. But why do the policemen and soldiers mark these compartments? An interesting bit of psychology in itself, for according to the dream these compartments are due to the presence of policemen and soldiers. How do you explain that?

Dr. Schmitz: I would say that he is now so far that he understands that the police and soldiers are not enough. Now he makes his own

212

compartments, and the soldiers and policemen are merely marionettes hanging there. To have one's own compartment is objectionable, but it is better than to believe in police authority. He has
made progress.

Dr. Jung: Yes, marionettes are dead things, save for their manipulation by a living hand. The soldiers and policemen are no
longer important, and the unconscious sees that fact. But my question is, why is conventional morality producing compartments, for
obviously that is what it is doing.

Dr. Schmitz: But that is the idea of bourgeois morality. It says,
"Have brothels, but keep them in compartments away from your
wife, your sisters, and your daughters"; and moreover, the police
protect the brothel.

Dr. Jung: Yes, it is a well-known fact that the police are in
alliance with brothels and such places. Compartment psychology is
really due to conventional morality, which says that certain things
are provided by the state. Being a citizen under the law you are
allowed to use that instrument. I remember a long time ago meeting
an American on board a transatlantic steamer. He was a conventional married man, who had fallen in love with a young girl, and
he wanted to fire his wife and marry the girl. He asked my opinion
about it, and I said: "Is your wife objectionable?" "No." "Have you
any children?" "Yes, five." "And you are just putting her out into
the street?" "But," he said, "I married her under the law, and the
law also stands for divorce. I can divorce her under the law." That
is compartment psychology all right. As long as you are under police
protection, such morality produces a perfectly soulless condition.
Where there is no soul there is no synthesis. A perfectly sane man
once said to me: "You can do anything you please as long as the
police do not know about it." However, he had terrible nightmares
and neurotic symptoms because he did as he damned pleased, and
he did not connect the two facts. There is a law in ourselves which
allows certain things and not others. The expediency of a persona
attitude in a conscious person can be conventional morality for one
who is unconscious. I have no use for a man who believes in conventional morality. He can be a criminal just as well, but be within
conventional morality and consider himself respectable. The man
who does wrong and knows that it is wrong can change. He is not
wronging his own soul. It is murderous for the human soul to help
people to make these compartments. It is a sin against the Holy

Ghost to have such a morality. There is no development under the law of conventional morality. It leads to compartment psychology, and how can a man develop when he forgets what his compartments contain? Such a man can do anything under the law, he can say, "Oh yes, but that was years ago."

Dr. Bertine: Doesn't an orgiastic scene imply conventional morality? Animals are not orgiastic.

Dr. Jung: Yes, the police and the orgiastic scenes are one and the same thing, but the orgiastic scenes are in compartments safely divided from the other compartments, in which other things happen. After these scenes in the dream he goes downstairs with his wife and hunts for his hat, which he cannot find, so he takes one of a strange design; on the way out he looks in a mirror and sees that he is wearing a funny brown cap and not a hat. That scene indicates a change. Something must have happened in the last dream, so his outward appearance is changed, this is symbolized by the peculiar hat. The patient has no associations with it so we cannot trace it. In such a case we must use our own wits. The symbolism of the hat must be something impersonal, if it were something personal he would have plenty of associations. The lack of associations in such a case can prove that it is a matter of impersonal symbolism, a sort of generally accepted metaphor. Do you know anything of these caps?

Dr. Schmitz: The cap of Siegfried.

Dr. Jung: Yes, the peculiar cap of Siegfried which he took from the dragon to make himself invisible. Do you remember other material?

Mrs. Schevill: You told us of mysterious little boys in brown leather caps appearing in a small German town, and the effect they had on conventional morality.

Dr. Jung: That was from a German book, the name of which I have forgotten.[1] I myself have never had this kind of symbolism, but it is very striking. It was only when I came across that symbol again and again that I began to feel its importance. My patient had never read this book. It was a story of a highly respectable German town in which these mysterious boys with brown caps appeared and then strange things began to happen. There were Vereins in those towns. Wherever there are three Germans, there is a Verein.

[1] See above, 27 Mar. 1929, n. 4.

Twenty Vereins come together and have an annual ball. It was all very respectable, all the young girls there lined up for the marriage market. Everybody was there but the parson, and later that proved to be fatal for him. Everything was going on as usual, when behind a column in the gallery there appeared a youth with a brown cap. Then things began to get gay. The band began to play with pep, a flickering flame poured through the place, everyone got wild, and the ball finally became the wildest kind of a primitive orgy, ending in complete promiscuity. Then the boy disappeared and tableau! Everybody came back to consciousness. There was the burgomaster with the waitresses, etc. Now, our dreamer has the same symbolism, the brown leather cap. He has never read the book, but he has obviously tapped an underground conduit of symbolic material, as did the author of this book. We discover the boy in the brown leather cap who is probably responsible for the wild night in the story. Such a ballroom in a respectable town is like the background of this man's consciousness. Suddenly a hole opens in the wall, and there he is with his wife in a terribly shocking place. That is what these boys do, suddenly open up horrible possibilities like the magic bottle with the images of the lovers, which was so shocking to all the people at the party; the bottle simply revealed the secret fantasy of those people. This is what has happened in the dream, a piercing of the veil, of the compartment wall, and this is due to the boys with brown leather caps. Do you know anything further about these boys?

Mrs. Crowley: Dwarfs.

Dr. Jung: Yes, and brownies. In the history of this symbol the cap is the peculiar head-dress of all sorts of people, the pileus of Mithras or Apollo, the Phrygian cap of Attis or Adonis;[2] and then the Greek Cabiri[3] were adorned with pointed caps. I think it was Pausanias who reported that two statues of Cabiri were placed out on the rocks at a particularly dangerous spot, to protect navigators. Ordinarily the Cabiri were little things, and were kept hidden in cases, and always wrapped up carefully. The *spiritus familiaris* of Aesculapius was also such a one, and was always found on the

[2] See *Symbols of Transformation*, index, s.v. "pileus" (as in 1912 edn.).

[3] The Cabiri or Kabeiroi were miniature hooded gods, whose chief shrine in classical times was on the island of Samothrace. They were also called "the great gods." For their occurrence in *Faust*, Part II, see *Psychology and Alchemy*, CW 12, par. 203. Also see below, n. 10.

monuments of Aesculapius as his guardian. He was a special god of doctors—Telesphoros, the one who brings perfection or accomplishment. They all wore pointed caps, usually brown. You may have seen on the arms of the city of Munich the "Münchner Kindl,"[4] who wears a long monkish robe which covers his feet, for you may not see the feet of a dwarf. There is the story of a miller's wife who was especially favoured by the dwarfs. They did all her work. She just left everything in the kitchen, and during the night she heard noises and knew that in the morning everything would be cleaned up. She knew it was the dwarfs, but she was curious and wanted to see them, so one night she sprinkled flour on the floor. In the morning there were the marks of duck's feet all over the floor, but the dwarfs never came again, she had to do her own work. She should not know of the feet of the dwarfs! There is a profound idea here. This material should give us a clue as to what the cap really is. The dreamer exchanges his ordinary hat for what seems a similar one, but which turns out to be this peculiar brown cap. What is the *hat* then, his ordinary hat?

Dr. Bertine: The headdress of a conventional gentleman.

Dr. Jung: Why express it by the hat?

Mrs. Schevill: Very often a hat can stand for an attitude.

Dr. Jung: Yes, but why use it for conventionality?

Mrs. Sigg: The man goes into the street with it.

Dr. Schmitz: It is his roof, his covering.

Dr. Jung: A man wears his hat in the street, where other people see him, when he is respectable, which means when he can be seen. Therefore he is presentable. If anyone should wear a Cabiri hat on the street now, we would think he was drunk, or some kind of a crank, or a musician! A gentleman cannot allow himself any fantasies about hats. In San Francisco if you appear on the street in a straw hat after a certain date, they will take you right off to the insane asylum. When I went to America I wore my usual European hat, but a friend said at once, "Your hat won't do. You must wear a bowler, because everybody does."

Mr. Gibb: Dr. Baynes[5] had to do the same thing.

---

[4] A small figure of a monk in the coat-of-arms of the city of Munich (founded by monks in the 12th century).

[5] The British psychiatrist and analytical psychologist Helton Godwin Baynes (1882-1943) was a close friend of Jung and translator of several of his works, including *Psychological Types* (1923). During 1928-1929, he and his wife Cary were living in Carmel and Berkeley, California. Gibb was also a friend of Baynes.

Dr. Jung: Exactly. The hat is a symbol. In a man's dream it usually means that he is especially concerned with his street appearance or with publicity. It represents a man's particular prejudice or grievance. Now, when the dreamer leaves the house he cannot find his hat, his outward appearance again, a serious loss for him, for he realizes that he cannot appear in public as he used to do, something must have gotten under his skin! He finds another hat, one that he thinks is similar to his own. This is again the soothing element in the dream. The dream says, "Never mind, it is not quite yours, but it is a hat like everybody else's." To his amazement he discovers that instead of a hat he is wearing a peculiar brown cap. So one could say that he leaves the house no longer the conventional gentleman who entered it, but one of those metaphysical naughty boys, or a Cabir. That proved to be such a shock that he woke up.

Dr. Schmitz: The cap is the sign of the peasant, so he is no longer the gentleman he thought he was.

Dr. Jung: Sure enough, but that idea of the cap does not suit our views any longer. A gentleman in a golf suit can wear a cap but with our gentleman it won't do, he is exceedingly meticulous about his outward appearance, he dresses very carefully, his tie, handkerchief, and his socks must always be of the same blue. The wearing of this common cap lowers his opinion of himself, he immediately becomes like any common person on the street, the butcher for instance. A man so conventional must have some distinction, a fastidious appearance, otherwise he would not be different from his butcher. So the wearing of the cap lowers him in his social standing, that is the first thing that troubles him. Why is he lowered?

Mrs. Sigg: He is first identified with the father and son, then with the Puer Aeternus. He is too high so he must be lowered.

Dr. Jung: Perfectly true. When we are unconscious of a thing which is constellated, we are identified with it, and it moves us or activates us as if we were marionettes. We can only escape that effect by making it conscious and objectifying it, putting it outside of ourselves, taking it out of the unconscious. That is exceedingly difficult for him to do. Not knowing the Puer Aeternus, he could not remove it, concretize it, or objectify it as outside of himself. I often see how hard this is for my patients. I find it hard to see a thing that has been a most intimate part of my own psychology as objectively as this match-stand.

But the patient was identified with the Puer Aeternus, and this identification removed him from the human sphere. How can I prove such identification? I can only say one thing: a man who is identified with conventional morality is not himself, he is the police, he is the brothel, he is the penal code, he is everything else. He is always regulated by laws, therefore he is always using that famous statement: "If you believe that sort of thing then any man or any girl could do so and so! What would become of our civilization?" I always answer, "You are not concerned with the fate of the eleven thousand virgins,[6] but with your own problems," but of course it is much easier to be concerned with the case of the eleven thousand virgins than with your own case; one is then a sort of Saviour concerned with the welfare of the world. But the real thing is to look to your own Self! Henri IV of France said, "My ideal is that every French peasant has his chicken in the pot on Sunday." I say, "Every man must be concerned with his own morality, and not with the welfare of other people." He cannot solve the problem of the eleven thousand, for he could move a whole lifetime along that line and nothing would happen, he would always be safe.

Since the man is the penal code, he is also conventional morality; and since he is secretly moved by the Puer Aeternus he is the Puer Aeternus, and also the boy with the brown cap, the opposite of the Puer Aeternus, a brownie thoroughly brown, coming from the earth, the colour of the earth. He is no longer in the world of beautiful general ideas, he is now under the earth, covered by the brown earth cap, by dirt. As he was above himself, now he is below himself, hopelessly caught by the magic power of the earth. This naturally has a lowering influence on his psychological constitution. He comes down to the primitive man, the caveman who is literally living under the earth. We come now to the important question, what is the meaning of the whole dream? I want to have your opinion of what it conveys, how it functions? What should the dreamer conclude from this dream?

Mr. Gibb: Doesn't it mean that he is beginning to know more of himself? To see all the compartments at once? He takes his whole party with him in the dream.

Dr. Jung: That is highly important. How would you value that?

[6] See below, 26 Feb. 1930, p. 498.

What does it mean that he takes the whole crowd there, family, friends, and relations?

Mr. Gibb: They are parts of himself.

Dr. Jung: Yes, a man is never represented by himself alone. A man is only something in relation to other individuals. You only get a complete picture of him when you see him in relation to his set, as you do not know about a plant or animal unless you know its habitat. So when the dream says he is going with his whole set it means going together and putting them into his life. In our conscious language we would say that he calls all these people together and for twenty-four hours there is nothing but the truth. It is a sort of feeling statement of his whole psychology, of what he ought to do. So in the beginning of the dream we have this sweeping criticism of his compartment psychology. It is as though the dream said, "Now take your whole bunch, and go into that well-known show and let them see the whole thing."

Mr. Dell: Are the compartments like a panorama side by side?

Dr. Jung: Yes, and that means he should look objectively at the whole of his life, put the compartments together and sum up. It is just what such people do not do, they keep things well apart, so that there will be no short circuit. The dream then gives him a panoramic view, an account of his whole life, lets every side of himself become acquainted with his life as a whole. That is pouring all the different contents into the melting-pot and seeing what will come out, then he can have a synthesis.

Mr. Dell: The short circuit gives the nightmare quality?

Dr. Jung: Certainly, and the shock here is that the dreamer comes out with a brown cap! He is lowered, he comes down from his respectable position where nobody knew what his life was, not even the police. He wears the brown cap, and now he gets an idea of what he really is. Many people never realize what they really are, because of their compartment psychology. They always have the marvelous good conscience of the criminal; they do not sum up, do not contemplate their lives as a whole. I have often heard people listening to accounts of themselves from friends or rereading their diaries say: "I was dumbfounded when I heard all that!" But more often people won't let it come to that—they fear it too much. For instance, a man who was very extraverted came to me. He always kept busy from early morning until late at night, and I said to him, "You should sit still for at least an hour every day, and consider what you are doing." He replied, "Well, I could play the piano with my wife, or read to her, or play cards." He couldn't get away from the idea that someone should be with him. Finally when I made him see that I meant he should be alone, he said, "Then I get quite melancholy." I said, "Now you see what kind of company you are to yourself. I want you to be quite depressed and realize what you are living." He wouldn't do it. That man was living an amazing life in compartments. When he was alone with himself he was in the worst possible company, one part of his life after another came up and he simply could not bear it. There are people who just funk their whole lives.

Mr. Gibb: Wouldn't you say the dreamer is beginning to do something toward giving up his life in compartments?

Dr. Jung: Yes, I should say that something was happening. He evidently got something from the brown cap. There are cases in which neither the doctor nor the patient can do very much, the analysis must depend on the goodwill of the unconscious, and the final realization must come from the strange world of the unconscious. You may be sure that, when things come up out of the bowels of the earth like this brown cap, something has happened, though nobody understands it. The greatest ideas of mankind have happened for years and years and no man has understood. I can give you a simple example: When I asked the Elgonyi in Africa about their religion they denied any belief in a god or ghosts or spirits or anything of the sort. They could tell me nothing, and it took me three weeks to discover why every morning just at sunrise they came out of their huts, each man put his hands to his mouth and blew into them, then stretched them up to the sun and after that they went off to work. I asked, "What is that?" They answered, "I don't know, my father did it, my grandfather did it, so I do it." I asked many of them and they all gave me the same answer. I persisted and grilled them. Finally I asked an old man what it was, and he said, "Our fathers did it; we are glad that the night has passed." That kind of forced breath is called *roho*, corresponding to the Arabic *ruh*, which means "rushing," hence "wind" or "spirit." In the New Testament wind and spirit are both expressed by the same word, *pneuma*. "The wind bloweth where it listeth"(John 3:8). At Pentecost *pneuma* descended on the disciples as a great wind which filled all the house. In Swahili there is an onomatopoetic word for the death-rattle—*roho* (related to both the Arabic *ruh* and the Hebrew *ruah*).[7] The breath that escapes the dying man is his spirit, and therefore the eldest son must put his lips to his dying father's in order to catch his last breath. So the Elgonyi custom means that they are offering life-breath or spirit to the sunrise. It is a thanksgiving, they offer their souls to God.[8]

So we express it in words, but they don't know why they do it. That idea is operating in them in a prepsychological state. I know that they have many ceremonies, circumcisions, markings, etc. and they do not know why. We say, "Aren't they primitive and unconscious? These people don't know what they are doing."

Dr. Leavitt: In modern religious symbolism, do people know any more?

Dr. Jung: I could ask you, "Why do you have a Christmas tree? Or what does the rabbit laying eggs at Easter mean?" No one knows what these things mean, we must go back to folklore to find it. Now, you know how the unconscious works. It is the spirit or the Heaven-born thing! The spirit was there before man's consciousness. It makes people do certain things in certain ways that you can never explain. Animals do not lift their paws to the rising sun, but men do. The Elgonyi call it a spirit that moves them; the concept of spirit does not exist for them, they simply do it, a spiritual agency moves them. Only on our plane do we give our souls to God.

Mr. Gibb: In northern India the natives must always die where the air and water are "right." They call it "Ab o hawa," which means "at home." "Climate" is our translation, but it is much more important to them than that. They must go where the air is right, *is theirs.* Even in epidemics, we could not prevent them from travelling and thus spreading cholera and plague, this idea was so strong in them.

Mr. Dell: Do they spit on their hands or just blow?

Dr. Jung: They blow hard; it is the same thing as spitting. Saliva is the water connotation of the spirit. Christ used spittle in making the ointment, mixing it with clay to heal the blind man. Spitting or blowing has a magic significance all over the world. Mr. Gibb's example uses wind and water, both symbols for the life-spirit, the

[7] For discussion of these words, see "Spirit and Life" (1926), CW 8, par. 601, and "Basic Postulates of Analytical Psychology" (1931), CW 8, par. 664. According to A. C. Madan's *Swahili-English Dictionary* (1903; used by Jung), *roho* may also mean "soul," "spirit," "life."

[8] For other versions of the same material see *MDR*, pp. 266/249, and "Archaic Man" (1931), CW 10, pars. 144ff. Also see below, 30 Oct. 1929, n. 1.

pervading thing. Earth is not moving, not spirit, but wind and water are. In astrology, for instance, the sign for Aquarius (a spiritual sign) has been taken from the Egyptian sign for water. Originally it had a denser part and also a more ethereal part, the upper part being the more spiritual. Are there any questions connected with this dream?

Mrs. Sigg: This is the third dream that says the dreamer's ego is not in accord with his wife's. At first it was the sewing-machine which he could not give to the poor girl, because it belonged to his wife; then in the dream of the Puer Aeternus, where he said that his wife did not bring the right kind of food; and now in this dream his wife asks him to wait for the others and he does not. Three times she is a hindrance. I don't know the connection unless it is her objection to sexuality. He seems to have something against his wife, he doesn't have the right attitude, he does not realize the anima.

Dr. Jung: Surely, there is much real trouble between himself and his wife, but we can only discuss the main issues of the dream. He is not yet ready to take up the anima problem.

Mrs. Sigg: Is it not dangerous for him to identify himself with the brownies?

Dr. Jung: That is not for him to say. I had to make him see that now he identifies himself with the earth, as before he identified himself with the collective idea. It is far better to go under the earth than under the conventional code.

Dr. Binger: Has he no conception of the anima?

Dr. Jung: No, not yet. It is very difficult to have the conception of the objectivity of our psychology. To objectify the anima would seem a mystical thing. Most people have not the faintest capacity to see what a psychological non-ego can be, or what degree of autonomy or reality certain facts have. They have never given it any consideration. Formerly the so-called autonomy of psychological phenomena was denied entirely. This permits of the projection of figures which leads to spiritism and theosophy. You get such figures as "the guardian of the threshold" and all such hobgoblins. That won't do either. There is a middle path of psychic autonomy, a conception that has not entered the philosophical mind of our time. To make people understand this "middle way" has been my particular effort.

Dr. Leavitt: These are all dreams, aren't they? Not fantasies?

Dr. Jung: They are all dreams. If the patient were able to lift all that material up into active fantasy, he would not dream it. He cannot do that, for he would be too much hampered by the idea that he was producing it. The idea "I am making my own mind" is a Godalmightiness! That is his prejudice.

Dr. Schmitz: Could the patient not learn something from this dream? The dreamer says, "If you go to this brothel, then you are a man who goes to such places and you must know it."

Dr. Jung: Yes, he must see that he is below his own estimation of himself. After a while all these things became disgusting to him, he felt he could not afford it anymore. He has tried several times since to raise hell, but somehow he finds that he always falls down on it. The sensation type has to learn by actual experience. He has sometimes thought that analysis conveyed nothing to him, but then certain things happened, and he had to admit that his dreams did something to him. He had to realize that he had changed when he discovered that he could no longer go to a brothel.

Mr. Dell: The spirit is working in us without our consciousness?

Dr. Jung: Even though we do not understand the dream, it is working and causing changes. If we understand, however, we have the privilege of working with the timeless spirit in ourselves.

Mr. Dell: This allusion to the cap as a sign that he has lowered himself is very indirect; without analysis he would have missed it completely. Is there anything in dream psychology that would prevent a direct allusion? He might have dreamed that he fell into the gutter, or something of that sort.

Dr. Jung: He just dreamed it like that.

Mr. Dell: Freud would speak of the censorship in the choice of the symbol, wouldn't he?

Dr. Jung: Yes, and I see your point now. The dream could say, "Now you are lowered," but what it does say in this case is "Now you wear a brown cap." Whether we analyse it or not, the spirit is operating in us without our consciousness. Something has happened to the man. I myself have had dreams that I could not understand until later events happened. The dream does sometimes prepare for a concrete event. So it does not matter if we do not understand the cap symbolism, but it matters if we do we get a chance for a tremendous widening out of our consciousness. That is why we analyse dreams. If we are unconscious we are always running the risk of being manipulated by unconscious factors, in an enantiodromic way,[9] as winter follows summer, etc. The unconscious is not really concerned with human aims, with the building up of our civilization. It has a peculiar movement, as though there were no such thing as time.

Mr. Dell: The change in the personality is always accompanied by consciousness, is it not?

Dr. Jung: You can be made to change by unconscious factors. You can wake up in the morning a different man, but such changes have no merit, you cannot gain anything by it for our civilization. Our aim should be to increase our consciousness. Things happen to us whether we are conscious or not, but when we are unconscious, life has no meaning; so many people come to me without any idea of what it all means. People need an understanding of things, of why they live.

Dr. Binger: The store of unconscious life is limitless, is it not?

Dr. Jung: Yes, there is no end to it. You can say—never mind the Einstein theory—space to us is as good as infinite.

Mr. Gibb: You would say that many things happen without dreaming, or is the dream itself the happening?

Dr. Jung: I think you are wise to take the dream as a happening. Then you can say, "I am so glad to have had this dream, now things have happened."

Mr. Gibb: But must one not allow that things happen even if one does not dream of them?

Dr. Jung: Of course, but we must allow that all things of fundamental importance are probably dreamed of. Dreams are messages sent up from the unconscious and show what is actually going on there.

Dr. Binger: Do you think that this is something like a character transformation? Do you think it is directional, moving toward an end?

Dr. Jung: I am inclined to believe that only where there is consciousness, awareness, can this prove to be true. In the dreams of the incurably insane you will find the same quality as in those of normal or neurotic people. The dreams of the insane are full of colour, very hopeful, and contain symbols of growth, so you feel that if you could talk about them, there is no reason why the patient

[9] *Enantiodromia,* a term used by Heraclitus to convey the idea that everything changes into its opposite in the course of time. See *Psychological Types,* ch. XI, def. 18.

224

could not be helped. But you cannot talk, they will not listen. These dreams reach a certain summit and then begin to go down, all the symbols become destructive, and you see that everything is going dead wrong. If a normal person had such dreams you would say, "This is very bad." But with the insane, after a while it begins over again. It is just a process of nature, with no intervention on the part of consciousness. So I conclude that for such a process as the building up of the individual, consciousness is indispensable.

Dr. Binger: It is like making a garden out of a jungle.

Dr. Jung: Yes, like making a garden out of a jungle. Only man makes a garden, nature never. So you see how our development depends on the intervention of the conscious. There is the factor of development, of evolution in nature, but it is slow, it takes millions of years. See how the primitive has for centuries remained in the same condition, while civilized nations have made enormous strides in a short time by the intervention of consciousness.

Dr. Binger: Can you dream and derive the benefit of consciousness without understanding the dream? Is it of constructive value?

Dr. Jung: To a certain extent. It is the tidal wave that lifts you up, but you are in danger of being swept down again with it. If you can cling to a rock and stay up, all right.

Mr. Dell: If the dream is a picture of a psychic situation, of something that has happened, how can it also be a compensation? What does it compensate?

Dr. Jung: The dreamer's idea of respectability.

Mr. Dell: The dream reports a change in attitude, but I don't quite see the compensation.

Dr. Jung: That is simple. He is a conventional man and having had this panoramic view something is changed in him. Before he had this dream he was too high and nature won't stand for that, and she has pulled him down. Now he is lowered. That is compensation. It is peculiar symbolism, why doesn't the dream say he is lowered?

Mr. Dell: Freud would say it was disguised by the censor as a protection to the sleeper, but as a matter of fact he wakes up.

Dr. Jung: Freud would say it was disguised by the censor, I would say that we have not yet arrived at the full explanation of the soothing character of the dream nor of why it expresses it in such a cryptic allusion. If the dream said, "Now you are lower down, before you were higher up," it would not be quite true, for from a spiritual point of view he is higher up, he is a far better man than he was when he was too high. When nature uses that peculiar term, a hooded figure, like a brownie, something earthy that must be hid away, something lowered, disreputable, it can also mean like a spiritual being, a monk with the Cabiri hood. The monks took on the brown hood of the Cabiri. It is a double-edged symbolism; when he is lowered, he is really being lifted up. *Cabiri* is from Arabic *el kabir*,[10] "the *great* one," and Cabiri are really quite small, the "small ones yet so great in power." The Dactyl, or thumbling, the size of the thumb, is small but very powerful. In Hindu philosophy he is Purusha, the small mystical man dwelling in the heart of everyone yet covering the earth, "smaller than small, yet greater than great."[11] When you pursue the symbolism a little more closely you will see that the man's unconscious is trying to bring out the relativity of things. When you understand this you will see that the unconscious is going to put him into the centre of things, that is what it is after!

[10] *Sems.*: "Cabura." The Arabic for "great" is *kabir* (cf. *gabir* in *Psychology and Alchemy*, par. 203), but ancient Greek *kabeiroi* could not have been derived from Arabic. Some scholars have held that it is a Hellenized form of the Semitic *kabirim*, "the great," through a Phoenician source, but this view is now in doubt. See Kerényi, "The Mysteries of the Kabeiroi" (1944), in *The Mysteries* (Papers from the Eranos Yearbooks, 5, 1955), p. 48; L. R. Farnell, article "Kabeiroi," *Encyclopedia of Religion and Ethics*, ed. J. Hastings, VII (1920), p. 628; and Liddell and Scott, *A Greek-English Lexicon*, rev. H. S. Jones (1940), s.v. Kabeiroi.

[11] See *Symbols of Transformation*, pars. 179-184 (as in 1912 edn.), where Jung quotes from the Upanishads concerning the thumbling Purusha and discusses in detail the connection with the Cabiric dwarf-gods.

LECTURE III

29 May 1929

Question by Miss Hannah: Has the brown cap got anything to do with the necessity of not feeling absurd in the collective unconscious? I mean getting such an attitude as a child has to the objective world?

Dr. Jung: Please explain. I don't quite know what you mean.

Miss Hannah: I mean such a thing as you said about Faust feeling a fool when he talked to griffins and sphinxes. The man in wearing the cap felt like a fool, not in the aquarium, but when he came out into the visible world. How would you explain that? In coming out of the unconscious one feels a fool.

Dr. Jung: But why should one feel a fool? Have you ever seen people coming out of the movies, tears streaming down their faces, still obsessed by what they have seen inside? Just so our man is obsessed by a peculiar idea, something has gotten at him. You will see in later dreams how he felt. Caps and head-dresses have the meaning of a sort of general idea which covers the ground—to put it in philosophical language, a concept that unifies a number of smaller ones. The German language has a saying which covers that: "Alles unter einen Hut bringen."[1] So this man wears the cap of the brownies, he has been in the underworld, he looks at things from underneath, and has the point of view of a brownie, so he is not "a fit" in the outside world. He is now covered by that general idea, and that of course makes him feel foolish.

Dr. Schmitz: He is not yet adapted to the real world.

Dr. Jung: The point of view of the collective unconscious has no relation to his world. That uniting of the two points of view will be the result of a long analysis. In this dream he gets into something

[1] Lit., "to bring everything under one hat." Cf. *Psychology and Alchemy*, par. 53: "Just as in summing up we bring ideas 'under one head' (*unter einen Hut*) so the hat ... covers the whole personality and imparts its own significance to it."

that would not fit into his world, something that could not be understood there, something that has estranged him to a certain extent. You will see from his next dream what the idea of the cap really works in him.

Next dream [14]: He dreams of a certain Greek merchant (he is half a merchant and half a planter) who has a cotton plantation on which he is growing a new species of cotton. He comes to the dreamer in order to bring him a number of immature capsules (cotton fruits in which the cotton is visible inside, but which have not yet opened) and he reports that in the country where he has his plantation, a new worm, a sort of cotton pest, has appeared and is causing immense damage. The dreamer asks him to show him the worm. He opens one of the capsules and the dreamer notices on one side a caterpillar-like worm and a sort of jelly-like substance similar to that which one sees on plums that are worm-eaten. The dreamer has some knowledge of the pests that destroy cotton crops, but this worm is like nothing he has ever seen before. It wriggles along and produces a black excrement. He is rather frightened, for evidently the worm has appeared in great numbers and has destroyed much of the crop. He thinks he should telegraph his agents, because this damage will injure the price of the crops, so he looks for his code-book (which will enable him to inform his firm without the knowledge of other agents) but finds that he has another book in his hand. His brother enters, while he is looking in the book, and the dreamer asks him for the code-book, saying he needs it to cable the condition of the crops. His brother laughs and tells him that he has already cabled a report of the crops. The dreamer is angry and thinks he should have been shown the cable, so that he would know what message had been sent.

Associations: Concerning the planting of a new kind of cotton and the worms: It is very important in the cotton business that one cuts open a great number of bolls before the harvest to see the number of worms and to calculate the percentage of damage in order to reckon the probable value of the crop. *Plantation:* It exists in reality, but it is not a Greek who has charge of the plantation. This particular country where the plantation is located is supposed to be relatively free from such pests, so it is a shock to the dreamer to learn that they have appeared in such numbers in a region supposed to be safe from them, and that the crop is damaged to an unknown extent. He knows that this black excrement colours the cotton and makes it quite useless, so there is probably much damage. *Cable:* He says that he is not quite satisfied with the way he managed the information. The logical way would have been to stop all business at the exchange until he knew the extent of the damage. Instead of that he simply wishes to send information to his agents, without giving them orders about buying and selling. When it becomes known that there is such an amount of damage to the cotton crop, it will influence the price of cotton, and there may be a sort of panic at the exchange. So he feels that he has been a bit lacking in forethought. It is also astonishing to him that he should have taken another book instead of the code. He says, "In reality I would not have made such a mistake, but in dreams we do things we would never do in reality. It is true that my brother, who had already seen my mistake, is more practical than I am, but when it comes to complicated business affairs where one should have a calm and rather superior manner, I have seen him in trouble."

So the dreamer feels superior to the brother because of his own greater business experience. He continues, "The cables in regard to the condition of the crops are a very difficult task that I always took upon myself when I was still in the firm. It is absolutely incredible, in reality, that such a cable could be sent without its first being shown to me. I am impressed by the fact that in this dream quite a number of illogical things happen and that I cannot see their meaning."

This is again a business dream. I think we will begin by trying to establish a connection between this and the previous dream. The cotton dream presents a fact very shocking to a man interested in cotton speculation. In a great firm where he is chief, he feels an enormous responsibility, for he is dealing in many millions. The reports from agents regarding the crops were his concern for quite a while, so when something happens in that sphere of his life it means something of extraordinary importance. The report that worms have appeared in great numbers in a district where the crops were considered to be perfectly safe, thus upsetting his whole calculation, would naturally appeal to the mind of a business man. You have an analogy in the case of a surgeon who performs an operation and then gets a report that the patient is dying. It would give him a terrible shock. The information is symbolic and means a worm has appeared! That fact is to be linked up with the dream before. The brown cap has appeared again. We said that something must have happened to the patient when he came out of the show with the queer hat; he was not the same man. You must put yourself in the place of that man. He is a sensation type, of the strictest common sense, there is no mystery in his world, it is all perfectly explained, so much cotton at such and such a price. Hence when something happens to change the aspect of his world, it is most upsetting.

Women usually allow for unexplained happenings in their world. In the world of women certain things can happen that are excluded from a man's world. A man believes absolutely in his picture of this world. He must have a true picture of his world because he is going to do something with the world, but the world is going to do something with the woman. If a woman is going to do something with the world, she must develop a definite idea of the world. It is natural that the woman's picture of the world is not too definite. Occasionally it might happen that water rises higher than the source, or that the barometer might go up when there is a cyclone. A man finds it hard to adjust to this, he thinks there is something a bit queer about her that she is ready to let things happen to her. The man has always been up against strict reality and has faced the obvious facts of life. He cannot have a fantasy about the price of cotton; he would endanger his whole existence if he made a mistake. A woman might say it is a trifle, nothing has happened. He cannot understand. To a woman it is possible that a match might rise by itself from a match-stand. If it happened to a man, he would report himself to an insane asylum and say, "I have seen a match rising by itself from a matchstand!" I knew a man who went to an asylum because he read in a paper that he was reported missing.

The dream before must have gotten under the patient's skin. When I was actually concerned with that dream I could not say what it was, but we can make a hypothesis when we go into the symbolism of the worm which eats the cotton-bolls. Something has happened in his world that has upset him, something that has never happened before. It makes him feel as foolish as though he had fantasized a price on the New York Exchange. I insist upon this as his psychology, for not all human beings have such a psychology. His is that of a mind trained for a special purpose, and we can only see what it means to such a man to dream of an unforeseen happening when we realize his psychology. He left in the brown cap, and now the worm in the cotton seed shows that something very serious has happened to him, as upsetting as though that worm had begun to spoil the cotton in a hitherto safe part of the country, and he had discovered it in reality. Only by understanding this can we get the full value of his emotion and astonishment. He takes a book and mistakes it for the code. Things are happening in an incredible way. His world is disturbed somewhere. You must first understand the patient as a man before you can get the meaning of the dream. It is enormously important, for these things give you a deeper insight into the evolutionary process than the dreamer himself can get. He is unconscious of what is going on. I say to him, "Didn't you feel anything at all?" "No." "Didn't something get under your skin?" "No." On the other hand, patients can say "Oh, that was a marvellous dream, so much was accomplished!" and one knows from the next dream that the effect was just a ripple on the surface, the deep waters were not moved at all. For six months they may have dreams of submarine volcanoes, but on the surface you see no change. Yet submarine volcanoes are facts. My patient went on for half a year after that dream without its touching him at all. He found it tedious to write out his dreams, etc. It was all an interesting pastime, but he saw no change. He didn't want to be a doctor or a psychologist, so he made up his mind to discontinue his analysis. He made the experiment of not coming again, then he had a hell of a time, he got depressed and miserable. Only then did he realize that something happened at the time when he had these dreams.

As to the actual symbolism, a great deal of the trade in the East is in the hands of Greeks. There is a saying in the Levant that the Armenian is the cleverest of all, and in the second place comes the Greek. To a business man in the East the Greek is the go-between; on the one side simple, primitive, and on the other sophisticated enough. You find Greeks all over the East. Even up along the Nile in the most God-forsaken country, you will find trading posts run by a Greek. He is on relatively good terms with the native and with the white man. He is tricky and equally disliked by both, so the Greek means to the dreamer a go-between. It is not nice, but you must have such a fellow. Here he is not a real man, but a collective figure who brings the report. Now what is your interpretation?

Prof. Schmaltz: My idea is that the cotton crop represents the dreamer's self. He discovers that this crop, which he believed valuable, has a worm in it, and he who felt himself to be on a higher plane is not so reputable and respectable, for he has some worms in himself. But the dream says not the whole crop was spoiled, but only a part of it. All the capsules have not matured yet, hence there is a possibility that part of the crop will not be infected. That is the hopeful side, but it is a bad discovery to find this in the unconscious part of himself, and he feels that he cannot act as he used to do in his conscious life, so he cannot act clearly and he makes one mistake after the other. The cable must be sent by code because it is a secret, a disagreeable thing that he does not want other people to know. On the other hand he does not take the consequences, the responsibility, and give his agents definite orders to stop buying and selling. He simply tells them that there is a worm and leaves them to decide what to do with it. That I should think is the meaning of it.

Dr. Jung: That is practically the meaning, but we must now go into the technical details. Sure enough, he makes a series of mistakes; for a business man there is a most conspicuous lack of attention. The fact that the brother sends a telegram, which only he himself as the chief should have sent, shows that already something has happened. The brother was working while he was upset; that points to the fact that often when we are distracted something happens that we should have controlled.

We are first concerned with the Greek. Why is it a Greek who gives the dreamer that information?

Dr. Binger: It is the eastern side of himself, the low side of his character, the go-between.

Dr. Jung: Yes, he has a low side to his character, part of him is close to the soil, native, and this somewhat dubious figure comes up, a go-between, to inform him of things going on in the lower strata. Why does he have such a low character as the go-between, so morally dubious?

Dr. Binger: Because many things from the lower strata are dubious.

Dr. Jung: Yes, so the unconscious uses a dubious character to represent it. He thinks of himself as a perfectly respectable man, quite incapable of wrongdoing, but there is a back door through which this dubious character comes in as a go-between and says there are such secret places. It is amusing to see these characters in the East. When I was in Tunis[2] I usually took my coffee at a

---

[2] In spring 1920. See *MDR*, ch. IX, i, and Appendix III.

small café, almost entirely patronized by business men. Every day a man would come up to me and secretly whisper in my ear, "They are selling wheat at such and such a price and you could do business." Always I said, "I am sorry, but I am not a business man." But he did not believe me, since I was there—what other possible reason could I have for being there? And every day he continued to inform me about the price of wheat and oil. So it takes a bit of a Greek to nose up these things for him. The Greek is a sort of function, a sort of intuition, who is nosing up these things in secret places.

The *worm* in the cotton as a symbol of something rather destructive that has made its appearance in his world can be explained quite rationally. It is the fact which a planter would fear the most, as it might destroy the value of his crop. A new destructive thing has happened, just as the fact that he wears the brown cap is very queer and upsetting. You remember the boys in the brown caps in the German town who upset the parson and the respectable society. It is exactly the same with this man. He is suddenly informed about certain immoral things in his unconscious, and it upsets him. Why should it be a worm? It is vermin. People are all a little rotten inside. Why should that evil thing be explained by a worm?

Mrs. Schlegel: Invisible things, a secret trouble, under the earth—it could be a worm or a snake.

Dr. Jung: Yes, but mice might be that.

Dr. Schlegel: The snake is often called a worm.

Dr. Jung: Yes, Sin in the Bible is the "undying worm."[3] It is the poisonous thing, eating into you. Why?

Mrs. Sigg: It is something that comes up from the earth.

Dr. Jung: Yes, the worm or snake is supposed to be a chthonic thing, from within or beneath. It has to do with the earth. It was invisible and then appears in the fruit. What does this mean psychologically?

Dr. Schmitz: It comes from the instinctive side of life.

Dr. Jung: It comes from the body, our psychological earth. Our body is the nearest thing we have to do with the earth. But why a *worm* especially? What is a worm?

Mrs. Sigg: A low stage.

Mr. Dell: An invertebrate.

Dr. Jung: Yes, a worm has no brain, just a sympathetic nervous

[3] Cf. Mark 9:44, 46, 48: "Where their worm dieth not, and the fire is not quenched," referring to hell fire.

system, which is the most primitive form of nervous life. So when we are quite bold we can say that the worm has to do with the sympathetic nervous system. This means the deepest layers, the simplest form of life, absolutely preconscious, a life that is not even centered somewhere. It consists of separate ganglia in a series, hence it represents what form of life?

Dr. Binger: A disconnected life.

Dr. Jung: Yes, disconnected, in compartments, in segments. You see that in the tapeworm. A forestage of worm symbolism is that each segment of a worm is an animal by itself. So this simplest form of nervous life, the original form, is a life in compartments, in segments. If life is completely in segments it is absolutely uncon-scious, there is no synthesis, so if life is nothing but a sympathetic nervous system, there is no consciousness at all. When a worm comes up, then, the absolutely unconscious form of life comes up, and it may be most destructive for our consciousness. The worm will dominate our psychology, and life will be lived in compartments as we have it in schizophrenia. The danger is always a disintegration and dissociation of consciousness into compartments. It is a fasci-nating study. The patients hear voices speaking out of one com-partment in one way and then out of another, differently. There is a famous autobiography by Schreber,[4] who became insane after having been a great lawyer before. He differentiates his voices, they give names to themselves, such as "those that are hanging under Cassiopeia," a social group or society which speaks in one style. Another group belonged to the bookkeeper, and they speak as if reading from a book where all new facts are recorded in Heaven. This man was very musical, and when he sat at the piano, usually a voice would say, "We have that already," but if he had a new warm feeling, then those voices in Heaven shouted down, "Got it." Then another set was made up of quite small people floating in the air. Every time he bumped into one, the little fellow went into him, said, "Oh damn!" and vanished. There were little compart-ments that exploded in him and melted into him, but later on as his illness progressed these compartments became air-tight. The

[4] Paul Daniel Schreber, *Denkwürdigkeiten eines Nervenkranken* (Leipzig, 1903), tr. Ida Macalpine and R. A. Hunter, *Memoirs of My Nervous Illness* (London, 1955). Jung evidently read Schreber's memoirs around 1905 and brought them to Freud's attention. They are often mentioned in *The Freud/Jung Letters*, from April 1910 to Dec. 1912; see index, s.v. Schreber.

little fellows sat on his eyebrows, but the compartments did not explode any more and let them in. That is the danger, that is what people are afraid of when they first touch the collective unconscious. They are afraid that a worm might get into their brains. It is uncanny, not that a worm is very amazing, but a disease in the brain is bad. Many people dream that they must eat something very impure. A patient of mine had a dream in which I led her up to a tree coated with a sort of glucose, where snails had gone up. She was disgusted, but I produced a plate with a knife and fork and said, "Help yourself." She had to collect and eat those snails. That means she had to assimilate the brainless animal—something like the worm.

Now, you are informed about the worm and why one is afraid of it, and that peculiar effect of an unforeseen apparition from the unconscious in our world. The dream gives us more details about the peculiar functioning of this worm. It is producing a black excrement which injures the cotton even in that part of the capsule not devoured by the worm. That must be something particular. Have you any idea about it?

Dr. Schmitz: If there is a neurotic element in the unconscious, it will have a fouling influence on the conscious.

Dr. Jung: The idea is that a number of these immature capsules are cut open to test the probable damage to the crop. When you find quite a number infected, a certain part not eaten by the worm should be in good condition, but all of it is spoiled by the excrement produced by the worm. The unconscious lays particular stress upon this fact. There are two causes of spoiling the crop. Why isn't the worm itself enough?

Dr. Binger: Could that be a fantasy product?

Dr. Jung: In order to interpret this part of the dream we must first know what the capsules mean, for they are the fruits of the plant which develop out of the earth. We have interpreted the worm, therefore we must also interpret the capsules. The plant has not even a sympathetic nervous system, there is no relation between that form of life and any nervous life at all. It is a prenervous condition, absolutely unimaginable to us; there is no possible connection in our consciousness, but the functioning of that vegetative condition produces a fruit which serves as food for the worm, for our sympathetic nervous system. It is very important symbolism. The capsule is a sort of flower (flower is better than fruit) that grows from nowhere, from absolute unconsciousness and invisibility, and the worm lives on that flower. It is as though our sympathetic nervous system were based upon a vegetative process out of which it draws its existence. That completely unconscious vegetative process is partially destroyed by the worm.

Dr. Bertine: Doesn't the fact that the cotton-boll is snowy white and the worm is the first thing that spoils it correspond to the infantile in us, the child-like innocence?

Dr. Jung: Yes, the cotton-boll is completely innocent of colour, snowy white, and that worm is the first thing that spoils it. Now, you remember the myth of Adam and Eve, the whole history of the trouble in the world begins there. The worm appears in the Garden of Eden and ruins it, that hell of a worm! That throws some light on the nature of the worm. We can go even further, we can compare preconscious life with the vegetative life of the lower animals, for all this fulfil itself in the individual in uterine life. What is merely vegetative at first later develops into the sympathetic nervous system, then the spinal cord, then the brain, so we almost repeat that growing up from plant life into human life. The plant corresponds to that very early stage of human existence, then there is a stage of dim mental life, not capable of consciousness, and in that stage trouble begins, the worm begins to live inside the capsule and destroys the innocent condition. The beginning of mental life, psychic life, is, According to the symbol, the beginning of evil. How do you feel about that?

Dr. Bertine: It means conflict, and the beginning of the breaking up of the "Golden Age."

Dr. Jung: But why conflict, why should that be? Why not development from something else? Why couldn't the worm eat something else?

Dr. Binger: The myth of Adam and Eve seems to be concerned with knowledge. The snake was connected with the tree of knowledge of good and evil. Ganglia life is not knowledge.

Dr. Schmitz: The worm is not yet a snake.

Dr. Jung: You know that the sympathetic nervous system is connected with something psychic "seeing with the eye of the depths."[5]

---

[5] James Kirsch, recalling discussions with Jung, comments on this passage: "Jung's understanding was that the sympathetic nervous system, i.e., the actual living anatomical system, was actually an organ of perception, comparable to the eye or ear. It had a modality connected with the unconscious, just as the capacity of the eye to see is connected with the brain." (Personal communication.)

The plexus solaris plays the role almost of the brain, a sort of counter-brain, so this would go even further back than the fatal facts of paradise.

Dr. Schmitz: The beginning of something individual, an attempt to relate two centres, and thus an attempt at integration.

Dr. Jung: The nervous system always makes an attempt to relate centres, no matter if one or more, and centres mean something individual. It is no longer a primordial soup. It is the first beginning of the dissociation of the perfect continuum of undifferentiated life, and so the first beginning of differentiation is the beginning of destruction. It is apparently the source of evil. You can say this dream is a narrow ledge to walk on, but this symbolism always repeats itself; I do not speak here of just this dream but of many dreams present in my mind. This symbolism is very old, it is the problem of the beginning of evil or suffering, and in a way the beginning of knowledge. It is as though such a dream would answer that eternal question of man, "Why do I suffer, what is the cause?" Genesis says that it is that damned snake that has bitten you. You are no longer a child, you have eaten of the evil, and you are conscious of knowledge, but for the unconscious that is not enough. It goes much deeper, back of paradise to the beginning of differentiated beings. Even there it is "I am I and you are you!" Marriage trouble is just the same thing. It is because "I am I and she is she!" If this were not so there would be no trouble; at the dawn of psychic life there is trouble, there is suffering. This dream is very negative. Of course you cannot convince the dreamer that worms are a particular blessing, he will say, "Oh, a hell of a nuisance!" He can't accept the fact that something has entered his world that he hadn't foreseen. He tried through his rationalism to get rid of all this stuff, all these problems; only women have such problems. But now he is confronted with it, he can no longer deny that he has such a conflict, he has such a problem, and he cannot see of what use it all is. I must say that I had no courage to tell him anything nice about the worm when I analysed the dream. If the dreams are not soothing, surely I should not be, so I did not tell him about metaphysical worms. But here in the seminar it is different, we can look at things objectively, and ask why the worm?

Is that worm really destructive? Did God create such pests just for fun, like flies, lice, malaria, sleeping-sickness, and all that stuff? Is it merely original destructiveness, cruelty, foolishness, or is there a deeper meaning? In other words, has that beginning of his psychic life, in all its destructiveness, a certain aim? No one gets conscious if he does not suffer! If you are always in the maternal waters at 35° C. you need nothing, but you are not conscious. It seems as though nature tries very hard to bring about consciousness in us. So if you decide that consciousness is a marvellous, divine, and desirable thing, you must be very grateful to the worm that eats those flowers. He eats to produce consciousness in the long run. Hence if you assume that consciousness is good you must say that it is a good thing that we have the worm. But the great question is, is it a good thing to have consciousness? Many people say, don't you think it is dangerous? Some men say, "Don't you think it is a very dangerous thing when you make women conscious of themselves?" I say, "Yes, dangerous for the men!" In reality the men who talk in this way are all soul-virgins, trying to keep themselves unaware, afraid of their own innocence, men who have never gone through a soul-defloration. When you consider consciousness as a great achievement the worm is very important. The early Gnostic philosophers thought that the worm was made by God to create a spiritual world—Yahweh[6] had created the material world and then God took pity on it and sent down his messenger, his son, the snake to take pity on his creatures, and to give them knowledge. The snake, a blessing in disguise, told them to eat from the tree of knowledge that they might see how imperfect was the work of the divine Demiurgos. This was the first step towards their liberation. When you recognize that a thing is imperfect, you can do something about it.

The Gnostics assumed the snake to be the Messiah, the son of the spiritual God who teaches people how to escape the curse of unconsciousness.[7] That teaching played a great role. The Catholic Church almost got into this channel, but the early fathers recognized its danger. In the second and third centuries Christianity was like a huge tape worm with no synthesis whatever and they had to get out of that state at all costs—so they could not accept a theory in which higher understanding, higher consciousness, was an ideal. They could only admit obedience to authority, as the main ideal in order to gather all the dissenting elements together, and so form the unity of the great Catholic Church. It was the only thing to be

[6] In certain Gnostic sects, Yahweh was identified with the demiurge, an inferior creator-god whom the Gnostics distinguished from the Supreme Deity. Cf. *Aion*, CW 9 ii, par. 118. [R.F.C.H.]

[7] Cf. ibid., pars. 298-9.

done at that time. The Gnosis therefore remained a bud that never unfolded, but in our day we are beginning to understand that out of evil comes good and out of good comes evil, the relativity of things.

We cannot stand the darkness any more. We cannot endure unconsciousness. For instance, we have psychological symptoms and we must know where these bewildering things come from. We cannot see who is running this thing inside of us. There are most canny arrangements that we cannot see; it is as though someone had invented them for us, to force us into certain activities. There must be a very clever fellow inside, inventing a scheme; he catches us here and there and eventually pushes through his own ends. When we make such a discovery we feel that we must understand what is going on in our own house. It is as though we lived on the first floor, and mysterious things are going on in the basement. We smell funny smells and we hear queer noises. We cannot live that way, we must know what is going on. It is exactly what people were concerned with two thousand years ago, but mankind got stuck. Our way of finding out may get us stuck too. We may run up against a higher necessity. The immaturity of the great majority of the people may cause them to get into a panic, and then up comes the great worm. Any kind of development of the human mind can only go as far as it is supported by a certain body of the population. If a certain limit is trespassed the movement will come to a standstill for social reasons, because of the danger of the disintegration of society. At the beginning of Christianity it almost went too far. The people split up into individual, dissenting factions, but before complete chaos is reached instinct creates a limitation beyond which we cannot go and things can be organized.

For the time being we are concerned with the understanding of the unconscious, because we cannot decently live any more without consciousness. That understanding is gnosis, but the modern translation is that the worm is not the Messiah, it is the symbol of the beginning of psychic life, a new unfolding of the mind. No matter how destructive that worm seems in the beginning, it will be your greatest benefactor, for it will bring you the germ of life, the gnosis of life. One of the last Gnostic groups, the so-called Mandaeans, have a concept for the Saviour which means "understanding of life," *manda d'hayye; manda* = "gnosis" or "understanding," and *hayye* = "life." These people are living now, the sect of the Suppas or

Subbas (Baptists), near Kut-el-Amara in Mesopotamia.[8] There are about three thousand of them, famous as silversmiths. Their books are known but difficult to translate. A German scholar, Lidzbarski, brought out their *Book of John*.[9] It is highly interesting in parts. The Manda liturgies are also known. This sect eats only drowned animals, they never kill them in any other way. They are followers of John the Baptizer, who, according to the *Book of John*, violently disagreed with Christ as to the policy of publicity. Christ believed that the teaching should be revealed to the world, but John the Baptizer said one should not reveal it because the world would destroy the truth. Mead has given an English translation of parts of the *Book of John* in *John the Baptizer*.[10] There we get an atmosphere that explains a mentality like Christ's. The *Book of John* called him the "Deceiver" because he betrayed the mysteries. There is a long discussion between Christ and John which was never decided. Their arguments are from the introverted and extraverted points of view. John the introvert said, "Don't give it away, they will spoil it." Christ as the extravert said, "But I can work miracles with it."

Dr. Bertine: *The Friend of Jesus*, by Ernest S. Bates,[11] gives the modern Gnostic point of view. The friend of Jesus is Judas.

Question: What are the modern Gnostic churches?

Dr. Jung: The new Gnostic churches are all new inventions of old things, like soup warmed up again, they have no direct relation. The last trace of the Gnostic teaching probably died out with the Cathars and the Albigenses.[12] They were Manichaeans, Gnostics, called Bougres in France. "Bougre" derives from the word for Bulgarian and came into southern France. The Rosicrucians probably represented a half-baked attempt to make up for the dry Protestantism of that day with its lack of imagination.

King's *Gnostics and Their Remains*[13] and Mead's *Fragments of a Faith Forgotten*[14] are two books dealing with the old Gnostics.

[8] Present-day Iraq.

[9] Mark Lidzbarski, *Das Johannesbuch der Mandäer* (2 vols., Giessen, 1905-1915).

[10] G.R.S. Mead, *The Gnostic John the Baptizer: Selections from the Mandaean John-Book* (London, 1924), pp. 35-93, partially translating Lidzbarski's text.

[11] New York, 1928.

[12] Concerning the Cathars and other heretical sects that sprang up in the 11th century, see *Aion*, pars. 139, 225-235.

[13] Charles William King, *The Gnostics and Their Remains, Ancient and Mediaeval* (London, 1864).

[14] London, 1906; 3rd edn., 1931.

LECTURE IV

5 June 1929

Dr. Jung:

As there are no questions we will go on with the dream. We got as far as the deeper meaning of the worm which is destroying the fruit. In the last part of the dream there is the question of how the dreamer will cope with the situation. The discovery of the worm is of great importance, though of course it is an entirely unconscious perception. The patient's consciousness is rather remote. In spite of the far-reaching explanation I gave him, he is still far from understanding the importance and scope of the dream. He would never have arrived at the explanation I am giving you. Here we are trying to go further in order to understand the whole theory and principle of dream expression. Each dream is like a short drama. At the beginning is a sort of exposition, giving a statement of things as they are, just as is shown very beautifully in the Greek drama. First there is a demonstration of the situation from which things start; then comes the entanglement or development, and at the end the catastrophe or solution. The second part of the dream usually consists of the problem of how the dreamer is going to deal with the situation. This may seem a bit arbitrary, but the unconscious really does work in such a way. First, the statement of the unconscious point of view; second, the possible way the dreamer will deal with it. We are inclined to say, "What the dreamer ought to do under the circumstances," but except in very rare cases, the unconscious does not say what one ought to do, never except when it is very obvious. Usually several solutions are possible, hence the dream simply presents a choice of possible solutions.

It is the same as in the *I Ching*, where the first hexagram you cast gives you the present situation, a picture of things as they are. This may be static, meaning that it will last a long time, and in that case you have no second hexagram. But if you are in a state of movement the numbers indicate a second hexagram which is derived from the first by transposing the lines. Thus the second hexagram gives the prognosis, an idea of the possibilities of future transformation. There is no certainty about it, for there may be unforeseen changes in the conditions, and also much depends on what conclusions you draw from the first hexagram. For instance, the first hexagram might show you how you should behave. If you pay attention to its intimations and follow them in the best sense, then if the prognosis of the last line is unfavourable it need not come off. There are all sorts of possibilities according to what you do with the first. This dream is built almost like an *I Ching* hexagram.

In the second part of the dream the dreamer says, "I want to inform our agents by cable, and therefore I take the code in order to keep the information secret." You see here the beginning of the activity of the dreamer. He wants to do something about the report of the worms. He has the right idea of informing his agents, and secrecy is perfectly fair in that part of the business. Translated into psychological language, the idea in the dream is that something has happened, a new worm has suddenly appeared, the worm which seemed to be a terrific danger; yet we saw that it also has a very positive meaning, the beginning of higher consciousness. That is why so many people are afraid of higher consciousness. For it appears as a greater responsibility and danger. Can you give me some examples?

Dr. Bertine: Prometheus who stole the fire from the gods and then was punished by having a vulture tear at his vitals for years.

Dr. Jung: Yes, the discovery of fire, that is a good mythological example. It is like the doctors who paid with their lives for carrying on experiments with x-ray. But you have historical examples.

Dr. Kirsch: Galileo.

Dr. Jung: Was he in danger? Yes, he got into trouble with the Inquisition.

Mrs. Sigg: Luther?

Dr. Jung: The Reformation, yes, or the much more impressive example of the advent of Christ which upset civilization and caused great slaughter. Think of the hundreds and thousands of people who went into the desert to lead the ascetic life; whole towns were depopulated, and the monasteries were filled to the top, and even the graves were used as shelters. It was devastating! Also there was the upsetting of individual families. That was the real reason the Romans hated Christianity so much, because it split up families, and thus threatened to rip open the foundations of the Roman state. The Romans were tolerant of all sorts of religions, but Christianity, that was too devastating. This is a good example of what a new thought can do.

Mrs. Sigg: Freud.

Dr. Jung: Yes, how many are cursing psychoanalysis.

Dr. Schmitz: But not Jung.

Dr. Jung: Oh yes, I could tell a long story about that, and you all could furnish the material for it. A thing of blood was the explosion of Islam in the East. Think of the Crusades, the Reformation in Germany and the upheaval of the peasant wars. A new thought makes a road paved with blood.

Dr. Deady: What about the situation in Russia? Is that a widening of consciousness?

Dr. Jung: Surely.

Dr. Deady: It is hard to think of the Communists as being an example of widening consciousness.

Dr. Jung: But the Communists are only a thin layer. It is the muzhik. There is a very good book by Maurice Hindus, *Broken Earth*,[1] showing why Bolshevism is a widening of consciousness. The muzhik is beginning to grumble with fate, with the Government, to swear and to complain, that means he is beginning to think. That is the miracle in Russia. Russia has remained unconscious for thousands of years beside Europe and nothing has filtered into it. The muzhik remained just primitive, but now something begins to move in his brain. To us the Communist means nothing, but to the muzhik it means that he might think. I am quite convinced that in the long run the muzhik will be stung into action and made to think socially and politically, and this will be the positive result of Bolshevism in Russia. Up to now the peasant has been willing to have anything on top of him, but if he begins to think something might come of it.

Now the danger of increased consciousness stirs our dreamer into action. The dream says symbolically that he is going to inform his agents secretly. How would you translate that psychologically?

Mrs. Sigg: In the last dream he wore the cap of the earth, and

[1] London, 1926.

now the fruit of the earth is spoken of. The agent might stand analytically for the analyst.

Dr. Jung: I refuse to be the agent of the patient. He is going to inform his agents. The agents are surely not the analyst but the man's own subordinates.

Dr. Schmitz: His functions.

Dr. Deady: His superior function that keeps him in contact with the world, his tools.

Dr. Jung: Yes, of course, he is informing his consciousness, his agents are his consciousness, they are all the threads that go from his brain into the world. He wants to inform consciousness; to realize it. Now the code, what does that mean?

Mrs. Sigg: Shortened language.

Dr. Jung: No, not shortened but hidden language. He could send a cable saying, "The cotton crop in such a part is infected with a new pest," but what would be the mistake in that?

Dr. Schmitz: Everybody would know about it.

Dr. Jung: Yes, in such an important matter with millions at stake, he could not risk sending an open telegram to his agents, the news could be too easily betrayed. It is funny that he could not inform his consciousness in a direct way, Why couldn't he?

Mrs. Kirsch: To do it in a direct way would be too shocking to him.

Dr. Jung: Yes, that is a good reason, but there is another. He can inform his consciousness secretly in such a way that *he* only knows it, so the code must protect the message against betrayal. That can be due, as you say, to the fact that he wants to spare himself, therefore he does not put it too bluntly. It might have another consequence, he might be betraying himself. Suppose you have a feeling that something is not quite right, and you have a hunch that you had better keep it to yourself, and then another voice says, "Damn it, things *are* so and so and you had better tell it." So you go to your wife and your friends and say such a thing is so, as though you were very sure. That is the danger, you would get into trouble at once. So the code protects him against the clear knowledge, against any immediate manifestation of his conviction. But when he has only a vague hunch or "feeling" he can keep it in a compartment. That is the meaning of the code form. He must use the key, but now he finds that he holds another book in his hand.

His brother sees his mistake and smiles when he asks him for the code. And now it turns out that his brother has already sent the message, so that the agents are informed, but the dreamer does not know the text of the cable. It looks almost like pedantry to go into all this, but it is most important because it shows the exceedingly subtle way in which we deal with ourselves. We are most diplomatic. We have all shades of consciousness, dim, clear, half-clear, dark, and with each level we have a certain way of dealing with it. We say things to ourselves in a sort of hushed voice, and thus do not upset the compartment system. If we speak loudly they will hear us in the next room and it will upset them in there. It is practical to keep quiet about certain things, and that is the reason why I talk about these subtle ways. You can catch people at such tricks. The point is that he wants to inform his consciousness in a clever way, with no sting in it for him, but he makes a mistake. What is it?

Dr. Schmitz: He intended to send the cable by the usual code, but now he has found a new code, perhaps a book of yours. Psychoanalysis. The brother is the shadow.

Dr. Jung: It is exceedingly probable that if the brother has sent the cable, he has sent it in code, for, as the managing director, he is as much aware as the patient is of the seriousness of the situation. That means that the consciousness of the patient has been informed quite automatically by the shadow.

Dr. Schmitz: Since his experience in analysis he tries to do it in a new way. The book means a better code, as it were.

Dr. Jung: The very fact that it was done by the shadow proves that it was done in the old way. The shadow means shadowy ways. If we leave things in the dark then they go on in the old ways, or even a little bit worse, like a leaking conduit or an engine when nothing is done to it. When the dream says the shadow has done something, you can be sure that it has been done in the old way.

The dreamer makes a mistake in taking another book for the code, but really it is his first attempt to do things in the new way, although he is not at all aware how he could inform his consciousness in a new way. Of course the dream says nothing about analysis. The dream says "another book." The man has no associations, he has no idea how his rather scant analytical knowledge could be used to inform his consciousness in a new way.

There is an analytical way of information. When you discover a shocking truth in the unconscious, you sometimes realize it in that blind way of the code. But sometimes it comes to you so clearly that you can only say, "Well, it is so." It may strike you like a blow on the head, so that you are dazed by it and cannot understand it. Here analysis comes in. The analytical way is to understand when you realize it. Many dreams are quite dreadful. For instance, suppose you dream that you want to kill someone, your father or your husband; if you have no way to understand it, it is too horrible. That is because you have no analytical code, and do not take it in the context, so it falls on you like a block of lead and almost crushes you. Analysis tries to give the necessary context, to show the relativity of such situations. If you take the dream literally, that you want to kill your father. It is terrible, but it is by no means terrible when it is translated into analytical language. It is as a rule to be taken symbolically, so to kill the father may mean remove the father, or it might mean remove his influence so that he will be inactive. The drastic primitive language of the unconscious just says, "Kill him," meaning no more than we do when we say, "Kill time." It is quite innocent, it means just "stop his activity." If you can put it in such a way the conscious can accept it without being blown to pieces. You can say there is an instinctive murderous impulse behind it. Well, we all have murderers among our ancestors, and there are many among us who could commit a murder under certain circumstances with no particular qualms. The original blood-lust is in it, but the meaning is different, so you can accept it.

This is the analytical code that makes things possible instead of the old code, which, taken literally and without the context, would be destructive. The old code simply served to conceal a thing instead of bringing it into full consciousness. The dreamer wants to inform his agents, but according to the old code. He is shocked by the report of the danger to the crops and does not know what to do with it. Many of my patients say, "How could I commit a murder?" "What can I do about it?" The old way is just to repress it, but the new way, the analytical way, would be to digest it to a certain extent, making it manageable. I say, "It doesn't mean that you are going to kill your father literally. You can counteract his influence without that." That already shows the patient what to do; he gets the information in a digestible, manageable form, it fits into the picture of his world, there is no shock, he can assimilate it. But our dreamer is not yet prepared, not yet able to get it in this way. There is no indication of what the book is that he holds in his hand, nor any information as to how he can use it in a different way. All he gets is anger at his brother for not showing him the cable. The patient realizes that it was his shadow, his brother, who did it; what he himself could have done remains in the dark. That is the negative end of this dream. The new facts are presented in a disagreeable, threatening form, but the facts alluded to in the symbolism of the worm are not negative. The dreamer is beginning to discard the old ways and take up the new, so I would say that the dream is not at all negative, it presents positive contents in a negative form.

Next dream [15]: "I am standing under a young cherry-tree looking at the ripe, very big red cherries. I say to myself, 'It is worthwhile.' Then I see that my children are collecting the immature fruits that have fallen off the tree, in a little basket. I say to them: 'These cherries do not belong to us and they are not ripe.' I throw them again under the tree on the ground. I notice a little girl of about two years among the children. She says, 'I too have a cherry-tree of which I am very proud.' She wants to show it to me, and leads me through the bushes to a quite young tree, and she speaks with the same intonation that my wife has in her voice when she speaks to little children. She says, 'There are no cherries on it.' I talk soothingly to her and explain that the little tree must grow up before it has fruit on it."

Associations: The cherry-tree with fruit: "It is well worthwhile to plant these trees because in time they have such beautiful big fruit." *The children collecting the unripe fruit:* "I think of my former dream with the strange hat that makes me ridiculous. Just so the fruit of this tree is not my property. Therefore I shouldn't touch it, but I should plant my own tree. This little girl brings back to me the child in a former dream."

The "child of two years" brings back the little girl in his first dream, the little sick child of the anima who didn't want to pronounce the "a" at the end of Maria, the name of the dreamer's wife, so you see we have here the reappearance of the anima. He is particularly struck by the fact that the child has the same intonation that his wife uses when she is talking to little children. He says, "It seems now as if the little girl had made a relationship with my wife, because she speaks with her voice to me."

Analysis of the dream: It begins with the beautiful cherry-tree full of ripe fruit. The dreamer says, "It *is* worthwhile," as if someone had just said, "It *isn't* worthwhile." He has practically no associations because he is still under the spell of the dream before, where he was concerned with the unripe fruits of the cotton. I forgot to tell you what Mr. Gibb has just recalled to me, that when the cotton is infected by this worm, the fruit drops from the stalk in an immature state. I remember that my patient described this to me fully at the time. Here we have again the immature fruit. What do you make of this beautiful tree and the cherries?

Mr. Gibb: The tree of knowledge.

Dr. Deady: The thing growing from the soil and producing fruit.

Mrs. Crowley: Would it be a question of sex, the cherries?

Dr. Jung: Yes, we will come to that later. In the dream before, something was wrong with the crop, the fruits were not sound, but here is a beautiful tree with fruit. The first impression is of health, completeness; sickness is overcome. What has happened in between?

Dr. Schmitz: It is a compensation for the mechanical way of the business man. He would never think of planting a tree or a flower. He would say, "It isn't worthwhile, it doesn't pay." Analysis is like something of the earth, a natural growth. You must have the patience of the peasant who tills the soil, and be satisfied with small results, very different from those of the business man. This beautiful tree is nature, and he sees that "it *is* worthwhile."

Dr. Jung: You are describing the atmosphere of this dream. You see that the unconscious has shifted the scenery and insists on an entirely new aspect. In the dream before, the growth of the cotton does not interest the dreamer in the least, it is only a question of buying and selling. Now in this dream he is confronted with a new problem, the growth of a tree, in which he has never been interested because he can buy the fruit in the market. But it is as though he could not buy the beauty of a tree full of fruit. He says, "It *is* worthwhile." He must recognize that there is a practical virtue and merit in raising such trees, which to him as a business man would not be worthwhile, too small a business. So the whole psychological problem is expressed in a new language, one could say natural language, the language of the soil. The problem with which he is dealing can no longer be expressed in terms of business. The language of buying and selling is too rational, so the language of the unconscious now proposes a different symbolism. Here is a beautiful tree with fruit, and he must admit this is also worthwhile. It is something opposed to industrialism, his former attitude. Every

248

day I hear, "What is the use of it?" "What can I do with it?" "What is the result?" "One only spends a lot of time and money and can do nothing." Only a few days ago I said to a patient, "The only thing you want to know is what are the facts and what you can do with these facts. This is all on the surface. You never ask what comes up in connection with these facts or how you are affected or feel about it, or what *you* can do with *yourself*." We think nothing can be done without applying dynamite. We do not realize that much can happen through development, through growth.

Often we are led to a wall, it is too high, we cannot get over it and we stand there and stare at it. Rationalism says, "There is no getting over it, just go away." Yet natural development has led the patient up to an almost impossible situation to show him that this is the end of his rational solutions. It is meant that he should get there, and perhaps stay there, make roots and grow like a tree; in time overcome the obstacle, grow over the wall. There are things in our psychology that cannot be answered today. You may be up against a stone wall, but you should stay there and grow, and in six weeks or a year you have grown over it. The *I Ching* expresses that very beautifully.[2] A similar situation which looks quite hopeless is depicted thus: "a goat butts against a hedge and gets its horns entangled." But in the next line: "The hedge opens; there is no entanglement. Power depends upon the axle of a big cart." So if you could stop butting against the fence you would not get your horns entangled, and presently you would have the power of a cart with four wheels. There is another way in nature, the way of a tree. This is against rationalism and the impatience of the animal man. It is concupiscence that wants to leap like a tiger over things. The tree stands still and grows and makes roots, and eventually overgrows the obstacle. So this dream calls his attention to the other kind of symbolism. It is a way especially useful in dealing with psychological difficulties. Today he is surely quite unable to deal with his problem, he wouldn't know how to make a decent relation with his wife, he has no words, no manner for it, so he would just make a mess of the whole thing. His unconscious says, "Better shut up." Then his rationality says, "Better run away," make compartments. But the way of nature's is to be like a plant, a stable being,

---

[2] Hexagram 34, "The Power of the Great." The Wilhelm/Baynes version of the *I Ching* has been substituted.

and in time the tree will bear fruit. The only way in which he can be helped is through evolution. This idea goes right through the dream. The little girl leads him to her tree, proud of it although it is so young that it does not bear fruit, and he himself explains to her that in time it will grow up and bear fruit. Now what about the cherries which drop off and are collected in baskets? Obviously these are the immature fruits of the cotton that fall off, infected by the worm. Every cherry-tree produces fruit that does not mature. What does this mean psychologically?

Dr. Leavitt: Certain psychological processes are not meant to mature, they die before they reach maturity.

Dr. Jung: Yes, in everybody's psychology there are certain things that are meant to die, just useless husks that must be cast off. In the metabolism of the body certain cells die daily—living today, dead and ready to be cast off tomorrow. So in psychology we must build up certain things that never reach maturity. They are useful for a time then disappear, as for instance, certain gifts that are promising in youth; after a while they often wither and drop off. Why do you think the dream insists on such a banality?

Dr. Leavitt: Might it not mean unprofitable experiences?

Dr. Jung: Life is a laboratory, an experiment of nature, and many things fail. People say, "This failed and that failed," and they remain quite unconscious of what they *can* do, they are pessimistic and so are only conscious of what they *cannot* do. The dream says, "Everybody takes risks, nature takes risks, we are all experiments that might fail." The immature cherries drop off. But our dreamer cannot see it. If he were a little less rational he could play more with life, but such a rationalist cannot play with life, for play is irrational. We must be able to say of certain things, "I will try it even with the conviction that it might be an error." Only when you live in this way can you make something of life, perhaps today one way, tomorrow another. Every root in the earth has to find its way around a stone. It may take the wrong direction. As soon as you come to the idea of growth and development you are confronted with the irrationality of nature. Every rationalist hates this, for with him things must be safe, "no risks please."

Now the children are collecting the fruits which have no value at all! What would that mean? Where do the children suddenly come from? The children are the immature fruits, they represent his own childish tendencies, but what does picking up the immature fruit mean?

Mr. Gibb: Hanging on to childish values.

Dr. Jung: That is exactly the picture the dream presents. It says, look at children, how they play, they take life as it comes, they even gather the rotten fruits, they don't ask "Is this a valuable cherry?" This is the idea the dream shows to him. You have to live certain things in life as though they were meant to become mature fruit and if they do not ripen drop them; they must be taken in a playful way, a childlike way, without prejudice. As soon as you are prejudiced you exclude certain possibilities, and life is no longer full.

Dr. Schlegel: One could interpret it as the man's infantility, collecting these immature fruits as though they were valuable, and his unconscious criticizing him as childish for behaving in that way.

Dr. Jung: That is an interpretation that would be perfectly good for an irrational type, but we must take into account that this man is a rational type. He would say just that of his own dream. I interpret it my way, because one of those children is the child of his anima. With the dreamer's interpretation he would exclude his anima, hence he would exclude his soul, then he would be back at the beginning again. This is a good theoretical interpretation, but it does not take the psychology of the dreamer into account.

Often people whom I do not know send me their dreams, but without a knowledge of the dreamer I can only interpret them theoretically. You have no *point de départ* for the interpretation. Therefore, in contrast to Freud, while admitting that dreams use the same images, we must remember that they are symbolic of different psychological situations. A snake in one case may mean something favourable, "the wisdom of the depths," in another something unfavourable, such as a physical illness. Once a woman dreamed of a snake a mile long, as big as an elephant, which meant typhoid fever. The woman had said, "Always before I am ill I dream of a snake, but never of so big a one." A snake may have seven thousand meanings.

Dr. Bertine: Could you interpret the dream before her illness?

Dr. Jung: No, I didn't analyse her. I only met her and she told me about it, but I thought it meant a long illness. Whenever the unconscious is on top, whenever it prevails against the present, it grows heavy and important, and is pregnant with the past or the future. When the unconscious is full of the future, or is an activated form of the past which has not been realized, then it prevails over man, Therefore the snake can mean the past or the future.

Dr. Schmitz: What about types that are not defined, as the intuitive for instance, who can't live on intuition and who has thinking or feeling as a secondary exaggerated function? His new language is good, he seems very rational. When we develop a new language, we are more eager to use it than our own. So an irrational type may thus become an exaggerated rational type. Then how would you interpret a dream?

Dr. Jung: This is a complicated case. If the person is exaggeratedly rational, then the dream should be interpreted as I did. I am not sure in this case, in fact I almost think that the dreamer was originally an irrational type. He has developed his thinking and has begun to rationalize himself, so he overdoes it. Very likely he is a sensation type and has compensated by an exaggerated rationalism, so the dream has to break that up.

Mrs. Crowley: Doesn't that make it very difficult to interpret one's own dreams?

Dr. Jung: Yes, with my own dreams I am just as helpless as anyone else. The dream falls in my own shadow where my light fails. It is just as though I had never heard of dream analysis. That is, of course, the maddening thing, that you are never equal to your own dreams. I have to begin at the very beginning and come to the most painstaking analysis. That proves that our dreams are always just ahead of ourselves. We never grow into the divine stature, we are never with our gods. The essentially human thing is that man is always a little below, a little incomplete. He *must* be so! So you have to assume the attitude of a newborn babe. One must always be humble when it comes to one's own dreams. After twenty or thirty years I have learned this attitude, that the things that are worthwhile are ahead of me. There are things in us that are superior to ourselves, therefore we get the idea of a hypothetical new centre superior to the conscious one.

Irrational types are always putting their foot in it. They are nearly always on the wrong path, hunting spectres. If they gather fruit on the road they throw it away because it is an accomplished fact.

We come now to the important fact that one of these children in the dream is his childish anima, and why she is only two years old. Her age has to do with the beginning of his psychological studies. From earlier dreams we saw that his interest in philosophy and theosophy was rather morbid. He was inclined to take theosophy in too concretistic a way, so the child of his anima was sick. In the dream to which he refers, she could not say the name of the dreamer's wife, and now she speaks with the intonation of his wife's voice and is on good terms with her, an important change. So after a month of analysis the child is no longer sick, and she shows her beautiful young cherry-tree to the dreamer. Obviously he feels that the big tree does not belong to him, so he does not let the children collect the fruit. When his anima takes him to her tree he feels it is entirely her own. Where then does the big tree belong?

Dr. Bertine: Did he have an intuitive perception of the possibility of such a tree from talking with you?

Dr. Jung: Yes, it is the tree of my anima. He only intuitively perceives it, senses that the stuff we talked about seems to be worthwhile. Then comes the temptation to swear on the words of the master,[3] like the Pythagoreans, and to take every word I say for the eternal truth. I say a lot of nonsense during the day and there are certain people who pick up all the immature fruit and rotten berries and eat them and think they have dined well. That tree produced a lot of immature stuff, and this man might have been inclined to pick it up and value it without criticism, but the dream warns him and says, "You let that stuff alone, it is not your tree, you have your own job to look after." Then his little anima takes him to her own tree, and he is very paternal and says, "Just have patience and in time it will grow and bear fruit." He is too paternal when he talks to his anima! Why is she so young? He is forty-seven, she is only two.

Dr. Schmitz: She is newborn.

Dr. Jung: Now with more spiritual interest she begins to live. She is immortal, she can change her form, sometimes she is very old, an old witch; why is she so young here?

Dr. Deady: She is young because his relation to this child, which is his relationship to woman, is so young.

Dr. Jung: Yes, his relation to his wife, and also because his attitude in the conscious is too old, hence his unconscious compensates for that and makes it too young. Any rationalist tries to live as though he were two thousand years old, like an experienced

---

[3] Cf. Horace, *Epistulae*, 1.1.1f.: "jurat in verba magistri" (swears to the words of the master). In Horace, the reference is to gladiators who swore the oath.

great-grandfather. If we had agreed with old Pythagoras the whole world would, by this time, be rational. When we live from the rational point of view, the anima is a baby. Two years old is pretty young, so you can see what the age of that man is, about nine hundred years old I should say. What he needs, in order to become human, is an enormous dosage of youth. The difference between two and nine hundred symbolizes the gap in his own nature. Obviously the tree to which the little girl leads him is his own tree.

It is an old Germanic idea that every man has his own tree, his totem planted when the child is born; if anything happens to this tree something happens to him, but if it grows and flourishes he is well and happy. You could injure a man by driving a nail into his tree or you could kill a man by cutting down his tree. The tree is used as a theme in *The People of the Mist*, by Rider Haggard,[4] where each individual of the tribe had his own tree. There is a peculiar relation between each man and his tree, and when his tree falls the life of the man comes to an end. According to Caesar, the Druids used to cut a tree into the shape of a man with outstretched arms in the form of a cross.[5] Christ on the cross is another example, for the cross is also the tree of life. Then there is a Jewish legend in which Adam, just before his death, is allowed to look for the last time into Paradise. The tree is dead, but in its branches is lying a little baby.

[4] London, 1894.

[5] Cf. *Symbols of Transformation,* CW 5, par. 402 (as in 1912 edn.), where Jung attributes the story to Thomas Maurice, *Indian Antiquities* (1796).

LECTURE V

12 June 1929

Dr. Jung:

We have finished our dream of the cherry-tree. Are there any questions?

Dr. Deady: Why do you say the shadow always does things in the "old way"? I don't grasp the significance of "old."

Dr. Jung: I mean that as an average statement. The general truth is that the shadow represents the old ways. Of course, there are exceptional circumstances, as when the unconscious is in the ascendant over the conscious. Why do I say the shadow represents the old ways? The shadow is the inferior personality, the old personality, the easy-going thing. It is your most personal reaction, the way you always have reacted. For instance, you find the shadow in your personal resentments, your intimate impulses. These are pretty much the same throughout your lifetime. In childhood, when there was hardly any consciousness, you reacted in a perfectly natural way, as the result of direct impulses. Later on these reactions become covered up by education, by the whole process of becoming conscious. Most people hide their personal reactions and so they fall more and more into the shadow. It is a perfectly plausible idea that they would not be agreeable on the surface, for human intercourse demands and needs certain forms. So the old ways, the old reactions, are preserved by falling into the shadow, into the unconscious. If a thing falls altogether into the unconscious, there is no chance of its being corrected. A thing comes up from the unconscious as fresh as the first day it was put there. Things have not rubbed against each other, they have not been in the melting pot, they are like museum pieces in glass cases, nothing wears them out and the form remains the same. That is why I say the shadow on the border-line of the unconscious means "old ways." There are certain exceptions where apparently the shadow is not the "old

255

way," as when the conscious is unaware of some new thing coming up from the unconscious. Such people become aware of disturbances. Things which have been dealt with long ago suddenly become unmanageable. On the eve of an outburst of a psychosis, people are upset by things they have never minded before, but now they become a stumbling block and an obsession. Of course, it would be a grave error on the part of the analyst if he should take these things at their face value. He should carefully ascertain whether these particular reactions have always been unmanageable, whether they are relatively customary or whether they have only just now become unmanageable. For instance, suppose a man has had a resentment. He had been cheated thirty years ago, then suddenly the whole thing comes up again, and he gets in a rage about it as though it had happened quite recently. That is what happens in the beginning of a neurosis or a psychosis. You see that in venereal diseases that have been satisfactorily dealt with long ago, but inferiority develops, and years later the man may begin to worry about it like hell and it falls on him like a hundred-ton weight. When you analyse the weight in the recrudescence of that resentment, you find that it is not due to anything new in the resentment, but to something behind it, something which has never been conscious. It comes up from the depths hidden under the cloak of personal reactions.

Mr. Dell: Do you mean that physical symptoms actually recur?

Dr. Jung: It can be so, or the symptoms may be purely psychological. The unconscious takes these "shadow forms" for its expressions, because there are no conscious forms into which it could flow. These reactions are avenues into the unconscious. One can catch the anima or animus by the exaggeration of these reactions.

Dr. Bertine: Then the anima or animus is the archetype behind these personal reactions?

Dr. Jung: The animus is a function, it should not be so terribly personal; if it is, it is so by virtue of its content, because it carries a weight. A big fish has appeared in the collective unconscious and the animus has swallowed it. The animus becomes fat, his belly is inflated, and he begins to talk with big words. You do not hear those words, you hear nothing, but you get a prejudice somehow and handle things on unconscious premises. Suddenly you find your way is wrong, due to a certain peculiar bias. It is just as though

256

opinions expressed by the animus in an inaudible voice were fil-
tering through in your thoughts, and it works exactly in the same
way as though you had that point of view. It is like the story of the
pigeon who thought "they were walking," but she really never had
thought at all. It is the best animus story I know, silly but profound,
as silly things often are.

Once a horse, an automobile, and a pigeon met by chance. It was
a beautiful day, and they thought they would go to a certain inn.
To get more of a kick out of the excursion, they agreed to make
it a race, with the inn as the goal. The auto raced along, and was
of course the first at the inn; he ordered black coffee and waited.
Pretty soon the horse arrived panting and perspiring; it was a hot
day and he ordered a glass of beer. They waited and waited and
waited, but no pigeon came, and they thought, "Something must
have happened to dear old pigeon," so they went back to find her
and there only a little way from where they had started, they saw
a white speck in the road. It was the pigeon walking along in the
dust, all dirty and bedraggled. They said to her, "What are you
doing here?" "Oh," said the pigeon, "I thought we were walking."
Now why did the pigeon think they were walking? The auto was
on wheels, the horse on the hoof, so the pigeon had to be on foot,
her wings no use at all! Just nicely beside the mark, that is animus.

Mr. Dell: Why do you make the pigeon female?

Dr. Jung: Oh, the word for pigeon in German is female. Also
the dove is the symbol of love, of Venus, of Astarte, and a sign for
the Holy Ghost instead of the mother, etc., so you see I have other
reasons for making it female. Even if the pigeon were a male the
logic would still be animus logic, which becomes aware of premises
no one would have thought of.

Dr. Schmitz: Is it not possible that the shadow can receive an
education by life itself?

Dr. Jung: Yes, by analysis it could.

Dr. Schmitz: Not normally?

Dr. Jung: No, because it is in darkness, inferior, carefully hidden
away, a skeleton in the cupboard. You naturally keep him there,
and that is a guarantee that he will remain unchanged. You do not
introduce him to your guests, just as you do not wash your dirty
linen in public. Hence the shadow can't "just normally" be educated.
Even in marriage, a certain distance is maintained, people can keep

257

their shadows away from each other. They call it "integrity of personality," "Integer vitae scelerisque purus."[1]

Dr. Schmitz: As in riper years we become more familiar with life, more mellow, doesn't the shadow grow also?

Dr. Jung: In the long run you can hardly avoid bringing the shadow to the surface. It shows with people in particular circumstances. For instance, if you want to test a friend, get drunk with him and you may see a beast.

Dr. Schmitz: Sometimes you will find him more sympathetic then, and much nicer.

Dr. Jung: Oh yes, on the other hand the shadow may be very charming. Some people hide their best qualities under an animus opinion or an anima mood, or an inherited prejudice, the influence of the family, etc. These people live their shadow qualities. Some people, and particularly introverts, always put the wrong foot forward. They have a particular genius for putting their finger on the sore spot.

Dr. Bertine: Whenever the shadow comes up with overwhelming force, it is always reinforced by the anima or animus, is it not?

Dr. Jung: The anima or animus is always something behind the scene, but it is quite impossible to say that it increases the shadow volume. The shadow rather increases the anima. Sometimes it is incorrect to use the term animus or anima. It may be a new content coming up from the collective unconscious. Sometimes you get a thing more as a hunch or inspiration. To speak of the anima or animus then would be too precious.

Dr. Schmitz: If the introvert shows his worst side, is it because his shadow is extraverted?

Dr. Jung: Yes, he waits so long that his shadow has put the wrong foot out by the time he speaks. I had an introverted friend who always hesitated and waited, so that his mouth began to speak before he was ready, and always said the wrong thing. As a student he had to pay a call on the famous old Virchow.[2] He felt very nervous and thought of him as a rhinoceros with two horns. Tremblingly he entered the study, made his bow, and mumbled, "My name is Virchow." "Oh," said the old man, "you have the same

---

[1] "He that is unstained in life and pure from guilt."—Horace, *Carmina*, 1.22.1 (tr. E. C. Wickham, LCL).

[2] Rudolf Virchow (1821-1902), German pathologist and Liberal political leader, in Berlin.

name as I have." Then my friend saw that his shadow had spoken first and made a mess of the situation, and he went right down into the earth. The best movie I ever saw was *The Student of Prague*.[3] It shows the separation of the conscious man and his shadow, so that the shadow moves by itself. In this case the man had pledged himself on his honour not to kill his adversary in a duel. As he approaches the place he meets his double coming away, wiping blood from his sword on the grass. He begins to be suspicious and when he reaches the spot he finds his adversary already dead. The shadow, disregarding the intention of the conscious man, had killed his adversary.

Dr. Schmitz: Like Dr. Jekyll and Mr. Hyde.[4]

Dr. Jung: Yes, a good example, there are many in literature. Why did you make so much of the shadow I wonder?

Dr. Deady: I thought you were the one who did it.

Dr. Jung: You asked me questions. You see, the inferior man has far more possibilities than the superior man, and that is why we are all so interested in analysis. The really creative thing in man always comes from the place where you least expect it, from the small thing, the inconspicuous thing. Hence the shadow is a very important part of man.

Next dream [16]: "I see a machine, and in seeing it I know that I am telling Dr. Jung about it, as though I were reporting a dream. I say that some parts of the machine are out of order and these parts are marked with little yellow labels pasted on them. Dr. Jung advises me to pay attention to those parts of the machine that are out of order in the next dream. I want to look more closely at the machine to see what parts are out of order or injured, but at this moment the machine disappears and I see my little daughter in a skirt with big holes torn in front. I think, Ah! that is the solution of that obscurity to which Dr. Jung called my attention."

The dreamer returns apparently to the beginning of his analysis, and is again busy with the idea of machines. Those of you who have heard the former dreams will remember that the machine plays a great role in them, but apparently he is not conscious of his former dreams in his associations. He speaks of a peculiar innuendo. He says the machine helps you to move in a quicker way

[3] See above, 28 Nov. 1928, n. 6.
[4] In R. L. Stevenson's novel (1886).

than when you walk. It can produce the necessities of life in a less laborious way than can be done by hand. He says, "To me the meaning of the machine is the increase of human power; the increase of human power in the psychological sphere is the dynamics of our functions, the source, the tool, the instrument by which we increase our will-power." So he arrives at the conclusion that the machine in the dream is human will power. He says, "If Dr. Jung calls my attention to something wrong with my machine then something is wrong with my will-power, and I should find out what it is."

The yellow labels: "In great factories the injured parts are marked, so the repairer can see what parts need to be repaired or substituted." *The disappearance of the machine* shows that the machine is not to be taken as something very real, but rather as a symbol. It disappears because what it expresses is now exhausted and we need a new symbol. The machine is replaced by his little daughter. *Little daughter:* The dreamer says: "My little daughter in opposition to my wife expects something of life, she likes to enjoy herself, thus she symbolizes something of my own pleasure in life." *The holes in her skirt* convey to me the idea that something seems to be wrong in my sexuality. The position of the holes in her skirt suggest this. So something must be wrong in my will-power in sexual matters."

Before I saw this dream we had analysed the worm in the cotton-seed. For practical reasons I had called his attention to something I have not mentioned to you, namely, the jelly-like substance interspersed with the excrement of the worm, in the interior of the cotton capsule. When I asked him about his associations with the jelly-like matter on plums and the excrement, he said something not in his original associations, nor in his report of the dream. Often a patient leaves out certain things when telling a dream. Sometimes he thinks they are not worth mentioning, sometimes he gets a slight feeling of discomfort, and he is not sorry if that particular association should fall under the table. So it is with this excrement and plum business: he associates the jelly on the plum with the female genitals, and the excrement of the worm reminded him of the coffee-bean. The coffee-bean is an archaic female sex symbol. You find such a far-fetched analogy where there is stored-up sexuality, then it is linked up with all sorts of things to which it does not belong. The dreamer's whole human development is linked up with his sexual problem, so he sees sex analogies all over the place, even in coffee-beans! Only when we were analysing this dream did he bring the association with his former dream, and say that there had been something in the former dream which was the cause of this dream. The plum as a female genital was spoken of, as was the sexual analogy of the coffee-bean. As that dream was one of disturbance, of destruction, it meant either a disturbance of sexuality or a disturbance that caused a disturbance of sexuality. The real essence of the disturbance is the worm, so the worm produces sex symbols, and the worm is also in his sexuality. The female genitals (the *yoni*) stand for sexuality in a man and the phallus for woman. These sex symbols simply stand for sexuality, and anything that happens in or around them means a disturbance of sexuality. It is very involved and not clear whether his sexuality is disturbed and hence there is trouble, or whether there is a disturbance and hence his sexuality is troubled. According to the dream both issues are possible and probably both are true, for the sex trouble is the trouble to begin with. This man's sexuality does not function properly. On the other hand he has trouble that disturbs his sexuality. Neurotic sex trouble is Janus-faced. There can be another problem, a spiritual problem not yet developed, but in an embryonic state, which is expressed in sex symbolism. When man is completely evolved, then sex is a function. Here you have a paradoxical and confusing innuendo of the unconscious, but only so long as you cannot think in paradoxical terms. In ancient philosophy, mystical philosophy as one should call it, this problem was expressed in a Greek saying which means "The Bull is the father of the Serpent, and the Serpent is the father of the Bull."[5] That formulates it. You cannot beat that for marvellous clarity, only you must understand what the Bull is and what the Serpent is. The Bull is the month of May, the marvellous fertility of the spring. Taurus is the house of Venus, in its full male manifestation, the uncontrollable power. The Serpent is the cold-blooded animal, the earth deity, it means darkness, night, humidity. It is hidden in the earth, it symbolizes death, fear. It is poisonous. It is the very opposite of the Bull, hence this saying makes the father of the Bull the obvious opposite, and makes the positive the father of the negative. According to the Chinese, when Yang is reaching its sum-

[5] Cf. "The bull is the father of the dragon and the dragon is the father of the bull," from the Latin writer Firmicus Maternus (4th cent. A.D.), quoted in *Symbols of Transformation*, CW 5, par. 596 (as in 1912 edn.).

mit Yin appears in it. Yin reaches its bottommost place and Yang is created. Hence they can say, "At midnight midday is born and at midday midnight is born." It is just the same. That exceedingly paradoxical way is one of the intrinsic qualities of the unconscious mind, hence the language of the unconscious is very difficult and confusing because we try to translate it clumsily into our language where we believe in a positive or definite truth. Such an idea is barbarous from a higher point of view. "Nothing is really quite true and even this is not quite true," as Multatuli said.[6] We always want a thing to be quite true, but if a thing is quite true it is a terrible mistake. Be careful, disaster follows, and your whole midnight sentimentality is all bunk!

We must go back to the patient's earlier dreams of machines. The first form in which the idea of a machine appeared was the sewing-machine which he wanted to give to the seamstress, a sort of anima, who lived in an unhealthy dark room suffering from tuberculosis. The next form was the steamroller making a road which produced a pattern, a kind of primitive mandala. This led us to speak of the significance of the mandala as an individuation symbol. We saw that the machine, which was obviously his sexuality, on account of its automatic character, was leading him towards his original pattern, and if he funks it, he will also funk the way that leads to his individuation. That is the meaning of the dream. Now you see how he is returning to this problem and the ways in which he tries to escape it. You remember the dream of the aquarium, the upper storey, and how careful the dream was in introducing the subject of talking over his problem with his wife. Daring thought! Then the last dream, of the cherry-tree, where he so much admires the beautiful full-grown tree, full of fruit (not his, his own is very small). There is a tendency in this man to admire something outside of himself, to have a pretext not to return to himself. But the dream calls him back to his own problem, his sexuality, as also in the dream of the worm. Suddenly the worm appeared in the cotton-seed, threatening the destruction of the crop. He felt that he must take care of the new situation, that the seriousness of it could no longer be denied. Then came this dream saying, "Oh, it is by no means a disaster, your own little cherry-tree will grow up and bear healthy

[6] Pseud. of the Dutch writer Eduard Douwes Dekker (1820-1887). The quotation, a favorite of Jung's, turns up several times in his *Letters*.

fruit." This shows the positive aspect of the same problem. After this we have the new dream of the machine which reverts to the sex problem. The theme of the cotton-seed dream is again taken up, some parts of the machine are out of order and I call the dreamer's attention to it. I do it in a peculiar way. I am almost analysing the dream, in the dream. How do you explain that? It is not easy, but you know from your own experience that you can have a dream within a dream; or while you are dreaming, know that it is a dream. It is all like a trick box one inside another. What does this mean?

Mrs. Sigg: It seems that one part of his personality is identified with you.

Dr. Jung: That is quite possible. Which part would that be?

Mrs. Sigg: The part he has repressed the most, his fantasy side. You appreciate that rather than his logical thinking.

Dr. Jung: But he associated the large cherry-tree with me.[7] He preferred to have a hero do the work. It is easier to eat the fruit grown by someone else, and we are educated in that way. In Christianity we are taught to throw all our burdens on Jesus, and he will bear them for us, and in such a way we maintain a suckling psychology. This patient thinks that I can analyse his dream and he can look at it theoretically. Most people think that when a thing is analysed it can no longer harm them, they can go around it. The analysis will give them words of power, they say, "Oh, that is a father complex!" Then the thing has been given the right name and the complex is gone. Take the fairy tale of Rumpelstiltskin, a little wood devil who does a lot of mischief at night, robs the children, etc. No one knows who he is, but if anyone can guess his right name his power is gone and he will explode at once. It is an old idea and true to a certain extent. Names have a sort of influence, words are apotropaic. When you can name a thing the patient is already half liberated. Hence we use the healthy effect of name-giving to help abolish a thing. But the real essence of the thing is not touched by the name you give it. It is not thereby destroyed. Names also attract; if you call certain names the thing appears. So you say, "Do not speak of that," or you rap on wood, or you choose a word that is a euphemism, which covers the black thing. Certain

7 See above, p. 253, Jung's reply to Dr. Bertine.

names are most unfavourable, for instance, the Black Sea is called "the hospitable sea."[8]

Mr. Dell: In *The Psychology of Suggestion* Baudouin[9] says do not say "I don't sleep," say "I *did* not sleep well."

Dr. Jung: Yes, that is the same idea. My patient is infected by the power of words, what he supposes to be my power, but his unconscious is not blindfolded. When the dream speaks of me, I am really meant. In this dream it is really myself, not a part of him. It is not to be taken literally that I am analysing him in his dream, but it refers to analysis. The dream runs as follows: "I see a machine, and instantly I know it is a dream." He knows the machine is an image which in former dreams he interpreted as sexuality, hence the dream goes on: "I see it is sexuality but I know it is a dream (not quite real). I report this dream to Dr. Jung as a matter for analysis." So the dream would say, "This sexuality I am concerned with is only partially real, so I call on Dr. Jung right away, for I cannot disentangle it." Dr. Jung says something is wrong with his sexuality. It is not only a *mixtum compositum*, but also perverted in some way. We don't see the whole machine plainly, and only certain parts are marked with the yellow labels. The next thing is that when he goes closer, to inspect the machine more thoroughly, it disappears, it is only a symbol. That means that what appears to him as mere sexuality will vanish as soon as it is closely inspected. people often find that when they look closely into a thing, it disappears to a certain extent. Now we come to that important part of the dream. The thing is no longer a machine, but his little daughter. She expresses his pleasure in life, she is forward-looking and expects to enjoy life as he does. He identifies himself with her. What is the little girl?

Dr. Schmitz: His anima.

Dr. Jung: But can you say that right away? That would be to interpret her subjectively, but the little daughter is real.

Mrs. Sigg: He had at first looked on sexuality as mechanical, a machine.

---

[8] An example of apotropaism, which is the attempt to avert the effect of a bad thing by giving it a good name. The Black Sea was originally called Axeinos, "inhospitable," because of its stormy character. Later it was known as the Euxine Sea (*euxeinos* = hospitable). (*Sems.:* "the most profitable sea.")

[9] The Swiss psychologist Charles Baudouin (1893-1963); the reference is to his *Psychologie de la suggestion et de l'autosuggestion* (Neuchâtel, 1924). At first eclectic, he eventually followed Jung's school. See *C. G. Jung Speaking*, p. 76.

Dr. Jung: Yes, as an automatic sort of gland mechanism, with no psychic implications. Now the dream says: "What you looked on as sexuality and took as a mechanical device is a human being, your own little daughter." Why does the dream not say "your wife" or any other woman? It says just "your little girl." His little daughter is very real to him, she is with him every day, so when he dreams of her you may be dead sure it means his little daughter. That child is as real as I am when he dreams of me, even more real. What does the daughter convey? Why the long pause?

Mrs. Deady: The idea of incest.

Dr. Jung: Yes, we don't want to be guilty of incest

Dr. Schmitz: Our complex here in the seminar is an anti-Freudian one. I thought of the incest complex, but that is Freudian and I didn't want to say it.

Dr. Jung: Yes, just that. Here we are dealing with the Freudian incest complex, that is the truth. That is why the dream says *"your little girl."* For what invariably happens is that when a man keeps to his respectable form, all that dark stuff which he heaps up in the cellar is creeping out somewhere else. It creeps not only into incest but into his sons, his dogs, his furniture. We have no name for perversion with the piano, but it gets into that. It can even get into the central heating. There is a remnant of our libido so slowly flowing that it can get into the very next thing. If there is no little daughter and hence no chance for incest, then there is a little dog, for an unconscious sodomistic relation, or a little cat or a teddy bear. I know people who have teddy bears in their sleeping-rooms. If not that it must be some old heirloom, an old chest or grandfather chair which is watched with jealous care and given amazing attention. When anything goes wrong with it then one just dies! I knew a man who had so much of his libido in a tree that when the tree died he died too, That man had a tree incest. The sort of libido that is expressed in sexuality does not do without a body. If it does not go into one body it goes into another. It fills the immediate surroundings and makes them almost demoniacally important.

There are many people to whom objects are particular devils, yet we all take it as a joke that a German professor has written a book about the cunning of the inanimate object.[10] Among the Africans certain objects are devils and demons. There is a peculiar

---

[10] A reference to F. T. Vischer's novel *Auch Einer* (1884), where examples are given of the "mischievousness of the object." Cf. "A Review of the Complex Theory" (1934), CW 8, par. 202.

relation between the object and the men. In certain languages we still have genders, masculine, feminine, and neuter. The primitive language has other sorts of classes; trees, lands, rivers belong to the same class, but they cannot express a certain class without using a prefix or suffix implying "having to do with a place quality." It is as if you said "New York *pa*" to denote the place-quality instead of some other, for New York alone may mean anything else. The prefix also gives the living quality. In German we say, "Der Mann"; the primitive must say, "Der Mann living." In some primitive languages they go further and say, "Der Mann, living, upright, outside." Now you have it all, the man is living, erect, outside his hut. In speaking of an object they must say, "Der Tisch (table), upright, dead, inside," all expressed by means of prefixes and suffixes. When I speak of *my* canoe, I say, "Canoe, outside, living"—when I speak of *your* canoe, it is "Canoe, outside, dead." Yours is dead, mine is living, no one else can have it, there is the wrong life-power in it. My mana is there, so if anyone should take it, it would be dangerous to him. The primitives are so much aware of their blood relationship with objects that these things are living or dead.

Now we come to the point I really want to elucidate, that this is psychologically true. These things behave as if filled with the man's life, so the sword speaks to him. A man has an intercourse with his weapon. From mythology we know that the hero's weapons are magically vitalized, almost alive. You can speak of the soul of an object, and on the primitive level this means objects have a life of their own. There is a story about a house in which the furniture had a party when no one was at home. Chairs and tables moved around of themselves.—If you put your hands on a thing it begins to move, warmed by your mana, you simply increase its vital power. To the primitive there is nothing strange in this, for they believe that the object lives.

So you see that the life not lived, the arrested libido in our dreamer is simply flowing out indiscriminately in all directions, into the next object, into his daughter. If his libido is going into chairs and tables and dogs, there is not much harm done, but if it is going into the children you will see that it is very dangerous. The holes in the skirt in this dream give the hint of danger. The tearing of the clothes is common in those terrible sexual murders. The brute of a murderer has simply given way to the uttermost impetuosity, the complete senseless emotions of such a beast. Compare our dreamer with such a hint! You can't believe it! Yet incest and sexual murder are not so very far apart. You notice that whenever he approaches the complex, a danger signal comes up and warns him. Now you have it. There is a dangerous impulse that might break forth. Take his consciousness a little away, get him a little drunk, and you do not know what might happen. In very respectable families things sometimes come to very close quarters, and, with this man, I would not say that an outbreak was very far away. Sexual murders are never premeditated. The murderer is as if gripped by an epileptic attack. That is why Lombroso[11] took these criminals to be epileptics, for such people belong to epileptic types; they are seized by a fit and such things happen. When there is such an accumulation of libido with extraordinary unconsciousness, then suddenly a wave may leap up or an avalanche come, or a stone fall from the mountain. The weight suspended from above may produce such a catastrophe, and so the dreamer gets his warning, incest with the suggestion of sexual murder, and again it is I who call his attention to it.

Now, I will tell you something that is a technicality in the interpretation of dreams. When a patient dreams "I tell Dr. Jung that," or "He calls my attention, etc.," that is information for me personally, for the doctor. The patient's unconscious addresses me and says, "Now listen Dr. Jung." Then I have to say something to that man. I have to take an active part. It pushes the interpretation of that dream and I had to do it—I said, "Look here, this dream points to the possibility of incest, to sexual murder." Certain walls are so thick one can't pierce them. Humanly you cannot expect of a man that he could rape his beloved little daughter, so the analyst must step in and tell him that this is within the human scope, these sexual murders are in our blood. You may have had such a murderer among your ancestors. That is the horrible thing in a man. There is a certain percentage of murderers in a population, and we all have to contribute so that this number may be full, so statistically we belong to them. Perhaps we contribute through our decency, or indirectly through our assiduity in collecting the wealth

[11] Cesare Lombroso (1836-1909), Italian criminologist and physician, whose theories on criminality and epilepsy are presented in *Genio e Follia* (Turin, 1882), cited in *Symbols of Transformation*, par. 277 and n. 27 (as in 1912 edn.). German tr. (in Jung's library): *Genie und Irrsinn in ihren Beziehungen zum Gesetz, zur Kritik und zur Geschichte* (Leipzig, 1887). No English tr. has been traced.

which makes men robbers. On the one hand Nature makes you very virtuous, in order to give others a chance to be vicious, but if all were virtuous Nature would lose its balance.

Dr. Schmitz: What would be the consequence of revealing this to the patient?

Dr. Jung: I will tell you. It would give him the shock of his life! But I was very careful in talking to him and mitigated it as much as possible. His unconscious really meant that he was to be shocked out of his righteousness. It shows him that he belongs to the common stock of mankind, it gets back to humanity, down from the high twig on which he was crowing. He must say, "I am like the worst of them, then why do I hesitate in analysis?" It is with such shocks that the unconscious tries to make people human.

Prof. Schmaltz: I think it is quite interesting that the labels are yellow. Yellow is quarantine, smallpox, poison, etc.

Dr. Jung: Yes, and it stands for prostitution. We say "yellow streak" too, for cowardice. That patient had no associations with yellow, it means the unconscious to him, but the unconscious is his own language. You cannot imagine that the labels would be blue!

Prof. Schmaltz: So long as you have a label on it, you know that it is dangerous.

Dr. Jung: Yes, it is again the man's tendency to keep things tidy and safe. Yellow means danger, so he will not touch it.

Dr. Deady: It is said that men don't like yellow.

Dr. Jung: Yellow is the colour of envy, jealousy, anger, all things negative with us, but in the East just the opposite.

Mrs. Crowley: It would be the colour of their skins.

Dr. Jung: There is a reversal between the East and the West. The colour of mourning with us is black, there it is white.

Question: Isn't yellow the colour of the intellect?

Dr. Jung: I should say it was the anima flag!

LECTURE VI

19 June 1929

Dr. Jung:

As far as I can judge we have arrived at a satisfactory interpretation of the patient's incest dream. Are there any questions?

Dr. Gilman: How badly was the man knocked out by your interpretation of his dream?

Dr. Jung: Oh, he wasn't knocked out at all, because he did not realize it. In certain cases realization comes only after a long time. It is amazing how blind some people can be. This is the first time the man's unconscious has dealt him a knock-out blow—and I tried to hand him a sugar-coated pill. There is an anaphylactic[1] system in every one to protect him against a too acid realization; I have none of the Protestant feeling that I should rub things in. Only when I think that a patient should begin to realize certain things do I insist on his understanding. This patient's realization was carefully theoretical. Such people take a particular pride in their ability to understand. If I had said to him, "You have the murderous instinct," he would have answered, "Yes of course, we all have," but to think that he could actually break a bottle over his wife's head—impossible! A thinker is never struck by thought, only by feeling. No one is more impermeable to feeling than the feeling type in an argument. The feeling type gives no access to his feeling because he manages it. It is his faculty, he uses it to get into connection with other people. You reach a thinking type through his feeling, for there he is vulnerable. We are not vulnerable in our superior function. It is as if it were inclined to be lifeless, cheap,

[1] *Sems.*: "anaplerotic," a medical term for an agent that promotes the healing of a wound or ulcer. Perhaps an error in transcription for "anaphylactic," meaning an immunological reaction of the body to the introduction of foreign proteins or certain drugs which induce a state of "anaphylactic shock," comparable to the "knock-out blow" which the unconscious had dealt the patient. [R.F.C.H.]

269

containing too little blood; it is dull and thick-skinned, but very clever in attacking other people and producing certain results. It is a valuable tool but not very sensitive in itself. We make a great mistake in assuming that a thinker's thought is very profound. It is rather the opposite, and only profound when it is mixed with the inferior function; and for the feeling type, the corresponding truth holds good. Our patient realizes that there is something in this question of incest, but from that to bringing up his feeling about it is a long way. He is not a neurotic case and I only see him off and on. It took him about two years before he began to understand what feeling is. I told you how he almost stopped the analysis when he first approached feeling,[2] so he is far from a realization of feeling in his incest dream. He would say, "Yes, those facts are all right," but he would speak exactly as though they were printed in a book.

Dr. Deady: What would be the feeling realization of that dream?

Dr. Jung: Oh, a feeling realization would be profound horror, which would produce a tremendous impulse to change the situation at once. He would say, that shall *not* happen. He would talk to his wife about the dream and say, "By Jove! This shows a terrible situation and we must do something about it." But even yet he has not said a word to his wife. I don't press him; I told him we would go very slowly, no matter if it takes six or seven years.

Dr. Schmitz: What would be the result if you pressed him a little?

Dr. Jung: Oh, he would say, "I am not such a damned fool as to put my hand into boiling water." He would stop his analysis. As you know, I am not anxious for patients, but I am interested in this case as a quiet laboratory experiment.

Dr. Schmitz: Does it move at all? What if you pressed him again after a fortnight, or mustn't you press him?

Dr. Jung: Yes, it moves. He is not neurotic; if he were, his condition would press him. Why should I do it?

Dr. Schmitz: Why does he come?

Dr. Jung: He has an intellectual interest, he is an intelligent thinking man. It is not my duty to press him, that is no job for me. I am not his doctor in that sense, for he is not a therapeutic case. If he were a neurotic patient I should press him and say, "Now don't be a damn fool, go to your wife and do something about it."

---

[2] *Sems.:* "how he is almost stopped when he makes an enterprise toward feeling".

The original understanding between us is that this is a gentleman's game.

Dr. Schmitz: You say that the patient is not accessible to thinking, so must be struck by feeling, and that a feeling type cannot be struck by feeling. I thought a feeling type was struck by situations that leave a thinking type quite cold, such as seeing an overloaded horse carrying more than is good for it.

Dr. Jung: No, they only talk like that. They work through their superior function and talk the language of feeling. If one has to work with a feeling type one must use the same language. For instance, I was treating a woman who was a feeling type. Her son had just been engaged, there was a slightly incestuous game going on there underneath, but the mother was not able to appreciate that problem. I did not mention the situation, but I said to her with a subtle intonation: "It must be very difficult for a mother to lose a son." She took it right away at its face value, ate it up and said, "No, it is not so bad. I think it is worse to lose a daughter." Now if I had talked with her intellectually, we should have had an argument about all the mess regarding incest and ugly things like that, then *she* would bring out, "It is so hard for a mother to lose a son." She knows and I know that it is not real. It is a necessary make-believe. This woman is a bright feeling type, not a fool. If there are two thinking-type men who are not fools, they know that while they are talking their intellectual stuff, saying a + b = c, etc., they know very well that they are just wrapping up something else in a parcel. They are putting things in decent intellectual form to hand it over. It is a *façon de parler*. Each thinks, "he knows that I know," and so it is with the feeling type. My patient puts it very nicely, as if some tears were repressed in a corner, but we both know that the game is made up for the occasion. We know that things are not so very hot, not so hot as when they were cooked. That is the superiority of the superior function, things are not so hot, not so hard. The superior function is really aloof, the hard thing is underneath, inaccessible, but we have the illusion that we are getting at it, otherwise you strike the sore spot and that leads to a conflagration. With a thinking type you cannot talk feeling language, as with a feeling type you cannot talk thinking language. If I used a feeling argument with this man and said, "Isn't it terribly sad when two human beings who love each other, who have been living together for years, sharing the pleasures and pains of life, are not in mutual confidence? Just go to your wife, take her in your arms, etc.," he would think me ripe for the lunatic asylum, or he would swallow it and with tears in his eyes he would fall on my neck, and tell me that he would do it. Then he would go out and say, "Hell and damnation! What was that fellow doing with me, making a weeping willow out of me?" Treating a thinking type in that way and making him weep would arouse hellish resistances in him for half a year. If he has any guts he will not talk with his wife, for he has been lured and cheated. When you take a feeling type and begin to talk intellectual stuff to him, you lay the train for an explosion and something awful might come out, for the inferior function is not adapted yet. Give an orang-outang a gun and see what happens. Therefore in analysis we must adept to the superior function and be on our guard. Let the patient talk. When I have a feeling type I don't talk too much, for I don't trust my feeling. When I talked to that woman about her son, I thought she might see the cloven hoof, but she took it and swallowed it, so I judge that my feeling function is up to date. It is a proof that my feeling function works quite well. It is the right kind of introduction, a good morning to the incest complex. That is good form for the feeling function.

Dr. Deady: Good form for her superior feeling?

Dr. Jung: Yes, to establish a good rapport. To her it seems good form on my part; it is just an absolute swindle, but the intention is good, is decent. Formerly I would have been ashamed to use such means, but it is really just good form, no more dishonest than herself. Suppose you have a neighbour whom you think is the devil incarnate, isn't it better to greet him than to shoot him?

Dr. Deady: Suppose she could bring up her inferior primitive feeling?

Dr. Jung: That would be very bad. It is the last thing to do. That would give the push to her incest complex and make it evident. What happened was that at the end of the hour we arrived at the conclusion that a mother can have certain feelings for her son. If she were not far advanced in analysis, she could not stand even this thought. But she still lacks the inferior primitive feeling that is behind this incest. Bringing up her inferior primitive feeling would come later, and then she would be really conscious. Even though this man could understand what his feelings are in regard to his incest complex, even then the very last touch would still be lacking. That last touch would be the realization through his inferior thinking. Invariably I see that the last realization, the primordial stuff from which the superior function is made, is the last thing to be touched by analysis. A thinker, for instance, has a thought morality. The thinker will say, "Thinking cannot be wrong, it is sinful to think illogically, such thinking is impure, to think illogically is a sin against the Holy Ghost. Thinking must be instinctively right." So with a feeling type, feeling must be right; if it isn't, then he is lost. It gives one an idea of what an enormous effort it was for man to detach himself from the inferior parts of his superior function in order to become human, to establish himself as it were against nature. But this is a question of very advanced analysis.

Dr. Schmitz: Can the inferior part of thinking be anything other than thinking?

Dr. Jung: It is thinking, all right, but entirely impure; that is, thinking as nature would think, the worst kind of feminine thinking, like the thinking of an ignorant cook.

Dr. Schmitz: The natural mind of woman?

Dr. Jung: No, rather the thinking of the female worm. Let a man like Kant see his inferior thinking and he would hang himself right away. For me to admit my inferior thinking is the worst thing under the sun. I would admit anything, moral insanity, incest, any vice, first. That inferior thinking is the worst. But this would lead us too far away.

Before we go on to the next dream, I want to reconstruct the situation for you. Before the incest dream, we had the dream of the cherry-tree. The dreamer was led to see that an irrational growth is taking place in him and that he should pay attention to his own individual development, instead of admiring what is developed in me. Then he has the incest dream. Everything begins from below, so he must get at some basic facts in himself. St. Augustine said: "Between faeces and urine we are born."[3] He must understand incest before he can go forward. He must know that his feeling is low. It is like an old mystery initiation. "Give away all that thou possessest, and then thou shalt receive." He must humiliate himself, he must repent, then an incubation dream comes for the understanding of the mystery. It happens in our psychology in the same

[3] It has been impossible to trace this trenchant aphorism in Augustine. Freud also quoted it several times, attributing it to an unspecified Church Father.

way. Our dreamer must understand the idea of incest and as much of the feeling of the situation as he is capable of, which is very little. We are going now on the assumption that he understands it intellectually at least. Perhaps something is happening.

Next dream [17]: "I am walking on a road that is ascending." (The incest dream meant a humiliation, a going down, and now he is going up again. In the old mystery initiations after repenting, prostration, going down, there is often flight of steps, meaning in astronomical language the seven constituents of man, or climbing up through the seven spheres[4] of your constitution, the complete realization of yourself.) "The walking is very painful so now I leap; I get along very quickly, half flying and half leaping, just touching the ground occasionally. Thus I catch up with an old beggar with a staff, wandering on the same road. There are trees on either side of the road, and suddenly I find myself leaping into them and jumping from branch to branch like an acrobat in a circus. Then I see a woman and a little boy walking on the road. Apparently they belong to me in some way. As I am clinging to the lower branches of a tree the boy comes up and tries to beat me with a rod. I catch the rod and try to take it away; then I see that he is now holding it in his mouth. I tear it out and then I see that his mouth is bleeding. I say, 'There you have it, when you want to beat other people.' Eventually the road leads to a building of yellow stone, roughly built with two side wings and a sort of courtyard in front. Where the wings open there is a bar, a sort of gate. First I have the impression that it is a prison. The sun is very hot and is beating down on that yellow stone building. There is a sort of porch next to the gate that would lead into the garden, but then I see that it is only a low wall, about as high as a man's chest. I can look over it and see an old man lying on the ground. He is in rags, and stretching his arms up stiffly. He is quite immovable, and I do not know whether he is alive or dead. In the garden there is an Arab child of six or eight years who is mocking us. Then I jump and leap up to the bar of the gate, so that I am astride of the gate with my feet toward the garden. Then the Arab child begins to howl and says that we are not allowed to come into the court. But I don't mind him, I climb over and approach the door of the house. It is

[4] Cf. the ancient idea of the seven planetary spheres surrounding the earth, mentioned in *Psychology and Alchemy*, pars. 66 (orig. 1935) and 410 end (orig. 1936).

very hot, and along the wall near the house we find a number of pieces of new furniture, as if they had just been unpacked from a van. Among them is a sort of washstand, with a frame for a mirror but no mirror. I say it cannot be very good for the furniture to be there in the sun (ironically). Then I try to catch the Arab child with a rope and bind his arms to his body, but the child is howling like mad and I think I had better let him go. I approach the door of the house and see on a plate the name 'Dr. Bauer,' then I go to another door and ring the bell."

Associations: The road: The patient says, "I compare that ascending road to the evolution of mankind, also to the evolution of the individual, which can be expressed by walking on an ascending road. Such a progress can[5] be effected without pain. In order to move forward more quickly it is necessary to detach oneself from the earth, to use the earth as a *point de départ.* In taking the leap he uses the earth as though it were a jumping board. *The old beggar on the road:* "He makes me think of the Hindu fakirs, a sort of saint." *Jumping from branch to branch* "reminds me of monkeys and the way they travel from branch to branch in the trees." *Woman and boy on the road:* "It was an unknown woman, but I think of my anima, and the boy might be Eros in the dream of the Puer Aeternus. I feel that the woman and child belong to me, but in what way I don't know." *The boy beating him with a rod:* "For a moment I was not quite aware of what the boy was going to do and then he began to hit me." *The blood in the boy's mouth:* "The blood might be a castration symbol." *The yellow stone building* "reminds me of certain buildings in Africa, near the Libyan Desert, buildings that might belong to the Egyptian administration, but in reality there would be no garden."

In the dream his first impression of the building is that it might be a prison, and he says in his associations, "The body is the prison of the soul." *The porch beside the gate at the main entrance:* The dreamer says, "In Africa the entrance to an estate is watched by a porter at the gate, who usually lives under the porch or in a primitive sort of building near the main entrance. For us it would be called a gatekeeper's lodge. *The old man lying in the porch:* He is not sure

---

[5] Here, "can" may be an error in transcription for "cannot." It is, however, significant that there should be an ambiguity at this point, since pain is the central motif in the dream. It was to escape pain that the dreamer took to the trees and tried to climb the ascending road "without pain." [R.F.C.H.]

whether the man is dead or alive, and he reminds him of a Hindu fakir or yogi. He says: "Yoga has been of great interest to me, yet I must confess that the absolute introversion, with the complete loss of the external world, even the loss of the reality of one's own body, is not quite sympathetic to me." You remember that in the first part of his analysis he said that he felt that his interest in occult studies was morbid and didn't get him anywhere. Then he talks again of the woman and the boy who accompany him. He says, "Curiously enough, when I jump up and sit astride the bar of the gate the woman and child are actually sitting in the garden, as if it had been no trouble for them to get in. As soon as I put my foot over they are inside, so I conclude they must be part of myself."

Peculiarly enough, the Arab child arouses no associations. He says, "It is just an ordinary child such as one sees by the thousands in Africa, absolutely real. I have no access to that child." About the *new pieces of furniture* put up against the house in the full glare of the sun, he says, "it was cheap stuff, such as you often see in cheap shops. There was nothing individual or personal about it, nothing desirable at all."

From the patient's remark in the dream that it is not good for furniture to be out in the sun, I conclude that the pieces of furniture do not really belong to that building. *Trying to bind the Arab child with a rope:* The dreamer says, "I am not clear whether it is a boy or a girl. It is as if I were trying to show that child that I am not afraid of him. The child may belong to that house, perhaps to the concierge." If that house were a private estate in Africa, and the family away for the summer, naturally it would be watched by a caretaker, and these people always have retainers, so there are any number of dirty urchins hanging around. Suddenly he remembers that it is eight years since he spent a summer abroad. So he has been in Switzerland for the last eight years. *Inscription on door plate, Dr. Bauer:* "That reminds me of Dr. Faustus and also of the last two words inscribed on Pernath's breast in Meyrink's story of *Der Golem.*[6] I think this inscription means the entrance of magic or sorcery." The last two words to which the dreamer refers are the Hebrew words "Aur Bocher," meaning "light" and "disciple," referring to the one to be initiated, so his intuitive interpretation would fit it: "The youth to be initiated into the light."

[6] Leipzig, 1915; tr. Madge Pemberton, *The Golem* (London, 1928).

Now of the whole dream he says: "In order to be able to climb that ascending road of evolution, it is necessary to detach oneself from the earth, and to use the earth merely as a *point de départ*. One should not be troubled by Eros, yet his accompaniment is inevitable, or perhaps necessary. It is necessary above all to have introspection and introversion, but it is not the all-important thing. When one is approaching the gateway of the soul cheap things like that furniture should not be in the garden of the soul. I should remove them. I think these cheap things are certain prejudices. The door with Dr. Bauer on it does not seem to be the right entrance. I feel that is the magic way. So I leave that door and go to another to ring." About the Arab child he says, "I have not the faintest idea what it has to do with me."

I must tell you that this dream is somewhat influenced by his having read Meyrink's *Der Golem*. In the last part of that book, the hero Pernath is led up to the gate of vision, which opens into the unknown garden of a strange house. On the gate are the cult symbols of Osiris, depicting initiation and rebirth. Initiation always takes place in the underworld, and Osiris is the god of the underworld, so the situation in *The Golem* is in a way the stage setting for the dream, though of course it is translated into entirely different terms. This is a pretty difficult dream, and we must go step by step. In the beginning there is the road which leads him up to a certain goal. Since walking in the blazing sun is so painful he leaps from branch to branch in the trees like an acrobat or a monkey.

Prof. Schmaltz: I am pretty suspicious about his explanation. Is jumping from tree to tree the right way to reach the goal? The difficult road with the hot sun blazing down is probably the right way, and he evades this by taking to the trees, the easier way, the intuitive way. I should say that the explanation he gives is not quite satisfactory for the true meaning.

Dr. Jung: He himself was not satisfied with it.

Prof. Schmaltz: And I don't think the boy is Eros either, but a figure that wants to tell him the truth, and beat the truth into him. I don't believe there is any castration symbol. The rod in the mouth of the boy is truth and very disagreeable truth, the truth must bleed.

Dr. Jung: Yes, you can beat or lash a man with words. At first the boy beats the man with the rod, then when the dreamer seizes the rod it is suddenly in the boy's mouth, and he tears it out with blood.

The dream begins in the right way. We are starting from a situation which we assume the man has realized. He has humiliated himself, and now lifts himself from his prostration, in order to go on the ascending road, but on this road the walking is very painful, a sort of torture. The sun beats down like tons of lead, and the dream very aptly uses the language that the man knows well. He speaks of "la chaleur accablante"[7] of an African summer, still, when there are trees you can walk in their shadow. But if you are "un tricheur," a man who plays tricks, or a monkey, you might avoid the dust of the road by jumping from tree to tree. That would be a very intuitive way to go, the intuitive goes by leaps, just touches reality and then is off again. He sees the goal from the mountain top and assumes that he is there, just touching the earth now and then. His assumption that he can reach the goal by leaping from tree to tree is not true. He can only get there by painfully putting one foot before the other, climbing laboriously and painfully, hence we must be suspicious of his mode of travelling by leaps and bounds, while he lets the woman and the boy toil along in the dust of the road. They have to walk, but he does tricks and goes like a monkey—monkey tricks! So we must conclude that in the dream before, he did not come down to the real feeling situation. In spite of his confession and humiliation, he only partially realizes the truth, and so he tries to go ahead in the same old way. He has an intuition of the hot painful way of the ascending road, so he tries monkey tricks again. He is afraid to touch the painful reality. The dream shows that in the very beginning.

Mrs. Sigg: After the last dream I had an impression of the parallel between the dream of the little boy, the Puer Aeternus, who had to be fed with white bread, and of the little girl of the incest dream. In both dreams the realization is incomplete, so he must repeat the thing again and again until it is made clear to him.

Dr. Jung: Yes, that is true, as I have pointed out before. The dream thus far is a critique of his cheap ways of evading reality. The dreamer feels that the Eros boy of the former dream is again the same boy. In other words, here is the same problem, the problem of his relation to his wife, which of course is not settled at all.

---

[7] "the stifling heat".

If he would put the problem to his wife once, it would be pretty painful, but that would be the real road, walking in the heat and dust. He still flirts with the idea that the boy should be a sort of Eros. But the Puer Aeternus means really your most devoted attempt to get at your own truth, your most devoted enterprise in the creation of your future; your greatest moral effort. Only, the man must walk on the road, he couldn't jump from tree to tree. So when the dreamer comes down from the tree the boy is trying to lash him. This is again a critique, he ought to be whipped like a naughty boy for avoiding his problem. But he tears away the rod from the boy's mouth, which surely means that he tears away the word of truth that comes from the Puer Aeternus. His real essence or innermost soul and spirit of truth says, "Now see here, you are playing monkey tricks, deceiving yourself, cheating yourself. You know quite well what you ought to do." He doesn't want to hear himself, he doesn't want to see that symbol, His idea that it is a castration symbol might be true in a metaphorical way. He has "castrated" his God, his divine voice, he took the power away, as Kronos in the old Greek myth castrated his father Ouranos.[8] So castration might simply mean laming his best truth, destroying his guiding principle. It is the sin against the Holy Ghost, acting against his real conviction. *Au fond* he knows quite well what to do, but he prefers not to do it. This is a precious demonstration of how dreams work. It is difficult, in the face of such a dream, to say the unconscious has no moral function. This dream is the best kind of morality you can imagine, yet many dreams are not moral at all, so I finally came to the conclusion that we cannot speak of morality but only of the fact that dreams show that certain behaviour is inadmissible because nature will not stand for certain things. This man is more decent underneath than he is on the surface. I am pretty much convinced that if this man were a real criminal, meant to commit murder, his unconscious would say, "You must commit that murder, or you evade your own problem." The East knows this, so the East can say, "The perfect one will play the role of the king, beggar, criminal, or murderer, being aware of the Gods." The East knows a murderer must commit a murder, or he is immoral. This means

[8] *Sems.*: "ate his own children". The myth (from the *Theogony* of Hesiod) is summarized by Kerényi in "The Primordial Child in Primordial Times," in Jung and Kerényi, *Essays on a Science of Mythology*, 2nd edn. (1969), p. 56. Cf. below, 11 Dec. 1929, n. 4.

that the man who is meant to be a criminal, or murderer, must do it, or he does not fulfil the role given to him in this life. It is easier for the East to have this philosophy, because of the belief that one life does not exhaust the whole of a man's possibilities. We in the West are in such haste because of all we must get into our one unique life. In the East they can make up in the next life what they have missed in this one. Hence they have time enough to realize the profound truth that you shall play the role assigned to you. After the scene with the boy we reach the building. What about that? There is something of the story of the Golem here. The building symbolizes the goal he should attain, it stands in front of him with outstretched wings. Here again something happens that is not right. What is it?

Mr. Gibb: He is barred out.

Dr. Jung: Yes, but he climbs over as if he were a burglar. Again it is a monkey trick, like leaping into the trees. At the end of *The Golem*, there is such a building seen in a vision. I will translate the description:[9] "It is the same way that I have walked in my dream, and again I take the little road that leads up to the castle. I am afraid, my heart is beating, now the empty naked tree will come into view, whose branches reach over the wall. Now I see it, but the tree is white with blossoms and the air is full of the sweet perfume of lilac. At my feet is the town in the early morning light, like a vision of the Promised Land. There is no sound; perfume and splendour only. It is the quaint old Street of the Alchemists, the way up to the castle, but when I saw it in the night there was a little wooden lattice gate in front of the white house. Now I see a most splendid gilded gateway at the end of the road, barring the road to me. There are two sombre yew trees on either side of the entrance. I stand on tiptoe to look over the wall and am again dazzled by fresh splendour. The wall of the garden is covered with mosaics, with a beautiful turquoise-blue background and peculiar golden frescoes, which represent the cult of Osiris. The gate is the god himself, a hermaphrodite, the two parts forming a double gate, the right side the female, the left the male. He himself is on a throne of mother-of-pearl in bas-relief. His golden head is the head of a hare. The ears are cocked and touch each other, like the pages

[9] Jung's version, though accurate, varies from that of Pemberton, pp. 286ff. He cites the same passage in his commentary on the first serial dream in *Psychology and Alchemy*, Part II (orig. 1935), par. 53. See also 26 Feb. 1930, at n. 7.

of a half open book. I smell dew and the perfume of hyacinths coming from over the wall. I stand perfectly still, marvelling, and suddenly an old gardener, or servant, wearing an old-fashioned coat, with a lace ruffle, and shoes with silver buckles, appears from the left side and asks me through the bars what I want. Without a word I hand him the hat of Athanasius Pernath. (The hero got his hat by mistake, and because he wore it he thought he was Athanasius.) The servent takes the hat and goes through the great gate of the castle. As he opens the door I see a marble house like a temple. There is Athanasius Pernath and leaning against him Miriam (the heroine, anima). I see both are looking down on the town. Just for a moment she sees me, then turns and whispers into the ear of Athanasius. I am spellbound by her beauty, she is so young, just as I had seen her in my dream. Athanasius also turns his face slowly towards me, and my heart ceases to beat, for as one sees oneself in a mirror, so his face is like mine! Then the door crashes to, and I see only the shimmering hermaphrodite. The old servant gives me back my hat and says, 'Mr. Athanasius is obliged to you, and asks you not to think hardly of him if he does not invite you into the garden, but it has been for ever so long against the rules of the house. Mr. Athanasius also begs to inform you that he has not worn your hat, because he noticed immediately that the hats had been exchanged. He only hopes his hat has not caused you any particular headache.' "

That is the story of a man who inadvertently got into the role of himself. He saw it as a mistake. That is what people say who fall into a hole. "Hell and damnation, I have fallen into a trap and the trap is myself." They always treat themselves as the greatest mistakes ever made.

26 June 1929

Dr. Jung:

This is our last seminar this summer—I hope the next dream is a good one.

Dr. Schmitz: May I ask a question about the Puer Aeternus again? Isn't Euphorion, the son of Faust and Helena, such a child of the wise man and the anima, such a Puer Aeternus?

Dr. Jung: This leads us a bit far into the figures of the collective unconscious. Faust is identical with the wise man, the magician. It has often been said that he was Paracelsus[1] (or the son of Paracelsus). If you take Faust as a real individual, Paracelsus for instance, then it would be the man Paracelsus identified with the collective figure of the old magician; many geniuses are thus identified with their differentiated function, and these people nearly always have the figure of the great wise man. In the poem of *Faust*, the Puer Aeternus, Euphorion, would be the child of Faust and Helena. Helena is very clearly the anima, so the child would be the product of the wise man with his anima. That is of course one statement, one individual case. It remains to be seen whether it is correct under all conditions. There is a hitch here, for the Puer Aeternus would be the product of two figures in the collective unconscious. Where does the real man come in?

Dr. Schmitz: Yes, Euphorion flies away after his birth, and I would ask what is his relation to the man? When individuation[2] has been realized, and after the birth of the Puer Aeternus, doesn't the

---

[1] Pseudonym of Theophrastus Bombastus von Hohenheim (1493-1541), Swiss alchemist and physician, the subject of two essays (1929, 1941) in CW 15 and one (1941) in CW 13. Cf. also *Paracelsus, Selected Writings*, ed. J. Jacobi (2nd edn., 1958).

[2] *Individuation*: "the process by which a person becomes a psychological 'in-dividual', that is, a separate, indivisible unity or 'whole.'"—Jung, "Conscious, Unconscious, and Individuation" (1939), CW 9 i, par. 490.

Puer Aeternus take the place of the shadow, as the individuation takes the place of the man? Perhaps there is some analogy here in the relation of the Puer Aeternus to the man, his anima and his shadow. Is he a substitute for what the shadow was before?

Dr. Jung: That is an awful tangle. In *Faust*, as soon as Euphorion is born he begins to show symptoms of extraordinary desirousness, always after the girls, and eventually he vanishes in flames. Exactly the same thing is true of the Charioteer and of Homunculus who, flying about in his retort, hurls himself against the throne of Galatea, the beautiful one, where he explodes and is gone. These three identical fatal occurrences mean that the creation of the Puer Aeternus has had no long duration. They indicate that something is wrong in the generation of the figure. The mistake is probably that the creation is through two unconscious collective figures, and man does not come in. This describes what one so often sees. The wise man, when afoot in the world, occasionally hurls himself against the throne of a beautiful Galatea and vanishes completely! How many of you have not known such a man. As soon as there is such an obstacle in the way, as the throne of a Galatea or of some other beautiful girl, it will bring him to a premature end. It is rather too much for a human being that he should be such a perfect wise man. Therefore we must dismiss the idea of the Puer Aeternus altogether, or say that he should be created in a different way. Man should not be identified with the "Great Wise Man," but he must assimilate his own shadow. The usual characteristic of the great man, the genius, is that he does not know that he has a shadow, but he has, and a very ridiculous one. Wagner for instance never realized, while he was sitting there writing about Siegfried, that he was revealing his own shadow for any one who saw him to look at. He wore a crinoline while hammering out the sword of Siegfried! In a dressing-gown tied with pink ribbons he wrote the Niebelungenlied, and made himself a perfect ass. But such a man cannot admit he has a shadow. He is never grateful to God for giving him his mind, but he assumes that he *is* creative mind, that he has done it all himself. As soon as you see your own shadow and admit that you are not perfect, you cannot identify yourself with the "Great Wise Man" and create a Puer Aeternus with your anima.

Then the question arises, is it possible under certain conditions that man, completed by the consciousness of his own shadow and being individuated, is capable of creating something with his anima,

283

a real Puer Aeternus, eternal as its name implies? Through individuation you create something timeless and eternal, which carries the quality of immortality. That is what the East seeks, and it is amply confirmed in their texts. You can take it or leave it as you like. So the Puer Aeternus created thus has the quality of eternity. Mind you, I make only a psychological statement, not a metaphysical one, for we are in conditions of time and space. We call iron solid, but what is solidity? Iron is really flowing. The question is only from what standpoint you judge it. We think of sealing-wax as solid, but suspend it for some time and it flows, it is semi-fluid. Solidity is merely a psychological attitude relative to man and his time. So when you call something eternal, it means simply the quality of timelessness. The complete individuation brings something of that quality.

Dr. Schmitz: Does that mean something not in a man's work, but in his life?

Dr. Jung: No, not in his work nor in his life, but in himself. It is simply a mystical fact of inner experience. One can only state it. It is one of the inexplicable facts of life. Ask a pious man about his religion, his experience of God, he can only assert it. He has nothing more to say. You can add nothing to it nor take anything from it. So it is with that eternal quality.

Now we are concerned with the dream of the building and the garden, and the road leading to this place. We had finished the interpretation of the dreamer tearing the rod away, with blood, from the boy's mouth. Now the building represents the goal of the road. The road has been built exclusively for that building, and when you walk on the road you come up to the gate, with a bar across it. Have you any ideas about that building? It is a square sort of structure of yellow stone, with two wings. The dreamer emphasizes the fact that it is built of yellow stone and says that it reminds him of an administration building near the desert in Egypt, save that there, there was no garden. My patient had read *The Golem,* and I have told you that this dream is closely related to the end of that story, which I have translated for you, and in which there is such a building, representing the ultimate goal of the road. The gate is made out of a figure of Osiris with the head of a hare. Osiris is really never represented with the head of a hare. That has been invented by Meyrink, whether consciously or unconsciously we cannot know. There is something peculiar about this image that

Meyrink may be unconscious of. While Osiris is never represented with the head of a hare, his adversary, Set, the Egyptian devil, is represented with the head of an animal with long ears. Some say that it is the head of a hare, some that it is an ass, others that it is the head of an okapi (a kind of antelope recently discovered in the Congo, now quite rare, but possibly in earlier times more widely distributed). In antiquity it was associated with the ass. There is a Roman legend that the Jews worshipped the head of an ass in Jerusalem. This was because the Jews were opposed to the worship of Osiris, so it was assumed that they worshipped Set his enemy. Then there is a picture of the mock Christ in the military academy in Rome,[3] a rough drawing of a crucifix on the wall done in a very funny fashion. The figure on the cross was depicted with an ass's head, and the inscription in bad Greek runs: "Thus the young officer Alexandros is worshipping his God." It is making fun of Jesus as the God of the Jews having an ass's head.

Set is the Egyptian devil, the evil opponent of the sun-god Ra. Osiris is really a very old god, later superseded by Ra. It happened once, when Osiris was very old, that as he was walking over the earth, he suddenly complained of a pain in his eye. When his son Horus asked him what he had seen, he said, "I saw a black pig." "Then," said Horus, "you have seen Set." Horus took out his own eye and gave it to Osiris to restore his sight, with the fatal result, however, that Osiris became the judge of the dead in the underworld and Horus was the rising god. This is all symbolic of the second part of human existence. While we have no actual texts about it, it is quite clear that the eye of Horus leads directly to Christ. Early Catholic teaching mentioned Isis and Horus as anticipations of Mary and Christ. Horus is the "healer," he heals the old god by giving him his own eye (which always means vision, view, teaching). Horus is also the god of the Mysteries; he is generally represented in the centre of the picture with his four sons in the four corners, one with a human head, the other three with animal heads. This absolutely coincides with the Christian representations of the four Evangelists, three as animal figures and one human, the lion, ox, eagle, and the angel. The four Evangelists surrounding Christ in the centre form the Christian mandala; Ho-

[3] See *Symbols of Transformation*, CW 5, plate XLIII: graffito from the wall of the Imperial Cadet School, Palatine, Rome.

rus and his sons make the Egyptian mandala.⁴ These mandalas are individuation symbols. The old mystical meaning of Christ was the perfect man who was the realization of the gnostic Adam Kadmon,⁵ the Primordial Man, lifted up and perfected to the most perfect man.

This is a lengthy introduction to the gate made of the statue of Osiris with the head of Set, the coming together of Osiris and Set, thus making a union of opposites; but all this belongs to the interpretation of the dream, so what do you assume about the building now? Have you any idea? The interesting thing is that it is expressed in a very banal way, as a public administration building. One cannot associate any individuality with such a building, impersonal like a hotel or barracks. It has a social value, it is a centre for many people. It serves a multitude, and many people live in it, streaming in and out of it.

Mr. Gibb: It is a symbol for himself.

Dr. Jung: One would assume that the symbol for himself would be individual. Why is it so utterly impersonal?

Dr. Bertine: He probably has a special idea of himself and has to come at it through something that contains all the common human elements, as a compensation for the wrong idea.

Dr. Jung: True, it is a compensation for the wrong idea regarding individuation. People assume that the self contains simply the ego personality, "I myself!" So the dream says, "You make a mistake, it is not yourself, it is a public building, a collective institution."

Dr. Schmitz: It is necessary to emphasize the universality of the self, the self contains the whole of collectivity.

Dr. Jung: Yes, we all instinctively make that mistake; when we speak of "self" we mean to say "I myself." Many people think individuation is selfish and egotistical, but far from it. If you do not exist the crowd does not exist. There is no ocean without the drop of water. The whole of the Sahara does not exist without every grain of sand. Provided you are a good grain of sand you make the Sahara. The individual, besides having the quality of

⁴ Concerning the symbols of the four evangelists and the four sons of Horus, see above, 6 Feb. 1929, n. 3.

⁵ Concerning the multiple aspects of Adam Kadmon as Jung later interpreted them, see *Mysterium Coniunctionis*, CW 14, par. 44 and other refs. in the index, s.v. "Adam Kadmon."

eternity, is "smaller than small though greater than great." This dream compensates his individual error that the self is the ego.

In the philosophy of Swedenborg (whom most of you would not consider a philosopher) there is the teaching of the greatest man, the *Homo maximus*, in whose body we are all like cells. Some of us inhabit his soul, some his eyes, some his brain, so we all contribute to make him as a whole. People with good brains would live in his brain, those with good eyesight would be hunters perhaps, making his eyes. Even the genitalia were not left out, by which he explains certain peculiar temperaments. This is Swedenborg's doctrine of the *correspondentia*,[6] but these ideas remained in a metaphysical concretization. They were never fully evolved psychologically. They got stuck on the way to consciousness.

The dreamer says that this building gave him a peculiar impression of being a prison, and his association is "the body is the prison of the soul."

Dr. Bertine: Doesn't that explain the feeling of "being caught" when people are themselves? It is the net of the Gnostics.

Dr. Jung: I should say that is a very typical example. When people come to themselves they expect a peculiar liberation, to be free from responsibilities and from vices and virtues, but in reality it is quite different. It is like a trap, you suddenly fall into a hole. "Hang it all!" you say, and there you are, where you belong. We are all like a little liver cell that has wandered away from the place where it belongs. The little liver cell escapes and wanders through all the tissues. When he finds the brain, he says, "This is a nice high place, there is good air here" but his neighbours say, "Get out, you are no good here," so the little cell is pushed out and it wanders along to the lungs but the same thing happens there. It says, "The world is very hard, nobody understands me." If it understood itself it would know that it didn't belong there! Finally it wanders along through the tortuous passages of the blood vessels into the liver and there it falls into a hole, a fatal catastrophe. The little cell says, "Damn it, most unsuitable place, how did I get here?"

---

[6] Emanuel Swedenborg (1688-1772), Swedish philosopher and religious writer. The doctrine of *correspondentia*, much favoured by the mediaeval philosophers, is related to the classical "sympathy of all things." Jung regarded it as a forerunner of his concept of synchronicity; see "Synchronicity: An Acausal Connecting Principle" (1952), CW 8, par. 924. For *homo maximus*, see "Paracelsus" (1929), CW 15, par. 12.

But God says, "Hold it fast," and it turns out to be a liver cell! This is what you might call individuation! So the worst trap is the body. We have all been taught that our minds and other virtues are wings we put on, so we get to flying about above ourselves, and we live as if the body did not exist. This happens often with intuitives, with everybody in fact. The body appears to us as a most serious obstacle. It is heavy, and we have a feeling of helplessness about it, as though it were a terrific impediment. Through our mediaeval Christian education the body has gotten a bad name. The hole which one falls into is through the body, and its bodily limitations; then one accuses the body, and the body says "but this *is* you." All this is expressed by the prison, therefore the dreamer's association is "The body is the prison of the soul." The soul, in contrast to the body, is that winged thing that is free to fly above the earth. Here again he mentions that the sun is burning hot, that it is burning up the whole place. That heat is characteristic of the whole situation. This man has lived for many years in the tropics, and he knows the danger of the African sun.

Dr. Deady: His mind is in danger by sun-stroke. He would have to give up something of his intellectual attitude. The unknown thing he is going into is dangerous, the collective unconscious material.

Dr. Jung: I should rather think of the extraordinary *intensity* of the African sun. It is his association with the problem, he feels that he is labouring under a strain of extraordinary intensity. Thus when we get into a difficult situation we say we "get into hot water." The sun is painful, so he tries to escape it by monkey tricks. He seeks the shade, while the woman and the boy walk on the road in the full glare of the sun. When the dream speaks of the intense sun it means an intense situation, that is, much libido is involved. This man happens to be well aware of Egyptian mythology, so we might make a poetic interpretation and say that the building is heated up by the eye of the merciless God. That he is in the presence of the divinity is surely in his unconscious mind. This is again a quality of individuation which we should not fail to see. The individual wielding power, who thought he was all of the ocean, who thought he was the whole of the Sahara, is reduced by individuation to a drop of water, to a grain of sand. At that moment of hopeless smallness and futility of existence he constellates the idea of universality. The most supreme thing, the greatest idea, has always been called God. The smallest power is always confronted with the greatest power, the smallest space with the infinite, so always the inner experience of individuation is what the mystics called "the experience of God." That is a psychological fact and it is why the process of individuation has always been appreciated as the most valuable and important thing in life. It is the only thing that brings any lasting satisfaction to a man. Power, glory, wealth, mean nothing in comparison. These things are external and therefore futile. The really important things are within. It is more important to me that I am happy than that I have the external reason for happiness. Rich people should be happy, but often they are not, they are bored to death; therefore it is ever so much better for a man to work to produce an inner condition that gives him an inner happiness. Experience shows that there are certain psychological conditions in which man gets eternal results. They have something of the quality of eternity, of timelessness, they have the quality of reaching beyond man. The have a divine quality and yield all that satisfaction which man-made things do not.

Now we come to the second part of the dream. You will remember that the gate is locked, and apparently there is no way to get in except by climbing over the bars, cheating. Locked means not easy of access; one is not meant to enter right away. There is a sort of porch or lodge at the entrance to the gate. The dreamer sees within the gate an old man with ragged clothes. His arms are outstretched, and he is quite immobile, so it is doubtful whether he is dead or alive. In his associations the dreamer says that such a lodge is quite the usual thing, for the porter of such a house. With the *old man*, in his rigid posture, he associated a yogi in the yoga state of abstraction, what he calls complete introspection, even to the point of disregarding his own body. The dreamer says that such a state is unsympathetic to him. What would your conclusion be in regard to the figure of the old man?

Mr. Gibb: His interest in his former theosophical studies is not quite dead.

Dr. Jung: Yes, the old man surely represents to his former theosophical studies, the fakir stunts and philosophy which tend to get people out of their bodies. That was one of the reasons why the dreamer came to analysis, he was involved to a certain extent. The picture is not inviting at all, and as a matter of fact the old man disappears from the dream at this point, he plays no further role.

This is a sort of intermezzo in the progress of unconscious thought. The old man might evoke pictures in the unconscious of a yoga philosopher who would symbolize an individuation process, for the yogis have worked out a philosophy of "the way." So naturally the picture comes in here as he approaches the gate, it might be in this way the gate could be opened. But when you find the porter in a state of coma he cannot open the gate. It is useless to call to him, he is removed from his body in a trance, he is not a good door-keeper. Obviously the desire of the dreamer to get inside the garden is very great, apparently it is evident to him that he must get in by *any* means. He sees a child of eight years or so inside the gate in the garden—the Arab child who is mocking at the dreamer, the woman, and the little boy. What about that child? The man's association is that he is just an ordinary street urchin, such a child as one sees hanging around a porter's lodge, one of the many children of the porter's relations all living together while the owner is away. You must imagine that child is not very attractive, he is dirty and ragged, with inflamed eyes from trachoma. Probably he has eczema, sleeps on dirt-heaps, and is covered with lice and fleas.

Dr. Schmitz: Can he be a Puer Aeternus in a negative form?

Dr. Jung: Well, it is not certain whether the child is a boy or a girl. In a later dream there is a similar child, a girl, but with this child he is not certain, though we have another clue which is far more valuable.

Miss Chapin: The Arab child is a parallel to the porter at the gate, but in a youthful form.

Dr. Jung: Yes, surely. The old man cannot open the gate, while the child can, but he is such a dirty little urchin. You see such children by the score in that country,[7] and they are a plague like flies. Why is the young guardian of the gate presented in such an unattractive way?

Mr. Dell: He is the humble, very unattractive first beginning, a sort of hermaphroditic being.

Dr. Jung: Yes, the dreamer wishes to open the gate and walk right in, but here is this dirty little boy when he enters the final goal. The door is opened not by an angel with lovely golden wings, but by a dirty little urchin! What would you expect when you come up to Paradise?

---

[7] Jung had visited North Africa in 1920. See *MDR*, ch. IX, part i, and Appendix III.

Prof. Schmaltz: This is the humiliation he must undergo. He is not a nice man but a dirty little boy.

Dr. Jung: Yes, do you know what that means in the Orient— nasty, dirty little children? Christ tells us "except ye become as little children."[8] He didn't speak of clean little children in school in those days, but of these same filthy children in the street, just as Christ saw them.

Miss Howells: Far away from stained-glass windows.

Dr. Jung: When you have to pass over the bridge, sharp as a knife-blade, narrow as a hair, you meet all your sins, or all your virtues. Since this man is very virtuous he will meet all his sins, so a nasty little brat of a child opens the gate for him. If he does not accept his low-down condition, he will surely not enter Paradise, he will not take this step towards individuation. But he jumps over the gate and climbs into Paradise, "taking the Kingdom of Heaven by storm";[9] the way of intuitive thought. What about that?

Dr. Gilman: Monkey tricks.

Dr. Schmitz: The intuitive way.

Dr. Jung: As soon as he is inside, the woman and the boy are there too. The woman and the boy are a part of himself, his psychological family. As soon as the dreamer jumps into the garden the child begins to shout that he is not allowed to enter. As he approaches the building, he sees some new pieces of furniture exposed to the hot sunshine, and among them is a washstand in which the mirror is lacking; the frame is there, but no mirror. The dreamer's association is that these pieces of furniture are all in very bad taste, cheap and common, with nothing individual about them. Obviously they have just been unpacked and are waiting to be stored in the house. This must refer to a recent happening.

Dr. Bertine: I should think it means his domestic affairs. The furniture lacks a mirror, so that he cannot see himself at all.

Dr. Jung: Yes, there is no mirror. The intellect is often called a mirror. As the mirror is lacking in the frame so insight is not there.

Prof. Schmaltz: This man is very enterprising, so he has sent his furniture on ahead, being quite sure that he will be admitted.

Dr. Jung: He was particularly excited because the new furniture is left out in the sun where the wood will be injured. As he is not

[8] Matthew 18:3.

[9] Cf. Matthew 11:12: ". . . the kingdom of heaven suffereth violence, and the violent take it by force."

admitted, the furniture is not admitted. It is a parallel, it is left outside, and it is in the same position as he would be if he had not climbed over the fence. Furniture cannot climb over the fence, so it stays in the hot sun. It surely belongs to him, and he has no doubt that the place belongs to him, so if the gate is not opened he slips right over. One could call this enterprising! He has the idea that he is a very respectable and righteous man, and when he comes to the gate of Heaven, he will be admitted right away into the drawing-room and he will expect that God himself will receive him, but there is only the little dirty child. His furniture which he has sent to Paradise has been left outside in the sun and it is very cheap stuff. The mirror is not in the washstand yet (unripe fruit again). In this enterprise of taking the "Kingdom of Heaven by storm," he makes some very disagreeable discoveries about himself. In the last part of the dream, before he came to the furniture, he paid no attention to the Arab child, he practically stepped over him, and now he seems to have some resentment in the dream, he evidently realizes that things are going wrong. He says, "Here is that damn little urchin again! I must catch him." He binds him with a rope. The child cries out, and as he doesn't want to have too much fuss he lets him go again. What does binding the child with a rope mean?

Dr. Schmitz: He is torturing his own soul.

Dr. Jung: But you must take only his associations. He says, "It is as though I were showing that child that I am not afraid of it, and that I can suppress it, even if it does belong to that house." He obviously wants to incapacitate that child who says, "You cannot enter."

Mrs. Crowley: He wants to suppress that side of himself, his inferior side.

Dr. Jung: Yes, at all costs he must suppress that side of himself, this is his unpresentable side. No one can live in a country like Africa without absorbing something of it. Its uncivilized character gets into and influences the unconscious, so afterwards it may be very difficult to get rid of the relatively primitive element and adapt to civilization again. Europeans who have lived for a long time in the East discover this. Now that our dreamer is living in Europe again, this uncivilized element will cause no end of trouble to him. He tries to bind it but it is so difficult to handle that he has to let it go. You will see in later dreams how this side of himself comes up.

Mrs. Sigg: He must not identify with the child from Heaven, or with the dirty child from earth.

Dr. Jung: There is no question of identification in this dream. It might come up later, but now he is most emphatically disidentified.

Mr. Gibb: Was he before a little proud of the child of the anima, so this child is a compensation?

Dr. Jung: He has the pride of the white man, which would disidentify him.

Dr. Deady: His struggle is with what the boy represents. He tries to bind his conflict.

Dr. Jung: Yes, but he simply does not want that child to run about free, "I will show that child." This shows the power of the white man in Africa. If a Negro at the gate of a house should say, "No admittance," the white man would say, "You go to Hell, I enter." After the intermezzo with the child he comes to the actual door of the house and discovers the plate with the name of Dr. Bauer. His association is Dr. Faust or the two last words in the inscription from Meyrink's *Golem:* "Aur Bocher." Dr. Kirsch has looked it up so we can get the whole inscription. It is a sequence of cabalistic words partly unintelligible. The meaning would be community, or power, then an untranslatable word, and then the "light of the disciple." These are of course words and concepts which play a great role in the book. The "disciple" is the initiate led up the path to individuation, the "light" is illumination. It is quite possible that it is a quotation from some magic book in a sort of Hebrew. The Gnostics fabricated any number of them in faulty Syriac, Aramaic, Hebrew, and Greek, even inventing artificial words. These inscriptions were very powerful, because nobody understood the words.

"Power" and "community" play a great role in this dream and show how closely it was associated with the reading of *The Golem.* Let us look at the context of that quotation. It comes at the end of a series of exciting visions, during which the hero has lost consciousness. He fell into the bottomless depths, and finally he feels that his feet have touched bottom. There he sees a group of bluish figures who form a ring around him. They all wear golden hieroglyphs on their breasts and each one of the figures holds a red seed-pod in its hand. (He had refused to accept a handful of seed-pods and even struck the hand of the phantom who offered them, thus scattering the pods.) Now these figures hold up the pods again.

There is a storm with lightning flashes. He feels feeble and terrified, and he hears a voice say: "It is the Night of Protection" (the night of the exodus, when the Israelites were protected against the Egyptians). Then someone in the circle says: "He whom you seek is not here." (This was said of Christ when the women came to the tomb and found it empty.) Then the figure says something he cannot understand, he only gets the word "Henoch." Suddenly one of the figures in the circle comes up to him and points to the hieroglyphs on his breast, and when he reads the inscription, he feels that this is the end and falls into a deep sleep.[10]

Obviously these visions are a series of mandalas, not such as you would draw, but they could be danced or acted. Forming a magic circle means individuation. The offering of the seeds is just like the story of the crocodile that would eat the child whichever way the mother answered.[11] The seeds are the same thing, a sort of fatal question. So whether you say "I accept" or "I do not accept," you do not know what will happen either way, because you don't know what it means. The hero in *The Golem* refused the seeds, so they come up again in a threatening form. The meaning is that the seeds are his various parts. We consist of a lot of particles which must come together as in the magic cauldron or melting-pot where all the dissociated parts of our personality are welded together. So the hero is asked, "Do you accept all the grains as parts of yourself?" He answers, "No, I don't," but he cannot refuse, because these grains *are* himself. The result is that they come up against him, they form a magic circle around him, and a voice says, "The one you seek is not here." Meyrink knows what "Messiah" meant to the Cabbalist: "The one that unites, that makes perfect, is not here." Because he has refused the parts of his personality, the parts are now standing up against him. Then one of the spectres comes up and shows him the way of enlightenment. Undoubtedly the second part means that he is a disciple who receives illumination.

Our dreamer is in the same situation. He is also one who has

[10] Cf. *The Golem*, tr. Pemberton, p. 151.

[11] This "quaestio crocodilina" is given in "On the Psychology of the Trickster-Figure" (1954), CW 9 i, par. 486, n. 19: "A crocodile stole a child from its mother. On being asked to give it back to her, the crocodile replied that he would grant her wish if she could give a true answer to his question: 'Shall I give the child back?' If she answers 'Yes,' it is not true, and she won't get the child back. If she answers 'No,' it is again not true, so in either case the mother loses the child."

refused the grains, he does not want to bring together all his compartments, he wants to force his way into Paradise. So he is in the position of the disciple who must still learn. He is not a master, and he cannot enter the place where Dr. Faustus lives, because in a way Dr. Faustus would be the complete man, the initiated one. He must go to the next door and humbly ring the bell (quite unlike his monkey tricks and climbing over the fence and catching people). That in plain language would mean "Well, that was a bit quick, I had better go to Dr. Jung and ring his bell." He had better confess that he is only a disciple and has still something to learn. This is the last attempt of the patient to solve his problem in a magic way, by yoga or any other theosophical means. From now on he takes an entirely different road. In the next dream he takes an auto trip to Poland, he travels with a man who is a sort of acquaintance of his, famous as being a great *coureur de femmes*, a boulevardier. His associations with Poland are interesting also. In the dream after that he goes into a poor little hut in Africa where there is a crocodile. It is just like Parsifal, who, having come by chance to see the Holy Grail and being then quite immature, is turned away; he goes out into the world and after a long time and many adventures comes back to the Grail. So this man goes back, in a way, to the little urchin, the Arab devil, as though he had to assimilate the thing most disagreeable to him, the weakness and humility of his more or less primitive feeling. Therefore he first goes to a country of lesser civilization, Poland with its disorder and corruption, then he goes even further back, to a primitive hut inhabited by a crocodile, into the mouth of hell, into danger, for crocodiles occasionally eat people! From now on the dreams deal with the most inferior and rejected part of his personality, his inferior man. Only when he can deal with his inferior part and unite his two sides can he come to the whole man, and take the place that this dream hints at.

Editorial Note: For chronological sequence, the number 18 has been assigned to a dream of 28 July 1929, during the interval between the spring and autumn terms. The dreamer brought it to Jung on 21 November, and Jung discussed it during the lecture of 11 December 1929.

WINTER TERM

First Part: October / December 1929

LECTURE I

9 October 1929

Dr. Jung:

Ladies and Gentlemen: I am going to continue the series of dreams that we worked with last year, with the purpose of demonstrating their continuity, and the development which shows itself in the unfolding of the symbolism in the patient's unconscious. Each one seems to be a psychological entity, the meaning of which may not show at the moment. They are little dramas, each with its preamble, dramatic situation, catastrophe, and solution, and yet somehow static. But if we take a series of dreams we find there is movement, a circular or rather a spiral movement. Moreover, it gives one a much greater feeling of certainty and safety to know that a wrong guess may be corrected or verified in the dreams that follow; and one is able to get a much better impression of dream analysis when one can follow through a series of the same person.

I must give you some idea of the dreamer himself, since some of you were not here last term. He is a European but has lived a great part of his life in exotic countries.[1] He is a very intelligent man, he has had a successful business career, and has now retired and handed the business over to his brother-in-law, but is still the nominal head of the office. He is 47 years old, is married, and has a nice family, nice children, and a nice fortune. His problem is the typical problem of that age. If he were a Frenchman he would retire and go fishing, that would be the normal and wise thing to do. For after 45, things become rather difficult. Depressions occur at that age, usually because these men have not reached what they had proposed to themselves to reach, they compare the reality with their ambition and it is disappointing. They think they are unable

---

[1] See below, p. 326, where it is first mentioned that the dreamer was "not a born European, he was born in Africa."

to accomplish more than they already have, and a vague melancholy settles down on them; they begin to give way. One sees the same thing with simple people; the man may take to drink, mildly or otherwise, and he often becomes slightly effeminate, while the woman grows more masculine and takes on the responsibility; often she starts a small business very successfully, perhaps a shop, and he becomes a kind of employee of hers. This peculiar change begins to take place after forty, really, as though the wind were taken out of a man's sails; he doesn't know how or why, but it is a subtle fact. So normally the beginning of the new phase of life is characterized by a sort of revolution that may be slow or acute. There is often a sense of resentment against life, because either one has not accomplished what one might or one has not lived what one might have lived. Then people are apt to do something stupid in business, or, more probably, they fall in love, for that is the side they have neglected. Anatole France speaks of the "Demon of Midday," a sort of demoniacal possession through love.[2]

When time brought this man a chance, he found terrible gaps in his intellectual and feeling life. He had tried to be the respectable married man, but he could not live in that ice-cellar for ever—his wife eternally frigid, not interested in sex and he not too keen about it. They lived together in a kind of insulated condition. This lack led him into adventures with demimondaines, but all those things grew less and less interesting, and he said to himself: this is not the real thing. He is a refined type and expects a more complete experience, not only sex and money, but love, a higher type of love and real devotion which is not in such women—really a most decent tendency. But even if out for something decent, he was up against our institutions; in the case of real love, it is more dangerous, one is confronted with impossibilities in that line of life. So he turned away from that and landed in theosophy, he dreamed himself into an artificial world of images, a stupid place where one can lose oneself in all sorts of heavens, and since it was a substitute, it was like flirting with a sort of spiritual cocotte, and he got very tired of it.

---

[2] The phrase "le demon de midi" could not be found in Anatole France's writings, but Paul Bourget published a novel of that title (1914), whose theme is the ravages of love on the psyche of a man of middle age. The phrase derives from *demonium meridianum* in the Vulgate, Ps. 90:6 = A.V., Ps. 91:6, where it is rendered as the "destruction that wasteth at noonday."

Then he became mildly neurotic and came to consult me, not really for treatment. He had come to psychoanalysis through his studies, and thought it might be better "dope" than theosophy, for he had heard of the Freudian sublimation idea by which nature is transformed by magic into playing the piano or living a saintly life; one thinks in a marvellous way and sex is wiped out. I destroyed some of his illusions, the only thing I could do for him, but I told him I could not solve his problem for him. If I had told him to go on with any number of women, he not only could not do it but he would soon testify that it did not work. He had tried the spiritual way of theosophy with its promise of seven heavens and was disgusted, so I said to him, "We will see what your nature, physical as well as spiritual, will produce. You have to be patient, as I have to be. There is no prescription."

His dreams have shown that the unconscious has begun to weave a sort of pattern, a peculiar tortuous way, zigzagging through the ups and downs of the human psyche, slowly insinuating certain symbols of ancient cults, through which the mental attitudes of men have in the past been transformed—so the reports say.

One dream, for instance, contained very important individuation or rebirth symbolism. But whenever a dream promised a step forward, he had a regression; when he should have reached up and taken, he withdrew. He climbed up a hill near the sea, the waves dashed up and made it impossible for him to stay there. Every time that he tried to do something definite, to launch his particular psychology in life—in his case, it would mean an attempt at an understanding with his wife—each time that he tried to talk to her, he recoiled. And each time I had to admit that there seemed to be very good reasons for it, that it was not mere cowardice. I have not met his wife and it may be that something in her is the cause; there may be some fundamental incompatibility there. There is an abysmal gap in sex psychologies. We are still in a primitive state of *participation mystique* in the relation between the sexes; we have not discovered that only different things can enter relationship. I had to tell him to hold himself in suspense and see what would come, no matter how long it might take.

Dr. Deady: Are you still working with him?

Dr. Jung: I have not seen him since last July, but he then seemed to be nearing a solution. He approaches it in spirals. But he must have more psychological insight and more confidence to stand upon it. His progress shows in a more positive relation to the work. It is not quite certain whether psychology is a truth to him, whether he can admit of psychic reality as he admits of the truth of the books on this table. When he has risen to that degree of certainty, he will be able to launch himself upon it. It is a very long way for him. He is a sensation type, worldly, a man of the stock-market, and it is hard for such a man to take as real what cannot be seen with eyes nor touched with hands. The way is full of risks and dangers, for he might get panicky, and it is possible that there might be something remote, some latent trouble in his unconscious, like freight which had gotten loose; and that might lead to a local schizophrenia, a piece of ancestral stuff which doesn't fit in his psychology. This is frequent and makes work difficult and dangerous.

The dream today follows the dream in which he is approaching that building.[3] There is a sort of avenue leading up to it, and the building has a symbolic value, as the mansion of the Superior Man (Dr. Faustus). It was a more or less positive dream, where one might expect a decided movement forward.

Dream [19]

He is travelling in an automobile in Poland with an acquaintance, not a friend, a Mr. B., and another man whom he doesn't know. They suddenly discover that they have gone too far south and must return to the right road by an indirect way, that they cannot get back to the right road directly but must make a detour on a small country road, so narrow and bad that it is not even indicated on the special maps. But they arrive eventually and then drive furiously over a beautiful, broad straight road. They make a halt, and when they start to go on, the motor refuses to move. They find a mechanic, a short corpulent man who speaks with a South German accent, who finds that the trouble is in the magneto—the revolving part had exploded. He is able, however, to mend it and it works again.

Associations: Mr. B. is a *bon viveur*, a German business man, very interested in the fine arts, with a great circle of artistic friends. The dreamer does not like him, he is not sympathetic.

[3] The dream is reported and discussed above, pp. 274-79, 289-95.

About the third man, the *stranger*, he knows nothing at all.

Concerning the *journey to Poland*, he is reminded that soon after the war one of his business acquaintances came back from Poland and told him that good cigarettes were so rare that for a few one could have a cocotte.

He is unable to say anything about *too far South*, but that discovery leads to the association that, as *bon viveur*, he is not on the right road, and therefore it is necessary to take another road which is not even indicated on the map, a new individual way, unforeseen. This indirect way turns out to be excellent and straight. But it seems dangerous to stop, and he concludes that it made the magneto explode.

He says that the *mechanic* who happens to be there is the motor doctor and identifies him with me. His association is that he had heard a lecture that I had given and was surprised that my German had no accent, as I come from Basel, where the dialect is very pronounced. He says that the little mechanic is in every way a contrast to me, and yet as I am the doctor, it must refer to me. The *magneto*, he says, is the heart of the mechanism. One could compare it to the heart in the human organism, because it effects the rhythmical ignition without which the motor does not work. Now what is your interpretation of this dream?

Dr. Schmaltz: It is like the one before, in which he tried to go right in, so sure of himself that he sent his furniture on ahead where it was left out in the hot sun; he was not allowed to enter, so he tried clever tricks. Now he goes the other way, in spite of the dream saying that he must take the muddiest country road where the dialect is most pronounced.

Dr. Jung: You very aptly put yourself into the mood of the dream, as one should always do. Now, why must he take the dirty little country road? In the dream before, he was toiling in the hot sun. In this dream he is not received, apparently, when he goes south, so he swings over to the north, he goes to Poland. This is a peculiar movement within the four cardinal points of the horizon. Where did we encounter this same symbolism of the cardinal points?

Dr. Howells: It was in the steamroller dream.

Dr. Jung: Quite so. And you remember the drawing that illustrated it, the mandala, the magic circle. The mandala plays a great role in Eastern cults, used as a psychological aid to individuation. I have told you that it could just as well be danced as drawn; in

India there is not only the static mandala, like the Tibetan, but also a mandala dance. A patient once brought me a drawing of a mandala, telling me that it was a sketch for certain movements along lines in space. She danced it for me, but most of us are too self-conscious and not brave enough to do it. It was a conjuration or incantation to the sacred pool or flame in the middle, the final goal, to be approached not directly but by the stations of the cardinal points, symbolizing the way in which man tries to reach his goal eventually. So this dream belongs to the movements of the mandala our patient had drawn several months before. He is now fulfilling the movement from south to north; he went south, then comes the recoil, and he goes north. Usually the dance is done in pairs of opposites, north, south, west, east, and at intersections of the horizons.

There are three forms of mandala:

(1)   A static design, the magic circle. This underlay, for instance, the rites of the Roman city foundation. The first circle was drawn with a plow around the sacred precincts. In the centre was the *fundus*, a sort of storehouse for the fruits of their fields. In China, that is called the space of the former heavens, the house of the ancestors. Psychologically, the central point of a human personality is the place where the ancestors are reincarnated.

(2)   The mandala dance, *Mandala nritya*. Or the *circumambulatio*,[4] by means of movement.

(3)   The mandala in time, the performance through life.

The Pueblo Indians have rites in which they follow the sun's course for five hours, beginning with the rising sun and ending with the contemplation of the North at midday. By doing this, they are purified and become true children of their sun-father. This is not a dance, it is rather a mandala in time, symbolizing the fact that if you live it as you dance it, you purify yourself and return to the original condition, which Christian language calls being the child of God. One becomes the child of God only by carrying the cross; if the life is lived without neurotic nonsense, it will be seen as the accomplishment of the mandala in time. The dreamer foreshadows his life in the steamroller-mandala dream. One often finds directions in dreams, going north, south, etc., but not always as

---

4 A Latin term that Jung used to denote walking around and around a centre, gradually approaching it in a spiral.

obvious as this. It is a principle in life, not only in the structure of the unconscious. The whole course of the Christian life is symbolized by the carrying of the cross. In the cult of Attis, a living tree was carried to the cave which represented the womb of the mother, exactly the same idea as in the cult of Mithras, who carried the Sacred Bull, the burden of his life.[5]

One could say that after the patient's Africa dream he came from the south to the north, to Poland, but with a certain regressive movement to the south. Now he must return and choose a new way, not even indicated on the map.

Poland in his dream is characterized by the association that cocottes are so cheap there that you can get one for a few cigarettes. In Africa he was trying to get at the superior man, the most precious thing. Failing in that, he turns to the north and takes the opposite road, the opposite in every way; he takes now the way of the flesh, he is travelling with a *bon viveur* in a country where demimondaines are very cheap. This is to a certain extent a compensation. But the new tendency is undermined in the beginning by the fact that the *bon viveur* is not sympathetic, he doesn't like him. Here is the disgust that his worldly experiences gave him. An interesting fact is that, though in the dream of having gone too far south, he seemed to be seeking something rather high and legitimate, it meant the thing from which he must return. He went too far south, not too far north—the *bon viveur* is not his ideal.

Dr. Deady: He must make a compromise. He must find the middle way. What would it be with that man?

Dr. Jung: It is not entirely revealed. The ideal would be the straight royal road in the centre. This man is a *tricheur*, he is playing a game. If south, he is apt to be a bit dirty. If north, he makes concessions to idealism. If you are travelling with a *bon viveur*, it is no good to pretend that you are shocked and play the idealist.

Dr. Schmaltz: That is like the dream before, where he climbs trees to escape the hot, dusty road. Monkey tricks! He tries to take the mud out of sex, instead of behaving like other people who go to Poland. He does not go through with the business. The dream slyly tried to show this to him.

---

[5] Attis was the son-lover of the Phrygian mother-goddess Cybele, and the pine-tree played an important part in his cult; see *Symbols of Transformation*, pars, 659ff. Mithras, in the Persian cult devoted to him, carried the Bull to the cave; ibid., par. 460.

Dr. Jung: There is no use in telling that man he is a coward. He is simply not aware of the fact that he is playing tricks on himself all along the road. He is not a coward, he is very decent, but he brings in his idealism to save himself from the painful sensation of being a black sheep. It is too painful to be a lost sheep. Everybody has the tendency to seek good motives for their behaviour, instead of saying: I have been a pig. One rationalizes on the good side instead of calling things by their right names. People can say that they are great sinners—we have been educated to the idea of the joy in Heaven over the repentant sinner,[6] brought up to think that one is a fine chap if one can repent. It gives one a thrill. But the point is to see exactly where the trick lies, for it is quite unconscious and subtle and escapes one's observation.

There are very subtle spiritual sins. It takes painstaking analysis to show where the real sin takes place. Such a man can be educated to truth and honesty if one takes the trouble to show him all his little ways. He is in bad company but keeps an air of respectability—a sort of angel risking himself in Hell in order to paint the devils white. It is like a man trying to convert a prostitute; he eventually lands in slime, worse than the man who goes to a prostitute with a square purpose. The dream shows him that he has to correct that. He must take an indirect way, not even on the map. Up to the present moment, that man has remained within the frame of respectability, mildly protesting, squeezing out of the situation. But the dream shows *that* to be immorality—a funny kind! The little road is not on the map. It is the indirect way. Now what would be the way out?

Dr. Harding: A map is a collective symbol.

Dr. Jung: Yes, the map is the official way. You don't get out of such a situation in a collective way, saving appearances. The way out is the individual way. He should judge the situation individually. He should say to himself: having joined that trip, is it decent to skin out of it by idealism? Either you say you have made a mistake and retrace your steps, or you go ahead and do as the others do. Then Heaven has gained one good sinner at least. "There is more joy in Heaven over one sinner," etc. But you see his expectation of the individual road is an expectation of fear rather—an awful swamp, on no map. But to his amazement it turns out to be a

6 Cf. Luke 15:7.

beautiful road, a straight road, where he can move with rapidity. He is not the first man who has travelled that road. Perhaps it is a little oblique. A straight road would be to go farther north, deeper into that kind of experience. Now when the unconscious uses such an inviting road as a symbol, what does it mean? Why is it so beautiful? Always when the dream shows an inviting thing, it is to lure the instinct of man, to attract his libido. The beauty of it overcompensates for any doubt as to its being an individual road. What does that mean, the individual road?

Mrs. Crowley: His way.

Dr. Jung: In that situation, it would mean his way, the only way in which he can deal with it. But it includes something generally overlooked. When you look ahead and see a road leading to the left when you expect it to lead to the right, either you go to the left with doubts or don't go at all because it seems to lead where you didn't mean to go. Now that road to the left seems to keep on for an interminable distance because one can't see beyond, where the road turns to the right and up to the goal. This man is quite likely to think the road to the north is the wrong one, whereas the way might lead via Poland, make a curve, and eventually come to the right goal. The individual way leads in directions that seem absolutely wrong. One doesn't realize when one swings to the left that left exhausts itself and swings to the right again. Our roads still keep to the original trails. The Swiss trail is a long wave-like curve. When I was with my safari in Africa, I found that it was exceedingly irritating to follow the bearers at a fast pace, for the white man's idea is to walk straight ahead. But one finds that the curve of the safari is really much less tiring; they do about six kilometres an hour, swinging around the curves very easily.

The individual way is a peculiar serpentine way, and that is the way of the dream. If you could only let things go, you would see that wrong would be exhausted and right would assert itself. That man does not trust the primitive man in himself, it is difficult to trust the unconscious law. He always tries to interrupt with his rationalism. He should make the full swing and then he would not lose his consistency, for it is in the hands of nature, and when he has said yes long enough, he will naturally say no. His rationalism is playing a very bad trick on him. As a matter of fact, the serpentine way of the individual is the straightest way he can possibly go.

That is symbolized by the serpentine way of the sun through the Zodiac, and the Zodiacal serpent is Christ, who said: "I am the way."[7] He is the serpent, so in the early Christian church he is the sun, and the signs of the Zodiac, the apostles, are the twelve months of the year.

[7] John 14:6.

LECTURE II

16 October 1929

Dr. Jung:
We will continue our dream of last week. Are there any questions?
If too many people are afraid to ask questions, it produces a static
atmosphere. If you all join in, your co-operation creates a com-
munity of feeling, and this *esprit de corps* is exceedingly important.
An inhibited atmosphere is unfavourable.

We were talking last time, you remember, of that straight road
on which the movement was easy. When the unconscious produces
such a favourable symbol as this beautiful road, the dreamer is
agreeably impressed by it, his libido is attracted, the unconscious
makes it easy for him. But one must be distrustful in such a case;
if one traces that symbol to its conscious counterpart, one may find
that it is nothing agreeable. It may be something that he is afraid
of, something that he dislikes. He is a conventional man, he is afraid
of unconventionality, and that superb road may mean just the thing
that he would not like in reality. When such a symbol turns up,
when something is made so agreeable, painted in such beautiful
colours, it means that the unconscious is trying to make it accept-
able. But, beware!—here we have to be careful. One cannot trust
the unconscious absolutely, one can only say this is what the unconscious would naturally choose. It does not mean, when it states
a condition, that it is necessarily good or advisable, it merely shows
things as they are—important information as to the inclinations of
one's nature.

For example, I will tell you the dream of a man with doubtful
qualities as to his business conduct. His dealings were not permissible, they were even decidedly fraudulent. From the following
dream I drew my conclusions as to his real nature. He was walking
in the street, an ordinary street in his home town, when he noticed
on the opposite sidewalk a very dignified and refined old lady

309

beckoning to him. He did not know her, but he crossed the road, and in a friendly and intimate way she invited him to walk with her and led him to the gate of what was apparently a large garden. The lady stopped there and, to his utter amazement, he saw that it was a tropical garden, full of trees and beauty. She invited him to go in, but for some reason he was seized with fear and tried to withdraw; he had a peculiar feeling about it. But finally he could not resist, she lured him in. It was a nightmare, although it was not obvious why.

He associated the old lady with his own grandmother, whom he loved dearly, so why a nightmare? Of course the garden is a dream garden (he lives in the north), a garden of Paradise, the garden of desire, illusory, referring him to a fantastic world to which his unconscious is inviting him. But why a *grand*-mother, not even the mother? This dream is modelled on the old primitive idea that when the father dies and goes to ghostland, he is just an ordinary ghost; but when his son has a son and he becomes the grandfather, he is no longer an ordinary ghost but a sort of duke in ghostland, he is the grand-father ghost, and the son sacrifices a bull to him. So grand-mother refers to the "great" unconscious, while the mother refers to the "little" unconscious. It is as an ocean to a little bay, or a vast continent to a peninsula. The man was being lured on to the collective unconscious, the land of dreams. Shortly after this dream, he committed a terrible mistake that led him into prison. So if one had told him that the dream was positive because of its good appearance, one would have helped him to disaster. Such a dream can be terribly misleading. One should say, rather: since this is an impossible place, a tropical garden in a non-tropical place, it should not be in reality; you should not live in a dream world that cannot be fulfilled; it is a psychic world, a happy island, but it is the *inner* world. Then only would one give him the proper meaning.

So in this case the road is easy and agreeable, but we must look at the first part of the dream to decide whether the meaning is good or bad. Perhaps it is doubtful. Also, let us see what happens on that road. They stop, and when they want to start again the motor does not work, so they call a mechanic, who finds that the magneto has exploded. One concludes that it would have been better not to have stopped. It is a very awkward thing when the magneto does not work—to come to a standstill after travelling on that road. So it seems to say, why don't you keep right on, go ahead, because if you stop, you will not be able to go on again. Now you remember he says in his associations that the magneto is the heart of the motor. What is that?

Answer: The heart is the feeling, the feeling explodes.

Dr. Jung: But are we right in translating heart by feeling? You see, it is more or less figurative, the heart is the central and essential thing. He doesn't mention the feeling. One speaks of the heart of a thing, even the heart of a town, the central place, but that is not emotional.

Mrs. Fierz: It might be the ego.

Dr. Jung: Picture the situation. You see, he is really driving on the right road. For a moment he doesn't continue on the right way, the individual way, and at that moment the heart explodes. It is a metaphor. The heart may break, we say in German that it splinters, which naturally means an emotional fact. But if you take heart as the central thing, it is not the ego.

Dr. Deady: The heart also means courage. He associates the magneto with a rhythmic principle, integrating all the parts of the motor.

Mrs. Fierz: It is his individuality.

Dr. Jung: Exactly. In psychological terms, it is his individuality, his individual monad, from which all the regulating functions of life take their origin. The individual monad is always contained in the inferior functions, therefore "heart" also means feeling. And here the individuality explodes, giving dissociation. You see, the constituents of personality can dissociate from each other; such and such a person in me can separate from me. Someone with an artistic personality, for instance, who does not fit in with everyday life, has to adapt as best he can, the artistic temperament is just a nuisance; a constituent that is itself a person splits off, and that goes off by itself and forms a second personality which is more or less independent of the central government. So the magneto, the central government principle, can be split into any number of factors, which correspond more or less to the Mendelian units.[1] One's various physical characteristics are inherited from many different ancestors, perhaps from ancestors who lived two or three hundred years ago; certain traits may disappear and then reappear in fam-

[1] The reference is to the system of heredity propounded by the Augustinian monk Gregor Johann Mendel (1822-1884) in 1865 but recognized only in 1900 (the year Jung completed his University education).

ilies; the famous Hapsburg lip is such a unit. And it is the same with the mental constitution. In the Spanish Hapsburgs, there were many cases of insanity, which disappeared entirely and then turned up again two hundred years later. So an individual is a peculiar combination of mental units, ancestral traits, more or less loosely fitted together. As a rule, one begins life thus scattered, and gradually through life one gathers these parts together. People come to me with the greatest illusions concerning themselves, and only slowly do they become aware of their many sides, which are just as important but which are projected. It is as though these constituents of their personality had exploded and were only recognizable through projections: what they see in that person is a part of themselves. It is quite intangible, but during the course of analysis these different parts are reassembled, the object of analysis being to gather them together into one functioning centre.

Here we could say that the heart, the central point, is dissociated immediately when he stops going on the individual way. As long as you go on the individual way, you function as an individual, but if you stop, you dissociate again, for you function only as part of yourself—you instantly drop back into the collective way. This is a regression. This explains why the magneto explodes when the motor is at a standstill; it seems perfectly irrational but psychologically it is true. The pairs of opposites fall asunder. As soon as people come to a standstill, that which has carried them falls apart. Through the stop, it becomes visible that the thing is put together from incompatible parts. Often the standstill comes to pass because the parts can hold together no longer, but also, as in this dream, the thing may split because it no longer functions. That is the case in schizophrenia, which comes about like this: A person has learned a certain way of functioning, and then he comes up against something that he is not up to, though it may be quite easy for another person. For instance, he may have to do military service, or perhaps buy a house. No one would ordinarily go crazy over that, but he does, for the situation demands something that is beyond his level of functioning. He goes to pieces, he instantly dissociates into constituents that become definite people and begin to talk, he then hears voices and has hallucinations.

This condition in the dream must be helped, so an expert is called in, a mechanic, a small, corpulent man who speaks in the South German dialect. The dreamer assures me that the expert would be myself, who must put the magneto together, but the qualities do not apply to me, and he was puzzled that the unconscious should give me such a form. Here again is a case of importance for dream interpretation. Freud would not hesitate to say that this is of course the doctor, disguised by the censor. But he is *not* disguised. Why should the unconscious take the trouble to invent a disguise that doesn't work? Freud would understand that it was an attempt, an indirect way, with the purpose of making me obscure. But why should the unconscious want to conceal the fact? We have absolutely no evidence that the dream tries to disguise the doctor. Rather, the unconscious is emphatic in creating a mechanic who has nothing to do with the doctor. He is just a fellow from South Germany, a man one would find in a garage, who would say, "The Germans know much more than the Swiss!" The obvious conclusion is that the unconscious is trying to convey the idea that the man who puts the magneto together has nothing whatever to do with Dr. Jung, right in the face of the patient's conscious conviction that I am the one who can put him together.

Dr. Deady: He ought to do the job himself.

Dr. Jung: Of course. That man in the dream refers to nobody in the outside world, that is a factor within himself. One of his faculties, his mind for instance, might help him to put his machine together, but this he does not want to see. He always hides behind the fact of his ignorance, he says he is a business man, not a learned man like Dr. Jung. He has shielded himself behind me for a long time. Naturally many things would happen which wouldn't happen to a man like Dr. Jung: he favours that kind of psychology, to let things happen for which he need take no responsibility. He can allow himself so many little indulgences in that penumbra of ignorance. If he admitted that he had the knowledge, he would have to admit the responsibility—make his own efforts to pull himself out of an awkward situation. This part of the dream strengthens his self-confidence, the intimation that he has within himself the man to fix himself.

Dr. Harding: There is one part left out, the third man.

Dr. Jung: Yes, a third whom he doesn't remember, so we must conclude that that constituent also is a dark figure.

Dr. Deady: It would be his shadow, the other side of the dreamer.

Dr. Jung: We cannot be too sure of that.

313

Dr. Harding: There is the man himself, the ego, on the way; the *bon viveur* (perhaps a shadow figure); No. 3; and the mechanic makes the fourth, the completed individual.

Dr. Jung: How would you translate that?

Dr. Deady: The four functions.

Dr. Jung: Yes, the four functions, let us assume. That would give us a clue. Some of you will remember having dreams where the 3 and 4 play a role. It is almost an archetypal situation. There is an example in the second part of *Faust*, a very peculiar passage where the Kabiri appear, bringing from the depths of the sea a strange symbol, "a severe shape."[2] Goethe does not say what it is. The passage is: "There are three, where has the fourth remained?" The Kabiri are identical with the Hindu concept of the unconscious creative forces, the *samsaras*. And they would be the third and the fourth.

In conscious psychology, we know that we can speak of the four functions, ways in which we adapt to a given situation, and we know by experience that people as a rule possess one function that is really differentiated, and that they have some disposition towards an auxiliary function. For instance, take a thinking-sensation type. Such a man knows what he hears and sees. (Not everybody knows that!) Then besides these functions, there is also some consciousness of a third which might serve the superior function; in this case it would be intuition. But what doesn't appear among the conscious functions, or only occasionally as phenomena that one can't control, is in this case *feeling*. It is the last, the unreliable thing, the sore spot, where such a man is inferior, where he receives his shocks and wounds. For thinking and feeling exclude each other because of their contrary nature. When thinking, it is better not to feel, and vice versa, in order that the two shall not upset each other.

Here we have those three, and the fourth that is missing. It is quite possible that the four functions should be represented by four people, like the four sons of Horus, only one having a human head, the other three wholly animal, which would indicate that in the days of the old Egyptians only one function was conscious and three were missing. According to our philosophy intellect is the human-headed one. In our philosophical writings, only thinking

[2] Cf. *Psychology and Alchemy*, par. 203, where "a severe shape" (*ein streng Gebilde*) is translated as "a form severe." The words "There are three, where has the fourth remained?" are not quoted in the text.

has been allowed. Bergson[3] accepts intuition, however, and there is also a philosophy built up on observed facts, that allows sensation. In the progress of civilization, the periphery of consciousness has widened out and gradually included more functions. Goethe, being a modern man, was already aware of three, and asked where is the fourth? In Christianity, there is the Trinity, the three in heaven, and the other missing one is the devil in hell. It is terribly upsetting when he comes up. All these psychological facts express themselves in dogma. The Church says: there are three, and where is the fourth? But please keep away from him!

Therefore it is a problem in dreams to know what to do with No. 4. But here No. 4 is very helpful. When one comes to a standstill with the three, and it is important to know what is going to happen, then intuition is very necessary. Thinking tells you what things mean, feeling tells you what they are worth, sensation tells you what they really are, and intuition tells you the possibilities of a situation. So one can travel ahead with certainty. Here his inferior man, on whom he naturally would look down, comes in as exceedingly helpful. Of course, we can't just say that this mechanic is the devil, and I don't know how the dreamer might feel if I should say that in order to accept this little fellow he must give up certain prejudices. He might feel it to be quite immoral. It would wound his pride to descend to such a level, so he is prevented from assimilating his inferior function. He is navigating in heaven with the three, and No. 4 is in the hot belly of the earth.

Now we have the necessary material to interpret this dream as a whole and to place it in the sequence of dreams. His story, as those of you who have been in the previous seminar know, is the process of individuation. This is, of course, always the object of analysis. The goal is the same but the way is exceedingly different. This is one of the dreams *on his way* that shows him his lack or mistake. The dream before this showed him that he was not up to his goal. He saw his goal and wanted to get at it but didn't succeed; he used ways and means that are too cheap. So he has to return. He has been in Africa, in the hot sun of the South; now he goes north. As I said, these directions have to do with the mandala. The four cardinal points of the horizon are often associated with the

---

[3] Henri Bergson (1859-1941), French philosopher, Nobel laureate in 1927. Jung frequently cited him, especially for his concepts of "durée créatrice" and "élan vital."

four functions, or they may be indicated by special colours. Sensation is often identified with the South, and intuition with the North. Or the functions may be personified by people as in a drama. In the case of our dreamer, we have indications that South is to him associated with something spiritual—at any rate, it is full of spiritual symbols for him—and the North with sensuality, the *bon viveur*, the cheap cocottes. This is not usual, rather the reverse, but the man is not a born European, he was born in Africa, which may perhaps account for it.

This dream starts in the North, then, with the figure of the *bon viveur* indicating sensuality. The dreamer had made the mistake of going too far south. He is travelling with two others—they are three in all—personifications of constituents of the individuality that can be represented as people, or the four cardinal points, or four demons, or four gods, etc. The functions are often taken as characterological figures rather than as functions of consciousness, for these are more or less identical with characterological factors. If you are a thinking type, everything that is decent in you is linked up with that; in your thinking you are a decent fellow. In your feeling you show another character. Inasmuch as the actual problem of the dreamer would be a moral one, this character is emphasized, and the four are shown as persons. So here, the objectionable fellow, the *bon viveur*, is himself, for he does not distinguish him from himself except by a feeble protest that he is not so bad. Inasmuch as the *bon viveur* would be a contrast to his superior man, he would be the feeling man, but we are not sure whether in his feeling he is like that.

The third figure is unknown but must necessarily be either intuition or sensation. He might be sensation, but I wouldn't go too far in such an interpretation. Looked at theoretically, the dreamer is a thinking type with sensation as his secondary function, a man of reality. He has intuition to a certain extent. Obviously his blind spot is feeling; there he is paralysed, awkward, with no self-confidence, he envies anyone who has any certainty in feeling, so we obviously infer that that is his inferior function, No. 4, in this case the mechanic. This is a guess, a working hypothesis. No one would expect feeling under the guise of a mechanic, but he might engineer the ultimate reunion of all the constituents for it is always the inferior function that dots the i, that brings completion—as no man is complete without his shadow. Until one knows about his inferior function, one knows nothing about a man. So it is quite possible that No. 4, represented as a mechanic who puts the whole thing together, might be the feeling that would give him the right values. The dreamer is always getting into difficulties because of his lack of understanding of right values. His feelings fool him. He is always thinking that people are very nice and then finding that they are terrible bores. As for living the grand life in Poland, in his mind he knows it is all bunk, but his feelings give him the wrong values about it. If they were reliable, if only they would not play such jokes on him, that man would be all right. It would be the thing that would make him complete, safe, adapted, and there he falls down. But often our greatest weakness is just our last chance for redemption. If No. 4 puts the heart in order, his most central essence, then he can move on. Let us see how he moves on. Make a guess at the next dream; one should get used to that continual flow so that one could almost guess the next.

Mr. Henderson: He goes south.

Dr. Harding: He might go back to the chickens and put them in the cauldron.

Dream [20]

He finds himself in a hut in Africa, somewhere in the upper part of Egypt. In a corner he comes upon a crocodile and tries to chase it out, astonished to find such a beast, and somehow it disappears. Then his youngest son brings him a kettle containing all sorts of peculiar old things. He takes up a whole bundle of small scythes made, not of steel, but of sheet iron—simulacra, not the real thing. Below that in the kettle he finds handles of old swords, made of metal and other material, some made even of glass, but the blades were all broken off. Below that was a statue of Christ, made of sheet iron, with a sword as long as the figure, and he notices that one can easily remove it from the statue. He wants to carry the kettle away with all its contents, but a native suddenly appears and declares that one would use all those scythes, banked up on the wall of the hut between small lamps in a sort of ceremonial. Then it dawns upon him that the hut is by no means ordinary but a kind of mosque, and the scythes are crescent moons, and he also realizes that the handles of the swords are Coptic cross symbols.

317

So Mr. Henderson's guess that he would go south is right. So is Dr. Harding's suggestion concerning the chicken dream, which was closely linked up with the alchemical cauldron, because the chickens were boiled in it to bring the constituents together. It didn't succeed, because the chickens escaped by the hind wheel. In this case we again have the cauldron, and I think your guess has to do with the same idea here, because all these peculiar obsolete remnants thrown together in a kettle suggest raw materials to be cooked, melted together.

Associations: The *upper part of Egypt* (which, of course, means the more southern part) is to him a symbol of his own upper region, his most spiritual part, his superior man.

About the *crocodile*, he says that it is a remnant of prehistoric times. The dream itself emphasizes that it is an ancient prehistoric creature, a saurian. It must have to do with deep animal instincts, and it should not be in the hut in the upper regions, it should be chased out.

About *his youngest son*, he says that he has often dreamed of him and has taken him for a symbol of rejuvenation, his hope for the future. It was he who found the kettle.

Concerning the *contents of the kettle*, he says that scythes symbolize crops, production; and swords symbolize destruction. The crescent moon would be productive while the cross, the sword, would be destructive. Within the last years, he has often thought of the extraordinary intolerance of the Christian church, suppressing, even destroying, everyone who didn't share the same opinion. But he never consciously credited Islam with a great productivity. On the contrary, owing to its dogma of Kismet, the domination of fatality, he thought that Islam belonged to the old iron, something to be thrown away. He had a feeling in the dream that he was attributing an archeological value to those contents. The *lamps in the hut* he associates with those you see in Islamic countries, in the mosques at the feast of Ramadan and other nocturnal ceremonies. He is astonished that *this house is a mosque*, a house of God, with different religious symbols that seem to be of more archeological value than materials for a cult. They are as if out of use, thrown together in a pot, regardless of their origin; the cross and crescent would not be found together naturally, they exclude each other, but here they do not hurt each other through their incongruity.

318

LECTURE III

23 October 1929

Dr. Jung:

We have two questions to deal with. The first one asks whether the mechanic represents the function of intuition or feeling. Sometimes it is of a certain importance to know what function is represented by a figure, but in this case it is not so, because the dream is not concerned with the specification of the functions. It is far more concerned with the moral problem. It contains the important problem of taking the way of the flesh against the way of the spirit; it is more or less indifferent what functions come into play. In this case the mechanic is No. 4, and in spite of the fact that numbers are not emphasized, one could theoretically argue like this, though it seems a bit arbitrary and forced: This man is a thinking type with feeling as his least differentiated function, and sensation and intuition are auxiliary. Now when No. 4 turns up as a sort of *deus ex machina*, we can be certain that this figure has turned up from the unconscious. It comes suddenly, spontaneously, apparently from nowhere. It is autonomous, coming and going as it wants. That is one of the characteristics of the inferior function. The conscious can do nothing about it. So the mechanic would be the feeling function. Do you consider that we have any other indication why this should be so?

Dr. Harding: It is the heart that he is putting together.

Dr. Jung: Yes. He is the heart doctor, for he puts the magneto together. Feeling is typically represented by the heart. It is also most probable that the inferior function would be the first to give way. It cannot maintain the necessary concentration, the devotion and courage, on his individual road. It is as if his heart were failing him.

The second question is: Why is it that some men are never faced with the necessity of bringing up the feeling function? I am thinking

319

of a man over sixty, extraverted thinking type, who still goes on within his formula.

He must be a bad man, very bad! We can only say that it is so; certain people can go blundering through life in the most amazing way and apparently nothing happens. But something does happen somewhere, in their family perhaps; no doubt his children suffer and have to pay the damage. This hangs together with the fact that a human life is nothing in itself; it is part of a family tree. We are continuously living the ancestral life, reaching back for centuries, we are satisfying the appetites of unknown ancestors, nursing instincts which we think are our own, but which are quite incompatible with our character; we are not living our own lives, we are paying the debts of our forefathers. This is the dogma of inherited sin. So that man may be allowed to go blundering on till he is a hundred. But if one goes into the history of his family, one will see. We know too little about our forebears. We go on in a terribly one-sided way sometimes, because it makes sense as a historical compensation for ancestors who lived a hundred years ago or more, though we think they have nothing to do with our lives.

This corresponds to the primitive belief in ghosts; whatever is the matter, they say it is due to an ancestral spirit. I saw such a case when I was in Africa. Down by a water-hole near our camp a young woman collapsed with a septic abortion, and they brought her home in a high fever. They would not tell me, or their own medicine-man, no local man, but they called in a foreigner, a witch-doctor from another village. The great man is always abroad. He was trying to smell out the ghost by behaving like a dog on the scent of something. He went in spirals around the hut—nearer and nearer—till he suddenly stopped and said: Here! It was the spirit of her grandfather, whom she had always lived with because her parents had died early. He said in ghost language that he was bored and lonely in ghostland and wanted her with him, so he came down the trail at night to get the girl, and it made her ill. The doctor prescribed building a ghost-house, so they made one very neatly of stone, quite the opposite of their own wattle huts, and they put in a bed and food and water. Sometimes they also put in a little clay image of the sick person, but they didn't this time. And the next night the ghost looked in and thought it seemed very nice, so he went in and slept until very late. "There is the sun!—I must go," he said, and he hurried off to ghostland, leaving the girl behind him. As a matter of fact, the girl's fever went down and in three days she had quite recovered. Funny things in Africa!

I don't mean to tell you cock-and-bull stories about Africa, but it is psychologically interesting that they put everything down to the action of ghosts, with the perfectly logical recognition that we are tremendously influenced by ancestral facts. To those primitives, all children are reincarnations of the ancestors and are given ancestral names. And they must not be interfered with or disciplined; one must not be harsh to children for fear of offending the ancestors, so they are a terrible nuisance till the age of puberty, when they are reborn and become human. Then in the initiations they get it, a hell of a time!—all their education in one big lump. It may be so severe that they are completely crushed by it. But before that they are not interfered with, for the ghosts would be offended and the children fall ill, and then the kraal would be haunted. So that man is probably compensating for the lives of his parents. People do awful things, but if one goes back into the history of the family one understands.

Now, before we go on with the dream, I want to set you a certain task. I would like you to do some research work in symbology. Here is an excellent opportunity, for in this last dream very typical symbols occur—crosses and crescents, representing Christian and Islamic remains. These obviously point to the two attitudes of mind. That the patient has such a dream is of tremendous importance to him personally, but the symbols themselves are of great collective importance. So it is a good opportunity for an attempt at comparative symbology. I should like you to form two groups, one to discuss the cross and one the crescent, and then make a report. The symbolism of the cross was written by a Benedictine monk in three volumes,[1] so you have plenty of material! You should also consider the pre-Christian, the primitive, and the prehistoric crosses, and the history of late and early cross forms, down to primitive ornaments. Also the cross as part of the mandala. There must be somebody who understands Latin and Greek, and someone else must have a scientific mind to put together the results of your researches. You remember that the old Turkish flag showed a

[1] The allusion may be to a work by a German Jesuit scholar, Jacobus Gretser (1560-1625), *De cruce Christi* (Ingolstadt, 1605, 3 vols.) or to one by a Flemish scholar, Justus Lipsius (1547-1606), *De cruce Libri tres* (Antwerp, 1594). Lipsius alternated between Catholicism and Calvinism and was briefly involved with the Jesuits.

crescent and a star. And in digging up some Punic graves,[2] below the Roman remains, tombstones of the seventh and eighth centuries before Christ were found with the same symbols. This reminds one of the Swiss city Bern, where the cantonal coat-of-arms carries a bear and they still keep bears in a pit there—their totem animal; this used to be explained as a bad etymological joke, bear for Bern, but when they excavated the old Roman settlement nearby, they found a temple with a perfectly preserved figure of a Celtic goddess surrounded by bears. So the crescent and the star have also to do with Ishtar, Astarte, the Magna Mater, the mother goddess of Asia Minor, and the Egyptian Isis, as well as with Islam. Then it has to do with a pre-Islamic Sabaean[3] astrological cult, which leads to Babylonian history. That kind of knowledge is needed to have any safety in the technique of dream interpretation. Also it gives one a most precious impression of the universality of the human mind, our own little minds being reproductions of archetypal patterns.

Well now, our dreamer starts with the statement that he is in the South again, in Egypt. In the dream before, he was in the North. His feeling function gave way, the mechanic put it together again, and he quietly continued his journey south.

Mrs. Sigg: He seems obliged to go south to the place where he was born.

Dr. Jung: Yes, going to Africa has for him a spiritual connotation, while the North is sensual, and it is interesting to see that this is so to one born there; as the place of his origin it is spiritual. In China, the South is also spiritual, dry, hot and radiant, the Yang; while the North, the Yin, is female and material and dark. The Chinese mystical idea was really born in the South of China. This is rather suggestive of certain dogmatic teachings, the underlying conviction that man is really a spiritual creature, like the Christian idea, "Our home is in Heaven," and all that. Why does the place where he was born mean something spiritual to this man?

Mrs. Fierz: Because in his case it is not the concrete birth in the flesh but rebirth, a symbol of the new man.

Dr. Harding: There is a spiritual as well as a material creature.

Dr. Jung: Yes. And now why is he in a hut? He has no associ-

---

[2] That is, on the site of Carthage, near modern Tunis.

[3] *Sems.*: "Sabinian." Jung referred to the alchemical and astrological connections of the Sabaeans in, inter alia, *Aion* (1951), CW 9 ii, pars. 128, 129n, 190, 307n. Saba, or Sheba, was in southern Arabia.

ations. This is one of those banalities in dreams, but they are very important.

Mrs. Fierz: Christ was born in a hut.

Suggestion: Inside the house of the mother.

Dr. Jung: Yes, inside the womb, a place of rebirth. The hut is the symbol of an exceedingly simple place. Such huts are square in that country, the most frugal holes you can imagine, a stable is comfortable in comparison; often there is not even a roof because it never rains. This suggests the box, the belly of the whale, the house of the square foot and the house of the square inch in Chinese symbolism, the simplest place, like the cell of a monk, completely bare. As a matter of fact, this is a country where the rocks are honeycombed with cells of early Christian anchorites, so the atmosphere is particularly suggestive.

Now, in that house is a crocodile. His associations are that it is a remnant of prehuman, prehistoric times, a saurian belonging to a former geological period, symbolizing in himself something that is primitively instinctual. That is what Janet[4] would call the "parties inférieures des fonctions" as opposed to the "parties supérieures." The crocodile is the "partie inférieure" of his instinctive nature. (Read *Les Névroses* by Janet. It is good, a book you could buy.) The well-organized part, the differentiated part, is the "partie supérieure," the function as applied to some specific use. If there is a disturbance in the functioning of the "partie inférieure," it would be organic, something wrong with the brain cells, for instance. If there is a lesion in the "partie supérieure" it is psychogenic and neurotic. An example is hysterical dumbness, localized aphasia, where the person can talk but not in his mother tongue; or a disturbance in walking, where a person walks with a queer gait, sort of hopping along. This can be seen in horses and dogs, for animals can become hysterical and have the same symptoms as

---

[4] Pierre Janet (1859-1947), French psychiatrist and neurologist, who did important research on hysteria; author of *Les Névroses* (Paris, 1909). Jung studied under him at the Salpétrière, Paris, for one term in 1902-3, and they remained friends. "Les parties inférieures et supérieures" are defined by Jung in *Two Essays*, CW 7, par. 235: "the collective psyche comprises the *parties inférieures* of the psychic functions, that is to say those deep-rooted, well-nigh automatic portions of the individual psyche which are inherited . . . and are thus impersonal or suprapersonal. Consciousness plus the personal unconscious constitutes the *parties supérieures* of the psychic functions, those portions, therefore, that are developed ontogenetically and are acquired."

human beings. I once saw a mare who walked very unnaturally on the sides of her hoofs. All domesticated animals may have hysteria.

This crocodile, then, means the "partie inférieure" of our patient's whole instinctive nature. Now, how do you explain the fact that in such a place such an animal appears? Geographically, crocodiles are rarely seen there now, though formerly the Nile swarmed with them.

Mrs. Sawyer: When he is in the South his instincts come up.

Dr. Jung: You are right. The character of the place is connected with an ancient spiritual quality, and just there the most primitive instincts come up. Where there is a church, the devil is not far away. A person cherishing the qualities of a saint has a peculiarly close relation to the devil. Nobody has such hellish dreams as a saint; St. Anthony's visions, for instance. One must be a saint to have infernal relations. It is the pair of opposites, the law of enantiodromia. In such a place one is apt to become aware of tremendous opposition if one is holding strongly to one side. One becomes aware of very ancient animal instincts, for instance, which is a rather terrifying experience.

Miss Wolff: Was he conscious of the spiritual meaning of the hut?

Dr. Jung: Naturally, as a white man, he would hardly enter such a hut in reality, but he knew there was also the spiritual aspect of it; he is divided as all white men living in the colonies are. One is aware of the extraordinary filth, and on the other hand one can hardly deny that the place has an extraordinary quality. One finds there very interesting symbolic remnants of Coptic Christianity. The meaning is almost conscious to him: "Les extrêmes se touchent." But how else would you explain this crocodile?

Mrs. Sigg: Was not the crocodile a very holy animal for the Egyptians?

Dr. Jung: Yes, in Upper Egypt. There was a crocodile cult. So this is a sacred saurian.

Mrs. Fierz: Before he gets to the kettle mustn't he find his totem animal as the incarnation of ancestral spirits?

Dr. Jung: The totem animal is always the first, the original, ancestor. The next generation would be heroic animals or demigods, like the Homeric heroes in Greece. The heroic age follows the animal in Australian mythology also. Then comes man. So in the place of his origin he meets the ancestral animal, the divine crocodile. Now you can begin to speculate.

Mrs. Sigg: Would it be a feeling connection? He must somehow get into connection with nature.

Dr. Jung: To be in such a hut is to be isolated like an anchorite or like any saints who try to live spiritual lives; or like primitives when they are secluded in the bush in order to get into the community of ghosts. The whole thing is an archetypal situation where man is put in isolation in order to become aware of ancestral ghosts. There are striking examples among the North American Indians. After the manhood initiations, they have to go alone into a cave or little tent, where they sit all day and fast. Nobody talks to them; they are supposed to have dreams and intercourse with spirits, chiefly in the form of animals. In northern California[5] there is a sort of marathon race; a man starts early and races up the mountain to the Fire Lakes (so called because they are reached in the sunset light). It is a lonely place and there he must sleep, and in the early morning the first animal he sees is his totem animal. If the animal speaks to him he must be a medicine-man. When he returns the old men take him into their circle and sing songs of animals, and when they sing the song of the animal he has conversed with, he cannot help betraying it. He may try to conceal it because he doesn't want to become a medicine-man, it is dangerous, but if the toad has spoken to him, for instance, when they sing that song he cannot help sighing audibly, and then he is in for trouble.

So now we see that the presence of the crocodile has something to do with a spiritual origin, which confirms our conclusion that the hut is spiritual. And we see that this is an archetypal situation, it is the place of the spirit, such as one sees in the initiations of primitive man. That would generally be a ghost-house in woods or mountains, and there is often a pole with the blood-stained skulls hanging on it of prisoners of war who were put to death in a ritual way, the ritual consisting of everyone putting his dagger in the prisoner's body and then licking the blade for the health magic. This is very fortifying. It is comparable to our communion, the

---

5 Presumably the Achumawi tribe, of whom Jung probably had learned from the American anthropologist Jaime de Angulo, nine of whose papers are in the C. G. Jung Archive, ETH, including "La Psychologie religieuse des Achumavi," *Revue internationale d'ethnologie et de linguistique*, 23 (1928), 141-589. Jung and Angulo had met in 1923 (Zurich) and 1925 (Taos); Cary F. Baynes was Angulo's former wife.

tasting of the blood, and to the spear-thrust when Christ is on the pole. The Greek word for cross is pole; the primitive victim was hanging on the cross. And in an old Germanic ritual Odin was represented hanging on a tree, pierced with a spear.[6]

In this place of the spirits we see the totem animal, which symbolizes the beginning of man. With the primitives, not every animal has spiritual qualities, only doctor animals. There are ordinary foxes, but if one of them behaves in a funny way or if a coyote, ordinarily very shy, appears in a village, the natives say, "That is a doctor animal"—an animal with spiritual qualities, an exceptional animal like, say, a white elephant.

In the spiritual place, then, there are ancestral instincts, the stock of physiological life, and here there is the instinctiveness of a cold-blooded animal with almost no soul. Hagenbeck[7] of the Hamburg Zoo says you can establish an emotional rapport with all animals except reptiles. There a psychic rapport simply comes to an end. With the warm-blooded animals there is a certain similar quality of psychology which makes connection possible. The difference between monkeys and human beings is not great. Köhler, in his researches on anthropoids,[8] saw them doing ritual dances like the primitive tribes. Monkeys in the primeval forest have a very human quality. And dogs are very human. But the crocodile is beyond human reach. For us it would be snakes, since crocodiles are prehistoric here. In dragon myths they perhaps refer to dinosaurs. Whenever a snake appears, it symbolizes a piece of instinctive psychology in ourselves that is simply inaccessible, something of tremendous power, a thing that is inexorable and that we cannot make compromises with. A Nordic myth says you can recognize the hero by his snake's eyes, cold, not to be trusted. You can't influence the serpent thing in man, and this makes him a hero or medicine-man. The serpent in Oriental psychology is very spiritual, it symbolizes the treasure of wisdom. Yogis have an instinctive understanding

[6] Cf. *Symbols of Transformation*, par. 399, quoting the Hovamol Edda, where Odin says:

> I ween that I hung / on the windy tree,
> Hung there for nights full nine;
> With the spear I was wounded, / and offered I was
> To Odin, myself to myself.
> —Tr. H. A. Bellows, *The Poetic Edda* (1923), p. 60.

[7] Karl Hagenbeck (1844-1913), animal trainer, founder of the Hamburg Zoo.

[8] Wolfgang Köhler, *The Mentality of Apes* (1925).

of people with snake's eyes because they are in contact with that part of their own psychology. But snake's eyes of course mean the bad quality, too, something quite inhuman that you see in primitive medicine-men also. In Spencer and Gillen's book[9] there is a photograph of such a man; he has a peculiar, staring look, it is the evil eye that can charm snakes. So the hero is of a like nature. He reproduces youth by casting off his old skin and taking on a new, a continuous rejuvenation by overcoming the great dragon, Death. The inhuman quality that the snake represents is linked up with the lower centres of the brain and spinal system, into which fakirs occasionally penetrate, as when they are able to stop their own bleeding, or produce tears at will, as some actresses do; these are snake powers.

When such a monstrous animal appears in a dream, we know that something is coming up from the unconscious which is not to be influenced by will-power. It is like a fate that cannot be twisted. The primitive is sad, like a lost child, till he has a dream placing him with his totem animal. Then he is a child of God, a human being, he has a distinct fate. It is always a sign in dreams that now a level is reached where something is going to happen. I once treated an artist who went all to pieces, got in a terrible turmoil. I was afraid he might be going into a psychosis. Then after a number of unsatisfactory and confused dreams, he had a remarkable dream of a wide plain where big mountain-like molehills appeared. They burst open and out came a number of saurians, dinosaurs and so forth. I took that as a sign of the beginning of a new epoch in that man's life. And so it was, he started an entirely new style of creative work. There was a most amazing change in his life and art. He was a man of no education, an ordinary painter, but he then started to read, and the whole world of knowledge began to pour down upon him.

I have seen such a symbol in other cases when a man can no longer arrange his life arbitrarily. It might be a threatening symbol. For a man who has played with life, from now on it is serious. Animals of this kind can only be influenced by a superior demoniacal man of the order of snake-charmers and sorcerers and medicine-men. But such a one has to pay the penalty for his powers.

[9] The ethnologists W. B. Spencer and F. J. Gillen, whose *The Northern Tribes of Central Australia* (1904) Jung owned and cited. The picture mentioned here could not be located.

He suffers the most from his own magic; a medicine-man has to go through hellish tortures. Eskimos hang them up by their toes or immerse them in icy water till they are nearly mad. Such a series of shocks pierces holes through which the collective unconscious comes in from all sides. Now, provided a man can stand the onslaught of things coming from below, he can influence other people, he can have an almost hypnotic effect on his fellow tribesmen. So in this case the crocodile means that something serious is going to happen. The dreamer is touching something exceedingly primitive and primordial.

Then the youngest son brings the kettle containing old objects. The association with the youngest son is that he is the rejuvenated self, the hope for the future. So the wife who brings forth a son has given birth to the husband. In the Christian year there is a famous day, the day of the newborn, of those who are newly baptized, "Quasi modo geniti."[10] The youngest son is the dreamer himself in a future form. He is the son of the crocodile, the child of God; the dreamer's intuitive anticipation is bringing him the cauldron with many old things in it.

The cauldron is a Celtic symbol;[11] it is the crucible, or the alembic, in the alchemical apparatus, it is the womb, the vase of sin. Among the Gnostic gems in the British Museum, there is an amphora representing the "vase of sin," the womb with the ligaments on each side.[12] It is the vase of transformation, the womb into which Nicodemus would not go: "Can a man enter a second time into his mother's womb?"[13] It was the *krater* for the mixture of wine and water. There must have been a mystical society called the Krater, for there is a letter written by the alchemist Zosimos to a lady, advising her to go to the Krater to be reborn.[14] In modern language: "I would advise you to undergo some analysis in order to get a better attitude." In the place where St. Peter's now stands in Rome,

[10] On Quasimodo Sunday, or Low Sunday, the first Sunday after Easter, the introit opens: "Quasi modo geniti infantes," "as newborn infants" (I Peter 2:2). But cf. Jung's reference to the baptism ritual on Holy Saturday (before Easter) in "The Structure of the Psyche" (1927), CW 8, par. 336.

[11] On the magic cauldron of Celtic mythology and its relations to the originally non-Christian Grail motif, see *Psychological Types*, CW 6, par. 401, n. 149.

[12] Ibid., par. 396.

[13] John 3:4.

[14] The lady was Theosebeia, his *soror mystica* in the alchemical opus. See "The Visions of Zosimos" (1937), CW 13, par. 96.

the Attis cult celebrated the *taurobolium*.[15] The initiate was put into a cauldron, a hole in the earth; a grating was put over it and there they killed a bull so that the blood of the sacrificed animal streamed down on him. Then he was pulled out, washed, clothed in white, and fed on milk for eight days, for he was a baby, his own youngest son. The high priest, now the Pope, was called *Papas*.

Dr. Draper: Does the cauldron sometimes represent something undesirable, as in *Macbeth*, where it implies evil?

Dr. Jung: Positive symbols can always be translated the other way round. The womb that creates life can also create death. In one case it is white magic and in another, black. The holy mass can be used for the temporal power, or for the spiritual food of man. The black way works terrible evil; the white way works salvation. In order to cure a sick man primitive people put a clay image or picture in the temple to make him well, but it also can be used to make him ill. This explains the primitive's dislike of having his picture taken; he thinks it is black magic, that part of his soul is being taken away in a black box. So it depends on what you cook in the cauldron and with what attitude. In black-magic ceremonies one finds holy names written on it even if it is used for evil. The cauldron is the magic womb, in this case to pull together extraordinary opposition. *Coincidentia oppositorum.*

It is a bewildering thing in human life that the thing that causes the greatest fear is the source of the greatest wisdom. One's greatest foolishness is one's biggest stepping-stone. No one can become a wise man without being a terrible fool. Through Eros one learns the truth, through sins we learn virtue. Meister Eckhart says one shouldn't repent too much, that the value of sin is very great. In *Thaïs*,[16] Anatole France says that only a great sinner can become a great saint, the one cannot be without the other. How can man deal with this terrible paradox? He cannot say: "I will commit a sin and then I will be a saint" or: "I will be a fool in order to become a wise man." The question is, what to do when put into a complete impasse. Then the dream says, in the cauldron things are cooked together, and out of things strange to each other, irreconcilable, something new comes forth. This is obviously the answer to the paradox, the impossible impasse.

[15] = slaughtering of the bull.

[16] Novel (1890) set in 4th-century Egypt, based on a tale, from the *Golden Legend*, of a courtesan who became a saint.

LECTURE IV

30 October 1929

Dr. Jung:

We will continue our dream. The two committees are at work now digging up material for the next seminar, so I will refrain from discussing the cross and the crescent symbolism because we shall hear about that later.

We have already spoken of the cauldron, but we remained entirely within its mythological aspect, as an archetypal symbol—very concrete, and too objective. Now, what does it mean as a psychological fact? For instance, when we dream of the mystic four of Pythagoras and the Greek philosophers, we naturally ask, what is the four anyway? That it obviously refers to the four functions is as near as we can get to it nowadays, but a thousand years from now people will be much farther along on the way. It may mean something that we cannot conceive of now. Originally it was the four sons of Horus, later the four Evangelists, and in the twentieth century the four functions. "That was their concretism," they will say. These old symbols are inexhaustible. They are not objects of the mind, but categories of the imagination which we can formulate in ten thousand different ways. They are inexhaustible because they are *before* the mind, the basis of everything mental. If you ask how I know, I have no absolute evidence. Another example is the Pueblo Indians' four cardinal points of the horizon, but they were already very civilized, we did not catch them at a sufficiently primitive stage to show the original unconscious form in which it existed.

I mentioned a very good and striking example of such beginnings that I myself observed, the beginning of the idea of prayer among the Elgonyi in Africa.[1] . . . The living essence from the inside of

---

[1] The passage that followed here has been omitted because it repeats essentially the account of the Elgonyi custom (blowing or spitting on the hands, etc.) given above, p. 220. *Sems.* refer in a footnote, here, to *Contributions to Analytical Psychology* (1928), p. 113, a passage in the essay "Mind and the Earth" (1927), which was Jung's

330

their bodies is held in their hands and presented to the rising sun. To us it would mean, "I offer my soul to thee, O God." I concluded that the moment of the sunrise was their God, and at that moment they offer their souls. But they themselves were perfectly unconscious of the meaning. These things come out of the blue, out of nowhere. The further back one goes, to the Australian tribesman or to the Paleolithic man, one still finds the most amazingly complicated rituals, and there is no explanation. The unconscious nature of man forces him to do these things, they express the natural structure of man, as though Nature herself were offering homage to the rising sun. Every animal, every plant, every flower takes a definite position toward the rising sun, and man does the same not knowing why.

So symbols are in existence before consciousness. That is the reason why we are so deeply unconscious of our own rites. Many of them are inexplicable. Is there anybody here who could give me a satisfactory account of our Christmas tree? Suppose a Chinese dropped in and asked you what it meant. You would say, "It is to commemorate the day when our redeemer was born." "But is that prescribed in your holy books? Is there any record that in a stable in Bethlehem there was such a tree?" We are just as dull and stupid as the primitive who greets the rising sun.

In my native town Basel, every year on January 13th, three masked dancers, a griffin, a lion, and a wild man, come down the Rhine on a raft; they land and dance around the town, and no one knows why. It is an amazing thing in a modern town. These things originate before mind and consciousness. In the beginning there was action, and only afterwards did people invent opinions about them, or a dogma, an explanation for what they were doing.

And so with the cauldron. First it was a hole in the ground, and then a kettle into which they threw water, meat, and red-hot stones. A thinker among them asked: "What are you doing? — Is this instead of the hollow in the rock where our ancestors cooked things?" He connected the two. Why do we dream of the cauldron? The old witches had a kettle, and the alchemists had their crucible, so it goes right back to the hole in the ground. That was the first idea of the magic cauldron. In the *Psychology of the Unconscious* there is

---

first written account of his observations on the Elgonyi. That section of the essay is now in "The Structure of the Psyche," CW 8, par. 329.

an account of the ceremonial of the Wachandi, where a hole in the ground quite obviously represents the female genitals.[2] That is the primary place, the original cooking-hole where things are produced. The unconscious seizes upon the cooking procedure as a symbol of creation, transformation. Things go in raw and come out new, transformed—and they taste better cooked. The magic cauldron is a suitable expression for that which transforms things. As a rain charm, primitives sprinkle water on the ground to imitate rain. In an Indian tribe of northern California,[3] priests and medicine-men came together and sang the song of the frogs, an imitation of the chorus of frogs in the rainy season; in order to bring rain, they sang as if they were frogs in wet weather. It was through such analogies that they sought to bring about a change.

Now, one sees from this man's dreams that things should have began to come together, but always when he makes a step forward he regresses. One can't push him. Slowly a deep conviction dawns upon him that he ought to change, and in order to do so the unconscious makes a proposition. The conscious says, "Why the devil don't you move on?" He raises his arms, but a countermove follows. Therefore the unconscious comes in with the advice, "Now here is the kettle," just as, when nothing will help, the primitive turns to magic quite shamelessly. We have a modern explanation for the number four symbolism, have we for the cooking-pot? I should tell you that when they invented cooking-pots, they gave them faces, eyes, ears, human form. There is a marvellous collection of Peruvian pots in the Museum of Natural History in New York, and among them are personified pots, and as soon as they are given human form, one recognizes the analogy to the human body. Then one puts the cauldron into man himself, he becomes the cauldron.

Mrs. Crowley: Would the Holy of Holies be the same thing?

Dr. Jung: Yes, but thousands of years later, when the kitchen became the most sacred place, the place where the fire was always burning. The communion, the meal of love, really took place first in the kitchen. There were co-operative cooking societies, originating chiefly in Rome, a city of two million inhabitants at that time. The social conditions were difficult then. Streets were narrow, houses were inadequate, they had no room to cook, so in order not to

[2] *Symbols of Transformation*, par. 213 (as in 1912 edn.). The Wachandi are, or were, a tribe of Australian aborigines.

[3] See 23 Oct. 1929, n. 5.

starve, they made these co-operative eating arrangements, which guaranteed to their members one meal a day.[4] There was one kitchen and one man in charge who prepared the meal, and these societies were under the patronage of a saint or hero. Herakles was one of the heroes, and probably Hermes, the Thrice-Greatest Hermes, and Christ, another mystical god. And the man who prepared the meal read something to the members when they were together; the Epistles of St. Paul were first read under such conditions. . . .[5]

That the cauldron soon became a living symbol was in recognition that the cauldron is in man, man is the cauldron. But what part of a man? With a woman one can say it is the womb which gives rebirth, but how about the man? He seems to be a fool device anyway, what can he do? We creep along the history of the symbol. First the hole in the ground (Negroes smear the hole with clay still), then the cauldron was taken out, and then some fantastical artist gave a face to it, so why not give feet to it? Now where is the cauldron in ourselves?

Suggestion: Is it the brain?

Dr. Jung: No, never in the brain. I remember the Pueblo chief who said, "We hold that all Americans are crazy because they believe that they think in their heads, while we know that we think with our hearts." A Negro thinks in his stomach.

Dr. Harding: The Bible says, "Out of his belly shall flow rivers of living water."[6]

Dr. Jung: Yes, it is in the abdominal cavity of man. That is the next analogy. As you fill the cauldron, so you fill the belly; as food is transformed in the cauldron, so it is in the belly. So the next step was to concentrate upon the body. Therefore those holy men in India concentrated upon their navels. And mental processes of the belly play a tremendous role in dreams. Now what about the abdomen as a mental organ? There is a chance that things might be changed if a most important function is in the belly.

Suggestion: Would it be the solar plexus?

Dr. Jung: Yes, the *plexus solaris*, the brain of the sympathetic

[4] *Sems.*: Note added presumably by one of the original editors: "There were also co-operative burial societies which guaranteed a decent funeral."

[5] Several lines have been omitted which repeat essentially the statement about Zosimos given above, p. 328.

[6] John 7:38.

system; it is less concentrated than the brain, but it is the centre of all vegetative functioning. It is the main accumulation of ganglia, and it is of prehistoric origin, having lived vastly longer than the cerebrospinal system, which is a sort of parasite on the *plexus solaris*. If you really concentrate upon the navel, succeed in repressing consciousness, and press everything into the vegetative system, you can bring the functioning of the cerebrospinal system to a standstill, just as fakirs do. They go into a trance, they don't feel and they don't hear, they are as if dead. But life goes on, and digestion goes on, it can go on when a man is practically decapitated; it doesn't stop the heart, though an outside shock might. So the sympathetic system has great autonomy and is still alive when the cerebrospinal system is cut off. As to the mental part, there is no possibility of assuming that it has psychic life, but my idea is that all nervous life is psychological though it is not all conscious. A man who cannot speak or move may yet have psychic contents. So with the sympathetic system there are psychic contents, but they are not yet conscious and they express themselves only in symbolic actions. The contents of all the early manifestations of religion came, not from the mind, but from the sympathetic system. And it is the saurian, the original worm, that brings up the contents of the unconscious.

When man concentrates on the kettle down in his belly, he discovers that something happens. He pushes his libido down into the original primordial instinctive centres. It is just as if all the incompatibles in his consciousness, the raw materials, were gathered together and thrown down into the dark abyss of his sympathetic system, into the warmth of the body, well protected, and there begin to cook, to be transformed. Lovely perfumes arise which are intuitions of new contents, new birth. All the analogies of rebirth come then; the renewal of man is represented as childbirth; and the cooking-pot always figures in birth symbolism.

The alchemists were not trying to form a new man, a human being, but a new philosophy in terms of alchemy. They had to be careful, because it was heretical, and the social consequences might be rather disastrous. The Pope would have been glad to have any gold they might make, so he let them go ahead. It was less dangerous to try to produce the *homunculus* than to change man himself, for that would have meant competition with the Christian mysteries. The making of the *homunculus* in the cauldron of the alchemist was the symbol of the transformation of man in his own belly.

The sympathetic nervous system is an exceedingly emotional centre, and it rules to a great extent the emotional part of our psychology, not the mental part. The cerebrospinal system controls the mind. Emotions are often mixed up or obscure, they cause confusion, and may even make people lose their minds. The word "sympathetic" shows that it has to do with the emotions; it comes from the Greek word meaning to *suffer, to feel compassion, to feel together with,* so it has the connotation of connection or relatedness. A mental emotion is an isolated emotion, you alone get angry, but the sympathetic emotion has almost a cosmic character, as if you were suffering with many, as if you were connected with the whole world, your whole nation. That word "sympathetic" is an old intuition derived from a very clear perception of that particular kind of emotion, it must have that quality. It has nothing to do with individuation, but it has to do with the whole history of man, including animals; it is collective, out of yourself, as if a strange thing had taken possession of you.

Now we must mention again the youngest son, that future man, the one he is to become. He points to the kettle, the creative thing, which means that the creative instinct in our patient is pointing out that analogy charm. So it is not the conscious solution of the dreamer or something that he has been told, it means, look into yourself, push your consciousness down into your belly and all that is contained there. He already discovers that there are things there of which he was oblivious. The main contents are the cross and the crescent, symbols which in his associations he refers to the Christian and Islamic religions. He was born among the Moslems. That is a very showy religion, and in Cairo and the coast towns one still sees very impressive sights, the afternoon prayer, for instance, when traffic stops, and long rows of kneeling people bow low to Mecca.[7] Whole streets are filled with them. So it must have gone deep into him, particularly as his Christian education was so exceedingly pale and Protestant in comparison. The mosques are far more impressive than Christian churches, they are marvellous, as fine as the most beautiful Gothic cathedrals in the West. This religion has been

[7] Jung had been in Egypt in spring 1926, homeward bound after the trip to East Africa.

misrepresented by prejudiced teachers; we have a funny idea of Islam through bad education. It is represented by our theologians as dry and empty, but there is tremendous life in it, particularly in Islamic mysticism, which is the secret backbone of Islam. In Africa especially it is making rapid progress because it is far more suited to those people than Christianity, it is more reasonable. You must not mix it up with the bad qualities with Christianity. Since Christianity has produced the world war and poison gas, we have to look at that in a different light. So Islam to this man is far more positive and determining than with us. But he finds the symbols that are typical of both these cults in the kettle. Why is that?

Mrs. Sigg: They are already in his soul.

Dr. Jung: One would rather assume them to be in his consciousness, but they have been cast aside—broken scythes, disused rubbish, no good any longer. They have been thrown down into the kettle, below consciousness. This is exactly what is the matter with him, as with millions of Christians. The living symbols have already fallen into the unconscious and they don't know it. People say here, "I am not a Christian, I don't believe in those old things," and yet their whole psychology is Christian. They don't know that they are suffering from a lack of the religious function. These symbols are already in the kettle to be made over as soon as someone puts a fire under it.

Here, then, are two determining but contradictory factors. At one time in his life he had considered the justifications for both religions. Then he couldn't make them out, why should he bother? He threw them away, and they fell into the kettle. But it appears now that these things have to be recognized. They are incompatible things: swords, scythes, the figure of Christ, etc., all thrown together in disorder, and naturally they cannot blend unless they are put through a reconciling process. These two strong imprints, the Islamic and the Christian, should blend, there is an arrested development of personality because they *won't* blend—these two standpoints so utterly different that they cannot possibly blend. He is at a standstill, he cannot move forward, it is as if his legs were going in different directions, so he remains stationary. The irreconcilable nature of Christianity and Islam must be reconciled. He is unable to do it consciously, and I also am unable. Each point of view has its justification. If you knew the social conditions that brought about their development, you would say that each one was right. You would be in the position of the famous judge: One man made a speech, and he said, "Yes, you are right," then another man said exactly the opposite, and he said, "Yes, you also are right." But, you see, this man's intuition foresees the necessity of bringing these two objects together. The fact that they are broken is obvious. Now the figure of Christ with the long sword of sheet iron, as long as the figure itself, what do you make of that?

Mrs. Sigg: It is a symbol of the cross.

Dr. Jung: Yes, the sword has always symbolized the cross. Of course, it is a very pagan *arrière pensée* that the sword has a soul: because my sword is animated, the enemy's is not. So they prayed to the sword before a battle, made their vows, pledged their word by the sword, with the advantage of the old Germanic idea that it had a soul.

Miss Wolff: There is an old German poem where Christ is represented as the hero with a sword, doing great deeds.

Dr. Jung: Yes, he is represented there as the healer and also as the hero and warrior. It is peculiarly applicable to our Christian nations, just emerging from the Great War. We are most of us very unconscious about it. To one born in the East it is convincing and impressive that a Christian people could use the sword to that extent. It is the German warlike quality, the primitive berserker rage that is in the Western man in general. So this man's Christ is equipped with a long sword, that most peaceful redeemer Lord leading an armed host. And the sword is detachable, an impression that would not originate in the Western Christian mind, only in one born outside, to whom the European is not the model of virtue.

As soon as I was outside our white civilization, I saw what Europeans are like. We look awful. The Chinese call us devils and it is true, thin cruel lips, and our wrinkles are uncanny. And we are always intent on something no devil can understand. What are we seeking? Why the devil should we be seeking at all? To a Pueblo Indian, God in his completeness is walking over the heavens every day.

As you approach the coast of Europe from the great flats of Africa, and see the snow-capped mountains, the little bays, etc., you know that this is the country where the pirates live, where their raids start upon the quiet, cattle-like men on their grassy plains. From Europe, that half-island, the white man came in ships, bringing awful diseases and fire-water, and even intentionally selling infected clothing to destroy the population, as they did in the South Seas. Wherever the white man went, there was hell for the other nations; one has to be outside to understand. The white man is a very beast devouring the earth, the whole world trembles at him. Such Christianity is a compensation, a hellish lie. The missionaries told me how they shoot antelopes from their bedroom windows, and how they cheat the British Government for a game license. They complain of their lot, when actually there is nothing more interesting than life among the primitive tribes. Rockefeller has given a great deal of money to the missions, but the people of the countryside say, "Don't employ a boy trained in the missions—they all lie and steal." How can these primitives be impressed with our religion? They accept it as the old Britons accepted it, who took Christianity, trembling, from the lances of the Roman legions.

To understand the delicacy of that man's criticism, you must remember that he is half outside of Europe. So he deals only partially with the white man, he is exceedingly careful, he only half joins in our private lunatic asylum. He has the fear and also the inferiority of the half-primitive man, that peculiar spot which people have who are born in the colonies. Take an Englishman, an aristocrat, born in Australia or South Africa, send him to Eton and Oxford, and put him through the ordeal of English education, and he will still harbour a feeling of resentment. There is something wrong with that fellow, he has a standpoint outside, and instead of using that as a weapon he feels inferior.

We once had a great theological conference here, and I asked a Christian representative what his ideas were about Buddhism. He answered, "Since the Bible is the last word of God, we are not concerned with Buddhism." This is the standpoint of a fool, and it is the white man's point of view. It is as if the people of Zurich should say they were not concerned with Paris. I had another patient, a woman born in India, who could only adapt to European life on the most sophisticated level. She couldn't dream of marrying or having a child, for then she would have felt that she was going native, since that is a law of nature. The conflict suffocated her and she was at a standstill. So these people born outside of Europe have a critique, and a certain detachment; it produces a different situation.

This man was not lamed by being born among primitives. He was born among the Moslems, and there was a time when the

Islamic mind was the leader of thought, the only light of consciousness in the deep mediaeval gloom. We used to go to school there. (Universities of Saragossa and Cordova.) And now the native man is coming in, explaining that his symbolism is still alive: the scythes, the crescents, which are to be hung among the lamps in the mosques at Ramadan, the highest feast of the Islamic cult. Islam is living in the native side of him. The Christian religion is no longer alive to him. So this man consists of two, a native of that country, and, on the other side, a European, but with a strong emphasis on the native.

LECTURE V

6 November 1929

Dr. Jung:

Today, as I promised you, we shall hear the reports on the cross and the crescent. We will begin with the more familiar, the cross, which Dr. Barrett has prepared.

SYMBOLISM OF THE CROSS

That the cross has been of great symbolic significance to mankind for many ages is beyond dispute. We see it everywhere about us today, never thinking to inquire into the origins and significance of this familiar symbol, and it is quite possible that the everyday person of ten thousand years ago may also have seen it in all phases of his life and accepted it just as un-questioningly as we do. In this paper we shall attempt briefly to look into the usage and meaning of the cross in various lands and through many centuries, and to draw together, and bring a certain unity to, the opinions of several commentators of the past and present.

There are many material objects whose contours readily suggest those of the cross, e.g., birds on the wing, man with outstretched arms, trees with limbs on either side, etc. But these familiar objects seem in themselves inadequate sources with which to account for the vast significance of the symbol unless we can find some powerful underlying motive which will

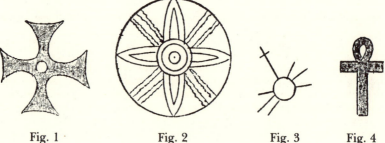

Fig. 1   Fig. 2   Fig. 3   Fig. 4

bind together the symbolic object, or the simplified representation of the object, which in itself becomes the symbol, in some deep relationship to mankind. Let us seek for this in a brief review of historical data concerning the cross.

The Assyrians (1)[1] represented their god of the sky, Anu, by the equilateral cross (Fig. 1). They also represented the sun and its eight regions by a circle with eight rays. By coupling these rays in pairs the radiated cross (2) was produced, which the King of Assyria wore suspended about his neck, in the same manner as men of our present day wear orders of knighthood (Fig. 2). This same figure appears on pottery of the period, its solar meaning being further assured by its alternating with the rayed disc. At times the two symbols appear in juxtaposition (Fig. 3).

In prehistoric Egypt we find the Tau, T , or gibbet form of the cross. This cross was used in its simple form and is thought to have been representative of the phallus. When the Tau cross is surmounted by a circle, or oval, we have the *crux ansata*, the magical key of life (Fig. 4). The oval is thought (3) to represent the sistrum (the musical instrument used in the worship of Isis, the goddess of the earth) or possibly to be a modification of the delta (those lands on which the gods played and produced all life, thus again connected with Isis, or Woman). The *crux ansata* becomes in this way the symbol of creation. We find this cross on the most ancient Egyptian monuments, frequently in the hand of a god, priest or king; Amon-Ra, Kneph, Isis, Hathor, and Osiris are some of these. It was also placed on tombs, presumably having the same significance as the phallus, which signified resurrection. In the paintings on tombs it is evidently employed by divinities to awaken the dead to new life. We see it thus in a twelfth-century bas-relief, where a goddess is holding the *crux ansata* to the nostrils of a dead king, the inscription reading, "I give thee life, stability, purity, like Ra, eternally." It was also held out towards the living as a sign of vital power. Both the Tau, T , and the astronomical cross of Egypt, ⊕ , are conspicuous in the remains of Palenque.[2] The Tau was the sign which Moses instructed his people to mark in blood on their door-posts and lintels so that the Chosen People should not be smitten by the Lord. According to Blavatsky (15), the cross was used in the old Egyptian mys-

---

[1] The parenthetical numbers refer to the entries in the bibliography, prepared by Dr. Barrett, at the end of the report. The footnotes are the editor's.

[2] Ruined Mayan city in Yucatán, southern Mexico. See *Symbols of Transformation*, CW 5, par. 400 (as in 1912 edn.); for the "Palenque Cross," ibid., pl. XLIa. According to Merle Greene Robertson, author of *The Sculpture of Palenque* (5 vols., Princeton University Press, in preparation), the Tau is especially conspicuous in Palenque art and iconography. It appears on pectorals worn by rulers from as early as the sixth century A.D. on stone tablets and stucco sculpture and as a windowlike opening in building walls. (Private communication.)

teries of initiation. The Initiated Adept was attached, not nailed, to the cross and left for three days in the Pyramid of Cheops. On the morning of the third day he was carried "to the entrance of a gallery, where at a certain hour the beams of the rising sun struck full in the face of the entranced Candidate, who awoke to be initiated by Osiris and Thoth, the God of Wisdom." This author also remarks that an ancient manuscript speaks of these crosses as the "hard couches of those who were in travail, the act of giving birth to themselves."

Fig. 5

Another familiar form of the cross in Egypt is found in conjunction with the solar wheel, giving the wheel four spokes (Fig. 5). The sun is often likened to a charioteer, and in Greece the solar wheel became the emblem of Apollo. It is also found in Assyria and Babylonia, and it is possible that the swastika was derived from it. The solar cross was widely distributed and, according to Inman (8), is still popular in Ireland. It was also found among the American primitives.

The ideogram formed by the *crux ansata* in hieroglyphic script, $\top$ (pronounced *ankh*), signifies life, living. Its abstract sense is not doubtful, it is a symbol of life, and not only of life but of rebirth, and thus of immortality—not without reason has it been called "The Key of Life." In spite of this rather obvious symbolism, various archeologists have contented themselves with describing it as the key of a canal lock, as a degenerate form of winged globe, as a phallus, etc., etc.

From Egypt the "Key of Life," now a magical and propitiatory symbol, spread to the Phoenicians and then to the whole Semitic world. It was everywhere present, from Sardinia to Susiana (that district of Persia occupied by an ancient civilization probably anterior to Babylonian culture), along the shores of Africa, Phrygia, Palestine, and Mesopotamia. It is seen on idols in India. On monuments of Phoenician or Hittite origin it is held in the hands of kings, as with the Egyptians, and is associated with the tree of life and the lotus flower. Some interesting variations of the ankh, as mentioned by Baldwin (13), are as follows (Fig. 6).

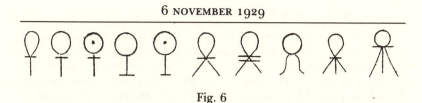

Fig. 6

It was, furthermore, combined with the emblems of the peoples who adopted it. In Phoenicia we see it combined with the truncated cone of Astarte (Fig. 7). The Greeks changed and amplified this symbol so that it came (2) to represent their goddess of life (Fig. 8). On early Phoenician coins it is seen attached to a rosary. The *crux ansata* continued to be used (4) as the Christian cross of Egypt before the Roman cross was adopted. It is even today sold in Cairo as a potent charm, according to Carpenter (5), confessedly indicating the conjunction of both sexes in one design.

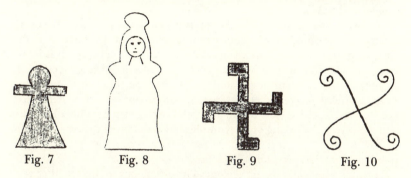

Fig. 7   Fig. 8   Fig. 9   Fig. 10

The somewhat complicated swastika cross appeared very early in the Mediterranean lands. It was found in the lowest stratum of Troy, which would place it at about 3000 B.C., i.e. in the Bronze Age. This was a simple swastika (Fig. 9). Later it becomes more complicated, having short spirals at the terminations (Fig. 10) and other variations. In the Cretan, or Minoan religion we find the double axe, a potent sign, arranged fourfold into a swastika composition. It appears frequently in Greece, being found on both pottery and coins in the Iron Age. Before the birth of Christ it had travelled practically all over Europe. Later the swastika was borrowed by

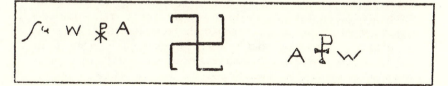

Fig. 11

343

the Christians, and towards the end of the third century we find it in the catacombs in company with the monogram of Christ (Fig. 11).

In India and China we have no evidence of the swastika before the fifth century B.C., and it seems likely that it was brought there from the Mediterranean lands. We see it in conjunction with various symbols, some of them solar, on the so-called footprints of the Buddha from the Amaravati stupa. It is thought that it was carried to China and Japan by the Buddhists, and it is a notable fact that the swastika enclosed in a circle was a new form of character introduced into Chinese writing by the Empress Wu (c. 704-684 B.C.) as a sign for "sun."

The swastika has been frequently found associated with sun worship, and through this association has been applied to signify astronomical motion in general. Perhaps it is through this that it has acquired properties as the sign of good omen, life, and luck. It is seen in America before the time of Columbus.

The swastika is most commonly regarded as a solar sign, its form being interpreted as signifying the rotary motion of the sun. In the light of the psychological interpretation it thus appears as a libido symbol. It is interesting to note that when the arms of the swastika are swung clockwise it designates the male principle and stands for sun, light, life. In India, however, the arms are sometimes swung counter-clockwise; it is then called the sauwastika, designates the female principle, and stands for night, destruction. While speaking of this complicated variation of the cross it might be well to mention the fact that in pre-Christian times a simple upright pole was sometimes spoken of as a cross.

Through Mortillet's (6) archeological investigations we find further verification for the existence of the cross in antiquity. In the deepest stratum at Terramares, he finds the remnants of a civilization far older than that of the Etruscans. In this layer, which belongs to the Bronze Age, he finds remnants of household utensils and other implements on which the cross appears in the most varied forms. In the burial grounds of Villanova, which belong to a somewhat later date (about the Iron Age) he finds much evidence that the cross was used as a religious symbol in connection with the worship of the dead. The tombs on Lake Maggiore are even more convincing in this connection. Each tomb contains at least one cross, mostly in the simple form $\times$. It is also interesting that what later became the sacred monogram of Christ, the ⚹ , is found here. Mortillet concludes from his observations that the worship of the cross was extant long before the coming of Christianity, and because of its development where living objects and idols are lacking, he believes that the cross was the most sacred symbol of a religious sect who rejected idolatry long before the birth of Christ.

In the tombs of Etruria were found crosses composed of four phalli. A

344

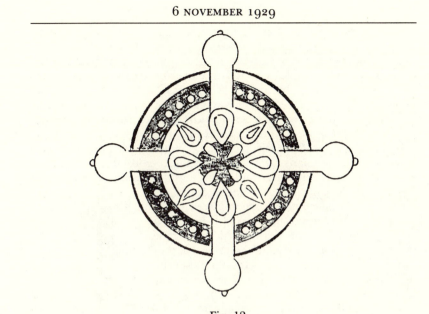

Fig. 12

Fig. 13

Fig. 14

345

similar cross appeared as an old Phoenician emblem and has been seen carved on a rock at Malta. This was the original Maltese Cross, which, however, has since been changed, although the phallic significance remains obvious. A good example (8) of this type of cross was found near Naples and is believed to have been worn by a priest of Priapus. It is composed of four phalli and a circle of female organs at the centre (Fig. 12). Inman (8) gives an interesting comparison with two Christian crosses which appear to be modifications of this (Figs. 13 and 14).

In Greece we find Plato saying (9) that God had divided the world-soul lengthwise into two parts, which he joined together like the letter X (Chi) and stretched between heaven and earth. This was the initial letter of their favourite god's name and itself one of the names for the cross. We also find that the sceptre of Apollo has at times the form of the cross (†). In ancient art Hercules was actually represented carrying the two pillars in such a way under his arms that they form exactly a cross. Here, perhaps (Robertson, 9), we have the origin of the myth of Jesus carrying his own cross to the place of execution. A symbol  Fig. 15 often seen in Greek churches and apparently of pre-Christian origin, is a cross surmounting a crescent (Fig. 15), the former the male, the latter the female, element.

The cross is also found in Mexico, Peru, and Central America. Its presence on religious monuments stimulated the early explorers to account for this apparent spread of the Christian teaching by assuming that Saint Thomas had once visited this land. It is now believed, however, that the cross arose independently in these regions. In Mexico the deity Inetzolcoatl was adored under the sign of the cross (4), which was called "Tree of Sustenance" and "Tree of Life." This deity also wore a robe covered with crosses. The hair of Toze, the Great Mother, was carefully arranged on her forehead in curls made to form crosses. According to Westropp and Wake (7), the *crux ansata* also is found in Mexico and called the "Tree of Life." According to Robertson (10) the Mexican god was represented by a tree stripped of branches and covered with painted paper. He also mentions sacrifices by hanging on a tree instead of on a cross. The Mexicans connected the sacraments with the symbol of the cross. In the sacrifice of a maiden to the maize goddess, the priests wore the slain victim's skin and stood with arms outstretched, crosswise. The sacred tree was made into a cross, on which was exposed a baked dough figure of a saviour god.[3] This was afterwards eaten. There is no question as to the pre-Christian antiquity of the symbol of the cross in Mexico.

[3] According to "Transformation Symbolism in the Mass" (1941), CW 11, par. 340, the dough figure that was eaten represented the god Huitzilopochtli.

According to d'Alviella (1) the cross in America amalgamates two cognate ideas: 1) As the symbol of the four winds emanating from cardinal points, and 2) as the symbolic world-tree, tree of life, tree of our flesh, analogous to the Scandinavian Yggdrasill, the cosmic tree whose roots surrounded the universe. In Yucatán, Cortez found crosses three feet high, and these are believed to have been connected with sacrifices to the sun and to the winds, a ritual wind belonging to each quarter of the heavens. The Aztec goddess of rains bore a cross in her hands, and in the spring victims were nailed to a cross and shot with arrows.

In North America various Indian rainmakers drew crosses on the ground, with extremities towards the cardinal points. The Blackfeet (1) arranged large boulders in the form of a cross which represented the "Old Man in the Sun, who rules the Winds." A cross found on shells in mounds in New Mexico is evidently solar or stellar in character (Fig. 16, upper). Other crosses of this type appear among pictographs of the Dakota Indians (Fig. 16, lower).

Fig. 16

As the world-tree, the Mexicans and Mayans had it standing in the centre of the universe, its roots in the waste-of-water, its branches in the clouds, as if searching for rain. The Mexicans worship it as "Our Father." The sacred pole of the Omahas typifies the cosmic tree, "centre of the four winds and dwelling place of the thunder bird." Tree burial among the western tribes of North American Indians probably bore a mythical (2) relation to the placing of dead in the tree of life, a symbolism which we

347

find so frequently in other lands. Offerings also (10) were elevated into trees. Missionaries (4) to the Hudson Bay region found the tree regarded as a magic talisman and symbol of fertility. The Hurons (4) tattooed themselves with the cross. The handled cross was also found in America (Fig. 17). An interesting detachment of the symbol of the cross from a concrete figure is found among the Muyscas[4] and Bogotá Indians, who stretch two ropes crosswise above the surface of a stream or pond and at the point of intersection throw into the water fruits, oil, and precious stones as a sacrifice.

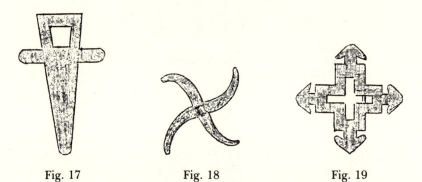

Fig. 17   Fig. 18   Fig. 19

In Central Africa copper ingots have always been smelted in the form of a cross. The cross was found among the Bantu Negroes before Christianity was introduced. Presentday Nilotic Negroes frequently shave a form of swastika on men's heads (Fig. 18). Among (10) natives of southern Nigeria who practised human sacrifice until the beginning of the twentieth century, we find again the use of the cross figure stretched on rude scaffolds in the form of St. Andrew's cross.

In India the equilateral cross alternates with the rayed disc. On an ancient coin we find a cross the branches of which terminate in arrowheads (Fig. 19). It is interesting to note in connection with this that, according to Carpenter (5), Krishna is said to have been sometimes shot by an arrow and sometimes crucified on a tree. It is also said that the birthplace of Krishna was built in the form of a cross and that he was buried at the meeting point of three rivers, which would, of course, form a cross.

Inman tells us of a very interesting old Buddhist emblem in the form of a swastika (copied from the *Journal of the Royal Asiatic Society*), Fig. 20, and embodying the creative idea in a way which recalls the *crux ansata*, but

---

[4] *Sems.*: "Muskhogean," as in *Psychology of the Unconscious* (New York, 1916 edn.), p. 300. (The Muskhogean family of Indians inhabited the southeastern United States.) In CW 5, par. 407, Jung substituted "the Muyscas Indians, of Peru."

Fig. 20

in a very much more complicated form. Each limb represents a phallus at right angles to a body and directed towards the barley-corn, a symbol of yoni, the female. Each limb is marked with the same female emblem and terminates with a triad triangle, beyond which is a conjunction of the sun and moon, as masculine and feminine emblems, respectively. The whole represents the mystic arba, the "Creative four." Copies of similar crosses have been found in what is thought to be the remains of ancient Troy.

The use of the cross (10) in India in human sacrifice was practised as late as 1855 by the Khonds, a primitive tribe. The victim was taken to a sacred grove and either fastened to a cross or placed in the cleft of a long branch of a tree, the arms outstretched, the body making the upright of the cross.

The Buddhists of Tibet placed the cross at street corners, in a fashion similar to the Hermaic pillars in Greece and Rome.

According to Robertson (10), the Chinese placed the equilateral cross within a square, this design representing the earth (Fig. 21). There is found in China the dictum "God fashioned the earth in the form of a cross." A Christian Father also writes, "the aspect of the cross, what is it but the form of the world in its four directions? The East on top, the North the right limb (looking from the cross), the South the left, the West the lower portion." The cross form is found also in the Chinese man-

Fig. 21

349

dala in connection with the representation of the universe, the gods being placed above the cross, and the demons of the lower regions below.

The cross appears frequently in pre-Christian northern Europe. We find it among the Gauls. The Druids (11), when an oak-tree died, stripped off the bark and shaped the trunk into the form of a pillar, pyramid, or cross, and continued to worship it. They also sought out oak-trees growing in the form of a cross, and when the configuration was not sufficiently convincing they fastened a cross beam to the tree or adjusted the limbs to form a cross. Churchward (4) tells of a Druid ankh-cross found in Cornwall and states that it is similar to those found amongst the dolmens of Brittany. A small Roman cross was later carved on its upper portion (Fig. 22).

Further north we find the Laplanders (16) marking their idols in the form of the *crux ansata* with the blood of the sacrificed. The *crux ansata* is also found on runic monuments in Sweden and Denmark.

On a statuette of a Gallic deity discovered in France, the tunic is covered all over with crosses, recalling the robe of Inetzolcoatl in Mexico. This god holds in one hand a mallet and in the other a jar. Regarding this mallet it is said (2) that with the Gauls the Tau cross came to stand for the hammer of Thor—not only an engine of destruction, but also an instrument of life and fecundity. This same symbol, the double-headed mallet, associated (9) with Osiris in Egypt, and also found among the Hindus (7), is but another form of the cross (Fig. 23).

The significance of the cross in Christianity is usually accredited to the crucifixion of Christ. In this procedure the Romans followed the example of the Greeks and Eastern peoples of nailing condemned criminals upon the cross until they died. Zöckler states that the crucifixion was primarily an insult to those condemned to death, their bodies being exposed as prey to animals and birds. The Tau cross was also used as an instrument of

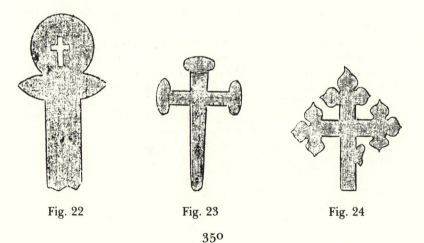

Fig. 22   Fig. 23   Fig. 24

torture and signified the infamy of the condemned. It could not be used upon a Roman citizen. Perhaps the idea of malediction we sometimes find associated with the cross derives from this usage.

Leaving aside the question raised by Robertson (9) as to whether or not the whole Christ episode is a myth, it is certainly true that the world was flooded with the cross in pre-Christian times, and it seems not unlikely that it should early have become the most potent symbol of the new religion; for the cross has always been, and its power was always only the power of the spirit which was poured into it as a symbol. It is perhaps unnecessary to point out that its use as the symbol of resurrection, the specific modern Christian interpretation, is in no way new. We have already spoken of this, but it might be well to mention here that there is a whole series of hanged gods preceding Christ, and these also were resurrected. We recall the hanging of Attis, Marsyas, and Odin, who were reborn after their ordeal. That these hangings had the significance of crucifixion is proved by the fact that the two words were used interchangeably in ancient and early Christian times. Robertson (10) tells of an effigy from the island of Philae representing Osiris in the form of a crucified god, wept over by Isis and Nephthys. When we remember that the tree is predominantly a mother symbol (12), the significance of this procedure becomes clear to us: the hero is delivered back to the mother for rebirth, thus becoming immortal. The tree is here clearly the Tree of Life. Bayley (11), in discussing the Odin myth, shows us an interesting reproduction of an old cross where the resemblance to the tree is very clear (Fig. 24). Jung (12) remarks that "it is not astonishing that the Christian legend transformed the tree of death, the cross, into the tree of life, so that Christ was often represented on a living and fruitbearing tree." Mithras[5] is represented as reborn of, or placed within, a tree, as were also Osiris, Dionysos, and Adonis.

Zöckler (14) tells us that during the first epoch of Christianity the following of the cross was still for the early Christians a very painful reality, and we find as yet no veneration or worship of it. It is a thing to be borne, not revered. The sign of the cross, however, was in popular use, as a method of driving away evil spirits and healing those possessed by the devil. Disguised signs of the cross were placed on ornaments, epitaphs, etc., and it was disseminated in the form of objects which recall its image as the trident; an anchor, or a ship with rigging; and in forms already employed by other cults, such as the *crux ansata* and the swastika. But the world was still too inimical to Christianity for the cross to be openly shown in a religious connection. According to d'Alviella, at the close of the third century the Christians designated Christ by the monogram of the first two letters of the Greek word ΧΡΙΣΤΟΣ, thus ⳩ . This was in the vision seen

[5] Cf. *Psychology of the Unconscious* (1916 edn.), p. 278; CW 5, par. 368.

by Constantine and brought about changes in the external meaning of the cross. Constantine's vision showed him a cross along with the above monogram, and the latter he adopted as his sign. It thus became a war flag, a sign of sovereignty over the world.

The addition of a transverse bar to the above monogram is supposed to indicate Christ on the cross, thus ☧ or ✳ or, by a process of simplification ⳨ or ┼. (We also hear of this monogram being derived from the *crux ansata* in Egypt and standing for the name of one of their gods.)

Constantine had the cross (2) on coins during his reign as well as, and along with, representations of Mars, Apollo, etc. Later the cross was everywhere. In the fifth century the *crux ansata* became rare except in Celtic countries. The swastika also appears less frequently in Europe at this time. The Latin and the equilateral cross were at first employed without discrimination. Only gradually did the former become associated with the West and the latter with the East. The crucifixion, the body on the cross, first appears in the seventh century. It is a somewhat remarkable fact (12) that in early Christian representations Christ appeared not nailed to the cross but standing before it with arms outstretched. It has been suggested that the crucifixion posture may derive from the Perso-Scythian usage of slaying a "messenger" to the god, flaying him and stuffing his skin with arms outstretched. This is analogous to the "ambassador" of the Jews, and in both cases the idea of the cross-form may derive from the fact that in the gesture language and picture writing of savages, that is the recognized attitude of the ambassador, or go-between. In so far as this posture is the least well adapted to self defence, it becomes the sign of complete submission and acceptance, where the individual throws himself upon the mercy of some greater power.

In the Middle Ages the crucifixion became one of the most popular themes for artistic representation. At this time also the cross became the symbol at popular rites, e.g., the market crosses in Germany, etc.

Constantine laid the foundation for the mediaeval conception of the cross as the sign of the missionary power of Christianity, the climax of which was reached with the Crusades. The erection of the cross in any district meant the proclamation of missionary work or the fact that the district had been joined to the Church. At last the cross became consecrated and venerated and prominent in worship of the Church. It was a sign of protecting grace.

Eventually the cross came to working miracles by itself, and legend was created around it as if it were a living thing. One of the most interesting of these stories appears in the thirteenth century mystical poem by Giacomo da Varaggio.[6] The religious art of this time was intensely symbolic and formalized.

[6] Also known as Jacobus de Voragine. The reference is presumably to his *Golden Legend.*

The Reformation brought about a great change in the interpretation of the cross. It came to stand for the suffering and affliction sent by God to call man to repentance so that he might recognize God's help and increase his faith. It is not the Cross of Christ that man must bear, but his own (Luther). The Reformed Church opposed all figurative representations of the Cross. Through this influence Christian art underwent a pronounced change in representations of the Passion of Christ: it became more realistic, less symbolic.

From the foregoing brief review we see that the cross has stood for many things. The figure of a man with outstretched arms, and all that this posture connotes, is imitated in the cross. We see it as a sign of rain and fecundity. It plays a role in the sun cult. It is an important sign for the keeping away of evil. It is a magic charm of fertility. Again we find it as the Tree of Life—not only the sign of life, but also the symbol of immortality. These manifold meanings of the cross can be brought to a unity only through realizing that the cross is a libido symbol. The Tree of Life and the cross have always been mysteriously identified as phallic emblems, but they need not be so considered necessarily, as a libido analogue may take a specifically phallic meaning, that is, it may be applied in a narrower sexual sense. Most authorities have questioned whether the cross has any relation to the two pieces of wood formerly used in religious fire production. Under the libido theory this relationship appears not at all unlikely, though it is too complex a relation to discuss here. The cross certainly does express the idea of union (particularly evident in the *crux ansata* form), for this idea belongs especially to the thought of eternal rebirth, which, as we have seen, is intimately bound up with the cross.

It seems clear that the cross in its fundamental significance, and also in its accessory functions, is unquestionably a libido symbol. We have assumed some understanding of the libido theory on the part of the reader, as it would be beyond the scope of this paper to go into the further psychological aspects of this question.

Bibliography[7]

1. Goblet d'Alviella, (Count) Eugène. *The Migration of Symbols*, 1894.
2. *The Encyclopedia of Religion and Ethics.* Ed. James Hastings. 1910.
3. Westropp, Hodder M. *Primitive Symbolism as Illustrated in Phallic Worship or the Reproductive Process.* 1885.
4. Churchward, Albert. *Signs and Symbols of Primordial Man.* 1913.
5. Carpenter, Edward. *Pagan and Christian Creeds; Their Origin and Meaning. n.d.*
6. Mortillet, Gabriel de. *Le Signe de la Croix avant le Christianisme.* 1866.
7. Westropp, Hodder M., and C. S. Wake. *Ancient Symbol Worship. Influence of the Phallic Idea in the Religion of Antiquity.* 1875.

[7] The entries have been checked and where necessary corrected.

8. Inman, Thomas. *Ancient Pagan and Modern Christian Symbolism.* 1874.

9. Robertson, John Mackinnon. *Christianity and Mythology.* 1900.

10. Robertson, John Mackinnon. *Pagan Christs. Studies in Comparative Hierology.* 2nd edn., 1911.

11. Bayley, Harold. *The Lost Language of Symbolism.* 1912.

12. Jung, Carl Gustav, *Psychology of the Unconscious.* Tr. B. Hinkle. 1916.

13. Baldwin, Agnes (Mrs. Brett). *Symbolism on Greek Coins.* 1916.

14. Zöckler, Otto. *The Cross of Christ.* Tr., 1877.

15. Blavatsky, Helena Petrovna. *The Secret Doctrine.* 1888.

16. Knight, Richard Payne. *The Symbolical Language of Ancient Art and Mythology.* 1876.

Dr. Jung: Thank you for your excellent and very complete report in the historical and ethnological field; there is really an overwhelming flood of material. I only wish that you had gone more into the libido theory of the symbol. It is such a universal symbol that it covers an enormous area of thought, and it is exceedingly difficult to make out what it means. As you say, it can be traced back to prehistoric times. Among the prehistoric remains in the Landesmuseum here in Zurich are sun-wheels, dug up in this vicinity, which would date from the Bronze Age. They are just ordinary small wheels, about four inches in diameter, circles with four spokes, the most ancient form of the cross. They were probably worn as a sort of charm.

Much earlier, from the Paleolithic Age, there are those remarkable rock-paintings (in the caves of Altamira in Spain, for example), naturalistic representations of animals—the horse, the reindeer, the mammoth, etc. And a wonderful rock-drawing of a rhinoceros with the tick-birds on its back has been discovered in Rhodesia;[8] there is also one of a charging rhino with muscles taut, that is most

[8] Jung evidently had seen a large photograph of the rock-drawing of a rhinoceros with tick-birds published in the *Illustrated London News,* 14 July 1928, pp. 72-73, shortly after its discovery in southwestern Transvaal (South Africa). Rock-drawings, or petroglyphs, of the wheel-like forms that he mentions a few lines further along were also reproduced in the *Illustrated London News,* 20 April 1929; they too were found in the Transvaal. These include what could be called star, cross, and sun forms. A petroglyph from the same area made up of concentric circles is depicted in *C. G. Jung: Word and Image,* p. 80. For comment on such artifacts see "The Tavistock Lectures" (1935), CW 18, par. 81, n. 6.

amazing from the naturalistic point of view. Then one occasionally notices in these animal paintings that there are no feet, and one can only assume that that was because they didn't see them, they were hidden in the grass; so those were the first impressionists, a modern artist could not do better. They are of an extreme age, dating perhaps from fifty to sixty thousand years ago. In Rhodesia, also, they have now discovered, besides the naturalistic representations, a circle with a double cross inside. Now supposing those people were able to naïvely produce such very naturalistic pictures, where did they see this cross to draw? The same race has produced this symbol, a most abstract idea. How do you explain it? One might say that the first philosopher sat down and began to think about the sun as a wheel rolling over the heavens.

But there were no wheels in existence then because the wagon was invented very much later, in the Bronze Age probably. Or he might have gone further and thought of the four cardinal points of the horizon. But one cannot project a late mentality into those primitive men, that is excluded, so we must assume that they have seen that thing, it was a vision.

The primitive has an unsophisticated immediate perception, not only of things without but also of things within, the subjective part of the process of apperception. One calls the external end of the process the real object, and then there is the subjective part which is within. You would be astonished if you could see yourselves as I see you, for instance, as I would be if you told me how I look to you. These primitive people had such a vivid perception that they were able to reproduce what they saw in an amazing way. Thousands of years had to elapse—it was only very late in the development of art that drawings of an equally naturalistic character could be produced again. With such a perception of the object, we must assume a keen faculty of seeing in general, things from within just as well. There is a well-known theory about the cave drawings, that they represent magic images, really the ghosts of animals that were assembled in the cave for magic purposes, probably to secure abundance of game, which was naturally of vital need to the primitive man.

One observes the same sort of thing in the primitives living today.

355

A missionary had a Negro boy who had recently lost his mother, and in the evening as they sat around the fire eating, the boy always put aside food for her and also talked to her. The missionary said, "Your mother is not here," and the boy answered, "But she is here, because she talks to me." He heard her voice and told the missionary what she said. That boy had a subjective perception. Now, if the man had told him to make a drawing of his mother, he would naturally have produced a human woman, and how would we know that it represented a ghost?

So when pictures date from such an age, where they have put no signs on them to indicate what they represented, we don't know whether those pictures in the Dordogne are real animals or ghost animals. It might be that they thought that the animals would gather where the ghosts were; by keeping the ghosts together, they assumed that the animals would also be in that region. Primitives do the same thing now; they do not dare leave their dwellings, inhabited by their own ancestral ghosts, and go to foreign countries where the ghosts would be hostile. So those men perhaps assumed that by guarding the ghosts, they would obtain all the mana, health, fertility, linked up with the idea of the ancestral spirits. We have no means to differentiate, to have a really valid opinion of the pictures of that age, as to whether they are of real animals or ghost animals seen from within.

There are two sorts of images seen from within: mirror or memory images of things to be met with in objective reality, which cannot be differentiated from pictures of real images; and besides those, we can see abstract pictures or designs from the unconscious directly, as triangles or circles or any other geometric sort of design. So we find the two perceptions also in primitive man—concretistic pictures and abstract ornaments. One often wonders where they found such complicated geometric figures, triangles and squares and circles, nowhere to be met with in nature, except perhaps in crystals. We derive them from the thinking process. Therefore I assume that this cross is really a ghost—a psychic reality in the Paleolithic Age. We can't say that it was merely a wheel; one would rather assume that the wheel was discovered through the abstract vision. This is a guess only, but there are certain evidences that things have probably gone that way. So the Paleolithic man saw the absolutely abstract, a true ghost, and it made a tremendous impression on him, exactly as it did on the Christian mystic in his vision of the cross or of Christ with his arms extended; or as it did on St. Hubert when he saw the cross between the antlers of the stag.[9]

The question is, what does that thing represent? It is surely the oldest symbol known to us, and so abstract that one would be completely at a loss to explain it, if there were no context, no surrounding material. But follow it up through the ages to modern times and then one gets, not only a full history of this particular psychological entity, but an almost complete insight into its tremendous importance.

Mrs. Sawyer: They might have gotten it from the rays of the sun.

Dr. Jung: It might be the sun, or a star. In Babylonia, such forms were used as decorations of kings. But if the natural man of those earliest days had represented just the sun, he would have made a naturalistic picture of it, like a globe or circle with an infinite number of rays. He would not see the cross in it. That would come thousands of years later, probably from the wheel. The interesting thing is that in just that naturalistic time such a very abstract symbol could be produced, with just those divisions.

There are other abstract symbols which can be explained as one can explain how the picture-writing of Egypt became the hieratic script and finally the modern Arabic, where hieroglyphs have degenerated into ordinary writing. Such symbols are sort of worn-out abbreviations; it is within our reach to see how certain things degenerate into the usual or the abbreviated forms. There is then a certain depotentiation of the symbol, it loses its original value. Formerly, in China, only holy men and priests could write, and so all scraps of paper were collected because writing was sacred. And it had a beautiful and venerable character, as one can still see. But there is nothing venerable about our present writing, it has lost its symbolic importance.

But this symbol, the cross, has not lost its value; it has increased in importance through the ages. It is not worn out, one cannot explain it by the degenerative process. On the contrary, it is an eternally living symbol. Those of you who are actually drawing

[9] St. Hubert (d. 727), of Liège, patron of huntsmen. According to legend, his encounter with the stag while hunting on Good Friday converted him from his worldly life.

your unconscious material[10] know how often it plays a tremendous role in our analysis, even with people who thought themselves a long way beyond traditional Christianity; it is quite astonishing to see them begin to draw its symbol, the cross. It started, as we have seen, in the remote past, and it has never lost its enormous importance. It can be found in all the four corners of the earth, even in Mexico before Christianity reached there. When the Spanish conquistadores and the padres arrived, they thought the devil must have preceded them, teaching men to worship the cross, as he was supposed to have done seven hundred years before Christ. The Christian fathers said that in Greece the devil anticipated the coming of Christ by the myth of Dionysos, so that when the real Saviour came, they could say, "Oh, the devil has taught us that already." The padres thought it was the same old trick, that Satan had again come and taught them to make crosses. That is one of the reasons that they destroyed that wonderful old Mayan civilization; only two letters of their alphabet now remain, for instance.

There is an extraordinary universality in the cross symbol, a never-failing mystical power, one may call it psychic, which again and again expresses a primordial psychic fact in man. To know what that fact might be, we have taken the trouble to follow it through history, through its ethnological distribution. From all these quarters you have had information from Dr. Barrett today. From this material, you know that it symbolizes the sun when it is surrounded by a circle; it is a symbol of life; also of sex; it is an abbreviation of the human form; it is a tree; it is the earth, and more abstractly, fecundity; also the wheel, the hammer, the axe, and much besides. This is a collection of disparate objects. How can they belong together?

It is like the famous series that Lumholtz made out in his book *Unknown Mexico*,[11] where certain Indian tribes have a peculiar idea of the identity of three entirely different things—the *hikuli*, the corn, and the stag are identical, for instance.[12] The same thing

---

[10] That is, engaged in what Jung called "active imagination," a psychotherapeutic technique involving a "conscious submerging in the unconscious, whose contents are then observed, pictured, . . . painted, modelled, sometimes danced . . . and meditated upon" (Aniela Jaffé, in *C. G. Jung: Word and Image*, p. 115).

[11] By Carl S. Lumholtz (London, 1903).

[12] For an elaboration of this statement see "On Psychic Energy" (1928), CW 8, par. 121 and n. 79. *Hikuli* is the (Mexican) Huichol word for mescal.

exists among the Brazilian Indians who call themselves red parrots. They are not birds and they don't sit in trees, but that makes no difference. They say, "Yes, we have human form but we are red parrots."[13] They must sense an internal identity, something beyond the form. We are of course dumbfounded by the suggestion that obviously different things can be identical.

It was the same puzzle with my primitive Negroes on Mount Elgon. I had assumed that they were sun-worshippers, and they laughed at me as if I had said some obscene nonsense. I was confused. God is called the sun, *adhista*, and not *mungu*, which in Swahili I had supposed meant God. To designate *adhista* as God, they said *adhista mungu*. But since they called it *mungu* in the east, why not in the zenith? I finally discovered that it was the sunrise, not the sun, it was the particular moment, and they themselves were *in it*, it is their particular subjective emotion connected with the sunrise.[14] So the key is that the most disparate objects can be brought together if they are compared from a certain subjective angle, such as their worth or value, for instance. You see, one can say that things that cost the same amount of money are the same, interchangeable. But take a primitive who knows only coins, tell him that one hundred gold francs and a one-hundred-franc note are the same, and he laughs at you. People had to get used to the idea. Coins and paper are absolutely different things, but we get the same subjective feeling whether it is in gold coin or a banknote. And so to the primitive whom the subjective is of immediate and the greatest importance, it doesn't matter that things are concretely different, it only matters that he gets the same emotion from them—the most different things would all range in the same field, so to speak.

Mana may be the voice of the chief, or his breath is mana, the wife of the chief is mana, his chair, his hut, all are mana. A spear, a canoe, lightning, a certain tree—all are mana. If they hear the gramophone, they say *mulungu*.[15] These different things are identical under the aspect of mana, they have the same attitude to them all. They bow to them, they are careful not to touch them, or they

[13] Jung cited this instance again only in his last work, "Symbols and the Interpretation of Dreams" (written 1961, published in *Man and His Symbols*, 1964), CW 18, par. 465.

[14] Ibid., par. 551.

[15] Ibid., where Jung states that Swahili *mungu* is a derivative of Polynesian *mulungu*. Also see above, 20 Feb. 1929, n. 3.

observe other ceremonies, because they are mana. When that is concerned, it doesn't matter what the objects are, it is only the subjective emotion that matters. Sometimes it is mana today and tomorrow no longer. It may again be merely a concrete object. For example, suppose a native comes across an old petrol tin and kicks it away and a fortnight later falls ill. Then he begins to think that tin was mana, and he shouldn't have offended it. So he sends his boy out to that thing in the bush with an offering of fruit and oil, in order to propitiate it, and now he is very reverential as he passes it.

Then there is the story of the old anchor cast up on the shore. A Negro broke off one of the pointed ends to use for a plow, and soon after, he became ill. Then he knew that the anchor had mana, so he took the broken end back, most respectfully, and after that, he always greeted it, bowing very deeply whenever he had occasion to pass by. As soon as they are mana, the most heterogeneous things are the same, all parts of the divine process. We can see the same thing in our own psychology. For instance, a man with a mother complex sees his mother in almost any older woman, or a woman of a certain kind, even in his own daughter. All are identical, there is the whole row, all alike, just the same. We are unaware of these things, yet they occur daily.

My Pueblo chief tried a long time to find a convincing simile to express his feeling about the sun. He finally said, "A man up in the mountains is not even able to build his fire without the sun." Wood wouldn't burn, no trees would grow without the sun, so naturally sun and life are identical. And sex is life, it produces children, so the sun is sometimes credited with a phallus as the symbol of generative power.[16] Life, human form, man, the living thing, the product of fertility, even the gods have human form. Also, the tree symbolizes life. It is alive like a human being, with head, feet, etc., and it lives longer than man, so it is impressive, there is mana in a tree. The cottonwood trees in the African bush reach a fabulous height, and as a rule they are regarded with awe. Trees talk, in any number of tribes men go out and talk with trees,

[16] For Jung's earliest account of the solar phallus hallucinated by a psychotic, around 1906, see *Symbols of Transformation*, par. 151 (as in 1912 edn.). This became a classic case for Jung in 1910, when he encountered a reference to a sun tube in an ancient Mithraic liturgy. Also see "The Structure of the Psyche" (1927), CW 8, par. 317-319, and "The Concept of the Collective Unconscious" (1936), par. 105.

they are identified with them. Formerly a tree was planted when a child was born, and as long as the tree lived the child lived—another case of identity. Trees through their fruits are nourishing, so they acquire a mother quality. There is a Germanic legend that the ash and the alder were the first two human beings, and there is the same story about a male and female tree in Persian mythology—they were the original human beings. Then there is the world-tree, Yggdrasill, with its roots in the earth and its branches in Heaven; the first life came from that tree, and at the end of the world the last couple will be buried in Yggdrasill; human life begins and ends in the tree.[17]

And so with the earth. It is productive, fertile, obviously a maternal life-giver, as the sun is life and sex. They are identical through the function. All these things have the same function, the same value, so they are the same. It was the application of the symbols to implements which gave the primitive his tools. The wheel, the hammer, the axe—these were the first tools, and they also are life-givers, they contain spirit. My battle-axe saves my life. In certain primitive languages a prefix or suffix is added to the name of my tool or weapon, designating it as being alive; my sword is alive, yours is dead. So all the tools are really living because they help our living. The wheel is such an important invention—try living without it and see! Live under primitive circumstances and see what happens when such a simple mother's tool as the needle is lost. One would gladly pay an exorbitant price for it. Weapons are life-giving protectors against the onslaught of wild animals. In the Minoan civilization they worshipped the double battle-axe as a most sacred thing. The Minoans were good at carving wood; the great palace of Minos was a wooden structure in its upper stories.

So we see that the sun, life, sex, the human being, the wheel, the hammer, the axe, all these and many more are identical because they function in the same way. And the cross symbolizes all of them, it contains all that, all are reproduced in the form of the cross. It directly represents the life one is spending, and because it is life, it is all important. Since the primitives were afraid that it was exhaustible, they sacrificed to the very centre where life comes from, and this was the centre of the cross. Indians make a cross of two

[17] Concerning Yggdrasill, the cosmic ash-tree in Norse mythology, see *Symbols of Transformation*, pars. 349, 367 (as in 1912 edn.), and "The Philosophical Tree" (1945), par. 461.

ropes over a pond and sacrifice right in the middle, because that goes down to the life-giving spring. They feed it so that the well of life may be flowing again. And the cross is an apotropaic symbol. It is used for protection, to ward off evil, which is death-bringing; if one is in possession of the life-giver itself, evil can't get one. People still cross themselves in danger or in a thunderstorm. During the recent upheaval in Jerusalem[18] the Christians put a cross on their doors to protect themselves against the Arabs.

Now we will wind up. Why is the giver of life represented by the cross?

Dr. Barrett: In man's tendency to anthropomorphize all his conceptions of life, he makes his own figure the form of the cross.

Dr. Jung: So you would say the cross is man as the source of mana? Do you mean something like this? Man certainly experiences himself as a creator in sexuality. Sex is the union of two different principles, the sexual act is the meeting of two opposing directions. The association of the cross and sexuality is shown by the phallic crosses which Dr. Barrett has mentioned, so in as much as life springs from sex, man feels himself a life-giver through sexuality.

Another source of life fertility is the earth. To early primitive man, the earth was flat, and they saw its horizon as a circle. In the more advanced civilization of the North American Indians, the earth is represented as a circle, and they put in the four cardinal points. The observer is naturally always in the centre of that circle or cross. Thus one arrives again at the symbol of the cross within the circle. If the figure of man represents a cross, the circle around it most probably represents the horizon. Or it might also be that it is a magic circle drawn around man as a mana figure. Mana figures are always in a way taboo. I fancy that in some such way the so-called sun-wheel originated. The mana of man, of the earth, of the tree and so on—life in every form—was represented by the cross and the circle, apparently on account of the similarity of the form of man and the tree with a cross, and concerning the earth, on account of the partition of the horizon. (In astrology, the sign of earth is ♁ and of Venus ♀.)

---

[18] A Jewish-Arab clash over the Wailing Wall in 1928.

But that would be explaining the symbol through its objectiva-tion, and my question is, why is the life-giver represented by the cross? It not only symbolizes the sun, it symbolizes sex, or the points of the horizon, or the human form, but they do not all necessarily suggest the cross. It is not very clear why it should stand for all these mana objects. Take peculiar electric phenomena, like light-ning, polar lights, and so on, they all have to do with electricity, but what is electricity? The cross designates the essence of all these objects, as electricity designates the essence, the force or power in all its different manifestations.

Dr. Barrett: Was there an intuitive idea that the cross would be the right symbol for all this?

Mrs. Baynes: Do you not have to go back to the original vision of the primitive man, to intuition?

Dr. Jung: Yes, it seems to have been one of the most original intuitions of man that the right form to express the source of mana would be the cross. Plato says in the *Timaeus* that when the Demi-ourgos created the world, he divided it into four parts, and then he sewed them together again, four seams in the form of the cross.[19] Here the origin of the world is connected with the sign of the cross, the original act of giving life. Pythagoras, who was earlier than Plato, says that the fundamental number is four, the *tetraktys*, which was considered by the Pytha-goreans as a mystical entity. In Egypt, the Eight was the most sacred company of the gods, the Ogdoads. There the origin of the world is watched by the *four* monkeys and the *four* toads.
Horus, the rising sun, has four sons. One finds the four in the paradise legend where four rivers flowed out of Eden[20]—the source of life. So since four is one of the primitive numbers that were first geometrically visualized in a prehistoric age, when abstract counting was not invented, people probably saw the cross in the form of four: ⋰ or: ⋰ . This figure suggests the typical crosses: $+$ and $\times$. So the number four and the cross are probably identical.

[19] *Timaeus* 36B. See "A Psychological Approach to the Dogma of the Trinity" (1940), CW 11, par. 190 and the related diagram, and *Symbols of Transformation*, pars. 404, 406 (as in 1912 edn.).

[20] In *Aion* (1951), CW 9 ii, par. 353, the four rivers are the Gihon, Pison, Hiddekel, and Euphrates.

My idea is that the symbol of the cross does not originate from any *external* form, but from an *endopsychic vision* of the primitive man. The peculiar nature of the vision expresses, as nearly as man can grasp it, the essential quality of life's energy as it appeared not only in him but also in all his objects. It is an absolutely irrational fact to me that vital energy should have anything to do with a cross or with the number four. I don't know why it is perceived in such a form; I only know that the cross has always meant mana or life-power.

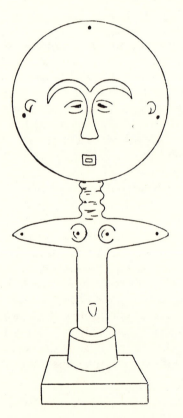

Wooden figure of a god.
From Accra, Gold Coast [present-day Ghana]

Ceremonial sword of wood.
From the Batak, Sumatra [Indonesia]

Mask (wood). Opaina Indians, Northwestern Brazil

Cap worn to influence the
spirits of the rice.
Celebes [Indonesia]

Design on a clay vessel.
Egypt, 1580-1350 B.C.

LECTURE VI

13 November 1929

Dr. Jung:
We will devote the seminar today to Dr. Harding's report about the moon.

THE SYMBOLISM OF THE CRESCENT AND ITS PSYCHOLOGICAL MEANINGS[1]

Before reading this paper on the crescent I should like to make a few remarks on the nature of the problem that the group found themselves confronted with. In the case of the cross, as we all realized when we listened to Dr. Barrett's paper, the problem was one of correlating an enormous mass of material. The cross as a symbol is relatively easy to trace. It appears everywhere, in almost every age and culture, in art and literature and on monuments. There was no lack of material, and the task the group had to perform was to go after it and hammer it into shape. The cross lends itself to this kind of treatment, for it symbolizes energy and is associated with the idea of weapons—the sword, the hammer, the axe. This is the truly masculine way of dealing with a masculine symbol.

But the problem of the crescent is exceedingly different. The material about it is relatively scanty. Nowhere does it appear in art and literature in the obvious and prolific fashion that characterizes the cross material. We found legends whose meaning was subtle, hidden, just as subtle and evanescent as the light of the moon herself. We could not go at it hammer and tongs in the masculine, academic fashion. So I ask for your indulgence if this exceedingly feminine subject is treated in an entirely feminine way.

Let us start with the reason for taking up the crescent symbolism at all. The dreamer has come to a place where he fully realizes his dual nature. On the one hand his intellectual and spiritual studies have left him in the

[1] Much of the material in this report was later incorporated in Harding's *Woman's Mysteries, Ancient and Modern* (London and New York, 1935; revised edn., 1955, with intro. by Jung, which is in CW 18, pars. 1228-1233).

air—they have proved quite sterile. On the other, his pursuit of the sensual side has left him disgusted. When he goes one way immediately the urge to go the other arises and he is at an impasse. Then he dreams of the cauldron. And in it are the symbols of two religious tendencies. I say tendencies, for although today these symbols stand for two of the most dominant religions of the world, namely Christianity and Islam, yet they predate these manifestations by many centuries, and have held for mankind progressively throughout the ages the secret of a *road* by which man perchance might solve the problem of his dual nature. For the problem of our dreamer is the great human problem, and for that reason it is of vital importance for each one of us to find if possible how a solution may be reached.

Man, by the very fact of becoming man and ceasing to be wholly animal, was precipitated into this predicament; he is still animal, but by becoming human he became also a conscious, that is, a spiritual being. The problem that our dreamer is up against is exactly this problem. It is the one that has concerned man from time immemorial; animal—spiritual—and somewhere man must find *himself*. This is the problem of man throughout the ages. He has seen in other spheres in nature incompatible forces at work, and there perhaps a solution has been reached which may for a little while give rest from this ever-recurring conflict. And out of that outer happening he has culled a symbol, whose validity consisted in the fact that by taking the external happening as a picture of the internal psychological conflict, man could, by a sort of identification or mimetic magic, really gain release from his inner conflict, and by virtue of the symbol could reorganize his energies on a different plane, solving the problem, as it were hypothetically, until bit by bit the energy released by the solution of the conflict served to create a new self for the man, which contained elements derived both parts of his nature.

So that when our dreamer finds in the cauldron these two symbols which have repeatedly formed the nuclei of a whole series of religions from the earliest antiquity up to the present time, it is as though the dream would say: "This is how the best and greatest of men in the past have found release from this conflict, the one group following the *cross* and the other the *crescent*." But these symbols go opposite ways. This man has been subjected to the influence of both, but neither holds for him that compelling power which, for other men and in other times, could solve the conflict and release them for life on a new plane. For him the problem must be carried a step further. But first he must discover for himself, and in his own terms, psychological, not magical, nor religious, what these symbols mean.

This was the problem that the members of the group put before themselves when they started on the task of studying the crescent and its sym-

368

bolism. One member of the group undertook to look up the primitive material; one the Hindu; another the religions of the eastern Mediterranean, with their cults of the Great Mother and moon goddesses; and so on. Then the group as a whole came together and attempted to correlate and if possible understand the large mass of material which had been accumulated. The following notes give a brief summary of their findings only. For the particulars of the material on which the paper is based I would refer you to the individual members of the group who went through the literature relating to the special field that they each individually took up. But it seemed to us best, owing to the nature of the crescent symbol itself, not to attempt to give a detailed account of the ethnological material, but instead to approach the subject as it were from within, so that we might reach as true a subjective comprehension of its peculiar character as possible.

I. *The Moon as a Man.* In the most ancient cultures, Iranian, Persian, etc., the moon appears as a man. In the earliest form he is the mythical ancestor of the king. For instance, Genghis Khan[2] traced his ancestry to a king who had been conceived by a moon-ray. In a later form of the myth the moon is a god. The typical story is that the moon-man begins his career by fighting the devil who has eaten his father, the old moon. He overcomes the devil and reigns on earth, where he establishes order and agriculture, and is the judge of men. In the end, however, he is again pursued by his enemy the devil, and dies by fragmentation. He then goes to the underworld, where he exercises the function of judge of the souls in the underworld.

The story of the moon-gods follows the same pattern. In their upper-world phase they are beneficent, with the attributes of Truth, Justice, Constructiveness, and Fertility. In their underworld phase they are destructive, they are also judges of the dead and mediators between man and the gods.

II. *The Moon as Woman.* A goddess of the moon appears as the central figure in many of the ancient religions, in Babylonia, Egypt, and Greece. She also appears in Rome under the guise of Diana, and in mediaeval Europe as the Virgin Mary. We have taken a typical example the goddess Ishtar of Babylon.

Like the moon-gods, Ishtar had a two-fold character. She is both the moon that rises in the sky and increases to fullness and the dark moon that creeps upon the full moon and overcomes it utterly. She has many lovers, but is always virgin. Her son Tammuz is a sun-hero. He is also the vegetation of the whole earth. He is the lover of Ishtar and is condemned by her to a yearly death. There was a religious fast of lamentation when

[2] Mongol conqueror (1167-1227).

the annual death of Tammuz was celebrated. Her later lover Gilgamesh[3] reproached Ishtar for her fickleness, for she had loved in turn Tammuz, a bird, a lion, a horse, a shepherd, a gardener, and then himself. She was early connected with springs, which are the source of life in the Arabian desert.

In her bright or upper-world phase Ishtar is worshipped as the Great Mother, bringing fruitfulness to earth. She was known as "Queen of the dust, and Mistress of the Field." She promoted the fertility of man and beast and was the goddess of wedlock and maternity, and the moral governor of men. In her underworld phase she destroyed all she had created in her upper-world activity. She is Goddess of the Terrors of the Night. She is the Terrible Mother, goddess of storms and war. She plays all possible feminine roles. She is invoked as "Virgin Mother, Daughter of thy Son."[4]

Her rites were orgiastic. She was served by priestesses who were also sacred harlots. She was known as the "Ship of Life" who bears the seed of all living things. She is related to the shape of the crescent resting on the water. There was a Chaldean goddess, Nuah, who carried the seeds of all living things in an ark. (Compare the Hindu word *arka*, which means crescent.) This links her to Noah and his ark, in which the animals were preserved, one pair of each species, when the world was destroyed by flood. These animals carried the seed of life and from them the world was repopulated, as though they were the parents of all life on the regenerate earth.

III. *The Moon in its Three Phases.* The moon appears in art and symbols in three forms: a) The crescent or waxing moon, where it is generally associated with a star. This is the commonest form in art. It is the symbol of the moon goddesses, is the form used in the Islamic religions, and also forms the national standard of Turkey and Egypt (Figs. 1 and 2).[5] It was

Fig. 1   Fig. 2

[3] See above, 30 Jan. 1929, n. 4.
[4] Dante, *The Divine Comedy: Paradiso*, XXXIII, i.
[5] On the Turkish and Egyptian flags the crescent is displayed vertically at the left.

also found in early Christian catacombs as a symbol of the Land of Heaven (Fig. 3). (b) The full moon is occasionally seen. In certain Indian pictures it is on the left hand of the Buddha while the sun is on the right. There is such a picture in Dr. Jung's library. We have here a picture of a Chinese sage from the fifth century B.C. He is shown as a learned doctor, with his bundle of scientific remedies, minerals, and herbs which he has gathered from all over the earth. But still men die and his wisdom is not sufficient to save them. In the picture he is seen struck by the sudden realization that if he could only obtain the wisdom of the moon also, he would be able to cure all disease and bring immortality to mankind. (c) The waning moon. In its waning the moon symbolizes the fear and inevitability of death. We have illustrations of this in pictures of Time and Death, who are represented with the inverted crescent of the scythe.

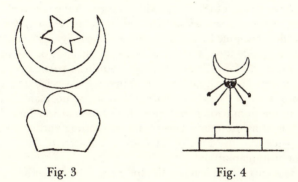

Fig. 3   Fig. 4

IV. *The Moon as Bringer of Ecstasy.* In the Vedantic Upanishad the moon is magical power, the mana which brings ecstasy. The same idea is shown in the moon-tree, from whose fruit the gods extracted the soma drink which gave them immortality. Here is a picture (Fig. 4) of the Chaldean moon-tree. The earthly counterpart of the legend is a tree or bush called the moon-tree. From the fruits of this tree a drink is extracted which is called "soma." This drink contains a drug which produces a state of ecstasy, for which purpose it is used in certain religious rites. We find the same method of producing ecstasy employed in many other religions, for instance, wine in the Dionysian mysteries, and peyote, a drug used for the purpose in a particular cult in North America. The moon is still said to have this effect. It is recognized today, albeit perhaps unconsciously, in the use of such words as lunacy, and in the superstition that if you sleep in the light of the full moon you may become crazy. You may even hear lovers give as an excuse for their indiscretions that it was a moonlit night.

V. *The Moon as the Dwelling Place of Spirits.* In Persian, Hindu, and Egyptian literature the moon is represented as the place where the soul goes after the death of man. On the moon the soul is judged, and goes either to the upper world or back to the earth. On the moon-barge the dead travel to the underworld and await their regeneration. The moon is thus a place for birth, for death, and for rebirth.

VI. *The Moon as Giver of Fertility.* In many primitive religions the moon is held to be the giver of children. Offerings are made to her on this account by childless women. Her aid is asked in childbirth. And on the other side it is considered dangerous for a young girl to sleep in the moonlight for fear of becoming pregnant. The primitive people of Nigeria think that the Great Moon Mother sends the Moon-Bird to bring the babies. This is perhaps related to our own myth of the stork. In this category belong the moon's relations to springs and the weather. The moon is a giver of moisture, and rain charms are generally made in relation to the phase of the moon. We still have the same idea when we associate the changes in the phase of the moon with changes in the weather.

VII. *The Moon as Regulator of Time and Moral Governor of Men.* Moon-time preceded sun-time by many centuries. The religious calendar of the Jews and of Christendom is still reckoned on the basis of the moon. For instance, Easter falls on the first Sunday following a particular full moon.

The tides were known quite early to be in some way related to the moon. So that our saying, "Time and tide will wait for no man" is really an assertion of the dominating character of the moon order. That the moon was thought of as the moral governor is interesting and accords exactly with the place that the Eros order does as a matter of fact take in the regulation of human affairs.

In all these myths and legends we find certain facts standing out. First, the changing character of the moon struck man's attention, in its contrast to the sun. The sun either shines or does not shine; it is either here or not here. But the moon is not like that. The moon may be partly here, she changes continually. From this come such ideas as that the moon is changeable, the fickle moon. These are terms that are also applied to woman. She also is said to be changeable and fickle, and from the man's point of view it is so. That is the way her moon-like character appears to him, for it is hard for him to understand its nature. But to a woman, that her life should flow in cyclic phases is the most natural thing in the world. For her the life-force ebbs and flows not only like the tides, coming up and going down in a nightly and daily rhythm as it does for a man, but also in moon cycles—quarter phase, half phase, full moon, decline, and so round to dark moon. During this cycle her energy waxes, shines fully, and then wanes again. The change affects not only her physical life and her sexual life, but also her psychic life. To a man this seems very strange. But he experiences the same law in his own inner life of the unconscious through his anima, and if he does not understand it, it irritates him and

372

makes him moody. Such a feeling may become so obsessive that the man may get completely out of touch with the external reality and present to the world only his moods, which are his reaction to his own subjective inner reality. But that is the extreme. In the ordinary case where a man finds this strange unaccountable thing happening inside himself, he does not realize that he has to wait till the right phase of the moon comes round. The ancients understood this when they said that certain things must be done at particular phases of the moon. If a man wanted a love-charm or a rain-charm or an artistic inspiration, and the ritual prescribed that the rites or magic must be performed at the new moon or at the full moon, or perhaps even at the dark of the moon, the man must curb his impatience till that time arrived. This is a lesson that a woman is compelled to learn. She has to submit to this law of her nature whether she will or not. But for a man it is much harder to submit. It is his nature to fight for a thing he wants and strive to overcome all obstacles by force. But when he comes to dealing with the moon, whether within himself as his own anima principle, or in the woman he is closely associated with, say his wife, he is compelled to submit to an order that is different. His nature is like the sun. In the daytime it shines, and man works and accomplishes. Then at night the sun is not there and man goes to bed and is not there either. But with the moon—sometimes when it is in the sky at night it is full moon, in a few days it has waned and gives only an uncertain light, or it may be completely dark. A man meets a woman. It is full moon with her, and he says, "Ah! At last a woman who is bright." He meets her again a few days later and to his dismay he finds the moon has waned and she gives only a feeble and uncertain light, or it may be that she is completely the dark woman. This is the bewildering fact. He tries to extricate himself from the incomprehensible situation by blaming the woman, saying that it is she who is incomprehensible, fickle, unreliable. But then the next phase of the problem comes and he finds that exactly the same thing happens in regard to his own feeling. A man under the sun, in a world of reality, would expect his feeling to be stable, accountable, reliable. He either likes a thing or he dislikes it; he either loves a woman or he does not love her, as the sun shines or it is night. But he finds his feeling is as erratic and unreliable as a woman. He finds he loves one day and is indifferent the next. This is terribly disconcerting, and so he decides to get along without feeling, to disregard it, to base his conduct on those things that can be relied on— *facts*, with no nonsense about them. This disregard of the moon principle of relatedness through feeling has led to a great deal of conflict and unhappiness between men and women. For the man disregards it, while it is the woman's basic principle. On account of this disregard of feeling a man can live in the most unattractive surroundings. So long as his furniture is solid and useful, he does not care if it offends the eye. But for a woman this is exactly the thing that matters most. If a chair or a table has a feeling-value for her she will keep it even if it is most impractical, so that it is always being knocked over or is too delicate to be sat on. But to her facts are of little importance when it is a question of the atmosphere of a room! In the more direct matters of relationship between men and women even more havoc has been wrought by this disregard of the moon, or one might say of the Eros side, which is the principle of relatedness through feeling. In our Western civilization we pay no attention to this. In other civilizations, however, recognition has been given to this difference between men and women. There is an old Persian book on the Art of Love, many hundreds of years old. It contains much of the old lore on the subject of lovemaking, and great attention is paid in it to the correct ways of approaching the lady. Regulations are laid down for each day of the moon. Only by following these directions minutely could the lover hope to gain the favour of his beloved. On one day of the moon a caress with the tips of his fingers on her right cheek was prescribed. On another she should be kissed this way, on a third that, and so forth. This old book contains a drop of profound wisdom. In the ancient Persian ritual it was projected to the outer world, so that these regulations were referred to the moon in the sky. But we must understand them psychologically. A man should woo his own feeling with as careful a regard to the particular phase of his own inner moon as this Persian book prescribes. Further he should observe as strict regulations about his approach to the woman. For the phase of the moon that she happens to be under is not a matter that she can control, however willing she may be, but nevertheless it dominates the situation.

Closely associated to this aspect of the moon-symbolism is the difference in quality between the sun's light and the moon's. The sun's light is bright, warm, glowing and dry, while the moon's light is soft and cold, giving warmth to no man; further the moon is moist, for on moon-light nights dew falls. The sun shines by its own light, the moon but by reflected light, just as we hear the constant complaint that woman has no ideas of her own, she only reflects man's thoughts. But the moon *is* and we have to reckon with it. These characteristics of brightness, heat, and dryness on the one hand and coldness, darkness, and moistness on the other have been gathered up by the Chinese into their great concepts of Yang and Yin, male and female.

One of the men members of the group writes, "The moon seems to me an especially feminine being. This impression is produced by its smooth light and the fact that it is to be seen in the night, that is, in mystical circumstances." This is a strange remark, for women are to be seen in the day just as much as men are. Yet we all know what he means. The thing that is peculiarly feminine does shine only in the night, that is to say when the light of the sun is removed, and man's work and activity are laid aside.

374

That is why it is so difficult to talk about the moon-symbolism. For, as the Chinese sage Lao-tse said about Tao, "The Tao that is talked about is not the true Tao,"[6] so one might just as well say, "The feminine essence, when it is talked about, is no longer the true feminine essence." As Dr. Jung once put it: "Yin is like a mother-of-pearl image hidden in the deepest recesses of the house."

The moon's light is cold. But we are not accustomed to think of a woman as being cold and a man hot. We generally think of a man as being relatively without feeling, that is, cold, and a woman warm. But we have to remember that while a man can be cold and calculating on the thinking or business side, there is also a type of woman who can be terribly cold and calculating while apparently living on the feeling side. It is relatively rare to find a man who is not touched to warmth on the erotic side, but there are whole classes of women who are as cold as icebergs and as calculating as stock-brokers even while they are living on the erotic side. The moon symbolizes this aspect of woman which, in spite of its lack of warmth, is so terribly attractive to men. The more the woman is outside the game of love, playing it as a game, the more effectively does she play her role of siren, and the more likely is it that the man will get hopelessly enmeshed.

It was, of course, known from the most remote times that woman in her actual physical makeup is in some way related to the moon, with her moon-cycles of menstruation. Thus we find menstrual taboos that have been put upon woman throughout the ages. Primitive man felt that at such times the woman was peculiarly under the influence of the moon and was there-fore especially dangerous. At that time even her shadow falling on a man's path could lure him away from his business. So that it was said among the North American Indians that the shadow of a menstruating woman would destroy the efficacy of the war bundle, or cause food to go bad, or frustrate the object of a journey.

The taboo on women is carried to its greatest extreme under Islam, where the crescent moon stands as the symbol of the whole religious cul-ture. Here women are not only secluded during menstruation, but must live their whole lives behind the veil. It is as though in the Islamic system woman is only known in her moon aspect and is therefore dangerous at all times. In accordance with this we find that Islam teaches that woman has no soul of her own. The Prophet says: "The woman is a man's gar-ment." That is, she is recognized only as the personification of the man's anima, and is accorded a place in heaven only as the spouse of her husband. It is interesting to note further that, whether as cause or effect, women

---

[6] Possibly a paraphrase or another version of the opening words of Ch. I of the *Tao Tê Ching*, which Arthur Waley (*The Way and Its Power*, 1934) translates: "The Way that can be told of is not an Unvarying Way; the names that can be named are not unvarying names."

375

in seclusion in harems and zenanas do as a matter of fact live only for the erotic side of life.

The next quality of the moon that we notice is her ability to give men strange ideas. She insinuates ideas, intuitions, and fantasies which are not at all in accordance with intellectual standards, but are strange, bizarre, and are filled with a peculiar emotion and intoxicating delight. This is seen in the soma drink, which came from the moon-tree and caused intoxication, ecstasy, and fantasies of a compelling charm. This is the Indian and Iranian form of the legend, but we have the same thing in our own language, where we speak familiarly of lunacy, or of being moon-struck, or of a thing being moonshine when it is the wildest fantasy. In slang speech we even speak of moonshine liquor, a spirit which generally contains wood alcohol, whose chief characteristic is that it produces a crazy drunkenness which may even go on to actual madness.

So that besides standing for woman in her harlot aspect, the moon must stand also for that other strange kind of thinking, which is not to be controlled by man's rational laws. For the moon, even as the sun, is high in the heaven and is not amenable to our commands. This kind of thinking which goes of itself, which is not under the sway of logic, does not originate in a man's head. Rather it rises from the lower depths of his being and befuddles his head, like the intoxicating drink, soma. Such thinking comes from those centres in the abdomen which Dr. Jung was talking about in connection with the cauldron. A man would say that such thinking is a sort of womanish thinking, and that that is the confused way a woman thinks most of the time. But a woman would say that when she thinks this way she is likely to be right, while when she thinks in her head, the way a man thinks, she is likely to be wrong or at all events unproductive. But a man feels that when he thinks this way there is something awfully inferior about it, something uncanny and somehow not quite clean. But these ideas, formed under the moon, have a power and compelling quality that ideas originating in the head rarely have. They are like the moon, they grow of themselves, they demand an outlet, and if you do not give them a suitable one they may well produce moon-madness. For the children of the moon must come to birth just as surely as physical children.

The next aspect of the moon that we must consider is her dual quality, which has already been brought out in the myths of the dark moon which replaces the light moon, and even more clearly in the stories of the moon-goddesses, who on the one hand are the mothers of vegetation and all living things, and on the other hand destroy their own productions with unfailing regularity and callousness. This aspect is most clearly depicted in the many stories of the virgin mothers whose sons are their lovers and are condemned to die each year, often by the mother's own edict. This dual quality is shown in certain old pictures, where we have the crescent moon, or a moon-goddess flanked by two animals, a pair of opposites, who are either worshipping her or fighting for her. I will pass round a sketch of a Phoenician sacred moon-tree with its animal worshippers and its legend, "There is the home of the mighty mother who passes across the sky." And to compare with it a reproduction of one of the Cluny tapestries. There we see the Virgin or Diana with her animals all around and the two animals who attend her with their crescent standards. The tapestries represent the senses, hearing, seeing, tasting, feeling, and smelling, and this one of which I show you the picture. It is called "Mon seul désir" and obviously refers to the sixth sense, sexuality.

We get the same idea of the dual quality of the moon in a more metaphysical form in the various legends that the dead go to the moon when they die. From there, in one form of the legend, the redeemed are carried on to the sun, from whence they pass in the eternal flame to the highest heaven, while those who are not accounted worthy are returned to earth for another incarnation. In this legend the idea is expressed that man's judge will not be a reasonable logical Being, whom a man could trust. On the contrary man will be judged by just this irrational, unaccountable factor that he strives so hard to ignore. For man is not complete without that other side that is represented by the moon. This has already been illustrated in the Chinese picture of the sage that I passed round at the beginning of the paper.

But to go back to the moon's dual quality. She is dark and she is light; she is good and she is evil; she is source of all the earth and she is destruction of all; she brings health and she causes sickness. As was said of Ishtar, "She is the divine Astarte, the strength, the life, the health of men and gods; and at the same time she is Evil, Death, and Destruction."

When we seek a modern interpretation of this material we recognize that the upper world ruled over by the white moon belongs to our conscious life, while the underworld where the black moon is queen is the unconscious. The moon-gods and goddesses who move between the two worlds function as mediators. Their two-faced qualities of fruitfulness and destruction, of justice and truth offset by fickleness and deceit, reappear today in the personifications of anima and animus described by Dr. Jung as functions of relatedness between the conscious and unconscious world of man. But this is one aspect of the problem only. For while to the man the moon may be considered as a symbol of his anima, who so often carries his Eros values, to the woman the moon represents her very inmost being. So that we need to go a stage further in our attempt to interpret the meaning of the symbol. For we should fall into the same error as the Mohammedans if we consider woman only as a personification of man's anima. The majority of you will, I am sure, agree with me when I maintain that a woman has a life in her own right, and that, to herself at any rate, she is by no means only the reflection of man's unconscious qualities.

The Great Mother-Moon-Goddesses were all considered as the givers of sexual love. They were served in their temples by sacred harlots. Their rites were dark and unspeakable, and were generally celebrated at midnight with orgies of intoxication and sexuality, and sometimes with infant sacrifices. To us this sounds anything but religious. What were the ancients after? What did they mean by all this? We catch a glimpse of its inner meaning when we turn to the mystics of Islam. They took love in its various stages of Rida, Satisfaction; Shavq, Longing; and Uns, Fellowship or Intimacy, as the outwardly lived dramatic representation of Union with God—just as we in our Christian ritual have sacraments of Baptism, Communion, yes, and even marriage, which are outwardly lived dramatic representations of the stages of initiation, whose goal is Union with God. There was a great woman mystic of Islam, Rabi'a, who lived about the eighth century A.D. She said in regard to the third stage of love, namely Intimacy:

> "I have made Thee (God) the Companion of my heart,
> But my body is available for those who desire its company,
> And my body is friendly towards its guests,
> But the Beloved of my heart is the guest of my soul."[7]

This is the attempt to obtain transformation from the concrete, the material, into the unseen, the spiritual. As the sacred book of the Chinese says in the homily on the Cauldron: "All that is visible must grow beyond itself, extend into the realm of the invisible. Thereby it receives its true consecration and clarity and takes firm root in the cosmic order. Here we see civilization as it reaches its culmination in religion."[8] But this attempt to obtain transformation is made by the approach of the downward-going road, while the cross leads us by the upward-going road. As Christ said: "If I be lifted up I will draw all men unto me."[9] But this road of the crescent leads downwards. Yet it also leads to transformation. As has been said by the Gnostics: "To go up or to go down, it is all the same."[10] Or as William Blake said: "It matters little whether a man takes the right road or the wrong one, provided only that he follows it sincerely and devotedly to the end, for either road may lead him to his goal."[11]

[7] Margaret Smith, *Rabi'a the Mystic and Her Fellow Saints in Islam* (Cambridge, 1928), p. 98.

[8] *I Ching*, tr. Wilhelm/Baynes (3rd edn., 1967), hexagram 50. The passage Harding quotes is part of the commentary on the Judgment.

[9] Cf. John 12:32.

[10] Cf. Heraclitus: "The way up and the way down is one and the same."—John Burnet, *Early Greek Philosophy* (4th edn., 1930), p. 138, frag. 69.

[11] *The Concordance to the Writings of William Blake*, ed. David V. Erdman (Ithaca, 1967; 2 vols.), does not yield a source for this quotation.

So we see that the moon stands for the great *principle of transformation through the things that are lowest.* Things that are dark and cold and moist, things that hide from the light of day and from man's enlightened thinking, hold also the secret of life, that renews itself again and again, until at last, when man understands, he may grasp the inner meaning which has been till then hidden within the very texture of the concrete happening.

In the past when a transformation of this kind was sought, the mystery religions prescribed a ritual of initiation. In Egypt the initiate was ritually put to death and was reborn through the power of Osiris and proclaimed "Son of the Sun." A similar transformation may take place under the moon, only here the rebirth is on the Eros side, not on the Logos side, and the initiate will be called "Daughter of the Moon."

I can give you two modern instances of this type of initiation, both cases of young men. The first was a young man who dreamed that there was a crescent-shaped piece of land which belonged to his father and which had fallen back into a condition of wilderness. The task was laid on him, in his dream, to redeem this piece of property. He knew it would be an exceedingly difficult task as it was marshy land and the haunt of dangerous snakes. He awoke with the sense of a weighty task ahead. Before the end of the week he was suddenly stricken with a serious illness. During his delirium he was continually concerned with the reclaiming of the piece of land. He was also most anxious to be told about the phases of the moon during the three or four weeks that he lay at death's door. There was as a matter of fact a new moon on the night he was taken ill. When he finally recovered he had gained an entirely new attitude to life both on the erotic and creative side. This was his initiation under the moon.

The second example is illustrated by a picture. (On account of the difficulty of reproducing this picture, Dr. Harding supplies this description.) Above is a temple. In the middle is the Holy Stone of the Highest, represented by a greenish square. Around it are the inscripions of ancient priests, who formerly sacrificed in the temple. A sacrifice has just taken place there, and the blood-stained fleece of the sacrificed animal is stretched on the ground before the altar. Below is a dark cavern. "That is the place where no one goes." On the floor is the blood-stained dagger with which the sacrifice was accomplished. Below this is a river which leads to a deeper, unknown underworld. The picture was drawn by a young man of 17 who was in bed after a painful operation performed without an anaesthetic, which had caused a good deal of both physical and emotional shock. In the days immediatly after the operation his relation to his mother was quite peculiar. It was almost as if he had become a little boy again. He could not get on without her and clung to her for support in this rather terrible experience. Then one day he asked for pencils and paper and made the drawing which I have just described. He was quite naïve about it. He did not know that it had any psychological meaning. At first he would not talk about it, but later he gave the following explanation. He said: "It is all inside a mountain. Above is a temple. A sacrifice has taken place there, and the fleece of the sacrificed animal is stretched on the ground before the altar. Below is a dark cavern, that is the place where no one goes." After he had drawn this picture his relation to his mother underwent a complete change. He came out of his regression and was himself again. That was all he said about it. But clearly the operation has appeared in the unconscious as a sacrifice. While he himself is the victim. He has been slain as a lamb and his skin is stretched out on the ground. Psychologically that means he, as his mother's little lamb, has been slain. This is his initiation into manhood. From now on he can no longer take refuge behind her skirts, he is a man, she can no longer make excuses for him. During the period when he was dead as it were, he went again into his mother's womb to be born. This shows in consciousness as his regression to childlike dependence on her. But what will be born out of this ritual death? That we see in the depths of the mountain—the place where no one goes—the deepest levels of the unconscious. Here we see a crescent moon arising, with the star between its horns. That means that out of this initiation experience he will gain a new light in his sky, the light of Eros. No longer will his mother carry all his Eros values and his anima—these he must seek for himself, individually, in his relations to women outside the family. It is as though for him woman was born out of this experience. And to himself there comes a single star, unity, the star that is between the sun and the moon. The promise of the solution for him of the problem of man's duality with which we started this paper.

In the woman's psychology the moon plays a somewhat different role. Here the problem is not one of grasping by conscious effort and strife the Eros values projected in the outer world, but rather of accepting the moon principle within herself, and of being accepted as Daughter of the Moon. It is a question of getting her own Eros principle into its rightful place as the ruler of life. For in our Western civilization women are brought up under masculine laws and ways of functioning, while the moon and all she symbolizes has fallen into disrepute. So that, with women, to be brought under the moon by initiation (or analysis) resembles a sort of re-crystallization of her whole being. In this picture drawn by a woman you get the idea that her whole structure is changing into the direction of the moon-rays, which are passed through her almost like lines of force, so that for the future she will function as a moon-woman. She will not try to solve her problems as a man does, after the pattern of the sun with its hours of conscious effort followed by hours of sleep and oblivion, but will accept the fact that even while the moon is there in the sky it may be only partly there, or even entirely dark. So that her solution will always have something equivocal about it. It will be both dark and light. She will solve the problem of duality in a fashion that differs from the man's solution, for she must make manifest in her own being the dual character of the dark-light moon.

Dr. Jung: Now that you have heard Dr. Harding's most interesting report, you can realize what an extraordinarily difficult chapter in our psychology the moon represents. The last time, we dealt with the sun and reduced it to a positive principle. Outwardly this symbol is embodied by the visible sun and inwardly by the cross, the most ancient vision of man. Today in discussing the moon, we approach a sphere infinitely dark, not only figuratively, but really. The moon is the ever-changing light of the night, the nocturnal sphere of human experience.

You remember that I told you last week of the African Negroes greeting the rising sun. In the same way they salute the waxing moon, that first silver hemicycle in the evening sky. They offer their souls to the waxing moon because that is also a hopeful sign, while the waning moon is the reverse. Primitive man has a marked day-psychology and a night-psychology, as well as a religion of the day and a religion of the night. Day is benign while the night is fraught with evil. In the majority of primitive religions, there is a pale deity of a beneficent kind, perhaps even a trinity, but that is a bit far away and usually there are minor gods, more humanized and closer to them. Then, besides, there is always a nocturnal cult to which magic belongs. The nocturnal element has sometimes been taken up into a very severe ritual form, as in the Catholic Church, where the "dark" magic is transformed into "white" magic. Night is felt as dangerous and full or fears. One sees nothing and cannot defend oneself. The night is peculiarly animated by things that one only vaguely senses and that one would not feel in the daytime. There are ghosts and witches and sorcerers about—nocturnal uncanny influences. That fear of the dubious things in the darkness is to a certain extent banished by the waxing moon, which rises as the sun sets. The night is illumined by the benevolent moon, milder and less impressive than the sun, but beneficent.

On the other hand, the waning moon is felt as unfavourable. It predicts evil and destruction. It is the time of ghosts, when all is dark, it is an opportunity for ghosts and fear. It rises later and later, and the night sets in without light, so that everything undertaken under the waning moon is appointed to decay, it is sterile from the beginning. One finds this feeling everywhere in the customs of the people. The Swiss peasants won't plant their crops in the time of the waning moon because the seeds won't grow; seeds must be put in under the waxing moon. Even my mother never washed the mother of vinegar[12] in the time of the waning moon, for then it would die: there must be a waxing moon for it to be favourable. Rationally, all of this hangs together with the millions-of-years-old impression of primitive man that fear is banished by the rising moon. While on the wane, it means extinction and death, a time when ghosts have power, and man is perfectly defenceless. So, from the very beginning of time, the moon has had a double meaning, it is exceedingly ambiguous in character, while the sun has only the one meaning.

The moon has, then, both a beneficent and a malevolent aspect, as Dr. Harding has mentioned. It produces illness and healing, and it produces madness and healing of the mind. And not only has it a good and a bad influence on the health, but it has a double sex character. You see this duality in languages, it would be quite a study in philology to classify the moon as to sex. In the majority of cases it is felt to be feminine, but there are a good many exceptions. The masculine moon-god has a particular geographical distribution, he is found chiefly in Asia Minor, from the Black Sea down to Egypt, and also on the Greek islands. There is evidence of one in Greece of the third century B.C. but he had also feminine attributes, he meant water, dew, rain, and moisture; he was the god of oracles, of ripening fruit, and also he was helpful in war, a healing god, ruling over health and disease. There was a temple in Karon[13] where the moon-god was worshipped and, connected with that, a medical academy under his patronage. One of his functions was to gather souls after death. He was termed "the gate of the soul after death." These qualities are not only characteristic of the masculine moon-god but of all moon ideas, and it is interesting that, even in the etymology of the word "moon," some of these peculiarities come out in different languages.

The word is derived from three different roots:

[12] A stringy, slimy membrane, composed of yeast cells and bacteria, that forms on the surface of alcoholic liquids and produces acetous fermentation. It is added to wine or cider as a starter to produce vinegar.

[13] Unidentifiable place. Among many works consulted, Frazer's *Golden Bough* did not contain a reference.

1. *leuk*, a word that appears in the Greek word *luka*; German *leuchten*, to light; Latin *luna*, Iranian *lou, luan*.

2. *men*, as name for the moon—in Iranian *mi*; North Breton *miz*; Sanskrit *mas*, Greek *mēnē*.

3. *men*, a different root meaning "measure"—Gothic *mena*; Assyrian *mano*; Anglo-Saxon *mono*. The German word for "month," *Monat*, comes from this root, as also the French *le mois*.

Here one sees something very characteristic of the moon, namely, we must assume that such root-words date from time immemorial, from primordial man, who connected the changes of the moon with the idea of measure. Primitive man connected the moon with mental activity also, and so he thought of the mind as coming from the moon. The first notion of measuring time comes from the phases of the moon. The solar measure came later. We must think about this first connection between the moon and mind, which Dr. Harding has pointed out. I would like to give you other instances. Some light is to be found in Hindu and Sanskrit literature, where the old philosophers obviously found out about this peculiar connection. There is a Sanskrit text: "Then in the centre, with 'This one, above, the mind'; above, doubtless, is the moon; and as to why he speaks of him as 'above,' the moon is indeed above, and as to why he says: 'the mind,' the mind doubtless is speech, for by means of speech everything thinks here. The moon, having become speech, remained above."

This is an example of the peculiarity of the ancient Hindu mind, which was always in doubt whether things were, or whether it thought they were. They said: if you think a thing, it *is*. The moon-mind, in other words, creates; or, as Dr. Harding has put it very poetically, moon children are as real as real children. Man's mind today is not that at all. We could say that our minds formulate, but we couldn't say that the products of the mind are facts, nor that something definite has been created because someone thinks something. To a primitive, when he thinks a thing, then it is, or becomes. His mind is not abstract, it is not yet differentiated.

Here is another Sanskrit text: "Now when that fire goes out, it is wafted up in the wind, whence people say of it, 'it has expired,' for it is wafted up in the wind. And when the sun sets it enters the wind, and so does the moon, and the quarters are established in the wind, and from out of the wind they issue again. And when he who knows this passes away from this world, he passes into the fire by his speech, into the sun by his eyes, into the moon by his mind, into the quarters by his ear, and into the wind by his breath, and being composed thereof, he becomes whichever of these deities he chooses and is at rest."

From these examples you can see that we are not just making a conscious analogy, even these early philosophers realized it.

Mrs. Fierz: What is "mind" in German?

Dr. Jung: Ah, there is a great difficulty. We have no word in German to express the equivalent of the English word "mind." I often use "mind" when talking German. The word *Verstand* does not render the meaning, that is not really Germanic, it is half a Latin word, it is the intellect. There is no such word in the German language; to translate this word "mind," you must give a whole definition. Our only help is the Latin *mens*, from which is derived the French *mentalité*.

Miss Wolff: The word *Vernunft* from Kant's *Critique of Pure Reason?*

Dr. Jung: That means reason, not mind.

Dr. Harding: One might say mind or consciousness on the ideational side.

Dr. Baynes: In mind there is a connotation of purposive activity.

Dr. Jung: Yes, that is perhaps the best suggestion—the intellectual process, consciousness with purposive contents. It is not emotional, nor mere imagery. When you take the German word "Sinn" in its poetical form "Du bist im Herzen, du bist im Sinn,"[14] it gives the concept of mind. In dealing with psychological subjects, one gets into tough places with the meanings of words. So in that connection of the moon with mind, one mustn't understand mind in the modern philosophical sense. It is the mind purely in its original meaning. We can use that hint of purposive content that Dr. Baynes has given us, Primordial man projected this upon the moon.

Now, this most important conception comes from the fact that man had the best opportunity to discover mind in the night when impressions of external reality vanished and when his own subjective functions could manifest themselves unaffected by objective stimuli. So the moon is naturally connected with fantasies, with lunacy. Hence the old superstition that the poisonous rays of the moon pierce the brain, and one wakes up with a mad dream, or

---

[14] = "You are in my heart, you are in my mind." In ordinary usage, *Sinn* = "meaning."

one is mad. In the Middle Ages, the witches used a magic mirror. They put it out in the moonshine for a certain number of nights that it might be impregnated by the moon's rays. Then they gave it to some one whom they wanted to harm and the reflected evil rays drove him mad.

This connection of the mind with the moon is very puzzling and of extraordinary importance for our psychology. I don't want to enter into it now, it is pretty complicated, but we can speak of other aspects, namely, the peculiar changes of the moon, which were most impressive to primitive man. He attempted an explanation for the changes in the heavenly light, and sometimes these stories are quite interesting psychologically, though usually they have no value for us. He was so impressed by the moon changes that he projected into the moon something in himself which is analogous, the anima. But of course the concept of the anima is a very late and a highly abstract one, so we must try to go more to the primitive roots of these things.

I have here a picture of a woman standing in the moon's rays.

There is a tell-tale line of red reaching from the genitals to the head. It shows very well the connection of the moon's rays with blood, linking up the genital to the mental region. And this picture has another peculiarity. What is that?

Dr. Draper: The curved rays of light.

Dr. Jung: Yes, also an irrational phenomenon. The sun's rays are always straight. What is the explanation?

Dr. Harding: Artistically, it carries out the curve of the moon.

Dr. Deady: It conveys force.

Mrs. Fierz: It suggests a wave.

Dr. Jung: That is right. The moon permeates the being with a wave. Now, what effect of the moon do we know that has that wave-like character?

Mrs. Baynes: The tides.

Dr. Jung: Yes, a fluctuation like the tides, which are an expression of the changes of the moon, a sort of tidal wave. Now the woman who made that picture didn't associate her mystical experience with the waves of the sea, but nevertheless she produced a wave, like the effect of the moon's rays. Man has a peculiar perception of waves within himself. This is illustrated in an English metaphor, "a brain-wave" or "a brainstorm." These are alternations of mood that have a wave-like character. In French they are called *les lunes*, in German they would be *Launen*. Mood is equivalent to *Mut* in German, which means courage, but *Gemüt*[15] is the exact opposite of what we mean by mind today. It is an emotional reacting mechanism, and so, if not etymologically, surely psychologically, it is linked up with the waves or tides of the moon, causing mental or emotional upsets, peculiar moods. These are among the most original perceptions in man which he could compare to changes of the moon. To the primitive man it was far more obvious than to us, and also he was more impressionable.

As to the relation of the moon to the menses in woman, we know that they no longer synchronize with the phases of the moon, although the period is a lunar month. How that came to pass we don't know, unless we believe in astrology, which says that our structure is connected with the sun and the moon and the planets. But that is an hypothesis which we cannot prove. Why should

---

[15] *Gemüt* can be variously translated as "sentiment," "emotion," "feeling," "heart." [R.F.C.H.]

women have a lunar period? An old teacher of mine, a distinguished professor of physiology,[16] made desperate attempts to connect the periodicity of menstruation with the tides and the time
when all life was in the sea. He went back to the amphibians who
lived on the seashore and found very rich food at low tide and very
little food in the high spring tide. The connection was not too clear,
and he always got into a bad mood when he was too closely pressed.
The moon was on top of him, he was not on top of the moon.

Science cannot explain this, but that shouldn't hinder us in following up the peculiar connection. If we follow the idea a bit further, we find that astrology is the psychology of the ancients projected into the heavens, into the most remote bodies. There are two
main principles in a horoscope, the sun and the moon. The sun
has the psychological quality of man's active nature, the moon of
man's reacting nature. In his active nature one would designate his
character as willed, voluntary. In his reacting nature he is passive,
merely responding to stimuli. As a matter of fact, when you meet
a man in his lazy hours, as he is at home, for instance, when merely
reacting to circumstances, you find that he is quite different from
the man in his business hours. They are two different men; astrology would say that one was his sun character and the other was
his moon character. And the action of the sun and moon are determined by their position in the so-called "houses."[17] If the sun is
in a warm fiery sign, the man is characterized by warmth, impet-
uousness, sudden anger—an especially vigorous active nature. When
the moon is in a strong position, it points to the more personal,
the intimate and unguarded side of the person, it indicates one
who is in a very passive condition. So people's character or fate was
read in a very literal way through the position of the sun and moon.
Of course, the more ancient the horoscope, the more projected it
was. Where modern astrology would say, "This man is violent,
impetuous, heedless of danger, will plunge into all sorts of indiscretions and will regret it afterwards," the ancients would have said:
"This man will commit murder and his head will be cut off"—or
make voyages and be drowned, or he is likely to be assailed by bad

---

[16] Possibly Friedrich von Müller (1858-1941), German internist, who was Jung's
teacher at the University of Basel. See *MDR*, p. 107/110.

[17] In astrological theory, one of the twelve parts into which the heavens are divided.

people. So what today is taken as a mere psychological factor, in those days was held to be fate.

I have a collection of old fifteenth-century horoscopes written by the last professor of astrology at a German university,[18] which today would be interpreted quite psychologically. He made a record of what happened to the men whose horoscopes were drawn. One was drowned trying to reach England, another was killed by pirates, and others murdered while travelling through a forest, etc. In those days, a rash word led to manslaughter, but now we gather up our instincts until we have a great bunch of them and then we do something big with them—like a great war! In former days, they gambled them away in drunken street fights. We are much worse today as a matter of fact. So from certain phases of the moon certain fates were derived, and these correspond to reacting attitudes in modern man.

People having such reactive natures are passive, they are parts of nature in mind or mood. They play parts in which they are surely not the active leaders but more or less the victims, managed by circumstances or by other people, by external and internal stimuli. They are not quite free. They are under a dark law. That is what man feels most in the night, so the moon became the exponent of that side of man's psychology, quite different from the sun psychology. And because it is so difficult to deal with, the moon is an appropriate symbol; the contradictions and paradoxes of night psychology fit in well with the moon. As Dr. Harding has pointed out, it is exceedingly difficult to deal with this psychology in rational language, it seems to be violated by that approach. It is as treacherous as moonlight in masking forms. Such a psychology represents an indefinite, peculiar condition of mind where a thing may be so and not so at the same time. All our attempts to define it refer to a condition that is semiconscious, nocturnal. In the night, when the sun goes down, another principle begins to work, and one's whole psychology becomes influenced by factors not active in the daytime. So when we speak of the unconscious in terms of the moon, we are really talking about the psyche in a semiconscious state, where things are unclear and contradictory, as unclear as objects seen in the moonlight where a dog may be confused with a cat. In the

[18] This collection could not be identified in Jung's library.

388

unconscious, opposite things are lying close together. Peculiar tides are coming up and sinking down. An approaching unconscious condition can be felt; I have known patients to be sea-sick when the unconscious was activated, or to have vertigo, because of what seems to be a strange wavelike motion, a moon-motion.

LECTURE VII

20 November 1929

Dr. Jung:

Today we will continue our discussion of the moon. Since the problem is infinitely complicated I would like the individual members of this particular committee to tell us their impression of that subject.

Mr. Henderson: I studied the Greek material and found Selene was the original Greek goddess of the moon, but she never attained the rank of major deity. The Greeks seemed to find her too dim and were dissatisfied with her, so most of her power was usurped by Hecate, who was more useful, more of an entity. She was a more positive goddess and was in close relation with humanity in practical matters.

Dr. Jung: It is true that Hecate was more considered, but who was she in her own right?

Mr. Henderson: She had two functions. She was the goddess of birth and fertility, but she was predominantly a witch, a goddess of black magic. Her cults were underground, and linked up with Ishtar and Aphrodite, with infant sacrifices, and sacred prostitution.

Dr. Jung: You link her cult up with Ishtar and Aphrodite, but she is neither of these. What aspect would Hecate represent? How does she differ?

Mr. Henderson: She represents the destroying power of the moon.

Dr. Jung: Decidedly destructive. And the name itself tells us something. It means the one that reaches far, hits far, farther than an arrow. The primitives believe that the magic causing of illness is worked by throwing out something substantial, like a pebble; certain American Indian tribes believe it is an icicle. To sum her up then, you would say that she was chiefly destructive and so had to be particularly propitiated. But destruction was not her only

390

quality, we must characterize her more closely. Take all her qualities together: She was a deity of black magic, of childbirth, and of the crossroads. The main feature is the underground character, that gives you the picture. She represents a psychic power, a factor that has all these connections—exceedingly mysterious, underground, helpful but at the same time destructive, uncanny, and working from the unconscious in a way man cannot understand. This is a witchcraft particularity that is especially in woman's unconscious. In a man one can see that his ray reaches far, it is a continuity; but in woman one simply can't account for it.

I want to give you a very interesting example. A member of our seminar has given me permission to tell you this. After our discussion of the cross and crescent symbolism, she went home, with the moon and the sun in her mind. Her boy of seventeen was sick in bed, unoccupied, and she gave him his toothbrush to mark to prevent its being mixed up with his brother's. She left him at work and was talking with her husband downstairs about everyday matters. Then she became conscious that she was listening and had the feeling that something might be happening to the boy, so she went up to him and found that instead of signing his name, he had made the following picture. Look at it in the light of our seminar. The mother had said not a word to the boy about it. Reading it from the bottom up, there is first the cross, then the crescent, then "Tau," and he made the remark that it could just as well have been a cross like this ✕ or a human body. The star above we have not spoken of. It is from the collective unconscious, yet it is from his own unconscious just as well. This is not merely a thought transference, it is a magic effect, a Hecate dream, the language of the collective unconscious. It is the answer to the dream we are actually concerned with. I make use of this particular instance to illustrate the effect. It also shows you a most precious piece  of symbolism, and how things synchronize in a radius of several miles. Perhaps the people upstairs or our neighbours over there are having queer dreams, we don't know. This is a power centre, and they are within the radius.

This hieroglyphic writing explains the sequence of our thoughts.

We shall reach the same results that this boy of seventeen has reached, but the state of our affairs at present is around the crescent. This is a most interesting case. Of course we can't assume that it was insinuated by the unconscious of the mother; it was simply released by the mother's attitude. It is the same conclusion that man always has reached and always will, and this process was released in him as in our dreamer. If touched upon, it comes up. Compare the fantasy material of the most different patients and see how they come to similar symbols and conclusions, of course with an enormous amount of individual variation. I have hardly ever seen such a neat result as this, it is quite amazing. Now this Hecate aspect of the moon, was that what impressed you most, then?

Mr. Henderson: No, the cult of Artemis—the predominantly productive goddess, the goddess of the fields and childbirth, the waxing moon—balanced the cult of Hecate.

Dr. Jung: Then you would explain Hecate as chiefly destructive, the waning moon. And we found that there was some justification for this, things don't thrive under the waning moon.

Dr. Barrett: A friend of mine in the railway-tie business tells me that they will buy no wood cut under the waning moon. The scientific explanation that he gave was that wood recently exposed to polarized light doesn't last as well.

Miss von König: In Sweden the wood cut in the waning moon is exposed to wood-worms, while in the waxing moon it is not.

Mrs. Sawyer: In France, before the Revolution, the forestry laws prohibited the cutting of wood except during the waning moon. Otherwise it was so full of sap that it would not dry.

Dr. Jung: These are practical concrete evidences of the influence of the waning moon, which fit in with what we hear about planting in the waxing moon. I know a man with a great estate in South Africa who, on principle, plants everything under the waxing moon because he has always observed that only so did they flourish. I didn't just trust that notion, but all these primitive beliefs seem to be true somehow, although we do not understand them. A meteorologist will prove to you that the weather does not change with the moon, and yet the idea keeps on occurring, so I am by no means convinced that the weather has nothing to do with it. A rational explanation is no explanation. We just have to wait till these things become confirmed through experimentation. Astrology, for instance, presents amazing suggestions which would be important if verified, but that has never been done. They ought to work out their researches statistically.

A Frenchman, Paul Flambart, made an attempt to verify certain irrational statements.[1] He has done some scientific research work in connection with the so-called aerial trigone: If the whole zodiac is designed in sections of a circle, then the three points, the months represented by Gemini, Libra, and Aquarius, form the aerial trigon. These are air-signs, and air means mind or spirit. The old saying was that one born under these signs was apt to be spiritual or intellectual; that quality was given him at birth. So Flambart took one hundred nativities of men remarkable for their intelligence, and he found that, though the birth-dates were everywhere on the circle, there  was an extraordinary accumulation on each point of the trigon, so one could say that the majority of such nativities were associated with the corners of the aerial trigon, with intelligence. This is of the nature of a scientific truth, but astrologers are proverbially reluctant to make such researches. They prefer to swim in intuition. To work scientifically is too much trouble; each horoscope would take three hours and one would need thousands of them. Astrology is a dark science, a Hecate science. Now we are emphasizing the waning moon. Have you anything more to say about Artemis?

Mr. Henderson: The two, Hecate and Artemis, were practically interchangeable, but Artemis was more the waxing moon with the idea of fertility. They supplanted Selene, who was not defined enough, so her cult was split up into the cults of these two goddesses, Artemis and Hecate, who were more practical and nearer to the people.

Dr. Jung: Yes, Selene is a bit dim. The moon is exceedingly paradoxical, and so one has to split up the conception of its personality. It is too upsetting to think in paradoxical terms. That is the sign of a differentiated mind, only very advanced philosophers think paradoxically. Few can stand it. So the Artemis side of the

[1] Flambart's researches were published in his *Preuves et bases de l'astrologie scientifique* (Paris, 1921), pp. 79ff. Cf. "Synchronicity: An Acausal Connecting Principle," CW 8, par, 869, n. 64.

moon goddess was bright and positive and the dark side hushed up; or the dark uncanny Hecate side was expressed and the good side hushed up. It was as if poison might produce some very good effect; or, if God wouldn't help, surely the Devil would lend a hand. I think you have here a valuable picture of the double character of the moon. What was your material, Mrs. Sawyer?

Mrs. Sawyer: What impressed me the most was the double meaning of the moon—on the side of life, and on the side of death.

Dr. Jung: Yes, and that coincides with what I know of primitives. One sees this lack of definition especially in the central conception of mana that we were discussing. Modern explorers are bewildered at their way of applying the terms *mana* and *taboo.* No distinction exists to them, because their dreams are like reality and their reality like dreams. Any concept is like any other concept. In Egypt one finds contradictory myths in neighbouring villages, or even in the same temple about one and the same god. Their way of thinking is utterly incomprehensible to us. The primitive consciousness is so dim that they simply can't see differences, they are quite naïve, they can only feel very keenly how they are affected. So very different things become as one to them, because they produce the same effect. They are astonished, for instance, with no reference to what astonishes them, the word "astonish" becomes a dynamic conception and they say it is astonishing, *mulungu.* I gave you such examples. So we don't find differentiated views of the moon in primitive beliefs. Later, when we do find it in Greek mythology, it represents the progress of the human mind through many thousands of years.

Mrs. Crowley: Did not moon worship precede sun worship in the Semitic religions?

Dr. Jung: Did you read the Babylonian literature? There it is true that the worship of the moon goddess is exceedingly ancient, but I think that Shem[2] may be just as old.

Mrs. Crowley: I wondered if the moon was not very important to them because of their nomadic lives? The moon might be as important to nomadic tribes as the sun would be to agricultural people.

Dr. Jung: Yes, though that is difficult to confirm because nomadic tribes leave no culture and no temples. The pre-Islamic cult

---

[2] Noah's eldest son and the eponymous ancestor of the Semites.

was of the stars and the moon. The nocturnal sky is exceedingly impressive to one who travels by night, as you say, but in the oldest Babylonian temples, one finds sun worship as well as moon worship. One sees the sun god at one end of the temple against the wall, and a statue of the king of equal size just opposite. Man and god opposite to one another, of equal value, it is very interesting. In Egypt, also, Pharaoh is the equal of the gods and is depicted in the form of Osiris and of Ra, and identified with the sun. Naturally, he wouldn't identify with the moon.

Mrs. Fierz: It struck me as strange from the point of view of development that first you have a dragon like Mummu-Piamut, or a heavenly cow, the mother of the moon goddess, who creates the world and eats it afterwards. Then later came the various different moon goddesses, and then in the course of development, comes a unifying principle again, as for example in the *Golden Ass,* 11th chapter. Again they are the same, they are unified. Even if the names are different, the meaning of these goddesses in all countries is the same. So in the late Roman times, they could take up the worship of any foreign goddess because the underlying meaning would be identical. I think that here is a parallel to individual psychology.

Dr. Jung: Your view has more to do with the psychology of the moon symbolism in general. You would reduce the specific moon goddesses to the conception of an original world animal, a heavenly cow who produces and then eats the world. Well, that is perfectly true, an extraordinary conception of something even back of the gods, something that is doing and undoing. But this doesn't enter our actual discussion; we must keep to a differentiated concept of the moon deity. If we go behind the moon, then we must go behind the sun; the story of the heavenly cow has no more to do with the moon than the sun, it is back of both. It is a profound intuition similar to the idea of Osiris, Isis, and Nephtys in the same womb. Osiris is the sun, Isis and Nephtys are the moon. There is also the Egyptian idea of the primordial mother Nu or Nut, also called the primordial waters, in whose womb were the sun and the moon before any created thing. That is still more primitive and also a more advanced idea. Later perhaps humanity will see that these most primitive superstitions were the intuitive perception of a most accurate truth. Scientific ideas are always transitory, because they are based on theory. Modern physics is crumbling. When I was a student "emanation," for instance, was ridiculed as completely absurd, but now we are coming back to it. Here we are with the Einstein theory, which is understood as a sort of cosmic emanation. Now, Dr. Draper, won't you tell us what you got from your researches about the moon?

Dr. Draper: The thoughts that were started by the researches were tinged by the mechanistic puzzle I have been in and so they took a biological trend. It seemed to me that there was an interesting analogy between the bisexual character of the moon and the bisexual character of animals. There are reversals of sex in the cock, fowl, and pigeon, as if things were adapted to self-fertilization in order to secure permanence, and that this suggests the means of overcoming death. I was also interested in the soma drink. The gods drank of it and revived.

Dr. Jung: Did you look up the Hindu material for that, Dr. Harding?

Dr. Harding: There are two sets of myths. In the moon there grew a soma-tree from which the gods extracted a drink which gave them immortality. And there is also the myth of Varuna, the moon who churned the cosmic ocean and produced the soma. Then there is a moon-tree that grows on the earth from which a drink is extracted called soma.

Dr. Jung: Yes, soma is a mythological drink in the Vedic religion, magical like the wine in the Christian sacrament, or in the Dionysian mysteries. It is a revivifying drink which is also intoxicating. If I were a good Christian, I should be against the substitution of a non-alcoholic for a spirituous wine, for the touch of intoxication is absolutely indispensable. If Christ, the founder, had intended that the wine should be non-intoxicating, he would have said to drink water. In the Manichaean mysteries, the holy food was the melon. The communion table was laden with gorgeous fruits, especially the melon, which was the sacrificial fruit because it demanded the sun in order to ripen and therefore contained the most particles of light. So when man ate the melon, he was likely to assimilate an enormous amount of light, and then the black substance, the devil, was overgrown. Christ chose wine, and the Catholic Church would never allow the wine to be non-alcoholic. As they would not allow the communion bread to be of any other kind of flour than wheat. And holy oil must be olive oil, and the candles must be made in a certain way. But the war brought a change; because of the scarcity of olive oil, by a special permission of the Pope they were allowed to substitute little electric bulbs, but that was only because of the misery of the times. The Catholic Church is very reasonable in such a case, but in the major things she would hold to tradition most faithfully. The point is that when one modifies these things, when one protests, it becomes just heresy; the Protestants without knowing it upset tradition in its most essential points. That wine is the blood of the Lord. When they let these beliefs go it means that they are on the point of disintegration; the Protestants are split up into more than four hundred denominations as a matter of fact. Catholicism, on the other hand, is linked up with the inviolability of such principles; it must be wine, it must have the touch of intoxication.

One of the oldest ideas of the intoxicating drink is the Vedic drink, soma. The Rig-Veda is of an amazing age, it is supposed to go back to 5000 B.C., and the idea of soma already occurs there. And now we hear that it is linked up with the moon; the moon-tree provided a drink for gods and man. This is very important symbolism.

Dr. Draper: Perhaps the exhilaration produced by the soma drink was the same as that which follows deep rapid breathing. The subjective effect of quick superoxygenation of the blood is almost the same as that which follows drinking alcohol. Is there some analogy here?

Dr. Jung: Yes, all these things have also a physical basis. Primitives sometimes know things ahead of the scientists. The modern theory of malaria was known by the natives in eastern Africa before the white man knew that it was the *anopheles* mosquito that caused it. So they had probably found out the connection between deep breathing, the accumulation of oxygen, and alcoholic effects. Hatha Yoga has particularly to do with breathing exercises, they try to spiritualize themselves through deep breathing. In Chinese Yoga there are rites where breathing is suppressed; there is a standstill of respiration, which is replaced by inner breathing.

Dr. Draper: The North American Negro is not happy unless he has a razor in one pocket and in the other the left hind foot of a graveyard rabbit, caught in the light of the moon. Is it man's attempt to solve the death problem?

Dr. Jung: It is the animal instinct that they want, and the foot is part of the animal. That it must come from the graveyard means

397

that it must be impregnated with the qualities, or the mana, of the dead, so it is a charm that has to do with the whole complex of questions that we are concerned with under the heading of moon symbolism. It is an apotropaic charm because it comes from the dead; if they inherit some amulet from their forefathers, for instance, it is good against spirits and against their own death. Just as rain is produced by pouring water, or a wind by sailors' whistling or hammering the main-mast, making a noise like sails in a wind. They say, "Stop your whistling, or there will be too much wind!" Inoculation is the same principle, simply a piece of moon symbolism in practical application. The soma drink is an apotropaic drink against death—when one drinks this, one cannot die; that medicine comes from the land of the dead, moonland, the moon-tree, it is the medicine of immortality. Gilgamesh travels toward the Westland, to the land of the setting sun. Then there is the myth of the Babylonian Utnapishtim,[3] which antedates the Noah legend by a thousand years. They both cross over a great flood and are removed to the Westland to live an eternal life. They are seeking immortality in the land of the dead. Anything that comes from death protects one from death. So our holy communion wine comes from the dead; we eat the dead body of Christ and drink his blood, and it gives us life. It is exactly the same as the primitive idea of soma.

Then there is the other side of the moon, the lunatic side, which Dr. Harding has mentioned, the moon madness which has to do with the moon as mind. Intoxication is artificial madness. A small dose is exceedingly important in order to bring up one's irrational side; a little madness is good—to be a bit upset—but more is dangerous. In the soma ceremonies, if one gets very drunk one falls from grace. St. Paul in writing to the Corinthians complained that they ate and drank too much; it was a terrible misuse of something sacred.[4] The temptation is to drink deep gulps. In the asylums, the insane are permitted to take communion but they ask for a whole bottle full, and one has to rescue the chalice.

That middle line suggested by the mystery cults is exceedingly critical and delicate. Drink more and one comes down into the flesh

---

[3] Utnapishtim figures in the epic of Gilgamesh. As Jung recounts in *Symbols of Transformation*, pars. 293 and 513 (as in 1912 edn.), Gilgamesh's quest for the herb of immortality "takes him across the sea to the wise Utnapishtim (Noah), who knows how to cross the waters of death." See above, 30 Jan. 1929, n. 4.

[4] I Corinthians 11:23-29.

with a bump; drink too little and one is not irrational enough. The purpose is to do away with our ordinary cramped consciousness. Even the primitive is just as intent as we are on our daily habits, our routine. The real purpose of the religious ceremonial is to revivify. It was created to lift man out of the ordinary, to disturb his habitual ways, that he may become aware of things outside. Many a man, from his accursed circle, has drunk to escape, and discovered the extraordinary beauty of the world and embraced the world, when ordinarily they are terrible beasts. They have discovered the beauty of drunkenness and embrace wine for the divine quality of it, opening their hearts, opening up avenues to mankind. One real moment like that may be a moment of revelation. The primitives needed it as much as we do. The original idea of the *Agape*[5] was a mild orgy, eating together, feasting, drinking the sacred wine, the blood of the earth. They kissed each other in a brotherly and sisterly fashion, and this was also the reason why St. Paul had to complain. They took it too literally—it lost some of its spiritual flavour. But it was an attempt at real communion.

Now compare our communion with what it was originally. It destroys the whole meaning to substitute non-alcoholic wine. There should be a cult licence that, under the restriction of the taboo, one can do certain things otherwise impossible. In the *Agape* one might kiss his neighbour's wife and feel like anything. One could choose his place I suppose. Otherwise it would be awful, so we have to allow for human nature. People were doubtless as they are to-day—one is careful to lean to the right instead of the left. It is really not blasphemous if we enter into the psychology of all these moon and soma ceremonials. Those things were done in the light of the moon, it might have been very dazzling. The nights of the dancing were relatively safe, and then, within the framework of a taboo, man could do what ordinarily he could not do. For instance, the primitives in performing a ceremony do not do it as they would themselves, but as their ancestors might have done it. They identify with those ancestors—the heroes—and perform ceremonies which were perhaps very obscene. Then they would be normal citizens again—perfectly all right.

In our day, a certain Christian sect, I forget what they call themselves, nominate a board of trustees who are called evangelists and

---

[5] A "love feast," usually preceding the Eucharist, celebrated by the early Christians.

apostles, even angels and archangels.[6] They symbolize the heavenly hierarchy on earth and are in a wonderful new condition—Mr. Jones and Mr. Smith in the daytime and archangels in the evening. I suppose they also identify with the heroes, one stage on the way to the very original carnival when they changed into animals, their totem ancestors.

In the cult of Dionysos, the Corybantes were a wild, orgiastic band of dancers. They wore animal skins and goats' horns, to be as much like satyrs as possible, and the girls were nymphs in their lovely nakedness, like maenads, and then things really happened. In Athens it was rather obscene; a huge indecent phallus was carried in the parade. Even in Rome as Goethe saw it, during the carnival in the ecclesiastical state, the old Priapus god, in the form of Pulcinello, walked about disturbing the women. This was in the eighteenth century, in the very heart of Christendom, and that symbol was intended to suggest animal increase, animal sexuality. It was a survival of the old religious festivals though of course no longer connected with the church. . . .[7]

But now only the intoxicating wine is left. In our rituals, even in the Catholic Church, no space is left for orgiastic licence. Now, more than in any other time, man has no chance whatever in that respect. We need that ceremonial licence. When we get drunk, we become pigs and lose our respectability, we have no taboo-frame in which to do it. We haven't served God, we have only been intoxicated. In those days, a man could keep his respectability and serve God a bit too much and then it was a grand thing; I pity the people who don't know what wine means in that aspect. There are no taboo forms under which we can get safely and religiously drunk, not to speak of kissing our neighbour's wife.

Well, I wanted to give you some aspects of the peculiar grotesqueness connected with the moon, a twisting of all the sacred elements. It is more difficult to sum up the symbolism of the moon than of the sun. The moon has an extra twist.

[6] The allusion is to the Church of Jesus Christ of Latter-day Saints (the Mormon Church).

[7] A half-dozen lines are omitted which repeat what Jung said about the *jeu de paume*, etc., in the lecture of 14 Nov. 1928.

LECTURE VIII

27 November 1929

Dr. Jung:

Before we discuss further the cross and crescent symbols in their relative aspect, I want to demonstrate to you how symbolic facts leak out in families. A little girl four or five years old has made a drawing of the things we have been talking about. The mother is in the seminar. Obviously she has not discussed symbols with her, yet that the child got it in a very extraordinary way is shown in this drawing.

It represents a mother's breast, and also a house, and up at the left is a crescent. Inside is a woman, and here are windows depicted in a strange way though the mother tells me that she knows how to draw proper windows. Evidently it is a combination of the cross and crescent symbols with the human mother figure crouching here in the centre. It is not an ordered drawing, it still has the peculiar chaotic disorder of early psychic functioning. The elements are there, but they are not in a cosmos or state of order, but in a primordial or cosmic chaos. That expression is contradictory, however; we use the word "cosmos" for the universe, but one could think of the universe not as a cosmos but as a chaos, for this is the chaos in the collective unconscious of a child, the primordial chaotic condition where things are only beginning to take orderly shape.

In the child's mind this original chaos becomes projected into human figures. In the adult mind, particularly in the second part of life, the cosmic figures, sun, moon, stars, etc., as well as other archetypes, begin to detach from the human being. The human being becomes less important, depotentiated. But the child, at first entirely non-personal, wakes up from the primitive chaos to the condition of relatedness, and this goes on till late in life, as the human being becomes increasingly more important. Until puberty, the father and mother and family circle mean everything to the child. The mother has the first place; it is as if all the suns and stars and moons had entered into the mother. Then at puberty the detachment begins, first the social, and then the spiritual separation—the last would only be at the time of the culmination of life.

I thought it quite worth while to demonstrate this case because it shows how such things can leak out—far more than personal secrets, for instance, which are unique and are not reinforced by collective figures. The collective symbols are in the child, so he has the necessary foundation to receive that stimulus. Personal secrets have less power—today they are most important, but tomorrow they may vanish, because they are not backed up by that terrific force of the collective unconscious. An unconscious personal secret has a tendency to exteriorize itself; it has a piercing quality because contaminated by the collective unconscious; and as soon as it is conscious, it is likely to get out, for most people with a conscious secret can't hold their tongues, they babble. Nature doesn't like secrets and forces us to talk, everything comes to light sooner or later.

Today our seminar will be devoted to the question of the interrelation of the cross and crescent symbols; we have discussed them separately so we have a certain idea of what they mean. The sun is the main representation of the cross symbol. One assumes generally that the cross expresses the sun, but I would put it the other way round, the sun expresses the cross. The cross is that inexpressible background representation of unrecognizable forces of creativeness, and because that background or source is of an unrecognizable nature and expressed only through manifold representations, man has forever used that abstract symbol.

The moon is the same, it is a symbol, quite apart from its real existence. For instance, the phallic symbol is a very definite thing, it is a symbol for generative power, but many other things represent that—a river, fruit, a tree, wind, etc. There is no end to the symbols for generative forces. So the moon is one of the symbols, like the cross, for different psychological factors. In all its different attributes it points to the collective unconscious, which can be expressed in many different ways—as the ocean, a lake, a jungle, a cloud, mist, the forest—all these symbolize one and the same thing, the unrecognizable collective unconscious. Here again is the very interesting difference between the two symbols that we have remarked before. The cross is definitely dynamic, and the moon is not; it is more a form into which one can pour one's contents. Hence the definitely female quality of the moon. It is linked up with the idea of the virgin and the harlot, or it is a receptacle for the souls of the deceased. It is a passive receptacle and yet not merely passive, for no matter how dead and quiet it is, it always has a definite effect, the effect of forming and giving definite limitations to a thing. It catches a dynamic element and solidifies it, transforms and crystallizes it, so that it has apparently attained almost a dynamic effect; it is merely that pouring certain contents into it gives it a different quality. It is like a wine-glass: Pour a noble wine into a crystal glass with a red thread in its stem and you feel that it is in the right form, while to drink that wine from an earthen milk-jug is not right—it is no longer the same thing, the containing form has done something to the wine. So the moon seems to be dynamic too because it has that formative effect upon the dynamic quality symbolized by the sun or cross.

The more we talk about the cross and the crescent, that is, the activity and the passivity of the collective unconscious, the more we approach certain concepts of Chinese philosophy expressed in Yang, ♂, the male principle, and Yin, ♀, the female principle. The definite interrelation of the two symbols corresponds to the Chinese concept. Yang is male, dry, active, fiery, creative, and is represented by the south side of the mountain, also by the dragon. Yin is female, cool, nocturnal, humid, and is represented by the north side of the mountain. It is the passive side of matter. (The words matter and mother are derived from the same word, *materia, mater*.) Our idea of spiritual and material is exactly parallel excepting that Yang is not entirely spiritual nor Yin entirely material. The Chinese philosophers project these ideas out into the universe and assume that the universe consists of these two agencies, the dynamic and the receptive, and that these constitute heaven and earth and all that is between.

Now, our Western idea would not be that exactly; that is not congenial to us. We cannot grasp the Tao unless we have psychological understanding, so it is only psychology which opens up the concepts of Chinese philosophy. But with this knowledge we can admit that there is an active and a passive aspect, a masculine principle which is generative and a female principle which is receptive. These are understood as psychological factors, but when it comes to the physical universe, we meet great obstacles in our mental make-up. Psychologically we can understand, and it doesn't seem entirely strange, so to us these symbols have something to do with the structure of our minds. Those of you who are drawing and painting know that we are still reproducing those symbols over and over again, showing that they are still expressive and alive. One discovers in analysis that they function in the same way as in the mystery religions and Chinese philosophy, only we do not assume that they are world principles. We merely assign psychological importance to them, we say that the crescent refers to one's feminine nature and the cross to one's masculine creativeness, without assuming that they are universal symbols at the same time.

But, as I said, we have the testimony of the old mystery cults and Chinese philosophy, which independently hold that they also have to do with the constitution of the world, not only with our subjective prejudice concerning what the world consists of, and that they are responsible for the operation of the "Heavenly Laws," as they would say. We should not consider such a statement as a metaphysical assertion, or as a fact of natural science, but as though it were the program of a party in a democracy. It is a view and it may be wrong, yet if we want to solidify the state or put up a reasonable government, we must take into account that there are so many fools who hold these opinions. A considerable number of people think in a foolish way. That is what man is like, and we are human beings too, and we have to consider the fact that many people, and even our ancestors, also held the belief that man is only one case among many, in which these general laws manifest themselves. Now we cannot scientifically prove that our functioning is coincidental with the functioning of the sun and the moon. We observe the similarity between the periodicity of woman and the moon, but they do not coincide, it is merely the same rhythm. So also, metaphorically, we could say that the active principle in man is like the sun.

In astrology we have another consideration, a bit uncanny and therefore particularly hated by scientists. You remember my telling you that birthdates of important men tended to accumulate around the three points of the aerial trigon.[1] If this were confirmed, we might go further and make statistics about suicides, lunacy, epilepsy, etc. That might lead to tangible results, and then astrology would be a very serious consideration. I have suggested to astrologers that we should have more scientific statements. Sometimes people without knowing one's birthdate can make remarkable guesses as to where one's signs are. Twice it has happened to me, once in England and once in America. I was told that my sun was in Leo and my moon in Taurus, Aquarius rising. This made a great impression on me. How the devil did they know? Did they see it in my face? But when one once knows a little about these things, they do not appear so mysterious, and one can easily discover certain characteristics—anatomical, for instance. Or sometimes things come out in a negative way. For instance, I think a certain man is quite certainly not Scorpio, and then I find that he is just that. So I have often heard some one say, "Surely I will not marry that one!"—and then he does. Or a patient will say, "All that you say is true, but this is not true," and then I find it to be the closest truth.

Now that is where astrology is today. It enables certain people to make verifiable diagnoses; and sometimes certain guesses, intuitive shots, are peculiarly adequate, quite astonishing. For instance, I was in touch with an astrologer who knew my birth-date but nothing about my personal life, and I got reports from him occasionally—"on such and such a day you must have felt so and so"—but always in the past, so that I could verify the truth of it. Upon one of these occasions he wrote that on the 31st of March, let us say, two years ago, I must have had the feeling of being reborn, for such and such a planet passed over such and such a place in my nativity. At that time I had in my psychological diary

[1] Gemini, Libra, and Aquarius.

405

accurate records of everything that happened. So I looked up that date and I had written, "Today I have a most unaccountable feeling of being reborn." I could tell you other irrational facts, certain evidences. But if one once takes it for granted that these things are true, one is confronted with the terribly serious question, what have *we* to do with the stars? Is there any connection between our miserable little everyday condition and these stars, great Jupiter and Saturn travelling through incredible cosmic distances? Moreover, the moment of birth is so accidental, the doctor is late, the midwife is clumsy, the mother is a little too impetuous. How could one assume such a connection? If you put it like that, it remains unanswerable. Astrologers are influenced by theosophy, so they say, "That is very simple, it is just vibration!" One astrologer after reading *Psychology of the Unconscious* wrote me, "Why do you bother about developing a libido concept? It is only vibration." But what is vibration? They say it is light energy, perhaps electricity, they are not quite informed. At all events the vibrations that could influence us have never been seen, so it remains just a word.

Now I will give you another wrinkle which is quite horrible. I hope you will be able to follow. You see, the astrologer says one was born when the sun was in such and such a degree of Libra, and the moon in such and such a degree of Scorpio, etc., and he bases the reading of one's horoscope entirely upon that position of the planets. For instance, he says, "Today Jupiter is passing over its own place in your nativity, therefore it is in the same degree in which it was at the moment of your birth." You take your telescope and you find the zodiacal constellation and Jupiter is not there at all! Then again the astrologer will inform you that the spring equinox is in zero degree Aries and you naturally expect the sun to be rising at six o'clock in the morning, precisely at zero degrees Aries. But you find something entirely different, it is perhaps at 28 degrees Pisces. In the spring equinox the sun doesn't rise in Aries. You look it up in history and find that in 100 B.C. the sun left the constellation of Aries and went into Pisces. Then the astrologer royal of Ptolemy said, "Now, we can't let that happen, we will fix that fact for always as it was in 2000 B.C. when the sun did the same thing—left Taurus and crossed over into Aries." You see, the spring-point moves back, there is a regression. That is the so-called precession of the equinoxes, moving 55 seconds each year, going back from the spring signs into the winter signs. Now this astronomer stopped that. He simply made it consistent. Otherwise the clocks would all go wrong each year by 55 seconds. So since·100 B.C. (Academy of Alexandria) we call the spring-point zero degrees Aries. We have kept our astronomical faith, but the heavens have moved on and we are simply out of time with the universe. If a man in 2000 B.C. said one was born in 25 degrees Sagittarius, it was true, but a hundred years later it was not quite true for it has already moved on 100 × 55 seconds and the horoscope is no longer exact. An astrologer perhaps says, "No wonder you have such a temperament, or such a royal gesture, because your sun is in the beginning of Leo; when the sun looked at you out of its own house at the moment of your nativity, naturally you were made into a little lion." But it *didn't* look out at you from its own house, for in reality it was in Gemini. Nevertheless you can prove that the man whose sun is said to be in Taurus gets the bull neck, or the woman in Libra gets the qualities of the sun from the heights of Libra, or the one whose sun is in Sagittarius has intuition, and you are quite right. Yet the sun was not in those positions. So that destroys any hope of vibration! I told you of the statistics connected with the aerial trigon, and yet those men of superior mentality were not born when the sun was in those signs. It is an extraordinary puzzle, and there are astrologers who don't even know it; they are theosophists and they say, "It is quite easy, it is just vibrations." But, you see, when it comes to our Western mind, we must think. How then do we account for the fact that our peculiar characteristics can be explained by our planets? One says, "Venus is very clearly your sign." How do you explain that *as if* when it is not?

Here is another paradox. In order to solve that puzzle, we should say, the thing that matters is not the position of the stars, the thing that matters is time. You can call time what you like. It is quite indifferent whether you say the spring-point is zero degrees Aries or 28 Pisces; that is a convention; it is nevertheless the spring-point. So you see, these old designations of time were not taken from the heavens, but given to the heavens. Spring and winter, for example, were projected to the heavens. Man has created the constellations. So obviously the constellations were not intended by the creator of the world to be an astrological text-book to us. In different systems of astrology the constellations are differently arranged. On the calendar stone of Mexico, or the famous Denderah stone in Egypt,[2]

[2] A stone bearing in relief a zodiacal chart, from the Temple of Hathor (1st cent. B.C.) at Denderah, near Luxor. It is now in the Louvre.

the constellations are grouped in a different way. We are even in doubt about the "Great Bear" or the "Wagon"; the ancients called it the "Shoulder of the Heifer." There was a time when there were only four signs in the Zodiac. The Romans had eleven. Libra originated in the time of the Caesars; because it was invented so late, it is the only one that is an instrument. They made the scales by cutting off the claws of the Scorpion. All the other signs are mythological creatures, or human. Man gives the names to the stars. The lion does not look like a lion, but man called it that because the sun was really at its culmination in that devastating time of the year when the heat is insupportable and everything is dried up and burnt. It is like a destroying power, so they said the sun was raging like a mad lion. This is the way the signs go:

Aquarius	Five thousand years ago, 3000 B.C. when the sun was in winter, there were floods of rain. Aquarius walked about pouring his water out right and left.
Pisces	Then the fish swam in the floods.
Aries	The little ram, the time of little shoots and buds.
Taurus	The Bull, the great push of nature.
Gemini	The fertility of man. One seldom does better than twins.
Cancer	A drawback, the summer solstice. The crab walking backward when the sun descends again.
Leo	After the first inkling of solstice it dawns on man that the sun will really be going, from the 22nd of July till the 21st of August, just when all is most glowing.
Virgo	When man is roaring like a lion there is nothing better to tame him than a virgin. She will cut the hair of the lion and make it short, like Samson and Delilah. It is not nice, the whole symbolism is somewhat obscene. But at that time of the year, the 15th of September in the Egyptian calendar, the left eye of the goddess is prepared to receive the god Ra, who is to walk into it.[3] The eye is a womb symbol. The female element takes the lead. The god enters the womb of darkness, Yang is under Yin. Woman is on top.

[3] "It [the first day in autumn] is the day on which 'the goddess Nehmit completes her work, so that the god Osiris may enter the left eye.' "—Heinrich Brugsch,

408

Libra	The balance after the virgin has done her job.
Scorpion	The fatal self-sacrifice of the sun. The sun gets cornered by the virgin and when the forces are equal (Libra), the sun commits suicide, and then comes a clear descent into the mother. There is a legend that when the scorpion is surrounded by fire it kills itself.
Sagittarius	The death of the sun. Death is a sort of river or gap. There is a life beyond, but one is here on this bank of the river and cannot get there. Then comes the legend of the centaur, a good archer, who with his bow can send an arrow across. It is a means of communication. The archer Sagittarius with the arrow of intuition foresees new birth out of the unconscious. This is the advent season, when ghosts begin to walk again, when the unconscious begins to manifest itself.
Capricorn	The goat-fish. (This was the imperial sign on the coat-of-arms of Augustus Caesar.) After the dead man contained in the sea, the next sign is this goat-fish. He is half fish and half goat, meaning that at first, as the fish, he is deep down in the sea, out of sight in the unconscious. Then he rises to the surface and climbs to the highest peaks and valleys. This is the sun, the promise of the new year, so some astrologers call the time after Christmas the "Promise of the Year." It is the time of the birth of Mithras, the birth of Christ, the birth of the new light, the whole hope of the coming year. People born then have strong hearts. They are ambitious, but they have to work hard to achieve their ends.

But the new year has to be generated. The sun generates the year in Aquarius. Aquarius pours out the waters of fecundity. He is also shown as a phallic god like Priapus. After the generating water the Fishes come again, and so on around.

This is how the Zodiac came into existence. It is really a seasonal cycle with particular qualities of climate—winter, spring, summer, autumn, qualified by the fantasies and metaphorical imagination

---

Religion und Mythologie der alten Aegypter (Leipzig, 1885), pp. 281ff., quoted in *Symbols of Transformation*, par. 408 (as in 1912 edn.).

of the human mind. And so man has called the stars that are synchronous with the seasons by names expressing the qualities of each particular season. The active principle is obviously the time and not at all the stars, they are merely incidental. If, at the time when astrology came into conscious existence, other constellations had been in the heavens, we would have had different groups of stars but they would have been called a lion or a man carrying a water-jug just the same. They are not at all like their names, even the most striking constellations. It is a tremendous strain for the imagination.

So, as I said, it is obvious that the active element is time. People born at a certain time of the year may have certain qualities. The relative position of the stars is only the means for counting time. Then here is a new paradox. What is time? How can it be an active principle? Time is an abstract conception of duration and is perfectly arbitrary at that; one could make an entirely different division. A second might be half a minute, why is a minute sixty seconds? It is not at all convincing, it is merely a conventional arbitrary conception. Then if one tries to boil it down, one comes to the conclusion that time is the flux of things, like the water-clock or the sand-clock, it is the running down, dividing the day into four parts, each part being one quarter of that day, between sunrise and sunset. To observe time, one observes the movement of things lasting a certain time, as the hands of a watch; it is the duration of a certain flux. This is abstract, but the flux of things is not abstract, it is perfectly concrete and tangible. That is what we term energy because nothing moves without energy. One must wind one's watch or turn the hour-glass. It takes energy to produce the flux, and what we measure is energy; and this is another abstract conception in so far as it means a changing condition of things. When one says time is merely an aspect of energy, one makes it more tangible, because everyone can observe it and measure it. Time and energy are correlated concepts. If there is no energy nothing moves and there is no longer any time. They are identical, a certain movement of time is a certain movement of energy. When we observe energy we really observe time, because it is through energy that we measure time. So I say, with no time there is no possibility of measurement.

Take a stone just before it rolls down hill. It is in a particular position of energy, it will crash but it hasn't. It is latent energy, the energy of position, *potential* energy. It may break loose at any time with terrific vigour. Then it crashes down manifesting *mechanical* energy. It lands in the valley, crashes, splinters, and then where is the energy? It is in the *warmth* of the stone and the stone against which it hurled itself. It has been transformed. This is a new movement of energy. Now, you can describe that whole transformation in terms of time. If nothing happens, there is no time. Time begins when that thing gets loose. There is a certain amount of time until the warmth is dissipated again, and then it becomes unobservable. The specific warmth has completely vanished, so time is only between the breaking loose of the stone and the last trace of warmth of the splintered rock.

Energy was in three forms, latent energy, mechanical energy, and warmth. You can translate this into the terms of water falling on a turbine and creating electricity. As long as the process lasts, there is time, simply different moments expressed through different forms.

Now consider the universal energy of the world, the life energy. It is unknown to us, but we must understand it under those terms. It is not observable if nothing happens. For instance, an egg is latent, nothing moves, but if it develops, time develops, age begins. Now take the energy of the universe and the solar system. In winter there is less radiation, in summer there is more. So someone who was born at a certain moment of the year naturally has a certain quality, because his origin was in those conditions. Nothing to be done about it, it is just so. The peculiar thing is that one should be able to trace the age of a thing to the exact time of its origin.[4] There are certain archaeologists, for instance, who have such a refined sense of the age of an object that they can tell it within ten years, just as an antiquarian knows by the print, quality of the paper, etc. of a book that it suggests a time between 1460 and 1470, let us say. So an etching can be traced. The expert will tell you that it is of the French school but influenced by the Dutch. He judges by the actual qualities of the materials used—the paper, the ink, the objects depicted, etc. When you see an old man, white-haired and decrepit, you say he was born about 1850. Often I guess age within two years. One can do that without any trouble, it is the same as saying that one was born under Aquarius but a bit more accurate. This is

[4] "Carbon dating" in archaeology became possible only in the mid-1950s: cf. W. F. Libby, *Radioactive Dating* (1955).

merely a technical method, like looking behind the screen of a clever antiquarian who has certain little helps—for instance, he knows when a certain varnish was introduced into Europe, or that the first pipe is not older than the discovery of North America.

Astrology consists of all these little tricks that help to make the diagnosis more accurate. So the astrologer, though he does not know the year or the month of your birth, may guess by your qualities. Now, the unfortunate thing is that we can designate the condition of energy, universal energy, in no other way than by time. Instead of saying the time of the falling stone, we say it was ten seconds ago that the stone has fallen. We call this year 1929, because once upon a time we began counting, assuming that we knew when Christ was born—though there is a controversy about that, Christ may have been born 100 B.C. Mead has written a very interesting book about that.[5] In China the years have names. In Rome they were named for the consuls, reckoned from the beginning of Rome in 750 B.C. After the French Revolution, they began to count the years as if it were the beginning of a new epoch. We indicate the conditions of the times by a number. For instance, 1875 might be called the time of crinolines, the first railways, newspapers twice a week with pages, corsets for ladies, top-hats for men, bad taste generally. They knew nothing of Nietzsche, Schopenhauer was the most recent news. Chicago was then the most ridiculous little place, and imagine New York in 1875! Four years after the Franco-German War, everything was moving in a different way, the way that was characteristic for that year, and nothing before or after will be like it.

So, in 1929, everything has the cast and brand of this year. And the children born in this year will be recognizable as part of a great process and marked by a particular condition.[6]

[5] G.R.S. Mead, *Did Jesus Live 100 B.C.? An Inquiry into the Talmud Jesus Stories, the Toldoth Jeschu, and Some Curious Statements of Epiphanius* (London and Benares: Theosophical Publication Society, 1903).

[6] Some of the ideas Jung was trying out in this lecture reappeared in his memorial address for Richard Wilhelm (1930), CW 15, pars. 81-82, where he first published a reference to "synchronicity," his theory later developed in the monograph "Synchronicity" (1951-52), CW 8, pars. 816ff., but first mentioned (as "synchronism") in the lecture of 28 Nov. 1928 (above, n. 1). See also the next lecture, at n. 8.

LECTURE IX

4 December 1929

Dr. Jung:

I find no questions today, so I assume that everything is clear and understood. You remember that we were discussing energy and time, and I suppose you must have wondered why I talked about such abstruse matters in connection with the cross and crescent symbols. It would be quite understandable to me if some of you had asked today why I had pushed that question so far, to fundamentals—as far as the stars, one could say. There were certain reasons. I found as I was thinking over the material for the next seminar, that my thoughts were developing towards the stars and the problem of the identity of time and energy or libido, and then I asked myself what the justification was for enlarging the scope of our problem to such an extent. I became curious to know what the patient's subsequent dreams said on the subject. I looked into my records and found that the very next was one that we could not deal with without this preparation. It contains this particular problem, as you will soon see. So you can believe me, that I am not just losing myself in idle speculation when I talk about time and energy. It is not a metaphysical problem, it is psychological, even astrological, for astrology was the first form of psychology, which is an extremely young science, dating from the end of the nineteenth century only. Of course, there was a beginning of psychological technique at about the time of the decay of Christianity and the period of the French enlightenment. Voltaire would be one of the first psychologists, and La Rochefoucauld, and Fénelon.[1] But it was not yet science. It consisted more of intellectual aphorisms.

[1] François de La Rochefoucauld (1613-80), whose *Réflexions et maximes morales* was first published in 1665. François de Salignac de la Mothe Fénelon (1651-1715), churchman and theologian, wrote mystical and quietist works.

413

It was essentially a critique. One might say that Nietzsche had a psychological approach to his material.

But inasmuch as the human soul has always existed, there must have been at all times an equivalent of psychology. Philosophy would be such an equivalent, but it is merely intellectual, or a metaphysical projection. Religion would be an equivalent also, one could say, yet it is metaphysical concretism. Then there was astrology, which was legitimate up to the seventeenth century and was used by doctors in universities, together with dreams, as aids in diagnosing disease. Palmistry also was so used. I have a little text-book of medicine written by a famous Würzburg professor towards the end of the sixteenth century.[2] It deals with astrology, phrenology, palmistry, and physiognomy, and was especially for the use of doctors. The author was practically the last of the official professors of astrology, which was a sort of psychology but with the qualities and peculiar character of projection. It was our psychology in its oldest form. Our modern science began with astronomy. Instead of saying that a man was led by psychological motives, they formerly said he was led by his stars.

In Schiller's *Wallenstein* there is a conversation between Wallenstein and the astrologer in which the latter says, "In thy heart are the stars of thy fate."[3] That is a translation of astrological into psychological terms. But this was very late, in the beginning of the nineteenth century. Until then, people assumed that it was not psychological motivation but the movement of the stars which caused the personal reactions, as if the direction of their lives was created by the vibrations of the planets. The puzzling thing is that there is really a curious coincidence between astrological and psychological facts, so that one can isolate time from the characteristics of an individual, and also, one can deduce characteristics from a certain time. Therefore we have to conclude that what we call psychological motives are in a way identical with star positions. Since we cannot demonstrate this, we must form a peculiar hypothesis. This hypothesis says that the dynamics of our psyche is not just identical

[2] Rodolphus Goclenius, *Uranoscopiae, chiroscopiae, metoposcopiae et ophthalmoscopiae contemplatio* (Frankfurt, 1608), cited in Jung's foreword to Julius Spier, *The Hands of Children* (London, 1944; 2nd edn., 1955); in CW 18, par. 1818.

[3] Friedrich von Schiller (1759-1805), *Wallenstein* (1798-99), which is divided into three separate dramas; the quotation is from the second, *Die Piccolomini*, II, 6. Cited in CW 5, par. 102, n. 52 (as in 1912 edn.).

with the position of the stars, nor has it to do with vibrations—that is an illegitimate hypothesis. It is better to assume that it is a phenomenon of time. In the concept of time the two come together. Time, or the moment understood as a peculiar form of energy, coincides with our psychological condition. The moment is unique, so that whatever has its origin at a certain moment has the energy and qualities of that particular moment. It must be so, because a thing originating a hundred years ago has the character of that age. In this conception of time we have a mediating concept, which helps us to avoid the irrational explanations of astrology.

The stars are simply used by man to serve as indicators of time, and our psychology has as little to do with the stars as a clock, which is merely an instrument used to measure a certain moment—say 10.45. It is exactly the same as if one said the sun is in Aquarius, the moon in Sagittarius, and Gemini is coming over the horizon with an elevation of 5 degrees. This is a particular moment. Four minutes are necessary for a degree of a sign to rise above the horizon. You can even find the very instant by dividing that degree into seconds. Such a constellation during a very long space of time is unique. In the lapse of 26,000 years we have one such position, the year, the month, day, hour, and seconds. The important fact is that it is this particular situation and not that the stars indicate it. One could use other constellations to establish time. The thing that matters is that the present moment is what it is—the particular moment and the actual condition of the world, and its energy and its movement at that moment. Whatever originates at that time will be marked by that particular moment, so the psychological factors are determined by the actual position and all its qualities.

To return to the cross and crescent, we found the best way to conceive of those two symbols was in the Chinese terms Yang and Yin, meaning by them the conception of the opposites needed to explain energy. Energy can exist only where the opposites are at work. When there is an equal warmth everywhere, as if all the world were reduced to a plane, then nothing happens at all. If every contrast is wiped out, if there is no chemical tension, then there is no higher level, no potential. Energy is dissipated, and we have what the Germans call "Wärmetod," or death in an equal temperature—entropy.[4] There is a speculative idea current that

[4] Entropy is the progressive loss of energy potential in the universe, leading to an ultimate state of inert uniformity.

the end of the world might be like this. Things might get into a state where all energy is wasted, where the temperature of surrounding things is equal to the temperature of the sun, for instance. So two opposing principles such as the Yang and the Yin are unavoidable premises for the concept of energy. The world cannot move without conflict. This throws light on the theory of complexes. Benevolent people assume that analysis has been invented, divinely ordained, to rid people of their complexes. But I maintain that without complexes there can be no energy. They are the focus and very mother of energy. So that cannot possibly be the task of analysis—if God invented that he would bring the whole thing to a complete standstill.

. . .[5] Complexes are due to passion. So Yang and Yin are not only physical and metaphysical but also psychological principles. They are quite unlike our concepts because it is a peculiarity of Chinese thinking that makes the Chinese take what happens within and without as being indissolubly connected. We, on the other hand, cannot assume that the position of the stars or something that happens on the planet Mars has anything to do with us. There seems to be no connection. We are unable to mix up two things, our minds have that bias. But the Chinese have the fundamental conviction that everything is connected with everything else, so that the most intimate things are in their eyes world principles at the same time. They would say that the Yang and Yin operating in us is at the same time operating in the heavens, in the great movements of the stars and the planets. This is an essential Chinese conviction, and so they understand human psychology as simply a special case of, one could say, spiritual principles. As the great, so is the small; as the small, so is the great. The same force works within as well as without.

This is the theoretical explanation of the *I Ching* and the explanation of the way it works an oracle. When one casts the sticks,[6] they behave exactly as one's psychology and the general conditions of the moment happen to be, no matter what is concerned; whether it is an individual or a group that is involved doesn't matter. The

[5] Several lines are omitted which repeat a summary of the Jewish legend about the Evil Spirit of Passion, which Jung gave in the lecture of 12 Dec. 1928, at n. 7.

[6] For the two methods of consulting the *I Ching*, by dividing a cluster of yarrow stalks and by casting three coins, see the Wilhelm/Baynes edn. (1967), pp. 721-724.

Chinese look upon them all as subject to a part of one and the same energy that moves everything. It is as if our discriminations were only valid as far as consciousness goes, but when it comes to the unconscious, it makes no difference whether a thing happens to you or to me. We are all affected by the same thing, for all these things are one and the same energy when it comes to the unconscious roots of our psychology. How far this is true you can judge from the two drawings of those children which I showed you,[7] as examples of the way of connection by the common roots. They took up the symbolism as if they had been here with us. Since I have seen many other examples of the same kind in which people not concerned were affected, I have invented the word *synchronicity*[8] as a term to cover these phenomena, that is, things happening at the same moment as an expression of the same time content. So the fact that the principles of our psychology are principles of general energic phenomena is not difficult for the Chinese to accept; it is only difficult to our discriminating mind. But this also has its value with its fine sense of the details of things, and this is where the East decidedly shows its incapacity, for they cannot handle facts and they allow themselves all sorts of fantastic ideas and superstitions. On the other hand they have a far more complete understanding of the role of man in the cosmos, or how the cosmos is connected with man. We must discover this and many other highly interesting and marvellous things known to them.

I hope that you see now why I have laid so much stress on this concept of the identity of energy and time. In order to understand the peculiar workings of the unconscious, we have to go far afield in theoretical speculation, and without such facts we would be unable to understand the development of these symbols in the unconscious. It is not in vain that in the dream the crosses and crescents are thrown together in the same cauldron where they should obviously blend, and that for a certain purpose. The purpose is the important thing. If the Yang and the Yin come together, the result is a release of energy which might be symbolized in different forms. It might be emotional energy in the case of the dreamer, or it might be a burst of revealing light, an inspiration or a great

[7] One drawing is reproduced above, lecture of 27 Nov. 1929.
[8] See the preceding lecture, n. 6.

417

vision. It is interesting to see how the unconscious, operating in the group, has already anticipated the vision. I have here a picture by a member of this group made beforehand, and so not influenced by our discussion concerning the union of the symbols. It contains a representation of what will happen when cross and crescent meet. In the drawing of the young boy on his toothbrush, we have very much the same thing. Here is the cross, then the crescent, and they are peculiarly together, and then instantly comes a tremendous outburst, a release of energy in the form of an enormous sphere of light. Such is the energic phenomenon. Here is the whole theory that when the opposites come together there will be a great manifestation of energy of some sort.

Now, that peculiar light engendered by the cross and crescent is a new enlightenment, a sort of revelation. If the truth of the crescent could be united with the truth of the cross, it would produce that enlightenment, the combined truth of Islam and Christianity. If it were possible to extract the essential truth of each and blend them, then out of that clash would come an enormous illumination which would amount to a new conviction.

Both Christianity and Islam are psychological methods of treating diseases of the human soul. They prescribe methods of living, attitudes, moral codes as well as dogmatic explanations of why things are as they are—how man misbehaved and God saw himself forced to do something about it, sending sons or prophets to cure the evils of man. Christ was essentially the Healer. The sect to which he belonged, the Essenes, was known as the Therapeuts. We cannot see now how our actual Christianity could possibly heal, since we cannot establish a connection between Christianity and a neurosis. If I told a patient that his religion ought to cure him, he would think that I was stark mad. But in the beginning it was effective. In the time of Augustus, the old gods were dying or dead, the old religions and the old temples were going fast. There was great confusion, the world was neurotic, and it became necessary to have a new therapeutic system. There was the Stoic system, for instance, with its theory of the happy, right, and complete life. Innumerable cults from the East were introduced. I have already spoken several times of the letter of Zosimos to a certain lady advising her to go to the *krater*, the mixing bowl, to find rebirth. It was just as if a modern man wrote to a friend: "I strongly advise you to go to the krater at Zurich for analysis—to the *Jungbrunnen!*"9 It is essentially the same idea.

In the beginning these methods are quite simple. Then they become more and more removed from the human sphere. The more they don't work, the more it is necessary to heap up miracles and all sorts of complications. The moment that a new light ceases to be a light, people make dogma of it; the less it works, the more it has to be enhanced. Whereas a true religion is exceedingly simple. It is a revelation, a new light. But one can hardly talk of it without blushing, on account of the false ideas that have been pumped into it, big words hallowed by two thousand years of suggestion. For a long time now, the Christian religion has not worked, so it became a Church of great splendour and power in order to increase its influence by suggestion. But neither does suggestion work in the long run. The church decayed. Protestantism was a symptom that the light had become so feeble that people felt it wouldn't do any longer. They were seeking a new light then, and they found it in Luther for a time, until he hurled himself against politics and had

9 = "fountain of youth," with pun on Jung's name.

to make his compromise with the world. Again the light grew dim and a religion of the usual dogmatic kind was the result.

Now this picture shows a new light. Such an outburst is in anticipation of new understanding, new vision, a unity which gives new expression to the world and to man. Everything appears in a new light. That is a renewal, a rebirth. But it must not be assumed that producing such a picture means that one has that light, that one experiences it consciously. Such a vision is quite impersonal. For the time being it is in the unconscious. It is as if the man in the fourteenth century who invented gunpowder said, "As you can drive the ball out of the cannon by the explosion produced by the tension of gas, so you can make the ball rebound into the cannon and recreate the explosive motor." He could have deduced all that, but he did not go so far. Nor did Hero of Alexandria[10] dream that he had discovered a potential steam-engine when he invented the first simple steam toy; he had no idea of its potential value. Those old Romans didn't realize that they had the principle of the steam-engine right under their noses. Perhaps a lunatic also had the intuition, for often it is they who have the first intuition of the things we later discover. It takes people a tremendous time to realize the simplest deduction.

You have seen how the pattern of these dreams is developing. The next one shows an extraordinary revelation. But before we go on, I would like you to bring up any questions that you have. I want a clean desk before proceeding to the next dream.

Dr. Baynes: My difficulty is with your statement that time and energy are identical. It seems as if time were an expression of energy but not identical. It is like the relation of speech to thought.

Dr. Jung: Time is the essential identity with creative energy. There is a Greek aphorism, "Wherever there is creation, there is time." Chronos was the god of light, creation, and time. Also the Stoic concept of primordial warmth is practically identical with time. The Greek *Heimarmenē*, meaning astrological compulsion, is identical with primordial warmth, the primordial creative force. I admit that this is strange, and if you are not sufficiently acquainted with the facts, it is not easy. Our Western mind refuses to function along Chinese lines. It is difficult to feel intuitively the creative wave of

[10] Greek mathematician and inventor (dates unknown; between 2nd cent. B.C. and 3rd cent. A.D.).

time that moves the winds, the clouds, the birds, and even the streetcars. We should realize the tremendous importance of everything that is *now*. To the Chinese this means everything, but to us it is nothing but chance—chance that we are here, chance that the bird sings and the dog barks. It is the unique characteristic of this moment. Whatever takes its origin in this moment carries the mark of this moment for ever.

I have been asked about the incident I described of the astrologer who told me that on the 31st of March, in such and such a year, I had a feeling of rebirth. He said it was due to the transition of a certain planet over the place it occupied at the time of my birth. There is a fact, which he got at through the old rule that when a planet does this, something happens more or less—it is always more or less.

Mrs. Baynes: I understood you to say that a planet was not in that position at the moment of one's birth.

Dr. Jung: No, it was not, on account of the non-identity of time and astronomical position.

Dr. Baynes: But the place where you were born must be mentioned—the here and now must be emphasized. So in order to diagnose your temperament he must have been guessing, for he doesn't know the place.

Dr. Jung: That is contained in my horoscope. It was necessary to tell him the place for it must be on a certain meridian implied in my horoscope.

Dr. Deady: Is it as though it were two thousand years ago?

Dr. Jung: It was true two thousand years ago. There are very few verifiable horoscopes. The material is scarce, and it has not been done in the spirit of modern science. I have told you about the aerial trigon. That Frenchman made such an attempt. The whole trouble has been caused by the sun that refused to work reasonably. It is very bewildering.

Miss Wolff: Perhaps you could make it clearer by showing it on the blackboard.

Dr. Jung: Suppose we are in the year 2200 B.C., on the 21st of March, and Aries is just coming over the horizon at 1 degree. This is the spring-point, that is, the intersection of the line of the ecliptic with the equator of the sky. Each one of the zodiacal signs represents 30 degrees. Slowly, through the precession of the equinoxes, the spring-point shifted through the sign of Aries toward that of

Pisces until in 150 B.C. Hipparchus[11] observed that Aries was gone and the sun was coming up in a new sign.

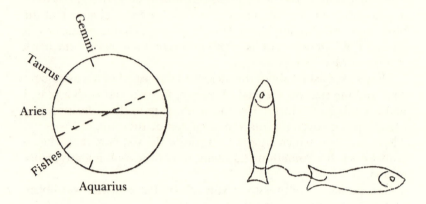

In those days tremendous things were happening. The gods changed when the stars changed. Here the Ram changed into the Fish, he died as a ram and was born as a fish. The gods had bull's horns when the sun was in Taurus, and they had ram's horns during the Aries period. Then the Fish became the symbol. The Christian baptism in water has to do with this symbolism. The Pope still wears the fisher ring—a gem that represents the miraculous draught of fishes, symbolizing the gathering of all Christians into the womb of the Church. So a new psychology began to make itself felt. It was the dawn of Christianity, and we can follow its course in the astrological picture. The fishes are represented in a peculiar way in the zodiacal sign. They lie almost tail to tail, joined by a commissure. This double arrangement is supposed to indicate Christ and Antichrist. That curious legend can be traced back to the first century—the idea that Christ had a brother, the Antichrist. When the spring-point has progressed to the whole length of the first fish, we are in A.D. 900—about the climax of Christian influence. Then it declines, and the spring-point is in the middle of the commissure, which would be in about 1500.[12]

Mr. Bacon: A curious fact is that the temporal power of the Pope and the power of the Dalai Lama reached their highest points

[11] Greek astronomer, discoverer (130 B.C.) of the precession of the equinoxes.

[12] For a discussion of the constellation of the Fishes in relation to certain temporal events and the Christ-Antichrist legend, see *Aion* (1951), CW 9 ii, pars. 147-149.

within fifty years of each other, and they also lost it within fifty years of each other.

Dr. Jung: Yes, that is very interesting, and there are other parallelisms of that kind. Now in about 1500, we have Luther, and the Catholic Church was right in saying that he was the Antichrist. When we come into the tail of the second fish, we are in 1750, the period of the French Enlightenment, when for the first time Christianity was dethroned and replaced by the Goddess of Reason. The spring-point leaves the fishes before the head of the second fish is reached. For the time being we are headed for the utmost destruction of that principle. About 1940 we strike the meridian of the first star of Aquarius. That would be the turning point—about 1940 to 1950.¹³ So we may look for new developments at about that time. It remains to be seen, I shall make no predictions.

Now we can go back into the past and verify some of these astrological peculiarities. At the time the sun was in Aries, about 400 to 500 B.C., there were particularly brilliant stars, and that time coincides with the greatest development of philosophy in Greece and China.

About 2000 B.C. Hammurabi¹⁴ announced himself as the great lawgiver. He declared himself the Ram. It was the time when the sun was just coming into Aries. Probably we are dealing here with unconscious laws of creative energy, of how things develop, which we only now begin dimly to divine. It is a very pale spectre still, but things begin to take shape.

Each spring sign is, of course, balanced by an autumnal sign. For Taurus, when the Zodiac was first made, it was Scorpio foretelling the suicide of the sun. The hero Gilgamesh passes through the autumn gates guarded by the Scorpio giants in going to the Westland. In Roman times, Scorpio had ceased to be the autumnal sign, it was Libra. When the sun came into Pisces, Virgo became the autumnal sign, and astrology has connected that fact with the worship of the Virgin Mary. When we get into Aquarius, we shall have Leo opposite, so we would have a deification of lion attributes— the worship of the sun or sun-like personalities. I hope that by the next seminar, you will have all this clearly in mind, because you won't be able to understand the next dream if you have not.

¹³ In *Aion*, par. 149, n. 84, Jung corrected these dates, calculating that the beginning of the Aquarian Age would fall between A.D. 2000 and 2200.
¹⁴ King of Babylon.

LECTURE X

11 December 1929

Dr. Jung:

I have here a question by Mrs. Sawyer which I rather expected and which shows that we are not yet finished with this exceedingly intricate problem about astrology and the connection between time and energy. As I told you, I never would have ventured into such an abstruse subject if it had not been indispensable for the understanding of the dreamer's material. This is his universe, and if one dismissed the problem, it would be saying to him that one was not sufficiently concerned with his psychology. For him, as for most men, the Logos side of his material is the most interesting. It might be less important in a woman's case.

Mrs. Sawyer's question is in regard to the relationship between ordinary astrology and the precession of the equinoxes. I will state the problem again. You see, ordinary astrology suggests that our life is dependent upon the so-called vibrations of the planets that are in a certain relative position at the moment of our birth and, they say, actually influence that moment and all our life. So if a planet crosses the same place it was in at that moment, perhaps twenty years later, it produces a special effect. Astrologers still hold to the actual place of the planets, but here we are confronted with the fact that today there is no correspondence between the positions ascribed to them and their actual position in the skies. Since 100 B.C. the spring-point has been artificially fixed at zero degrees Aries, but astronomically that is no longer true. In reality, on account of the precession of the equinoxes, the spring-point has passed from Aries to Pisces and it is shortly to enter Aquarius. So our calculations are simply arbitrary, having to do only with time and not with the actual position.

Now, the last time I told you something that was apparently quite contradictory. Having stated that the position of the stars had no

424

influence upon us, I then drew certain conclusions about the effects of the sun on the earth as it passed from one zodiacal sign to another. I told you, for instance, that in A.D. 900, when by actual astronomical calculation the spring-point was at the point of greatest extension of the Fishes, Christianity was coincidentally at the height of its power. Then by 1500, the spring-point was in the commissure, the ribbon connecting the two fishes, and at this point began a mental and spiritual revolution and the decline of the Church. The second fish represents the Antichrist and the decay of Christianity. The Gothic movement was vertical, and then began the horizontal age of materialism, a time of great intellectual extension, voyages of discovery, etc., but winding up with the World War, the moral defeat of the spirit of Europe. I said, too, that we might expect a peculiar change in the mentality of the world in the next fifty to one hundred years, in the time when the spring-point proceeds into Aquarius. So I seemed to be linking up the astronomical positions with human affairs and with peculiar changes in mentality. The problem is an exceedingly difficult one, and it took me years before I understood, so I don't expect you to solve it at once. An astrologer told me that the ephemerides, that is, the position of the planets, are exact as to time but not as to the actual position of the stars. Now I will read Mrs. Sawyer's question: "I understand that astrology has been projected into the stars, and that it does not matter whether the stars are actually at the spring-point, the time element being the important thing. But when you say that the spring-point is now actually in the Fishes and prophesy about 1940, you are following the actual movement of the stars, are you not? Was the whole projection in the first place really made with an intuition of the backward movement so that the projection works both ways—that is, that it works from a static standpoint and also at the same time from the moving standpoint?"

Well, the important point is that the horoscope is true only in the time sense, not astronomically. It is independent of the stars. We see that menstruation has a moon period, yet it does not coincide with the phases of the moon; otherwise all women would menstruate at the same time, and they don't. It simply means that there is a moon-law in every woman and likewise the laws of the stars are in every human being but not in the relation of cause and effect. The fact that the spring-point changes does not mean that it is the cause of the changes that ensue on earth. Life has changed

425

and will change, as the spring-point is changing, but the apparent connection is a coincidence; that is, the two things occur together in time but not in a causal sequence.

In an ordinary horoscope, one is not concerned with the spring-point. In the life of the individual the spring-point doesn't matter, but in the life of the tree of mankind, it matters very much. An ordinary year is to us what the Platonic year of 26,000 of our years is to the race. The precession of the equinoxes is making its way backward in a circle from Aries to Pisces, to Aquarius, Capricorn, etc. When the cycle is complete, it covers 26,000 years. That is the Platonic unit in the life of the tree. The fixation of the spring-point is an arbitrary measure for our arbitrary use, the same condition having prevailed in 2000 B.C., when the astronomical conditions actually did coincide with the statements of the horoscope. The precession of the equinoxes might be said to be the clock-hand that marks the great spaces of time, the hand that measures time for the tree of mankind. On our clock, the hand moves forward, but with the clock of the race it moves in the other direction. Each zodiacal sign then becomes a [Platonic] month, and we call a certain period of 2,150 years the [Platonic] month of the Fishes, for instance, which is of course again a projection. So for us, our whole historical life, the length of human consciousness, is only three months. But man has gone through those 26,000 years many times. Divide 1,000,000 years (the probable age of man) by 26,000 and you will know how many Platonic years there have been. Paleolithic man might go back many hundreds of thousands of years to the *Pithecanthropus erectus*, and from that to the apes and, still further, to the saurians.

So when we speak of the coming up of the saurian in our dreams, we mean that the impressions of an infinitely remote time are making themselves felt. In the course of the innumerable revolutions of the Platonic years we have received imprints of conditions of which we are not conscious, but they are in our unconscious. Only three months in power is so little, it makes a poor showing. One is embarrassed intellectually, for one does not know; human consciousness is much too young. There are certain symbolic evidences in our dreams and fantasies, but that is far from scientific. All that remains to us, for instance, of the "months" of Taurus and Aries are bull gods and ram gods. Perhaps by a further elaboration of the unconscious we may sometime get further back; we may get the feeling of what Gemini and Cancer meant to mankind. At all

426

events, we have the Zodiac, which is the naïve projection of unconscious imprints through numberless Platonic years. Mankind
has projected intuitive memory into the stars as he moved through
the cycle in remote ages I don't know whether in those days he felt
the exceedingly historical character, but relatively primitive man
has made those projections.

Then time progressed, and slowly the spring-point wandered out
of Aries; and then they felt the need of getting it fixed, and since
then it is simply the law in ourselves that accounts for the validity
of astrology. It has the same validity as the connection between the
monthly period of woman and the moon. So we can think of the
underlying laws of our unconscious as star laws. But the artificial
spring-point has nothing to do with the life of the tree of mankind.
At the time when the Zodiac was invented, man was in the spring-
time of consciousness, so the falling of the spring-point in Aries, a
spring-sign, was appropriate; it is as if the horoscope of humanity
had begun with the dawn of consciousness. The essential point to
remember is that the precession of the equinoxes does not prove
the identity of astronomical facts with periods of human psychology. It is just that our consciousness began in the spring-time of
mankind, and that happens to fit the zodiacal sign of that time.

But here is a little mistake. Hipparchus should have fixed the
spring-time in Taurus instead of Aries. At that time the Zodiac had
only eleven or ten signs. In Roman times there were eleven, Libra,
the twelfth, was made by cutting off part of Scorpio.[1] That had to
do with the fact that the spring-point moved from Taurus into
Aries. This is very complicated, but you must get the peculiar fact
that the flow of energy, the libido in ourselves, is the flow of energy
in living nature and in the universe, although the two worlds are
not causally connected in their energic phenomena. The energy in
both is identical in essence, but in each plane it is following different
causal sequences. And the flow of energy in ourselves and in the
universe has to do with time. How can we best catch time, in itself
such an abstraction? Well, in the flow of energy we have something
upon which to hang time.

Our modern idea of time is highly abstract, we have definite
notions about the divisions of time into hours, minutes, seconds,
etc.—very fine distinctions about time values, in other words. To
the primitive, however, time is a very nebulous thing. One feels

[1] Cf. above, pp. 407-408.

this as soon as one is out of the reach of civilization, and of course the whole East has no notion of time in our sense. So we can't expect primitive man to produce symbols with the specific time character as we know it. He is much concerned, however, with the flow of energy, as is shown in his conception of mana. We have plenty of material that shows us that energy symbolism. But the question of time symbols is abstruse and more difficult, and I want to confine myself now to those that appear in language. We are constantly using metaphors, for instance, in which time appears as a river, a wind, or a storm—"the stream of the hours that pass"— or "Tempestas horarum"[2]—devouring quality of time. In mythology it may be the dragon that eats everything that one loves— father and mother, all that one has. Therefore the hero who overcomes the dragon brings into existence again all the ancestors, the crops, even whole nations that have been eaten by time. He redeems all these precious things from the past.

So the quality of eternity has been attributed to the religious hero. Before Christ, it was immortality that the hero possessed, not eternity. In the Babylonian myth of Gilgamesh, the hero was two-thirds divine but one-third human, and in order to be wholly divine and gain immortality he must cross the great sea to the Westland. Now in these symbols—dragon, wind, river, etc.—we have energy symbols. It is the flow of life, the river of life, wind, spiritual energy. So we see how the concept of time gets mixed up with energy concepts. As a river is a fertilizer, so time has also been understood as productive. Bergson has this idea in his *durée créatrice*,[3] which is really the Neoplatonic idea of Chronos[4] as a god of energy, light, fire, phallic power, and time. The material for time symbols as they appear in language is very scattered. The concept of time is so abstract and merges so with that of energy that it is difficult to detach, in order to show that time is really meant. It soon becomes

---

[2] *Tempestas*, Lat., = "space of time," "passing stream of time," as well as "weather" and "storm."

[3] See above, 16 Oct. 1929, n. 3.

[4] There is a confusion here and in the next par. between two entities in Greek religion. Kronos (or Cronus) is one of the Titans, youngest son of Ouranos the sky-god; he castrated his father, married Rhea, and fathered children whom he devoured at birth, except for Zeus, who survived to vanquish Kronos. The name Kronos is unrelated to the word *chronos*, "time." The personification Chronos is, in Orphic tradition, the name of a cosmogonic deity from whom emanated Ether and likewise Chaos. (C. Kerényi, *The Gods of the Greeks*, Penguin edn., 1958, pp. 17-20, 100.)

energy. Mana at first seems only to have to do with energy, but later on it takes on time qualities.

Now let us take Chronos, the god who ate his own children, the word having the meaning of time. *Chronos* is from the Greek root *chre*, which later becomes the Indo-Germanic root *gher* (where there is a reversal of the *r* and the *e*), and they have the peculiar connotation of a verb, activity. The word *chre* has the meaning of passing over like wind. In German it is *hinstreichen über*. *Gher* gives the idea of taking in, holding. From the root-word *chre* comes *chronos*, and from the root-word *gher* comes *geron*, a Greek word meaning old, in German, *Greis*, old man; so time takes on the guise of an old man. With the primitives, the notion of time is expressed by an old man, or by a visible sign of old age. In seeing an old man, it becomes visible that there is time. My Africans thought I was a hundred years old because I had white hair. One hundred means untold ages. Chronos is the oldest of the gods.[5]

Then there is an Iranian word *zrvan*, usually found in connection with another word, *akarana*, meaning a god, and *Zrvan Akarana* means unlimited duration that contains all that happens.[6] An old French scholar once made a shrewd guess about this phrase, but unfortunately it proved to be not the right one. He guessed that since it meant an immensely long time, it contained the idea of Ormuzd (light) and Ahriman (darkness). In other words, the pair of opposites. But this cannot be, because one version has it that Zrvan, the devil, made time and another that Akarana, the god of duration, made it, so opinions are divided about the origin of that awful thing, the flow of energy. One can never make out who is responsible. Nowhere is there such a marvellous dualism. One could make a diagram of it like this: Do you see that it makes a cross? I have a book with a picture that I would have liked to show you. It is a crucified god hanging on the cross, and on the right is the sun and on the left the moon. The blood from all his wounds is flowing down as grace to the world—divine energy. The clash of the sun and the moon, unified by the suffering man on the cross, brings the energy. The thing that flows is time.

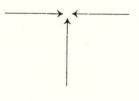

---

[5] According to Kerényi (ibid.), Kronos was the youngest of the second generation. Also cf. above, 19 June 1929, n. 8.

[6] Cited in *Symbols of Transformation*, CW 5, par. 425 (as in 1912 edn.).

Then in the old Persian religion there is another very interesting symbol, a real mana concept. It is *Haôma*,[7] which means grace. It really means fiery splendour, but it is what the Christians called grace, the gift of the Holy Ghost, like the fiery tongues that fell upon the disciples—fiery tongues of heavenly grace, mana. It is quite possible that there is somewhere a connection between the Persian and the Christian idea. You see, besides the time, there is also the energy concept.

I would like to discuss also another Greek word dealing with time, *Aiōn*, meaning the time of life. *Aiōn* has interesting connections. The equivalent in Latin is *Aevum*, meaning eternity, also the duration of life, or an epoch in history. There is a wonderful verse in Horace,[8] about the river that is flowing and flowing, fleeing past into all eternity, (*aevum*). Again we find here the peculiar union of energy and time. The old High German word *ewa* meaning "always" is close to the Anglo-Saxon and modern English word *ever*. Then concerning *Aiōn* there is the interesting fact that the Persian *Zrvan Akarana* became in later times the god Aiōn and played a great role in the Mithraic cult. This is rather difficult to understand. He also is called Deus Leontocephalus, or the lion-headed god, and statues of him have been often found in underground caves. The cult of Mithras was chthonic in character, so all the churches were at least half underground, and originally they were in caves. (It is said that the cellar where Christ was born had been a grotto-temple of Attis.) In the statues, the god Aiōn is represented as a man with a lion's head, about whose body is coiled a serpent, the head of the serpent projecting over the head of the man.[9] Another Mithraic symbol is the amphora with the lion and the serpent battling for its possession, and often a flame is coming out of the amphora.[10] The lion is July, the fiery heat of summer, and the serpent represents the darkness and the coolness of earth, so it is the Yang and the Yin again. Aiōn is the god of the union of the opposites, the time when things come together. Now, I think I have said enough for the

---

[7] Cited in "On the Psychology of the Unconscious," *Two Essays*, CW 7, par. 108.

[8] *Epistles* 1.2.43: ". . . labitur et labetur in omne volubilis aevum" ("yet on [the river] glides and on it will glide, rolling its flood forever").—LCL, tr. H. R. Fairclough.

[9] Such a statue is reproduced as the frontispiece of *Aion* (1951), CW 9 ii, and as pl. XLIV in CW 5 (described in par. 425, as in 1912 edn.).

[10] Depicted in ibid., pl. LXIIIb.

present about the peculiar connection between time and energy and psychology, we have had rather a profound discussion. Let us return to the dreamer.

One of the members of the seminar asked me if our discussions here had not affected the dreamer himself. I think they have, I must say that during the summer he made a decided step forward. His feelings became very positive, and up to that time they did not visibly stir. Four weeks ago for the first time he wrote a spontaneous poem about the birth of the new sun, which is a spring festival celebrated in the north of Africa. On the 28th of July he had a dream which he brought to me to analyse on the 21st of November, three weeks ago.

Dream [18][11]

He dreamed of a Buddhist monk, a little old man who led him to a fissure in a Cyclopean wall, and inside he saw the wall-people, who were like a secret society doing mysterious things. Once inside, in a sort of temple, the old man changed into a beautiful little boy, and the dreamer fell down and worshipped him as if he were a divine being. He wore three capes one over the other and a sort of cap. He was something like a *Münchner Kindl.*[12]

This puzzled the dreamer, but I explained to him that the Cabiri are usually represented like that, the one on the arms of the city of Munich is a little monk. He is like the Cabiri of Aesculapius, the inspiring familiar spirit of the doctors, who is often represented as holding a scroll and reading wisdom to Aesculapius, and he is always cloaked from head to foot with a hood over his face. His name is Telesphoros, meaning the one that brings completion, perfection, or initiation. That is what I told him, and somehow that worked in his mind, for during the last seminar, he produced a picture of a boy in the cross position. In one of his outstretched hands he holds a sun, in the other the sistrum, or the crescent. Mind you, he knows nothing of what is going on here, and yet he was doing exactly what we were doing. The dream is interesting but the symbols would not have come from what I told him, they

[11] See above, p. 295, for an explanation of the numbering of this dream.
[12] See above, 22 May 1929, n. 4.

probably would not have come without our seminar. I think he was stirred from within. I must draw your attention to the design on the robe. It is like a fleur-de-lys but it is also a Buddhist symbol for the thunderbolt, or collective energy, which the dreamer did not know. When I asked him for an explanation of the picture, he said that as he painted it, he constantly had the words in his mind, "I am the Resurrection and the Life."

Now we will take up the dream that directly followed the one concerned with the union of the pairs of opposites, the sword and scythe symbols.

Dream [21]

He sees a vast grey plain approaching him, and the closer it comes, the more the monotonous grey dissolves into multicoloured stripes, some wide and some narrow, and they move in a peculiar way through each other, uniting and separating. And then he sees that many people are occupied with those stripes, as if to shape or canalize them or to change the direction or to blend them. The work is hampered through pressure that comes from other stripes. So on account of that interference, the activity of the people is hindered and the results are often quite different from the original intention, and he says to himself, "Cause and effect." Then he tries to help them and in working on them he becomes aware that they are nothing but the surface of a vast mass, like a huge river flowing in a given direction, and the movement is due to the mass flowing along like a lava stream, the stripes coming up and disappearing again. At the same time, he becomes aware that it is all transparent and luminous, that not only the mass itself but the atmosphere and the people and he himself are all permeated with something that he compares to fluid light, and he knows that this has a tremendous influence on everything that it permeates. He says to himself, "The Fate of Man, the Fate of People, the Fate of Worlds," yet still he remains preoccupied in shaping his stripe.

Associations: Of the *grey plain*, he says that grey contains all the colours because it is a mixture of all.

Concerning his remark *"Cause and effect,"* when he sees the people remodeling the stripes, he says, "That is indeed quite illogical.

People couldn't hope to make any effect on that huge mass. They would have no effect on the total thing."

Then he says that he is quite unable to get at the meaning of the dream. He thought it must have to do with impressions he got from a book by Künkel, called *The Great Year*,[13] meaning the Platonic year. I have read that book and it is not particularly important, but there is a pretty good description of the outlook on the Fish age and the age of Aquarius. There are some ideas in it that are interesting. The dreamer happened to read it. Now, how can we prove that it was an astrological dream?

Dr. Baynes: By his saying, the Fate of Man, the Fate of People, etc.

Dr. Jung: Yes, that shows the three stages, the individual man, mankind, and the world. It is exactly what we were talking about— the identity of the flow of energy and time, which contains the great Platonic years and his individual fate too. Now, what do the stripes suggest?

Mrs. Sigg: Shaping his individual life.

Dr. Jung: Yes.

Mrs. Fierz: It is the same idea as the thread of the Parcae.[14]

Dr. Jung: Yes, it stands for the extension of time, the thread spun by the goddesses of fate. Now what are the colours?

Dr. Baynes: The colours are the individual elements of the spectrum.

Dr. Jung: Yes, and that peculiar fluid that permeates?

Miss Wolff: It is clarity, light, the spiritual principle of consciousness permeating everything.

Dr. Jung: Yes, everybody and everything is permeated by it. That flow of compact substance like lava is the idea of physical matter, and it is permeated by light, the spiritual principle, which is not only inside but above. There are the two things, substance or the material body, and the mysterious unsubstantial principle of consciousness. They interpenetrate one another. We think we know something about matter, but what is consciousness? We have no idea. We have no standpoint outside of consciousness from which we could judge its quality. Now each individual is represented by a stripe, and Mrs. Fierz has compared the stripes in the dream

[13] Hans Künkel, *Das grosse Jahr* (Jena, 1922).
[14] In Roman religion, three fate goddesses.

433

to the threads spun by one fate, decorated with roses by another, and cut by the scissors of the third, which would be death. This is a similar kind of extension symbol.

It might be interesting to go deeper into it. We can say that human life is a long stripe like a long river. Looking down at it from a mountain, one can see perhaps a hundred miles, the whole distance of the river from its source to the sea. One can see it all in one or two seconds, yet a ship on the river needs a long time to cover that distance, and it takes the actual water a long time to flow so far. It is time or human life seen from very far away, the beginning and the end at the same time. It is seeing time in space. Now, supposing that from a very high Swiss mountain you see two horses and wagons coming up, and you know it will take two days for them to meet. From above we can look into the future of those two fellows. So in such a dream we see human life as a stripe, as the river of time, and a person having such a dream is on a high standpoint, seeing the past, present, and future all at once. From such a point, human life would look like an extension of man, and then man himself would no longer be a definite figure, he would be extended in time. To his present body would be added all the other bodies he has ever had. The body I had yesterday and before that, when I was cheese high or like an embryo, down to my death, form a stripe, a long series of bodies. This makes man into a snake, and time is a snake. In the fourth dimension, man is a worm, and our length is not measured by metres but by the number of our years. One might say that that was a perfectly crazy notion, but I will give you an illustration full of religious dignity. Christ is represented as a great serpent who carries twelve signs on his back, meaning the twelve signs of the zodiac and also the twelve apostles. He says, "I am the vine, ye are the branches."[15] He is the zodiacal serpent and they are the manifestation of the months, so the idea of man as a serpent is not so unique.

The serpent was the original form of the physician's god. There was an enormous serpent in the temple of Aesculapius, and in the third century, the huge beast was brought to Rome to combat the spirit of pestilence. For centuries, there was a serpent in the sanctuary. It was snake worship. A staff with a snake wrapped around it was the doctor's symbol, the caduceus. It was also the symbol of

[15] John 15:5.

434

Hermes the Sorcerer. There was originally an idea that Aesculapius himself was a serpent, so it conveyed the idea of healing, as Christ was the healing one. Saviour and serpent are used interchangeably. Moses lifted up the serpent and Christ said that so he must be lifted up to draw all men unto him. The Gnostics say that Christ was a serpent sent by the really spiritual God who had pity on mankind when he saw what poor half-conscious things they were. He sent Christ as a serpent into the garden of Eden to teach people to eat of the fruit of the tree, to know good from evil, and to become conscious. It is a peculiar idea—that we ought to became wise like a serpent.

WINTER TERM

Second Part: January / March 1930

LECTURE I

22 January 1930

Dr. Jung:

You remember that in the last seminar we were interested in three or four cases of exteriorization of our discussion of the cross and crescent symbolism, the cases of children who produced drawings which precisely expressed that subject. I have now another example to tell you about. In Berlin I saw a patient whom I had seen only eight or nine times before, but in that time I had started her drawing, at which she was very quick and quite efficient. The other day she showed me one which she said her husband criticized as artificial. She had drawn the same picture that Mrs. Sawyer showed us here, the cross and the crescent and the great light, done on the same date. That is especially interesting because I had seen her so little. I had received in the meantime two or three letters of an official character from her husband, but there was no direct connection.

Then, in looking through the cellars of the East Asiatic department of the Museum in Berlin,[1] I was able to get these examples of seal cylinders, which are of great interest in connection with the same symbolism.

[Here Dr. Jung showed us several photographs and plaster impressions of designs, seals, engraved on the surfaces of Babylonian cylinders made of amethyst and jade. Among the most striking was a Maltese cross, with the crescent in one corner and the sun below with the cross in the centre. Another contained the idea of the pair of opposites—two male figures on either side of the sacred tree of the Babylonians. The trunk of the tree had a peculiar segmentation and it carried the light on top, in the shape of the

[1] Staatliche Museum, Berlin: Vorderasiatische Abteilung. It is now within East Berlin. The Berlin visit Jung refers to is not otherwise documented.

winged disk of the sun. The disk was divided into four parts by the cross form and the wings made it resemble an Egyptian symbol. Another example was a segmented tree with the amphora on top, out of which appeared the winged disk. Still another of a similar pattern had human heads on top equivalent to the winged sun.][2]

The sacred tree played a great role in the Babylonian cult, and it is very frequent on seals. Sometimes it is like a date palm, usually with two priests in adoration, or giving water to the tree. Our Christmas tree is really a parallel, the light of the new year. Then there was the idea of the birth of the sun out of the top of the tree; Mithras and Ra have both been represented in that way. Mithras is sometimes shown with three heads, a trinity, rising out of a tree. It is also a medieval idea, like the family tree of Adam, with the roots in the sleeping Adam, the Kings of Israel in the branches, and Christ crowning the top as the last descendant—again the light-bearing tree. I have a drawing by a patient of a segmented tree with a winged disk on top, and around the roots are four heads. The segmented trunk stands for the spinal column, or the Ka or bodily soul of the Egyptians, while the sun-disk between the two wings at the top would be mind or spirit.

At my request, Dr. Deady and Mr. Henderson have made a synopsis of the dream material of the past seminars, which will be read for the benefit of the new members. It will be almost impossible for you to grasp all the detail, but it will be an advantage to the class to pause and if possible take note of what may be called the musical movement of the unconscious in these dreams, a sort of rhythmical movement. It is a way as yet unknown. We are far from understanding the dynamics, the laws of the movements of the unconscious; it is perhaps like a sort of symphony. A friend of mine has worked out an interesting scheme from a series of his own dreams extending over three years; he extracted the motifs and arranged them in a system which he invented, making a notation for degrees of intensity also. One makes out from it a sort of counterpoint. Certain motifs take the lead and others disappear. I noticed, for instance, that when the anima motif was up, the sex

[2] These seal engravings, or others very much like them, were published in Anton Moortgat, *Vorderasiatische Rollsiegel, ein Beitrag zur Geschichte der Steinschneidekunst* (Berlin, 1940); cf. nos. 630, 535, and 667. According to Professor Edith Porada, the identifications of details given here by one of the editors of the seminar are largely inaccurate. (Personal communication.)

motif was down; and when the sex takes the lead, the anima recedes. So one might from this report get an impression of a peculiar musical character in the flow of dreams. I have a feeling that music has much to do with our unconscious; perhaps it is the music of the future. Schopenhauer's idea of the movement of eternal ideas might be with us the movement of archetypes. That remains to be seen, it consists chiefly of question marks so far.

[The report was read by Mr. Henderson.][3]

Dr. Jung: I suppose you could not follow entirely the mass of condensed material that has been read, you must have rather a blurred impression. It is very important, nevertheless, that you heard the flow of images represented. Now I am going to set you a new task. I should like you to try, with the aid of this report and the fuller reports of the former seminars, to reconstruct, in a sort of abstract way, this movement of the unconscious through the series of dreams. I want to find out something about the laws of this peculiar melody. Perhaps there are musical people among us who may get a hunch; I am too unmusical to manage it, but I can give you suggestions for this kind of enterprise. I suppose you have seen that there are certain motifs which occur from time to time— a machine, or the mandala principle is hinted at, or the cauldron, the anima, etc. These are principles, motifs, of worldwide frequency and great stability of meaning and interpretation. And these motifs can be grasped: here is something rather concrete, a fact, like a hard handle which one can take hold of. Of course I admit that there is a vague fringe where one doesn't know exactly how they should be taken. Sometimes it is very clear, sometimes thin and tenuous; there are many shades of meaning. In such cases one might classify them as doubtful or definite. In any science here are doubtful facts. But as a whole one finds a certain number of very definite themes, such as directions in space, spiritual symbols, sex, which do not escape one's grip altogether. If one has such tangible themes, so that one can say this is a rebirth dream, or a regressive dream, etc., it makes a working basis; if one possesses detail one can perhaps establish certain rules according to which the movement takes place. One might invent a method by numbers, or by drawing, let us say, by which these motifs would become visible. I will show you the method my friend used.

---

[3] This report has not survived.

1, 2, 3, and 4 represent dreams.
A, B, C, and D are motifs.

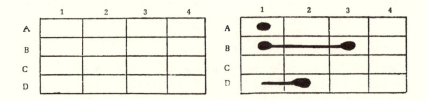

The presence or absence and the intensity of the various motifs is noted for each dream. In working with a patient one has two methods of measuring the value he puts into his material. If he talks a lot about a certain theme, it is obvious where his libido is; or he may not talk about it at all—his libido is there, but he is unconscious of it. The other method is the number of associations and the feeling-tone.

Here is another possibility similar to the one above, where we will try to map the intensity of the various motifs. We could say in dream 1 that C is lacking altogether. A, which is marked in 1, diminishes in the next dream, and B also, but B goes over into 3 and A does not. D increases from something very slight in 1 to something very pronounced in 2.

This is research work for you—new land. Anybody may find gold. You may see something which nobody has seen before. Perhaps you would use different colours to show how the threads move, similar to the dreamer's great vision of the river. You had best follow the suggestions of the unconscious, and you may arrive somewhere. It looks as if it were feasible. Those peculiar stripes in his dream would be the different motifs. In his dream they meant individual lives, but perhaps we are each but a complex in a greater mind, as, in our own minds, complexes are individual autonomous attempts. We think we are supreme somehow, some finality about us, but it is quite possible that we are merely such complexes, which move about, discuss things, perhaps have rows together, they might fight as we do, make a hell of a noise. We must allow such speculation, allow ourselves to open our minds and cast away all prejudices—search for the truth. In finding the truth it is always necessary to throw away everything that one has thought before. Why not? I tried to make a pattern myself and it turned out rather funny, like a river with oil on top. But it looks quite aesthetic, and when a thing suggests beauty or harmony in its form, it always has more to do with the truth than when it is ugly.

LECTURE II

29 January 1930

Dr. Jung:

The last dream we dealt with was that great philosophical vision.
This next one is entirely different.

Dream [22]

The dream begins with the vision of a peculiar kind of machine,
which the patient feels that he himself ought to control. It seems
to be for grinding something, but he doesn't know what substance.
It is a sort of vehicle which can be driven either by horses or by
motor and it is provided with a peculiar roof. His interest is chiefly
concentrated in a big cylinder, around which revolve a number of
small cylinders with apparently irregular, globular surfaces. The
main cylinder is not entirely globular, it has indentations, and as
the small cylinders rotate, they always fit into the indentations of
the big one, and also into those of the small ones on either side,
like the action of a cog-wheel, or perhaps a ball-and-socket joint.
(We call them "Kniegelenke." In French it is "rotule.") He says that
he is at once aware that the machine is not working well; something
does not function as it should. So he tries to move each cylinder
by itself, to turn each one so that the main globular surface is visible
on top. Then he calls a mechanic, and explains to him, speaking
French, that he has changed the position of the *rotules* of these
cylinders and that now the machine will function better.

Associations: Concerning the *machine*, he says that it seems to be
a device for grinding something and that it is to him a sort of
metaphor. It is the treadmill of daily routine work, and he adds
that this is actual because at that moment his analysis was interrupted by a business trip to a distant country. His business still

444

requires a certain amount of attention, and it is his duty to look after it. He says that he is, in a way, in the relation to his former business as he is in relation to this machine. The business is like a machine which works, but occasionally does not work, and then he must take over the control. So quite obviously the main aspect of the dream is a sort of metaphor which expresses his business, and the language is more or less taken from his business preoccupations.

Then he says that the peculiar *arrangement of the cylinders* makes him think of a sort of division of time, that time is the same, consisting of a series of units which are all linked up together, but each differing from the others, as days, hours, years, etc. The main part would be the year, and all the little irregularities would be the days, which are long or short or have other different qualities. Then he says that the irregularities remind him of how teeth behave. When a tooth is pulled out, the teeth opposite have a tendency to fill out the gap. Obviously he means the fitting into these indentations.

Now the *mechanic*. He says that in spite of the fact that there is already a mechanic busy at that machine, he himself tries to get it into working condition. He speaks French with the mechanic, which is not astonishing because, particularly in his business, he speaks as much French as German or more. He calls the cylinders *rotules*. In reality it makes little difference whether one speaks of a cogwheel or a *rotule*, but to him it made a difference, so much so that he mentioned it in his associations.

That is the whole dream, a very difficult one. Those who heard the dream before might have a point of view. Where is the link?

Mrs. Fierz: The link is in the end of the last dream. I think there is an analogy between each man working at his own stripe and the fact that the dreamer himself is putting the machine in order.

Dr. Jung: Yes, that is one link. And his business occupation is a perfectly conscious thing to him, so we can safely assume that his dream has taken the language of that business, according to the old adage that the dog dreams of a bone and the fishes of water.[1] What is another link?

Mrs. Crowley: The time element is in both dreams.

Dr. Jung: Yes, here we find the time element again in his as-

[1] In "The Practical Use of Dream-Analysis" (1931), CW 16, par. 318, Jung quotes "the old tag, *Canis panem somniat, piscator pisces*" ("The dog dreams of bread, the fisherman of fish"). It has not been possible to trace the Latin source of either version of the proverb, which occurs in various cultures.

sociations that the irregularities of the small cylinders symbolize the months, days, etc., revolving around the year. Is there another analogy?

Mrs. Sigg: We have had several dreams of machines and we know that there is a gap in his life. His sexual problem is not solved. The fact of his sex being out of order is the nucleus round which he revolves through all his dreams.

Dr. Jung: Yes, the last dream of a machine was the one where the motor went wrong, where the magneto exploded. In that also is the idea of revolving around a central nucleus. Before that there was the steamroller dream, also grinding. It was grinding gravel into the road, and it also was provided with a roof over the engine. It was making the road, moreover, which turned out to be the mandala design, as the ground plan of this one would be if one imagines it complete. It would be the flower-mandala motif, like this: So there is again the identity between his own life and time. I did not stress that analogy to the patient. In practical analysis one is concerned with immediate things, so I only hinted at it. It seemed more important for him at that time to get his own machine into working order. He is a very practical man, and his interest in philosophy was a side issue, a sort of pastime. That is the reason why the unconscious insists again  on this, because it is necessary for him to see that peculiar identity of life and time and energy. When a dream emphasizes a motif, one must go back and pay attention to it. Of course, there are certain motifs, certain thoughts, that are so profound and far-reaching that one can talk for months and not come to the end. Psychological identity is one of those ideas, and it is better that we go into it.

Mrs. Sigg: It seems natural that the machine cannot work as long as it is only thought of as being a physical mechanism. The dream seems to say that he is a child of his time to dream of his life as a machine, but in reality it is more like a flower, which is organic in its arrangement.

Dr. Jung: There is, of course, the idea of the irrational in it, though it is a machine, and it is sure that this man looks on life in too rationalistic a way. The dream calls his attention to the fact that life is by no means rational and symmetrical, it is very complicated and irregular. That is surely a point he would overlook because he always tried to arrange his life according to certain principles and not according to irrational facts. Therefore his machine is again and again out of order, and he has to return to it. But this is a side-light, and we must go again to the general situation.

You see, this dream came after a great vision, which suddenly opened his eyes to the real size of his problem. He never suspected that his dreams would lead him as far as that. Practically nobody realizes that one has to climb to a very high standpoint in order to see the full extension of the psychological problem. We all start with the idea that psychology is one small aspect of life. One even thinks in derogatory terms of it as "nothing but," only this or that, but when one follows up the royal road of dreams, one after a while discovers that the problem of human psychology is by no means small. One is impressed by the fact that the unconscious of man is a sort of mirror of great things. It mirrors the totality of the world—a world of reflex images. Looked at from the standpoint of the conscious, this world is the reality and that the reflex. But the reflex is just as living and real, just as big and complicated. There is even the standpoint that the external world is a reflex of the unconscious. It is only the Western minority who believe that this is the reality, and that other the mirage, the world of images. While the whole East, the majority, think the only reality lies in those images, and what we say in reality is just a sort of degenerate phantasmagoria which they call the veil of Maya. That is Plato's idea—that the original things are hidden, and the realities of our own conscious life are only imitations of the real thing.

So mankind is split in its judgment about the final point of view to take in these matters, and Western consciousness insists on looking at the unconscious products as merely mirror images. But if we study the dreams we see that the unconscious conveys its own right, it conveys the idea that that side of reality is not to be neglected. Otherwise everything goes wrong, and we have all sorts of neuroses which we cannot account for. Apparently one is living in a perfectly rational world, and then it is practically wiped out by one mood that comes up from the unconscious. It is there, and there are absolutely no means of removing it. Even the philosopher who explains it away as "nothing but" might have a neurosis and suicidal fantasies like anybody else.

Now our dreamer, as I said, was at that time still very much

447

under the influence of his rationalism. That is an egocentric point of view—because *I* believe, *I* think, things have to behave according to this law. If a stone should defy the laws of gravity and suddenly begin to rise, the police would be called because a stone had broken the law, and everybody seeing it would be sent to the lunatic asylum. Look at the physicists when it was discovered that the atoms didn't behave according to rule. The whole learned crowd was so upset that every idea of matter dissolved. Evidently when a certain degree of smallness has been reached there are no laws. Human experience is only three months old, and when it is six months old it may be that the stone will rise instead of fall. The recognition of the essential irrationality of the universe hasn't yet filtered through into our Western *Weltanschauung*. We are still convinced that things are going according to rationalistic rules. Therefore this dream again insists upon the thought that is contained in that great vision of the river. The unconscious says to him that whatever he does is illusion, that it is all the play of that great river and his life is but one wave on the surface of it. He may think that he is changing those stripes, but his life means nothing. That is the Eastern point of view, where the magnitude of man is instantly dissolved. He might feel as if he were the whole ocean, but of course he is as little the ocean as one grain of sand is the whole of the Sahara. Such a vision is apt to annihilate human life to such an extent that one just gives up. Anybody believing that as the ultimate truth would ask himself what was the use of attempting anything. One would suddenly feel manipulated by greater forces and think it was simply useless to struggle, that it was all perfectly futile. This is the reason of the Eastern quietism. The life of the Great One is all that matters, it does not matter whether *I* am alive or dead. And that leads almost to a state of semi-consciousness. Nirvana is being in non-being, or non-being in being, a paradoxical state in which consciousness of self is absolutely extinguished, assimilated in the Great One.

But now the same unconscious, in its unprejudiced natural functioning, leads the dreamer right back to his own life, choosing images in the terms of his daily life, bringing him back to his particular task. It shows him that his machine is not in order and that he should be busy on it. The two dreams are inconsistent, yet this one is full of allusions to the former, which it seems to contradict. What was the main theme is now somewhat in a corner, as a more or less irrelevant detail; it is now merely contained in his associations that details of the machine are related to divisions of time. From this we conclude that the Eastern standpoint is no more an absolute truth than the Western. Our individual life is not an illusion, it also is valid. And there you have the enormous conflict between the two *Weltanschauungen*, the two great aspects of our own psychology.

So in this dream he is taken away from the mood of the world vision. It is as if the unconscious had reached a culminating point in that great picture and then dropped him to the level of his most personal problem. One often finds that in dreams—a sudden leap from the heights into the greatest individual misery, perhaps, as if it said, here is a vision a law of life, and, by the way, your machine is out of order. This is the counterpoint in dreams. After the most general theme, one suddenly hears the individual note as a sort of contrast. And since even the unconscious recognizes the necessity of the individual standpoint, brings it in with the same insistence as the general motif, gives it the same value and dignity, that we may therefore assume, I should say that the smallest thing is just as important as the greatest thing. There would be no Sahara without the grain of sand, and the molecule of water is absolutely indispensable for the ocean. The individual man is indispensable to the existence of the cosmos, and when we return to the ridiculous shortcomings of his personal life, it is just as interesting a problem as when we are led up to those heights from which we catch glimpses of the full extension of universal life. Now, you remember that the machine has played a role in former dreams. What conclusions did we reach then?

Dr. Baynes: It is concerned with sexuality.

Dr. Jung: Yes, a mechanism in dreams means a mechanism. And we speak of a mechanism in man when it functions automatically, in a mechanical law-abiding way, when after this comes that. One knows exactly how it will take place. It is a perfectly reliable and regular connection of facts, which of course is what one finds in the realm of automatic processes, of instincts. One would not find it in the realm of will.

Yet sexuality is not only a machine. It is connected with many processes of the conscious mind, which are directed by free will, as we call it. Things are far more complicated. We would never be able to explain the functions of the human mind as mechanisms

449

alone. Apparently in this case, however, it is the mechanical part, the organic part, which is out of order. Now that former dream, by expressing sexuality through the symbol of the road-making machine, gives it a certain meaning which we should not fail to see. The making of the road formed the mandala pattern, which meant that the road of sex is the road of fate, the road of the completion of the individual. So we could say that without that mechanism we would not be in the clutch of fate. As a matter of fact, if man were liberated from the compulsion of sexuality, he would not be fastened to the earth, he would be always free, like a bird on the wing. He never would be limited to any definite fate, because he would escape any obligation. Sex is the power that binds everyone, and therefore it is the most important and the most dreaded thing. The neurotic tries to escape it because he wants to escape a fate which doesn't agree with his childish wishes or his egotism. The dream, by choosing the symbol of the steamroller, conveys the idea of a Juggernaut, a tremendous weight, an inexorable crushing thing which rolls over man and grinds him flat.

In this machine something is out of order. In his sexuality this man is not right. There is something which upsets him, and in fact he is lacking in his relation with his wife. There you would all agree with him in assuming that such a thing should not be, but be careful in drawing such conclusions. One can say of nothing that it is right or wrong. How can one judge? Human life and human fate are so paradoxical that one hardly can make a binding law. The average truth is that if a certain woman marries a certain man there is a sex relation between them, but there might be something stronger than the power of sexuality bringing them together for entirely different ends. We must allow for such things, because they really happen, and when one treats those cases one learns an extraordinary tolerance for the manifold ways of fate. People who have to live a certain fate get neurotic if you hinder them from living it, even if it is appalling nonsense in relation to statistical truth. It is truth that sometimes the water runs uphill. It may be wrong from the rational point of view, yet such a thing will happen and we must submit. We see that these things have a certain purpose, for we have really no standpoint from which we could hinder them. They contribute to the fullness of life, and life must be lived. One must not try to teach a tiger to eat apples. A tiger is a tiger only when he eats flesh; a vegetarian tiger is perfect nonsense. In this case, however, the lack of relationship with his wife is evidently disturbing, for from the beginning his dreams have pointed out that there was something wrong. The point is brought up again and again and for one reason. This man has philosophical interests and is inclined to make them a refuge into which he withdraws to shield himself from this most painful problem. At first he tried occultism and theosophy, and then he hoped I would have discovered some palace of ice where he could hide from this uncanny thing. After the heights of the last dream, where naturally he would have been only too glad to stay, the dream puts him down into his own reality.

In the magneto dream, the mechanic had to repair the motor and he himself remained passive. But this time the dream says he must manipulate the machine himself. The mechanic is again the doctor from the conscious standpoint, but this dream shows me up as a *quantité négligeable*. When people have not only the necessity but the ability to help themselves, they are quite apt to put the analyst into insignificant roles. But that is not to be taken as enabling the patient to step over the analyst. The conscious standpoint must be very carefully studied. Suppose somebody with megalomania comes along, thinking I am a funny chap who is giving him a good time for a while, and then he dreams that I am an ordinary barber or a tailor. In this case it would have an entirely different meaning. To him I would say, "Your Highness, I am your most obedient servant and only too glad to tie your shoes," and by that he will learn where his mistake lies. Or a woman patient might dream of me as a concierge, whom she tips as she goes out. In consequence I am something beyond the Pope, God himself, to her conscious mind. The concierge is presented in compensation for an enormous overrating. So there is no absolute rule in interpreting a dream, it is always relative to the patient's psychology. It depends on the conscious point of view; one must know what the dream is trying to compensate. In the former dream he took me as the master mechanic, while in this one he is a step farther on; before he has even noticed the mechanic he finds that he can put the machine into order himself. So I am completely depotentiated.

This would be a wish-fulfillment, if you like—what we call in German "Zukunftsmusik"[2]—for the dream impresses him with the

___
[2] = "Music of the future"; figuratively, dreams.

role that he might play but which he is not yet playing. It is obvious that the unconscious has the tendency to make me the *quantité négligeable* and to make him the important man who understands machinery. That is a great step forward because it helps him to realize his own activity and to rely on his own judgment and his own skill. lt shows that the unconscious is so far in its development that it enables him to take over a responsible role, and we may assume that if this development continues, he will be able to take the solution of his problem into his own hands. When he first came to me he wanted to be told what to do, he wanted a prescription. If it turned out to be the right one he would make a god of me, but the next time he blundered, he would say, "Why have you given me such bad advice?" It is either a failure or I am a god. Therefore I face him with my utter ignorance and refuse to give him a prescription. I impress him with the fact that it must be worked out. Consciously he doesn't know a solution, he says there is none. But there are no insoluble problems. His own unconscious is the great river, and if he can only get into that river the problem will be solved somehow. Sometimes it does not solve itself with the agreement of the conscious, sometimes a problem knocks one flat and the river rolls over one. That is also a solution, though naturally one dislikes it. If he trusts his rational mind only, the river will surely roll over him. It is in a way reasonable to take a modest place and try to work it out with me. But now, in the development of his analysis, it dawns upon him that he must take the whole problem into his own hands, and he has a certain confidence that he can do something with it. He feels a profound willingness to tackle it in the artistic way in which an expert would handle it—not impulsively, like a Negro who hits the motor to punish it, but wisely, like an expert. So this is what he is doing in fixing those cylinders.

It is very difficult to elucidate this symbolism, especially the peculiar connection with time. But if one can express psychological facts in terms of days, months, years, etc., one can say that these units mean psychological constituents, parts of the great river, and then one understands this peculiar arrangement. Such a mandala would be a sort of map or ground plan of the structure of the psyche or self, the expression of what man is as a psychical entity. The East would understand it in this way. The main body or the virtual centre would express the self, and the parts around it would be constituents of the self, as the months or the days are the constituents of the year. There is an analogy in the early Christian idea that Christ's body was the Church year; each year repeats the events in the life of Christ. As Christ has twelve disciples constituting his body, so the year is constituted of twelve months, and so the zodiacal serpent is constituted by twelve zodiacal signs, and this is said to be the Christ again, because he himself said, "I am the vine, ye are the branches."[3] The vine and the branches are indispensable to each other, and so the Church minus the twelve apostles is non-existent, as the year without the twelve months would be non-existent. So man is like the year with its twelve months and so many weeks and days and hours. He has, let us say, four seasons, four constituents, like the four gates of consciousness in the East and the four functions which I have discriminated.

Again and again we find this system of four turning up. The typical mandala in Buddhism always contains the square, the so-called courtyard of the monastery, with the four gates of consciousness, portrayed by the colours red, blue, yellow, and green. And that is what I see every day when my patients begin to draw. The number of constituents can be increased to any amount, usually it is four, or it may be twelve or twenty-four, but it is always an equal number. One is quite safe in assuming that something is wrong when a mandala has only three corners. That would mean that one function was quite lacking. I saw such a mandala drawing once, made by a man who was in fact almost entirely without the function of sensation. The *quadratura circuli* was the problem of the Middle Ages, the problem of psychological completeness. And this idea of the mandala expressing the totality of the human being and the right position in the universe, is the fundamental idea underlying the motif of the machine. It is the central fact, the underlying pattern, and it can be nothing else. Therefore the steamroller, which makes the road, reproduces this pattern.

Now, these constituents of the personality—which one may call functions, or Mendelian units, or the primitives would call them remnants of ancestral souls—these constituents don't always fit. They may be irregular, perhaps, on account of some inner friction. But through the development of life, in the course of years, these constituents ought to function in such a way that there will be in the end a complete synthesis, the integration of human personality.

[3] John 15:5.

So many neurotic conditions are due at the beginning to certain incongruities, temporary tendencies that simply won't blend; fire and water won't come together, and upon that split the whole neurosis is based. The neurosis has the purpose of hiding or bridging over that gap. Analysis has the task of filling it up by a peculiar experience, which might be the cement for fire and water and hold the two resisting things together. The difficulties in life are nearly always based upon such fissures or incompatibilities, and it seems as if the purpose of psychological life was to let them function together till the irregularities have rubbed off, like the irregularities in the facets of the cog-wheel, so that in the end all the incongruities shall adapt themselves in a smooth functioning. Our dreamer is trying to do this; his constituents obviously do not work together. Where have we met this idea before?

Answer: The chicken dream.

Dr. Jung: Yes, one chicken always ran away, One constituent has an evasive tendency and tries to escape. There is ample reason in his case for such an evasive element, for this is a typical example of the inferior function. The inferior function is not a welcome fact. You agree to the superior function and you admit the auxiliary function to help the superior one, but if there is something in you which won't fit in your machine, which causes you trouble all the time, you naturally help that thing to run away. Your machine then apparently functions all right, but from time to time there is a crash and you are upset, and that is of course the neurotic condition. The neurotic condition means a state where one is functionally, chronically interfered with. A little wheel has gone loose in his head, we say in German, or perhaps it has only slipped a cog. He uses the word "rotule," which etymologically is perfectly correct. It comes from a Latin word meaning "little wheel," but it is the French technical term for this kind of articulation. A constituent of his personality does not function with the others. It should come in somewhere, so now he is giving every cog-wheel such a position that the main surface will show; he is mending the trouble, apparently. What is the meaning of that?

Dr. Deady: A differentiation in consciousness of the elements of personality.

Dr. Jung: Yes, he has apparently done the right thing. I would myself say that the sex question was not really the fundamental trouble, but the dream says that it will function much better. It is, in a way, a disappointing dream, we would naturally expect something more startling. Nothing at all and yet it begins to function.

Mrs. Sigg: He puts the functions in the order of their greatest differentiation.

Dr. Jung: Yes, he tries to arrange these constituents in such a way that they show their most differentiated surfaces. He takes them at their main value.

Dr. Deady: He arranges them simply so that each cylinder shows.

Dr. Jung: Exactly. He establishes a consciousness which is aware of the main value of the constituents of his personality. Merely a change in consciousness. It looks like nothing, but it is the most important thing. It is like balancing the accounts in a big business. Before, he was constantly deceived by irregularities, he never had the right idea. Now he will know that each constituent has such and such an importance and give it due consideration. What is disturbing him will now come in under its own name. That is a guarantee of a relative smoothness of functioning. He will function much better in future.

LECTURE III

5 February 1930

[In answer to a question by Mrs. Sawyer concerning the interpretation of the figure of the mechanic in the dream of the exploded magneto, and in the last dream of the grinding machine, such an animated discussion followed during the first part of the seminar and the notes taken were so confused that only the following fragment could be reported properly. The subject was taken up again and clarified in the beginning of the next seminar.

In connection with the statement that the repair of the motor was delegated to an unconscious figure, this example was given as an illustration of the independent nature of an autonomous complex.]

Dr. Jung: We find it exceedingly difficult to realize that there are autonomous factors within us which actually do things. One can see that objectively in cases of somnambulism, where people, quite unconscious, get up in the night and accomplish certain things, discovering in the morning that it has all been done as if by brownies. I had an uncle to whom it happened. He was a rather well-known expert court-accountant, and he had to clear up a tremendous case of fraudulent manipulation. He was unable to clarify a most important item, until once, at about three in the morning, his wife saw him get up and go into his study without dressing. He sat working at his desk for about half an hour and she noticed when he came back that he had a staring look, his eyes wide open and glassy, and realized that he was in a somnambulistic condition. In the morning he felt low and heavy and complained that he could not find that damned mistake and would have to look for it again. Of course he was amazed to find that he had written in his sleep a long statement clearing up the whole case. There were even some quite astonishing details, such as a hole in the paper, which showed the figures underneath. His conscious did not see it but the un-

456

conscious corrected it; it was the automatic function which decided the case. That would here be the mechanic. It is a daily occurrence in analysis, that I say to my patients, "I don't know what the answer is, but we shall see what the unconscious has to say about it," and then the next dream brings a most amazing solution, as if I had submitted the whole thing to a higher supreme authority.

Dr. Deady: How far is that interpretation of the mechanic dependent on the man's conscious attitude? When you first spoke of the magneto dream I think you gave it a characterological interpretation.

Dr. Jung: Naturally it is a requirement that one knows the character of the dreamer. Dreams have no general meaning, one cannot translate them as one can a text. They are compensatory to a particular conscious and unconscious situation in a particular individual. Mrs. Sawyer's difficulty is really a great theoretical stumbling block. You see, originally Freud said that when you dream of your father, it *is* your father, or when you dream of Mrs. So-and-So, it *is* Mrs. So-and-So. I remember very well discussing this with him, when I said that one had better call it an *image* of the father. One cannot assume when one dreams of a person that it really is that person; that image may be entirely symbolical. For instance, when a patient dreams of me as the Pope or Jesus Christ or the waiter in his restaurant, I know I am not all that. That simple fact forced me to use the term "image." Freud has now adopted that idea. It is obvious that the people one dreams about refer more or less to real people, so when one dreams of somebody with whom one is in close relationship, one is fairly safe in assuming that it means that particular object. But there are restrictions. For instance, if a wife dreams of her husband photographically as he is, I would assume that she had really dreamt of her husband. But suppose she dreams in a roundabout way, a close analogy, yet he is not quite her husband, what is one to do in this case, which is fairly common? The unconscious has a tendency to say, "Not exactly." Certain traits appear which do not belong to the husband, peculiarities which belong to the wife perhaps, and then the image of the husband is ornamented with these projections. Or it might be that these qualities undeniably belong to him, but she has brought them out by her behaviour and is quite unconscious of the fact. It is important to learn to make these distinctions.

In this case of the mechanic the patient dreams of a figure who is not even symbolically connected with him, nor is he an odd chauffeur or garage man whom he might have encountered. And he is utterly unlike myself. The only analogy is that he is an expert at motors and I am an expert at psychic motors; that is the only bridge, so the dreamer grabs at that, he thinks it must be Dr. Jung because he is repairing the motor. But it is all-important that this man learns how to repair it himself, and it would defeat one's ends to teach him that it is I who figure in this dream. The greatest wisdom an analyst can have is to disappear and let the patient think he is doing nothing at all.

Dr. Baynes: There was one point in the dream which I think is liable to lead to confusion, and that was the different meaning which could be attributed to expressions in English. A mechanical thing is something which repeats itself, as for instance, a gramophone, whereas the principle of a machine has the connotation of continuity of energy. Yet in the dream this machine has very much the character of a new kind of invention, or new kind of idea, so that some sort of transferring process seems to be implied.

Dr. Jung: Another bewildering detail—that it might give the impression of a new invention used to transfer energy. That is true and not true. If we keep strictly to what the dream says, then it is not a new invention, but a kind of grinding contrivance. Moreover, this dream is associated with the two former dreams of machines, and there is nothing new about them either, so we really have to start with the assumption that the unconscious is choosing a motif more or less well known. But, on the other side, this machine serves a purpose which is very mysterious. The purpose of the steam-roller was obviously the making of a road. The purpose of the automobile was to transfer him somewhere, to get him into a different situation. Now, this machine has no such purpose. Why should he be grinding something? He says it is grinding something and it should function properly, but he is vague. So its significance is mysterious; one is left guessing. In the first dream, the steam-roller, we have the indication that it was associated with the function of sex, energy in a sexual form. In the second dream it had to do with the heart, energy in the form of feeling, and we had sufficient reason to assume that it referred to the absolutely organized part of the sexual function. In French we say the *partie supérieure* and the *partie inférieure des fonctions*. The *partie inférieure* is the well-organized part of an action. For instance, when one is learning to ride a bicycle, at first one learns to balance consciously and then it becomes automatic, but if one thinks about it, one falls off. That is the *partie inférieure* which functions perfectly by itself so long as it is not interfered with. Like swallowing—if one tries consciously to swallow, one can't, and that is typical of the inferior part of any function. The well-organized automatic part goes perfectly if one doesn't disturb it with untimely attentions. But Janet[1] is perfectly right in saying that disturbances in the *parties supérieures* are always psychogenic in origin. Take the function of eating. Anybody can eat, animals can eat, there is no difficulty whatever about it, it is a complete mechanism. But to eat under certain circumstances, to react properly at a diplomatic dinner, let us say, where one must listen to the speeches and the ladies on either side while one eats the wing of a pheasant, to do that is not easy at all.

Now, we cannot assume that there is something organically wrong with this patient, organically he is all right. But it is possible to get organically wrong from psychogenetic disturbances; an apparatus may get rusty. One might choose not to drink water perhaps, and then one would get organically wrong; an organic disturbance would be caused by the psychic connection, there would be a disturbance in the *parties supérieures*. There are many functional diseases like that which result in real physical illness. For instance, if anybody remains in a certain resistant mood too long, it is quite possible that the effect will be so bad that the person may have an angina, or his stomach may not function properly, he may acquire God knows what. If he is apprehensive all the time, if on account of certain assumptions he does not breathe properly, he may destroy his own machine, he may have tuberculosis. With the decrease of immunity the antitoxic factors disappear and he becomes perfectly defenceless.

So in this case one could easily imagine that our patient gets out of order somehow from psychological reasons. People who get wrong psychologically are often health fanatics. They are always seeking the right food and the right drinks, they don't smoke and they don't drink wine, they need a lot of salts and are drug-store fiends. Always some new scheme and never very healthy. It is a fact that the sinner generally feels better than the righteous one,

[1] See above, 23 Oct. 1929, n. 4. For the view mentioned, see *Les Névroses*, pp. 386ff., cited in *Symbols of Transformation*, CW 5, par. 26, n. 26 (as in 1912 edn.).

for the weeds always thrive better than the wheat. All virtuous people complain about that. Those people who take such care of themselves have always a tendency to become morbid. That amazing energy for drinking a certain water, for instance, comes from a continuous fear which is in them, and that is the fear of death. It is because something in them says, "For God's sake don't let me die because I have not lived." This man has a bit of that health mania, and the fact is a symptom of something not being right. He also is afraid of death because he hasn't lived, or it is as if he said: I must die if you don't allow me to live. He doesn't look unhealthy, but it is easy to imagine that something might go wrong—if not with him, perhaps his wife or children will suffer. It is often the case that the health mania is extended to the children, the poor worms are sometimes made extremely ill through the fears of their parents.

The idea that something is going wrong in his body is rather confirmed by this dream, because the mechanism refers to the physiological mechanism: his sexuality, which does not function, and, naturally, that can cause a certain disturbance. This is especially true of a man, in whom sex is far more impulsive and stronger than in a woman, it must force its way through or there is trouble. For a woman sex may remain quiescent for a long time, she may even go through all sorts of sexual experiences and not have the faintest idea of it. For instance, I saw a Russian girl—a cocotte—in a Paris hotel and I made a record of her experiences. She had had over fifty lovers, but only out of curiosity, she was always frigid. But once a man came along who produced a sexual feeling in her. She was astonished and said, "Oh, is that it!" She then married him and became a respectable little bourgeoise. She had talked sex and she had read it, the vilest stuff one could imagine, she lived a life that was completely foul and did not know what she did. It was like oil and water. There are many women who continue in that unconsciousness, which shows that in woman sex has not the piercing quality that it has in man.

If this man had not felt that something was getting organically wrong in his body, he wouldn't be disturbed, and there would be no motive for bothering about his life. He could be a wonderful theosophist, for instance, if it were not for that boring little instinctive devil that keeps on nagging—that inexorable thing. One might say to him, "Thank heaven that you had that great vision, but here

460

is the immediate truth and it is necessary for you to face that problem; for how can that light be luminous if you don't function right?" He must force his nose to the grindstone. Whereas formerly in his dreams, in his psychological development, the magneto mechanic had to do it, now he himself must take an active and responsible part in the shaping of his destiny. This really was the first dream in which I got a glimmer of hope that this man would tackle his own problem, that he would develop perhaps such a love of fate that he would pull his courage together and take the wheel into his own hands, because it means just that. Hitherto he has thought, as every man and woman think: well, I married and my wife is here to take care of it, I can't bother. The man expects it of the woman and the woman expects it of the man. If it doesn't go, they complain that something wrong has been done and blame somebody else, the wife's mother or some other member of the family; nobody thinks of the necessity of having to take the wheel into one's own hands. Such an efficient man knows how to steer in his professional life, but in his personal life he collapses completely; just as a woman can steer the part of her life that has to do with etiquette and social matters, but when it comes to an important situation in the world, she collapses and delegates it to her husband or to somebody else.

Now the great necessity of this man's life becomes evident to him, and he tackles the job, which means that in a more or less remote future he will choose that path of life which will settle his sexual problem. He can follow no principles. He must follow his individual choice, his individual fate, and that cannot be foreseen. If he asked me, "How do you think I can ever get out of this dilemma?" I could only say, "If you put yourself right, you can be sure that everything will go right; that is my conviction." Thus far the problem is, what shall he do with his sex? Very simple and very complete. But we have seen in former dreams that the steamroller produced the design of the mandala and that when we make a drawing of the working of this machine, we arrive at practically the same result. This gives an entirely new situation. The mandala is a circular symbol which no one would associate with sex.

Some of the new members have asked that the mandala should be discussed further, so I will repeat here that it is a universal symbol in the East, where they are considered to be exceedingly important. In the West it is found only when "heretics" make use of it. (Mandala is properly a neuter noun, *mandalam* meaning "image.") It is used for the transformation of energy, as in certain rituals the *yantra* is used, also for the transformation of energy. *Yantra* simply means a figure, an image of the god, or of something belonging to the god, like an icon. Hindus in the Shiva or Vishnu cult form images of the god every day—little clay images. And they make a dish of fibre or of palm leaves to use for the ritual morning meal of the god, and then throw it away because the god has used it. It is to remind you that in your innermost self you are that god, he is within. That you are alone is only an illusion. When you produce that image, you are through contemplation transformed for a moment into a god, and so purified, and your health power increased. You are in the great river. Certain temples have the form of typical mandalas, like the famous temple of Borobudur in Java,² which is a circle in a square.

² Monumental Buddhist stupa of the 8th-9th cents. A.D. See Heinrich Zimmer, *The Art of Indian Asia* (New York, 1955), vol. 1, pp. 298-312 (description), and vol. 2, pls. 476-494.

LECTURE IV

12 February 1930

Dr. Jung:

Before we continue I want to go back for a moment to our famous mechanic. As you have probably noticed there are some doubts still. The great difficulty naturally is the paradoxical explanation one has to give in such a case. We are always concerned with two sides in dealing with such a symbol, namely, the conscious standpoint of the dreamer and the standpoint of the unconscious. Then there is another difficulty which I have spoken of several times, and that is the method of interpretation which Freud has followed, that the dream symbol is a more or less concrete façade which is a sort of cheat, something which tries to lead you astray, and which therefore has to be destroyed in order to find out the real meaning of the dream. That point of view is in everybody. We are all acquainted with it, and it forms a prejudice which I am always having to fight against. It forces me to say that the dream is not a façade, it is a fact. It is like an animal—what is the name of that curious animal in Australia? The duckbill?

Miss Ordway: The duckbill platypus.

Dr. Jung: Yes, that's it. Well, that animal is not a duck, nor a mole, nor yet a rabbit; moreover it has a marsupial pouch. It is a most monstrous mixture of elements, a thing which should not be. If somebody dreamt of such a thing, the analyst might say, " 'But there ain't no such bird,' it is surely a most damnable thing, a mistake of nature that must be destroyed, there simply is no such animal, so you cannot have dreamed it." But there is such an animal. One cannot say that it is a mistake. Among primitives, when a woman brings forth a monster, a child with three legs or two heads, they kill it right away; it is dangerous and should not be allowed to live; they are always afraid of anything abnormal. So the abnormal paradoxical surface of the dream has led Freud to for-

463

mulate the idea that it was merely a façade for something rational and understandable and that therefore he had to tear it down. This is the prejudice we have to labour against. But I hold that when nature made that hell of a duckbill, she really meant to produce that thing. It is really in existence and is as little a mistake as a man or an elephant. It has been born, and the dream with all its paradoxes and unexpectedness is a fact too, so one has to take it as it is, and when it speaks of the mechanic, that man is really meant to be the mechanic. I never thought that he would become such a famous fellow!—We are having to spend more time on him than if he were a well-known historical character. The dream says it is that unknown mechanic, but as long as I am actually repairing his machine, naturally I am also the one who is doing it. The dreamer, the conscious point of view, says that the man who is repairing the magneto is Dr. Jung, yet the dream says the unknown mechanic is not Dr. Jung. A paradox, I grant you. One can hold a certain conviction in the conscious while the unconscious holds a completely opposite conviction which is equally true. As one can think to oneself, "I am all right, I am a fine sort of fellow," whilst the unconscious is saying that I am a perfect swine.

Well now, my chief opponent in last week's discussion, Mrs. Baynes, has acquired the great merit of having worked out a definite statement with which I agree. She says: "In the former dream where the magneto explodes, the conscious says the mechanic is the doctor, but the unconscious says the mechanic is an unknown man. In this dream of the grinding machine, the conscious standpoint remains the same, but the attitude of the unconscious has shifted. The unconscious now says, 'Although a mechanic is present it is you (the dreamer) who are taking the place of him as an expert; it is you who are mending the machine.' Thus the dream shows the doctor up as a negligible quantity, and for the dreamer, this marks a distinct progress."

The dreamer is naturally disconcerted that his most appreciated doctor should be so depreciated, that he should have made him into a porter or a chauffeur or a waiter whom he tips, for instance. Freud would say, "Ah, a resistance! You represent me as a waiter." But that is wrong. It is a mistake to take it like that, for you then kill the perfectly legitimate attempt of the patient's unconscious to liberate himself from the yoke of the analyst, who, whether he wants it or not, takes the place of God and is expected to perform miracles and to heal him. The patient should learn that there is another mechanic within him who will eventually be himself, even if the doctor is still mending his machine. It is still a conviction separated from the dreamer, but in time will become himself when he has acquired the capacity. Now I think this should be clear, and we will continue.

You remember I began to talk to you last week about the significance of the Eastern mandala. The different forms of the Eastern mandalas are dogmatically fixed, varying according to the different religious standpoints. The mandala plays a great role in the Tantric and the Buddhist religious systems in India, but there are innumerable sects, and it is sometimes very hard, even for a connoisseur, to make out the particular differences. One group with an especially dogmatic and definite creed is the so-called Tibetan or Lamaistic Buddhism, and I shall bring you next week a mandala from that sect.[1] The outer circle is usually a sort of fringe of fire, symbolizing the fire of desire, or *concupiscentia*. The concept of St. Augustine and of the Christian church, describing the arch sin, or the fundamental quality on which sin is built, as the desirousness of man, is exactly like the Buddhist conception—that all the senses are aflame, that the whole world is surrounded by the fringe of desirousness.

Then comes the black circle, which often contains little golden thunderbolts, symbols of continuous energy; this is a magic circle which denotes, "I contract my energy, I hold myself in, so that I do not burn up in the flames of desire." Then comes the gazelle garden, the lovely garden of the courtesans, in which the Buddha taught and where there are beautiful plants and birds and flowers. There is also a circle of petals before you enter the garden; they are the petals of the lotus on which the Buddha was standing when he appeared and announced the law. And inside the garden is the courtyard of the monastery temple or the "pagoda," and there are the four gates. Then you must realize that it is not only a flat thing, but is also thought of as having body, relief, so there is a sort of higher terrace. In the book that we published together, Wilhelm speaks of the "Terrace of Life."[2] The temple of Borobudur is built according to that scheme, and also the old Mexican or Mayan tem-

[1] Below, facing p. 479.
[2] *The Secret of the Golden Flower*, 1962 edn., p. 22 ("terrace of living"), in Wilhelm's tr. of the text; cf. p. 101, in Jung's commentary (= CW 13, par. 33).

ples, which rise from the ground in pyramidal form by steps at the different levels. There is a very ancient one at Sakkara, in Egypt,[3] which is on raised terraces, and probably expresses more or less the same idea. We have no texts that give a sufficiently clear interpretation of their symbolic meaning. The only access we have to such symbolism is in China.

Now, upon that terrace of our mandala is a central circle, again raised above the level of the courtyard, which is filled with symbols of emanation or contraction, thunderbolts of bilateral extension called diamond wedges. And within is the innermost circle, in the centre of which is again the diamond wedge. That symbol had originally a yonic and phallic significance. For instance, in our day, this is a very obscene gesture which an Eastern cocotte makes to

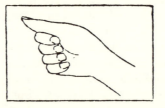

attract a man; it means sexual intercourse. And it meant in Babylonia the worship of the god; priests made that gesture to the idol or to the Tree of Life. The thumb has a phallic meaning, so the gesture would mean life. And those of you who heard our discussion of the cross symbolism will remember that the disc of the sun, with the cross in the centre, had also the meaning of life. Holding the ankh to the god meant, "I bestow life upon the god"; or the gods held the sign before the king, meaning that they bestowed life on the king. So that sign means generative power, because generative or creative power is only manifested where man is the victim. He offers himself to the gods as an instrument, and whatever he is creating, the will of the god is superior to his own desire, despite the fact that he identifies himself with the god and thinks he is the hell of a fellow to create such a thing.

You see, this symbol meaning life, right and left, above and below, is checked in itself. One finds it everywhere, meaning life emanating from the centre and going towards the centre, systole and diastole.

[3] The Pyramid of Zoser, IIId dynasty, c. 2900 B.C., the first large stone structure known to history.

It is like the movement of breathing and suggests the rites of Hatha Yoga; the rhythmic performance of breathing is part of the Yoga ritual and can be compared to the vacuol in the amoeba. Therefore the central place to which the four directions in space converge is called the germinal vesicle; it is the field where extraversion and introversion are symbolized.

Extraversion means going out through the gates of the courtyard. The inside square is divided like this: ⊠ and each of the triangles is characterized by a different colour and represents particular philosophical conceptions. Red is in the north below, the cardinal points of the horizon being all reversed: A most interesting book, the *Bardo Thödol*, or the *Tibetan Book of the Dead*, has been translated recently by an American named Evans-Wentz.[4] There the coloured triangles are explained, and one can identify them with the four functions as we know them in our Western psychology, the basis of our consciousness, the four qualities of our orientation in space, and therefore identical with the cardinal points of the horizon. One leaves the gates through the different functions or habitual attitudes. The man who leaves through the south gate will live in the southern world, and the man who goes out through the gate of thinking will live in the thought world. But when they return, the functions do not matter; only as long as they are outside are the functions important. When he enters the courtyard of the monastery, he approaches the place where all the functions meet; in the very centre he goes into the void where there is nothing. We cannot say it is unconsciousness, it is a consciousness that is not.

We come here to the famous Buddhist paradox, the non-existent existence, the being which is non-being, or the consciousness that is absolutely void. That idea of the void of consciousness is explained in the book which I published with Wilhelm. It is really, as the Buddhists always try to explain, not an empty consciousness as we would understand emptiness, but a consciousness that is not dominated by its contents. These contents attack our consciousness

---

[4] *The Tibetan Book of the Dead, or the After-Death Experiences on the "Bardo" Plane*, according to Lama Kazi Dawa-Sandup's English rendering, ed. by W. Y. Evans-Wentz (London, 1927). Jung wrote a psychological commentary to the German tr. (Zurich, 1935), which was tr. by R.F.C. Hull for the 3rd Anglo-American edition (1957); in CW 11, pars. 831ff.

with the fire of desire and we become possessed by them. The Buddhist idea of liberation is that we should not be devoured by them, we should rather be their masters; therefore one has to empty the conscious, as it were, of those overpowering contents. Or if anything is there, it should be like fishes in a pond; they are not masters of the pond, they are simply contents and so they cannot rule it. The pond is the very reason for their existence, it is the vessel which contains them, they don't contain the pond—though there are always fishes suffering from megalomania, who think that they contain the pond, that they are able to drink all the water and have it in their own inflated bellies. So that consciousness of the inner circle, that void, is perhaps better described as a vast unconsciousness, holding so many contents that there is nothing there because nothing matters. That is the nearest approach I can give you to the idea of Nirvana: positive non-being or non-existent existence.

Now, that paradoxical thunderbolt in the centre of the mandala I have been describing symbolizes a supreme state of revelation, a state of potential or latent energy. Everything is possible, but it is still, as before the dawn of the world; everything in suspense, yet the next moment there will be a world. This expresses the most gigantic feeling of a god, a Demiourgos that exists before anything exists; or of a god who suffers from a tremendous headache and hopes to be delivered soon. For I suppose he must have suffered terribly when he was in this state of pregnancy. That is not my invention, there are old esoteric ideas that God was very lonely, bored beyond words, and the desire was simply unspeakable to have someone who would be not himself. And that was the origin of the world: he had a terrible headache and wanted to get rid of it. We really have all been in the same psychological condition, so we can feel at those moments that we are exactly like the Creator with a creative headache.

This gives you a general idea of the Eastern mandala, and while I have been explaining this symbolism, you may have been thinking that it had some likeness to what we ourselves feel or experience. That is perfectly true. As a matter of fact, productions of similar structure are quite naturally made by many patients when they get to problems that are beyond the personal. There comes a certain moment or climax in any analysis when, at least for a time, the personal simply collapses, it no longer matters, and where something impersonal forces its way in, which is felt to be far more important, even against the will and purpose of the individual. And then these symbols appear. I learned about the Eastern mandalas after I had become conscious of our Western ones.[5] When I first saw one I thought, now what is this?—for it seemed to be just what I had seen with my patients. Then I went deeper into the study of them and found the most amazing parallelism.

Of course, the Western mandala has no dogmatic form yet, because it is completely individual; it is still as if played with. The Eastern form is a ready-made machine into which one puts oneself to be transformed, but the European drawing is not ready-made, it has still to be made, it is a most individual expression and anyone making such a thing has the feeling that he is producing something which is entirely himself. He believes it to be an individual variation or fantasy, not assuming that it could be of any general importance. So the Western mandala, being a means of self-expression, functions entirely differently from the Eastern way. It is not a finished temple in which there is a definite ritual, it is only an attempt. There is no ritual and no priesthood. It is as if many people were trying to build temples. That is the way these things come into existence. The Eastern stupas were once individual attempts, and so were the pyramids. Some king had a fantasy, or it was a high priest, or anybody who was in power and could afford to build such an enormous thing. There is always the individual attempt on the primitive level also; they build their ghost-houses according to their own plans. Nobody has yet felt the urge to produce a Terrace of Life in the West, to buy a piece of ground and build a mandala, instead or drawing it and bringing it to me in an analytic hour. A fellow with plenty of time and money might say, "Why, I will build that!" and there would be a peculiar monument which might become a national monument later on, simply because it expressed something which was of the greatest importance. If people take to it, it will remain; that truth will be convincing because it appeals to the general imagination. The great audience hall built by Akbar[6] was also a mandala, a most individual expression of that particular man, and it became extolled as a historic monument because it was built on generally convincing lines. That is the way

[5] Jung first published European mandalas (including, without attribution, several of his own) in the German edn. of *The Secret of the Golden Flower*.

[6] See above, 13 Feb. 1929, n. 1.

such things come to pass. With us, as I say, they are in the making, but I shouldn't wonder if something came out of it, it is possible. Out of these Western mandalas something will be created when one understands that it expresses something at the same time artistic and fundamental.

Dr. Draper: Will you explain what appears to me at the moment rather paradoxical, that the primitive people of whom you were just speaking are collective in their reactions, and yet at the same time more individual than we are?

Dr. Jung: Yes, that is a paradox, I grant you. They are more individual and less so. They are like animals. A complete thing, unhampered, simply what it is, identical with the laws of their species. That is my idea of the complete individual, not perfect, but individual. Complete in their virtues and in their vices. Fulfilling the meaning of the species, utterly collective, and at the same time individual. I say that you cannot be a really collective being without being completely individual, because only when you are humbly the thing that nature intended you to be, fulfilling decently the experiment nature is trying to make, only then are you a decent member of society. Not society with a capital letter, you might well be a holy terror to that society. Now I want to show you how the mandala enters in our dream. Are there any questions?

Mrs. Baynes: I would like to know if it is possible for the Western mind to get into that interior circle without falling into the Christian Saint psychology—that is, making a lust of renouncing lust.

Dr. Jung: Yes, it is quite dangerous to talk about Eastern psychology, because we Westerners are so imitative, particularly about things we don't understand. We try at once to ape the thing, assuming that we are thus getting it. We would like to transport Western psychology into Eastern form, but that would be a tremendous mistake. It would be the same mistake the missionaries make with the Negroes. Christianity is the religion of a highly civilized people, it is not expressive of primitive people. The missionaries spoil the native religion completely, and they themselves get spoiled. That is what happens when Western people identify with the East. It is really regrettable, a complete failure. They do it in order to escape their own problems, it is nothing but a cheat, a lie. That thing in the East is no lie, it is very sacred, but it is not for someone coming from a Western city, with that Western life in him.

470

The East reaches the Inner Court by a ritual which is collectively valid; there it is real life, but for the Westerner it is simply lying. He does not come from the life which that thing in the East presupposes, namely, a man who is low and also perhaps noble, a man who is perfectly acquainted with his vices as well as his virtues. Along comes a pale Westerner, very respectable, and enters the gates to be still more respectable. But he makes use of it only in order to increase his specific lie, and the result is that such people are perfectly empty. They walk about with glassy eyes, dead, every scrap of imagination gone, completely sterilized. They use that ritual to remove themselves from life. In the East they use it to increase life, life spent luxuriantly, like the jungle; all that is guarded and fathers intensity. The Westerner uses the very same means to mutilate his life still more. His left hand is already cut off and then he cuts off his right hand as well, so that instead of completing his experience, he completes his ignorance. Quietism has a meaning in the East, because if one is not quiet one goes to pieces; if one worries one goes mad. We live on time. Their watch is eternity. To ignore, time is useless and fruitless for us; we live in the actual moment, and if we ignore it we mutilate ourselves still more. Much of what goes on in Eastern rituals is hushed up. For instance, in certain Tantric systems, at the crowning moment when the initiant has entered the central place on the Terrace of Life, he performs a ritual cohabitation with a woman. That fact is not known, or it is just whispered. Westerners think the centre is a great void. Only when a man is capable of thinking of that act as a sacred nuptial can he understand the East. Christianity originally ended in the circus, wild animals in the arena and death. It is the idea of totality which is the necessary ingredient, not an artificial two-dimensional being. So it is absolute nonsense when Western people try to get into such a shape. They simply cannot do it.

But what the unconscious is surely trying to bring about is the building up of that temple, which means that it has a tendency to create the idea of the totality of man. That idea will get stronger and stronger as we get more oriented in our moral values—the more we learn that there is nothing very bad without a bit of good, and nothing very good without a bit of bad. We shall be improved by that truth, by that relativity, and get a little of the attitude of the Eastern man, who was always close to the earth and never dreamed of being absolutely superior to the laws of nature. They worshipped the laws of nature. You can see that in every Indian, in their worship of the phallus. They know it is a phallus, and the sterile woman brings offerings to it, often a little polished stone like an ash tray and in it an oblong stone. It is an olive mill to press out oil, a fertility symbol. One can see it in the streets and buy it, and there are huge representations of it in the temples. In Roman times no woman was in the least *gênée* to wear a phallic symbol as a brooch. Even in the early Middle Ages they used phallic amulets. It is only lately that it became indecent and completely hushed up. Now these things are discussed quite openly again, but that leads into a sort of disorientation of our morality. If you read about the conditions prevailing in certain countries now, especially the condition of the young people, and their point of view, you get an idea of what we are up against in our times. One understands why the unconscious is trying to bring up a new stability, a new order.

To return to the bearing of all this on the dream, we had come to the peculiar fact that the machines were connected with the mandala. The first machine made a road which very clearly amounted to a mandala. And in this dream the structure of the machine is again something like one—a revolving central part, suggesting a complicated device, with its constituents or parts working in perfect order. As far as I can make out every part is rotating, and in the mandala there is rotation also; the rotating idea is in fact necessary to bring about the magic circle around the sacred place within. In the foundation of a Roman city, for instance, they moved in a circle, the *sulcus primigenius*,[7] around the *fundus* in the centre, they went with a plough in the way of the sun, making a furrow around that central place. Not far from Zurich, at Irgenhausen, near Pfäffikon, are the remains of an old Roman castle with the *fundus* right in the centre; it has been excavated and repaired to a certain extent. It is always a good idea to see these things in reality, and it is easy to reach—there is an omnibus line from Zurich.

Still more interesting psychologically as an illustration of the rotation movement is the temple at Borobudur, which I spoke of before. That is a pyramidal mass consisting of circular corridors decreasing in size, like a spiral, till one comes to the central point on top. One walks in a spiral round and round, and the walls of

7 = "magical furrow"; *fundus* = "plot of land." See Jung's commentary on the *Golden Flower*, CW 13, par. 36.

these corridors are decorated with bas-reliefs representing former incarnations of the Buddha. It is a pilgrimage of initiation, and one is surrounded on either side with the images of the many lives of that perfect man. The pilgrim is taught that he lived as a plant and as a locust and as a monkey. That is not like our Western ideas, we would see a bill on the wall with *Verbot*.[8] But there he sees the life of all nature, including every mistake one could make—all the 576 processes the Buddha had to go through, working through the spiral way till he reached the centre. Then only was he the perfect man. Utterly unlike our idea of the proper kind of living! The rotating movement has the particular significance of the completion of life; if one covers the whole ground one cannot fail to complete oneself. If one remains on the East side, one is developed only on that side and absolutely atrophic and non-existent on the other. This is our psychological situation; we are a one-sided product with an unknown shadow side, which may cast a cloud over us at any time. The Buddhist creed, the spiral movement, gives one a chance to become the all-around man. The Platonic idea of the first man was an absolutely globular being, hermaphroditic, because the idea was that one must pass through the lives of women as well as men to grow into the perfect man. Through such an initiation an almost complete consciousness would be produced, in which there would be nothing left to take possession of one. In the Westerner, that side forms autonomous complexes which roll over him, and then there is a darkness and he doesn't know himself any longer. It is that other unknown side. The idea of rotation really means an evolutionary movement, a rounding out, a consciousness of the whole extension of one's life.

So the dream of the patient obviously means to put his machine in order and to let it rotate. And we see that the mandala symbolism comes in to show him that it really is his own individual *yantra*, that mechanism which ought to function and to transform him—as if he were walking round and round at Borobudur. By being identical with the machine he would arrive at his goal. The Eastern idea is demonstrated by its chiefly circular character, in which the cross is not so obviously represented; the idea is that man should enter the centre, and there he should become identical with the god that occupies it. Our Western mandalas on the other side show a tend-

8 = "forbidden."

473

ency to represent the cross in the centre in the following fashion: ⊕. This would mean a differentiation of the most central thing, and that does not exist in the East. It is probably what they criticize in us because it is missing in themselves, and that is why the East is coming to the West; as we go to them in order to get away from that spikey torture instrument and come round by the circular movement. I say this with reservations, but I have by now seen so many European mandalas and have been so impressed by the fact that the centre is preferably characterized by the cross that I think there must be something in it. It is not coincidence or mere chance. It is a Western characteristic, as working round in a circle is characteristic of the East, the *circumambulatio*. They work around, always having the centre on the right side. To go the other way would be absolutely wrong or regressive, and black magic would result.

Dr. Draper: Does the whirling dervish dance have any relation to that?

Dr. Jung: I don't know. There might be a connection. There is a mandala dance, which is beautiful because of the rotating movement and the position in space, the centre establishing relations with the figures on the sides. Sometimes there is a vessel of gold in the centre with flames rising from it and four pillars around it. Anyone with a motor imagination could make a very beautiful dance out of that motif.

Now in the dream of our patient, the mandala has to do with sexuality and that is linked up with his inferior function; it is a curse, a taboo, arising perhaps from his colonial inferiority. It is as if, in the mandala, one had blotted out a part. He should get himself together and then that damned thing would function. He must acknowledge the inferiority of his relatedness, which has hitherto been his stumbling block. When he came to the place where the whole thing should function together, he collapsed and had to begin again, for sex cannot be left outside. One can imagine that when the Buddha was a monkey he was a real monkey, he was just that thing; otherwise he would not acquire merit. For instance, in the East, when a man wants to be a holy man he is allowed to enter a monastery. Then if the life of a *célibataire* doesn't suit him, he can step out of his monastery and marry and is none the less a monk, only he doesn't live in the monastery. That is perfectly logical. He hasn't lived that phase enough, he has not burned out all that needed to be burned out, and one can overcome a thing only when it is burned out. Otherwise one is bound to it for this life and many others. One has to work that way, and then one comes to the place where there is no more. The Buddhist idea is a perfectly natural one, so natural that it has been called the religion of pure reason.

Dr. Deady: What did the patient get in his conscious out of your handling of the dream?

Dr. Jung: I really did not tell him all that I have told you, only hints. He was aware that these machines have to do with sex and are also an expression of human will. The mandala is really an effect of some fundamental idea in man for which I find no explanation. It is like asking why a certain thing should be beautiful—people call it beautiful and so it is. So this machine represents an underlying fact of an ideal nature and is the means by which he can transform himself. I called his attention to the fact that the revolving machine had to do with clockwork, time, a libido machine, and that it meant the complete functioning of his life energy, and I told him he must put it right. The dream says, now go and do it if you dare. But perhaps it is not the right time, as the Chinese would say. Therefore we cannot foresee what the next dream will show us. What we might expect, if the time is ripe, is that he will start something along the locust line or monkey line or certain human lines, but in any case that he will go a step further and come to a new chapter of his psychology. But if the general situation is not favourable, we may expect a catastrophe. Something may interfere. Perhaps somebody has an intuition.

Mrs. Deady: Are these all his dreams?

Dr. Jung: Practically all. He is not a very prolific dreamer. This one was seventeen days after the one before. What would you expect to be the next move?

Mrs. Henley: That he tries the machine.

Dr. Jung: Fine! You are an optimist.

Mrs. Baynes: I think he looks over the field in his conscious mind.

Dr. Jung: I hope he will do that because I told him he ought. And then what?

Mrs. Baynes: He might try to avoid it again.

Dr. Deady: This is the most positive constructive dream that he has had. Something ought to happen.

Dr. Jung: That is what we really could expect. We even must expect it. When a thing is ready it is very important that the expectation of the analyst is positive—*now* things are all right! He must have that self-confidence, he must go out into the world and say, now the motor is perfect. But the great question is, has he been in such a situation before? If not, unless he takes it very seriously, there might be a Tartarin[9] result—when he assumed that the glaciers in the Alps were all brought up there by the Anglo-Swiss Corporation and arranged so that he was in no danger in climbing them. It is quite possible that, never having been as ready as now, he probably also never realized the nature of the dangers and doubts which he might encounter when taking the hypothesis seriously. It is now possible that, though ready, he will hurt himself against an obstacle which he hasn't seen hitherto—a subtle snag of a rather unexpected nature. When I analysed that dream I remember thinking: now everything is ready, start the motor. And then came the thought, there might be a snag somewhere!

Dr. Deady: A snag outside? The motor is bound to act.

Dr. Jung: He starts his motor in the garage and he may get stuck in the garage, without letting his libido out at all!

[9] See above, 6 March 1929, n. 1.

LECTURE V

19 February 1930

Dr. Jung:

I have brought you today the picture[1] of which I spoke last week, the reproduction of the Tibetan mandala. It is a *yantra*, used for the purpose of concentration upon the most philosophical thought of the Tibetan Lamas. It shows in the innermost circle the diamond wedge or thunderbolt, that symbol of potential energy, and the white light symbolizing absolute truth. And here are the four functions, the four fields of colour, and then the four gates to the world. Then comes the gazelle garden, and finally the ring of the fire of desirousness outside. You will notice that it is embedded in the earth region exactly to the middle, with the upper part reaching to the celestial world. The figures above are three great teachers, the living Buddhas or Bodhisattvas, two yellow and one red. That has to do with the Tibetan Lamaistic doctrine. They correspond to the mountains on the earth below. What the mountain is on earth the great teacher is among men. I have another mandala where, instead of a thunderbolt in the centre, there is the god Mahasukha, one form of the Indian god Shiva, in the embrace of his wife Shakti. Today I think we will continue our dreams.

Dream [23]

Our patient says that he is at a sort of festival celebration in a Protestant church, in which the benches are not all arranged in the

[1] Jung published the yantra as a frontispiece to *The Secret of the Golden Flower* (in orig., 1929, and tr., 1931) and again in *Psychology and Alchemy* (1944), CW 12, fig. 43 (described there as a Tibetan painted banner, formerly in the China Institute, Frankfurt, and destroyed in World War II). He published it again with "Concerning Mandala Symbolism" (1950), CW 9 i, fig. 1, analyzed in pars. 630-38.

same direction but in the form of a square, so that they all face the pulpit, which is in the middle of one of the long walls of the church. A hymn is being sung, a very well-known one, typical of our Christmas festivals: "O du fröhliche, O du selige Weihnachtszeit."[2] (One hears it everywhere at that time of the year.) He joins in the singing of the hymn and suddenly hears somebody behind him singing the same words in a peculiar soprano voice, exceedingly loud and the melody quite different, so that everyone around that person gets completely out of tune. Our dreamer immediately stops and looks back to see who the singer can be. It is a man sitting on a bench at right angles to his own and wearing, strangely enough, a sort of woman's garment, so that he feels unable to make out positively whether it is a man or a woman. Then the service comes to an end, and on going out, he finds he has left his hat and overcoat in the wardrobe. (He was thinking naturally not of the word "wardrobe," but of "garde-robe" which is of course really a French word, but in French one would say "vestiaire". "Garde-robe" is used in German, taken over from the old French word, which originally meant the man who takes care of the wraps.) On the way back to the wardrobe, he wonders whether the word "garde-robe" in French is a masculine or feminine noun, and he comes to the conclusion that one should say "le garde-robe," and not, as it is used in German as a feminine noun, "die Garde-robe." While thinking of that, he suddenly hears the singer talking to a man who is with him, saying that today he has shown for once that he too can sing. Our dreamer again turns back to look at him and has to restrain himself from making a disagreeable remark to him. He notices that he appears more masculine this time and that he has a Jewish type of face, and then seems to know who he is and remembers that his son is a friend of his. Then the son suddenly appears and violently reproaches his father because he upset the hymn.

Associations: As a child he had been *forced to go to church* every Sunday. On account of that compulsion, he developed an antipathy to churches and parsons, which is the reason that he almost never goes to church except on special festivals. The church in which the benches are arranged as he described, all facing the pulpit, is the church to which he had been made to go as a boy.

---

[2] Sung to the tune "Sanctissima," usually with the English words "O thou joyful day, O thou blessed day, Holy, peaceful Christmastide."

Concerning the *hymn* he says, "When I think of that hymn, I think of the end, the refrain, 'Freue dich O Christenheit,' meaning 'Rejoice, O Christendom.' "

Then he associates with his joining in the hymn the fact that he *cannot sing*. He is quite unmusical, and if he tried he would probably upset the melody as much as the man who sang an entirely different melody in a high woman's soprano.

With the peculiar *singer, whose sex is uncertain*, he associates the fact that he, as a boy, read a book called *Der Golem* by Meyrink.[3] (That is quite a remarkable book; I think it has now been translated into English.) You remember that in a former seminar he dreamed of a square building where he climbed over a fence. We spoke especially of his associations with the end of that book, *Der Golem*, where the hero comes to the locked gates. Here again he associates just that last scene, where the hero arrives at the supreme moment when he really should find the answer to all riddles, the supreme solution of the whole problem, but then comes to the locked gate upon which is the symbol of the hermaphrodite. The dreamer says that this symbol of the hermaphrodite means, as he would interpret it, the alchemical nuptial, that is, the blending of the male and female in one indivisible whole. He says that he can't help feeling that that song would sound very different from the hymn in the Protestant church—in other words, that such ideas would not fit in with the ideas of the Protestant church and would prove most disturbing. Obviously!

Concerning the word "garde-robe," the uncertainty whether it is masculine or feminine refers naturally to the same thing as the dubious sex of the man, and again he associates the hermaphrodite symbol.

As to the discovery that the *singer is Jewish*, he says that he thinks Meyrink must be a Jew; he is convinced that even if he does not confess to it, his creed would be Judaic, he would be reserving in the secret room of his soul the Judaic conviction. That would explain, he says, why Meyrink in his book *The Green Face*[4] sends the hero to Brazil to save him when the continent of Europe collapses. You see, that book has a somewhat unsatisfactory ending. Apparently Meyrink got very involved in a complicated plot and did not

---

[3] See above, 19 June 1929, n. 6, and text following.
[4] Gustav Meyrink, *Das grüne Gesicht* (Leipzig, 1916).

know how to find his way out of the tangle; then by divine providence, a great storm came up and devastated the whole Occident and got him out of the difficulty of a satisfactory solution. His hero, Sephardi, the Jewish scholar, having foreseen it, had collected his family and friends and emigrated to Brazil unharmed, as it is a local storm in Europe only. Obviously the dreamer means that Meyrink, being a Jew, saves his tribesmen in the fatal moment and nobody else, a sort of exodus out of the cursed land.

You probably would not have expected such a dream after the ones before, I certainly would not have guessed it. That is the wonderful irrationality of the unconscious which always beats us. I would not have foreseen it—except in one respect: that last mandala dream would upset certain Occidental convictions, and as this man has had a definite religious education of a narrow kind, he cannot help preserving certain prejudices which would be cruelly hurt by the ideas of the mandala psychology, because that brings a new ethical orientation. It is a point of view that does not fit into the Christian standpoint, which divides the world into good and evil and does not allow any reconciliation. The whole of Christian eschatology follows this line of thought in teaching about the ultimate things—that at the end of the world there will be a Last Judgment where good and evil are divided definitely and forever by those two remarkable institutions Heaven and Hell. All the evil ones will be cast into hell and will cook there forever, and the good ones will attain that blissful condition where they are allowed to make music during all eternity. This is a dogmatic statement of the irreconcilability of good and evil. Nothing to be done about it, just give up, no choice. But the mandala psychology is of a very different kind: an endless chain of lives moving on through good and evil, through all aspects of things. The eternally revolving wheel of existence, now in the shadow, now in the light. This is an extraordinary relativation of the ethical problem—that having been high you will be low, having been low you will be high. Out of the darkness comes the light, and after the light comes again the darkness, so evil is not so bad and good is not so good because they are related and only together by a mistake which remains inexplicable. Why, after all, is it not perfect since it is the work of a perfect Master? The Occidental answer is: because the devil put some dirt into it, or man was such an ass that he spoiled it somehow, this work of an omnipotent and omniscient Being. The fact of evil was the cause of the invention of the devil, who double-crossed the good intentions of the perfect Master.

In the Eastern mandala psychology, all this takes on an entirely different aspect. Relativity is rather shocking to a Westerner. It intimates a certain indulgence even, and to a puritanical mind that is almost unbearable. That is the case with this man. It would not be so much so in theory. He does not go to church, he does not follow the traditional creed; but when it comes to practical life it is a bit awkward, because our church views are all linked up with our real god, which is respectability, the eyes of the community. When he comes to that, the real god, and his fear of those eyes, he collapses into a terrible conflict.

Now, if he has really understood the meaning of the last dream, that the machine is now going to function, it would indicate that he is about to enter life in a new way, where every wheel is in place and where the machine will yield the all-around life which it is meant to yield, a complete life, with light and shadow. But no sooner is he at that point than he hurts himself against traditional convictions, and this next dream contains obviously the problem of the offended Western values. Therefore he is brought instantly back to his childhood, when he was forced to go to church. It is as if a voice from within said, "Remember the days when you were still in the church and believed these things. How can you get away from that? You are still there singing the same song as the whole Christian community." And then comes the first disturbance, that soprano voice. Now where does that soprano voice come from?

Miss Howells: It is the feminine side of himself, the anima.

Dr. Jung: Sure! It is Madame Anima who suddenly begins to sing too. He was singing the song of the community as if he were a perfectly respectable member of that church, and then the anima breaks in with an entirely unsuitable song. And what does that melody express? Not the words, but the melody. What is the value of that?

Answer: Feeling.

Dr. Jung: Yes, nothing is more impressive than an organ. When you are reminded of a Protestant church you just yawn, a terrible bore, but when you hear the music, you cannot help having feeling, it stirs you. Perhaps not if you go regularly, but a man like myself, who has not been to church for an eternity, will naturally have a sentimental feeling—a beautiful remembrance which appeals to one's feeling. It is wrong not to acknowledge it. A sermon is tedious, while music pulls at the heart. So it is very typical that the dream speaks of feelings, which are really dangerous in a man's case. In his thinking these ideas have no hold on him any longer; he is firm in his convictions. But the music gets him, and he is ground under. He is drawn in and cannot help singing, so he gets into a situation or mood that is quite opposed to the intention mentioned in the dream before. Then the conflict arises in his feeling sphere, and that is why his anima begins to sing. The anima is always connected with the inferior function. As he is an intellectual, his feelings are somewhat inferior, and she is like a personification of his inferior feeling function. Why does the anima not sing the church song? Why an entirely different melody?

Mrs. Baynes: To tell him she is there.

Dr. Jung: But what for?

Mrs. Baynes: Because she wants to make trouble.

Dr. Jung: That would be almost a depreciation of the anima.

Mrs. Baynes: He does not appreciate her, so she wants to make herself felt.

Dr. Jung: But if she only wants to make herself felt or to make trouble, she could just as well be a dog that barks, or an automobile that begins whooping outside the church.

Mrs. Sigg: The anima has a different taste. It is not the taste of the Church, it would perhaps be more like the Indian style.

Dr. Jung: You mean more in favour of the mandala psychology? That is exceedingly probable, because the anima has to be excluded from the Christian frame. She is eternally a heretic and does not fit in at all, a perfect pagan, in more or less open revolt against the Christian point of view. Perhaps you are astonished that I speak of her in such a personal way, but that has forever been the way of taking her, that figure has always been expressed by poets in a personal form. Usually she is projected into a real woman, who thereby becomes more imaginary, like the Lady of the Troubadours and the Knights of the Cours d'Amour,[5] slightly divine. Then you know how Rider Haggard speaks of "She who must be obeyed";[6] he makes her a very definite figure. So to give her the right quality we must describe her as a personality and not as a scientific ab-

---

[5] These concepts belong to the chivalric tradition of medieval Western Europe.
[6] See above, 12 Dec. 1928, n. 8.

straction. In zoology you can speak of the species, the *whale*. But there are many different kinds of whales, you must say *which* whale, and then it has a specific value. The anima represents the primitive layer of man's psychology, and primitive psychology shuns abstractions. There are practically no concepts in primitive languages. In Arabic, there are sixty words for types of camel and no word for camel in the abstract. Ask an Arab the word for camel and he does not know. It is either an old, or a young, or a female camel, etc., each called by a different name. In a language more primitive still there are thirty different words for cutting—cutting with a knife, a sword, string, etc.—and no word for the act of cutting.

My particular friend Steiner[7] supposes that there were pre-stages of the earth, one a globe of fire, another a globe of gases, and on one of them, he says, there could even be observed some sensations of taste. Now, whose were the sensations of taste? There is no such thing as abstract sensation, some sensation suspended in space to the Big Dipper or Sirius. In one Negro language there are fifty expressions for walking, but not one for the act of walking; one cannot say, "I am walking." Nor is there a word for *man*. We have all these abstract concepts, and in a way they are misleading, or rather, not informing. We can say a man or a woman or, even more indefinite, a person wants to speak to you, and how little we know—whether he or she is outside, inside, standing up, alive or dead. A primitive telling you the same thing by the very nature of his language would inform you, for instance, that an alive, erect man was standing outside your door. There are no words in their language for a man without an almost complete description. They have the most curious expressions for walking which describe exactly how it is done, each specific case of walking, with knees bent, on his heels, etc., so if you hear of him at all you can fairly see that man moving. It is an almost grotesque description of each subject. This absence of collective notions is absolutely characteristic of the primitive mind.

Now, concerning my concept of the anima, I have been reproached occasionally by scholars for using an almost mythological term to express a scientific fact. They expect me to translate her

[7] Rudolf Steiner (1861-1925), German occultist, first a Theosophist, then the founder of Anthroposophy, an offshoot of Theosophy. The reference here is perhaps to his book *Wie erlangt man Erkenntnisse der höheren Welten?* (1922) (= "How does one attain knowledge of higher worlds?"), a copy of which Jung owned.

into scientific terminology, which would deprive the figure of its—or her—specific life. If you say, for instance, that the anima is a function of connection or relationship between the conscious and unconscious, that is a very pale thing. It is as if you should show a picture of a great philosopher and call it simply *Homo sapiens*; of course a picture of a criminal or an idiot would be *Homo sapiens* just as well. The scientific term conveys nothing, and the merely abstract notion of the anima conveys nothing, but when you say the anima is almost personal, a complex that behaves exactly as if she were a little person, or at times as if she were a very important person, then you get it about right. Therefore, chiefly for practical purposes, I leave the anima in her personified form, just as I would in describing President Wilson, or Bismarck, or Mussolini. I would not say they were specimens of *Homo sapiens*, I deal with them specifically as they are. And so the anima is personal and specific. Otherwise it is just a function, as intuition or thinking are functions. But that does not cover the actual facts, nor does it express the extraordinary personality of the anima, the absolutely recognizable personality, so that one can easily point it out anywhere. Therefore I quite intentionally keep to the very personal term, meaning that she is a personal factor, almost as good as a person.

Naturally there is danger on the other side that people think she is a sort of ghost. Sure enough, to the primitive mind she is a ghost. She is a definite entity, and, if you are in a very primitive mood, you might see her in the form of a ghost—a smoke figure or a breath figure. She may become an hallucination. One sees that, for instance, in lunatics when they are possessed by the anima. Not very long ago I was called in as consulting physician to see an insane boy in a clinic in Zurich. When I came into the room he greeted me very politely and said, "You will probably not believe it, but I am my sister and I am a Buddhist." He has actually a married sister, but she plays no role in his life. He thought it was just a mistake that people took him for a man, and even declared that it was a malevolent invention on the part of his mother. To him that anima sister was absolutely real, more real than himself, he was identical with her. She was a Buddhist and therefore initiated into the mysteries of the East, and she had an Indian name, which was an extraordinarily clever contrivance. I don't remember it exactly, but it consisted of three syllables, and the middle syllable was *dava*, which is a Hindu word for divine. It was half Italian and half Hindu or Sanskrit and a bit of Greek. It was a typical designation, and the meaning was divine-mistress-sister. I have known many other cases where men have felt the anima as an extraordinary reality. I am quite certain that Rider Haggard could not possibly have written such an interminable series of novels if the anima had not been extremely real to him. That is the reason why I stress the personal character so much. We have to deal with the figure in a form that is entirely different from the usual because it designates a living factor, despite the fact that this factor, under certain conditions of development, may lose all that personal character and transform into a mere function. But that can only be the case when the conscious attitude is such that it loses the quality and characteristics of a human being—that is the mandala psychology.

Miss Howells: Is it common for her to take on the quality of the Orient or an older civilization? Here she is a Jewess.

Dr. Jung: It would seem so. In *She* the anima is an Oriental being, and in Pierre Bênoit's *Atlantide.*[8] The animus also. But we had better not talk of the animus now. It just scares me, it is much more difficult to deal with. The anima is definite and the animus is indefinite.

Question: Is the anima definitely a part of every man and every woman?

Dr. Jung: No, she is the female part of a man's psychology, so she would not naturally exist in a woman. When she does, she is absolutely identical with the woman's conscious principle, and then I would call it Eros. The same is true of a man reversed. Animus in a man is not a person, it is his conscious principle, and then I call it Logos.

In Chinese philosophy they speak of the masculine and feminine souls of a man. Therefore Wilhelm uses animus and anima exactly as I would. The terms animus and anima correspond to the Chinese *hun* and *kwei,*[9] but always they apply to a man. The Chinese were not concerned with women's psychology—as I unfortunately am! Even in the Middle Ages women were said to have no souls worth

[8] The novel *L'Atlantide* (1919), another work often cited by Jung, as early as March 1920; see letter quoted in *C. G. Jung: Word and Image* (1979), p. 151.

[9] In Wilhelm's discussion of the Chinese text (*Golden Flower*, 1962 edn., pp. 14f.) and in Jung's commentary (ibid., pp. 115ff.; CW 13, pars. 57-60), the Chinese word for anima is *p'o*; *kwei* is said to mean "demon" or "ghost of the departed one." Cary Baynes's footnote to Wilhelm (loc. cit.) aims to clarify the use of the terms.

mentioning, or only "little souls," like the story of the penguins in
L'île des pingouins, by Anatole France.[10] Since St. Maël had baptized
them, it became a question whether they had souls or not, and they
at last called in St. Catherine of Alexandria to decide. "Well," she
said, giving the final word in the celestial discussion, "Donnez-leur
une âme immortelle, mais petite!" So in the Middle Ages women's
psychology was *chose inconnue*, and similarly the old Chinese philosophers had the concept that the masculine animus was meant
for heaven, while the female soul would become only a spectre, a
phantom, who sinks into the earth after death. One goes on into
Eternity and the other becomes a sort of haunting ghost, a demon.
Therefore the Chinese meant by the animus in man what we mean
by the Logos principle, or the conscious principle.

But since I have to deal with women's psychology as well as men's,
I have found it better to call the conscious principle in man Logos,
and the principle of relatedness in women Eros. The inferior Eros
in man I designate as anima and the inferior Logos in woman as
animus. These concepts, Logos and Eros, correspond roughly with
the Christian idea of the soul. And the thing that does not fit in,
the thing that sings the wrong tune, would be in a man the anima
representing the Eros principle, and in a woman the animus representing the Logos principle, but in a sort of inferior form, a minor
position. The reason why the anima is here playing that role of
diabolos in musica is that the exclusive Logos principle in man does
not allow for the Eros principle. He must discriminate, see things
in their separateness, otherwise he is unable to recognize them.
But that is against the principle of relatedness. A woman does not
want to have things segregated, she wants to see them almost syn-
chronized. A man who is possessed by his anima gets into the most
awful difficulties, for he cannot discriminate, especially among
women. While a woman under the law of the animus cannot relate,
she becomes nothing but discrimination, surrounded by a wall of
spiky cactus laws. She tells a man what he is up to and that chills
him to the bone and he cannot get at her.

Now in regard to the particular role of the anima in this dream,
that she is feminine is probably quite clear to you, but why is she
masculine too? This is a very unusual case. And mind you, after-

---

[10] Jung relates the story in *Mysterium Coniunctionis* (1955), CW 14, par. 227, and
briefly in his commentary on the *Tibetan Book of the Dead* (1935), CW 11, par. 835.
Concerning Anatole France's novel *Penguin Island*, see above, 23 Jan. 1929, n. 2.

wards she becomes a man, a Jew. What do you think of the conditions under which a man's anima would be either male or hermaphroditic?

Answer: Homosexuality.

Dr. Jung: That is true. One often encounters anima figures of very doubtful sex, or quite indubitably masculine, when the conscious mind is feminine. But in the case of our dreamer there is no question of homosexuality. He is perhaps not quite free of perversions, everybody has the statistical amount; we all have that percentage of murder in our being, the whole population. But in him there is no trace of anything like repressed homosexuality. So why has he a masculine anima?

Mrs. Fierz: The anima is so incapable of making the man accept her that she has to play that role, use a sort of mimicry, to do so. It is the unconscious approaching the conscious.

Mrs. Sawyer: Isn't he identified with her and therefore she is masculine?

Dr. Jung: You mean since he cannot approach her he has to identify? Mrs. Fierz takes it from the unconscious side, that the unconscious is trying to make itself heard. Mrs. Sawyer sees it as the conscious trying to connect with the unconscious—his conscious possessed by the anima and so hermaphroditic. In either point of view one must detach her in order to establish a connection.

Mrs. Henley: Might it in this case simply express lack of development, because homosexuality is an attribute of youth?

Dr. Jung: That is also true, since he is undeveloped on the side of religion; from that point of view he could be expressed as a sort of homosexual boy about ten or twelve years old. That would be symbolic homosexuality. It is a fact that certain apparent sex perversions are merely symbolical; expressing an undeveloped state. In this case, there was no conscious manifestation of homosexuality that could be pointed out, so we may assume that this is symbolical homosexuality and not a disturbance of the normal. There have been traces of this feeling in some of his former dreams, in the dream of the Puer Aeternus, for instance, where he called the boy Eros and had a decided feeling of tenderness towards him.[11] And again in a dream which he had during our last seminar, that case

[11] Above, 13 Mar. 1929, p. 170.

of synchronicity, where he was worshipping the boy Telesphoros[12] and had doubts then also whether there was something homosexual about it. But it was merely symbolical, a certain immaturity, like the twelve-year-old condition. Such mental immaturity may be very local, it may refer to a specific expression of it, or it may go so far that a man is capable of believing that he actually is homosexual, in spite of the fact that he never had the experience. I have had men come to me complaining that they were homosexual, but when I say to such a man, "How was it? Did you get into trouble with boys," he exclaims indignantly that he would not touch a boy. "Men then?" "No." "Then why the devil do you call yourself homosexual?" And then he explains that a doctor said he was because he had had dreams where something homosexual happened. This simply means that the man in certain respects is not mature, and his immaturity may express itself in different ways—that he is not up to women, or not up to life, or not up to spiritual things. That must be the case here: that he is definitely immature in certain respects is expressed in the dream by his being brought back to his boyhood. Now in regard to what is he immature? Where is he unconscious?

Mrs. Deady: He can't manage his sexuality.

Dr. Jung: But you must keep in mind that he is a man who has allowed himself all sorts of things with fast women and who is not at all unaware of sexuality. His sex is wrong but not concretely. Now what is the trouble with him?

Dr. Deady: He has the sex of a boy of sixteen without feeling.

Dr. Jung: That is the point, no feeling. His sex is perfectly normal but it is unrelated sex, a sort of auto-eroticism, a kind of masturbation. There is no relation to the object, and that is probably the reason for the frigidity of his wife, and the reason of his other adventures. Eros is undeveloped, not his sexuality. That is by no means undeveloped, but his relationship to sexuality is wrong. In the last dream he was going to set his machine in motion, and the question came up whether the parts of the machine were properly related to the central part. All these functions, particularly his sexuality, have to be worked into the total mechanism. If unrelated, he naturally cannot function as a total personality. His sexuality must come into complete consideration, and he must have feelings

---

[12] Above, 11 Dec. 1929, p. 431.

about it. In other words, the Eros principle must be recognized. The reason why the anima appears is that she *is* Eros. And when he has the old point of view, singing the old song, Eros is repressed forever and the very devil. Therefore she comes up in church and disturbs the church hymn. His immaturity is expressed by the fact that he is back in his childhood and also by his symbolic homosexuality. If a man's anima is masculine, he is absolutely possessed— obsessed—by her, and he cannot establish a relationship with her until she is feminine. To say he is effeminate means the same thing—that she has power over him. The fact that the dream expresses is: you are effeminate, you are possessed by your anima.

LECTURE VI

26 February 1930

Dr. Jung:

Today we will continue our discussion of the dream. Are there no questions?

Mrs. Sigg: I could not find anything about the yantra in the library.

Dr. Jung: I can well believe that. Yantra is a term from Tantric philosophy,[1] designating any kind of device or symbol that serves the purpose of transforming or centering the libido of the one who is concentrating upon it. It has been explained by a German scholar by the term "machine." The word is used for mandalas and for other ritual symbols instrumental in the transformation. To speak of transforming energy through a rite may seem strange to you, but this is an exceedingly primitive idea. The most original form of yantra is the churinga used by the central Australian natives. That is either a stone slab or oblong board, which is given to a man after his initiation. Each man has his individual churinga, which he keeps concealed in some hiding place. Then from time to time, when his libido gets rotten or wrong, his health power exhausted, he takes it out, places it on his knees and rubs it with his hands for a long time. Through that procedure the bad health is supposed to be absorbed by the churinga, which releases at the same time its good health power, its good mana, and that enters the man's body; then, the ceremonial being accomplished, he conceals his churinga and goes away. After a couple of weeks or a couple of months, according to his need, he returns to again renew himself. This is perhaps the most primitive form of worship and the most primitive form of yantra. Naturally, in subsequent ages and stages of civili-

---

[1] For a fuller explanation of yantra, see Heinrich Zimmer, *Myths and Symbols in Indian Art and Civilization* (1946), pp. 140-144.

zation, it has become far more differentiated and meaningful, although even today there is an example of a similar nature at the shrine of St. Anthony in Italy.[2] The pilgrims there press their whole bodies against his marble sarcophagus and rub it with their hands, in order to get the good health power. We call it grace, a release from the suffering of the soul as well as the body.

Later on this rubbing was replaced by a sort of mental rubbing against a thing. In my book *Psychology of the Unconscious* you will find the development of this idea of the transformation of symbols and libido in etymology and history. I speak there of Prometheus, the fire-bringer (from the Sanskrit root-word *manthâmi*, from which is derived the word *mathematics* and also the word *thinking*).[3] That was the original rubbing, shaking it to and fro in one's mind, constant movement, rhythmical movement; but translated now into the needed spiritual form, meditation. So when the believer is meditating on the yantra, it is the same as rubbing the churinga. I must again point out that when I call the mandala a yantra, as it is in the East, it means something quite different from its meaning to us. The mandala has to us the meaning of a product, an expression, and its specific value is that it is an expression, and not that one uses it as a finished instrument, a traditional dogmatic form sanctioned by time, and serving as a ritual symbol or yantra. Its importance to us is just the reverse. There is a tremendous difference between the symbols of the East and the West. To produce them is all-important for us, it is a means of expression; and it would be poisonous for us to use the finished products of the East to bring about a transformation of our libido. If it works at all it is not for the good and it has a sterilizing effect, because first of all we have to build our unconscious up to symbolic expression. Perhaps in two thousand years or so we shall use these symbols when they are in a finished condition as yantras, but there is no possibility of that for the present.

Mr. Holdsworth: I should like to know whether this rubbing of the skin is a deep-rooted thing, because animals do it such a lot. Does a sick soul produce an irritation of the skin? A cow rubs herself until an irritation is produced sometimes, and it seems to me that

[2] St. Anthony (1195-1231), whose tomb in the basilica at Padua is the reputed site of miracles.

[3] *Symbols of Transformation*, CW 5, pars. 208, 248 (as in 1912 edn.).

it is all connected up and a cow is practicing this symbol when she rubs herself quietly and happily against a tree.

Dr. Jung: That is perfectly true. It is certainly an original form of worship when they rub up against a stone. We have the same idea in the lingam symbols; they take butter for the purpose of rubbing them. It had its origin in animal instincts, which surely could take on a spiritual meaning. We don't know what ecstatic feelings a cow may have!

Dr. Baynes: In England they used to erect the rubbing stones in a ceremonial way for the cattle to rub against. There are any amount in Cornwall.

Dr. Jung: Exactly. Those menhirs were no doubt for that purpose and for nothing else.

Mrs. Crowley: Would the rubbing of beads by Orientals be like it?

Dr. Jung: No, that is really different, that comes from a kind of nervousness. You lose the traces when you follow it up. For instance, the handling of the rosary is extremely primitive and it is almost habitual, that rubbing of the little beads. Or the peculiar custom that certain people have of always holding something in their fingers; or when you are thinking hard, you are apt to scratch yourself behind the ear. It means something which seems to have to do with sexuality, that rubbing produces courage. I saw a peculiar scene once when I was travelling in North Africa. A Bedouin mother came down to the train with a little boy about two years old. I had a spare piece of bread which I tried to give to the child, but he was afraid to take it from a white man. The mother smiled and said he was too frightened. Then suddenly she took his penis and rubbed that little thing, and then the boy got up his courage and took the bread with a smile. That was one means to produce courage, which is the same mechanism. Of course we could talk about these things at length, many things would deserve attention from this point of view.

Mr. Holdsworth: Does alcohol irritate the intestines?

Dr. Jung: I wouldn't say that alcohol rubbed the intestinal tract. After a fall we rub the place with ointment, but it is not the ointment which is effective, it is the rubbing. In German we speak of "Behandlung," the putting on of hands. The Old Testament is full of it. Magnetism, hypnosis, however one explains it, one can at least say that it increases the circulation. Mothers have very nice little charms or mantras when children hurt themselves; she takes the child's hand and rubs it and says a little verse.

Dr. Schlegel: I think the effect consists to a certain extent in the fact that you centre the attention upon something else, you take away the morbid attention from the spot that is painful. As when one is dealing with a delicate business affair, one often smiles and it relieves the tension of the situation.

Dr. Jung: That is true.

Dr. Deady: Does the Westerner, in making a mandala, ever use the Eastern form?

Dr. Jung: They seem to quite instinctively concentrate upon a form that is more or less an analogy of the Eastern form, but only more or less. The number four is an example. I must say that I have seen by now many mandalas and the number four is by far the most common. I have seen it with five, and some with six, and only one with three as far as I can remember, but in that case, it was perfectly obvious that the man who made it was lacking in one function, that of sensation. The Greek mandala cross, for instance, the swastika, is the four-footed sun rolling on four feet. The original

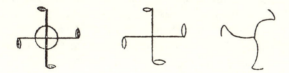

form of it was really the disc of the sun with four little legs, as among the red Indians. But on pre-Christian Greek coins we find a three-legged symbol, which is called a *triskelos*.

Miss Pollitzer: Which function did the Greeks leave out?

Dr. Jung: I don't know. Speaking of it in those terms it is difficult to say. Greece is altogether a puzzle psychologically. Our ideas about Greece have undergone great changes. We used to think of it in terms of pure beauty, wonderful temples gleaming against blue skies, splendid gods, Olympians living a courageous sort of life. Old Greece seemed to be absolutely on the surface in blazing sunshine. But that is all wrong. There is a very dark, tragic, mystical Greece hidden in the past, an entirely different aspect that was discovered only in the time of Nietzsche. Before that, people thought only of Attic beauty and paid no attention to the dark side. Especially in reference to Greek mentality we are not quite clear, at

495

least I am not. It was a very peculiar mentality, and you may have noticed that when you read Greek authors at different periods of your life, you get quite different impressions. For instance, I read the classical Greek tragedies when I was in school, and then I read them again twenty years later and was tremendously impressed with their extraordinary primitivity—murder, incest, and blood all over the place, which did not impress me at all when I was in school. It is perhaps that Greece is too close to us—it is specifically Western.

Well, we began to discuss this dream and did not finish it. It is a pretty involved situation. You remember we spoke of the fact that after the dream before, one could expect something to happen, and one assumed that *now* things were ready, now the machine could function. But instead comes an entirely new situation. Evidently the dreamer has begun to function more or less, and then an obstacle—an obstacle in the church to which he went as a little boy. He has gone back from the present moment to his eleventh or twelfth year, so we may expect that there is a reason why he cannot move on, why the machine, despite the fact that it is ready, will not function yet; there seems to be something in his path which prevents it. Sure enough, there is a certain attitude which probably originated in about his eleventh or twelfth year.

There is a detail in that church to which I call your attention, namely, that the benches are so arranged that they surround the pulpit on three sides, and thus the parson, in delivering his sermon, would have the whole community assembled rectangularly around him, with his back against the wall of the church. It is an unusual arrangement, but I should not pay much attention to it, as it is a detail certainly derived from the church of his childhood, if it were not that it is again mentioned when the singer turns up. He is on a bench around the corner at right angles to his own, so, as it is a detail that goes right through the dream, it must have a certain symbolic importance. One must always keep in mind the psychological situation of the dreamer, which is very complex. You would probably be inclined to assume that he is exclusively concerned with his own problem—what he is going to do with his machine. But that is not true. He is of course concerned with his specific problem, but he is concerned with it looked at from the angle of the analytical situation. A patient never dreams absolutely apart from that. It may happen in the beginning perhaps, where there is no rapport and the patient is entirely within his shell, looking into himself in a sort of autoerotic way, but this man has done a lot of analytical work and has a good rapport with me, so we can assume that whatever the solution of the problem may be, that will always be included. The dreams must always be in a certain rapport with the analyst. Looked at with that in mind, then, what about the benches?

Mrs. Deady: In his first dream, the benches were arranged in such a way that there was no communion. Here there would seem to be.

Dr. Jung: Quite so. You refer to that early dream, but there it was not a church, it was really the *jeu de paume,* and there the benches were arranged in such a way that the backs were all turned to the centre, where the preacher or any central figure would have been. In that dream there was practically no rapport, you see. That was a very early dream, and he was still in himself. But here we have an entirely different situation. The audience is turned towards the speaker. Now who or what is the audience? There is a whole community in that church.

Mr. Holdsworth: He is making a demonstration, he is showing some attitude to the rest of the world; and the audience consists simply of the people who receive the demonstration.

Dr. Jung: Well, he doesn't demonstrate in the right way, he is as one among many. That is a motif which often occurs in analysis. Patients dream that they come to me for consultation and when they enter my office, somebody is already there or people are continually passing through my room. They are never alone, so they never say what they mean to say because they are all the time occupied by other people. Or they are told that a patient is with me and I cannot see them. Now all these dreams mean that the patient does not come alone. He comes in the form of many people; his point of view is not one, it is many. Under what circumstances do you think that would happen?

Dr. Schlegel: When a person is identified with other people.

Dr. Jung: Of course. That happens very often, particularly with women. When we are speaking of a certain problem, there is no question of what *she* is doing, but what *one* is doing and what *they* are doing. I always call that the problem of the eleven thousand virgins because it usually has to do with a discreet problem. But if any discreet solution would recommend itself, she begins to talk about what the 10,999 virgins should do, but carefully avoids dis-

497

cussing what she, the patient herself, might do or think. She appears as an overwhelming host and that kills all possibility of an individual solution.

The animus has the peculiarity of thinking gregariously. He thinks how that problem would be solved if ten thousand other people had the same problem. But social problems are always individual problems. Five thousand people may be actually sick with typhoid fever, but each patient has his own specific typhoid fever. So these people in all modesty identify themselves with legions, and naturally there is then no solution. I cannot solve the problems of the eleven thousand virgins in one heap—I can perhaps do something for one, but not for a legion, it is impossible. So the dream says: you cannot solve your problem when you are dealing with so many people—the father, the mother, the grandparents, friends—they all interfere, this one saying so-and-so and that one something else. Therefore I say to such a person: leave all that stuff alone, appear on the stage and say *I*, and not as *they* opinionate.

That is the dreamer's case. His attitude is as if he were one of a battalion, as if he were just like the whole community in that little respectable church, where they all have the problem of being married and don't know what to do with it. Mind you, there are people who are not married yet, people who have been divorced, very old people of every social stratum, and he assumes that all have the same problem. But that is impossible, that is *participation mystique*. He projects his own problem into the crowd and therefore it becomes impracticable and he cannot manage it. Many of those people would firmly deny that they had such a problem, but he naïvely assumes that everybody has it and takes the whole community as an expression of himself. He tries to handle it from the standpoint of the many, as if it could be answered by legislation, as if a law had been passed in Parliament that each person should do this or that. Now, all this gregarious thinking is centred around the parson. What does that mean?

Answer: The parson means the analyst.

Dr. Jung: Yes, I would be the parson. He is nonexistent here, but it is obvious that I would be he, and our dreamer's gregarious thinking is now perfectly willing to listen to the enlightened words of the parson. Here again is a mistake. What would that be?

Answer: The parson does not say anything.

Dr. Jung: First of all he says nothing, there is no sermon, so they would listen in vain. And besides that?

Suggestion: He is projecting his problem into the parson?

Dr. Jung: He assumes that he would say suitable words, and as he heard it in church it must be all right; he would surely carry the advice out because they were the words of the parson. That is a very characteristic and specific attitude—that one listens attentively and takes the words of the parson, and dismisses one's own individual attempt, thereby hindering one's own advance. Then you remember his saying that he was forced to go to church as a child, which he disliked extremely, and he never went later for that reason. So the dream seems to suggest, since he hates to go to church, why then does he go? Why does he have that attitude? It takes the negative example as a symbol for his attitude. Then comes the singing. It has been pointed out that there was no sermon, but the community was singing. Of course singing is an expression of feeling, so he is now using his inferior function. Here we get a light. You see, whenever one is unable to deal with a complicated psychological situation, then very often, on account of the lack of one function, one tries to deal with that situation using functions that are simply not applicable. There are certain predicaments in life which one cannot intelligently deal with by means of thinking. This very delicate erotic situation demands feeling. He has thought about it—to his complete dissatisfaction—and obviously he should bring out his feelings. That has been the case in former dreams already. Now when that expression comes in a dream, what would you conclude from the fact? What has been the omission of the dreamer? The dream points out a singer.

Mrs. Sigg: He omitted to express his feelings to his wife.

Dr. Jung: How can he express his feeling to his wife in company with the whole community?

Suggestion: His feeling for the analyst?

Dr. Jung: That is right, but he expresses it in a peculiar way—a Protestant is a peculiar thing. They all sing some hymn to God and turn their faces to the parson thinking that is the way of God. His relation to me has been chiefly technical, I am the intellectual mechanic, and feeling in connection with me has played no part in his dreams. His feeling is entirely collective, so he certainly cannot apply it to his wife. How can a whole battalion love Mrs. So-and-So? He can apply it here for the first time, he can sing Hosanna.

499

By putting me in the church as the parson and he himself as part of the crowd, he can express his feeling in a gregarious way, he also can sing because all the others do. And now he is singing a Christmas song. Why just that? And, mind you, it is one of the best known songs of this country.

Miss Howells: It is the birth hymn he is singing, the birth of his feeling.

Dr. Jung: Yes, it is a birth hymn, but we must see about its feeling value. He is quite informed about symbolism, he has read a good deal, the intellectual side is no trouble to him. But the feeling here is infantile. This is a song that we have all sung as little children; it is perhaps the first song which would make any impression upon a child's heart. They may not understand the words—they sometimes twist the words into the funniest things. "Christ, our hope" they call "our grasshopper"! There are funny things in childish prayers. Here, you see, he brings out the first solemn recognition of feeling when the whole community sings this Christmas song. Here a lot of very genuine childlike feeling comes to the fore, and that is in connection with what we might call a *sous-entendu* in the dream. I am the *sous-entendu.* So here you see the possible value of that community singing. What would that be?

Answer: Unity.

Dr. Jung: Not only that, though that might be the effect of it.

Mrs. Sigg: Strengthening of the feeling.

Dr. Jung: Quite so. Strengthening. You must understand the feeling of that man as something that creeps on its belly, unable to lift its head, something weak and soft which needs strengthening. He needs a whole audience to help him bring out his feeling expression. He could not get up and sing this song alone, as he could not express any kind of individual feeling for me. He might quote the words of somebody else about me—"as he says." He might say that the *Zürcher Zeitung*[4] had written thus and so about me, but he could not do it himself, even if he felt much more. I emphasize this point because later in the dream that man gets up suddenly and sings an entirely different song alone, against the whole community. That would not happen if it were not so tremendously important for the dreamer to sing his own tune. It has a definite positive value, but there is a catch.

---

[4] Principal newspaper of the city, now called the *Neue Zürcher Zeitung.*

Dr. Schlegel: It is not individual.

Dr. Jung: Exactly. It is done collectively, he can have his feeling without any responsibility, and that is what such a man absolutely needs. The slightest trace of responsibility crushes his feeling right away, so that crowd is almost necessary to help him realize a feeling with responsibilities. But naturally no sooner does that happen than up comes a new problem, and that is now the singer. What does the fact that he sings an entirely different tune suggest to you?

Mr. Holdsworth: That somebody does not believe in the tune that the others are singing.

Dr. Jung: Obviously. Almost like a protest.

Dr. Baynes: A minority report in Parliament!

Dr. Jung: Yes, and it is again a feeling expression, it is not an opinion. It is really the same song but an entirely different tune. What would that mean?

Dr. Schlegel: It is the individual attitude that is coming up.

Dr. Jung: Yes, one could say it is now individual, an individual voice in the dreamer that stands up for itself against the utterly gregarious situation which prevailed before. The singer is now a very interesting figure. You remember that he is characterized as somewhat Jewish in type, and he is hermaphrodite—at least there is great doubt about his sex—and the dreamer associates the hermaphrodite in Meyrink's novel *Der Golem*.[5] Now we have to go into a part at least of that story, which is really a very big attempt at dealing with figures of the collective unconscious. Of course Meyrink does not know anything of my theories. He deals with it in an entirely literary fashion one could say, with all the advantages and disadvantages of that method, yet the figures are perfectly recognizable.

First there is an anima figure called Miriam, a Jewess. Then there is her father, Hillel, an old Cabalist, who is a typical wise man, also a figure of the collective unconscious. That is a very sound connection, the wise old man is often in a father-like connection with the anima—either physical or spiritual. In the case of Haggard's *Wisdom's Daughter*[6] there is no actual father, but an old Egyptian priest instead, and *She* would be his medium. It is a well known fact that priests often used young girls as seers or for casting oracles.

---

[5] See above, 19 June 1929, nn. 6 and 9.

[6] H. Rider Haggard, *Wisdom's Daughter: The Life and Love Story of She-who-must-be-obeyed* (New York, 1923).

Now, these two figures play the main roles in the story. Then there is that fearful thing, the Golem. And there is besides a mysterious character called Athanasius Pernath. He is a peculiar figure who enters in the beginning of the novel as the lover of Miriam, in whom the hero of the story (which is told in the first person) is interested too. They meet somewhere and exchange hats, so the hero walks off with the hat of Athanasius, whom he does not know at all, and through this hat he gets fantasies and ideas into his head, which do not belong to him but to Athanasius. The name Athanasius is in itself a most valuable hint, it means the immortal one, so he is the immortal part of the hero. In terms of the mandala, that would be the "centre," the "diamond body." That has been expressed in other speculative philosophies in many different ways, such as the "spark of eternal fire," the "sea-hawk:" or that precious immortal body, the *Nous*, that descended from above into the sea and through which all things came into existence. Man is like that— a chaotic sea into which a divine spark falls. The baptism of Christ in the Jordan, when the Holy Ghost descends upon his head as a dove, is the same idea. Also, the descent of the Holy Ghost upon the disciples at Pentecost in the form of little flames—the creative spark that comes from above. That is age-old symbolism.

It is revealed at the end of the book that the whole story is due to the fateful mistake of the hero in getting the hat of Athanasius. He suddenly has visions of things that he does not understand, a sort of psychosis, and the story deals with different phases of this. The Golem is an entirely negative figure, the complete shadow of the immortal one. He began as a lump of clay and was brought to life by black magic, by writing the holy name on his brow. So he is a living being that has no soul, a mechanism which can be killed only by wiping out the holy name. The figure occurs in many ancient Jewish legends, and Meyrink used it as a personification of the horrible troubles which befall the hero through those visions. Then at the end of the story he has a sort of clarifying vision. After many adventures he comes to the house where Hillel and Miriam are supposed to be living—a simple white house in a garden, with a wooden gate in front. As this is the place that the dreamer refers to in his story, I will give you a rough translation of the way the author puts it:[7]

[7] For Jung's different tr. of much the same passage, see above, 19 June 1929, pp. 280-281.

"The night before it had been the same place, but now in the morning I see that it is by no means a simple place. There is a very beautiful golden gate, quite an elaborate thing, and there are two yew trees which rise above low bushes or flowering shrubs, flanking the entrance. I see now that the wall around the garden is covered with a beautiful mosaic made of lapis lazuli. The god himself, a hermaphrodite, forms the two wings of the gate, the left side male, the right side female. The god is seated on a precious throne of mother-of-pearl, and his golden head is the head of a hare; the ears are erect and close together, looking like the two pages of an open book. The air is full of the smell of dew and hyacinths and I stand there a long time, astonished. It is as if a foreign world were opening before my eyes. Suddenly an old gardener or servant in the costume of the eighteenth century opens the gate and asks me what I want. I give him the hat of Athanasius Pernath, which I had wrapped up in paper. The servant disappears with it, but in that moment before he shuts the gate behind him, I look inside and see not a house, but a sort of marble temple, and on the steps leading up to it, I see Athanasius with Miriam leaning on his arm. Both are looking down upon the town. Miriam catches sight of me, smiles and whispers something to Athanasius. I am fascinated by her beauty. She is so young, just as young as I saw her in the dream. Athanasius then turns his head toward me and my heart almost ceases to beat. It is as if I should see myself in a mirror, such is the similarity of his face to mine. Then the gate shuts and I only see the resplendent figure of the hermaphroditic god. After a while the servant brings my hat which was in the possession of Athanasius and I hear his voice, deep, as if from the depths of the earth. He says, 'Mr. Pernath is much obliged and asks you not to hold him inhospitable that he does not invite you in, since it has always been a strict law of the house that guests are not invited. He also says he has not used your hat as he noticed at once that it was not his own, and he hopes that his hat has not caused you headache.' "

But it caused a tremendous headache! Here we get into very deep waters, because this figure in the dream is obviously taken from that symbolism. We naturally would not be able to see it from the form of the dream but from the associations. It is valuable, in such a case, to have the associations, from which one discovers all sorts of things of which the dreamer is not aware. We are forced to bring in all these considerations that are in this passage from

Meyrink. The Jewish element certainly comes from this book; the dreamer associates that he is reminded again of the hermaphrodite of Meyrink and mentions that he thinks he is half a Jew. The main figures of the story are also Jews, but these do not appear in the dream; the only one that occurs in the dream is that man who seems to be a hermaphrodite. Now what would you say was the meaning of that figure after considering all this material?

Mrs. Crowley: It has the monotheistic idea. Jehovah was considered to be male and female in the Cabala.[8] There is an analogy with the hermaphrodite there.

Dr. Jung: Mystics in general have had that point of view, and that would fit in with the idea that this figure might be God himself. Is that your idea? What would you assume the hermaphrodite and Athanasius, Hillel, and Miriam to be? In the dream, the immortal one, Athanasius, and Miriam are practically one figure, they are drawn together, which would almost allow us to say that is God because such a condensation would be called God on theological grounds. What are the historical instances for such a composition?—are there no theologians here to tell us? The Trinity, of course: the Father, the Son, and the female figure, the Holy Ghost. The dove, the symbolical bird of love, was the bird of Astarte. And originally in the Oriental church, the Holy Ghost was looked upon as a female figure, Sophia, the wife of God. That idea is found in the "Pistis Sophia" and in other Gnostic manuscripts.

Mr. Holdsworth: Did the Coptic churches cut out the Virgin? Who is going to be the husband of the Virgin?

Dr. Jung: That also leads to the idea of the hermaphrodite, but at the moment we are considering the idea that this condensation figure, two male figures and one female figure, is based on the idea of the Trinity. We are now arriving at the interesting conclusion, following out Mrs. Crowley's suggestion and according to the associations of the dreamer, that this figure is God. The hermaphrodite in Meyrink is very clearly a god, three persons in one. But don't you think it is awkward to be confronted with such peculiar conclusions? It means that God is singing a different tune from the people in his own church. It suggests the famous story of the rich peasant to whom the people went to collect funds because the

---

[8] Cabala (or kabbalah), the Jewish mysticism of the Middle Ages, embodies the belief that every word and letter represents mysteries understood only by the initiate. It is a form of gnosis based on scriptural interpretation.

old church had been destroyed by lightning. He said: "I am not such a damned fool as to give to one who has destroyed his own house!" Now what are we to conclude about this God singing a new tune?

Mr. Holdsworth: That God has a sardonic sense of humour, which I have always suspected.

Dr. Jung: We must not get blasphemous. When it comes to psychology we must stick to facts.

Dr. Schlegel: The Church belongs to the old collective God, but now comes a new God.

Dr. Jung: It might be so, for God is not allowed to have a word these days, the Church has taken it all out of his hands. It is quite possible that he has changed his views in two thousand years; anybody would change his views, even if he were eternal. So it is quite possible that he sings a different song now. We are not informed. When we go back into history and remember what he said to the Chinese and the Hindus and the Jews and the Egyptians, it is hard to reconcile. There are many very justifiable points of view. To make them agree—that is a job for a superior mind.

We must be serious about this matter, for our dreamer is not at all an irreligious man, he has convictions. And if I should say that miserable sinner sitting on the bench opposite him was God singing a different tune, it would be rather startling; when I reach the conclusion that the voice is God's, according to all our wits, that is a pretty big statement. If I were to say it was Mr. Smith's voice, well and good. But if I say that every minute we are in the presence of God, that he must collect his senses and realize that just as all our remote primitive ancestors have believed that the voice of dreams is the voice of God, so here the voice of God has spoken—well, if that man has any realization one would expect him to cock his ears at least. But it is as if I said to you: I have disagreeable news—a phone message from the Observatory that at a distance of perhaps seventy million kilometers, a meteorite the size of Africa is headed for the earth, and those seventy million kilometers will be covered in no time, in a few days perhaps or a few weeks. You would say that that would be startling news, but I tell you that people would be entirely unable to realize it. We must wash, shave, have patients, have lunch, to hell with that stone. Yet it is certain that within ten days our whole earth will be blasted to atoms. I have seen time and again that people are unable to realize certain truths. So when I

505

say to this man that this is the voice of God, he takes it like a metaphor and just thinks it is a poetical way of putting things. In this case it is of the utmost importance that his feeling should be touched; one should be careful to see in how far he can realize it through feeling. Something must happen to his feeling; it is so soft, so weak, that divine intercession must take place in one form or another. If I say to him that this singer is a compensatory phenomenon he will make an intellectual joke of it. While if I make the flat statement: this is the voice of God, quite simply, that means that in such a feeling situation he almost invites divine intercession, and that a superior force will step in to help him where he is weak. It has always been tremendously helpful when people could realize that just where they were the weakest and lowest; there intercession takes place.

LECTURE VII

5 March 1930[1]

Dr. Jung:

Last time we came to the strange conclusion that the hermaphroditic figure of that singer in the church really could be a symbol for a god, and today we have to discuss the conclusion still further. It is rather unexpected, but we have to admit that there are plenty of good reasons for it. I told you that when one reaches such an extraordinary conclusion it is difficult to realize what it means, and it would be particularly difficult in this case to make the dreamer see that it was justified. As a matter of fact when I analysed this dream with him, I did not point out such a possibility; I saw that it was indicated but I refrained from discussing it with him. Do you know why?

Dr. Deady: There has been no indication that he was prepared for it in the previous dreams and it would be liable to start a resistance in him.

Dr. Jung: Yes, that was the reason which forbade it, for from the dream itself, one can see that he is still under the influence of his memories, he still has a fixed idea about all these matters, so necessarily if one used the word god, he would at once compare his former conception with it and then one would be up against a tremendous resistance. It is not because he would be offended intellectually of course—from that point of view he has long since criticized his old concept of God and laid it aside—but because he has no other. He remains, therefore, simply identical with whatever he was taught, the traditional ideas. Moreover, to some people today, even talking of religion almost amounts to obscenity. It is exceedingly unpopular to discuss religious matters with people who

[1] Though not alluded to in the transcript of this lecture, the death of Jung's friend Richard Wilhelm had occurred on 1 March 1930.

are in any way connected with science; they are shocked and one risks being condemned as utterly unscientific. One can say anything one pleases about sexual matters and be considered surely scientific, but religion is discredited. I remember a story in that connection, under the title "Things One Should Not Talk About." The writer was dining with a Colonel. It was a man's dinner, a very good dinner, and they had arrived at the cigars, at which point, he says, one can talk about anything under the sun, any obscenity, with the exception of one thing. He said to his host, "Tell me, Colonel, what is your relation to God?" and shocked that man out of his wits. There is a peculiar taboo on these matters, and in dealing with such a man as our dreamer, who is perfectly decent, intelligent, and well-educated, yet under the prejudice of our time, one must be exceedingly careful.

But here where we are concerned with an impartial discussion, we must go into it at length because it is no small matter to use that term which has received such an extraordinary valuation in the course of time. If I called it the voice of a demon to a Greek audience of two or three thousand years ago, there would have been no trouble. They would have immediately accepted it, because the concept of the individual daimon was perfectly familiar to them. Socrates had his daimon. Everybody has his *synopados*,[2] the one who follows with and after, the shadow, understood as the individual daimon. The very word I would have used—demon—would not have suggested anything mysterious and evil any more than divine. But divine did not have the connotation that we give to it. It was the daimon, something tremendous, intensive, powerful, neither good nor bad necessarily; it simply did not enter the category of good and evil, it was a power. At a more primitive level, the term *mana* would be used, with more the connotation of the animus or the anima—a soul. Or the soul-serpent, who speaks to you, or has command of you, at times helpful and at times a nuisance perhaps. That is the original conception of divine, the daimon, a power that may be superior, or may quite violently interfere with one.

Even the more properly divine Olympian gods were not removed to a place of sacred inaccessibility. They were thought to be powerful and holy, but outside all our categories of good and evil. They often behaved very scandalously, they had most obscene, even sod-

___

[2] See above, 28 Nov. 1928, n. 4.

omitic love affairs, but that did not disturb people in the least. That a God should take the form of a bull or a swan to carry out his love designs did not shock intelligent humanity in those days. But when civilization had developed to a certain extent, and when the categories of good and evil had become more distinct, then people made a joke of the gods, who became ridiculous chiefly on account of their love affairs. They behaved in a shameful way, which surely would have been offensive to mortals if they had indulged themselves in the same way. That was one of the most powerful weapons of the Christian Apologists, which practically broke the necks of the old gods, and from that time on, the concept of a god developed chiefly on the side of a more sacred inaccessibility, until the absolute God was discovered, who was absolutely good, absolutely spiritual, all the evil sides being removed to a dark corner where devils dwelt. So the term demon became a term for evil beings. Not only the Greek gods were removed but the old gods of Genesis, and the Germanic gods, Wotan, Thor, and all the rest of them. We use the names of the gods for dogs' names now. So the concept of God became exceedingly one-sided, and that is the situation in which our dreamer finds himself.

Of course, as I said, he has not the dogmatic idea of God, he does not believe in the Church God, but that does not change the concept, only the validity of his belief. The concept itself remains the same with nothing to take the place of that depreciation. I would have had to go into a long dissertation about the history of that concept, and for practical purposes it was perfectly sufficient to say: Here is a voice that asserts itself individually. I pointed out that he only believed in collective values, and that the voice stood for individual values. That is all I told him, but the material which he gives in his associations shows clearly that the unconscious was attributing divine values to that voice, which means theoretically that the figure of the singer is in the place of his depreciated concept of God. Here we see something exceedingly interesting happening under our eyes, namely how the historically depreciated concept of God is replaced by the ancient individual daimon. We might call it a sort of regression to a time from two to six thousand years ago when the idea of an absolutely supreme god had not yet arisen, and where the divine element was only the voice within, the voice of the dream.

In this man, then, the religious process begins three or four thousand years ago, at that stage where the individual daimon, the soul-serpent, speaks to him and clearly says: This is your god. It is pretty awkward and if I should rub it in too much, he would naturally be scared, because he would assume that such a god—that thing, that hermaphrodite—might tell him something shocking which would interfere with his collective values. If I were to insist upon the importance and divinity of that voice it would simply scare him and he must not be scared, or he never will dare to stand up for himself—providing that he believed me. But I am fairly sure that he would not believe me because we are utterly disinclined to believe that anything can happen in our psychology which would amount to a superior power. We are all naturally disposed to believe that our psychology is "nothing but," that there is nothing in us which we have not provided for, which we have not acquired. This idea naturally starts from the fact that the contents of our consciousness are certain acquisitions, individual experiences, and among them there is nothing that would prove the existence of a superior power. It is everyday life; strange things happen perhaps, big experiences, but one has some sort of an explanation for them, and if not criticized too carefully, one can say it is nothing but one's own subjective psychology. One can say, with the lunatic whom I once treated, "Tonight I disinfected the whole heavens with corrosive sublimate[3] and no god was discovered!" You see that is our conscious standpoint, or perhaps one says: "Je n'ai pas besoin de cette hypothèse."[4]

So if I should say to such a man that the voice in his dream was divine and should be taken seriously, as the command of a superior power, he would not believe me and he would not trust it. The main objection that people make is: "But what is the authority of the voice? Anybody can have fantastic dreams, but to what would it lead if everybody listened to that voice which they hear? If you think in terms of the eleven thousand virgins, all listening to their voices, the world would become a lunatic asylum, everything would become impossible in the next minute." This is our prejudice. Mind you, this man is the son of a clergyman, so he had the theological

[3] Corrosive sublimate = bichloride of mercury.

[4] Pierre Simon de Laplace (1749-1827), French astronomer, who, when reminded by Napoleon that in his treatise on *Mécanique céleste* (1799-1825) he had not mentioned God, replied, "Sire, I had no need of that hypothesis."

vein in him. He may be quite liberal and enlightened, but there is the Protestant Christian.

Mrs. Henley: This man was interested in theosophy, so why should he be such a sceptic?

Dr. Jung: That is all very well when you read it in books, but when you are confronted with that voice it is a different matter; if it should say to our patient, "Now undress and give all you have to the poor, take your bank account and give it to the poor of Zurich," he would be scared out of his wits, and he assumes that the voice might say that. Or the voice might say, "Go to your wife and tell her you are in love with that girl." Sure enough he would rather die than do it. There is the trouble—when it becomes reality. It is all very well when you read in books about the incarnations of the Buddha and the spiritual life, because that doesn't hurt the bank account, but when it gets in to the family, there is nobody there, a clear field, then to hell with the whole philosophy. You see I have had many discussions with theologians and they all accuse me of psychologism, of relativizing God as a psychological factor, assuming that I represent God as nothing but a psychological factor in people which they can take out of their pockets and put in again whenever they like. They all assume that psychology is a rational sort of game in which metaphysical facts are handled as merely psychological combinations. They do not know that I look at psychology as a field of facts. For instance, if it were a science of the stars, of their movement according to such and such laws, I would not assume that I could give different laws to the stars, that I hold them in my pocket, or that I could pull Saturn down and approach it to the sun. That is what theologians do and therefore they assume that I do the same. Psychology to me is an empirical science. I observe but I do not invent. As astronomers painfully observe celestial bodies in their law-abiding movements—facts in the heavens—so I observe psychological movements, where one is dealing with autonomous factors of extraordinary power and where one simply studies the ways of those powers. One cannot assume that one ought to change their course any more than the stars in the heavens. The psyche is greater than myself; it is not in the hollow of my hand. If I could observe the Olympian gods in their movements, I would not assume, because I discover some little detail of their behaviour, that I have them in my pocket, and no more do

I assume that I have any kind of power in relation to psychological facts.

You see in our human life, psychology is a supreme factor. If it happens that a majority of human beings get a new idea in their heads, they can turn the whole world upside down. Look at the Russian Revolution. Look at the outburst of Islam. Who would have thought that such a thing could start in those Bedouin tribes of Arabia? But it did—bringing people into the foreground who had never played any role in history before, and it spread over half of Europe, nearly as far as Switzerland. Yet it was nothing but an idea, a psychological fact. Look at what Christianity has done to the world. And what brought about the Great War? Surely not economic factors alone. It was an idea, and what power was in it!— an extraordinary thing, lunacy without parallel. Now those are psychological facts. Sometimes you see it in the life of an individual, a perfectly good intelligent person; but one crazy idea gets hold of that person, one little inherited factor which obsesses the whole machinery and destroys that life completely; and not only that life but the life of the whole family. And then one complains of psychologism! But the theologian is used to giving orders to God, he tells him how he should behave. He has got him in writing, and he says: You are not God any longer if you do not behave as you did two thousand years ago. He has taken God's freedom away from him.

That point of view plays a considerable role in our patient too, so that he is in many ways disinclined to assume that such a voice could be divine. Yet from our theoretical point of view it is indispensable that we see what the unconscious is doing, and here is a case where we have to admit that we are attributing divine values to the voice within. Now what does that mean? The divine voice, as I said, is simply a mana value—a powerful voice, a sort of superior fact which takes possession of one. That is the way in which the gods or any superior spiritual facts have always worked; they took possession of man. And where there is a demonstration of divine power, it does not come under the category of natural phenomena but it is a psychological fact. When human life is inferior, when conscious intentions are disturbed, there one sees divine intercession, intercession through the unconscious, through powerful fact. Naturally one has to dismiss moral categories altogether. The idea that God is necessarily good and spiritual is simply a prejudice made by man. We wish it were so, we wish that the good and spiritual might be supreme, but it is not. To arrive again at a primordial religious phenomenon, man must return to a condition where that functioning is absolutely unprejudiced, where one cannot say that it is good or that it is evil, where one has to give up all bias as to the nature of religion; for as long as there is any kind of bias, there is no submission.

My Somali friend in Africa gave me very good teaching in that respect. He belonged to a Mohammedan sect, and I asked him about Khidr,[5] the god of that particular cult, about the ways in which he appears. He said: "He may appear as an ordinary man, like myself or like that man there, but you know that he is Khidr, and then you must step right up to him, take both his hands and shake them, and say, 'Peace be with thee,' and he will say 'Peace be with thee,' and all your wishes will be granted. Or he may appear as a light, not the light of a candle or a fire, but as a pure white light, and then you know this is Khidr." Then, bending down, he picked up a blade of grass and said: "Or he may appear like this." There is no prejudice, there is supreme submission. God can appear in any form he chooses. But to say God can only appear as the spiritual one, as the supreme one, according to the rules of the Church, is man-made bias, inflation; to prescribe to that phenomenon what it ought to be, and not accept what it is, is not submission.

So I say that our dreamer would only be able to accept our interpretation on the basis of complete submission, leaving all his prejudices and accepting that whenever and wherever that voice speaks he has to submit. Of course, that scares people out of their wits—the idea of a fact outside of them, or inside if you like, that could suddenly come up and say, "not what *you* want but what *I* want!" In the Church they are very careful to judge the case first and see whether such a command is convenient, whether it is in accordance with the rules of good behaviour, or respectability, etc. If it is all that, *then* you obey. But if the voice says something that is against all your cherished prejudices, against your illusions, against your wishes, then it is a different consideration. So you had better

[5] Khidr (or Chidr), "the verdant one," figures in the 18th sura of the Koran as an angel, the eternally youthful archetypal friend. See *Symbols of Transformation*, CW 5, pars. 282-293 (as in 1912 edn.). In Jung's 1939 Eranos lecture, "On Rebirth," CW 9 i, which is based on the Khidr legend, he relates the same anecdote of the Somali headman (par. 250). Khidr is also a symbol of the self.

assume that there is no such voice! But that is not submission, and where is the superior guidance? Our ambition is to be masters of our fate. And why should we not be able to make our lives according to our intention? Sure enough, it would be most desirable if we could arrange our lives to correspond to our desires and ambitions, but it does not work. Now, why cannot people take their lives in their hands and arrange them according to their own ideas?

Mrs. Crowley: Because they cannot see clearly enough. They cannot get outside.

Dr. Jung: You would say because our consciousness is too restricted? Too blind? That is a perfectly good standpoint.

Mrs. Sigg: It could not be managed because there is always interference from others.

Dr. Jung: Naturally if there is too much interference one must consider means; one must act within one's limits. We cannot assume that everybody would have divine omnipotence. We would not accept and would not wish for that; we can act only according to our natural means. As Mrs. Crowley points out, our consciousness is naturally limited, we are only conscious of a little section of the world. Our sight only reaches to a certain distance, our memory is insufficient, our perceptions are insufficient, and many things happen which we are too blind to see—blind moles. Think of all the sense perceptions we cannot catch which would be important for our orientation. I remember a very good illustration of that: A man who was hunting tigers in India had climbed a tree in a place where game was plentiful, and sat there waiting quietly in the dark for his prey to come along. Then he felt a light breath of air, a gentle evening breeze, and he suddenly got frightened and began to tremble. He reasoned with himself that it was foolish, and the wind subsided and he lost his fear. After a time the wind rose again, this time stronger, and he was again in terror. There was no danger apparently, but he was sweating with fear and this time his panic was so great that, in spite of tigers, he just dropped down to the ground and started to run away. No sooner was he down than the tree crashed to the ground. He thought it was the hand of God, Providence, that saved him. But as a matter of fact a man who lived in that country could easily have seen that the tree would fall; it was unmistakably hollowed out by termites. If he had examined the base of the tree he would have seen it. His eyes *had* seen it probably, but the impression did not get through to consciousness.

Then his unconscious slowly began to work and told him that the tree was perforated by termites and that when the night wind arose there might be an accident. There is always danger when termites are about; even in houses one must be careful. In camp one must look after the tent-poles every few days for fear of the little tunnels built by those extraordinary insects. I know a case where a man had left some etchings hanging up in his house when he shut it up for a couple of months, and when he returned the etchings were gone. The glasses were there stuck to the walls, cemented, so that they could not fall, but when he touched the frames he found that they were only pulp. The termites had eaten them from within, everything was crumbling. That is what a hunter should know and what he surely did know, and yet in his eagerness he overlooked that dangerous possibility.

Our insufficient consciousness makes us overlook the vital necessities of our nature, if they interfere with our personal momentary desires which the next day will be entirely unimportant. And so we forget about the eternal things, the things that will be of the most importance in the long run. On the other hand, it is exceedingly necessary to be able to concentrate, or we shall be inept dreamers. There is the great dilemma. To drive a car, one must be conscious. An engine-driver cannot afford to dream, he must have tremendous concentration. In our daily life in our overcrowded civilization, we have to be conscious, and so we become blind moles on the other side.

Therefore those ideas of a wonderful and spiritual God become utterly insufficient because they give us no guidance. It is almost a philosophical concept; it has no life of its own, it is man-made, and our actual psychology realizes that. We need to find an orienting principle, a function besides our consciousness, which will give us warning as the hunter was warned; so that in case of deviation or danger we get some point of view which we would not have thought of consciously.

Obviously our dreamer is now at such a point; he is quite convinced that there is no way out and that he has only my authority to help him. I told him that I could not solve his problem, but I knew that such things could be solved in a peculiar way; I said that I had seen such cases and that if we analysed his unconscious we might find a solution. So he was willing to try. I said that because I was really convinced that after a while we would strike that factor outside our consciousness. I was hoping for nothing less than divine intercession. I did not know what to do, I only hoped that something would begin to work in him when our human intelligence could not find a way.

That voice was really the beginning of a sort of autonomous function to him, bringing out a point of view which he really did not possess at all. It was a tremendous manifestation of an unconscious function which formerly was called the individual daimon, or the individual guide, or an oracle, or an ancestral spirit. Or on a very primitive level this voice was projected into objects, animals spoke to people, the soul serpent, or the totem animal, or a tree gave a command which had to be obeyed. If that voice is listened to, one will have a chance of a more complete life, because one lives then almost as if one were two people, not one alone, and there will be a whole sphere of knowledge and experience in which all functions, all ideas, will enter besides our ordinary consciousness.

To go on with our discussion of the hermaphrodite, we are coming now to the consideration of the fact that he has a Jewish facial type. The associations in connection with that are, as you know, chiefly the Jewish characters in *Der Golem* and also the fact that he thinks Meyrink himself must be a Jew. So there is ample evidence that this divine figure has a Jewish character. But when I use the word divine, you must never connect it with the ordinary use of that word, I mean it in the antique sense, a *mana* figure. Have you any idea why that figure should be Jewish?

Miss Howells: I think it takes on the quality of the inferior man. It represents a shadow figure.

Dr. Jung: And why should that be Jewish?

Miss Howells: Because it represents a much older civilization, or perhaps it represents a race to which he has an antipathy. Before, it was a Greek.

Dr. Jung: But why should he not take the character of Greek or any other older civilization? Why just a Jew?

Mrs. Sigg: On account of his own religious teaching.

Dr. Jung: Perhaps you do not know that all Protestant Europeans have the Jew in their unconscious, just as the American has the Negro, and still farther down, the Red Indian. We can explain that through the fact that the Jewish element in our population is a minority and that the minority represents the minor qualities of our character. Then, moreover, we have not only the Jew in reality as a minority that lives with us, but we have the Jew within as well, in the fact that our religious teaching is derived from the original Jewish religion. We have been brought up on the Old Testament and believed in the Old Testament, so we might expect to be consciously Jewish. Why is that only in the unconscious?

Mrs. Sigg: Because Christians are not clear, they have not thought it out that the Semitic element is so strong in our religious teaching.

Dr. Jung: Yes, but how would that Jewish element show in the Protestant?

Dr. Deady: In the Torah, the Law, rationalism?

Dr. Jung: Yes, one could say they were expressed by the standpoint of the law.

Dr. Deady: That is what our Puritans did with the Old Testament.

Dr. Jung: But it is not only a Puritan affair, it is a Catholic affair just as well. Where there is a trace of anti-Semitic antipathy, one can be sure that there is a Jew in the unconscious.

Dr. Deady: Is it true that the Jew has ever become christianized?

Dr. Jung: In a way it is true, the Jew today is quite christianized, his psychology has taken on an absolutely Christian quality. He has not remained behind the times, he has developed as much as we. The European Jews are quite different from the North African Jews whom I have seen and studied. I analysed a Jew from Baghdad, for instance. Now this peculiar fact that the modern European contains a Jew in the unconscious is much emphasized under certain conscious conditions. Do you know what those conditions would be?

Mrs. Sigg: In Germany, when they put too much libido into their business projects, they project all that into the Jew.

Dr. Jung: That is quite right. You find this unconscious figure of the Jew chiefly with those Protestants and Catholics where the real god is the yellow god. But you find it also in perfectly idealistic, nice people whom one could not reproach as being particularly money-lovers. Who are they?

Dr. Baynes: People in love with law.

Dr. Jung: Yes, just those people whose standpoint is the law, because the law is not given by God, it is made by man. That standpoint was essentially overcome by early Christianity. In the Epistles of Paul, one is impressed again and again by the fact that the law does not come from without, they were redeemed from that law, reborn; there was a revolution against that law. But now, see what our people have done, Catholicism is built up exclusively upon the authority of the law, and Protestantism also.

Dr. Deady: More Jewish than the Jews!

Dr. Jung: Yes, they called their children by Jewish names. My maternal grandfather,[6] for instance, who was a great Puritan, gave Jewish names to his children. His conviction was that they spoke Hebrew in heaven, so he became a professor of Hebrew in order to be able to read the newspaper there.

Dr. Deady: The Puritans in New England gave such severe punishments. They had no milk of human kindness.

Dr. Jung: That is the reason why they have a Jew in the unconscious. Because they believe in the Law, believe in authority, they quietly slip back to the standpoint of the Old Testament, only they call it something else. They call it the Church—Protestant or Catholic. But the real God is respectability and law and there is no freedom at all. Naturally our dreamer is of that kind. To express myself in the words of St. Paul, "He is the child of the unfree one of the lower city and not of the city above."[7] He is still in the Old Testament condition. Yet now we see that that voice in him which really disturbs the hymn, which sings a different tune, is of the Semitic type. Here is apparently a complete contradiction. One would assume that, being Jewish, he would believe in the law, yet here is an individual of that type who upsets the community by singing a different tune.

Mrs. Crowley: I think it is not so strange when you remember the prophets. They were also against the law.

Dr. Jung: Yes, in that prophetic element the other side of the Semitic comes out. You see, when a Christian speaks of the Jew he sees one side only. He sees the ten tribes that were really criticized by God, and not the two that were holy, who contained the prophetic element. (That is a Jewish saying, not my invention.) The dreamer's point of view is that the voice is a discreditable one and should not be, he has the racial resentment against it, it looks to him as if the Jewish element should be depreciated. While as a matter of fact it may have a different meaning, that may be a

---

[6] Samuel Preiswerk (1799-1871), of Basel, clergyman and Hebrew scholar, father of thirteen children. See *C. G. Jung: Word and Image*, p. 12. (Emilie, the name of Jung's mother, is, however, not a Jewish name, but originally Latin.)

[7] Cf. Galatians 4:22-26.

prophetic voice, and then it would mean: "You will sing a different song!—you will upset that community singing!" For the time being it is only delegated to his shadow, but it is prophetic and means: that is what *you* will come to!

Now there is still a detail that we have to deal with. In the latter part of the dream he encounters the singer again and hears him remark that he just wanted to show for once that he could sing. He remarks this to a new man who joined him, the son of the singer and a friend of the dreamer, who steps in and reproaches his father for disturbing the community. Now what about that? The son, a friend of the dreamer's, blames his father, the singer.

Mrs. Sigg: It seems to me that in Germany the old Jewish God is taught in the churches and so the children do not sing, "O du fröhliche." For children the psychology is not clear. It kills every belief of a good God.

Dr. Jung: They are impressed with the fact that they are sinful from the beginning. But tell me, why does that son reproach his father? Who is that friend of the dreamer?

Dr. Schlegel: If the singer is God, the son would be Christ.

Dr. Jung: Yes, and he would be the friend of the dreamer, and would reproach his father when he sang the wrong tune. Is that clear? The question is: is Christ the son of the God of law or the son of the God of the prophets?

Dr. Deady: The son of the God of the prophets.

Dr. Jung: Of course. The real Christ is the God of freedom. But how do you explain his reproaching his father for upsetting the community singing?

Dr. Schlegel: He is the mediator between the conscious and unconscious points of view. It is too difficult for the dreamer to accept this new melody for the moment.

Dr. Jung: You think that Christ says to his father: "Hush! don't sing such things! Too upsetting!" Or one could make another kind of *raisonnement*, that Christ, as he is preached in churches and ordinarily understood, would surely be the son of the God of the law and not the son of the God of freedom. Listen to what the Catholic Church has to say about Christ, and what you hear every Sunday in a Protestant church! So here is the son who is against the father, and there is the element that he appears as a friend of the dreamer, the friend of man. But in writing the dream-text, our patient puts in brackets, "Yet I do not know that man in reality at all." Something put in brackets in the report of a dream is like a violent protest—a sort of exclamation shouted from the gallery. The dreamer exclaims against the idea that this man should be his friend, he says he is a perfect stranger. So we must doubt the quality of that man. We are probably safe in assuming that there is something doubtful and ambivalent about that figure, and that is true of the figure of Christ, because we have two entirely different conceptions of him. There is the Church conception of Christ, and then another which has more to do with the truth, namely, Christ as the illegitimate son of a woman named Miriam, by an Egyptian soldier, Pandira. Therefore Jesus was called "Jesu ben Pandira."[8]

That is only one legend, but they all coincide in the idea that he was an illegitimate son and as such was a sort of outcast and naturally had a tremendous feeling of inferiority. "What good can come out of Galilee?" He was in the wrong corner anyway, and that would produce an enormous amount of ambition, particularly in an intelligent boy. His first fight with the Devil was with his own power-devil, his worldly ambition, and he had the greatness to renounce it. Thus he achieved spiritual greatness. So he went to one of the schools of the Therapeutae,[9] a religious sect who left the world to live a contemplative life in schools or monasteries. They were teachers and healers, and they had a rather wide-spread spiritual and philosophical influence, and were also well-known for their dream interpretation. There is an instance of that in the history of the Jews by Josephus. A prefect of Palestine called in one of those men to interpret a dream. They were rather like analysts. One of them was John the Baptist, and Christ went to his school and he was initiated by him, as we know from his baptism in the Jordan.[10] Then somehow he disagreed with him.

Now, happily enough, the writings of John have been discovered; it was always known that they existed, but it is only recently that

---

[8] For Jesus ben Pandira or Pandera, see Joseph Klausner, *Jesus of Nazareth: His Life, Times, and Teaching*, tr. H. Danby (London and New York, 1925), pp. 23-24, and Morris Goldstein, *Jesus in the Jewish Tradition* (New York, 1950), pp. 35-37. In CW 5, par. 594, Jung mentions another Jesus ben Pandira, said to be a founder of the Essenes, c. 100 B.C. (In 1912 edn., Pt. II, ch. 7, n. 126.)

[9] A pre-Christian sect, syncretizing pagan and Jewish elements, confined to the neighborhood of Alexandria (1st cent. A.D.). The Therapeutae are known only from Philo, *De vita contemplativa* (LCL Philo, IX), rather than from Josephus.

[10] Matthew ch. 11. John was not, however, one of the Therapeutae.

they have been translated.[11] In the book of Johānnā we find the whole discussion between Johānnā and Jesu ben Miriam, the deceiver. That is the title under which he is introduced, because he betrayed the mysteries according to their point of view. John reproaches him for having handed out the great mysteries of life to the people, and Jesus defends himself, saying that he is right in doing so. Curiously enough that discussion ends without any final agreement. There are two opposing standpoints, neither one yielded, and the scales remain in complete balance—John is right and Jesus is right. One says: do not spread it abroad, the people will spoil it. The other says: I give it for the sake of the people, for love. So Jesus became a great reformer and a great healer, and then he got into trouble with the official Church, which in that time, of course, meant political trouble, so they had to do away with him. Like Socrates. The ordinary human life, one could say, and if you look at it that way, you see that he was a man of great freedom of mind, who was working for the betterment of humanity. He was a man who wanted an increase of consciousness, a better understanding amongst human beings, more love and more knowledge of the heart. And see what the Church has done with it! If Jesus should come back today and have an audience with the Pope at the Vatican, they would say: "It is awfully nice, anything new, but it is really awkward!—With the best of will, we couldn't change it."

Dr. Deady: Change it! They would give him three months in prison!

Dr. Jung: Well, there are these two evaluations. There must be order, there must be tradition, there must be law, because man is really evil. Probably the majority of people here in this room would not need the police. I consider myself above stealing my neighbour's apples and I would not burn down his house, therefore I need no police. But the police are necessary because at least half of mankind is really rotten, and they need the Church because they would make bad use of their freedom. The majority of people must live in prison, otherwise they can't live at all, and that is the reason for laws and organizations. So one could say that the bringer of freedom, Jesus, was really calling for the law, and John, who preserved the light from falling into the blackness of the masses, would abuse it. For if one doesn't let the light into the darkness, what is the use

[11] See above, 29 May 1929, nn. 9 and 10.

of the light? The followers of John[12] are reduced to about three thousand people, and I doubt if even the priests understand their holy writings now. They are mostly silversmiths and they only eat drowned meat; it must not be slaughtered, they must drown whatever they eat, their chickens, goats, or sheep, and they eat with averted faces. That is all that they got out of it. And when you read the original text you are amazed at its extraordinary beauty. But if you look at what they have done with Christianity, it is equally ridiculous. So, you see, we have two different conceptions, an ambivalent figure. On the one side the traditional Saviour, and on the other a man who meant something quite different from what the Church means today. One realizes that in reading Paul, who expresses himself clearly enough; one can see that his conception of the spirit was absolutely different from the spirit of our Protestantism.

So we can understand that the figure of the friend who silences his own father is a very ambiguous one. On the one hand it could mean that it is very nice of him to reproach his father for having upset the community song—it really should be hushed up, that different voice, because it is damned awkward. On the other hand it is almost treachery to try to deprive the dreamer of the primordial religious phenomena and the real solution of the problem. So here again is that same terrible dilemma. Shall it be the law? Or shall it be freedom? It must obviously be both. There must be law and police because human beings are devils, and there must be freedom because there are decent human beings also. Therefore there will eternally be doubt. Shall it be given out, or shall it be concealed? Christ said, you should not put your light under a bushel. But if you let it shine what will happen?

Mr. Holdsworth: It will be put out!

Dr. Jung: Yes, or perverted—made into power. So the dream touches on a very delicate problem. Of course this is not very convincing and I did not mention a word of all this to my dreamer, but when it comes to a theoretical discussion we must bring in all that material. I know his subsequent development, and it took him two years to realize such thoughts. He would not have had the necessary knowledge at first, for many of the things I mentioned just now are relatively unknown. You see, the best things are always

---

[12] The Mandaeans, or "Christians of St. John." See above, 29 May 1929, p. 240.

kept back. For instance, theologians would not speak of those say-
ings of John, though they are more authentic than the Gospels and
of a time previous to the Gospels. To mention one example, there
is the Gospel text: "When two or three are gathered together in
my name"[13] etc., but the rendering in the original text is: "When
there are two together they are not without God, but when there
is one alone I am with him."[14] There, you see what the Church has
done.

[13] Matthew 18:20: "For where two or three are gathered together in my name,
there am I in the midst of them."

[14] From Oxyrhynchus Papyrus 1, discovered in Egypt by B. P. Grenfell and A. S.
Hunt and published by them in *Logia Iesou* (Oxford, 1897). As translated by M. R.
James, *The Apocryphal New Testament* (Oxford, 1924), p. 27: "Wheresoever there are
(two, they are not without) God: and where there is one alone I say I am with him."
(Restorations in parentheses.) Bruce M. Metzger, of the Princeton Theological Sem-
inary, comments: "In view of the subsequent discovery of the full text of the logion
in the context of the Coptic Gospel of Thomas, the saying is quite different from
that in Matthew: '. . . Where there are three gods, they are gods; where there are
two or one, I am with him' [sec. 30, Gospel of Thomas; tr. Metzger in appendix to
Synopsis Quattuor Evangeliorum, ed. K. Aland, Stuttgart, 1976]. . . . This can certainly
not be the original behind Matthew's text." (Personal communication.)

LECTURE VIII

12 March 1930

Dr. Jung:

Today we shall hear the report about the different attempts that have been made to get at the composition of dreams or the melody of their motifs—the task which I suggested at the beginning of this term.[1]

Dr. Baynes: There are seven attempts here. The general difficulty, according to the feeling of the committee, was that any attempt to find a rhythm in the motifs of the dreams was almost impossible in such a short series, that there was not sufficient length to allow repetitions to come in regular rhythm. Also it was felt that the actual condition of the dreamer's consciousness was required to give the contrapuntal effect. That contrapuntal effect would be between the position of development of his conscious attitude and the growth and the realization of his dreams. The whole development of the dreams necessarily involves the question of realization, and the chart made by Miss Ordway represents the curve of that realization process; but no one, as far as I can make out, has a really contrapuntal design.

[Here Mrs. Deady's artistic design in colour was shown.][2]

Dr. Jung: The idea here would be the spiral, showing the attempt of the unconscious to penetrate the conscious. In the progress of the dreams, you really see that attempt to impress the conscious with the unconscious point of view. The final fact would be the complete blending of the unconscious attempt with the actual quality of consciousness. In colour that would mean the mixture or the

---

[1] Above, 22 Jan. 1930, p. 441.

[2] *Note in Sems.:* Unfortunately the reproduction of the charts was found to be impracticable.

sum of all colours, which would be pure white. Also, by intuition, you have something here that suggests the Taoist symbol. In the black you have the white spot, and in the white the black spot, indicating that when Yang has reached its culmination, Yin is born in it.

[Dr. Howells showed a chart which was not made out in pictorial form.]

Dr. Jung: The method used here does not speak to the eye, it speaks to the thought, but it yields a decidedly interesting result, in that you have such a comprehensive list of the archetypes occurring in the dreams. It probably seems to you very difficult to make out the archetypal motifs or symbols, but it is not really so difficult, because the mistakes you make in discrimination are not very important. If you give the motif a wrong name, it does not matter much, because the archetypal motifs are so exceedingly vague that there is nothing very definite about them. Any archetype is really perfectly indescribable, something perfectly empty, but capable of assimilating a certain kind of material of tremendous variation, yet always pointing to a certain archetypal quality. For instance, the archetype of a house, a hut, a cave, or a temple. These are all very different, but it doesn't matter by which name you call them, because all these names or concepts are merely attributes of the underlying thing, which is really indescribable. In this chart, you can see that, in the beginning of the sequence of dreams, a set of archetypes is shown quite different from the ones that appear later. Those that are conspicuous until about the middle of the series more or less disappear later on; one sees a decided change. From that, we can draw an important conclusion, namely, that the whole process of development is slowly moving into a different atmosphere. I don't want to qualify it, but I think we are safe in the assumption that the later development of the dreams chooses a new language, as if creating a sort of superior superstructure overlying the original primordial motifs, as if a new building were going up upon the basis of the original archetypes. This is a working hypothesis, a point of view, and it remains to be seen in the following dreams whether it really holds good, whether it amounts to a law. In that case we would have gained an important point of view, only we should then find a suitable method by which it could be presented to the eye. If you could combine your faculty of abstraction with the pictorial faculty, that would make a perfect blend. I recommend that marriage.

[Mr. Henderson's chart.]

Dr. Jung: In this we see something rather remarkable. At first things are quite fragmentary, not well characterized. The stronger characterization takes place after the middle of the series. So we see here the great advantage of the graphic method that speaks to the eye. We see, for instance, that the motif of analysis actually undergone is definitely increasing in volume, and in the end there is a tremendous increase of religious feeling. That shows again a new aspect.

[Miss Ordway's chart.]

Dr. Jung: The advantage of this method is that it would show the degree of conscious realization, and also whether the dreamer is moving towards or away from his goal. One gets from certain dreams decidedly the impression that they are on the upward climb, while others seem to show regression, and of course it is very important in working on dreams to take into consideration the amount of conscious realization shown—not only the operation of the archetypes, but also their relation to consciousness. I have the impression that the demonstration of their actual behaviour is better shown in the charts by Dr. Howells and Mr. Henderson. In this one it is difficult for my imagination to see the statistical frequency of their occurrence, but on the other hand we get a better idea of their importance to consciousness, which is surely a point of view which has to be kept in mind.

[Miss Hannah's pictorial diagram, in which she made unconscious pictures to represent her conceptions of the dream motifs.]

Dr. Jung: You invented these!—you did creative work on his dreams! That is, instead of thinking. It is nothing to laugh about, there are many things that I have to do instead of thinking. There are certain unconscious things that you can get at only in that way because thinking destroys them. For instance, I found something fundamentally important through carving. My hands did it, not my head. The central idea here is the spiral, and consciousness is in the centre. Mrs. Deady's temperament, in her spiral design, puts consciousness in the centre with rather the idea of intensification there, while Miss Hannah's is just the other way around, the consciousness is moving out of that central spot into wider and wider spirals and finally widening out to the cosmic dream of the river.

This difference has to do with types. One gets consciousness from without and the other from within. I am very glad that these two attempts towards the spiral have been made, because it shows that there is a temperamental inclination to produce a graphic demonstration on that basis. I had really never thought of that, and it seems to me an idea quite worth considering, though I think it would be exceedingly difficult to show the continuous flow of dreams through that method. My imagination is not very helpful to me there. My temperament would rather incline to see it in the way Dr. Howells and Mr. Henderson have worked it, which would probably be the more intellectual and abstract way, while the other is more dynamic, a method chosen by people who are more impressed by the peculiar dynamism of dreams.

If I may make a suggestion, it would seem to me interesting to try to combine the methods of Dr. Howells and Mr. Henderson. Dr. Howells' archetypal motifs are more exact, more statistical, while Mr. Henderson's general outlines are more suggestive. If you could do that, then let Mrs. Deady try her hand at the dynamism of the whole thing, we might get at something in that way. These attempts are worth while. To myself personally, the fact that the later dreams chose new motifs is enlightening. I foresee the possibility that one could demonstrate how the unconscious gradually develops and produces archetypes which eventually might catch the conscious. Of course, we have not followed up material enough to see whether the unconscious eventually joins the conscious, whether the two blend, and by what kind of archetypes they finally are joined. For the sake of completeness we should write records of all the conscious states of the dreamer during his analysis. That is a task for the future—that somebody should make a diary of whatever occurs in his conscious, and thus we would have the two sets of material to work with.

Dr. Howells: There is a discrepancy in my report. I could not tell in the steamroller dream whether to put the steamroller under the head of mechanism or sex, because the dreamer himself had no sex awareness in that dream.

Dr. Jung: No, but to my mind the sex mechanism comes out quite clearly in his associations. I would record it under *sex* and *mechanism* and also the *way.* One sees the motif of the *way* there, though it is a peculiar way. That would make an accumulation of motifs, but several archetypal attributes are nearly always contained in one picture.

Dr. Howells: But that would be putting it from the point of view of your or my consciousness rather than the dreamer's consciousness.

Dr. Jung: You cannot possibly put it from the dreamer's consciousness. Things may have unusual connotations, but he never mentions it, he thinks it is indifferent or he forgets it; yet it would be exceedingly important for the qualification. In this case he does not mention that there is a sex nuance, but it will come out somehow in his associations. So I would rather proceed in a more or less arbitrary way. The motif of growth or increase can be demonstrated in many ways; for instance, by the symbol of the tree, which has the meaning of growth and many other connotations besides. One finds that vagueness of concept not only in mythology but to a certain extent also in philosophy. Schopenhauer made an interesting chart,[3] a whole network of intersecting philosophical concepts, showing how they overlap so that no concept is ever quite by itself, all are connected. Otherwise we would not be able to think. It is only by those bridges which overlap that we can think; if we have to do with irreconcilable concepts which nowhere touch, it is impossible. So that overlapping and intermingling is indispensable for the thinking process, and probably that peculiarity is in the unconscious itself. The more we approach unconsciousness, the more indistinct things become, till finally they are only dimly visible and everything means everything else. We see that in primitive psychology—the most extraordinary paradoxes, like the famous story mentioned by a German explorer which I told you last term, of the Brazilian Indians who call themselves red parrots. They say that the only difference between themselves and red parrots is that the parrots are birds and they are not; otherwise they are exactly the same. Just as we would say we are all human beings, but some are English and some are German, showing that we have advanced far enough to discriminate between man and man, but they even fail to notice the difference between man and animal. That coincides with other primitive ideas; for instance, that they do not place man on top in the scale of animals, but somewhere around the

[3] *The World as Will and Representation*, tr. E.F.J. Payne (1958), vol. I, book 1, par. 9, facing p. 49.

middle. First the elephant, the lion, the python, the rhinoceros, etc., and then comes man, by no means on top.

We are now proceeding to the next dream, but before I read you that, I want to sum up the situation in the last one. We have seen that it shows a hindrance to further progress. The machine seemed to be in order and able to work, and then obviously it did not work because of a considerable hindrance, namely, the Church and what the Church implies, the traditional Christian point of view. I emphasize this point once more because in a later dream we shall come across this motif again. As I told you, when I analysed this dream with the patient I did not tell him half that I have told you. There must be a foundation upon which to place certain ideas; one simply cannot begin at once to pour them out into the head of the poor victim. There are so many fallacies, cherished illusions, and sensitivities there that it is better to stick to the simple and obvious. So when the obstacle of the Church comes up, it means that the solution the unconscious is trying to find is hurting him on account of the traditional Christian ideas. He is way back in his childhood, and it seems as if his religious point of view had not developed since. I pointed out that you would never suspect that from his conscious presence; in his intellect he is way ahead, but in his feeling and the greater part of his shadow personality, he is still under the sway of the old prejudices. Temperamentally he is still a Christian of the particular creed in which he was brought up. The Jewish type of man who upsets the communal singing is the voice of all that material which has been stored up in the unconscious, and which would have formed a continuous development of his religious feeling, if he had made any progress in that respect since his childhood.

You see, the religious spirit is not one and the same thing always. It changes a great deal, and therefore suppositions concerning it change a great deal. One hears the most extraordinary differences in the definitions of religion or the religious spirit. There is a Church standpoint and there is a very liberal standpoint—two absolutely different points of view, almost irreconcilable, and here we have the contrast between the two. While he is still clinging conservatively to the traditional Church in his feeling life—I am not speaking of the intellectual—the progress in his feeling that would correspond to the progress of his mind is simply stored up, and that unconscious accumulation finally forms a personified something, a person. The peculiar fact in our unconscious psychology is that any accumulation of energy has always a personal character; it is always a thing to which one could give a personal name. One sees that in insanity, where unconscious thoughts or feelings become audible or visible; they become definite people. A lunatic recognizes the different voices, yet they are nothing but thoughts. The idea of inspiration and even certain ghost theories are based upon that. In this case, the progressive feeling corresponding to the intellectual development appears in the form of a person of Jewish type. The dreamer is not in reality anti-Semitic, but he cannot help having that anti-Semitic feeling which expresses the negative aspect of the figure. But on the other side there is the prophetic element in the Jewish character, which is indicated in his associations by his reference to Sephardi in Meyrink's book, who leads his people to a land of safety. There is the prophetic and guiding quality.

Now, the intruder is for the time being a doubtful figure. Not in its purpose—it is definitely the new thing, but no matter how good, useful, or wonderful the new thing may be, it might have a bad effect if it hits upon an immature condition. It is always a question in psychology whether one strikes the right word at the right moment. Saying the right thing at the wrong moment is no good. Always the two must come together. We assume that the right word cannot do harm, that the truth is useful at any moment, but that is not so, it may be perfect poison, and nowhere does that become so clear as in analysis. Such an intruder, no matter how true it is, no matter how valuable if the patient could realize it, is nevertheless perhaps inopportune and therefore nonsense. There have been very great people who indubitably told us the truth but it was not the right moment and they had to be wiped out. The right moment would have been seven hundred years later, perhaps. The great question is, is it the right moment or not?

Mr. Holdsworth: Do you think that if Christ had lived today and preached what he did, that he would have been crucified?[4]

---

[4] Jung was asked much the same question 28 years later, in connection with a symposium published in *Cosmopolitan* (New York), Dec. 1958. His reply: "It is absolutely certain that if a Christ should reappear in the world he would be interviewed and photographed by the press and would not live longer than one month. He would die being fed up with himself, as he would see himself banalized beyond all endurance. He would be killed by his own success, morally and physically." (CW 18, par. 1461.)

Dr. Jung: No, he would have been sent to the lunatic asylum or to prison. But it would not be the right word now. He was crucified, but nevertheless he said the right word at the right time; that is why it worked to such an extraordinary extent. Somehow it went home, it was *à propos.* In our dreamer's case it would not be *à propos* to tell him all that we have concluded here about the nature of that voice. It would not hit the right condition.

Now, after our exploration into the field of religion, we will return to the actual human reality of our case. "Tout est bien dit, mais il faut cultiver notre jardin."[5]

Dream [24]

He was doing gymnastic exercises in a sort of child's bed with high sides—a crib—and beside it was his wife on a mattress on the floor, watching him do his stunts. He was doing these exercises in such a wild way that the whole crib broke down, leaving one of its high sides in his hands. At that same moment he saw a mouse jumping away from under the bed. He tried to kill it, beating down on it with the iron wall in his hands, but it ran away through the open door into the next room where usually their boys were sleeping, though he did not know whether they were actually there then. He took the matter rather lightly, thinking there was no importance in it and that they could let that mouse go. But when he told his wife about it, she instantly got terribly excited and thought it might injure the boys. She took a stick and went into the next room in order to murder that little mouse.

Associations: Concerning the *exercises,* he says that usually in the morning he does gymnastic exercises, thinking that it stimulates the circulation of the blood and also improves his mood. "At least, as far as my experience reaches," he adds.

About the *child's bed,* he says that his children all slept in such white iron cribs with movable walls which one could remove at will.

Concerning the fact that *his wife was beside him but lying on the floor on a mattress,* he says that fact seemed to mean that he was doing his exercises beside her bed, and he compared her bed to a child's bed. This is entirely wrong; he is in the child's bed, but he mixes himself up with her, not seeing it.

[5] See above, 5 Dec. 1928, n. 4.

About the *mouse* he says that a mouse always has the effect of producing a state of fear in women. He thinks that there is a sexual analogy there, because when a mouse is about, a woman always jumps up and tucks her skirt around her legs so that the mouse cannot run up. Once in a hotel I suddenly heard the most terrible scream so that I thought there was surely a murder. Then I saw a woman jumping and screaming at the top of her voice for help, and thought it must be a bad case of epilepsy; but it was a mouse. The dreamer continues that he thinks that this mouse might symbolize the fear his wife has of sexuality, or her resistance to it.

Then he returns again to his *gymnastic exercises* and says that they might be his intellectual activities which his wife is watching, "and I think," he says, "that if I practice such mental exercises, it might drive away her fear of sexuality." A very complicated thought! He is now mixing up gymnastic exercises with chasing that mouse. He says further that the fact of the mouse running into the next room would indicate that the fear of sexuality is transferred to their boys, and it might injure them, so he thinks it is quite necessary to go after it with a stick to kill it.

Now consider the amazing difference between all that material we have discussed and the actual situation of the dreamer. He is not even in church, but in a child's crib, and he is hedged in by high walls; those cribs have high sides in order to prevent children from falling out and hurting themselves. That means that he is still at an age when he has to be fenced in and protected. How would such a condition show in the conscious?

Dr. Baynes: He makes his wife the custodian of his instincts.

Dr. Jung: Yes, he arms his wife with a stick, but that is very metaphorical; things are not so drastic as that.

Dr. Schlegel: On account of his mother complex, he may have a childish attitude towards his wife.

Dr. Jung: How would that show in his mental behaviour?

Answer: In extreme conventionality in everything.

Dr. Jung: Exactly. No pep concerning moral problems, they are kept strictly in the crib as if he were threatened by a mortal danger if he should fall out. He has an abject fear of being incorrect or unconventional in trying to get out of that safe place. Now this is of course a very sad demonstration, and it makes you understand why I did not go into further discussion of the dream before. It would have been like talking to a baby in the crib, so how can one expect him to realize the great religious problems of the present time? With his mind, yes, but then he would have gone off in a balloon ten thousand feet above sea level, and after that he would come down into his crib and things would be as they were before— with one exception, we must admit one thing. He is doing gymnastics in the crib, and obviously he means it as something mental or intellectual, What would that be?

Mrs. Crowley: His analysis.

Dr. Jung: Yes, but it is not only analysis. He was interested in theosophy and various mental pursuits of a more or less occult nature, and also he has that hygienic streak, eating the manna[6] and thinking the right thoughts, and so, most hygienic of all, analysis. So he takes exercises in the morning beginning with the bath, probably singing in his tub—that is exceedingly healthy—and then he would drink a non-alcoholic coffee and eat a particular kind of bread. And the same with his mind. These are exercises which are intended to be exceedingly healthy, but they are too violent and the bed breaks apart, which is extremely awkward. Of course the breaking up of the childish crib would not be so bad if something else did not happen, the mouse; and the mouse does not bother him, it bothers her. That is the trouble. Now, what do you assume these violent exercises express?

Mr. Holdsworth: A very great anxiety to get on terms with his soul.

Dr. Jung: Yes, I should say it was that. He started in on analysis in the usual hesitating way, with many objections of an intellectual and moral nature, but he became quite serious. When he had once grasped the idea he fully applied it. So he obviously did his morning exercises with great force of belief, and when one goes into analysis thoroughly, the crib goes to pieces after a while and one cannot hinder the mouse from escaping. The cat is out of the bag—a most lamentable fact! Obviously he thinks the mouse is connected with his wife. He supposes that it is the cause of fear to her and also implies that it is the reason of his wife's resistance to sexuality. But we should speak first of the fact that his wife is watching him while lying on a mattress on the floor. What is the reason of that peculiar position?

Mrs. Baynes: She is waiting for him to grow up.

[6] *Sems.:* "mana."

Dr. Jung: She seems to be in the form of a mother, but why is she on a mattress on the floor?

Mrs. Sigg: At least he would not run the risk of falling from the bed to the floor.

Dr. Jung: That is a point of view. That is what is done with lunatics.

Mrs. Baynes: I think he did it because he was in a crib, so she had to be in a worse position—lying on the floor. He wanted to reduce her power.

Dr. Deady: He could not carry on in his attitude if she were in the same bed with him—they would have to be grown up.

Dr. Jung: It is said that there is room in the smallest hut for two loving souls, but not in a child's bed! Well, I think the most impressive point about their respective positions is that he is higher up and looking down, as Mrs. Baynes points out. He is obviously admiring himself in his intellectual stunts, for most people who do physical gymnastics are a bit narcissistic, in love with their own bodies. It is a sort of autoerotic business, and he has that quality a little too, he would admire his wonderful spiritual process. That bit of vanity is not very disturbing. It does not hinder his seriousness of purpose; it is just a little human touch, like, for instance, the vanity of the man who is very modest. One must allow for that, it is altogether too human. So his mental superiority is probably expressed in his looking down on his wife on that mattress. It is not a very comfortable position for her, the mattress on the floor must be hard, so the dream insinuates that she is rather uncomfortable; moreover she is in the position of the mother and yet looked down upon. We must take note of these possibilities, because here comes an intricate bit of psychology—the next thing is the escape of the mouse. Well, we have to detach ourselves here for a moment on account of the confusing associations which he produces. Obviously he is trying to clarify the situation, but he gets hopelessly muddled, and the confusion starts already with the fact that he compares his wife's bed to a child's bed. His bed is a child's bed, not hers, he can't make out which is which. There must be a peculiar entanglement, *participation mystique*, and for the time being he cannot make out what his part is. That really is the case in *participation mystique*, one doesn't know whether it is oneself or one's partner. It is as if I called my brother by my name, unable to make a difference between him and myself. Or as if a Catholic accustomed to a Father Confessor called me Father Jung, making me identical with the priest. Patients call me Dr. So-and-So after explaining to me what a terrible man that doctor is! So our patient is very obviously muddled, and therefore we cannot take his associative material at once, but must look at the mouse from an abstract point of view and ask what the mouse is in general.

Mr. Holdsworth: It is the woman's sexuality, I suppose.

Dr. Jung: When we are interpreting with no regard to the patient's associations, we must be careful to be as naïve as possible, to have no prejudices in connection with the associations. Take the thing literally, concretely. How would you describe a mouse to somebody who had never seen one? It is a tiny grey animal, hardly seen in the daytime, which disturbs one at night with disagreeable little noises; they eat all kinds of things and one must always be careful that they don't get at the good things in the kitchen. They live in houses, parasites, and one tries to catch them by means of traps and cats because they are generally a nuisance in any house. Then the mouse appears often in folklore and typically in fairy stories. Now what would it represent psychologically?

Dr. Baynes: Repressed instinct.

Dr. Jung: Yes, but what instinct?—because any animal, taken psychologically, represents instinct in man. In as much as we are automatic and instinctive we are nothing but animals, because our behaviour is then in no way different from that of an animal. We can say it is an instinct whenever an animal occurs in a dream, but, mind you, it is always a very particular instinct, by no means *the* instinct. A lion or a huge snake would mean something quite different.

Mrs. Crowley: Fear? A mouse is terribly afraid.

Dr. Jung: Yes, it is really a terrified animal, but they are quite fresh too.

Dr. Deady: They are always tolerated. The household never makes any attempt to eliminate them really.

Dr. Jung: That is a perfectly healthy point of view.

LECTURE IX

19 March 1930

Dr. Jung:

Here is a question concerning the archetypes. We were discussing the possibility of representing dreams by the method of crystallizing the archetypes, and Dr. Schlegel's question is whether one could enumerate them. He is of the opinion that it would be impossible to do so. That is one question. There is another to which we shall come presently.

The question as to whether archetypes are limited in number is almost impossible to answer, for it depends upon a more or less arbitrary decision. In trying to extract archetypes from a dream, one sees that there are a number of indubitable archetypes which are more or less analogous to each other. Take for instance the cauldron. It is analogous to the baptismal font, the underworld, the volcano, the depths of the sea, and many other things. Now shall we call them independent, or are they describing one and the same thing? If we assume that all archetypes describe one and the same thing, we renounce their discrimination and the whole thing becomes perfectly unmanageable; in that case we practically wind up with the fact that there is only one and that is the collective unconscious. If we do discriminate between them, we find no limitation to their number. One's imagination simply would not yield representations and images enough to characterize them or to name all their possible variations. Theoretically, then, we arrive at the conclusion that every archetype is absolutely unlimited in characterization, but only theoretically, because our language is definitely limited. There are instances where we can make innumerable variations, yet they refer to practically the same thing. So the question cannot be answered. We can only say that they are theoretically unlimited, as the numbers that one can count are interminable, but practically they soon come to an end, or are quite unmanageable.

But we can say that there are a reasonable number of archetypes which can be clearly discerned and which are not mere analogies of each other. For instance, the archetypes of the hero and the cauldron are certainly not identical, in spite of the fact that the hero is in closest connection with the idea of the cauldron. In primitive myths, the hero always enters a cave, or the underground world, or the belly of a whale, where he makes a fire, etc. In other words he enters the cauldron, thus bringing about the miracle of renewal or rebirth, which is the most characteristic quality of the cauldron motif. So despite the close relation between the image of the hero and the image of the cauldron, we can discriminate these two things—even though the cauldron and the hero are really identical in the fact that it is one and the same process. Entering the cauldron, or a condition expressed by the cauldron, is an involution of energy, and rising again from the cauldron is an evolution of energy. Therefore one could call it simply a certain movement, a transformation of energy, represented by these archetypal figures; it is always the same energy—two different states of the same energy. But you see that, as soon as the thing is made into a scientific or philosophical reduction, it becomes absolutely abstract and unimaginable and therefore impracticable. To call a rebirth dream a transformation of energy is so abstract that it means absolutely nothing. So we need archetypes, we need that picturesque language to express this peculiar kind of transformation.

It is the same with the idea of the anima. When we speak of her as a function it conveys nothing, but by making it personal, she becomes a personal reality. If we make an abstraction of it, it is simply a figure in our head, an artificial abbreviation, and not the thing itself. Even in science, when we make abstractions from facts, we are left with nothing to deal with; we are not dealing with the real animals, only with stuffed animals, or perhaps an ideal construction of an animal, conveying more and more nothing. And so it is with the archetypes: the more we treat them scientifically, the more they evaporate. If we restrict them to what we think to be their essence, we arrive at one principle expressed in terms of transformation of energy, which means nothing and which is absolutely lifeless. Therefore we have to talk of archetypes, and when one begins to discern them, there is no limitation apparently. How many did you extract from the dreams, Dr. Howells?

Dr. Howells: I got 38 out of 20 dreams, and I did not get half of them.

Dr. Jung: I think you abstracted a number from your own dreams, didn't you, Miss Flenniken?

Miss Flenniken: I got 62 out of 90 dreams.

Dr. Jung: I remember that in your case I made the observation that you could have restricted the number because you had several archetypes, the prophet and the magician, for instance, which were obviously one. In another case, however, one might be forced to separate them. The prophet, the magician, the old king, and the priest are all independent figures, yet they are all together. In a particular problem there might be an important difference between them, and then one would naturally differentiate them, but in most cases it is better to draw them together, to let one contaminate the other. There are so many to deal with that one has to restrict their number by applying a sort of contraction, summing them up in one figure. That arbitrary decrease cannot be considered theoretically but is dependent upon one's particular purpose; for instance, in making a statistical statement of the frequency of the flow of the archetypes, only a limited number can be chosen. Otherwise one simply cannot represent them, one's colours wouldn't last out, and the whole picture would become too confused. It would be possible to differentiate them into such an infinite number that practically every word would become an archetype, because every word has its history. Every word goes back to something which has been repeated millions of times before and therefore acquires an archetypal quality. So in how far one has to limit the limitless archetypes is entirely a matter of the particular end in view.

The other question that Dr. Schlegel asks is whether archetypes would be created in our day. For instance, what formerly was expressed by fiery chariots rising up to heaven would nowadays be aeroplanes. When railways were new in France, Victor Hugo said: why not make engines and trains that look like something?—and he suggested the form of a huge snake and the engine was a dragon's head with fire glowing out of its nostrils and spitting smoke. He was assimilating a new collective phenomenon to an archetypal idea. Dragons are in our day great machines, cars, big guns, these are archetypes now, simply new terms for old things. These new things are just as valid as the old ones; as the new things are merely words for images, so the old things were words for images. The

538

mythological idea of the dragon is probably derived from the idea of huge saurians; it is really quite possible that the dragon myths are the last vestiges of ancestral memories of the saurians—the terrifying thing of which man in the dim past was afraid. Of course, to be afraid of dragons, even in historical times, was futile because there were no dragons. They have become a psychological fear because those beasts don't exist in reality; as a father or mother complex can keep on being operative in psychology even if the father or mother are long since dead. They can be still alive in the form of symbolic images, as the dragon is still alive in the form of an image, although it is in reality nothing but a name. So when we express an archetypal idea by a machine it is as though we were talking of a time when machines did not exist, as though there were still saurians. There may be a time when we no longer talk of machines, but the ideas and fears will persist long after the actual machines are obsolete, and so it becomes obvious that these images are simply names for the things we are afraid of, names for *fears* quite simply. Even in the days when there really were saurians, they were a name for that fear. So the operation of archetypes is naturally going on, only today we don't talk about dragons but about cars and machinery and big organizations. Sure enough, all the little merchants in America and Europe who have been crushed by the Standard Oil Trust must feel that to be a great crushing monster.

Mr. Holdsworth: Were there any men in the world in the time of the great saurians?

Dr. Jung: The mammoth was hunted by man, and those huge lizards on the island of Cocos[1] are saurians, so they are still alive in the tropics. And one reads in Caesar, in the *Bellum Gallicum*, about a unicorn in the Black Forest that could not lie down because its joints were stiff, so it slept while standing, leaning against trees; and the people cut the trees down so that it would fall and they could kill it.[2] That unicorn was undoubtedly a rhinoceros. There

---

[1] Evidently a transcribing error for the island of Komodo, near Java, where a monitor lizard, sometimes called the "Komodo dragon," can reach a length of ten feet. It does not occur on the Cocos Islands, in the Indian Ocean.

[2] *The Gallic War* 6.26-27. The interpretation here of Caesar's account of the beast is rather free. Jung later became learned on the subject of the unicorn: see "The Paradigm of the Unicorn," *Psychology and Alchemy* (1944), CW 12, pars. 518-544 (not in the 1936 Eranos version).

have been no rhinoceroses in Europe for a long time, but just recently they discovered the remains of one again somewhere in the petroleum fields of Silesia, where the whole body was preserved.[3]

Dr. Schlegel: Do you identify the idea of archetypes with the idea of symbols, so that everything which has a symbolical value can be considered as an archetype?

Dr. Jung: No, the symbol is an entirely different conception. I would call an archetype a symbol when it was functioning as a symbol, but it doesn't necessarily function in that way. The word *symbol* has been very much misused. Freud calls things symbolical when they are only semiotic.[4] If he had had a philosophical education, he could not mix up those terms. For instance, railroad employees have a design of a little winged wheel on their caps, and Freud would call that a symbol of the railway, but it is a *sign* of the railway. If it were a symbol, it would mean that the men who wear it had been initiated into a secret cult symbolized by a winged wheel, and the devil knows what that might mean, perhaps something divine. One uses the word *symbol* for something which one can only vaguely characterize. A symbol expresses something which one cannot designate otherwise; one can only approach the meaning a little by using certain designs. For instance, the Christian faith is symbolized by the cross, which means that the cross expresses something which cannot be expressed in any other terms. The Greek word *symbolon* means creed, and the term *symbol* in its original use also meant the creed. The original idea of the creed was not that now God is caught and we know exactly what he means. The actual creed is the nearest approach in a human way to certain intuitions and beliefs—the belief that God is the Father and in the same person the Son and the Holy Ghost, for instance. The great mysteries of life and eternity could be expressed only by symbols, and therefore they were always sacred.

The archetype when functioning can be expressive of a situation,

---

[3] According to C. O. Dunbar (*Historical Geology*, New York, 1949, p. 31), "a remarkably complete carcass of the woolly rhinoceros was excavated from the muck of an oil seep in Poland in 1930. . . . The woolly rhinoceros was a contemporary of the woolly mammoth." The find was documented in the *Science News-Letter* (Washington, D.C.), 17 May 1930.

[4] For a fuller account of this distinction, see *Psychological Types* (1921), CW 6, pars. 814ff., def. of "symbol."

and one can call it symbolic inasmuch as the situation is more or less unknown, but the archetype can also function in a situation which is entirely known to you. For instance, we say a woman suffering from bad temper is like a fire-dragon. That is an archetype, but one wouldn't call it a symbol; it is simply an exaggerated metaphor. But when someone makes a peculiar design in order to express something which he cannot express otherwise, and in so doing uses an archetype, you would then call it a symbol. If a person makes a drawing of a snake, and above that a cross, and above that a moon, and you ask what that may be, you will probably see him begin to stammer, a jumble of words and vague conceptions; there is nothing to do but guess, and then he informs you that it is the only way in which he could characterize his thoughts and visions. Now that is a symbol, and he has used the archetypes of the cross, of the snake, and of the moon, but in this case it is not semiotic, it is symbolic. That difference was always known in philosophy but Freud mixes up the two, his use of the word *symbol* is really meaningless.

Dr. Baynes: This question of making new archetypes seems to me problematical because, in relation to the dragon, no one could believe that he had any part in making a dragon nowadays, whereas the modern man knows that, with engines, we are on top. We can make them.

Dr. Jung: Yes, but suppose an age when the machine gets on top of us. Then it would become a dragon, the equivalent of the old saurians, and really, when you look at New York, it really is on top of man; he knows that he has done all that and yet it pulls him down.

Dr. Baynes: Hasn't it something to do with the attitude of a man towards it? Wouldn't it be like the churinga, which he knows he makes, yet it has a kind of power over him? It is both above and below him.

Dr. Jung: Yes, but that would prove that he could make archetypes—because we have that ability to make something into a dragon. I should say that we could transform that power which is embodied in the image of the dragon into something else, yet that something else is equipped with the power of creation too. The old rabbi was capable of making a living thing, the Golem, from a clod of earth by black magic, but that thing had a tendency to grow and grow and finally it fell on him and killed him. So the churinga is made

541

by man, yet because it is a symbol, it is also the abode of divine power. All idol-worshippers know that the image has been made by man, yet it is chosen as an abode of the god because it is his symbol, and inasmuch as it is inhabited by a god, it is sacred, it is taboo. In building a machine we are so intent upon our purpose that we forget that we are investing that machine with creative power. It looks as if it were a mechanical thing, but it can overgrow us in an invisible way, as, time and again in the history of the world, institutions and laws have overwhelmed man. Despite the fact that they were created by man, they are the dwelling-places of divine powers that may destroy us.

Dr. Baynes: The point I tried to make was that in making machines we are transforming irrational into rational power. It therefore seems to me that the shaping of the archetype should be according to this function of rationalizing—like harnessing the Nile, which would be rather different from the dragon.

Dr. Jung: Yes, but when we speak of the transformation of the dragon into a machine, we are in a certain stage of that development only. We are actually in the stage of inventing the machine, we are just about to transform that primitive energy into the machine. We have ideas about the godlikeness of man and forget about the gods. After a while, when we have invested all our energy in rational forms, they will strangle us. They are the dragons now, they became a sort of nightmare. Slowly and secretly we become their slaves and are devoured. New York has grown to overwhelming proportions and it is due to the machine. And it is such a devouring monster that Dr. Draper[5] tells me that the average life expectancy of people in New York is forty years. In Switzerland it is sixty years.[6] Why do we have psychology? Because we are already strangled by our rational devices. One can see that also in enormous machine-like bodies of men, armies or other organizations, which all lead to destruction. Think of the tremendous power of Napoleon I and how completely his army was wiped out. And Alexander the Great,

[5] George Draper, M.D., of New York, a pioneer researcher in psychomatic medicine, was the brother of Ruth Draper, the monologuist, whom Jung also was acquainted with.

[6] According to the Office of Population Research at Princeton University, the life expectancy of a human being in New York in 1930 was 60 years, and the same for Switzerland. In 1980, in both the United States and Switzerland, it was in the low 70s.

whose army was crushed in India. Think of the history of Babylon and Assyria. It took two thousand years to reach the climax of their glory, and in the next thirty years the whole thing was destroyed. It is always so. Great organizations eat themselves up.

Mr. Holdsworth: Would you say that, when the farm labourers started to break up the machinery in the industrial riots,[7] they were working under the fear of the dragon?

Dr. Jung: It is difficult to discuss that question because it is too near to us, but perhaps those riots in England arose from the fear of the dragon in machines.

Well, now we must get back to our dream. We got as far as the mouse, which we really must tackle seriously. You have heard the dreamer's associations about it, and we decided that it must be an instinctive thing. In what way would it be characterized? We must be as specific as possible in dream interpretation; we must bring theory down to reality.

Mrs. Sigg: A mouse comes up unexpectedly very often. It seems to be a symbolic representation of man's sexuality, and this man's sexuality is not so connected with the whole of his being.

Dr. Jung: But why think of sexuality at all?

Mr. Holdsworth: He is a child in his crib. When it breaks he has outgrown it. Then naturally his sexuality appears.

Dr. Jung: It is often the case that when a man comes of age his sexuality does not work.

Mrs. Sigg: Women sometimes say of sexuality that it is only the animal part of their nature.

Dr. Jung: It is the word only that points the way. That is really an important point because the mouse has always been "only." You remember perhaps about the mountain being in labour pains and then appears a ridiculously small mouse. That is the "only." It is tiny and not important, a nuisance but not dangerous in any way. One has to take care that it doesn't eat the cheese and the bread, soil the food, make holes in things, but it is not very considerable. We have to take that point of view. Where have we evidence of that in the dream?

Mrs. Sawyer: Where it runs away and he thinks it is of no importance.

[7] The reference is presumably to the Luddites, workmen in English manufacturing towns who rioted in 1811-1816 and wrecked machinery, which they supposed to have caused unemployment.

Dr. Jung: Yes, the evidence is in his associations. But his wife has a different view. She gets very much excited and goes after it with a stick, assuming that it might be dangerous to the boys. Now, what is that mouse? There seems to be a general suspicion that it means sexuality. And the mouse is instinctive; instinct, like sexuality, is under a strong taboo. Let us discuss that possibility. In that marriage the difficulty, as we were saying, is the fundamental difference that exists between the viewpoints of husband and wife concerning the importance of what we call Eros—sex or relatedness. He is confronted with the sex problem, that is the point in ligitation. There have been discussions about it, and his wife holds entirely different convictions from the dreamer. He thinks of sexuality as something very important and indispensable, and she thinks it is futile and can be dispensed with except for the purpose of producing children; she has the puritanical idea that sexuality only serves that purpose and has otherwise no justification whatever. That is a hint for us. He would say, "Oh, let that little thing go, it is not so important," and she would say, "No, it is terrible. It should not be." Well, we guess that the mouse is sex, but there is another consideration. It is surely an instance of a secret nocturnal instinct, because mice show themselves in the night. They live in dark holes, parasites, outcasts, outlaws, and we trap them or poison them whenever we can. So it must be a form of instinct under a strong taboo. What is that instinct? Will only sexuality cover it? There is another conclusion.

Dr. Draper: To be quite irrational, it might be that the first part of this lecture about archetypes and dragons had the occult purpose of preparing us for the interpretation of the mouse symbol. Thus the mouse might be a diminutive dragon which in the dreamer's life is actually significant, really a dragon. We can look at the mouse as an inverted dragon. It may refer not only to the physical but to very much broader concerns in life.

Dr. Jung: That is true. Sexuality is not only a little mouse, it is a very big thing, a most upsetting problem; but the dream speaks of a mouse, and we assume that it has a purpose in so doing. We would expect far more powerful symbolism, but instead of a dragon we find only a little mouse. That would be no argument against the idea that the mouse really means sexuality, but I should say it was definitely the purpose of the unconscious in this case to belittle it, to make it quite small so that it appears as nothing. It is like a sort of deceit. The wife makes a fuss about it as if it were a much bigger thing than it is in reality, because she would represent the figure in the dream that knows more about the importance of that mouse or sexuality than the dreamer himself does. One might say that he relegates realization into his wife, as if he said, "You would make a fuss about it but to me it is nothing." The question is, why is it belittled? Why is it not represented at its full value? It is really the fundamental problem in the dream for the time being.

Mrs. Sigg: To encourage him.

Dr. Jung: Yes, that is really the idea. Often we see that certain things which in reality seem unimportant are tremendously emphasized in dreams; something is given an extraordinary size to impress the dreamer when he undervalues it. And the reverse occurs where a thing which is enormously important is belittled. It is like the instances we were recently talking about, where the analyst is decreased, depotentiated, in order to give a chance to the dreamer to assert himself. Otherwise he is obsessed by the figure of the analyst. In this case, the man is consciously quite aware of the importance of sex, and the purpose of the figure of the tiny mouse might be to encourage him. Now, to encourage him to what?

Mrs. Sigg: To try to find a way to manage the problem with his wife; he might ask the reason why his wife was afraid, for instance.

Dr. Jung: But he often asked her that and it led nowhere. All women have that fear of mice, and it is always ridiculous to a man. So it is even ridiculed, obviously the unconscious wants him to think of it as a small matter which his wife makes a fuss over as if it could injure the children, which is nonsense. The tendency of the dream, then, is to decrease the importance of the problem in order to encourage him. But encourage him to what?

Dr. Baynes: To follow the libido which he is so scared about.

Dr. Jung: When the bed breaks apart, away runs his libido. He is not afraid of running after it because he delegates the fear to his wife, but what would he do with it? He tries to kill the mouse with the wall of his crib and fails to hit it—a case of turning big guns on sparrows. Now to what is the dream trying to encourage him?

Mr. Holdsworth: To get to it with his wife. He should take a stick according to the old proverb about a woman:—"The more you beat her, the better she'll be."

Dr. Jung: No, he would never do that. There would be no attraction to him in beating her up, he is too refined. Naturally, if he were deeply in love with her and lived several degrees nearer to the East he would take a stick, but for an educated Western man it is not attractive to beat a woman down and then have intercourse with her.

Mrs. Sigg: But I think it would be an important thing for them both, for the benefit of their children, if they got all right again. They could discuss the question and what effect it might have on the children.

Dr. Jung: Obviously the wife is of the opinion that the mouse might injure the children somehow, but that is all bunk. We are concerned now with the fact that the dream encourages him. But to what? I want you to continue.

Dr. Baynes: He is in a crib, in a kind of corner fighting the bogey in the mouse, and he has to come out in the open.

Mr. Holdsworth: Isn't it that there isn't so much in all this copulation business?—it is only a mouse.

Dr. Jung: I want to force a lady to say what he ought to do. It is a sweet sadistical question. I want to see how they continue their sentences. Now please betray a secret. You see that we have to discuss things *à fond*. Where are the ladies who can tell us something enlightening about it? We men are poor judges of human feelings. It would be a splendid opportunity for the ladies to have a word in this discussion which concerns them. Mrs. Sigg is perfectly right to assume that he is to be encouraged. Don't be afraid. Don't be so fussy. What would that mean?

Mrs. Baynes: Perhaps he is becoming discouraged by his wife's repudiation of him and that is why his libido is on such a small scale.

Dr. Jung: Yes, in his conscious. The situation between this man and his wife has become terribly uninteresting in a way. His wife was petering out. He would have wished that she had been more interested, but since she was not, he occasionally stepped aside and had foolish adventures with very ordinary women. Then he tried theosophical studies, but he could not settle his problem in such a futile way, and so he came to analysis and is making a serious attempt at it. He now tries to hold himself together and to be superior to this problem; he avoids trips to Poland[8] and tries to be

[8] Poland: cf. dream 19 and the association for *journey to Poland*, above, 9 Oct. 1929, p. 303.

reasonable. But there is the mouse, that nocturnal nuisance, and naturally in his conscious he thinks this is terribly important and something must be done about it.

Mrs. Deady: Hasn't he built up a tremendous mountain of fears in himself?

Dr. Jung: That is what she has built up, not he.

Mrs. Sigg: I understand quite well Mrs. Deady's meaning, and I think it is true that if there had been such a long separation, there might be an invisible wall in the man too.

Dr. Jung: Sure enough, there is an invisible wall, but we cannot make it visible. What we see in this dream is only the tendency of the unconscious to decrease the importance of the problem. We might even say that he kept himself within four walls as if he were a baby, behaving like a baby, fulfilling his functions as a baby, doing what he was told to do, and in the course of his exercises the bed breaks apart and the mouse runs out. When it held together in infantilism the mouse didn't appear. But now the problem appears. He is inefficient and does not succeed in killing it, it escapes, and his wife rages because she thinks, if his sexuality comes out it will injure the children, which of course is always an argument with wives—they say it injures children.

Miss Hannah: Is it that he should, like the Buddha, try living as a monkey?

Dr. Jung: Try living as a mouse?—imitate the ways of the mouse and escape? The appearance of animals in dreams often means to imitate the ways of animals. In fairy tales there are helpful animals. Now what would that mean practically? I wish particularly that the ladies would use their wits on such a question.

Mrs. Baynes: I think that one very important point is that he has got to get out of the crib before he can manage anything.

Dr. Jung: He is out of the crib. No help any longer—no sheltering behind infantile walls. Something is now en route, just leaving the precincts, but we should know what it is.

Mrs. Deady: He should not think about it so much. He should have the suddenness of the mouse—just one leap.

Dr. Jung: Just one leap—like lightning, silently? Yes, that would be imitating the mouse, but we are too metaphorical, we should be more specific. We have the consideration here that this mouse means a separate autonomous factor, something instinctive that has left its hiding-place and appears on the scene. No use trying to kill that thing, the mouse is quicker; no use trying to kill it even if his wife holds that it might injure the children. Something in the mechanism is loose now. We speak of a screw loose when one does things one didn't intend to do, says things one didn't intend to say. An autonomous factor has appeared on the scene that takes on a very small form but that asserts itself just as a mouse asserts itself. It will be a nuisance in the night and in the day, and it will make holes because nothing will hold it for ever; it will creep through walls and doors, it cannot be locked in; whether he wants it or not it will work.

That is the obvious meaning of the dream, but naturally the man will ask me, "What is it?" and I will say that it is his sexual problem, which neither he nor his wife can control, it will find its way through. "But why just a mouse for a big problem?"—to which I would say that obviously the importance is greatly decreased and that it literally means that the dreamer should not make such a fuss about his sexuality. He can leave it alone because that mouse will take care of itself. He worries all the time about what one should do, not what he should do; he seeks a formula or something that is generally acknowledged to deal with the situation. But he should completely dismiss it, he should simply say that he can't manage it and doesn't know what the solution is. If that thing wants to live it will live, and he should let it go. What is left alone takes care of itself, it works out according to its own laws. The cat is out of the bag, and if the problem is working like that it will keep on working, making ways. Provided that it is real, it will produce certain effects, and naturally one is more or less at its mercy; it goes on even if one does not know when or where. It is most important that we assume nothing. There are many problems with which our rational mind is quite incapable of dealing, apparently impossible situations, and I am very careful not to mix in. There are people who at thirty-five go into a monastery, for instance. People sometimes choose strange lives which the average opinion would say were wrong, but it may be right for them, how do I know? If his unconscious should say that this man's sexuality had disappeared completely, that it was absolutely unimportant and did not exist, it would be unexpected, but I would say, well, perhaps this is true. Here, then, I would say to the dreamer, the mouse has escaped, and now it can do something if it really is alive, if it has strength. It will take care of itself and something is going to happen.

Do you understand? I mean that I really believe in autonomous complexes. I really believe that autonomous factors can produce something and help settle an unmanageable problem in a way that is not repressing it nor neglecting it. It is as if you sent your servant with a letter of credit to cash: you cannot go so you delegate your powers, you send that problem away into the desert, into the unknown, and it will find the way. I cannot tell how to solve it, but if you dismiss a problem it will work out along the lines of general law. You see, I can talk very definitely about this case because I know by what *péripéties*[9] he went and how it has developed since, and I know that here things began to move. You remember that the former dream said that the machine was ready to work, and you know what the difficulty was—that he came up against church prejudices and moral laws. Then he recoiled and found himself in the crib. Now the crib breaks apart. The machine becomes the mouse. He recognizes that it is a living mechanism able to work out its own salvation. It is the first time he has discovered that it can take care of itself. I don't know how. It is left to the grace of God, but I can tell you that it was very alive. It worked itself out.

[9] From Greek *peripetia* = "a sudden change in the situation."

LECTURE X

26 March 1930

Dr. Jung:

Before we enter upon our discussion today, I have a proposition to make concerning the next seminar. There are several among you who are going to be here for the summer term, and probably there will be a number of new members. For them we should have a short résumé of this term's proceedings. The actual dreams need not be mentioned, but it would be important to have a general exposition of the problem, how it evolved and with what variations—a psychological abstract of the general movement of that long serpent of our dream problem.

Then I should like to make another suggestion. We have recently been making attempts at formulating archetypes in the dream material and we had considerable difficulty about it. Now, since archetypes were originally derived, not from dreams, but from mythological material, like fairy tales, legends, and religious forms of thought, I think it would be advisable to try first to classify the archetypes from such matter. I think it would be an interesting enterprise if some of you would choose different mythologies to work on—if one took Germanic mythology, and another Graeco-Roman, or primitive folklore, and so on. You get an idea of classification by looking through the index of *Psychology of the Unconscious*, and there are English books along that line. That rather uninteresting book "Cinderella" is nevertheless very valuable from the psychological point of view; there one sees how the archetypes are worked out. There is a parallel in German literature called *Astralmythen*, by Stucken, and also *Das Zeitalter des Sonnengottes*, by Frobenius, where you find an enumeration of archetypal motifs and the methods by which these scholars have attained their re-

550

sults.[1] I make this proposition in the hope that some of you will be interested. Are there any questions?

Dr. Baynes: In reference to your first suggestion concerning the résumé of this term's proceedings, do you propose that various members should make an abstract and then submit the report and have the best or most comprehensive one multigraphed?

Dr. Jung: One person could make the report, simply a general abstract, like the report Dr. Deady made only less specific.

Dr. Deady: In what way would it differ from that?

Dr. Jung: I would not go into the detail of the dreams. I would simply try to describe the general development of the thought. It would be a résumé of the thought, not the actual dream material.

Dr. Baynes: I should think that your book would be the best for looking up the archetypal motifs.

Dr. Jung: I don't want you to confine yourself to that. The Cinderella motif is an exceptionally clear case. Then exceedingly interesting material is to be found in Indian mythology. It would help you to see the same motifs occurring as in dreams.

Question: Do you want everyone to do it?

Dr. Jung: Not everyone. Only the people interested.

Suggestion: *Orpheus, the Fisher* is an interesting book which is in the library here. There is one by Bachhofer too, but that is not translated.[2]

Dr. Baynes: *The Holy Grail*, by Jane Weston,[3] shows the motifs in quite a scholarly way.

Dr. Deady: A new book has just appeared in England called *The Lore of the Unicorn*, by Shepherd.[4] The writer seems to have read every book in the world which other people have not read. The bibliography is extraordinary. He covers everything from legends to dreams—a remarkable piece of research.

Dr. Jung: Yes, but I am afraid that would be a monographic

---

[1] Eduard Stucken, *Astralmythen: Religionsgeschichtliche Untersuchungen* (2 vols., Leipzig, 1896, 1907). Leo Frobenius, *Das Zeitalter des Sonnengottes* (Berlin, 1904).

[2] Robert Eisler, *Orpheus—the Fisher* (London, 1921). For a comment on Eisler's work, see *Aion* (1951), CW 9 ii, par. 147, n. 75. Bachhofer is perhaps a transcribing error for Bachofen: Johann Jakob Bachofen (1815-1887), Swiss jurist and writer on symbolism and mythology. See *Myth, Religion, and Mother Right: Selected Writings* (Bollingen Series, 1967).

[3] Jessie Weston, *The Quest of the Holy Grail* (London, 1913).

[4] Odell Shepard, *The Lore of the Unicorn* (London and Boston, 1930).

discussion of one motif, which is not exactly what we are after. We are after a method of discerning archetypal motifs from wider material. Of course, Cinderella is only one motif, from one point of view, but the method is excellent, and of course your unicorn book might have a good method also. Silberer's book on mysticism[5] is very good indeed. You will find there the cauldron motif and a number of others.

Well now, I find on my desk this *document humain*, but I don't know the author, as it is not signed. I will read it to you.

Some Suggestions about the Dream-Mouse

The discussion of last seminar has created a certain amount of ill-feeling in the world of mice. In order to clear it up the mice have taken the liberty to send in the following conciliatory proposals.

Dr. Jung has said that when an animal appears in a dream, we must take it exactly as it is in reality, and try to find its meaning with the help of its own characteristics. So we have stated that the mouse is small—shy—lives in holes—comes out at night mostly—is greedy for lard and can disturb orderly households. What was not pointed out besides these characteristics is the extraordinary fertility of the mouse, which is equalled perhaps only by the guinea-pig. Every child who owns a couple of white mice knows this—knows that only massacres after the Herodian fashion will do anything against a growing crowd of continuously produced offspring. It really seems as if the males also must bring forth.

It might be useful not to overlook this extraordinary fertility of the mouse—perhaps it will lead us somewhere. Let's say then that the mouse is an animal of darkness, of night, and of fertility. This shows plainly its connection with moon-life, with all the symbolism of the moon, which the seminar will remember from former discussions. But within this moonlit circle the mouse has its own special place, and what that may be we can find out best by considering woman's behaviour at the sight of a mouse.

There is an old saying that a girl who is not afraid of mice has lost her virginity. And it is certain too that women at the sight of a mouse show their fright in a very peculiar way—as if their virginity were attacked. This is very curious, as a mouse is surely no danger for woman's chastity.

Now, we must take our courage into both hands and say this: when in a room there is a man and a woman and a mouse—when the woman

---

[5] Herbert Silberer, *Problems of Mysticism and Its Symbolism*, tr. Smith Ely Jelliffe (New York, 1917).

screams and the man thinks it doesn't matter, it is in spite of all appearances very probable that it is the man who is frightened, and the woman is not.

Every man present may now come down on us and declare triumphantly that this would only be another proof of the falsehood and hypocrisy of woman—just another crocodile's tear in her deceitful eyes. And at that one would have to say yes. But after the men had enjoyed their triumph one might go on and say that we had better not stop at that. When from Eve's time on through the ages women at the sight of a mouse have always behaved in such a queer deceitful way, this way itself must mean something. The sham perhaps has a good reason—perhaps it is no sham after all, but a sort of symbolical behaviour—as symbolical as the mouse itself.

The mouse, we believe, is a symbol of woman's wish for fecundity. This wish in all women is deeply rooted, because it is only by giving birth to children that woman fulfills her natural task and lives according to her destiny. And one may not restrict this statement to the material and physical world of woman's body and sex only. It is just as true for the moon-mind of woman, which all the time also longs for the seed of the sons of light, in order to bring forth the spiritual children of the moon in dark but ever fervent creativeness. The wish for physical and for spiritual conception is even so closely connected in women that often they mix the two up and must leave it to the discrimination of men to decide what they really want. It can happen that a woman gives birth to one child after another, because she does not know that her moon-mind suffers from neglect, whilst on the other hand many a wife troubles her husband with her imperious wishes for spiritual relatedness, when in reality she ought to have some babies.

But however this may be, it seems very probable that the mouse is the symbol of the Yin principle in its readiness to conceive.

Just as in the material world it is only the womb that creates in woman, so in the spiritual world it is not intellectual or rational life which contains woman's creative power. On the rational side woman is the guardian, the mother. But it is the warm, brown earth of irrational Eros that must receive the spiritual seed of man. Now, Eros in its nature being so irrational, it lacks language completely—it can speak neither English nor French nor German. And as it does not know the logical word at all, Eros can never say clearly what it wants and why it wants just this. Therefore when Eros is at work in woman, all she can do is to act or talk in sometimes very queer symbolical ways, in order to attract man's attention. What Eros wants is to make man ask a question, because to questions Eros can answer. The answer will always be a child—in the material world it will take nine months, in spiritual matters it can come much quicker.

Only man does not know all this. Whenever Eros is concerned, man, who has not developed within himself all his female side, is as ignorant as

Parsifal. He really does not know—he is not even aware that at bottom he is frightened. As Parsifal before the Holy Grail, so man stands before woman's Eros. And just as Parsifal was accepted to the Holy Grail only when he asked the question, so it is only at man's question that woman's Eros can be revealed.

The difference is that the Grail—being holy—remained silent and waited for the question, while short-lived, earth-bound woman cannot wait quite so well. So great is her longing to conceive that she uses the most astonishing means to make man speak.

In the case of the mouse it is as if woman would adopt all the outward signs of man's inward fear in order to awake his chivalry and courage and in order to make him see how superfluous fear is in this case. When a woman screams at the sight of a mouse, it does not mean: "I am afraid." It means: "Do you see the mouse? Don't you understand it? Please ask now!—ask a question!"

It seems to us that the mouse is a very excellent symbol for the longings of Eros. As the mouse lives almost unseen in all countries and climates, so woman's Eros, even if hidden in the deepest mousehole, is omnipresent. Like the mouse it prefers the friendly shine of the moon to broad daylight, and feels best in the quietest room of the house. And like the mouse it promises numberless offspring. About these offspring the French law seems to be valid in all cases, namely: *La recherche de la paternité est interdite*. Only the children of Eros can resemble their fathers so absolutely, that it's sometimes almost a joke.

Perhaps one ought also to know why man at bottom is so afraid of the mouse. In a way man is very right there, his fear is a pious fear. Logos must be afraid of Eros, because in Eros he meets his opposite. And when the opposites don't meet in exactly the right way, great harm is done. So man's fear works like an inward warning not to misuse woman's blind, unreasonable wish.

We must not forget to state that also for our symbolical mouse—as for all mice—there exists a cat. And this cat has destroyed many mice during the ages. When the mice grow too noisy and fresh, it's right that the cat should eat them. But no cat should be allowed to eat more mice than is good for its stomach. And yet one can see many a cat that swallows mice till it gets indigestion—or what's worse, grows so fat with mouse-food that it becomes clumsy and bad-humoured. The cat which eats the dream-mice is called Anima. Therefore it is very nice and a good sign indeed that in our dream it is the dreamer's wife who chases the mouse—and no cat anywhere near.[6]

---

[6] The Seminars index issued in 1939 reveals that the writer was Linda Fierz-David, and Barbara Hannah so confirmed (1980). She wrote *Der Liebestraum des Poliphilo* (Zurich, 1947), tr. Mary Hottinger as *The Dream of Poliphilo* (New York and London, 1950), with foreword by Jung.

Dr. Jung: This is excellent. I congratulate the unknown writer. That the anima is the cat that eats the dream-mice is decidedly a new consideration.

Mrs. Baynes: You admit the truth of that?

Dr. Jung: Well, I am so surprised that I have to think about it.

Mrs. Baynes: Why do you suppose the mouse that wrote the article remains hidden? She deserves some cheese, I think.

Dr. Jung: I am not so certain! Well, are there any questions concerning the mouse that has been so exhaustively dealt with? One would not have supposed that such a little thing could have caused such comments—caused the mountains to move, one might say.

Mrs. Sawyer: Why did the mouse go into the boys' room?

Dr. Jung: It is true, we didn't speak of that. Are there any suggestions?

Dr. Howells: A woman's reaction to the sexual problem is that it can get into the children.

Dr. Jung: That is obviously her idea in the dream—that the mouse could injure the boys. There is an accent on the boys. It might have been a girl—the Eros of the dreamer escaping into the girls' room, but it is the boys' room, which is quite remarkable. What would you assume?

Mrs. Sawyer: How old are the boys?

Dr. Jung: Eight or ten perhaps.

Mrs. Sigg: It seems as if when parents give too much or too little libido to a certain part of their lives, the children are inclined to act the other way.

Dr. Jung: But we are concerned with the question of this Eros which goes to the boys. When it goes to the girls' room, it is perfectly evident that it would be incestuous libido, and when it goes to the boys' what would it be?

Dr. Baynes: Homosexuality.

Dr. Jung: Yes, incestuous homosexuality. Such a repressed libido naturally reaches out for the next object—sometimes a daughter, sometimes a son. Of course it is quite possible that the boys are also symbolic, but here we are in a pretty delicate situation, because the boys are just as real to him as his wife. His wife is not symbolic, she is literal—we are clinging to the fact that the dream definitely means his wife. Then here are the boys, his sons, no getting away from it; we are forced to admit that the dream really means that Eros escapes and goes to the boys and might injure them. It is perfectly clear that if such a repressed Eros should take the form of an incestuous relationship, the fear of the wife would be justified. The question is, why the boys and not the girls?—and I should say the answer was that in a former dream, under similar circumstances, it was the daughter. The mouse—the libido—escaped to the daughter and brought about an incest situation. When I analysed that dream, it gave him a severe shock; he saw it immediately, and that has probably blocked the way. But the way to the boys is open. He is absolutely disinclined to assume that he could be homosexual, and therefore it is the loophole for the devil. When we say that such a thing is quite impossible, just there is the place where the devil can come in. Our dreamer does not dream of the possibility, it is too utterly unlikely, and that is just the way of the mouse—the invisible way. So the right instinct of the wife comes up and realizes the danger.

Mrs. Henley: Why doesn't he try to kill the mouse if he has that strong feeling of sexuality about it?

Dr. Jung: He did try, but how could he kill a mouse when he was holding half a bed in his hands? His wife had a stick, which is more practical, but his weapon was too unwieldy, it was not the right instrument. That, of course, has a psychological meaning too, which hangs together with the meaning of the crib, where he was a child and could not injure himself or anybody else and could play safely. Now the thing falls apart, and he still holds the means by which he has been fenced in. He uses the same means to kill the mouse, the same infantile measures, but naturally such a thing is much too clumsy.

Dr. Deady: Could it not mean that he puts the Eros into the boys, passes on the responsibility, and so it remains at a low level?

Dr. Jung: Well, there is nothing conscious, so in this case we could hardly talk of responsibility. If the homosexual incest should come off, if the mouse should ruin their lives, that would be in later life but not now. It would mean merely indulgence now, sentimental love for his boys, or an identification, which is simply homosexual incest. Then later on, the son would inherit the sins of the father and have to compensate for that inherited sin.

We are coming now to the next dream. As you probably have noticed in the course of this seminar, it is very often the unexpected that happens, and a certain characteristic which we have left entirely out of consideration is the next point to turn up, namely, the fertility, the generative principle, of the mouse. In the dreamer's conscious mind that characteristic was the most remote. Therefore this next dream dwells on that side.

Dream [26][7]

His wife is giving birth to three children at the same time—triplets (which is of course for a human being a somewhat unusual fertility), but the two first children are dead when born, only the third child remains alive. He says that this dream repeated itself in the same night, yet despite this fact, he cannot remember any other detail. He only remembers that he assisted at the birth, that the midwife was there, and that she took the two dead children away with her.

Associations: He says that triplets, or even twins, give him the impression of too much of a blessing all at once. It seems to him quite sufficient if only the third child remains alive. He dwells now upon these dead children and says that spiritualism and Yoga seem to him to be such unnecessary children which are removed by the midwife—associating me with the midwife notwithstanding my sex. The third child seems to him to be a development of the relation between man and his anima or soul. (That part remains dark.)

Now, in this dream we have an extraordinary fertility. For mice, who are accustomed to producing many more, it is very little, but for human beings it is remarkable. What would you say about this dream, aside from the fact of fertility?

Dr. Deady: Is there a psychological connection between his hygienic attitude, which is repressed sexuality, and his theosophical attitude of mind?

Dr. Jung: There is a close association between his vegetarian, so-called hygienic interests, and his Yoga and spiritual interests.

Dr. Deady: I thought of him as exercising in the crib as a part of his hygiene, while the mouse, sexuality, repressed by the hygiene, is the real thing he wants.

Dr. Jung: Naturally, spiritualism and Yoga kept his interests aloof from the realities of life, and also the food craze—eating lettuce, or locusts and wild honey, is a very good means of repressing sex.

[7] See below, 7 May 1930, p. 573, and 14 May 1930, p. 597, where this dream is shown to be no. 26 in the chronological sequence.

Dr. Deady: They are all methods of repression?

Dr. Jung: Yes, repressed below the bed, hidden away. He is performing hygienic stunts on top of the bed and the mouse is underneath. The more he practices those apotropaic cults, the more the crib breaks apart and the mouse escapes, so the whole thing has been in vain. Now, between that dream and this new one the mouse has obviously accomplished something. There were five days in between, and in those five days something has happened. The mouse has caused an extraordinary fertility—caused his wife to bring forth triplets. An astonishing fact. Naturally that has no reference to reality, she has never had triplets, she is quite normal in that respect, but she is clearly herself in the dream. We cannot say it means his anima, for instance. It is really his wife, and she is fertile. He is inclined to think of her as perfectly sterile and to take that fertility as his own, because there is nothing of the sort visible in his wife's case, and the only thing that has changed in the last six or seven years, he thinks, is that he has changed from his cult for spiritualism and Yoga to analysis. His wife has apparently not lived at all, and therefore he is impressed with her absolute stability, her static condition of doing nothing. But the dream says she is capable of producing triplets, which is a striking compensation. That was an amazing blow between the eyes. It was so unexpected that I didn't discuss that aspect with him. It would have passed him by, because he was so convinced that his wife could not be different from what he believed her to be, that it was perfectly futile to suggest it, so I left the thing practically in the condition in which he represented it—two still-born children in his development and one that lives on. That was the only point of view which was then accessible to him, I felt very clearly. The dream came as a tremendous surprise to me too, for I was so impressed by his description of his wife that I thought one hardly could assume triplets.

But, as subsequent events have shown, a tremendous change has taken place, most unexpected, so we do not know what the ultimate outcome will be. At all events, the change brought about in her was so remarkable that one could at least speak of twins. So I think it points to extraordinary happenings in the future—a case of psychological anticipation. It is as if I should prophesy that now his wife would bring forth, like old man Abraham and his wife Sarah; her womb was already dead within her and how would it be possible?—and he doubted the word of the Lord.[8] That would be this man's condition, and I found no heart to support the dream because I myself was quite doubtful whether this could be true. Yet according to all the rules of the game I should have said to him, "We cannot get away from the fact that your wife is your wife, and, sure enough, something is going to happen to her." As a matter of fact, two years later, it came off in a most astonishing way—I was surprised I must say. One always is making the mistake of not counting on miracles. But there are miracles only we don't believe in them. The fact that he associates the dead children with his occult investigations and the living child with his psychological interests is of value too; it is a parallel. It would mean that, just as he has made rather an astonishing transformation from spiritualism, through Yoga, to psychology, so in the same way his wife could change. You might criticize me here for taking his wife not as a reality but as a mere projection, as his own feminine unconscious, and to a certain extent you would be perfectly right. Here I break through the rules of the game, apparently. But we cannot make these rules so strict that when a husband or wife appears in a dream in their proper form, they are *nothing but* that husband or wife. It is also the *image* of that husband or wife. When he dreams of his wife, it is his wife, but also what his wife is to him—it is also an expression of himself.

We came here to a most important consideration: the fact that when one is analysing married people, or people who are in very close relationship even if it is not marriage, then one simply cannot deal with their psychology as a separate factor; it is as if one were dealing with two people, and it is exceedingly difficult to disentangle the individual belongings from the relationship. One finds invariably that the so-called individual psychology of such a case is only explicable under the assumption that another human being is functioning in that mind at the same time; in other words it is relationship psychology and not the psychology of an isolated human individual. It is even very difficult to isolate the individual parts from the related parts. So we can hardly consider such a dream as his own property; it would be his wife's just as much. His psychology is in her as hers is in him, and every dream that each one has is more or less an expression of that relatedness. It is as if

[8] Genesis 17:15-17; 18:10-15.

a human being in close psychological relationship had lost his two legs and two arms and one head, and now had four legs and four arms and two heads and two lives. The individual is permeated by the psychological sphere of the partner, and so the whole life problem, the whole spiritual problem, is directly interpenetrated. The main bulk of their psychological material is relationship material, it carries the imprint of two psychologies.

Therefore if I should say that the wife in this dream was *nothing but* his wife, it would not be exact. I would be neglecting the fact that she is an individual with her own belongings, and at the same time a piece of his psychology. For instance, when he speaks of spiritual interests, he could just as well say that his wife had first intimated that he should study Yoga or any other occult science, and that she further had led him on to analysis. That puts an entirely different face on the situation, but that is the psychological truth, because whatever he does is an expression of his relationship, to such an extent are we fused and interpenetrated. If he should assume that his wife means practically his own unconscious and that his studies are certain moods or phases of the longings of his unconscious, that would be right; but he does not realize this, and inasmuch as the unconscious is to him fertile, he naturally assumes that his unconscious has brought forth the triplets, or the interests, without seeing that his wife is fertile. Consciously his wife even repudiates those interests, but she has them all in her unconscious, and therefore she develops an unconscious resistance; she doesn't want to become aware of them. That a man should have those particular psychological interests is sometimes loathsome to a certain type of woman. She is really tremendously interested, but for certain reasons she represses it. But in the case of marriage things are so entangled that one could just as well say that his wife had led him to those interests, which is practically what the dream says.

Such a dream is only understandable when you take it as the expression of a relationship. It is as if he and his wife had come together in the night and concocted a dream, issuing a statement that was equally true for either side. He is perfectly satisfied with having brought forth so many interests, and she is perfectly satisfied that she has brought forth triplets. But her role is for the time being overshadowed. She is entirely unconscious of the fact that she is living in these interests and fertile within. That she represses these things may be because of a superior unconscious that is responsible for extraordinary tricks. We know by experience that when we want a thing consciously we kill it, but when we are perfectly unconscious, it comes through. It is as though we were blotting a thing out by staring at it or desiring it, but apparently if we fear it it will be magically brought about. Therefore people say one only needs to be afraid of things and they happen. The other fellow does it, the most amazing things can be insinuated—not only working for good, but also for evil. So the evil of which we are unconscious in ourselves will be insinuated into the surroundings and there it will work. We can produce just as many evil effects as good effects. Therefore we have to get away from it, yet it is so vast and contains so many hellish possibilities that we can hardly hope to exhaust that ocean of unconsciousness.

In this case, how could the dreamer know that his wife is only repressing her interests in these things and that there may be a superior aim in that repression. It is a tremendous game, an amazing plot, so when we discover a few threads, they are just threads; but if we could pull at them, we might pull out an extraordinary web with an extraordinary pattern on it. We cannot do it however, It is too superhumanly clever.

Now, that is what I have to say about this dream. Are there no questions? I am perfectly aware that it is a very difficult thought, this interpenetration through *participation mystique*. I understand that you cannot perhaps swallow it right away, but it is an hypothesis without which it is simply impossible to explain certain things, and according to my experience, a vast majority of the dreams of married people are of this kind. Also, of course, people who are not married but who are related to somebody. Or even if they are not closely related to anybody, they are still interpenetrated by external factors. For instance, it is quite possible in the case of a person living in a hotel that in the next room lives somebody with a peculiar kind of psychology, and a certain amount of that filters through the walls into his dreams. I know a man who had a terrible murder and suicide dream when sleeping in a certain room, and it turned out that he had got into the room where that happened, so he was penetrated by the atmosphere. We can get infected in the same way where living people are concerned. A mental contagion is amazingly strong; we hate the idea and repress it as well as we can. We like the idea that we are isolated within ourselves, that there is nobody on our wires, that nobody can tamper with our directions and decisions. But as a matter of fact there are certain doors which are open, and certain things can enter and disturb us, even where there is nothing which you could call a close relationship.

It is a sort of atmospheric thing in many cases, and it is not only peculiar to man. Animals also can be interpenetrated, they some- times behave according to men's psychology because of that inter- penetration, and if we do not admit such things, then we are the victims. Also there are people who take on evil animal smells; they smell like a zoo, so that I have to open the windows. That is no joke. I had a case once of a patient who developed a smell, not a real one, but I have an extra sense like the primitive medicine man who smells snakes. So I smelled carrion, and it got to such a point that I could not have her in my study at all. Fortunately it was warm weather, so I could take her to my garden house where there was a draft, for it almost made me sick. One day I had dismissed that woman, and in came another case, a very intuitive lady. She had not seen the woman leave, did not know her, and knew nothing about her. As she entered the room, she took her parasol and began to fan vigorously, saying, "Such bad air in here!" I said, "But all the windows are open, it cannot be stuffy," and she said, "You must have had a terrible case here!"—so I knew that she had smelt it too. The patient herself didn't know it, but soon after she had a dream in which the difficulty was brought up, and then we could solve it and the smell went away. Now it is quite possible that animals smell this. My own sense has degenerated; it is awfully weak in comparison with that of a dog, but I am quite certain that animals are able to smell those things. With us, it is a sense in between intuition, and one doesn't know whether it is something physical or something psychological, but there are surely cases where, under the influence of complexes, people develop evil smells. Are there any questions concerning this particular problem?

Dr. Baynes: There is one theoretical question that I should like to put, in reference to taking the wife on the subjective or objective plane. Would you not in practice interpret the wife here as rep- resenting that problem which held him up and brought him to analysis, with all the fertile results which have flowed from it, rather than taking her as the actual wife, insofar as you did not know at that time that the wife was herself functioning in a fertile way?

Dr. Jung: At that time I took it only subjectively, because the objective side of the dream would not have entered his mind. It would be too upsetting. You see, the comprehension of a living *participation mystique* necessitates a preparation, and we had had only about fifteen or sixteen dreams. That is not much, so it was best to wait for a later opportunity. At a later stage, I would say that we must now be accurate, and could then show him what had occurred, that his wife in the dream really meant his wife and she was fertile, and that she was mixed up with his progression from spiritualism and Yoga to analysis. Therefore, he must not believe that she is absolutely sterile.

Dr. Baynes: Then you would give a subjective provisional interpretation for the time being?

Dr. Jung: Yes. At this time, practically in the beginning of his analysis, he was impressed by it, yet he is of a very cautious and careful mind, and you will see from his later dreams that he gets the whole thing in the intellectual sphere, not trusting himself entirely. He thinks it is a very interesting sort of philosophy, but the question is, how far does it apply to reality? We must be exceedingly careful to make sure upon what ground the patient is standing, and it was then a very thin edge. He did not have the real feeling; it did not go deep under his skin. So I left it to his interpretation that the still-born children are his past interests, and that the other now lives and is helpful to him, and at a later opportunity all the other considerations will come in. It is enough, it is helpful. As a matter of fact it took him a long time before he could see the peculiar fact of interpenetration, and I am quite certain that if I gave him that dream now and asked him the meaning, he would interpret it in the same old way.

Mrs. Crowley: Would you say that the closer the relationship was, the closer would be the identity in the unconscious? It really reflects her almost more than him.

Dr. Jung: No, it would reflect his point of view just as much. I should say that this is a particularly strong unconscious relationship. It would be less strong in a couple where the conscious was more closely related. There is more distance between people who are consciously connected than between people who are unconsciously connected. In this marriage, where so much is unconscious, there is very strong interpenetration. In a case where there is an enormous interpenetration, people have an enormous need to mark the difference. I remember such a marriage, and a friend of mine made the remark that there were just twenty degrees difference between them. In summer when it was frightfully hot, he was sitting at the fire, and she was sitting at the window fanning herself. She loved sugar and he hated it. She loved brilliantly lit rooms and he liked dark rooms—all such differences that served the purpose of daily nagging because of their extraordinary *participation mystique*. He was a highly intellectual man and she was his housekeeper, an awfully stupid woman, silly and ugly, and the devil knows why he married her. She was the mouse who was formerly in the kitchen— the highly intellectual man and his cook. There was an unusual *participation mystique*, yet in the conscious there were miles of hopeless distance between them. No coming together at all.

Mrs. Henley: In the case of unconscious interpenetration, do people take on new relationships if there is a divorce?

Dr. Jung: It may cause extraordinary situations, great disturbances. If such a *participation mystique* is destroyed, it leaves an open wound, and most probably the same thing will happen again.

Mrs. Henley: Unfailingly?

Dr. Jung: Almost, because you are there. Whatever condition you create, you will create again. You do not change if you are a being without equilibrium; it doesn't matter where you are. In the long run, when a thing is unconscious, always the same pattern must be lived through; the unconscious things come through. But in a second marriage there might be the very great difference that this *participation mystique* had become conscious. When one is conscious, something can be done with one's little bit of personal will. But the unconscious things are carried out by seven devils.

Mrs. Crowley: What happens if that *participation mystique* is assimilated in consciousness by one and not the other?

Dr. Jung: That is a difficult problem which one often meets in analysis. Such a case creates a new potential. The one who becomes conscious says,"I can't stand this any longer. You must come along and get conscious too." Then there is also the possibility that something might happen even if only one of them is conscious, such as is happening to the wife of the dreamer. All the time she is in analysis too.

SUMMER TERM

May / June 1930

LECTURE I

7 May 1930

Dr. Jung:

We are to hear a report today about the problems of our dreamer, how they developed from the beginning up to the point where we left off in our last seminar.

Dr. Howells' Report

This is in no way a synopsis of the dreams that have been analysed in the seminar, but an attempt to give a glimpse of the patient and his unconscious, so that those who have just come, and have not had time to read the notes on the past lectures, can get a little idea of the patient who consented to give his dreams for analysis in the seminar.

The man is a European. He is not a patient, in that he is not ill nor even neurotic to any extent. He comes to analysis largely because he is dissatisfied—a bit surfeited with life, sex, and pseudo-philosophy—and like all surfeited people, he is starved. He is a wealthy retired business man, about forty-seven years of age. He is married and has four children.

To some it may be interesting to know that he classifies as a thinking-sensation introvert.[1] His life up to now has given him little chance to indulge any irrationality, so one might call him a hard-boiled business man, to whom the material aspect of life has been paramount. He has no real relationship with his wife, and probably with no one, yet he is a good collective sort, and very respectable, in the conventional sense of the word.

It must be understood by those reading the notes for the first time that in no case does that patient receive in his analytical hours half of what we do here. He is not ready for it, and to tell him as much as is given us would only enhance the man's tendency to continue trying to accomplish

---

[1] For the introverted type in Jung's classification, see *Psychological Types* (1921), CW 6, pars. 620-671, esp. par. 668, where he posits a situation in which *thinking* is the superior or principal function and *sensation* the secondary or auxiliary function. Cf. above, 13 Mar. 1929, n. 1.

his being by his thinking. It would also rather anticipate his analysis, and so rob it of that emotional attribute without which the process is void.

In all, twenty-four dreams have been analysed.[2] For the purpose of getting at them, I have divided them into three groups: the first, the second to the seventeenth, and the seventeenth to the twenty-fourth. This division is not entirely arbitrary, but as the patient might himself see them in retrospect.

The first dream rather characteristically unfolds his whole problem. This is not an accident, for in a strange way the unconscious cries out for recognition when it has long been stifled and abused by the demands of collective life. The dream, taken objectively, shows the man with no working relationship to his wife, and with a bondage to the conventionalities of life. Taken subjectively, it means no understanding of himself. He is so unconscious that, to himself, he is the correct and perfect gentleman. The shadow man, or the dark side of his own nature, has never been recognized. He is so one with his persona—that mask which he presents to life—that one might easily wager, especially since he is an introvert, that he is scarcely aware that he does consort with prostitutes and do other unseemly things. Besides this unawareness of the nether man, there is his anima, a little ill child of two years. I shall try to follow her through this abstract, for her growth and change is very interesting, and reveals the simultaneous growth and change of the man himself, which we can't witness, and which Dr. Jung tells us little or nothing about.

Now we approach the second division, the second to the seventeenth dream, which represents three and a half months of analysis. They are vivid pictures of what the average person goes through in analysis, except that since the patient's life has been lived in the midst of an old culture and the man has had great advantages, his dreams betray more colour and richer allusion than the dreams of those born in a newer civilization. Also, these very factors that have enriched his life have also made for an intense conflict, and hence lend to the dramatic quality of his dreams. This is best illustrated in the nineteenth dream,[3] where we see in his unconscious the struggle between the Christian and Islamic religions, by both of which he has been influenced. So, like all of us, what is his asset in life is also his hindrance.

In the course of the first seventeen dreams, we find the man doing what all of us tend to do—he swings from high to low, from a state of resoluteness to irresoluteness, from great universal problems to personal ones. There is a rhythm in them—a progression and regression. In fact, distinct up and down movements can be seen.

[2] If the dream of the triplets (now no. 26) is included, Jung has analysed 25 dreams.

[3] In the present enumeration, this is dream no. 20.

The second dream takes up the main issue of the introductory one almost as if the unconscious were saying: "Sir, you may not realize this, but your anima is more than an ill child of two years, she is a tailoress, ill with tuberculosis, and she lives in squalor and darkness." It isn't a very pleasant picture that this prosperous man of business, this model husband and fine citizen, has this kind of woman as a guardian to his unconscious.

Then the unconscious, having rubbed it in a bit, swings to its merciful aspect, and in the third dream shows him a way—that his life is not to go on like a machine, that it is to follow an individual path along which there are no glaring signposts and no traditional rules of conduct. It is a new view of life to him—no methods, no precepts, but a slow rather blind groping. Still, the unconscious says there is a way, a definite pattern, and as if to emphasize it more, a new picture is flashed from the dream world, in which all his scattered tendencies, which I suppose are largely his feeling relationships, are shown as chickens escaping in all directions, just as chickens always do. But the dream suggests also that they can be put into one pot, and go towards the making of a unified individual.

The next movement (the fifth, sixth, and seventh dreams) is a distinct regression, yet it is probably not as apparent to the patient as to one looking at his unconscious material as a whole. His unconscious delays him, puts obstacles in his way by suggesting magical cures, shows him that he is not giving his undivided attention to his analysis, and again lures him with the way most enticing to a rational temperament—that is, the mechanistic way. Machines of one sort and another and the mechanistic attitude appear rather often.

So, once again his unconscious suggests the way that has already failed, the mechanistic way of dealing with his love life, just as if it were a monthly bank balance, or a clock that wants winding on Saturday nights. He contemplates it all, no way out appears. Then the unconscious throws him back years farther in his life and into the very crux of the whole problem— that he has never lived his own feeling life. Why should he? His father was a minister—he carried the responsibility for all that sort of thing. Traditional religion, from the Protestant point of view, is largely a feeling matter. The patient was very proud of his father, and still probably had him put away in a pigeon-hole, automatically trusting all the feeling side of his own nature to this erstwhile preacher father. So naturally, the patient goes scot free of taking any responsibility for his Eros. It is exactly the same thing expressed by pious Christians when they say: "Christ died for me."

This is perhaps the most revealing dream of the whole series, and also the most ghastly, for here is our patient, who is forty-seven years old, with no decent feeling development because his father carried that end of life in his profession; and so here is the son at mid-life, fated to bear that subtle and serious lack of facing the responsibility for his own complete life. He had tremendously admired his father, who undoubtedly was an exemplary sort, and yet even having a parson father does not release one from taking the responsibility for one's own complete development.

In contrast to this sudden revelation of the deep-seatedness of his problem, the unconscious, in a merciful mood, if one can say it has moods, gives him a visitation from a "Puer Aeternus," something new, strong, and vital. But this is more than the man can assimilate. His dream anticipates him far too much, for immediately he swings downward again, and he is forced to look at further dark possibilities within himself, worse than the mechanistic attitude of adjusting his love life, and worse than living his feeling nature provisionally in his parson father. Now he has to see with his own eyes the abnormality of his sexuality, even to the extent of the possibility of incestuous relations with his daughter. This shows that this man must still treasure his old conception of himself as a correct and respectable gentleman. Otherwise the unconscious would not say to him, "You are a potential sexual criminal, you might even rape your own little daughter." He does not fully comprehend the enormity of his potential criminality. The full realization would probably only come in retrospect as he can view it from the standpoint of greater maturity.

Directly following this, the dreamer makes one more trick attempt to accomplish his development. He goes to a shrine, a "mansion of the superman," but he goes as a monkey swinging from tree to tree, and so avoiding dust and heat and fatigue. It is not altogether unique, for most of us do evasive tricks at some stage in analysis.

But from now on, after the seventeenth dream, his unconscious material changes. There are no more short cuts, and since the trick method is stopped, we may assume that the patient is on his way to individuation. However, he has not yet in any tangible way faced the matter of his relationship to his wife. One might expect him to, and yet he does not. It is difficult to keep in mind that this patient has been in analysis seven months, and yet outwardly he has done nothing. Dr. Jung remarked that one wonders if he really can—possibly he has in his psyche a detached and isolated area that cannot be integrated.

Now the new series of dreams begins, which marks the man's steady onward progress. The patient finds that within himself he has the person who can put his life in order. This is the first hint from the unconscious that he himself must do the work—not the great doctor—he must father his own life. So again we expect the man to face his relationship with his wife, but he does not. He plunges into that dream that I referred to early in the paper, which showed the conflict of the two great religions, Christianity and Mohammedanism. But, after all, this is only the objective conflict, for the symbols of these two religions—the cross and the crescent—

must also be interpreted subjectively. The real conflict in the man is not the opposing religions but the opposing principles of his own nature—the male and the female principles—for which these symbols stand. It is the Logos versus the Eros of his own nature.

After this dream comes a dramatic and very beautiful one [21]. I quote it verbatim, because it shows so well what Dr. Jung has emphasized—that analysis, if pursued long enough, takes one from the petty and personal problems into great universal ones.

"I see a vast, grey plain approaching me. As it comes close the monotonous grey dissolves into multicoloured stripes of differing widths. They move in a peculiar way through each other, uniting and separating. And then I see that many people are occupied with these stripes, shaping them and weaving them. The work is hampered through pressure that comes from other stripes. So, because of the interference, the activity of the people is hindered, and the results are quite different from the original intention, and I say to myself 'Cause and effect.' Then I try to help them, and in working on them I become aware that they, the stripes, are nothing but the surface of a vast mass, like a huge river flowing in a given direction, and the movement is due to the river flowing along like a lava stream, the stripes coming up and disappearing again. At the same time I become aware that it is all transparent and luminous, that not only the mass but the atmosphere and the people and myself are all permeated with something that is like a fluid light, and I know that this has a tremendous influence on everything that it permeates. I say to myself, 'The fate of man, the fate of people, the fate of worlds,' yet still I remain preoccupied with shaping my own stripe."

This dream must needs relax him, give him a chance to rest. One can almost feel the poor devil take a deep breath.

After such a vision of the universal principles of life, one feels that according to the ebb and flow af things the patient may drop into a psychological abyss, but the next move of his unconscious, while it does not keep him on the heights of a cosmic view, which would not be good for him, lest he should identify himself with cosmic principles, brings him with a thud into the realm of reality, and he finds himself manipulating a ball-and-socket joint. It's form takes one back to the third dream, where a steamroller made a pattern of a definite form, suggesting a mandala or a rhythmic centred design. But here there is a vast difference, for the ball-and-socket joint not only suggests something in three dimensions, which the mandala pattern did not, but it suggests the possibility of rotating—in other words, that the individual will get at, in his development, more than one side of himself. Formerly he has accomplished his life by his thinking. Now he is to accomplish it also by his feeling, and so the ball-and-socket suggests that all sides of his nature will be developed. It is a neat way of presenting to a stern materialistic man that one's being is not accomplished on a flat surface—that is, by thinking alone.

So we have come with the dreamer through the infinitely personal to a universal view of life, and to a whole attitude in regard to himself, but he apparently does not integrate it, for at the next turn his unconscious hurls him back into a church scene of his childhood, and there a queer hermaphroditic figure sings some familiar Christmas hymn but sings it in the wrong tune. This creature is his anima—she who at first was an ill child, then the wretched tuberculous tailoress, then a little girl gathering blighted fruit under a cherry tree, and here she is a weird mixed figure, not entirely woman, and not man. This is an uncanny figure. It suggests all sorts of things, but especially that the patient is still so identified with his persona, or his correct collective self—the man the world sees—that he still does not recognize his other half—his shadow—so here we find the shadow in the form of a Jew, united with the woman or anima figure under the guise of one person. Also, in as far as the patient is unrelated, he is immature, and so his anima appears immature—not a real woman. Hence we can assume that the patient is not a real man, or one might more kindly say he is effeminate, because he does not possess his feeling, but rather is possessed by it. It is like the tail wagging the dog, instead of the dog wagging the tail.

This dream closely links up with the eleventh, the one that I alluded to in which the dreamer's whole problem seems to go back to his parson father, who lived, at least professionally, the feeling life for his son. Here the patient is returned to the church, which represents a feeling connection to the twelfth year of his life, and he is reminded that he must notice that thing in himself that sings a tune not in accordance with what he himself sings. This strange creature says: "Listen to me, I'm not singing the sort of thing you are familiar with. I'm introducing you to something else, I am a new voice."

Following this comes an apparent regression, and yet it illustrates that no regression is as much a one as it seems, just as a progression is not always as much as it seems.

Now he returns to the humdrum of his own immediate problem. He is reminded again, through his unconscious, that it is necessary for him actually to face his sexual problem. This is presented to him as a mouse running from underneath a crib in which he is lying doing gymnastics, while his wife lies on a mattress on the floor, watching him. The patient, in giving his associations, though he is a sound thinking type, gets all mixed up, and even here, after a long analysis, he contradicts the very text of his dream and says that his wife is in the crib, and that the mouse, though it runs from underneath his bed, represents *her* sexuality. This simply shows how hard it is, even when one tries to keep mindful of one's own problem, not to see it as some one's else. It shows how frail is one's own psychological integrity.

However, even though he might fail to see his mistake, and continue to project his own difficulty onto his wife, the next dream corrects his error, for it states that his wife has given birth to triplets, and that he himself assisted the midwife. This dream has a twofold aspect. It is not only a prophecy of his wife's fertility, figuratively speaking, but it has a subjective meaning. For taking the wife as the anima figure, and not his actual wife, but rather the *wife in him*, it means that something is functioning in him that has the possibility of a living being. The dream not only prophesies the fertility and creativeness of his relationship to his wife, but more than that, it says that through rapport with the wife *in him* he can have a living child.

It is a long step from where the man began where his relationship with his unconscious was represented by an ill child of two years, then a poor tuberculous woman, then a little girl gathering unripe fruit, then a hermaphroditic creature singing the wrong tune, to *his wife*, who can give birth to triplets.

Dr. Jung: Thank you for your interesting report. I hope the new members got a certain idea of what we have been doing. Now we will continue. But I must first explain that the dream about our patient's wife giving birth to triplets, which Dr. Howells just mentioned, does not follow immediately after the one about the mouse. I brought it in then because it confirmed the famous paper in which the mouse was taken as a fertility symbol: triplets would be nothing for mice, but for a woman a great feat. The sequence in exact order, then, is first the dream of the hermaphrodite, then the mouse, then the dream which I am about to read to you, and then follows the dream of the triplets.

The hermaphrodite dream was a matter of religious considerations and symbolism in connection with his immediate problem, which was, as you know, that he had no personal relation with his wife. Then in the course of the analysis religious and philosophical problems have turned up. Dr. Howells has just quoted that extraordinary, almost cosmic dream—cosmic dreams are always philosophical in character—and then came the specifically Christian dream which brought him back into the church of his youth. The hermaphrodite is a very interesting religious symbol which we did not elucidate very satisfactorily because it is still a twilight figure. I don't know in how far you are aware of the very great role the

573

hermaphrodite figure played in the past, beginning with the primordial figures in Plato. It appeared in the Eleusinian mysteries, for instance, and in the mysteries of the Templars,[4] as we know from tombstones that have been found, and in the so-called Hermetic philosophy of the Middle Ages, where the idea of the *daimon* also played a considerable role.

After the dream of the hermaphrodite, which was definitely an attempt to introduce a new element into his religious point of view, came the dream with the mouse in it, in which the fact was shown that this time the mouse had escaped, meaning that hidden instinct had escaped, and this, according to the context, had a sexual connotation. It is no longer under control, no longer hidden under the bed, which has broken asunder on account of the dreamer's violent exercises—referring to his violent thinking in analysis. This fact would prove that now something is going to happen; something is out of his hands, and we may assume that it will now develop. This is obviously the effect of the dream before, in which the old religious point of view, which proved to be a hindrance, has been abolished to a certain extent through the introduction of an entirely new element. And it is on account of the new element that the sex instinct has been freed. Now comes the new dream which I did not mention before.

Dream [25]

He saw a man dropping from a sort of aeroplane. That was not quite clear, it was something between an airship and an aeroplane, it looked rather strange; it was a yellow triangular shape which seemed to be filled with gas, and it was not very far from the ground—only a bit higher than a house. The man dropped from it by means of a parachute into a meadow in the immediate neighbourhood of the dreamer's house. He went there at once and saw that the man got up rather slowly and painfully and was trying to move his right hand, which seemed to be injured. It began to swell at the joint and looked as if it might be broken. The dreamer asked him if he needed something to bandage it, but the man himself

---

[4] The Knights Templars were a religious order, fl. c. 1113-1314, contemporary with the Crusades.

opened a parcel that he carried and took out some stuff to bind it up. He obviously tried to help himself.

Associations: The dreamer is immediately struck by the peculiar look of the aeroplane and says that it is a symbol of the Trinity, the symbol of the Christian God. I have often seen that symbol in churches—a golden triangle somewhere above in the supposed heavens; sometimes the ceilings of old churches are painted blue and decorated with stars, in the midst of which the triangle is floating. He says that he was impressed with the fact that the man should try to drop from the aeroplane at such a short distance from the ground, for the parachute would not have time to open properly and he would probably injure himself by striking the earth too quickly. Despite that fact, the man came down on his feet, and he remarks about this that there is a proverbial expression which one applies to certain people: "He always falls on his feet like a cat." If you throw a cat out of the window, no matter how high, it always drops on its feet, and so one says of certain people that no matter how adverse their situation may be, whether they are bankrupt or morally injured, they always fall on their feet, they are never in a very bad plight. Yet the drop from the aeroplane was rather imprudent, and naturally the man was injured. Our patient says that he was probably somewhat stunned by the shock and so had some trouble in getting up—he got up rather slowly and painfully.

About the *injury to the right hand* he says that to him the right hand always means energy, the activity of man, his efficiency in material and practical life.

Then the dreamer himself makes an attempt at the interpretation of the dream, and I give you this with his associations, because the further people advance in the knowledge of dreams, the more they quite instinctively make attempts at their interpretation; it becomes impossible to think of certain dream symbols without thinking at once of what they probably mean. That attempt is not to be rejected, it should be considered as part of the associative material, though it must not be taken too seriously because it is *only* a part; it might be true, but we have to wait till we have seen all the material.

He says, then, that it seems to be a pretty dangerous enterprise to jump down from the Trinity—to jump down even with particular measures of precaution from the heights of the Christian religion. And then he says. "The Christian religion—or at least the concept of the Trinity, which is not just the same—looks almost as if, when

575

one jumps down from that level, one might become quite useless in practical life" (quite an amazing conclusion!). "At all events one has to carry some stuff so that in case of injury it can be treated properly and relations with external life taken up as soon as possible. While I am thinking about what the dream could possibly mean, suddenly it is as if I were hearing some verses in English." He tried to think where they came from, and he remembered that they were by the poet Lowell. Now I must confess that I do not know that poet, who is an American, it seems, and you will be astonished to hear that he found those verses in an American finance paper. I was quite impressed with the fact and thought, Well, well! they must propagate good literature at the same time! Now listen to them:

New occasions teach new duties: Time makes ancient good uncouth;
They must upward still, and onward, who would keep abreast of
    Truth;
Lo, before us gleam her camp-fires! We ourselves must Pilgrims be,
Launch our Mayflower, and steer boldly through the desperate winter
    sea,
Nor attempt the Future's portal with the past's blood-rusted key.[5]

How that might apply to some financial scheme I don't know, but with some effort of the imagination one can take it as a generally valid remark about human psychology. At all events these verses seem to have stuck in his mind as pretty good human wisdom and as being somehow connected with the meaning of the dream, and if you go through them carefully you will see that they really do apply to the last dreams in rather an obvious way. Referring to the old Christianity, there is a new truth ahead and we ought to keep abreast of it. "New occasions teach new duties"—we are sort of pilgrims and we launch our Mayflower and steer boldly, appealing to courage, and should not make the foolish attempt of trying the future's portals with the key of the past—we should not try to understand new concepts or new visions with the key of the old concept. And the "blood-rust"—well, it is a funny thing that our great philosophical concepts are rather blood-stained. To take a step ahead out of the great unconsciousness has always cost humanity a great deal of blood. The Inquisition[6] in Spain cost about

[5] The American poet James Russell Lowell (1819-1891), "The Present Crisis" (1845), in the Oxford edn. of *The Poems* (1917), p. 98.
[6] *Sems.*: "Reformation."

one hundred thousand lives, roasted at stakes, and we don't know how many have perished in the early Roman persecutions, to speak of those instances only.

This dream is not very difficult. It is a continuation of the religious theme, and it is one of the first dreams really where the patient's associations are highly satisfactory and his attempt at interpretation is quite good. The introduction of the new element in the old dream is obviously working now. One could say that the escape of the mouse had the effect that he returns to the earth, for the man dropping from the aeroplane is a mere reflex of his own inner experience—that he suddenly comes down from the Christian elevation, leaves that standpoint of the aeroplane above and comes down to earth with rather a shock. Now, it is interesting to me, and perhaps you also noticed it, that he insists upon the Trinity and that he has some misgivings about identifying the Trinity with the Christian religion. That seems a bit involved, he feels a doubt. You see, when such a thing occurs in a dream, it is like a sort of knot. Say a patient dreams of a door that is not very interesting, it doesn't seem to be very important or involved, but when he nags one about it, knocks at that door, asks why there should be a door, is it really a door, then one knows that there is something underneath, a knot. There may be several elements—a dark and tangled spot—so one had better have a good look at it, there may be something in it. Here he makes such a knot of that triangle. Whether it is connected with religion or not is indifferent to us, we are perfectly satisfied as long as he is trying to get away from the Church standpoint. Yet he makes a knot of it; he tries to make a certain difference between Christianity and the Trinity. But that need not be taken literally, it only means that in the Trinity there is something which is not clear. Of course, we know that it is the Christian formula for the supreme value, the supreme idea, the supreme motive, but the fact that the supreme value should be symbolized as a Trinity, as being three in one, is in itself mysterious. It has always shocked me. Now why should he speak of that?

Mrs. Crowley: Would it be a question of his own effort towards integration? It might apply to his three functions, indicating that the fourth, his feeling, was still missing.

Dr. Jung: You are on the right track, but that Trinity concept is extremely involved. When we speak of it, we naturally mean the triune God, somewhere in space, or transcendent perhaps, not even in space, at all events something quite definitely different from ourselves, and one wonders why that God should consist of three. Of course, that is by no means a Christian invention, the idea of the Trinity is well known in other religions in the East and even in primitive religions. The triune god is to be found practically all over the world; it is an age-old principle. And since we are accustomed to think of God as utterly different from ourselves, when we find such a triangle somewhere out in space we do not think of identifying with it. Now, you have heard in the dream of the hermaphrodite that a new idea has been introduced. One could say that instead of the church standpoint the dreamer got at least a hint of a divine being of an hermaphroditic nature, which appears in a disturbing inacceptable form, really a most disreputable character, and yet quite clearly made up from his own material. We asked ourselves then whether we were quite justified in assuming that such an ugly, unfavourable thing could be called by a divine name, but in the end we came to the conclusion that this figure must be some sort of demon or god, perhaps a personal demon, at least something to which we could give the attribute divine. Of course, as you have understood, it would not be in the traditional sense divine—that would mean something very high or valuable or wonderful—but in the ancient sense of the word, where it has the quality of the *tremendum* or *daimon*; or, in a still more primitive sense, of the mana figure, a figure that has prestige or influence and can be anything, good or bad, white or black, helpful or disastrous, at all events indifferent as to moral or aesthetic qualities— yet *efficient*.

Now, that element was introduced in his former dream, and it is that which has made him drop down from the Trinity. The Trinity, of course, is of an entirely different nature from that hermaphroditic being. It is abstract, detached from man, given an independent existence, and projected to the ends of the world. But even such a thing is a human projection, and it must have started somewhere in human psychology. We can say—trying to make a very careful and cautious formula—that it has represented an idea of the highest value, the highest meaning, the highest influence, the greatest energy, really the best thing we knew of. It was an absolutely valid guiding principle in our own psychology, represented in a very abstract way as a triangle. But naturally, the more these things were symbolized in such abstract forms, the more those forms would in the end necessarily lose their power through becoming detached. They became too dogmatic or philosophic, and through abstraction they lost their influence. And that is the fate of the Christian triangle; it is now too far away from man. Peculiarly enough, that has been its fate in the primitive religions also. There are several religions where one finds such trinities, in one or two cases symbolizing really high and spiritual gods. One finds it among the Bataks,[7] for instance; they recognize the existence of such a trinity but they say it is far away, they don't know whether he or they are concerned with them any longer, so they much prefer to look for immediate necessities from ghosts and sorcerers and witches because that is more practical. So these abstract gods usually play a very faint and insignificant role in primitive religions, while ghosts and devils play an exceedingly important role, and something of the same kind has happened to us. This abstract form of spiritual god or trinity has become intangible and inefficient, and in so far as we still cling to it we simply are not upon the ground. One cannot put it into real practice. Nobody on such a standpoint can really live the absolutely spiritual content of Christianity. He simply makes a compromise and lies to himself; he doesn't give up his worldly life but keeps something in himself aloof from life by the aid of that spiritual principle. Our dreamer clung to the aeroplane in order that it might carry him over the swamps, he wanted to avoid getting his hands or feet dirty. But that is just the hellish compromise, and they don't keep clean in spite of the fact.

Now, the idea of the Trinity is a symbol, not a sign—I emphasize that fact. That is to say, it is a form, a cipher, an analogy, an image, which more or less approaches the unknown thing which is intuited or felt; and it is not formulated in a more accurate way simply because one is unable to express it better. This fact comes from a condition which is characteristic of all symbols, namely, that the kernel, the real nucleus, the basic substance of symbols, consists of unconscious contents that make themselves felt, yet the conscious is unable to grasp their meaning—unable to analyse, to dissect them, to grasp their substance. They are felt as a dim but at the same time a very powerful presence. People feel that they should give a name to that incomprehensible presence, and therefore they

[7] A people of Sumatra (Indonesia), whose religion Jung discussed first in "The Theory of Psychoanalysis" (1912), CW 4, par. 512, and in several later works. His source was J. G. Warneck, *Die Religion der Batak* (Leipzig, 1909).

use a symbol. The symbol in itself, as a name, is a perfect futility, yet inasmuch as it designates the invisible presence it is exeedingly powerful. It is, then, an approximate designation of an invisible and powerful fact that influences man from the unconscious sphere. If it had come from the conscious sphere, it would have been analysed and understood, and it would have lost its fascination right away. But inasmuch as it is a fact from the unconscious which *cannot* be dissected by the conscious, it therefore remains an explicit and efficient factor with a definite function.

In this case, the function is the very doubtful one indicated in the dream; the Trinity is here said to be an aeroplane, that is, a very modern contrivance for carrying people and goods from place to place in a particular way, not touching the earth but going through the air. It is a machine, and you remember that I have often emphasized the fact that a symbol functions like a machine in our psychology. Not long ago I came across a book about Oriental religions by a German,[8] who speaks, among other things, of the influence of Yoga and of the forms of the sacred images in India, and I think I told you that he calls the *yantras* machines; he holds that they function exactly like machines because they are symbols, symbols being a means of transforming energy. You see, the dream has the same view, it represents the Trinity as a flying machine which lifts people up and carries them. That is the function of the symbol and its value to man. If he could not designate the thing, it would function without him, it would function by itself. I mean, it could seize upon a man, suddenly land on him, like Yahweh in the Old Testament—it took the prophet by the neck and forced him to his will. Without the symbol the divine factor cannot be invoked and worshipped. We use it as a sort of magic means to force the gods; in calling them by the right name, we make them come, we reach their ear and we influence them. So in antiquity it was exceedingly important to know the right name of the god, the

[8] Heinrich Zimmer (1890-1943), German Indologist, formerly at Heidelberg. Jung and Zimmer first met in 1932 and subsequently became close friends through their common participation in the Eranos conferences. Zimmer died in New York three years after going to the United States as a refugee from the Nazi regime. In Zimmer's first book, *Kunstform und Yoga im indischen Kultbild* (Berlin, 1926; 2nd edn., Frankfurt a.M., 1976, p. 46) he characterized the yantra as a tool (*Werkzeug*), device (*Apparat*), or mechanism (*Mechanismus*), and he elucidated the idea of yantra as machine in his posthumous *Myths and Symbols in Indian Art and Civilization*, ed. Joseph Campbell (New York, 1946), p. 141.

secret, sacred name that the god should be called by in order to have his ear. The true symbol, the true expression of the psychological fact, has that peculiar effect on the unconscious factor that is somehow brought about by giving it the right name.

It is as if you wanted to recall very clearly the image of someone who was absent, either to yourself or to an audience: you imitate that person, how he speaks, how he laughs, what he says, or you call his name, and by that means you evoke his image. By the same method this unconscious factor can be invoked, provided you give it the right name. We ought therefore to have symbols in order to control the unconscious factors. Otherwise they are absolutely beyond our control and we are their victims, and whether their influence is beneficial or disastrous remains in their hands. So it always has been of the utmost importance for man to have a certain magic control of the gods. You are probably rather shocked at the idea, because the Christian always assumes that we cannot force God, that we depend entirely upon his grace, but the sacraments in the Catholic Church are magic devices, magic methods, of forcing the grace of God—like the marriage or baptism ceremony, for instance. You remember the famous story from *L'île des pingouins*,[9] how they baptized the penguins, and St. Maël said that if the sacraments were exact, if the rite had been performed in the proper way, it must give souls to the birds; if it did not produce the desired effect, it meant that some mistake in the form had been made. It was really believed that people could not sin any longer after having been baptized. Yet there were cases where people were still sinning, which would mean that the grace of Heaven had not worked, that there must be a flaw—the rite had perhaps not been correctly performed and must be performed once more. There were even cases where people received baptism twice and still sinned, and then probably the priest thought up something else—that they were children of Satan, meant for eternal baking in hell, and that closed the thing.

I quote this psychology to show you how strongly mankind believed in the efficiency of the invocation by the true name. You can say that it is the most appalling nonsense, but that there is such an extraordinary belief in mankind shows that it is not nonsense, it shows that it represents a psychological fact. And if no such in-

[9] See above, 23 Jan. 1929, n. 2; and 19 Feb. 1930, at n. 10.

vocation were possible, it would be useless to have symbols, that is, to give names to unconscious facts. The point that I want to emphasize is that the real substance of a symbol is always an unconscious fact. So the real substance of the symbol of the Trinity is an unconscious fact, and as long as it is unconscious it works, the effect being that it lifts people up, manages their lives, rules their existences. As long as a symbol is alive it works, and it is alive as long as we are unaware of the meaning of the unconscious substance behind it. For instance, this man no longer believes in the Trinity, yet the psychological fact of the Trinity is still working in him, as we see in this dream. It is only now that he descends from the aeroplane, which means that up to the present moment the Trinity has worked in him—an unconscious fact. Now we come to the question, what is this unconscious fact and what has happened to it that he can now jump from the aeroplane? We find this partly answered in the dream of the hermaphrodite and the dream of the mouse. In the first, the idea of the demon has been introduced, the word "demon" being used in the antique sense of something different, powerful, mana. In the second, the mouse dream, we learn that something from the dark world below has escaped from control. Now, how could that influence the Trinity? You see, we might be able to conclude from that what the nature of the Trinity is. You have heard Mrs. Crowley's remark and that should give you an idea. Will you repeat it, Mrs. Crowley?

Mrs. Crowley: It occurred to me, as you have suggested, that the triangle or Trinity was a projection of man's effort towards self-integration, or realization, and that the symbol used by the dreamer indicated that he remained fixed in the trinity of his three functions, the fourth not yet emerging into consciousness.

Dr. Jung: That is right. It is a question of the four functions. "There are three, where is the fourth?" A new figure has been introduced in the former dream and the mouse has escaped. Now how can we get that whole thing together? Obviously the efficiency of the Trinity is injured. It is flying rather low, just over the houses, already attempting to land.

Dr. Draper: Could it be the introduction of the feminine element in the hermaphroditic figure, representing the first appearance of his feminine component, which he had hitherto repressed?

Dr. Jung: It is an unconscious male side with the unconscious female that creates the hermaphroditic figure. That hermaphrodite is something disreputable, a monstrosity that really should not be, but it is unavoidable.

Dr. Draper: But I thought you emphasized the fact that acceptance of this feminine component was essential for the male.

Dr. Jung: Well, it is a necessity or an ethical postulate to integrate the feminine side. But it also can be a hellish weakness, inasmuch as one falls into it. We avoid being possessed by the anima, the dark thing that belongs to the unconscious, and we all try to get away from it. It is uncanny, it smells of defeat. That thing is coming up in him and therefore the mouse runs away. That the mouse escapes is quite good for the mouse but perhaps not so good for him. Now, what has that to do with the Trinity?

Dr. Baynes: Is it not the development of the autonomous chthonic factor which depotentiates the Trinity symbol?

Dr. Jung: Yes, it depotentiates the Trinity symbol right away. Perhaps it is also projected to earth. Anyway, because something has happened in the underworld the power of the Trinity symbol is taken away. The landing is the critical moment naturally, and to drop from an aeroplane with a parachute is not the easiest way to do it.

Dr. Schlegel: But is there any reason to assume that the Trinity was an efficient symbol for the dreamer?

Dr. Jung: It was efficient in that it kept him alive. But it flew over everything, so he never faced his real situation, as he is now forced to do. He always escaped somehow into the mind, into all sorts of interests. Yet always the dreams led up to that dream which showed him that it was his church belief, of which we thought to be free altogether, that was really at the bottom of his trouble, holding him under somehow, giving him certain convictions or conceptions which proved to be inhibiting. That hindrance was responsible for his not facing the fact, which is quite understandable. If one has a belief or a religious conviction which helps one to escape the dark interests of one's own nature, one will cling to it.

Mr. Henderson: From the collective aspect, could you say that the chthonic element was lacking to the Trinity and is now about to be returned?

Dr. Jung: We can say at all events that the thing which comes up in the two last dreams is quite clearly from the dark side. Also the sex factor, which is exceedingly chthonic, escapes from his control; that constitutes itself as a factor which is already influential, which is already mana, and that has to be given a name. He must now create a new symbol. In one word, it is the inferior function which comes up now; that is not contained in the formula of the Trinity, because the Trinity represents the three powerful functions not yet realized in the conscious mind. The primitive man possesses only one function, he is only capable of one thing, so three are unconscious. I do not give it as evidence but I always use, as a very striking example of the three unconscious functions, the earliest form of Western mandala, Horus in the centre with his four sons in the corners; three of those sons have animal heads and only one of them has a human head. And there is the same symbolism in the early Christian mandala, Christ in the centre and the four Evangelists in the corners; one only is an angel and the three others are animals.[10] The animals are the unconscious functions, so the Trinity is really built upon the three animals in the unconscious, which makes it so exceedingly powerful; one can conjure three animals by the machine, the symbol, of the Trinity.

Now, if the fourth function comes into play, it means that the Trinity has lost so much of its power that it cannot hold that other function in check. Do you remember those chickens?—the one that escaped? You see, the one function which is conscious would be very weak (not in modern man but in the man of two to four thousand years ago) and therefore he would feel inferior and sinful, his unconscious would be more efficient than he. But the moment he acquires more functions, more differentiation of consciousness, the Trinity suddenly loses its efficiency. It is always a Promethean act of revolution, it is always man's self-assertion over against the gods, that increases his consciousness. It is as if he were wresting a new insight, a new light, from the hands of the gods, and this tremendous process is here in this dream and is the actual problem of the dreamer. He has come to the point where he cannot avoid recognizing the shadow side of himself, an important factor which cannot be controlled any longer, something divine; and that recognition will upset the Trinity symbolism, since he is now confronted with the fact that the powerful thing, the divine thing, is not three but four. Do you understand?—in the Trinity something was lacking, and now he discovers that it was the devil, Prometheus, the fourth, Lucifer rebelling against God. I express myself naturally

[10] See above, 6 Feb. 1929, n. 3.

in Christian language here because he himself feels it like this. Now he has to recognize that the mouse has escaped and that the Trinity is no longer all-powerful, that symbol is now depleted.

Many people have had evil experiences in life, so for them there is no such thing as a good God, or perhaps they have no God at all. So God is quite certainly not all-powerful, he seems to have a very restricted power. He probably tries to do good, but the devil is always sowing some seeds of mischief in between. We find that in the Persian dualism,[11] in the constant struggle between the dark and the light, and it is quite uncertain which will win out. That is the recognition that God is very restricted in his power because of the evil God beside him. The Christian teaching is that the devil is allowed to play his part for a while, to test human beings, and then he is locked into hell again and made inefficient. The Church says that there is always a devil that cheats God or destroys God's good intentions, which of course is a perfectly inadequate explanation, because the power for evil is perhaps just as great as the power for good. The importance of the dark side is now realized by this man— he can repress it no longer—and that is enough to deplete the Trinity symbol, and he has to give it up. The Trinity symbol, then, as far as I understand it, is really due to the fact that it symbolizes the three unconscious functions of relatively primitive man, of the man of antiquity, and inasmuch as it still holds good in our day, we are in the same state of relative primitivity, a state of childhood. The more advanced our consciousness, the less are we able to project such an idea as the supreme being consisting of three persons. In religions that have had a chance of greater philosophical development, like the Eastern religions, man is not so inferior— he is really in the centre of creation; at all events, a counterpart to the supreme being, a part of the divine process, or he himself the supreme being perhaps, in the form of a Buddha—or a grain of sand. Our Western idea, however, is that God can do just as well without these worms here, and it is only by his grace that he doesn't let us rot away. That is the primitive belief, with no recognition that the gods are really parts of our psyche. And people are still so primitive that when told that fact, they say "Only that," as if they knew what the psyche was. It is always a sign of progress when a man realizes that the supreme being is relative to himself, as he is relative to God.

[11] Zoroastrianism.

Now, the descent of this aeroplane means that the three functions are no longer the exclusive possession of the unconscious. The Trinity becomes part of the conscious, and thus it loses its character as a symbol and becomes a mere idea or concept. The Trinity is now in the situation of becoming psychological. The same process brought the ancient Greek gods down to earth, and they became ideas or emotions—Eros, Phoebus, Aphrodite, Mars, etc.

Through the extension of consciousness, the predomination of the unconscious becomes depotentiated. The one conscious function detaches an auxiliary function from the trinity of the hitherto unconscious functions, and by the aid of this auxiliary function, the conscious is enabled to acquire a new standpoint over against the one function that is conscious. From this standpoint man is now capable of looking at his former consciousness; the new function is like a mirror, in which he can reflect the picture of his former consciousness. It means that we are now capable of saying: I see myself as this inferior, unfree, and foolish being, and I am also the one that can look at it and say: I am two, I am the one conscious function and I am another function also, that can look at this prostrate figure as if I were a god. We have acquired the divine quality of being able to look at ourselves, which the primitive man cannot do, we have acquired a second observer. The primitive man has only eyes to see the object, he has nothing behind his eyes. But we have acquired a mirror in ourselves which says: that is yourself, and in saying that we have a superior point of view. I look down upon myself as if I were a god, as if I were superior, and I *am* superior, that is my superiority. And if I acquire another function I have two mirrors and can say: I see that miserable figure and I see the man who observes that figure; that is function No. 3. And if I acquire a third function I say: I see that man, who sees that man, who sees that miserable human being; and that is completion, that is the No. 4. That would be the acquisition of the complete divinity of man, namely, a complete self-criticism through man himself. Therefore Schopenhauer quite truly says: the only divine quality that I attribute to man is his sense of humour.[12]

[12] Cf.: "Because of the lack of the faculty of reason, and thus of the lack of universal concepts, the animal is incapable of laughter as well as of speech. Laughter is therefore a prerogative and characteristic of man."—*The World as Will and Representation*, tr. E.F.J. Payne (1958), vol. II, p. 98.

LECTURE II

14 May 1930

Dr. Jung:

Here are questions from Mrs. Sawyer and Mrs. Crowley. I should like to settle Mrs. Sawyer's question first because it is more general. She says: "You mention two mandalas, one Christian and one Egyptian, in which three functions are pictured with the heads of beasts and one function with a human head. The human-headed function is the conscious superior function and the other three are unconscious. Did you also say that in Christian psychology the three superior functions are carried by the Trinity and the inferior function by the devil? In such a case, is there practically no consciousness at all—all four functions being carried by symbols?"

I said that the three unconscious functions are carried by the Trinity and the one conscious function by the devil. I spoke of the three animals, and that these three unconscious functions play a superior role. But that means superior in the sense of power, not in the sense of differentiation. For the primitive man is always under a superior guidance, something is on top of him, because it demands an extraordinary consciousness, an extraordinary self-control, to say, "I will." The primitive cannot say, "I will"—he is driven; the primitive is almost completely under the spell of his moods. There is no question of choice, things decide themselves. And that fact is portrayed by the superior power ascribed to their gods, who are, for instance, of powerful and gigantic size and demoniacal influence, against whom man is just nothing. That is a portrait of the psychic situation of relatively primitive man, or in other words, of the relation of his conscious to his unconscious. His unconscious is paramount to his conscious, and he projects that fact into metaphysical space in the form of tremendous gods. While as soon as a man increases his consciousness, the gods decrease in size and in power.

587

One sees that very beautifully in the development of Buddhism, where an entirely new point of view is introduced. There we see that the gods appear even at the birth of the Buddha, as they appear when he dies, and that even the gods have to become men to be redeemed. They still have desires and fight each other like human beings. And so the ambition of the Buddha was to liberate his people from such beliefs and to show them the higher degrees of consciousness, to give them release from the contradictory power of the gods. You see, as long as there are three gods against one man, it means that man is completely inferior and of the devil. Of course, it is obvious in the Christian dogma that man is bad from the beginning and would be entirely lost, were it not for the grace of God, which might eventually save him. But that is an awfully uncertain business, you know, and if by chance you do not become one of the honorary members of the Church, back you go to hell where you came from—no chance at all. I have mentioned before the fact of that famous passage from the New Testament: "When two or three are gathered together in my name, I am with them."[1] The original form, which was found in an Egyptian papyrus, was: "When there are two together, they are not without God, but when there is one alone, I say I am with him."[2] The Church interfered and separated man from grace when alone. There must be several together in order to have a chance, and if you are outside the Church there is no redemption. That consciousness of man's utter inferiority is portrayed in the Trinity, as I said, three against one— simply more powerful—and naturally our dogma supposes that this Trinity is infinitely perfect, although it is obviously not yet so good that the devil is abolished. The devil is still moving around like a bad dog. My father was a clergyman and I used to argue with him about that. I said that when a person has a bad dog, the police interfere. But when God or the Trinity lets such a dangerous devil roam about amongst quite nice people, nobody is there to punish God for it, which is an outrageous thing; what is not allowed to man should not be allowed to God.

Well then, three functions are represented by the Trinity. One is obviously human because it is designated by a human head; that is man's consciousness, the one function that he has succeeded in

[1] See above, 5 Mar. 1930, n. 14.
[2] Cf. M. R. James, *The Apocryphal New Testament* (1924), p. 27: Oxyrhynchus Papyrus I (discovered 1897), x.

detaching from the eternal sea of unconsciousness. Naturally when he has only one, it would not be to him a superior function. We have a psychological approach and so now we call it that, but with only one, there is no comparison, so why call it superior? We should say rather the one function differentiated from the general unconscious, and that one function is a very miserable inferior thing in comparison with the unconscious. Moreover, that it is stolen from the gods makes man feel inferior and sinful, and therefore we have to purify ourselves from the diabolic admixture of nature. You can read about that in the text of the Catholic mass, where they even exorcize the salt that is to be mixed with the baptismal water, and the incense, because everything is supposed to be contaminated by the devil. The smoke at the altar is in order to disinfect it spiritually. "So may be absent all diabolical fraud,"[3] the Latin text expresses it. Circumcision is a rite of exorcism, to enable one to escape from impure natural elemental influences. As long as we have not undergone these ceremonials, we are impure and contaminated and unacceptable to the grace of God. That is the beginning of man. He feels his utter helplessness and misery in every respect; he knows how much depends upon his efforts, and he knows that all sorts of devils are against him. Therefore the primitive symbolized his becoming a man by his ceremonies of initiation. Now, I say that when he succeeds in detaching another function, he is about even with the gods. Then he begins to have a psychology and realizes that, if he should be able to detach a third function, he might create for himself a sort of divinity. That is really the case in the Eastern religions, where we see that the gods become more and more illusions. The Easterner will admit that the gods are real, that Shiva, for instance, is a reality to inferior people; but with increase of consciousness, they also are illusions. That is shown very beautifully in the *Tibetan Book of the Dead*, the *Bardo Thödol*,[4] where the dead are instructed by the priests that the gods are illusions which have

[3] The rite of blessing the salt occurs in the Missal at the beginning of the Order of Blessing Holy Water (*Ordo ad faciendam quam benedictam*), which is performed not during the Mass but just before it, in the sacristy rather than at the altar. It includes the words "et effugiat a loco . . . versutia diabolicae fraudis," as translated by Jung. The Order for Holy Saturday includes (at the church entrance) the blessing of the fire and the incense.

[4] See above, 12 Feb. 1930, n. 4.

to be overcome. It is one of the neatest pieces of psychology that I have ever seen.

Now, I hope you understand what I said about that acquired divinity. It doesn't mean that you are going to be gods. The most confusing thing seems to be that people think the three functions must be specific functions. That is not at all the case. You see, there are always the types, and for certain people a certain one is differentiated and three are unconscious; that is, the *majority* of functions are unconscious. That is what the Trinity means; it is by no means three specific functions. Is that plain? For those among you who don't know why we speak of four functions, I must explain that they are the four sides of our orientation in the field of consciousness. I am unable to add anything to that. The four functions are based upon the fact that our consciousness says there *is* something in the unconscious. Sensation is a sort of perception, it knows the thing is there; thinking tells us what it is; feeling says what it is worth to one, whether one accepts or rejects it; and intuition tells us what it might become, its possibilities. I must confess I don't know what more I could include. I could discover no other. With that everything is said. And the peculiar fact that there are just these four coincides with the fact, which I only discovered much later, that in the East they hold the same conviction. In their mandalas, the four gates of consciousness express the four functions, and the four colours express the qualities of the functions. You can see that very well in the text I mentioned, the *Tibetan Book of the Dead.* Are there other questions concerning the functions?

Mrs. Henley: I think most of us are clear as to thinking, feeling, and sensation, but we are least clear about intuition. Could you say something more about that?

Dr. Jung: Sensation simply tells you the visible, tangible, sense qualities, while intuition is a sort of guess about its possibilities. Your senses tell you that here is something, and your thinking tells you what it is, but it takes a lot of intuition to tell you what is behind the walls. If you allow an unbeautiful way of expressing it, intuition is a sort of elephant's trunk put into someone's spinal cord—to go into and behind it and smell it out. Therefore good intuition is often expressed by the nose. A primitive uses his nose, he smells out thieves and ghosts, and it is the same with mediums in our day; they go into a house and sniff and say "ghosts" if it is haunted.

One may discover a peculiar psychology by smell, as I told you recently. You smell a rat—that is intuition.

Dr. Deady: What is the condition of the differentiation of the three functions still in the unconscious of the relatively primitive man? Could you say that they were differentiated?

Dr. Jung: No, they are not differentiated. Anything that is in the unconscious is contaminated with everything else. Only the conscious function is differentiated, That is the split between man and the pleroma, or God, or the universal unconsciousness, whatever you like to call it. He stole one function from the gods. That is beautifully illustrated by the myth of Prometheus stealing fire from the gods. Whatever consciousness man has acquired he had to steal from them. He emerged from the thick cloud of general unconsciousness, and it was only by tearing loose one of the functions that he was enabled to become detached. How that was brought about I don't know; it is a peculiar quality in the psychological structure of man; animals have not that ability to free themselves from the original psyche. It is a kind of dissociability. That is mysterious, one can speculate about it; we do not know how that came about, but it was so.

Dr. Baynes: I think that some of the confusion which I have happened upon comes from the question of the auxiliary functions, that is, when any of the functions have actually appeared and operate as auxiliary functions but have not attained the *per se* character of a major function. From your point of view you would use the term "differentiated" only for that function, or functions, which has gained a *per se* value, wouldn't you?

Dr. Jung: Yes, quite.

Dr. Baynes: For instance, when you find thinking acting as a trace-horse to intuition, you would not give that the quality of a differentiated function?

Dr. Jung: The function which has the *per se* character, the superior or differentiated function, can really be handled, but the auxiliary function is only relatively manageable; with that, already the trouble begins.

Dr. Baynes: Like those figures, half animal, half man.

Dr. Jung: Yes, one figure is human-headed, another ape-headed, and when one begins to base oneself on the ape-headed function, there is trouble; one contacts the animal kingdom and in comes the unconscious. It has happened to everybody that he meets a problem which he cannot settle with the superior function—say a thinker who discovers that he needs feeling. Then his sensation or intuition will lead him to a new world. In the famous dream of the mouse, that could be called just as well the intuitive function, since this man is no longer able to settle his life-problem through his intellect. No sooner has he discovered this than the mouse runs away; the autonomous factor begins to rule because he is no longer at the head of the show. Then life begins to unfold. That is the reason why we understood the mouse as a sort of sign or symptom that something new is due to come.

Mrs. Baynes: You said you thought of primitive man as being three against one. Do you think of modern man as being two against two?

Dr. Jung: That is very difficult to say, but I am inclined to think so from certain signs of the times. A very simple example is the peculiar fact that only in the course of the nineteenth century have attempts been made to rehabilitate old Judas. That means a sense of justice coming up over against the gods. Very respectable, well-meaning people have made desperate attempts at it, and they have their following, a large audience who appreciate that attempt at rehabilitation. That is only one small symptom, but there are many others, the fact of Bible criticism for instance, a scientific enterprise meaning that taboos are now checked, which can be due only to the fact that man feels competent to manage them. The authority that was formerly indubitable and unquestionable has now decreased in importance, and man has advanced correspondingly, he is able to criticize it, he can face it without fear of a thunderbolt. But there are other thunderbolts which come from below. We always look above, but we need no umbrella against thunderbolts—the devil comes from an entirely different quarter.

Now we come to the other question. Mrs. Crowley says: "Will you some time give us more of the symbolism and analysis of the hermaphroditic figure? You said before that you would go into it more fully."

The hermaphrodite is an important symbol that often occurs at a particular stage of psychological development. It is an archetype. A German scholar has recently written a book about it; he collected a lot of material about this being of two sexes that plays a role in all sorts of mystical beliefs, and also in the old Hermetic philosophy. I don't want to enter into the history of that symbol now, I will only call your attention to the fact that the Platonic all-round being is a hermaphrodite, a bisexual condition which means asexual, because the two conditions check each other. It is the symbol for the infantile not-yet-differentiated state, for as soon as the sexes are differentiated there is consciousness. Therefore in the analytical development the hermaphrodite is a symbol for the preconscious condition, when the definite thing that the person should become is not yet conscious. But since it is in the unconscious, such a symbol might occur in their dreams. In the case of our patient, it is the intimation of a superior guiding factor, of a superior self, but still in the hermaphroditic condition. You see, consciousness means discernment, separation; but here the pairs of opposites are not yet separated, so there is no consciousness. It is what I designate as a pleromatic condition, a very apt term which I take from an old philosophy to designate a potential condition of things, where nothing has become, yet everything is there. That is the condition in the unconscious; the functions are not yet differentiated, black is white and white is black.

I told you that interesting fact in the differentiation of words, that in both English and German, the adjectives *better*, *best*, come from the same root as *bad*. That is a case of the original state of identity of the opposites. It is the state of paradise when the wolf is still sleeping with the lamb and nobody eats his neighbour except for fun, where things are in the primordial peace together, the original unconscious pleromatic condition, symbolized by the hermaphrodite. It is an unconscious anticipation of a future ideal condition, as the history of paradise shows. You see, the original wonderful garden of paradise was lost forever, and, according to old cabalistic lore, when Adam and Eve were exiled, God put paradise into the future, which means that the original condition, an undifferentiated unconscious, becomes a goal, and the things which were separated after the first sin shall come together again. That is a bit of the history of the development of consciousness. For in the beginning man feels an exile, he is practically alone in his consciousness, and it is only by increase of consciousness that he discovers his real identity with nature again. Therefore the very culmination of Eastern wisdom is *tat tvam asi*, which means "That art Thou"—each thing myself, myself in everything, the final identity of all things again—yet conscious in that state of paradise. But in the hermaphroditic condition nothing is conscious. So that original condition of pleroma, of paradise, is really the mother from which consciousness emerges. The symbol of that original condition turns up again and again in different forms during the development of consciousness, always portraying a thing that is in the past, yet it is also a symbol for the future. For there will be nothing in the future that has not been in the past, because we can only work out of the material that is given us. The original condition is the symbol for the future condition, the idea of the kingdom of heaven is a repetition of paradise. One sees these symbols in the drawings of patients, in the circle or globe, for instance, expressing the all-round perfect being, containing, as it were, the other half, which is the idea of the primordial Platonic being.

Here is Mrs. Crowley's second question: "Will you suggest how the dreamer might have alighted from his air excursion had feeling not been the inferior function—had that been his superior function, for example?"

It would have been exactly the same, because it does not matter what the three unconscious functions are.

Mrs. Crowley: Would his reaction be the same? I was wondering how we could learn to differentiate more carefully, and in the case of an individual with whom feeling was the superior function, what the reaction in such a dream would be.

Dr. Jung: The reaction would be the same on principle, yet of course the dream would have been a little different.

Mrs. Crowley: I meant more from the angle of approaching reality from the feeling point of view.

Dr. Jung: Whether you rationalize the world through thinking or feeling comes to the same thing in the long run. The ultimate result would be exactly the same.

Mrs. Crowley: Yes, you really answered my question earlier.

Dr. Jung: Well now, we have not yet finished the dream. We still have not dealt with the alighting from the aeroplane. The man falls down and has difficulty in getting up again. And his right hand is injured, it begins to swell and seems to be broken. You remember our dreamer associates with the right hand energy, the activity of man, his efficiency in material or practical life. How do you understand that?

Mrs. Baynes: He must give up his rational attitude. He must turn to the left and find another way in the unconscious.

Dr. Jung: Yes, but what does that mean in practical life?

Mr. Henderson: It affects his business.

Dr. Jung: That is it. At about the time when he had this dream, he showed signs of unrest, which I thought might have to do with his finances, but it now slowly becomes obvious that he really is not interested in his business, it is no longer of importance to him. He says the only thing he is interested in is the human being and life in general. Well, he can afford it, that problem was not so bad. People who have to be interested in their business for their livelihood would not be so interested in the problem of the other side. For it is all balanced, all regulated. Of course, everybody believes that his problem is the worst, but in reality it is not the impossible that is expected of the human being. But that his power is broken is what a man of his calibre minds the most. You see, the right arm is always the symbol of power. Those of you who have read my *Psychology of the Unconscious* will have found there the motif of twisting the arm out of action; or the hip, like the legend of Jacob in the Old Testament, where he was wrestling with the angel of the Lord all night, and the angel twisted his hip.[5] That is the destruction of man's selfish power, and that is inevitable.

The differentiated function is nearly always misused for one's own selfish power. It is an invaluable means to have as a weapon in the beginning, but usually one uses it for too selfish ends and then comes the compensation of the unconscious. Then something will come up which takes the weapon out of your hands. Therefore in the hero myth, in the supreme struggle, the hero has to fight with his bare hands, even his usual weapon fails him; the hero who has overcome the monster with cunning from within finds his arm twisted. He is deprived of his superior function for the sake of the next function which is waiting for differentiation, for it seems that nature is continuing that desire to dissociate man from his original unconscious condition. As nature has pushed one function out into consciousness, so she seems to force man to become conscious of a second one, and for that purpose—because the next one has to be developed—the differentiated function suddenly becomes useless.

[5] Genesis 32:24-25 ("the hollow of Jacob's thigh was out of joint as he wrestled with him"). See *Symbols of Transformation* (1952), par. 524 (not, however, in 1912 edn.).

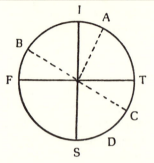

I think it will be useful if I make a diagram again, it helps to a clearer understanding. We always represent the four functions in the form of a cross, and as I put thinking in the East, feeling would be in the West, because feeling is opposite to thinking. One has to omit the standpoint of thinking very carefully in order to realize one's feeling, and vice versa. Then down below would be sensation and up above be intuition. Now let us assume that the differentiated function would be intuition and the auxiliary function thinking; then the division would be about here (A). That makes man largely conscious of intuition, and then the line of division (BC) between the conscious and the unconscious in a pure intuitive type would be as I have indicated. Now, if he gets into a situation in which his intuition doesn't help him—say, for instance, when he should think about things—then his intuition is of no use, it is the worst nonsense. When the necessity comes of his understanding what the situation is, instead of always running ahead chasing new possibilities, he has to suppress intuition to a certain extent; for intuition will go on overcrowding his conscious with new contents, and whenever he begins something new he has to run after it. Therefore he must twist out the arm intuition and give all that power to his thought, and that is usually done through an act of concentration, which is largely a matter of will. Or if a man is unable to concentrate, then something will happen to him that enforces it. Very often those intuitive types get a physical illness, tuberculosis or ulcers of the stomach and other abdominal troubles chiefly; also peculiar hysterical troubles, which may produce all sorts of symptoms that immobilize such people, lay them low, and force them to exclude possibilities. Then they have to keep still and cannot run after things; they are put into situations where they cannot escape thinking, where the only thing they can do is to think furiously. That is how a function is paralyzed or killed for the sake of another function.

In this case the individual moves on here (D), and here he approaches the sphere of unconsciousness. So here is terrible danger, the inferior function which is opposite to the superior one; that is the very devil. That neighbourhood becomes most uncanny, one shuns it as much as possible, one is afraid of all that might be behind that wall of the unconscious. Therefore we make a different move, we go to the lesser danger, in this case feeling (F), and only when we have the three on that side do we dare to attack that thing. There must be three against one, it is the acquisition of the triangle that fights the one. Now if you remember still those verses by Lowell which our dreamer has quoted (why do you laugh?), you will see that they fit in with the spirit at least of all our deliberations. It is as if his associations arose from his having overheard our discussion here, so we are well within the scope of the dreamer's feeling.

I think we can put that dream aside now and go on to the next one, which I have already mentioned, the dream about the triplets [26].[6] It was read in the last seminar, but I will go over it again as quickly as possible for the benefit of the new members. He says that his wife has borne triplets, two of them still-born, but the third remains alive. That is the whole dream, and he says that it repeated itself despite the fact that he can remember nothing else connected with it. He only remembers that he was present at the birth and that the midwife was there and took away the dead children.

In his associations, he says that twins or triplets give him the impression of too much of a blessing. It seems to him perfectly sufficient if only the third child remains alive. He thought a good deal about what they meant and came to the conclusion that they were spiritual children, as they certainly had nothing to do with his real children. The peculiar fact that two children are still-born he cannot bring down to concrete reality, so he makes the assumption that they are still-born *attempts*, because children as psychological symbols often have that meaning, just as every man is an attempt of nature. So he thinks the two dead children represent his spiritualistic and Yoga studies, which seem to him today to be perfectly superfluous spiritual abortions. He says that I am the

[6] See above, p. 557.

597

midwife who took the dead ones away, because after he came to me he saw no point in those other attempts, the theosophical interests. I never said a word against them, because there is something quite definitely interesting in those things. I know that if there is anything in them for him he will cling to them, and if not, he will leave them. He says he played with those subjects for a while, and the third attempt, the child that is alive, is the slow development of his relationship to his soul through analysis. He uses the German word *Seele*, which may mean the anima or the more Christian concept of the soul. He obviously means his relationship to the inner world of experience.

The dream seems to be very simple, but there is a theoretical catch in it. He is quite satisfied with his interpretation of it: that the triplets are three attempts at a new form of life, because to him it was an entirely new enterprise to seek spiritual development. Formerly he was the head of a big business, and when he withdrew he was left to face the question "And what now?" He was forty-five years old, and what to do becomes a very serious question when one is confronted with the problem of having nothing to do, yet having to find an outlet somewhere. He took up so-called spiritual things first, for people who are ignorant of psychology easily take an interest in ghost seances, telepathy, and occultism in general. So it was quite natural, and apparently what he says about the little dream is satisfactory, yet there is a catch in it. If you rigorously follow the principles of dream interpretation, you will know what it is.

Mrs. Sigg: It seems that these three children are born at the same time, but it was not at the same time that he began those studies.

Dr. Jung: Yes, that is really a bit strange, and he pays no attention to it, but that is a minor catch—a little mouse-hole in comparison to a trap-door. Where is the real tunnel?

Mrs. Nordfeldt: It was his wife who had the children.

Dr. Jung: Yes, and what did I tell you about that? I will repeat that famous rule of thumb which aroused the animus. If the dreamer dreams of his wife, then it is his wife. When you dream of a person who is in vital relation to you, either by actual blood relationship or in any really vital connection—anybody who has a hand in your psychological structure—then you must look at the person in the dream, at least for a while, as if he was really the person himself

598

and not a symbol for something in yourself. For instance, there is a pretty vital relation between the patient and the analyst, and when a patient dreams of him we can assume that the analyst is meant; if it should be something unfavourable, the analyst is confronted by the criticism, perhaps a new discovery about himself which is possibly true; at all events, he has to take that possibility as real, and only when it is duly considered and nothing has been found, even with a great deal of consideration, is he allowed to assume that it might be something rather subjective in the patient. Also, the analyst sometimes dreams of the patient with whom he has a more or less vital relationship. For the relationship between the analyst and patient is vital; if not, it is dead. Some are more vital than others—the most vital when he doesn't understand, when he has struck a snag somehow. Then he might dream of the patient, and the best policy is to inform him or her because there might be something in it which the patient would see right away. Naturally, it is only relatively advanced cases which give one such trouble. Otherwise one doesn't dream of them at all. I tell you that to show you how serious I am about taking such figures as real.

So when the patient dreams that his wife has brought forth triplets, I am in the disagreeable situation of having to explain why his wife should have brought forth triplets. If we had not such a rule of thumb I could be perfectly satisfied with his explanation of the dream; he was quite ready to go to sleep on it, leave it at that. Yet there is that string—he dreams of his wife and it must be his wife, I am confronted with that fact. Then Mrs. Sigg has brought up the fact that his spiritual children, Yoga and theosophy and analysis, were not born at the same time, and one couldn't call them triplets when one was born in 1927, one in 1928, and the other in 1929. The idea of triplets includes the fact that they must have been born at the same time practically, it is the same pregnancy. That is very difficult—where does his wife come in? Obviously we have to take his associations pretty seriously that these children are attempts, that is the most reasonable explanation. You see, it makes a tremendous difference when we say that it is his wife who brings forth. Can you explain that puzzle? You remember we alluded to it in the last seminar.[7]

Mrs. Crowley: It was a sort of psychic reaction.

[7] See above, p. 558.

Mrs. Baynes: You said about this specific case, when you discussed this phase of the dream, that it was as if he were in such close *participation mystique* with his wife that he could take her as himself subjectively, and it was true that she also was going to be productive.

Dr. Jung: That is it. As you know, this man has practically no relation with his wife, he cannot talk to her because she much prefers to cling to traditional things, to stay in a safe refuge against the chaotic possibilities of the mind, as many a man clings to a safe marriage against erotic possibilities. This absence of relationship is compensated in the unconscious. You see, when you are living with somebody with whom you have no real relationship, you are unconsciously connected. And that peculiar unconscious relationship produces a psychological condition which could be compared to a sort of continuum where both function, as if they were both in the same tank under water. They are under the same cover, in the same boat, which makes a particular kind of immediate relationship. This unconscious relationship produces most peculiar phenomena, such as dreams which clearly do not belong to the individual. So when it is a matter of husband and wife, the husband may dream the dreams of the wife, or the other way around; or one of them may be forced to do something which proceeds not from his own psychology but from the psychology of the other. Those are symptoms of such a *participation mystique*.

Obviously, that man's conscious relation to his wife is insufficient, so here we can assume an unconscious contamination in which he as well as his wife functions. You see, his wife has a marked resistance against any kind of thinking, as he has against his Eros side. She will not use her mind. A thing must be ready-made and safe, guaranteed for at least two thousand years, backed up by the highest authority, before she will accept it. It must be absolutely water- and air-tight and nothing to be changed. Of course, that is perfectly unnatural; it is abnormal and machine-like; something has been killed, and it has therefore been compensated in her unconscious, where she produces extraordinary things of which we do not know. There she thinks furiously, there she is busy with all sorts of radical things, perhaps with religion. If we had her dreams we would see all that. Her unconscious is in a real turmoil, and it is repressed and cannot boil over into the conscious, but in the night it creeps into the open canals of her husband's brains. His mind is open and he speaks it out and shocks her out of her wits, because it is her own stuff he is talking, the stuff she is talking in the night with the devils. And likewise, on the other side, what she says in the conscious is to a great extent brought forth by the unconscious feelings of his anima.

When the patient had this dream I didn't tell him all this, because at that stage it would have been wrong to preach too much wisdom. It was more important that he should learn to make his own way in analysis, catch the feeling that he could handle the stuff. At first it was very strange to him, but now we shall see his attempts to interpret the dreams coming to the foreground, and I did not want to interfere with that. In the case of such a man it is very important to be on good terms with his superior function, as in the same way it is wrong to put oneself in opposition to a woman's Eros. Otherwise one works against a great power, which is too much waste of energy.

Now, all this would explain that dream and also to a certain extent the strange fact that the triplets, the efforts, were born all at the same time. That is an intimation that when a thing happens in time it becomes history, but in the unconscious there is no time, it is eternal. The unconscious can speak of things which are absolutely separated through long intervals of time as being together; to us they are separated but to the unconscious they are not. They are like the pairs of opposites, like black and white, light and dark, the future and the past—in the unconscious there is no difference. So these triplets are all born at once, yet there are years between. The three attempts are really one attempt; it was one particular stimulation which probably came from his wife. It was the moment when he felt that he had come to an end with his rational intellectual attitude and when Eros came up in him. It was an entirely unconscious moment. I think that certain very intuitive people might be able to realize such a moment, but usually it happens completely in the unconscious.

In analysing dreams at such a time, one is confronted with the most disagreeable problems. Something tremendous has happened, and the patient says he knows nothing of it, that it is perfect nonsense. The analyst knows that something has happened but is not yet visible; it has happened in the pleroma and has not come through into time. It must have been a very definite moment when our dreamer unconsciously felt that thing had come to an end, and at the same moment in his wife, only the reverse naturally. And that was the moment when the triplets were born. It is like a child dreaming of his future. I have seen cases where children have anticipated the main points of their coming life in very simple terms; they were anticipations of a whole lifetime, everything together, and happening in reality thirty, forty, or fifty years hence. Even most extraordinary problems can be dreamt by children, when one cannot see at all how a child could conceive of such things. Is it that they get it through their parents? We still don't know. I think it must have to do with the collective unconscious, but that is another question which we will not go into now.

Dr. Baynes: There seems to be some connection between the depotentiation of the Trinity and the birth of the triplets.

Dr. Jung: Yes, that is the real interpretation of the dream, that there is a continuity. When the aeroplane comes down, it means that the Trinity is depotentiated, dissolved, and here it appears again; it is now born out of man. The Trinity that has been in an unconscious condition before is now reborn into consciousness.

Miss Wolff: In that case I should say that it is important that the triplets are born of a woman, because the Christian religion leaves out the woman, excepting the Virgin.

Dr. Jung: It is well that somebody stands up for the woman. You see, when good old Sophia became a member of the Trinity, as the wife of the Lord God, the old Fathers never liked it, and she was abolished except in the Coptic Church; they had only the Virgin Mary as a sort of spiritual midwife in the neighbourhood. Since then the female element has been absent from the Trinity, but now she comes back. It is a very remarkable fact that now the woman should bring forth the lost Trinity.

Dr. Draper: Why should two of them be dead?

Dr. Jung: That is a very serious question. We must know now who the dead children are. That dream is full of hooks. Keep that question in mind.

LECTURE III

21 May 1930

Dr. Jung:

We will continue our discussion of the dream. Do you remember where we left off, Dr. Draper?

Dr. Draper: We were talking about the *participation mystique,* that cross-transference.

Dr. Jung: That was not quite it. You asked something very awkward—why those two children were dead.

Dr. Deady: Miss Wolff asked a question concerning the woman having come into the Trinity.

Miss Wolff: It was not a question, just a remark.

Dr. Jung: Just a remark! That is exactly the point, we must establish the connection, otherwise we talk in the air. You see, in the dream before, the whole Trinity came down to earth, and in the next dream came the birth of triplets, obviously referring to the Trinity, which was reborn in a very peculiar way. We made the hypothesis that the three had to do with functions, which would mean that of the three functions of the Trinity, two are dead and only one is alive. And then came your question, why should two of them be dead if they are supposed to be living elements in the Trinity. Now I call that a very awkward question. Is there an answer? The associations are very important, that the children represent the three stages in the dreamer's mental development, two of those stages still-born. Moreover, the importance of that is emphasized by the fact that the midwife, whom he associates with me, is doing away with those dead children. So Dr. Draper's question is really very awkward, for how can a thing that is reborn be dead, and what is the use of being reborn when it is a miscarriage?

Mrs. Crowley: There was the point that his wife had borne the triplets.

Dr. Jung: But there was no question about the paternity; we

603

must assume that the dreamer has something to do with his own children. We have not heard of a secret lover.

Miss Sergeant: If they represented his theosophy and other occult interests, why should they not die when analysis is born?

Dr. Jung: Yes, that is what the dreamer clutches at, and there evidently would be the loophole to escape Dr. Draper's question. But in our interpretation we assumed that the Trinity meant the three functions in the unconscious. That was hypothesis, it is not guaranteed by the dream; the dream and its associative material does not speak of functions. We were discussing the Trinity in a very general way and not entirely in connection with the dream, where we had only to do with the three stages which the dreamer mentioned. But we left that point of view and spoke of the peculiar fact that we find these trinities of gods all over the earth, from which we may assume that that symbol must be based upon a universal psychological condition. And concerning such a psychological condition, we know that there was a time in the dawn of all history, in the beginning of civilization, when man first detached one function from the collective unconscious; that is, he succeeded in making a part of the unconscious psyche serviceable for his own purpose. The moment when man could say he had a purpose or the will to do so-and-so marked the birth of that detachment. Naturally, when one studies the psychology of the functions, one finds that it is not fully detached, that, in a differentiated type, there is still a part, a root, of the most differentiated function which is embedded and entangled in the collective unconscious.

That is the most difficult thing for people to realize in themselves—the thing they will admit last. Take a thinking type, for instance, who is completely identical with his conscious function. If you tell him that a certain part of his thinking is absolutely primitive, he jumps at your throat. He will not admit it, he must cling to the idea that somewhere he is divine and free. You can tell him that his feeling life is far below the mark, that his sensation is not good, or that his intuition is rotten, and he will admit all that. But never say that his thinking is impure. Yet even his thinking is at some point impure. One sees the same thing in a differentiated feeling type. He is apparently quite able to feel hypothetically, as a thinker can think hypothetically. Most people can only think concretely. I remember saying to such a person: Let us assume that Sydney is in Canada and not in Australia. Whereupon he immediately replied: That cannot be, Sydney is in Australia. Now, that is not a thinking type, for a thinking type is able to think that Sydney is in the moon; he can think anything. Just as a feeling type is free in his own function: he can assume that we are all perfectly happy, he can conjure up happiness for everybody for a while, the most wonderful atmosphere which everybody thinks is marvellous, but then comes the catastrophe. After a while the whole thing collapses. For even such a highly developed feeling type, who seems free from conditions within, has certain feelings somewhere in the background which are absolute slaves, the effects of dark causes, and he seems to be free of them only because he wants to believe in his divinity, his freedom. And it is true that in so far as you have succeeded in detaching a function you *are* free, free from conditions, beyond causes. But as a whole, you are never quite free.

What I said, then, about the Trinity being the three functions in the unconscious is a universal consideration not mentioned in the dream. And in such cases, where people ask awkward questions, one had better return to the actual text of the dream, which is that the Trinity has descended, three children are born, and the dreamer associates with them the three stages of his mental or spiritual development. For further explanation of the dead children, we have to refer to his associations. So in the very first place, even if we connect it up with the Trinity in the previous dream, before discussing the Trinity as three functions we must look at it in a different way, namely, as three successive stages. And we find that in reality the historical Trinity is also in three stages: the Father, the Creator; then the Son; and then the Holy Ghost. The Paraclete, the Comforter, is left by the Son. So we see that even in the dogma the Trinity is a succession, yet it is in eternity. What is to us separated is together in eternity because there is no time. In the light of the dreamer's associations, then, the Trinity is to be understood in this case as three existing not at once but in succession. His three stages are representations, so to speak, of his three successive conditions—spiritualism, the Father; theosophy, the Son; and psychology, the Holy Ghost.

Now, the fact that two are dead would refer to the first ones. The Father is dead, the Son is dead, and the Holy Ghost is alive. Spiritualism is dead, theosophy is dead, and psychology is alive. That would be the parallel, and it would be subjectively true in his case. You have heard enough about his attitude to the Church to know that his convictions in that respect are very definite; he can no longer believe in the traditional Church, Christianity is dead for him. Also he is probably aware through his theosophical studies of the belief, widespread in our days, that there are three stages of spiritual development, namely, the Old Testament, the Father; the New Testament, the Son; and the present time, the Holy Ghost, which is the new thing to come. That idea probably comes from the East, it is reminiscent of the successive incarnations of the Buddha.

Mrs. Fierz: The Cistercian monks of the twelfth or thirteenth century were the first to speak of it.[1]

Mr. Schmitz: I think it was in the eleventh or twelfth century. If I am not mistaken it was a current assumption in the time of Frederick the Second.[2]

Dr. Jung: I think you may be right, and it is quite remarkable that it came up so early.

Question: What was the idea?

Dr. Jung: The idea was of the three successive conditions in the evolution of truth: the Old Testament was the Kingdom of the Father; the New Testament was the Kingdom of the Son and so of Christianity in general; and the third would be the Empire or Kingdom of the Holy Ghost, that is the thing to come.[3] This idea of successive revelations, or periodical manifestations, has an Eastern character, and it is of course a fact that there were Eastern influences in the early Church. In the second century before Christ, there were already Buddhist monasteries in Persia; it is quite certain that there were Persian influences in early Christianity and probably

[1] The Cistercian order was founded in 1098 and was most active in Western Europe during the 12th cent. Cf. Jung's interest in the 14th-cent. Cistercian monk Guillaume de Digulleville and his visions in three stages: *Psychology and Alchemy*, Part II (orig. 1935), CW 12, pars. 315-322.

[2] The Holy Roman emperor Frederick II (1194-1250) "considered himself intimately bound" to the Cistercians and was received into a prayer-community of the Order. See Ernst Kantorowicz, *Frederick the Second 1194-1250*, tr. E. O. Lorimer (New York, 1931), p. 85.

[3] The idea figures in the writings of Joachim of Fiore (c. 1135-1202), who was first a Cistercian but eventually broke with the Order and began his own Order of Fiore. He developed his Trinitarian conception of history as passing through three great periods, or *status*, long after leaving the Cistercians. See Marjorie Reeves, *The Influence of Prophecy in the Later Middle Ages: A Study in Joachism* (Oxford, 1969), pp. 16-27. Jung discussed Joachim's ideas at length in *Aion* (1951), CW 9 ii, pars. 137-144.

Buddhist as well. At all events, the Catholic Church was influenced by the East. The rosary is an Eastern yantra, for instance. Thus it is possible that the idea of the successive manifestations of the Bodhisattvas penetrated early Christianity.

Mr. Schmitz: The Russian Church has accepted the idea of the three elements.

Dr. Jung: Yes, it is a general idea. In theosophical circles these three stages have also been widely discussed.[4] And now, people think that the coming of the new age—Aquarius—will be the third condition, the new revelation of the Trinity. I don't know in how far my dreamer has been influenced by such ideas, but I found that he knew about the three successive stages in human development, which coincide with, or are symbolized by, the successive stages of the Trinity. You see, this idea would rather bear out what we were discussing in the last seminar, namely, the successive incarnations, one could almost say, of the three different functions, the Father, Son, and Holy Ghost, and if that should be completed we would have the complete individual. At all events, when the Trinity comes down to earth we may expect a tremendous change, transformations not only in our own psychology but also in our psychological concept of the divine. It will make a great psychological difference because we shall no longer possess the necessary unconscious conditions for our conception of the divine factor. The necessary material was the three unconscious functions that formed a body of considerable energy, which was the basis for a conception of an all-powerful Trinity. Now, if that factor gets dissolved by conscious realization, or the detachment of these functions, it would follow that the psychological material already in our unconscious would be the sole structure for a new concept of the divine. So it would be an entirely different way. To finish this argument, have you an idea what the psychological material in the unconscious would be? If the three functions of the Trinity were assimilated, what would remain? That would again throw an interesting light on the dream.

---

[4] In H. P. Blavatsky, *The Voice of the Silence* (1889; edn. of 1971), pp. 6ff., the progress of the soul is symbolized as the passage through three halls, of Ignorance, Learning, and Wisdom, beyond which is the Vale of Bliss. Jung's library contains Blavatsky's *The Secret Doctrine* (1893, 1897) and her Theosophical glossary. His occasional references to Theosophy in the CW and Letters are mostly disparaging. In a letter of 12 Feb. 1959 (*Letters*, vol. 2, p. 186) he called it a "regressive -ism."

You see, as long as man has but one function, he is just aware that he can do something, but he is always up against an overwhelming psychological condition, the three in the unconscious, the majority, on top of him. Then he acquires a second function and becomes more complete. He gains more balance and acquires something like a philosophical consciousness. He can be aware of himself as such a psychological being. He can say: I want to do this or that, and he can also say: I see how foolish that is. While with only one function that is impossible, there is no reflection; it is only with the acquisition of the two functions that he has acquired a mirror. The left hand can then judge the right hand, and he has thereby gained a sort of divinity, a superior point of view. The third function makes a second mirror. He can say: I see this fellow here who is watching that chap down there, and I see how he thinks and that he makes a wrong conclusion. With a fourth function there would be still more consciousness. Obviously, it is a tremendous thing in the growth of consciousness that one can get behind oneself, that one can as a spectator again and again mirror oneself. Probably one can actually do it only to a limited extent, there are presumably certain restrictions to our consciousness, but one can see the possibility of infinite mirrorings and of infinite judgment. In that case, one would arrive naturally at a being who was so fabulously superior to conditions that it would be an almost limitless freedom, like the complete freedom of God that has not to obey conditions because it is the only condition that is. Therefore the more functions one acquires, the more one deprives the divinity, or the magical factor, the mana factor, of its efficiency. It is as if one were undermining it, or hollowing it out, because one takes away from it and adds to oneself with every new point of view. So one lifts oneself up above conditions. That is the path of redemption in the East, the attainment of successive conditions of consciousness which gradually liberate man from the pairs of opposites, from the qualities, from *concupiscentia*, from the wheel of death and rebirth, as they express it. Now, one would conclude that, through this detachment of the functions, we would arrive at a complete assimilation of the Trinity, in other words, a complete assimilation of the divine factor within ourselves. But then nothing would be left apparently. Or is that a wrong conclusion?

Mrs. Fierz: The devil.

Dr. Jung: Oh no, we would assimilate the devil. We could even check God. We could say: I see this is God and he thinks so and so, but I am going to play a trick on him, I am the devil. Or the reverse: I see the devil and I will play a trick on *him*. Our question is: suppose one arrives at the complete assimilation of the Trinity, would one still be only an inferior being? We are naturally of the devil, from the very beginning our hearts were black, we arose from the slime, and we would be perfectly convinced that we were bringing into the Trinity something terribly inferior. But with the acquisition of the Trinity we obviously rise to a higher level, to complete freedom from conditions, and if that is the case we would assume that God would not be objective any longer because he is clearly one with us. We would be in a way divine, which is of course the Eastern idea. Do you think that such a thing is psychologically possible?—that the divine object could disappear from man's conscious?

Suggestion: I think there would be a sort of entropy.

Dr. Jung: Then it would be a sort of *désintéressement* such as one sees in the East. That Eastern quietism is a kind of *désintéressement* so that people vanish practically. But we cannot say what that condition is inside, because nobody is inside such a condition—unless he is dead. It is like expecting a man to say how he feels when he is dead.

Mr. Schmitz: The tension of polarity would cease, and therefore it would be the same as death. At the moment when he reached his goal he would no longer be living.

Dr. Jung: Yes, one might assume that when he has reached the complete assimilation of all projections, he will have reached the stage of divinity, and then he is necessarily dead, because every thinkable form of energy has been turned in, assembled in the field of the square inch, or the house of the square foot, as Chinese Yoga puts it,[5] and there it is held in a form of duration where nothing happens at all. But as long as we live we are obviously incapable of withdrawing all energy from the world, of withdrawing all projections. We keep on eating things, smelling things, moving, and all that is psychology in projection. It is projection, it is giving out, something is constantly leaving us—as long as we live we are projecting. We are incarnating energy, and so energy is not completely withdrawn, it is not completely within ourselves, which means

[5] See above, 13 Feb. 1929, text at n. 3.

that an ideal condition of complete awareness cannot be reached as long as we live. But we may say that we can reach it approximately, so that one could imagine how it would be. We can assume such a condition, in which one has withdrawn the maximum projection. We can assume that the maximum energy is now within, gathered up in the so-called diamond body. Then what about the divine object? Is that still divine?—or is it depleted? What form would it take if there were one? Or is that a perfectly unintelligible question? I would not ask it if there were not a doubt in my mind. Naturally in analysis I have observed patients and have seen these things so often that I have formed certain ideas.

Now, there is still one important point in that dream which we have to clear up, namely, why his wife is bringing forth at all—why, when the Trinity comes to earth, does it not go into him? Yet the dream says it is his wife who brings forth—as if his wife were a sort of modern Mary, the Holy Ghost having come down with wings and fertilized her.

Dr. Draper: It is possible that notwithstanding his complete assimilation of his projections, he reaches the stage where there still remains in him the fact that he does go back to the mudfish. That forms a sort of matrix from which he cannot possibly escape. He still has something of the amoeba in him.

Dr. Jung: There you are on the right track. For the fact is, if we succeed in assimilating other functions, or in bringing our projections back to ourself, we do acquire a sort of divinity, and that has a peculiar effect upon our psychology, it removes us from the inferior man. People often get quite inflated and think they are acquiring a wonderful superiority because they are identifying with the next mirror. The more mirrors one acquires, the more divine one becomes, and the more also one becomes inflated—identical with the next mirror, that is, and again taken away from the ape-man, from everything that is low and weak, perhaps even dirty, that still is wet from the original waters, covered with primeval slime. We get away from all that, farther and farther away, the more awareness we acquire, but then a very peculiar fact happens. What would that be?

Prof. Hooke: Are assimilation and detachment the same thing?

Dr. Jung: The psychological consequence of the assimilation would be detachment, because only when one gets a superior point of view does one say, I am so-and-so. One doesn't identify with the fact that one is incapable or wrong, but with the superior point of view naturally. We all identify with our one differentiated function—I am myself, and then I find myself in my thinking. A great musician would naturally think himself a great musician. Do you think that Wagner suspected that he was anything else? He never thought that he was—I won't tell you what, I leave it to your imagination.

Mrs. Baynes: But I thought you were presupposing that you were taking all four functions together, and if you do that you could not forget that primordial slime.

Dr. Jung: You may not forget, but with each mirror you get a higher point of view and you naturally identify with it. In actual fact you are getting away, you won't stay on the level of the amoeba.

Mr. Schmitz: And then comes the revenge of the inferior man?

Dr. Jung: Exactly. The more we get away from our roots, the more we identify with mirrors, the more inefficient we become, because the mirror has no feet, it has no hands. It is complete awareness, perhaps, yet no effect except the effect which we can give to it. What is inside it means exceedingly little. I can tell a person that things are so-and-so, but he simply cannot make it true, because insight counts for little unless it is given hands and feet. The further we get away the less we are efficient.

Prof. Hooke: And yet we are the more divine!

Dr. Jung: Yes, that is a terrible paradox, but you must not mix it up with philosophy. This is psychology, where we really move in paradoxes. The more divine, the farther from earth—speaking psychologically, and from that you may conclude that God is a most inefficient being. But that is of course metaphysical. It may be true and it may not be true.

Mr. Schmitz: That is the reason why God incarnated himself in the Son. Empirically, he is not, he is incapable, and that is why he has created this terrible world. He must be not only *in potentia* but *in actu*.

Dr. Jung: Yes, that is why man is indispensable to God. Without man, God could do nothing. That is not metaphysical. I don't believe in metaphysics, I only own to psychology, and in our psychology it is surely so—that God finds himself in a very helpless condition. We find that idea in old legends, in that cabalistic legend, for instance, that I have told you, that God in the beginning was all alone, there was nothing except himself, and his loneliness grew and grew to such an extent that he got a terrible headache from it, and realized that there should be something that was not himself. In the beginning everything was in the form of a vaporous cloud, so he drew that together till it became more and more condensed, and suddenly a light burnt through, and that was the Son, the first ray of Light. (Cf. The Gospel of St. John.)[6]

Dr. Baynes: It is like Prajapati.[7]

Dr. Jung: Exactly the same idea—the extraordinary loneliness of God and his helplessness in that condition.

Well then, we make the statement that the more we increase our awareness, the more we draw back our projections and gather up our energy in ourselves, the more we remove ourselves from actual efficiency. The idea that God was perfectly helpless and lost in his loneliness and had to create man in order to become or to be is expressed in many myths or philosophical *parabola*,[8] and thus is explained how man is in a way the indispensable means of God's becoming. That is beautifully expressed by Meister Eckhart[9] where he says that God in his very divinity is not God, he must be born through the soul of man again and again. "Without me God cannot live."[10] So the condition of divine awareness is really a condition of infinite mirroring, and the more one lives in the mirroring, the more one is removed from the substance, whatever that is. One cannot help having a too superior point of view. Suppose one has a tremendous universal insight into things. One shrugs one's shoulders and says: better that I know nothing at all, for then I could do something. Knowing so much would keep one out of existence, one wouldn't know whether one was alive or dead, one would be simply universal. So *through* that awareness one would be aware of functions, but the interesting thing is that when one is mirroring a thing one does not possess it. It is like an old magic idea that

[6] John 1:9: ". . . the true Light, which lighteth every man that cometh into the world."

[7] The Hindu god-creator, "a personification of the all-containing life-matter and life-force. . . . He felt lonely, . . . and so he brought forth the universe to surround himself with company" (Zimmer, *Philosophies of India*, 1951, p. 300).

[8] Ecclesiastical late Latin, = "parables."

[9] German Dominican mystic (c. 1260-1327); Jung discussed this concept of his in *Psychological Types* (1921), CW 6, par. 428.

[10] In ibid., par. 432, Jung quoted from another German mystic, Angelus Silesius (1624-1667): "I know that without me / God can no moment live; / were I to die, then He / No longer could survive."

mirroring a thing means possessing it. That is not true. One gets the illusion that when one is able to mirror that fellow there, and from here to decide about him, that one possesses him. But he is not possessed, he keeps his original substance. He is there and one cannot take him in. One can only take in the images of things, but the things remain and one is removed from them. One doesn't keep the world in one when one takes away one's energy; the world remains there, one only removes oneself; and so it comes about that through a superior awareness one is peculiarly separated from the substance.

Then something happens. And here we come to our original argument, namely, what will happen when we assimilate the Trinity? Obviously we get an almost universal or complete awareness, mirrors after mirrors, and we apparently acquire divinity. Well, something in us, some remote vista, is divine, one ray of light is divine, but we have not undone our reality, this world. We have only removed ourselves from the world through that awareness, and we apparently have lost the divine object, the divine object from the regions of light, where it was before. All illumination came to us from above, and it was light which revealed itself to us as truth. But when we are identified with the mirroring, the divine factor changes its form altogether. In what form would it reappear?

Mr. Schmitz: The first thing is that the collective unconscious will take its revenge. The higher man climbs, and the more he identifies himself with those heights, the more he will get into a mess of ridiculous and childish casualties.

Dr. Jung: One knows everything with one's universal awareness, but that does not hinder matter from acting. It doesn't influence the substance in the least.

Mr. Schmitz: But is it not possible, if the sensation function, for instance, works well, if it is quite differentiated and free, that one might have a certain connection with matter in that situation of divine solitude?

Dr. Jung: It is more than possible, it is inevitable. You perceive reality, yet the superior insight removes you, and you are in solitude.

Mr. Schmitz: The insight through the four functions?

Dr. Jung: Yes, because what the mirrors reflect is not substance, only the image. Also, sensation is not what one usually understands—having sensations of touch, light, etc.—it is simply an awareness of things as they are, what the French psychologist Janet calls "la fonction du réel,"[11] a psychological point of view, an attitude.

Mr. Schmitz: If one has this "fonction du réel," is it conceivable that one would be as remote from matter?

Dr. Jung: Oh yes, one can see things as they actually are through one's awareness, and yet be absolutely removed from them. That is the great tragedy. The more one is aware, the more one is removed.

Mr. Schmitz: Then the conclusion would be not to be so aware!

Dr. Jung: If one can afford it. But we cannot afford not to be aware. Everything in us forces us to higher consciousness. We have to follow up that way, but on that way we lose connection.

Mr. Schmitz: The happy end is death!

Dr. Jung: That is the Eastern idea, Nirvana. The more one is removed—not that you are actually taken away into cosmic distances, it is the psychological situation—the more one says, what is the use of bothering. In two years or fifty years one will be dead and then one will disappear anyhow. Other people will come, other illusions will come, it does not matter. That is universal awareness, and it removes one. It is a psychological condition. One is here, seeing, shaking hands with people, saying how do you do, and yet one is ten thousand miles away, anywhere in the cosmos, but not here. Now if that is the case—and that will be the case with more complete awareness—then compensation will take place. Then, as the Chinese say, the lead of the water region will react.[12] One rebels against that removal, and then God, the divine factor, the overwhelming factor, appears in things. Do you understand?

It is very interesting to look at the development of thought psychologically in the nineteenth century, after the French Revolution, after the rational era of natural science. Then people began to believe in ghosts, in moving tables, materializations, etc. These are most primitive ideas, yet they had at that time the value of almost

[11] See above, 23 Oct. 1929, n. 4. For "la fonction du réel" see Janet, *Obsessions et la psychasthénie* (1903), vol. 1, p. 433. Jung variously explained the term as "acting up to realities" (1907; CW 2, par. 1066, n. 17), "psychological adaptation to the environment" (1907; CW 3, par. 19, n. 36), and "correct relation to the surrounding world" (1948, CW 18, par. 1232).

[12] Wilhelm, *The Secret of the Golden Flower*, tr. C. F. Baynes (1962 edn.), p. 21, and Jung's commentary (1929), CW 13, par. 35. "Lead" means the metal.

divine revelations. And, mind you, they were not altogether idiotic people, and there are many people today who believe in a valid origin for these things. It was the time when that famous book *Force and Matter* by Büchner[13] appeared, and was received with such extraordinary enthusiasm. It designates the height of materialism, just in the fact that in it matter becomes spirit. Look at the most modern facts in science and what is matter after all? Thought is matter, and matter is thought; there is no difference any longer. That is the Einstein theory. The latest truth about matter is that it is like thought, that it even behaves like a psychical something, that it is a psychical phenomenon. The whole concept of matter is dissolving into these abstractions. It is changing altogether, which has much to do with an entirely different consideration, a tremendous revolution in our whole outlook.

Mr. Holdsworth: When you spoke about God being unable to get along without man, did you differentiate man from the other animals?

Dr. Jung: Oh, I would include the whole tribe of animals. That is not an original idea. You may have heard of Jaworski,[14] who thinks that all the parts of the human being are derived from animals. He says that each organ of the human body is really a sort of conglomeration of all the different animal principles. There is a picture in one of his books which shows what part of the animal is associated with the various parts of man. The idea is, roughly, that all animals are contained in man. Then there is a German book by Dacqué,[15] who says that animals all come from that block which was hewn out to make man, that animals are particles split off from man. We are not derived from the ape-man, but the ape-man is derived from us—and went on making apes. There really might be something in it. Our idea about the descent of man is most peculiar. It might just as well be that a certain old gorilla was a by-product of man; that is perfectly feasible from a biological

[13] Ludwig Büchner (1824-1899), German materialistic philosopher. Jung called his book *Kraft und Stoff* (1855; tr., *Force and Matter*, 1864) "outstandingly stupid" (1945; CW 18, par. 1383).

[14] Hélan Jaworski (1880-19??), French writer on philosophy and science. Jung had several of his books, including *Pourquoi la mort?* (1926).

[15] Edgar Dacqué (1878-1945), German palaeontologist, who reversed the Darwinian theory of the origin of species, thus losing his scientific reputation. The reference may be to his *Urwelt, Sage und Menschheit* (1926), in Jung's library.

point of view. Such ideas are in the air nowadays, *I* cannot decide! You remember what Eckhart says: "All grain meaneth wheat, all metal meaneth gold, and all nature meaneth man."

So when I speak of man I mean creation, because in a way man is creation, for he only is aware of creation. If nobody is aware of it, it is as if it were not. That is Schopenhauer's idea[16]—that the world does not exist if man is not aware of it, and therefore man should extinguish himself in order to bring suffering to an end. It is also the Eastern point of view. And lunatics have the same idea that the world is chiefly a projection, that it exists only when they create it. They say: I make those people; if I don't look there is nothing there. Such tremendous exaggeration is, of course, due to the fact that their connection with reality has been severed, a fact which also occurs in the highest condition of Yoga, where a man feels the whole world as an enormous illusion, an hallucination. He speaks to a person as if there were nobody there, as if it were just a voice he has heard, and he feels it like that. These are peculiarities of people who have concentrated their thought within. I told you that anecdote of old man Schopenhauer standing in the flower bed. When one is removed to a higher level of consciousness, reality appears as a sort of illusion.

Well now, we must return again to the original problem—what takes place in the Trinity when it comes down to earth? The dream gives us the simple answer that it is reborn in the shape of triplets, two of them dead and one living. That is a pretty sad rebirth, I should say, not very complete. The only thing that remains from that whole process of transformation is a little baby, one perhaps divine but very human baby that should be taken care of.

Mr. Crowley: In a way it is the same, because it contains all the possibilities.

Dr. Jung: Well, yes, but from the point of view of Christian possibilities it is not even a very modest Saviour.

Dr. Baynes: Is it not that the depotentiation of the Trinity is bringing the action down from the abstract to the normal sphere of relationship, the human embodiment?

Dr. Jung: Yes. When we go back to the actual associations of the dreamer, which one must always do, mind you, we come to that theoretical conclusion. To him these three children are spiritual efforts, and his most recent preoccupation, psychology, is the

---

[16] Principal theme of Schopenhauer's *The World as Will and Idea.*

only remaining child of the Trinity. So that would be the divine child. And what is the divine child? *The honest attempt of man.* The last remnant of something divine is the honest attempt of man, made through that derivation to a sort of God. You will laugh that I bring in H. G. Wells, but in his book *God the Invisible King*,[17] God is *a youth*, and I know that figure from innumerable dreams. We have often spoken of it, the Puer Aeternus who represents the more or less heroic attempt of man, which becomes or, in a way, takes the place of a deity. A peculiar kind of deity, for what is weaker than a human attempt? What is more miserable, more helpless? It is an exceedingly small seed in the beginning. It has to grow, and one has to take care of it to enable it to grow, and that is, of course, not one's idea of the divine—a thing so helpless and weak. But if it is true, as Eckhart says, that God has to be born in the soul again and again, then God is born necessarily as—well, an embryo, a little child, absolutely inefficient, that has to become. So it shouldn't shock our religious feelings too much when we attribute the divine quality to the human attempt. But apparently it shocks us from the standpoint of rationalism or from our intellectual point of view. Why should it have the quality of the divine? One cannot see that, and I don't know why one should. I strongly advise you not to. To assume that your attempt is necessarily divine would be a terrible assumption.

I say that your attempt has the divine quality because, if you study these attempts of man, you will discover that they are not so much conscious decisions, not so much his own free will, as that they are forced upon him. He has to make the attempt, he cannot escape it. It may be the thing he is perhaps most afraid of, the thing about which he has always thought: For heaven's sake, I hope that does not come to me!—and afterwards he says: Oh, I wanted it! But he funked it for years. He may even think that it is his worst foolishness, his most miserable folly, and that he is a damned fool to try. Why expose himself to these things? It is because he has to do it, he cannot keep his fingers off it. A superior factor in himself, *Deus ex machina*, the divine thing in him, that tremendous power, is forcing his hand, and he is the victim of his own attempt—though he *says* his attempt was just his purpose. Not in the least! Therefore, when you talk to people like Mr. Goethe or Mr. Napoleon, they will frankly tell you that it was not so much their own choice, that

---

[17] See above, 27 Mar. 1929, n. 5; also 30 Jan. 1929, n. 1.

they had the feeling of fate in it, that they were following a sort of guidance. And all people who have really done something in the world have that feeling that there is much behind the screen, some real incentive in their choice and in what they have done. For, if told to do something important, one is terribly afraid and would give anything in the world if one had not to do it.

Now, the dream says to this man, you are without a God, you have dropped out of the Church and there is no God; the only thing divine is your honest attempt at this psychological business. I don't mean that analytical psychology is in any way divine, but it is the only way that he can make; it is his boat, his water, his sail, everything, and it is of miserable human make. There is no divine revelation in it but the fact is that he cannot leave it. There was once a time when I said to him, "You are not forced to do this kind of analysis, you can do what you please. It is an interesting intellectual game for you, and I admit it need not be anything more. And now, if you want to know how much the thing is worth to you, just give it up." I always say that to my patients as if it were a matter of belief. If you do not need clothes, give them up, go about naked, and if you feel better, so much to the good. But he can't give up analysis. Later on he will say that he clung to it with tremendous energy, made himself do it every day; yet in reality he could not give it up. There is the power, there is the mana, and it is wise to see it. That is why the dream speaks in such a way. It is extraordinary that these dreams look so simple, and yet we have to talk for hours to find out what they really mean. It is so simple to say that the Trinity comes down and a child is born, and yet it makes a. tremendous transformation in his whole system that he inadvertently gets into a divine presence. He is suddenly confronted with that tremendous factor, and how does it appear to him? As a little child.

Those of you who were in a former seminar will remember Meister Eckhart's beautiful story of the dream of Brother Eustachius, a monk of a Paris order, about the little naked boy whom he had to feed with bread, and no bread was good enough, and only afterwards he discovered that this little boy who had been with him was the Lord himself.[18] So my dreamer had not the faintest idea that his honest attempt, that little boy, was the God to come.

[18] See above, 20 Mar. 1929, p. 181.

Mr. Schmitz: Would you say that the divine in analysis might be the method of removing resistances against this honest attempt?

Dr. Jung: Yes, one could say that. For most people's attempt is not honest, it is an illusion. They make heroic attempts to escape the real attempt, because that is the thing of which people are most afraid. The honest attempt is the worst danger.

Mr. Schmitz: Why danger?

Dr. Jung: Oh, danger because one is afraid of it. It is a risk, one dies by living. There was a French soldier who was a very fine man, I mean a real man, and his principle was that he always followed his fear; wherever he was afraid, there he would go because he felt it to be his duty. Not foolishly, like climbing a chimney; one doesn't do that—it is too foolish. He was an officer in some garrison in France, and he met there a man who had been in the Foreign Legion on the border between Algeria and Morocco, who told him all kinds of terrible things about it, quite gruesome details, and this officer said to himself, you are afraid!—so he went into that African army. Later on, travelling on leave in the South of France, he visited a Trappist monastery. He knew nothing about that order, nothing about the rules of the monks, he only knew that they did not speak, that they only lived in order to die. Suddenly it struck him as a most fearful thing to do, it got him, and he said to himself: These fellows do it, go and be a Trappist. So he went; and as a Trappist he again had an experience. He heard of certain Trappist monks who had gone alone to Morocco to do missionary work among those tribes, and that some of them had been cruelly murdered. Again he felt fear, so he became a missionary and went to Morocco, and he was murdered. That was the end of it. There was a man who obviously had found out that, for him, following the fear was the honest attempt. I don't know how to value such a life, I have no means of knowing if it was wonderful or beautiful. I only tell you the story to show you how that man followed the thing he was afraid of. Whether that was right for him is not to be judged by us. I suppose if I had seen that man, if he had come for analysis, it is just possible that that might have turned out to be his life. I have seen many cases where people said: Do you really think that I have to go through this or that? I say: I don't know, we must find out.

Mr. Schmitz: In a female dreamer, would the symbol be a girl, or also a boy? Women very often dream of little girls.

Dr. Jung: That is a specific problem, and here it is a universal problem, because this man has really a philosophical mind. I have explained before that his wife doesn't think at all; therefore one could say that her mind is in the depths of the cosmos, and he gets that from her. It is just that which is so interesting, that it is his wife who brings forth his honest attempt, the triplets.

LECTURE IV

28 May 1930

Dr. Jung:

Here is a question from Mrs. Crowley about the decrease of efficiency through the mirroring process. You remember our argument about the psychological effect of what we called the mirroring process, namely, the discovery of a new standpoint from which one can judge oneself by means of a newly acquired function—that is, the function newly detached from the unconscious. And we discussed the interesting fact that the more we are capable of mirroring ourselves, the more we get detached and the more general our insight becomes. That relatively universal insight leads necessarily to a sort of quietism, as it does in the East. The principle in Eastern philosophy which is connected with this process is *wu wei*[1]—doing nothing or non-doing. That is the formula of the quietistic principle which is connected with the supreme insight. This comprised, formerly, not only this ethical principle but the Eastern political and strategic principles as well, though it is of course no longer valid since the East has become so europeanized. Now this "non-doing," or lack of efficiency, is not necessarily destructive. Of course, it hinders efficiency as we understand the word; for instance, the American concept of efficiency would surely be rather injured by the *wu wei* principle. One can hardly imagine a greater contrast than these two, but the American efficiency is far more destructive than the Eastern lack of it.

Mrs. Crowley: It destroys the individual?

Dr. Jung: Yes, but it is not only the psychological destruction of the individual, it is also physiological. Look at the men in Wall Street! At forty-five they are completely exhausted. Modern life in

---

[1] Cf. *Psychological Types* (1921), CW 6, par. 369: "*Wu-wei* means 'not-doing,' which is not to be confused with 'doing nothing.' "

America is more efficient than in any place in the world, but it completely destroys the man. Also it has a peculiar effect on the unconscious of the American woman; it stimulates her animus, as it likewise stimulates the anima in a man. When these figures prevail, it means just destruction. So if one added a bit of the Eastern *wu wei* to our Western idea of efficiency it would perhaps be helpful. Naturally our efficiency would suffer, but that is a monster, a dragon, which eats human life. *Wu wei* means a certain decrease of efficiency, but it is not as destructive to life. Up to a certain point it would be an excellent medicine for our psychological and also physiological existence.

Mrs. Crowley: I gathered from what you said the more removed you were, the less you could function.

Dr. Jung: Yes, according to the understanding of our Western world. But the East is not inefficient; the old Emperor ruling his Empire by *wu wei* was by no means inefficient in his own way, though he was very weak according to our ideas.

Mrs. Baynes: Could you say that the present situation in China,[2] where millions of people have to die, is due to this idea of *wu wei*?

Dr. Jung: That might be true, perhaps, for the principle is obviously not ideal. The East certainly needs more of our technique, and we criticize the East for its quietism because it is a one-sided point of view. I don't say that we should accept an Eastern philosophy. Many people do go in for Indian theosophy and such stuff, but I am an opponent of that because I know that for us it is not healthy. You see how this dreamer clearly develops in the direction which points ultimately to the East, but adding the East to the West does not suppress the West. The common result will be something quite different. It will be an effect of this mixture.

Question: It seems to me that if your formulation of the four functions as having existence both within and without must necessarily bring a dynamic factor into the functions, and would not that lead to introversion? I mean in a theoretical case?

Dr. Jung: One could say that Eastern psychology suffers from an introversion neurosis. All those terrible epidemics out there, or the awful famines, and the fact that the West is able to conquer those peoples, all that is a sort of rebellion of objects against their

---

[2] The allusion is to the long civil war between the Chinese Communists and the Kuomintang.

introversion. We have a Western neurosis based on extraversion. I speak of the East as a sort of compensatory symbol, but I would not identify our attempt at compensation with Eastern psychology as it actually is, because I reject the political and social conditions as they are in China or India, and I would not even like to have the same kind of mind. We speak of Chinese philosophy in terms of the highest appreciation but we forget how cruel the Chinese are. I am glad that such things do not happen with us, though since the Great War we can say nothing. We have organized cruelty; there they do it in a more dilettantic way.

Mr. Schmitz: I think we must make a point between the conscious and the unconscious application of the *wu wei*. In the great periods of Chinese philosophy, *wu wei* was a conscious purpose, but if *wu wei* works unconsciously it is nothing but a lazy and indifferent *laisser aller*, the kind of thing which has been going on in China for the last fifty years. But in Europe also a certain sort of *wu wei* has always been practiced. Of course, real statesmanship is not possible without it. What else is Talleyrand's dictum *pas trop de zéle*,[3] or in English "Wait and see," or "Never complain, never explain"? Especially the efficiency of English politics—I emphasize the efficiency—often comes from a very wise application of the principle of non-action. For instance, in the Great War, it is said that the sister[4] of the German Emperor gave him favourable astrological dates for starting attacks, and one supposes that the English knew that but could not help it. So they awaited patiently the end of the series of dates favourable to Germany and lost the battles and won the war. Psychology proved stronger than military efficiency. We can admit that, whether we believe in psychology or not.

Dr. Jung: That is very interesting. Well, I think we will now proceed with the next dream. You remember, from the dream we have just been dealing with, that we came to the conclusion that the child who remained alive was really the idea of the honest attempt—this man's honest attempt to do something with psychology, so we could almost expect that the next dream would be

[3] According to Ste-Beuve, the statesman Charles Maurice de Talleyrand-Périgord (1754-1838) was reputed to have advised his subordinates "Et surtout, pas de zèle" (and above all, no zeal) in order to avoid indiscretions.

[4] It has been impossible to document this rumour in the historical scholarship. The Kaiser's sister Victoria, Princess Schaumburg-Lippe, who had a reputation for eccentricity, was the conjecture of one specialist.

busy with that. For the question left over is, what will his attempt be, how will he go about it, how is this child to be brought into the world? Because when a dream speaks of a child it is always a new attempt, some positive manifestation of life, or a new idea. When someone has written a new book, for instance, it is often expressed metaphorically as a child. So we may assume that the next dream will deal with the reality of that attempt. Now we shall see whether that hypothesis is good or not.

Dream [27]

The dreamer says that his firm has opened a new branch, and they would now occupy themselves with the export of coffee. The real seat of the firm is in the Colonies, so it would be in a position to do that kind of business. It was decided also that this new branch should operate as a so-called *compte-joint*, a corporation or a co-operative firm, with a French firm called Michel & Jalaubout. The dreamer is in charge of this new organization and has had to explain to several employees how this *compte-joint* should be organized and carried out. Then the idea occurs to him that the new branch ought to have a separate room in the house of his firm, and he feels that this room should be just the one he is occupying. So in order to make it ready, he gathers together various bottles and boxes from drawers and puts them together on a sofa, and then gathers them up to carry into another room. He empties that room in order to make it ready for the employees of the new branch. Then he asks an employee who comes in whether everything is clear, and the man replies that it is, but he would like to ask whether the former branch of the business would be carried on too, or whether it would be given up now on account of the new foundation. The dreamer answered that it was quite self-evident that the former business must be carried on, and that this new branch was a side branch. The whole conversation, he noticed, was in French.

Associations: He says that much coffee from America is imported into the whole of North Africa, but that almost none is exported because there is practically no production of coffee there, although so much is consumed. So the export of coffee from a North African town would be really impossible; it could only be an importation.

Concerning the name of the firm *Michel & Jalaubout*, he says that the name Michel reminds him of Michelin,[5] the maker of French tires for automobiles, and that he had had some rather important business connections with that firm.

About the *name Jalaubout*, he says that it is unreal to him, he knows nobody of that name, but it reminds him of the French word *jalon*, which means a sign or a sort of token. For instance, one would call a pole that one puts in the ground to mark a certain place a *jalon*, as when one is measuring out a field, one might put in these *jalons* to mark the space. Then he says that the word begins with a J or an I, which for him has an extremely masculine character, so he is almost inclined to identify it with a phallic symbol. And then he remembers the well-known writer Schuré[6] (a pretty fantastic writer, strongly influenced by theosophy, but his fantasies are sometimes quite interesting, though apt to be a bit too wild), and he says that he remembers having read in one of his books about the name *Jahve* (meaning Jehovah) and that this name derives from the eternally female *Ehwe*, to which was added the masculine or phallic "I." That would be indicative of the mixture of the masculine and feminine in one figure, so here we see the relation to the hermaphrodite. Then he separates the word like this: *Jalon au bout*, the *jalon* at the end. The *jalon* is the phallic principle which clearly refers to his undying sexual problem so that would mean the phallus at the end.

Dr. Baynes: What is that word *Ehwe*?

Dr. Jung: It probably would be Hebrew, but one cannot rely upon Schuré. Can you tell us, Professor Hooke?[7]

Prof. Hooke: The Hebrew word for existence, *hawah*, from which the word *Jahve* comes, has no philological connection with the word to live, *haweh*, with which the dreamer associates his *Jahve*.

Dr. Jung: It would be very probable that Schuré had a wild fantasy here, he is not very careful. He is a poet. You may have read his book, *Les Grands Initiés*.[8] He has some very good psycho-

---

[5] André Michelin (1853-1931), founder, in 1895, of the rubber-tire company.

[6] Edouard Schuré (1841-1929), Alsatian writer on mysticism and the occult; he was close to Rudolf Steiner and Richard Wagner.

[7] Samuel Henry Hooke (1874-1968), professor of archaeology and religion, University of London; subsequently, he published scholarly works on Near Eastern mythology.

[8] *Les Grands Initiés; esquisses de l'histoire secrète des religions* (1889); tr. F. Rothwell, *The Great Initiates* (1912).

logical ideas but they are not his own, he can't help producing them quite involuntarily. That makes good psychological stuff for the analyst, but it proves nothing as to his other merits. This is merely our dreamer's associative material, and he himself has no particular confidence in Schuré. It would probably be more a reminiscence of his theosophical studies.

The next association concerns his removing those *bottles and boxes*, which remind him of a sort of house pharmacy. You remember he has hygienic tendencies, as such people often have, and so is also interested in all sorts of patent medicines. One sees that chiefly with rather one-sided business men; they are always inclined, when something goes wrong, to become hypochondriac. They become vegetarians perhaps and give up alcohol and drink a lot of patent medicines; and they read medical books for their particular uplifting, as a sort of substitute for spiritual development. Their spirits are to be bought at a drug-store. It is really astonishing how often such a one-sided business man gets hypochondriac. I don't know in how far that is true of my dreamer, but I suppose he has some secret penchant for these bottles and boxes and other prescriptions. Now he associates the fact that he is moving all that stuff from the room he has already occupied to another, with the change of attitude in himself; the situation, inasmuch as it is due to an attitude, is changed.

He associates with *the employee* who asked him if the new branch would now be the main interest of the business, first, that this employee is perfectly unknown to him, and then he says that obviously this question, whether the branch already existing would be neglected or even repressed, refers to the psychological functions, and that it seems, from the result of the discussion in the dream, that there exists no plan to change the main functions, but he should change his attitude to them, and the other functions should be developed. And, peculiarly enough, he emphasizes the function which seems to be illogical. That refers to the business of coffee exportation, which would be perfectly nonsensical in North Africa. Of course, he knew that these side interests, meaning inferior functions, had to become conscious. They had to take over that new room which he himself had held hitherto and which has been made ready for them. And then he says, in their attempt at bringing about the new arrangement, he had the aid of a well-known, very influential man named Michelin, who happens to represent one of the greatest French firms, and he had besides the aid of his own masculinity.

So our hypothesis that this next dream would be concerned with the life of the third child, the honest attempt, holds good. The dreamer represents that new attempt as a business attempt, which naturally would seem to him, as a business man, entirely feasible and legitimate. In the first part of the dream, the statement is made that this new branch of the firm will be for the exportation of coffee from a North African harbour; and you have heard his associations that he considers that perfectly illogical, since they would be unable to do anything of the sort. Much coffee is consumed in the country and none is produced, so there would be no business at all. Now what do you say to that?

Dr. Deady: He himself would have to produce the product in the land before he could export it.

Dr. Jung: Yes, but the country is sterile, North Africa would not do for producing coffee.

Mr. Schmitz: There might be a connection between importation and exportation, and introversion and extraversion.

Dr. Jung: I am doubtful about that. It is rather a question of production, creation.

Mr. Schmitz: Till now his soil was sterile and now he is obliged to produce something. He has imported theosophy and now he should export a new product.

Dr. Jung: Yes, we might assume that the sterile soil could be made fertile, though nothing is said of that particular version. But of course that is a very important motif; the Redeemer comes from a place where one never would expect it.

Mrs. Baynes: Didn't he say himself that he had to turn from the logical to the illogical?

Dr. Jung: Yes. The underlying idea of the former dream is, now what about that honest attempt? And this dream says there is perfectly illogical business in it, it is not at all a business proposition. When one thinks of a new attempt, one naturally seeks the possibility among reasonable conditions, along feasible lines. A business man would never seek his possibilities in a place where he was quite certain that nothing could happen. He would assume that there would be progress and that something reasonable would happen. That is what all people wish for naturally. But the dream prepares him for a shock, that his new attempt will be a perfectly illogical one. You must realize that he is a business man even in his dreams, so the idea of opening a branch for the exportation of coffee in North Africa is shocking to him, like a sort of obscenity. Yet his dream is forcing him to recognize the irrational possibility. He is actually in a position where rational means are exhausted, everything is blocked, he does not see a way out, so help can come from only the most impossible place where he would least expect it; the dream says, make yourself ready for an exception, a perfectly illogical thing that you wouldn't dream of in reality.

Mr. Schmitz: It is a mythological motif that one cannot have a thing without an impossible condition attached, as the wood coming in *Macbeth*;[9] or in another legend, flowers coming from stones. And then in a certain symbolic sense a flower will indeed come from a stone.

Dr. Jung: I am glad you made that remark. Such an initial condition is often found in prophecies or fairy tales, like the wood coming to Dunsinane in *Macbeth*; or the coming of a man not born of woman; or water running up hill—perfectly impossible conditions like those in this dream. You see, it really needs a shock in such cases because men of that kind are hard-boiled sinners. They believe in rational things because life has shown them what they are worth; they made a lot of money by rational means and naturally they believe in them; they believe that everything can be bought. Therefore they are so hypochondriac. Not long ago I saw such a case, a great business man who broke down and had hypochondriac ideas, and was continually travelling all over the world, seeking a physician who could cure him. He said there must be a cure for his disease because one could buy everything, so that great doctor must exist somewhere. He assured me he would pay any fee if I would treat him. I could demand anything. Money could do it, and if it didn't, it was that not enough money was offered. I remember another rich person who did not believe in death. He also believed that life could be bought, and that a relative who suffered from an incurable disease need not die, that if one would buy the best physicians and hospitals nobody would die because he could afford to live. A man might be shot in the brain, but if he paid a sufficient fee for it, surely it was impossible that our wonderful science could not cure his illness. And so such men build up a neurosis.

[9] *Macbeth* IV, ii.

Our patient's mentality is of course not as bad as that, but there is something of the kind in him. He naturally would believe absolutely in rational ways as such people are bound to do just because of their success. When one succeeds in making money from a thing, it must be good, because one sees it in one's bank account, one lives by it, enjoys it. Therefore he continued that rational method and naturally he came to the end of it. That the dream says now that the way to the new attempt will be perfectly illogical breaks through all his expectations. His secret hope has hitherto been: "We will analyse that stuff, we extract things here and there, removing complications, and though I don't quite see how logical the thing is, the doctor knows; he is a scientist, I pay him to be on the job, and in a certain peculiar way things come right." He thinks it is all perfectly good business which one can buy. Therefore such people must have paid authorities, experts, doing the job for them. Now, this dream breaks into that spider-web of assumptions and says it is as if he had to open such a nonsensical branch, and in the dream he takes it quite seriously.

Now we come to the second statement, that the new branch will be undertaken in co-operation, in *compte-joint* with the French firm of Michel & Jalaubout. You remember the associations. Let us take the idea of the co-operative relationship in that particular firm. I want to insist upon the question of the *compte-joint* now in this new business he is undertaking, the exportation of coffee, in which, as you know, losses and gains are divided. Naturally, that French firm, if things take a wrong course, will be just as much injured as his own firm. Now what do you think about this proposition to undertake such a co-operative business? It is a very important question. That observation in his dream will give you a chance to look into the business of practical analysis.

Question: Is it not a union of his rational and irrational functions?

Dr. Jung: Yes, if you could prove that Michel & Jalaubout are the irrational functions, but you cannot.

Dr. Baynes: There seems to be a French element. The French association is important.

Dr. Jung: Yes, but that rather belongs to the firm, and for the moment I am insisting upon the corporate relationship for the sake of clearness.

Mrs. Baynes: You said French had always been the language of his business.

Dr. Jung: That is perfectly true, but it has nothing to do with the *compte-joint* relationship. It has to do with the whole thing, but for the sake of clearness we must speak first of that relationship.

Remark: It means that not only the dreamer is involved.

Dr. Jung: Yes, that is important. His attempt will not only concern himself but other people just as much—that French firm of which we are not speaking just now. So his attempt is not an individualistic attempt. It may be quite individual, yet it is not selfish or egotistical, concerned with himself only. It divides his risks with other people.

Dr. Baynes: It concerns export, which has also the idea of giving out.

Dr. Jung: Yes, there is very much the idea of relationship between himself and the outside world. And the idea of the division of responsibility is a very important point, because when his progress has to do with a condition that is entirely his own, he would naturally think that, if he goes in for a nonsensical enterprise, it was his own individual nonsense and he would feel quite isolated. But the dream says it is a co-operative enterprise. The risks are divided between his own firm, his total personality, and another firm.

Mr. Schmitz: This illogical thing, if co-operative, is not only his affair, it is acknowledged by the collective world.

Dr. Jung: Naturally, because that firm Michelin is one of the most important of French tire-makers, which means a lot to him. He has very important business relations with the firm already, and of course the dream indicates that he is not at all astray in such a nonsensical enterprise, when even that greatest firm, supposed to be very efficient, is dividing risks with him. What we have made out from our discussion, then, is that such an illogical attempt, which would isolate an individual with feelings of inferiority, is counterbalanced by the statement of the dream, that a firm of unquestionable authority is taking the same risks as himself, which is of course exceedingly important to him as a business man. Naturally one supposes his firm is a good one because Michelin is not supposed to have relations with just any *arriviste*, any kind of speculative fool. So that aspect is surely a compensation for a feeling of inferiority which he would necessarily have when confronted with the indispensable condition that he should attempt something perfectly foolish, an illogical enterprise. But that is not the whole thing, we must go a little more deeply into it. We will discuss the firm. Let us take Michel.

Miss Wolff: Did he know that Michelin was the inventor of the tires? The wheels mark a creative element.

Dr. Jung: That is true.

Mr. Schmitz: But is there actually a firm called Michel & Jalaubout?

Dr. Jung: No, there he associates only Michelin.

Mr. Schmitz: That is a strange collaboration, Michel et Jal-au-bout. Even such a firm as Michelin has a secret collaboration with the phallic element of the world!

Dr. Jung: It is no secret collaboration. The firm of Michelin is a most important manufacturer of automobile tires. But it is a funny mixture!

Mr. Schmitz: An automobile has very often a sexual symbolism.

Dr. Jung: Oh yes, anything can have it—the chair upon which you sit. One can have sexual intercourse with almost anything; it depends upon the dreamer. Now what about Michelin? You see there is a change in the name, the "in" is left off. Such a thing in a dream is a hint that it is not exactly Michelin. For instance, if you dream of your father, and see him in surroundings or conditions in which he never would have been, it means your father but not exactly your father, he wears unlikely clothes perhaps and is slightly somebody else. So when he dreams of Michel—provided he knows nobody named Michel—his next association will surely be Michelin. That name is in red letters in his book as one of his most important business connections, so we could say that as in reality he shares mutual risks with the firm of Michelin, so in a psychological enterprise he shares risks with a Michelin firm, but it is not exactly Michelin, only approximately.

Mrs. Sawyer: Has it nothing to do with the auxiliary functions?

Dr. Jung: Yes, but that is a bit too far away. We are here concerned with something in his immediate experience. That name Michelin means so many numbers with so many ciphers behind, endless zeros, hundreds of thousands—money, and tremendous tensions, hopes, and fears. Perhaps he has an important order every year and the question is whether that order comes or whether another firm is getting it. His very existence depends upon such combinations, they make the whole tension of his life. Nobody can get so one-sided as a financier. So we cannot get away from that very important personal factor, Michelin, that means highly important business in prospect. As a business man he would go up like a skyrocket, of course, because it means the whole passion of speculative and business life. Then our next commonsense conclusion would be that, if the dream refers to the Michelin firm, it probably symbolizes an equally important collaboration in his psychological life. And that is the collaboration with the analyst, of course. I am his Michelin and therefore the "in" is left off, because it is not exactly Michelin.

Now, Michelin is the inventor of tires, and here one can speculate about the symbol of tires, automobiles, etc. He looks upon me in the psychological sphere as a great authority, but since the psychological sphere is perhaps to him not so awfully important, the unconscious insists that it is important, just as important as his connection with Michelin. Of course, he would not consciously believe that. Naturally he has the necessary respect for me, but he doesn't assume that I could be of such extraordinary value to him. I don't want to convey the idea that I forced my importance upon that man. I put it exactly as I have done here. I said that his business connection with Michelin is the symbol for an important connection with me; for the time being that association was just as important for his psychological welfare as it was important for his business to be associated with Michelin. Now that would cover Michel, but how about Jalaubout? That puts me in the same firm with Jalaubout.

Mrs. Baynes: A very dangerous combination!

Dr. Jung: Is it dangerous for me or for him? You see, we have divided risks.

Mr. Schmitz: Michel is the killer of the dragon, and you are the dragon-killer in analysis; and now Jalaubout has also something to do with the dragon.

Dr. Jung: Well, we should realize now the associations that he gives with that word Jalaubout. You remember he divided it into three words. First "Jal," where the "on" is left off because *jalon* would be too much like the phallic pole. One of the most primitive forms of the phallic emblem is a pole, but because it is not exactly a phallus, the "on" is left off. The phallic symbol is an important hint, yet in such a case where part of a name is altered or left off, we must expect another determinant which caused the removal.

Another association of equal importance in the case is *Jahve*, where there is the inference that the J of *jalon* was in itself, through its vertical form, a masculine symbol, and there was the fantasy which he got from Schuré about *Eweh* being the symbol of the female. Then two together made the hermaphrodite. Now again from this association we get a whole world of ideas and possibilities—you remember our former discussion of the hermaphrodite[10]—joined in a curious way to the phallic symbolism. It is like a charade, the whole thing making one form, obviously two sides of one and the same thing. On the one side would be his psychological relation to me, symbolized by Michelin the dragon-killer, or the inventor of tires; and on the other side the divine hermaphrodite and the phallic symbol. What is your idea about this?

Dr. Schlegel: "Au bout" means that in the end he must do it himself, helped by the hermaphrodite power.

Dr. Jung: Well, literally, we have the Jal, and the divine hermaphrodite, and the phallic pole, and both together in the end, and that suggests a peculiar meaning.

Mrs. Crowley: Individuation evidently.

Dr. Jung: Yes, but that is too abstract now. We must elucidate that peculiar fact of the phallic symbol with the divine hermaphrodite, which is a difficult problem. The fact that "Michelin" refers to his psychological association with me as being one part of that firm means that his relation to me shares the risks of the enterprise. The enterprise is his psychological attempt at analysis, which is half my risk and half his risk, as if I were directly connected with his attempt, so that if he fails, I fail, and if he wins, I win. Now how about that? I could say: it is my venture, and whether it succeeds or not, he has paid my fees, I have made so much money; and if it is a failure, well, I am sorry.

Dr. Baynes: There is the superior man that he recognizes or projects into you and through that comes to the goal—by relation with the superior man.

Dr. Jung: Of course, Michelin is much the greater firm, so one could speak of a certain superiority, but I should say that this symbolism tends rather to put us on an equal footing. You see, we have equal shares in the gains and losses. The dream decidedly makes the psychological enterprise a co-operative business. That is

[10] See above, 19 and 26 Feb. 1930, passim.

to my mind a very important point of view, because usually it is assumed that the patient appeals to the doctor, who sits upon a throne and hands out black pills of wisdom, and the poor little patient swallows them as well as he can and the analyst is not concerned—or only as a seller of drugs or something of the sort. You see, that would be his attitude. One pays so much and gets the stuff. Now against that assumption, the dream says, no, it is a co-operative business, gains and losses are divided, and Dr. Jung is just as much concerned as you are, it is as much his attempt as yours. Do you see the implication of such a symbolism? It changes the atmosphere altogether. He is no longer the little patient who crawls on his stomach to the grand authority to get his pills. He is now a co-worker, and I am a co-worker, and we share all the risks of the situation. The dream lifts him at once out of his atmosphere of a rabbit being experimented with, and shows him that he is concerned with the business we are sharing. And he not only shares it with myself, he also shares it with Jalaubout.

Mr. Schmitz: I can see that more clearly because a *jalon* is used as a sign where a new way has to be built. The analysis is the new way, and if it is a long business, the first thing would be to try the export business, the wrong way. Yet you have to go there first. The *jalon* sets the mark for you.

Dr. Jung: You could say a *jalon* was a sign. You might put a pole somewhere as a direction to a distant goal, or if you were building a road, to designate the line upon which you want it to go. That is beautiful symbolism for working out one's psychological way, the line of one's life. There is also an aspect of the *jalon*—as *jusqu'au bout*—that it will mark the goal. But his associations go to a deeper thing, to the phallic symbol on the one side and the divine hermaphrodite on the other.

Mrs. Sigg: When the dreamer first came to analysis, he thought that sexuality had nothing whatever to do with religion, so no divine element was in it, but now the dream says that if he works together with Dr. Jung there will be a combination with the divine.

Dr. Jung: That is perfectly true. To this man the unexpected thing is the peculiar connection between religion and sex, and the second name contains religion and sex. In his rational mind he would divide the two altogether. That sexuality has been shut off in an air-tight compartment has been the great trouble in his life. We know how he tried and failed to get away from the whole thing

634

with his theosophical attempts. Then came a dream where he was made acquainted with the different compartments of his mind, and suddenly there was a crash when things which did not seem to belong that way came together. So that second name contains his idea of sexuality and his religious ideas, and one could say that the phallus as a symbol, and the divine hermaphrodite, the deity, mean one and the same thing; and at the same time the element of "the way" is in it, as a *jalon* is really used to show a certain direction, to mark a certain way. This idea of the "way" is a very important one in the East. Where does that occur?

Dr. Shaw: Isn't it an idea in Protestant theology: "I am the way"?[11]

Dr. Jung: Yes, in the dogmatic form, but the rule is not applied there.

Dr. Baynes: The Way is the symbol of the Tao.

Dr. Jung: Yes, the Taoist idea of the way is given in the union of the opposites, namely, sexuality, the pole, and the divine hermaphrodite; the cross of the two together makes the way. Sex below, religion above, and, in between, the way. For whenever pairs of opposites come together, when two opposing conditions meet, something will happen in between which is equal to energy. Water falling from a higher to a lower level means an energic process resulting from the clash of opposites; from above to below, from tension to relaxation. The energic process only goes one way. The symbols of Tao are symbols of energy, or reconciliation of the pairs of opposites. Always between the two comes the one who opens the way, creates the way. So that *jalon*, that *jal-au-bout*, gives the idea of the way between the pairs of opposites, the phallus and the divine being.

Now that is a peculiar firm, that Michel and that Jalaubout. Mr. Jalaubout shares the risks too. If we fail in our honest attempt to get that man somewhere, then I fail to get myself somewhere. I make my way only when I make my patient's way. That is the connection, and that is what the dream tells him. For there is something else connected with that business, the gods of the earth and the gods of light. On the one side sexuality and on the other side the deity, the creative forces of the universe combined into one figure; the phallus below, the radiant God above. These two are

[11] John 14:6.

635

one and the same, and that person or whatever it is also shares the risks. If you succeed, that great mystery of life succeeds. If you fail, God also fails. Now that is pretty strong language, but it is exactly the meaning of that symbolism. It is again compensatory. As I already pointed out, the name Jalaubout is in itself a compensation for his rational division between the phallus below and the heaven above. That is the division that everyone would naturally make, for we are no longer used to the idea that the universal creative force above is connected with the phallus. Therefore the phallus has always been a symbol of enormous creative power. So the ugliest thing in the world, being creative, embodies the greatest creative thing in the world. As it is formulated in the *Upanishads*: "smaller than small, yet greater than great"[12] or, "small as the size of a thumb, yet covering the whole earth, two handbreadths high."[13] That is the personal and the superpersonal Atman. In India they were able to think these paradoxes. We are not far enough along, so this concept of the union of opposites is terribly shocking to us. To the Eastern mind it is too little shocking; they should be shocked a little more.

So this rather inconspicuous symbolism of Michel and Jalaubout reveals not only the whole process of analysis but also its divine implications, one could say its almost cosmic significance. It shows what I said before, that the honest attempt is what one would call God. That is confirmed in this dream. It is on the one side the human attempt and on the other side a very burning question for the gods as well—whether man succeeds or does not succeed, whether the gods succeed or do not succeed. Well, that is about all I have to say about this Jalaubout.

Miss Wolff: That other dream where the hermaphrodite appeared was an unsuccessful attempt?

Dr. Jung: Yes, this is an entirely positive answer to a negative intuition in the former dream.

[12] *Brahman* is so characterized in the *Katha Upanishad* 2.20021, cited in *Psych. Types*, par. 329.
[13] Likewise *purusha*, in the *Shvetashvatara Upanishad* 12.15, cited in *Symbols of Transformation*, CW 5, par. 178 (as in 1912 edn.).

LECTURE V

4 June 1930

Dr. Jung:

We got as far with our dream as the meaning of the names Michel and Jalaubout, and now we come to the next point, the arrangement of this new enterprise, this branch business. You remember the dreamer said that he was explaining to an employee that the firm would be arranged as a *compte-joint*. A joint account is, as the name expresses, a very close connection. The new branch is almost integrated into his former business; the two firms, that is, are partially incorporated with each other. That gives us a certain hint. You may remember a former dream in which it was indicated that his psychology was split up into what we called compartments. Here he joins another firm and incorporates a new branch into his former business in a very intimate way, and you can be sure that this new enterprise has been in him for a long time, but in a sort of air-tight compartment which has now to be opened up. The two different tendencies are coming together; we have here the first sign that they are blending. He is a man who likes to have compartments for different parts of his psychology; he puts certain things in one drawer and other things into another, in the hope that they will never touch. But in that former dream he already began to show these different compartments to his wife, in other words, to make her acquainted with the different sides of his own personality. And he here makes a new and very serious attempt to organize those different sides in a business-like manner.

The dreamer says, then, that he is explaining his plans to employees—what he is going to do about it. It often occurs in dreams that there are indifferent or obscure people about, and when one asks patients for their associations concerning them, they say they don't know, there are just people about, quite unimportant. But obviously they are on the stage, playing a role, and we therefore ought to know what they are. Have you an idea what employees would be in such a case? Are there no theosophists to tell us something about it? Theosophists know everything! Well, when one doesn't know the meaning of a symbol, one had better take it quite naïvely and say they must be something like what employees really are in a business, that is, subordinate forces, sort of delegated powers, psychical factors that can be personified. You see, our minds have the peculiarity, which we see in the whole structure of the nervous system, that certain ways of functioning become reflexes. For instance, when you are learning to ride a bicycle, you have all the trouble in the world to keep your balance, till suddenly you get it; it has entered your system, you have delegated it to one of the employees who is now trained to do that job for you, it holds the balance for you without your knowing it. Of course, you would feel it as a subconscious factor, yet every part of the human psyche has a personal character.

One sees that quite easily in such experiments as table-rapping or table-turning. These subconscious contents come to the surface then, and are produced by things that resemble persons. When one asks who is writing or manifesting through the table, invariably that thing says, *I* am doing it. And who are you? And then it says, Aunt Mary or Uncle So-and-So—somebody who has died. Now, we cannot assume that it is always just ghosts. There are stupid people and perhaps there are stupid ghosts, and whether they get more intelligent I don't know. But at all events, there is one very important case published in the reports of the Psychical Research Society, where a man took immense trouble to find out who the thing was that talked, and it got quite embarrassed in the end and finally confessed, "I am you, you should not ask any more, I am yourself." And that is very probable. It is an unconscious delegate that says things occasionally which the conscious would not say, sometimes quite commonplace, and sometimes in symbolic form, like typical dreams. These are the persons who produce dreams. Also we are dreaming more or less during the day, and whenever we lower the glare, the acquired intensity, of our conscious for a moment, up come those things and we hear voices. Of course, we do not hear them exactly as voices—we are not crazy—and when one studies the hallucinations of insane people, one can see these minor telephone apparatuses at work much better. But they make all sorts of trouble for us.

For instance, if you have to walk across a floor in a big assembly, you naturally get self-conscious and you hear voices: "There he goes!—he is terribly self-conscious and is probably going to fall over the feet of somebody. People think he is ridiculous!" That is what you feel, though you will not get it in definite words. An insane person would hear a stentorian voice shouting: "There goes that fool and sure enough he will show that he is an ass!" And you will get the same, practically, when you analyse the feelings you have in such a moment. Or at a funeral, when you are expressing your feelings in an appropriate manner, the voices may say you are not so sorry, you are rather glad the old man died, and that gets so much under your skin that you may find yourself congratulating the mourners. Perhaps you are walking in a funeral procession, knowing that you should have a sad face, yet you can't help smiling, all sorts of jokes occur to you that you would like to whisper to your neighbour, and you will do so if you have a chance. The parson says the old man is now sitting at the right hand of the Lord but you know that is all bunk—he is burning in Hell. All such phenomena are due to those employees who are perfectly aware of the real situation. There are a host of them—we don't know how many—probably a perfectly unlimited number that represent our thoughts and feelings. They amount to reflexes, and if one splits off any part of a psychical function and gives it a chance to live by itself, it will take on the character of a person. It will be a little personality, but a restricted personality, with only a very partial realization of its own existence; the smaller the personality, the less the realization.

One gets very little from such things. If one asks the ghosts that are manifesting in the table what their condition is, they cannot tell very much, mostly platitudes, they seem to be very unaware of their surroundings. Perhaps some of you have read Sir Oliver Lodge's book about his son who died, *Raymond*.[1] He asked him all sorts of questions and the replies were peculiarly meagre. The boy was very intelligent and one would expect of him much better answers. The father asked him, "Do you live in houses?" and he answered vaguely,

[1] *Raymond, or Life and Death, with Examples of the Evidence for Survival of Memory and Affection after Death* (New York, 1916). Lodge (1851-1940), English physicist, was interested in reconciling science, religion, and spiritualism. He was prominent in the Society for Psychical Research, to which Jung read a paper, "The Psychological Foundations of Belief in Spirits" (1919), CW 8, pars. 570ff.

"Yes, we have houses," as if he didn't realize that they lived in them. He answered as if he were in a dream. It is the psychology of a very fragmentary person, and that may come from the fact that it is only a psychical phenomenon; or if it is a ghost—which I don't know, as proofs are impossible—then ghosts must live in very fragmentary forms. One sees the same thing in lunatics. I remember an old woman who had formerly been a tailoress, and when one said good morning and asked how she was, she would reply, "Oh, I have just had a telephone." "But I see no telephone." To which she would explain that it had been fixed through the wall, she didn't know how, but nearly every day God sent her special messages. She might say she was empress of the whole world, or that she possessed an island that consisted of pure silver—nonsensical things.[2] They have no realization of their surroundings.

These minor figures in our patient's dream are like that. They are unconscious creative forces and they are perfectly normal, because in dreams we are dissociated anyhow. But if one sees such figures in one's ordinary conscious life there is trouble, for that is an indubitable symptom that one is dissociated. People in that condition walk out of their houses as if it were already printed in their biography. It is as if a voice were repeating what they were doing, with either appreciation or criticism. For instance, a voice tells them that what they have just said was wonderful, and then they have a peculiar backwash of feeling in their faces. And then naturally that other voice comes up, for these voices are always balanced. In cases of insanity one finds that there are always favourable and unfavourable voices—employees who are working for your interests and against your interests, pairs of opposites.

The next thing in the dream is that he is making a room ready for that new branch. He takes all sorts of bottles and boxes out of drawers and puts them together in order to carry them into another room; his association was that they remind him of his own little drug-store at home. I have already spoken of his hygienic interests. Although this seems a ridiculous detail and one would assume that these bottles and boxes were terribly uninteresting and meant nothing, yet it is typical for this man's particular psychology. Now, what do you see in that symbol which is so typical? Be naïve about it,

[2] This is the case of "B. St.," a patient in the Burghölzli, which is the principal paradigm of "The Psychology of Dementia Praecox" (1907), CW 3, pars. 198-314. The "telephone" instance is at pars. 309-313.

please, then you get at the truth. Try to picture the man handling his boxes and bottles.

Dr. Deady: His life depends on them and he is going to sacrifice them.

Dr. Jung: Oh no, why should he get rid of them?

Miss Hannah: He just loves keeping things in boxes.

Mrs. Deady: It is compartment psychology.

Dr. Jung: Exactly. He has everything neatly in bottles and boxes and drawers. People with such a psychology always have these little drug-stores, and there is always a fuss about them. Like people with tender reminiscences who cherish certain divine remains— pressed flowers, or the teeth of the grandmother, or all sorts of little books and bric-à-brac tucked away in drawers and chests because it expresses their compartment psychology. This man is like that, each content divided from the other and each neatly labelled; one uses at this moment such a drug and at another moment such a pill. Now, that is a well-ordered mind of a sort, it means a regulation of the whole feeling or Eros system. If he should liberate all the contents, it would be an indiscriminate flood, and that is exactly why he bottles them up. The flood would be too interesting, that is the trouble. Now, emptying these drawers and sorting the contents suggests that he is cleaning out and stowing away things in order to have a whole room ready for the new business. That is a decidedly important step forward. He is now proceeding in a very businesslike way. But naturally, when going into such an enterprise, he will hear voices, and here is the employee saying: But what about the rest of your business? You see, doubt comes up in him quite inevitably, because the new business seems to be a very interesting enterprise which he has been avoiding for quite a while. You remember how, whenever he touched it, he at once fell away from it again, but here it seems to become a very real and serious thing. The fatal question is asked. In such a moment it is quite inevitable that some reaction should take place, so here comes the employee who asks the question about the main business. What is his main business?

Dr. Deady: His intellectualism, his whole attitude, a regulated system of life, as opposed to the irrational thing he is going to take on.

Dr. Jung: Yes, it would be the totality of his psychological situation, his complete life, and there would lie his natural fear. If

641

he begins a new business, it might interfere with his former business or with the functioning of his total life. So the fear that there might be some disturbance is not unreasonable, and he hastens to explain to his employee that it will not affect the main business, it is only a branch. He uses that term, just a branch business; it does not affect the whole. Here he is doing something in the dream which you can discern in everyday life when such an objection occurs to you. You even talk to yourself, you say: now don't get excited. People talk to themselves as if they were talking to an excited horse, or somebody else has to do it for them. It is a sort of fragmentary consciousness.

Now, that is the whole dream, and before going on to the next one we should realize the exact situation. The mouse has escaped, which means that something is going to happen, and his church resistance has been broken down. He went through a very complicated unconscious *raisonnement* about his religious philosophy, and he came to the conclusion that his psychological enterprise is the really vital thing for him. It is the enterprise upon which he is going to embark for good, and that is the third living child, you remember. That child has to become a reality somehow, and now in this dream he is ready to create it in reality in a very businesslike way. Therefore his unconscious chooses the methods of his own business life in order to emphasize the absolute reality of his enterprise. So we are now in a situation with the dreamer where we could expect a continuation—the beginning of that business. The branch is not yet fully organized; this dream contains only the preparations. The following dream came five days later.

Dream [28]

He was called by the voice of a child to go to a swimming-pool. The child said that there was a big animal in the water. He goes with the child but instead of a swimming-pool, he comes to a large bed. The child pulls away the bed-cover, and there is an enormous tortoise. He finds in his hand an iron tool, a chisel with a wooden handle, which he takes by the iron part. He beats the head of the tortoise with the wooden handle—not with the iron part, mind you—whereupon the animal opens its mouth and spits out a living child.

Associations: The dreamer says that man is not in his habitual element when he is in a *swimming-pool*—in the water, that is. He thinks that swimming has something to do with living in the unconscious, it is something like dreaming. He wonders that the swimming-pool is not a bathing-place but a bed, really the place where one dreams.

The *tortoise*, he thinks, is like a crocodile, a relic of prehistoric animals, and he says that it looks as if he were not intending to kill it (as he had no feeling about it) but apparently only wanted to overcome it, because he was beating its head not with the iron part of the chisel but with the wooden handle. He says, concerning the child that came out of the tortoise, that it looked like an embryo in the womb, that is, it came out with the arms and legs all drawn up in the embryonic position. He says that this is obviously a birth, but he doesn't know what to think about it.

This dream is not simple. I think we will start with the first sentence. He hears the voice of a child calling him to the unconscious, the swimming-pool. What would that mean? You see, it is not his own child, he doesn't know it.

Mr. Schmitz: His honest attempt.

Dr. Jung: Yes, one thinks naturally of that third child, the honest attempt, his new business which is also a sort of child. And the new attempt, the new life, is calling him to a certain place. We had that child symbolism in the second dream before this one,[3] and the question left over from the last dream was how the new enterprise was to continue, so it is obvious that this is the new attempt. Then his associations show that he has found out the analogy, the immediate relationship, between the bed and the swimming-pool. It is a movement in the unconscious. Water generally means the unconscious, and one's movement in the water is not the habitual movement, like walking in the air, but a new way of locomotion, as the conscious life is naturally different from our psychic life in the unconscious. Dreams have a different kind of movement, and in his associations the dreamer insists upon comparing the bed and the swimming-pool—what is swimming in the pool is dreaming in the bed. I think we can hardly add anything to his associations. That is perfectly plain.

Now, something is hidden in that bed—in the unconscious—

[3] See above, p. 557.

which he discovers in pursuing his new attempt. Naturally, the new attempt would have no reason if one were not going to discover something new—have an adventure. Such an enterprise always means a wish for new discoveries, and the first thing he encounters is a tortoise. We don't know why he should find such a prehistoric animal on his way to the new enterprise, that is perfectly irrational, we simply have to accept the fact that it is so. Now he links up the tortoise with the crocodile. Do you remember about the crocodile in a former dream?[4]

Mrs. Sigg: The crocodile was a holy animal in Upper Egypt.

Dr. Deady: The saurian brings libido from some very great irrational depths.

Dr. Jung: You remember I said that when a crocodile or any saurian turns up, one may expect something quite unusual to happen. This is again such a case. As I explained at that time, the crocodile, as well as the tortoise and any other cold-blooded animal, represents extremely archaic psychology of the cold-blooded thing in us. Schopenhauer said: "the fat of our brother is good enough to smear our boots."[5] That is the thing we never can understand— that somewhere we are terribly cold-blooded. There are people who, under certain circumstances, would be capable of things which they simply could not admit. It is frightening, we are shocked out of our wits and cannot accept it. I gave you examples of the natural mind of woman; there you see the cold-blooded animal. And naturally the same thing is in the cold-blooded man; they will confess it to each other, but never to a woman, because it is too shocking. It is like an awful danger very far away. It used to be in the Balkans, but now it is much farther away—in the moon. It would be a moral catastrophe, but since we are so far away we can laugh about it. But when it touches us, we don't laugh, it drives people almost crazy. Once we were quite certainly cold-blooded animals, and we have a trace of it in our anatomy, in the structure of the nervous system. The saurian is still functioning in us, and one only needs to take away enough brain to bring it to the daylight. Let a man be wounded very badly in the brain, or have a disease that destroys it, and he becomes a vegetative and utterly cold-blooded thing, exactly like a lizard or a crocodile or a tortoise.

4 See above, pp. 317, 323.
5 Untraceable.

I told you that Hagenbeck, the famous connoisseur of animals, said that you can establish a psychic rapport with practically all animals until one comes to snakes, alligators, and such creatures, and there it comes to an end. He told about a man who brought up a python, a perfectly harmless and inoffensive animal, apparently, that he used to feed by hand when it was quite big, and everybody assumed that it had some knowledge of him and knew that he was its nurse; but once, suddenly, that animal wound itself like lightning round the body of the man and almost killed him. Another man had to cut it to pieces with a hatchet in order to save the man's life. That is a typical example of the untrustworthiness of these creatures. Warm-blooded animals have an idea of man; they are either friendly, or they avoid him and his habitations because they dislike or are afraid of him. But snakes are absolutely heedless. So we must assume that cold-blooded animals have an entirely different kind of psychology—one would say none, but that is a little arbitrary. These cold-blooded relics are in a way uncanny powers, because they symbolize the fundamental factors of our instinctive life, dating from paleozoic times. If constellated by circumstances, the saurian appears. For instance, a terrible fear or an organic threat of disease is often expressed in dreams by a snake. Therefore people who understand nothing of dream interpretation will yet tell you that whenever they dream of snakes, they know they are going to be ill.

During the war, when I was in charge of the British interned soldiers, I became acquainted with the wife of one of the officers, a peculiarly clairvoyant person, and she told me that whenever she dreamt of snakes, it meant disease. While I was there, she dreamt of an enormous serpent which killed many people, and she said: You will see that means some catastrophe. A few days later, the second of those big epidemics of the so-called Spanish flu broke out and killed any number of people, and she herself almost died. The snake comes up in such cases because there is an organic threat which calls forth all one's instinctive reactions. So whenever life means business, when things are getting serious, you are likely to find a saurian on the way. Or when vital contents are to appear from the unconscious, vital thoughts or impulses, you will dream of such animals. It may be the hindrance that comes up, and it will block your way though you think it is perfectly simple. Up comes an invisible hindrance, and you don't know what it really is because you can't see it, or symbolize it even, and yet it can hold you. There is something hidden. Perhaps your libido drops, it appears usually in that well-known form; one loses interest suddenly, and the dream expresses it as a dragon or a monster that appears on your way and simply blocks the path for you. Then in other cases, such a monster is a help: the tremendous force of organized instinct comes up and pushes you over an obstacle which you would not believe possible to climb over by will-power or conscious decision. There the animal proves to be helpful.

Now we do not know how vital the coffee business will be for our patient, whether it really is important or dangerous to him, but this dream tells him: Look out! Here is the saurian—this is serious! At all events, the decision he obviously has made means that it will be a situation touching his instincts, the very foundations of his being. So the appearance of a tortoise is rather a startling discovery in this case. And it seems to have a very important function here, because it brings forth a child, which clearly demonstrates the fact that it is really a doctor tortoise, not an ordinary one, a thing that is a secret human being. The only association the dreamer gives is that he links it up with the crocodile. Now what about the tortoise?

Mr. Schmitz: There is important mythical symbolism connected with the tortoise. There is even a myth, I don't know where, that the tortoise is the mother of the whole world, that everything living is born from the tortoise.

Dr. Jung: You find it in Hindu myths chiefly. The world is carried on the back of an elephant that is standing on a tortoise.[6] A tortoise is a most fundamental being—the basic instinct that carries our whole psychological world. For the world is our psychology, our point of view. And as our point of view is carried by our instincts, so the world is carried by the tortoise. Now, what about the symbolic aspect of this animal?

Mrs. Deady: It is also very fertile.

Dr. Jung: That is true, but all lower animals are very fertile.

---

[6] Two mythological themes seem to be conflated. Sixteen divine elephants support the universe, according to the *Matangalila* (cited in Zimmer, *Myths and Symbols in Indian Art and Civilization*, 1946, pp. 104ff.). Vishnu assumed the shape of a tortoise to support Mount Mandara, for the churning of the ocean, in the *Bhagavata Purana*, and to support the Indian continent, in the *Markandeya Purana* (A. Daniélou, *Hindu Polytheism*, 1964, p. 167).

Miss Wolff: The tortoise has been a mother symbol.

Dr. Jung: Yes, the tortoise in mythology has that female character—maternal, underground. But these sex analogies are everywhere, and the tortoise has something very specific about it.

Mrs. Crowley: Its longevity.

Dr. Jung: It has a tremendously long life.

Miss Sergeant: It moves slowly.

Dr. Jung: It is not very temperamental!

Prof. Hooke: It only becomes vocal at the moment of coition.

Dr. Jung: That is also a particularity, but it is not so accessible to human experience. There is another very striking feature.

Dr. Howells: The amphibious side of the animal.

Dr. Jung: The amphibious side is exceedingly important as referring to the unconscious side; that has a symbolic aspect. But there is something else.

Dr. Baynes: There is its crustacean character.

Dr. Jung: Yes, it can withdraw into its own house. But the tortoise is a very impersonal symbol. The obvious features are that this animal has an armoured house into which it can withdraw and where it cannot be attacked. Then it is amphibious, it is apathetic, it lives a very long time, and it is highly mythological and mysterious. Remember that the *I Ching* was brought to land on the shells of one hundred tortoises.[7] These are all the qualities of a particular psychological factor in man—age-old, very wise, and manifesting in the conscious as well as the unconscious. This makes the tortoise very meaningful. What would it portray if you translated it into a sort of conscious function?

Answer: Introversion.

Dr. Jung: Yes, but only in an extraverted type.

Dr. Baynes: Sensation?

Dr. Jung: Only in an intuitive type.

Mrs. Fierz: Feeling?

Dr. Jung: Only in an intellectual type. If that thing should be fully developed, fully integrated into man, what would happen then? You see, if you translate the tortoise symbolism into the most differentiated thing man possibly can attain to, it always contains the thing that is in the beginning and also in the end.

Dr. Baynes: It is an irrational function.

[7] Untraceable.

Dr. Jung: Only in a rational type.

Dr. Schlegel: It has the ability to introvert and extravert, go in and out.

Dr. Jung: Yes, but it is more than that. It is the transcendent function. That is what the tortoise symbolizes, and therefore it is so important.

Mrs. Baynes: I don't see that.

Dr. Jung: The characteristics of the tortoise are the characteristics of the transcendent function, the one that unites the pairs of opposites.

Mrs. Baynes: I thought the transcendent function was created each time the pairs of opposites came together.

Dr. Jung: The coming together each time *is* the transcendent function. The term transcendent function is used in higher mathematics, where it is the function of rational and irrational numbers. I did not take that term from higher mathematics, I learned only later that the same term was used there, meaning the same thing, namely, the function of rational and irrational data in the functioning together of conscious and unconscious, of the differentiated function with the inferior function. It is the reconciliation of the pairs of opposites. From this reconciliation a new thing is always created, a new thing is realized. That is the transcendent function, and that is the tortoise. And the new thing is always strange to the old thing. A plant, for instance, may have fruit which is not at all the same, like the spores of the water algae. The mother is a plant, but the child is a little animal with a little head and a little tail, swimming about, and then it settles down and becomes a plant again.[8] So the result of the transcendent function is as strange to us as the turtle is.

Dr. Schlegel: Is it only the tortoise, or every cold-blooded animal?

Dr. Jung: Not so much as the tortoise, on account of its great age and its amphibious quality. The snake has a somewhat different meaning, it can renew itself by shedding its skin, which gives it the quality of eternity. But the snake comes nearer to the tortoise than the crocodile, in spite of the fact that there are enormously old

[8] According to the biologist John Bonner, certain algae (the "parent" plant may be male, female, or asexual) produce asexual zoospores (single-celled, with two flagella or "tails"), which can swim to a new location, settle, and produce a new, fixed plant. (Personal communication.)

crocodiles. There was one on the west bank of Lake Victoria⁹ which the Negroes fed because they said that crocodile protected the whole coast, it chased away all the others. It was tremendously big and fat—they fed it with fish, and it never ate human beings. It was the friend of man, a doctor animal. Usually the crocodile symbolizes the voracious quality of the unconscious, the danger from below which suddenly comes up and pulls people down. That is also a function of the unconscious, a very dangerous one.

Now we come to this very peculiar action of the dreamer, that he beats the tortoise on the head with the wooden handle of the chisel. He says that he obviously wants to overcome the animal, but has not the intention of killing it or he would have used the iron part. Now what about the chisel? An instrument is an important motif. Instruments often turn up in dreams with the same meaning that they have in mythology.

Dr. Deady: I think he said that it was a tool for opening boxes.

Dr. Jung: Yes, as if there had suddenly been an allusion to a locked box and it was necessary to pry open the lid, but that was not meant.

Dr. Deady: Striking the head, then, would be to bring about consciousness.

Dr. Jung: To beat somebody on the head?—Unconsciousness, rather! Although we have a nice story in this country of thieves who broke into a house and tried to smash a man's head with a hammer. But the man said, "Come in!"—as if somebody had aroused a slight interest in him by knocking at the door. In this case it is probably something of the sort. The tortoise is not killed, it merely got dizzy and delivered that child. But why such an instrument?

Mrs. Deady: It would help him to open all his drawers and boxes, his compartments.

Dr. Jung: That he must have it to open the boxes is quite possible, but what does the instrument mean?

Mrs. Crowley: In mythology it is a phallic symbol, so it might mean penetration.

Dr. Jung: Yes, and in the *I Ching* penetrating means understanding a thing;¹⁰ therefore we speak of a penetrating mind. And naturally when one speaks of a thing that is able to penetrate, one

⁹ Jung was at Jinja (Uganda), on the north shore of Lake Victoria, in January 1926, before descending the Nile.

¹⁰ *I Ching*, hexagram 57.

649

thinks of an oblong and pointed object. So there is the obvious phallic analogy, but it also symbolizes and expresses the penetrating will of man. In psychology, the action of the mind is symbolized by penetration. And we have figures of speech in other languages, in French and in German, where the action of the mind is symbolized by the idea of penetration—a ray of light like a spear, for instance. Later on, this man had a dream where he came to an illumined wall, and he knew that behind it was truth, and he holds a spear trying to pierce that wall.[11] There is the act of penetration. In this case he uses a penetrating instrument but not for penetration. He knocks the animal on the head just to beat it down without smashing its skull. What does that mean?

Mrs. Nordfeldt: He is overcoming it.

Dr. Jung: Yes, and where do you see that in folklore?

Mrs. Baynes: In the similarity of cutting the dragon open.

Dr. Jung: Of course. It is the fight with the dragon who holds the treasure inside, and when the hero has succeeded in beating the dragon down, out will come the father or mother, or he will get at the hidden treasure. In this case, the dragon or tortoise delivers a child. That is what the dream means exactly—the overcoming of the unconscious. He has to make it conscious, he has to wrench it loose from the original unconsciousness, to detach that bit of consciousness or that content from the unconscious and make it his own. Now what has he to make conscious by beating back the instinct that keeps everything in the unconscious?

Mrs. Nordfeldt: The honest attempt.

Dr. Jung: Yes, the child. And what child?

Question: The inferior function?

Dr. Jung: Sure enough, it has to do with the inferior function, with everything that is inferior in him, that is still to come, still to develop. But that is not specific enough. Could it not be that it is the same child again? You see, in the dream before we had a new enterprise, but are we sure that he was quite conscious of what that new business meant? If he were entirely conscious of the new attempt, of what it would mean and what its implications were, he would not have such a dream. He does not know it in the conscious, it is too obscure, and therefore he explains to his employee that the new enterprise is just a side business, and of course the main

---

[11] The dream is not discussed in this seminar.

business will not be interfered with. Then this next dream speaks of the birth of a child, the birth of the honest attempt, which he has to detach from the unconscious as if he were a new St. George who has to kill the dragon first in order to go on. He must first overcome his unconsciousness in order to continue with his purpose.

That seems strange to you but not to an analyst. One shows a thing to a patient and he says, "Yes, I see that perfectly, is it not wonderful?" Three or four weeks later it is as if he had not understood at all, and there must be a new recognition of the same thing. You see, a real recognition, a full realization, of these unconscious contents never happens all at once. It always comes in waves, wave after wave, with a pause in between before a new and more intense realization of what that thing is. There are cases where a dream in the beginning of analysis contains the whole analytical procedure. If one realized it one would possess everything that one needed—to get at it if one could. At first, you get only a very vague glimpse, it is as if you had never seen it. Then it comes again and you think, that is it, and then it fades away. And then comes a third wave and you think, is it not marvellous?—a perfect revelation. Then that ebbs away, and a fourth and fifth wave come, and many waves must come until we realize that what we call progress is really always one and the same thing, which we are simply unable to realize and which only dawns upon us very slowly. It is as if the sun, in order to become visible to us, must come up and go down again and again until we realize that it is the sun and it is day. We shall have other dreams where that problem will come up again. This man's first attempt at realization was not enough, he is still up against the old dragon, against the old unconsciousness. Therefore he must first overcome the dragon in order to detach the child from the maternal abyss in which it was concealed.

Mrs. Baynes: But didn't we say that the child that took him to the bed and turned down the cover was the new attempt?

Dr. Jung: Of course it is.

Mrs. Baynes: Is this new child the same?

Dr. Jung: One and the same! The first attempt was the effort to realize, but that was not enough. He is not fully conscious, which is demonstrated by the fact that he has such a dream. I can give you a practical example: I was once treating a man who was a doctor and by no means a fool. He was an alienist too—which of course does not prove that he was not a fool. He had a mother complex; he lived in his mother's house and she took care of him. He was a little husband. From the very beginning he had dream after dream about his mother complex, and each one told him that it simply would not do, that he could not live like that. After about six weeks—you can see that I am a poor analyst—I realized that there must be a special tie between the man and his mother, and I discovered that he was writing daily letters to her in which he explained his whole analytical procedure, every detail. So he remained in the closest connection with her all the time. And this was after six weeks of talking about that mother complex every day. It was six months before he came with a long face and said: "But, Doctor, do you really think I should *detach* from my mother? Is it possible that you think I should not live in the same house with her?" I said: "Exactly! That is what I expect of you, how often have I told you that?" And he said: "But I thought you did not mean it. You cannot possibly think that I should live in a flat of my own! What about my mother?" "Well," I said, "there you are! That is your problem. I mean just what I say, and it is extraordinary that it takes so long to realize what I told you in the first hour."

It is as if somebody said: "Hurry up, the house is on fire!" and one replied: "Do you really think that houses in Zurich can catch fire?" Perfectly unable to hear what is said. And that is very general. It is amazing what it takes to make people hear and see. The simplest thing will not get under their skins, and one can repeat it a dozen times or twenty times. The moment that that man realized that he had really to detach from his mother he had an awful dream. He dreamt that he was climbing a steep hill which was very slippery. He just managed to reach the top when, looking down, he saw his mother. He shouted: "For heaven's sake, don't try to come up!" But his mother started, and then slipped and broke her leg. Next day, in reality, a telegram came: "Your mother has broken her leg." That explained his stupidity, why he was so deaf. His unconscious knew that it might kill his mother. Those old bonds, cases of *participation mystique*, are exceedingly dangerous. One must not get impatient. Just say it again. So this difficulty in realization explains certain dreams.

You see how many attempts our dreamer has already made to approach the problem, and that is merely the difficulty of realization. He cannot make up his mind to see the thing exactly as it is, and to give it the right value. This seems to be a tremendous difficulty, and I never hastened him, never bullied him, because I know quite well that it cannot be forced. It is vital, there is a saurian in it and one must not push the thing. It needs to mature slowly. If you push it you might injure vital instincts. I have never made any conditions—if you do not do this, and all that stuff. That won't work at all. One has to be exceedingly patient in such a case. But we shall encounter quite a number of dreams where the wave comes on again and again and where he has a new chance to take it. One often finds that motif, the hidden treasure, or the blossoming of the treasure or the flower in mythology and folklore. It is supposed to blossom after a certain period, say nine years, nine months, nine days. On the ninth night, the treasure comes up to the surface and whoever happens to be on the spot on the ninth can take it, but the next night it goes down to the depths, and then it takes nine years and nine months and nine days before it blossoms again.[12] That is the demonstration in folklore of the difficulty of psychological realization.

Miss Howells: How long is it since he began till the time of this dream?

Dr. Jung: He began in May and this dream is in the middle of October.

[12] Cf. *Psychology and Alchemy*, Part II (1935), CW 12, par. 111.

LECTURE VI

11 June 1930

Dr. Jung:

Mrs. Crowley asks a question concerning the autonomous figures we spoke of last time. She would like to know how to distinguish such autonomous figures from instincts or very strong impulses. I am afraid I could not distinguish between them. Instincts that would appear in our psychology are chiefly personified as autonomous figures, inasmuch, of course, as the instincts are not smoothly integrated in the whole of the personality. As soon as one is at variance with them, they have a decided tendency to become objectified in some way, and then they oppose us. It is as if it were another person with a will that contrasts with one's own.

We will go on now to the next dream. The dream before was mythological, St. George and the dragon, and in this case the dragon was a turtle that was giving birth to a child. Now, after that mythological dream, the unconscious, by the law of enantiodromia, returns to a very businesslike proposition.

Dream [29]

The dreamer says that he is going to look into his business abroad. His brother-in-law, who is a director in the business, complains that the buying agents in the interior are buying a lot of high-quality cotton for high prices, and that there is a standstill in the selling of just that high-quality cotton at present. So the dreamer says to him that, in such a case, one should proceed energetically to reduce very much the buying power of the agents, as otherwise one would lose an enormous amount of money. Naturally, a great deal of capital would be invested where large quantities are bought at high prices.

654

Associations: He says that this dream can be interpreted on the objective plane, because he is really afraid that his brother-in-law, the director, is somewhat too slow in his decisions, and might lose control of the buying agents, or miss certain opportunities. But on the other hand, on the subjective side, it also is possible that his unconscious is complaining that he acquires far too much high-quality merchandise, which might lead to serious losses, as this kind of merchandise has no currency just now.

Well now, do you get anything from his associations or his interpretations? Do you understand the dream?

Dr. Baynes: Does it mean that he is doubtful, because he is putting more capital than he can afford into a thing of a very rare quality that has not much currency?

Dr. Jung: Yes, but how is that applied?

Mr. Richmond: His new value is getting into his old, into his main stream of life, and he is afraid of overvaluation of this high-grade material.

Dr. Jung: But what value would this particular high-grade material represent?

Mr. Richmond: The new value that he has been finding. It is becoming high-grade coffee.

Dr. Jung: Coffee is just a side branch. Here it is the main business. Do you mean he is afraid of putting too much value on, or of making too great an investment in, his new enterprise?

Mr. Richmond: Are they not coming together now?

Dr. Jung: That remains to be seen. I am not so sure. I think we had better go through the dream in detail in order to be certain of its meaning. The first thing of importance is that the dream takes a most objective and practical situation. It is exactly like his business where he formerly was the chief, though now his brother-in-law is in charge as director. That is all quite clear, the situation in the dream is perfectly real as he knows it. Of course, to a business man his business is just as much a reality as, say, his wife; it is sometimes a much greater reality than his family, so we cannot say that it is entirely symbolical. In all his associations the reality character is stressed, as in his anxiety lest his brother-in-law might buy a bit carelessly. So we are led to believe that the unconscious wants to accentuate the point of reality quite particularly. Sure enough, his business life is in the strongest contrast with what he is actually doing here in analysis. Practically all these considerations in his dream point to a former habitual way of life. So one could say that the difference between his daily, ordinary reality and his new enterprise is particularly emphasized, and there obviously must be trouble or the unconscious would not insist upon it. Therefore we must assume that there is some conflict going on in him about the relation of analysis to reality, expressed in terms of hard cash.

Now don't you think, Mr. Richmond, that the buying of cotton might be that new enterprise? I see no evidence in this dream which would speak against that assumption. It looks as if the dream had forgotten all about the coffee, because it views the problem obviously from an entirely different angle, that is, the new enterprise is no longer handled as if it were a branch or a sort of side issue. It is now expressed in terms of the main business; it has become, apparently, even the main consideration. It is interesting in this connection that Goethe, whenever he made an entry in his diary about the second part of *Faust*, on which he worked so long, wrote, "Have worked on the main business," *das Hauptgeschäft*. So as far as this dream goes, we have no reason to assume that the analytical enterprise is still a branch business. It has become identical with the main business and therefore can be expressed through the main business. But a fear is in the dreamer's mind that the buying agents might invest too much money in that indubitably high-grade merchandise.

Mr. Schmitz: The employees of the last dream are putting too much libido into this new enterprise, and he fears it will not be changed into cash.

Dr. Jung: Well, he recognizes in the dream that this merchandise is of high quality, excellent stuff, yet what could he do with it? That is the question. He acquires a lot of very good and interesting ideas, new interests and so on, in analysis, yet there is no selling; in other words, there is no application. Now why is that?

Mr. Schmitz: Because his shadow, his brother-in-law, is not efficient enough.

Dr. Jung: The brother-in-law is not responsible for the bad selling. It is a general condition of the market.

Dr. Baynes: No demand for it.

Dr. Jung: Yes. And who refuses to buy the valuable stuff?

Mrs. Baynes: His wife.

Dr. Jung: Exactly. He has no market for his good material because she won't buy, and so he, as a good business man, naturally

656

thinks: why the devil should I invest such a lot of money in that high grade stuff when I cannot sell it, when it does not work? Now that is a perfectly justifiable doubt. The condition of the market is a sort of atmospheric thing and decidedly an outside condition. His wife is his outside condition, and she is extremely reluctant to acquire that high-grade merchandise. He cannot talk to her about it because it hurts her somehow, and she does not want it. Of course, it would be putting a bit too much responsibility upon his poor wife if he should cling to that explanation exclusively. His wife is more or less an exponent here. Of course, she has her own dignity. She plays a considerable role in the game, but I would not make too much of her; she is an exponent in his own psychology, perhaps his anima, the feminine quality in him, his Yin quality.[1] And it may be a very tough and unwilling quality that refrains from buying good cotton and wants cheaper and perhaps worse material. As you know, the public does not always buy the high-grade merchandise, they want to have things cheap; so it is quite possible and even very probable that his own new realizing powers are more or less unwilling to acquire that high-grade merchandise. Now, what would that mean? Well, this is a precious piece of masculine psychology. We have so often spoken critically of women, and here we come to men. I shall not spare them.

Mr. Schmitz: He does not realize it enough. It is unconscious.

Dr. Jung: That is right, and that is a very important point about men. You see, a man knows exactly when a thing is wrong or what it should be if it were right, and he is inclined to assume that, when he thinks the thing, it is done, because he is convinced of it in his mind. Yet it is not done at all. A man can write a book or preach a marvellous sermon about how people should behave without carrying out the principle at all in his private life. He does not live it. That is an entirely different consideration. The spirit is strong but the flesh is awfully weak. The Yin power, the realization power, is very low, very inferior, it doesn't follow suit, it doesn't accept that wonderful thought and put it to work; it remains inert and passive and fails to move at all. The thought enjoys itself in itself, revolves in itself and goes on revolving in itself, and nothing comes out of it. Reality goes on as it always has and nothing is changed,

[1] In Taoism, "*tao* is divided into a fundamental pair of opposites, *yang* and *yin*. *Yang* signifies warmth, light, maleness; *yin* is cold, darkness, femaleness."—*Psychological Types* (1921), CW 6, par. 366, paraphrasing the *Tao Te Ching*.

yet the man who is identical with that wonderful thought up in the air thinks it has changed a great deal. He thinks: I have an entirely different view of things and the world, therefore everything is different. Yet when it comes down to hard facts nothing is different, everything is as it ever was. If such a man had a good Yin power, a good realizing power instead of an inferior one, he would feel at once that he thought but never realized, and therefore he had no right to think that way—that he shouldn't think those things. If he does think those things, he must realize that he has pledged himself. But that absolutism of thought and conviction is rarely to be found, as it is entirely a religious quality. Only a religious man has that quality, that Yin power, that puts his thoughts through into work. The mere intellectual has nothing of the kind, he has absolutely no realizing powers; it is air. Thus the most important thing he can imagine turns out to be just words; to say it is nothing but words is not far from the truth. And this is so common that nearly all men *believe* it is words and not reality. When they hear somebody talking, I say about ninety-nine per cent of all men surely assume that it is just words and not reality, because in ninety-nine cases that is true.

So the public that is somewhat reluctant to buy that high-grade stuff represents very probably this man's own inertia, his own low realizing power that unfortunately is backed up by the reluctant attitude of his wife. As I remember, I actually told him that this dream should be taken on the subjective side, despite the fact that his wife is truly resistant. Even in such a case, he should not use it as an excuse, he should not make her responsible; he should say instead: after all, that is my wife. She is the exponent of his psychology, and if he considers her as that, he is doing justice to himself as well as to her. For if he realizes, if he begins to put things into practice, the situation will change altogether, as we shall see. As a matter of fact this was the case. When he had worked up his impotent Yin power, things changed. He became suddenly quite different. Then even his wife changed, which is evidence of the fact that it was really in the first place his own inertia, his passivity, which was also hindering her. This is especially obvious since, when they reached a better relationship, she still did not give up her resistance to his interests. Yet despite this resistance, the situation became normal.

Mr. Schmitz: You said that the power of realization is the Yin principle. Is the realization characterized by the sensation function?

Dr. Jung: Oh no, not necessarily, for a sensation type has the same kind of psychology. It is a Logos and Eros question, which has nothing to do with the functions.

Mr. Schmitz: Then sensation would not be *la fonction du réel?*

Dr. Jung: No, because you can be absolutely detached from realization in your sensation. The point is that a man's psychology is chiefly characterized by what I call Logos or the thought principle. Whether he functions according to this type or that does not matter, the main feature is Logos, as the woman's is Eros, no matter what type she is.

Mr. Schmitz: But very often it is the same thing with women. They cannot realize what they feel. They feel very well but they do not realize it.

Dr. Jung: That is an entirely different question. In German one uses the verb "to realize"[2] chiefly with the connotation of concretizing things, and I was using it in that sense. In English one uses it in a much lighter way. It has more the meaning of "to see," "to understand." I should have said *concretize.*

Mr. Schmitz: For women is it the same difficulty?

Dr. Jung: Naturally, only the process is reversed. It is then not a question of a weak Yin, but of a weak Yang. Women with a perfectly good realizing power cannot put their minds into action. They may be convinced that they know a thing for a very long time yet they do not know it because the mind has no power; whereas a man can make up his mind every day to do a certain thing and yet never do it.

Dr. Baynes: Would you say that a man could think a thing and not give it, and a woman could surrender without thinking, but surrender constructively with thinking?

Dr. Jung: Absolutely. It is characteristic of a woman's psychology that she can do a lot of things without thinking about them.

Mr. Baumann: I have just seen a very nice example of not realizing things, and it happened to a famous psychologist. I spent a day with Mr. Forel, who has written a book about the sexual question.[3] He talked for about half an hour at breakfast about votes for women and the rights of women, and said the men ought to let the women do things. An hour later he went to the kitchen,

[2] *Verwirklichen.*

[3] Auguste Henri Forel, M.D. (1848-1931), Swiss neurologist and entomologist, who was director of the Burghölzli in 1879-98 (preceding Eugen Bleuler). His book *Die Sexuelle Frage* had been published in 1905 (tr., *The Sexual Question*, 1925).

where his wife was making peach marmalade, and proposed one pound of sugar to one pound of peaches, though Mrs. Forel said that half a pound of sugar was the proper amount. The marmalade was too sweet and Mr. Forel was extremely angry and smashed all the pots on the floor.

Dr. Jung: Exactly like him! Now the next dream.

Dream [30]

Our patient says: "I am walking in the street and a wagon is passing, a big sort of furniture van full of stuff, and I see that the driver, a tall, slender man, is doing acrobatics on top of the van. Then suddenly the wagon changes into a little house in which I find myself with the driver, who is now changed into a terribly uncouth and vulgar fellow, and he continues his gymnastics up on a sort of ledge running along the ceiling on one of the walls. He is quite naked. Several other people are in the same room, among them a boy. The atmosphere gets very peculiar, something like a spiritualistic séance, and one of the people says to the boy that he ought to call up somebody, meaning a sort of invocation, and another person, joining the conversation, says: 'Oh yes, we will call up his great-grandmother and we will rape her.' The boy now becomes quite rigid, as if in a trance, and suddenly an old lady appears, with grey hair but a very young and distinguished-looking face. The uncouth, vulgar fellow, who had been clinging to the ceiling hitherto, suddenly jumps down and catches her in his arms. She defends herself and succeeds in jumping out of the window, where, held by the arms, she shouts for help. People are coming and the man lets her drop and curses her for having broken the window. Now the lady goes away with the people who gathered in the street; obviously she is going for the police. One of the men present in the room says that he has succeeded in taking a picture of the whole situation with his cinematograph apparatus, he has made a film of the scene, and he is hurrying to get the pictures into safety before the police come. Then I am looking out of the window and I see that the house is standing near a river which is flowing past, and to my astonishment I see that artillery is coming toward us on the other side of the river. They are loading the cannons to shoot and aiming at our house, I call the attention of the other people present

660

and propose that we go into the cellar or into a neighbouring house, as a bombardment seems to be imminent. One of them answers that the neighbours would not like to have us, but we can go into the cellar, and the photographer says it is all indifferent to him as long as his pictures are safe, and he is sure they will be a tremendous success and that it will be a great business for him."

Associations: He says that the wagon or car is one of those big *furniture vans* that one sees in the street, especially at the time when people are moving in the spring or fall.

The *driver* reminds him of a photograph he had seen in an illustrated paper of a peasant, a particularly strong and powerful man. I remember having seen that picture. He was a woodman from the wine country near Lake Geneva and he was a very beautiful fellow, quite masculine. The dreamer says that when he saw his face, he thought: no more inhibitions!—a real *coq du village!* You know, nearly every village has one or two idiots, and usually one typical character who is always called the *coq du village*, and that man was evidently such a masculine beauty. But immediately afterwards the driver becomes transformed into an uncouth and vulgar fellow and the dreamer calls him a human animal, *an ape-man*, which explains his acrobatics—he is behaving exactly as a monkey would in a room.

The boy, he says, is obviously a medium, a link in a chain, and it is his effect in the room that makes the unconscious soul or anima, the great-grandmother, rise from the depths of the past.

In the *scene of the attempted rape*, the dreamer understands that the great-grandmother is obviously his anima or soul, and the instinctive ape-man is jumping on her in order to destroy her, a sort of violation. So the conflict is not solved through the occultization of the animal side of man, or through the subjection of the white soul, but only by the flight of the soul, her escape, which is brought about by her own wits and by the help of the environment.

Concerning the peculiar intermezzo of the *photographer,* he says that the fact that the whole scene has been perpetuated in a picture means that it should not be forgotten.

The next feature in the dream is the discovery of *the river that flows past the house*, and he says that the consequence of the flight of the anima into the external world is his separation from that world, which now is in a hostile attitude to the conscious ego—the ego which on one side could not be subdued (he identifies here with the ape-man) and on the other side was not strong enough to subjugate the anima.

He suggests that *going into the cellar* might mean retiring into oneself.

Concerning the last rather cynical *remark of the photographer*, that the whole thing is perfectly indifferent to him as long as his pictures are in safety, he says that this record, the pictures, seemed to possess a very great importance but he does not know why.

Now we will interpret this dream. It is very difficult to grasp it as a whole; it is so long and there is so much detail that one can hardly take it all in. Therefore the ordinary technique in such a case is to divide the dream into scenes or parts, and to look at each part separately. Only in the end shall we try to bring it all together.

The first picture in the dream is that furniture van and the driver performing his acrobatics on top. The driver seems to be identical with that *coq du village* that he saw in the illustrated paper. He says nothing about the acrobatics. As a matter of fact, he did not put that association down because it was so reminiscent of his recent dream when he was doing acrobatics himself, and the mouse escaped from under the bed.[4] Since that reminiscence points to the very vital moment when the mouse ran away, we may assume that he is again concerned with a similar problem, perhaps of equal importance. Then the last figure in this dream is the photographer who says that, having gotten his pictures into safety, the whole thing is absolutely indifferent to him, and there our patient observes that that seems to be of very great importance somehow. So we may conclude that he had a feeling of importance attached to this dream. Whether we can see the justification for it does not matter—we know that it is important, and it begins with a reminiscence from a former very important one. The acrobatics in that dream were associated with analysis, they were mental acrobatics. Naturally it meant a certain strain to him to follow my psychological arguments, a good deal of patience to become acquainted with that peculiar kind of thinking which seems so illogical and irrational at times. Now here again somebody is performing acrobatics, but it is no longer himself; here it is the driver who afterwards changes into an ape-man. Have you an idea about that?

4 Above, dream 24, p. 531.

662

Dr. Baynes: Was there not a dream in which a monkey was doing acrobatics in the trees?[5]

Dr. Jung: Oh yes, that was some time ago. It was not a monkey, but the dreamer performed acrobatics like a monkey in the branches of trees, in a sort of alley which led up the house with the square courtyard, where Dr. Faustus lived.

Dr. Baynes: There was also the motif of the moving of furniture there.

Dr. Jung: Yes, the furniture had been brought out of the house and it was cracking in the sun, indicating that it should be moved.

Mrs. Crowley: It might mean his shadow here.

Dr. Jung: Yes, the driver is what one would designate as a typical shadow figure. He is everything the dreamer is not—a *coq du village.* That conveys the whole meaning. The dreamer is rather inhibited and very correct, so he admires that lack of moral inhibition and envies him the faculty of playing the role. It is the typical shadow, the inferior man, and this time the inferior man is performing gymnastics, while in the former dreams it was the dreamer himself, the conscious ego, who was doing them. Also, in the dream of disporting himself in the trees in the alley, it was his conscious ego. This must indicate an important change. You see, he has dreamt twice that he was doing acrobatic stunts, which is obviously a sort of realization in the dream of how difficult it was for him to train his mind to a more psychological way of thinking. To his rational mind, this intuitive kind of thought, these fantastic analogies, were perfectly unknown, and he found it very difficult to deal with these evasive ideas, which would surely be considered perfectly fantastical vapours by nearly everybody. People always wonder how I can deal with them as if they were concrete things. When they get a glimpse of the anima, for instance, that intangible presence, they wonder how one can talk of it as if it were a concrete figure. And for many people it is extraordinarily difficult to deal with illogical concepts, which are much too abstract, and they feel perfectly lost in handling them. Well then, after this acrobatic motif has occurred in his dreams twice already, it is now the shadow that is concerned with these exercises, no longer the dreamer. What does that mean?

Mr. Schmitz: His conscious is interested but the unconscious is not.

---

[5] Above, dream 17, p. 274.

Dr. Jung: Yes, the conscious has mastered the thing. He got it more or less, that is perfectly true. Consciously, he was accustomed to it, but now comes the inferior person concerned with the same difficulty. It is as if the struggle were going on in a lower stratum; it is no longer his conscious but his unconscious which suffers. This may be a strange thought to you. You are perhaps inclined to think that when your conscious has mastered a thing, the difficulty is overcome, but as a rule that is not true. You can master a thing in the conscious quite easily, yet the lower man finds it exceedingly difficult and suffers from that trouble. For instance, take any kind of human relationship in your life, or any kind of painful duty. Your conscious knows it is necessary, you must adapt to it, and you really can do it; but if you get a bit tired or don't feel quite well, up comes the old resentment, and suddenly you cannot cope with it any longer. It is as if you had never learned to deal with it. The weak, inferior man comes up as soon as your conscious gets a bit soft. It only needs a little fatigue and all your beautiful faculties are completely gone—whatever you have learned completely gone. That truly can happen. I remember an occasion when it happened to me. We were making experiments in the Physical Laboratory and I was concerned with a pretty complicated case. I was about to explain to my pupils how the thing worked. It was perfectly clear to me how that whole phenomenon came to pass, I knew it quite well, and I said I would tell them after lunch. But after lunch I could not understand it, simply on account of the fact that there was not enough blood in my brain. That amount of after-dinner dullness was sufficient to disable me, I had not the clarity of thought that I had before eating. It often needs no more than that—like the philosopher who said that before dinner he was a Kantian and after dinner a Nietzschean.

This first statement of the dream, then, means that the difficulty now is chiefly with the inferior man in himself. The conscious has mastered that part of the problem more or less. It is only the inferior man who gives the trouble; he has begun to exercise himself also, which means that he is about to come up to the level of consciousness. Naturally one cannot expect the shadow ever to come quite up to that level, but one may expect it to be more or less adapted, to chime in, so that the two come together. That stage is not yet attained, it is still only in the preparatory stage, but it seems to be on the way. The inferior man is performing his arts on the top of the furniture van, which afterwards becomes a little house. That gives us a clue. You see, the luggage van always denotes a change, leaving one place for another, a state of transition. The dreams before have spoken of new enterprises. He is obviously going to find a new place, to create a new condition. Even in the dream where the acrobatics occurred the first time, as Dr. Baynes has just mentioned, there was already the motif of house-moving and furniture, and here the change is effected apparently. Now what does the luggage van suggest, apart from the idea of house-moving? It is a big and clumsy thing.

Dr. Baynes: Is it not a temporary container of his effects, his goods?

Dr. Jung: But what would the goods be?

Dr. Baynes: His psychological effects or values which he is changing.

Dr. Jung: Yes, but are you not impressed with what the dreamer particularly emphasizes, the clumsy bigness of the car containing a lot of furniture?

Mr. Schmitz: Impedimenta!

Dr. Jung: That is it. You see that these *impedimenta* (that beautiful Latin word which really means obstacles, hindrances) are a very typical symbol for a certain psychological fact. For example, you know those moments when you are hurrying to the station and you have three bags on one side and one on your back, and naturally you lose a parcel and have to go back for it, and then you remember that there are twenty more trunks which should be shovelled into your compartment and which are not yet at the station, and only at the last moment the porter comes hurrying along with them. That typical dream! Those are the dead things we have to carry, things which are no longer living, things which we are bothered with but which have to be carried along. They belong to our existence in the flesh, because we cannot travel without any luggage, and we cannot live on this earth without any furniture. And nothing wants to get lost, everything accumulates; old shoes and old trousers never leave you, they are always there just waiting for you, they are jealous of the new ones. One can't get rid of a single thing. And these impedimenta, which cling to us and which we have to carry along, are simply an exposition of our psychology.

Our psychology consists not only of an eye that is able to cover vast spaces, travel in the fraction of a second a hundred-mile distance and more. It also consists of functions moving in a much more clumsy way. For instance, you may understand a thing, know every corner of it, yet your feeling has not yet realized it; you know all about it, yet it is still not your property and only in time does it begin to sink in. You are in the vanguard of your mind, and the army, the greater part of you, is still miles and miles behind, not here yet. I see that very often in my American patients. They are here in the flesh, but they seldom dream of Europe, they are always dreaming of America. So they are not really here—everything is looked at through the spectacles of New York or Boston, only one-half or one-third reality. And only after some time trunk after trunk comes from America; it takes them I don't know how long. Sometimes they never arrive, a part of them always remains where they have been before, which is quite reasonable; surely if we Europeans were to go to America, it would take us very much longer to get across, for we cling to the soil still more than the Americans. This is simply a natural psychological law.

And so you may find a good friend, but after a while you discover that he has a sort of suite behind him and a lot of disagreeable things come in. Or you marry, and you think you are marrying just that woman or that man, but not at all. Their whole ancestry down to the ape-man crowds into your marriage and naturally into your psychological relationship. It takes time, because they have to travel up from the remote past, and so for quite a while, say for half a century, you keep on being astonished, and you are not through with it yet, mind you. Therefore, you see, when you move you cannot simply take your umbrella and step into the next house, it needs more than a toothbrush. You carry a bag, and then somebody comes after you with a trunk, and then comes a car, and then a van, and then you are not through with it, because memories of all sorts of things will still cling to the places where you have been. So a real change seems nothing short of an earthquake. You can change the conscious by a mere thought. In five minutes I can clear up a difficulty. I say: Well, it is so-and-so, and the fellow to whom I am talking, if he happens to be an intuitive, says: That is grand, now I understand. And he walks out all puffed up. But nothing has happened, he has heard nothing. He turns the next corner and collapses. There are such fellows who are born weekly, like the Buddha, who went through about 570 rebirths. That is a psychological truth too.

666

So here the inferior man is on top of a load of goods that never will do acrobatics; the only acrobatics they will experience are the acrobatics one has to do in managing all those trunks. It is good exercise for one, and they won't do it because they are dead contents which don't move unless one moves them. They consist of all the dead passivity and inertia of the deepest layers of the unconscious. We don't think of that ordinarily, but whatever we have to carry, well, they just have to be carried. One never can change them, one has to make up one's mind to travel with that whole load on one's back. Beneath the inferior man comes the load of things that are dead; they are an encumbrance, but one must carry them like a snail carrying his house on his back.

Mr. Holdsworth: What about the Europeans who go to America?

Dr. Jung: I just said that he would probably be less in America than the American is in Europe, I think that Americans are much more able to move than Europeans, but naturally a part of the American is so deeply rooted in the Indian soil that it will never leave America at all, as we would never leave Europe—or only in some generations. Then the colonial split occurs.

The furniture van, then, expresses the idea of moving, and that is probably the reason why in the next picture the van changes into a little house, and the dreamer finds himself in the house as well as the driver. What does that mean in psychological terms?

Mr. Schmitz: He has found a new place for all his stuff.

Dr. Jung: Well, yes, he has arrived here in the new space in which he is supposed to move. A new situation is reached.

Mrs. Deady: Doesn't he have to drop some of his impedimenta? The dream says it is a little house.

Dr. Jung: More modest than he is accustomed to, but I know that man and I am pretty certain that if he moves into a new house, he will carry all that stuff with him. He obviously arrives in a new situation, in a house which is not movable in itself, it is a settled situation. He arrives at a certain conclusion, a definite standpoint, one could say, a dwelling-place where he is meant to stay for a while apparently. That means a new psychological attainment, a definite step forward. And then something very peculiar happens— the transformation of that beautiful man, the driver, into a perfectly uncouth, primitive ape-man. How does such a change come about? We must see a reason somewhere.

Dr. Deady: The van contained the deepest layers of the unconscious.

Dr. Jung: Yes, but why should that affect the driver?

Dr. Deady: What is appropriate to the moving-van becomes inappropriate in a house. The nomadic animal-self is inappropriate when he is settled down.

Dr. Jung: You mean the fact of settling down is more or less offensive to the inferior man, and he instantly shows further bad qualities? That is a perfectly permissible point of view, because it is backed up by facts. One sees people, who, as long as they are on the move, as long as they can be nomadic, are manageable, but no sooner do they settle down than they develop all sorts of disagreeable qualities. They can't stand being stationary. Why is that?

Mrs. Crowley: A resistance to responsibility.

Mr. Schmitz: They are very repressed in a house. Having a house represses a lot of instincts which a nomadic life would allow them to realize.

Dr. Jung: But is that the only reason?

Mrs. Sigg: They must make a great effort at adaptation, and that comes slowly.

Dr. Jung: That is right. Do you remember that dream of the hut where this man found the crocodile, the saurian?[6] That was a similar situation. The hut was a kind of house, meaning a definite situation. You see, it is very typical of human beings that as long as things are suspended and they have a chance to move on and on, they always have hope of finding the good thing round the next corner, so they never insist on having happiness where they are. But when you settle down and assume that now it will come off, you are up against a brick wall. Happiness does not descend upon you, it is even a considerable strain to keep quiet. And then you think regretfully of former times when you could escape and disappear somewhere in the clouds on the horizon. So you promise yourself all the time new countries, new chances, wonderful things, and are lured on and on, living the provisional life.

That is very typical of the specific psychology of the neurotic; part of the neurosis consists of that suspended life, or rather, the provisional life. I learned that term from a patient who had a compulsion neurosis. He said: "The trouble is, I am living a pro-

---

[6] Above, dream 20, p. 317.

visional life, and the name of it is Happy Neurosis Island, where nothing has come off yet. I am now forty-five, and I know I began my provisional life—I went to Happy Neurosis Island—when I was seventeen. And I cannot be cured because, if I should remember again. I should wake up a boy of seventeen and have to realize that so many years had gone by wasted. Now I have hope and I can live." I told him in the beginning that he would not put it through, because he could not bring off the sacrifice of thirty years; it is a bloody sacrifice to cut away thirty years of your life. He could have done it if he had wanted to be cured, but he didn't. Such a case hardly ever does. That is an excellent formulation of the peculiar psychology of the neurotic. He lives as if there were no time, as if nothing had yet come off and everything were still to come. There is no here and now but an eternity of ten million possibilities, and because he is lured by a sort of imagination or dim feeling, every action which might lead to something definite is instantly checked and somehow made inefficient. The neurotic cannot or will not occupy the new place for which he must declare himself entirely responsible for better or worse.

Now, we see the great difficulty that my patient is confronted with. He might declare himself responsible for his situation, but to actually stick makes a tremendous difference. I do not mind at all when people say this is impossible, that they can't do it. I say: Of course it is difficult to put your neck in a noose, it is as if you were hanging yourself; but otherwise you are suspended on a possibility that gets fainter and fainter and is wasting away time and life. If you have to choose between the devil and the deep sea, it is better sometimes to choose one or the other than the state in between, where nothing happens. So it is a very great step forward for the dreamer when he can say: This is my house, I am here. It does not look very considerable, yet it is his own and he makes up his mind to stay. Then one expects that things will now be all right since he has made such a great sacrifice, but then the very devil begins. Spooks. The house is haunted by the ape-man, and the unconscious begins to play all the monkey tricks it can possibly invent. There is an enormous revolution in the unconscious. It is a wild animal suddenly and begins to raise hell with him. A door closes. Nothing else, there is food and water, but there is a closed door, and that is the typical moment. It is now in the house and the very devil, it becomes more ape than man and begins to climb

669

about. This climbing about is very much like the dreamer's former acrobatics. He is not very offensive, he is like a baboon or something of the sort.

I was once in the room with a baboon. I was sitting very quietly in a corner whilst he was turning over the pieces of furniture. The man who was with me—a famous educator of monkeys—said it was better not to pay any attention to him. Then it dropped on my head and shoulders, and I was pretty scared because baboons can bite like the devil. I didn't dare move, I just sat quiet, and presently he began to louse my head. The man said I had shown him the right monkey tact. You see, that monkey tact really works with children and apes, and you must show monkey tact to those ape qualities of your unconscious. Just ignore them for a while, and keep as quiet as if you did not exist, even if they sit on your shoulders. Then they will like you and befriend you, then nature comes to you. The mistake people make is to be shocked or frightened at the first animal, so that their conscious wants to make friends— cluck, cluck at them—and naturally the animal does not understand that baby language, and they have one enemy the more. It is the same with children. They hate people who talk baby language to them, and they despise them because they want to make friends. Adults are not expected to make friends with little children, children make friends with adults; they sometimes become quite obstinate when you seem to like them.

So with the unconscious, you shouldn't get panicky. Naturally the monkey raises hell. You must keep quite still and not get crazy, or the monkey gets crazy; if *you* keep quiet, after a while peace will permeate the whole room; it will see that there is no reason to get excited since that fellow with the peculiar fur is not excited. And so the driver, the ape-man, is not offensive. He is just performing his stunts as before and not very aggressively, though of course his person smells of the menagerie and that is not very agreeable for cultivated people. But now something terrible happens, somebody makes a suggestion—the great-grandmother! That decidedly means trouble. A new element is entering the situation. Up to the present moment this little house has been a man's house, only men in it and perfectly nice. A man can cope with his inferior man as long as there is no great-grandmother about, but if there is a great-grandmother the easiest things become unbearable.

Mrs. Baynes: Naturally the great-grandmother won't stand for the baboon.

Dr. Jung: The baboon is the shadow, we have located him. But this great-grandmother is not a figure that can be explained personally. This man's great-grandmother has vanished in the dust of ages. And this new figure, an entirely impersonal, mythological sort of figure, who would she be?

Mr. Schmitz: The anima.

Dr. Jung: Yes, but would you just say anima? That is too indefinite, we should make it more specific; we must pay attention to the very word. You see, the word "great-grandmother," which is exactly the same in German, means a very grand mother or the grand grandmother, as the primitives would say, which means a great intensity, the very grandest mother. That is a very high title of honour. She must be an extraordinary being. You see, the primitive idea is that when a man dies, if he leaves a son, he enters the ghost land as a father and only a hen is sacrified to him. Then his son becomes a father, and the father in ghost land becomes a grandfather, and instantly his rank is increased; he is then a sort of duke, and the son has to sacrifice, not a hen, but a bull. So the importance of the grandfather is much greater than that of the father. We do not realize that that is the origin of the word. It means that the further you remove the mother from the present moment into the past, the more her importance increases. She becomes more and more ducal, more and more an exponent of the origin of mankind. One could say, as the father comes nearer to the totem animal, so, the more generations there are between the mother and the present generation, the more she becomes a great grand power, for she then represents the totality of power of the human past.

Prof. Hooke: Why has she a young face?

Dr. Jung: That is the aspect of the great-grandmother as the anima. She is very old and at the same time very young.

LECTURE VII

18 June 1930

Dr. Jung:

We discussed the ape-man in the dream last week, and today we come to the next point, the boy. You remember that we have occasionally come across the boy in former dreams.[1] Of course, that symbol does not always mean the same thing. Sometimes it is repeated in exactly the same sense as before, and sometimes not at all. It always depends upon the context in the dream itself and also upon the conscious attitude of the dreamer. The best technique, therefore, is to take every dream as an entirely new proposition, every situation as entirely new, as if we had never heard of the meaning of symbols before. I recommend that technique in this case. The *dramatis personae* so far are the dreamer himself, the driver who has become the ape-man, and several unknown people only hinted at, among them a boy, obviously not very conspicuous to begin with. Have you an idea concerning these people?

Mr. Schmitz: They are those minor forces—sort of cabiri.[2] They were the employees in the former dream.

Dr. Jung: It would be the same, but in this case without the particular connotation of the employees. You see, an employee denotes a person who is in a certain dependent or cooperative position, but here they are mere presences, and it is not sure that they are in any cooperative relationship to the dreamer. They are just there, and we cannot even say whether they are hostile or friendly. That is, they represent subconscious figures that are not yet clear, not yet decided, but among them there is this recognizable figure, the boy. Naturally we must have the dreamer's associations in such a case, because we cannot afford to assume that the boy is

[1] Above, dream 12, p. 170, and dream 18, p. 431.
[2] See above, 22 May 1929, nn. 3 and 10.

672

exactly what he was in former dreams. You remember, for instance, a dream in which he had decidedly divine qualities, like a Greek god, Eros, as the dreamer said. Here the boy obviously functions as a sort of medium, for the dreamer says that he gets into a trance-like state and then that great-grandmother appears. This is the first time we have had such a figure in a dream. Now, that in itself is a symbol, because it is not reality; he is not concerned with any boy that would be a medium in reality, and therefore it is a perfectly fantastic symbolical creation. How would you translate that in psychological language?

Mrs. Sigg: The boy is young, so he suggests a beginning, a new attitude.

Dr. Jung: But what else?

Mrs. Fierz: Perhaps the mind of all those other subconscious figures.

Dr. Jung: If the dreamer were a woman, we might say that he represented a new thought in her, because the mind in a woman is usually represented by a male figure, but since the dreamer is a man, it would be something else.

Mr. Schmitz: A message from the unconscious to the conscious.

Dr. Jung: Yes, but that is a very positive interpretation. You can also interpret it a bit more reductively.

Mrs. Sigg: A boy also appeared in that former dream when the dreamer was doing acrobatics in the trees, and he tried to beat the dreamer with a rod.

Mrs. Sawyer: The dreamer pulled the rod out of the boy's mouth so that he was bleeding.

Dr. Jung: That is true, The boy was holding in his mouth the rod with which he had tried to beat the dreamer, and when the dreamer took it out of his mouth, he made the boy's mouth bleed. Well, here we have, as often happens, two motifs that have also occurred together in a former dream, in this case, the ape-man and the boy. So we are at once confronted with the question of what connection there is between them, and that leads us to the reductive interpretation of the boy. What is the boy?

Mrs. Crowley: The opposite of the man, the compensation for the ape-man.

Dr. Jung: That is again a very positive idea of the boy, but we could have a negative idea of him just as well. We might say, for instance, that he was the childish aspect of the dreamer, the dreamer

673

himself as a boy. You know real boys have very ape-like qualities, climbing where they should not climb and playing all sorts of monkey-tricks; boys are known for that, they often behave like monkeys. We have absolutely no reason for thinking little boys are angels. So men who still have the boy in them are by no means charming human beings, they can be beasts. You see, when he turns up in connection with the ape-man, we have to look at the other side; the boy is a very ambiguous symbol. I hope you remember the German book which I quoted when we were speaking about this motif, *Das Reich ohne Raum* (The Kingdom without Space), by Goetz.[3] That is about the negative side of the Puer Aeternus, the story of the boys with the leather caps who played the most amazing tricks on people, by no means nice. In the former dream, then, we have the ape-motif, climbing in the trees, and the boy, and here again this ape-man appears, and immediately after comes the boy. So we must pay attention to the connection.

As a matter of fact, the childish element in a man naturally leads down to ancestral figures, ancestral life. That is why the primitives have such peculiar ideas about education. They hold that the ancestral spirits are incarnated in the children, and therefore they are very loath to punish them; the children must not be beaten, because if one offends the children one would offend the ancestors. But when they reach the age of puberty those spirits go away, and then there is violence. The spirit of the young man is broken in as a horse's spirit is broken in. Before that there is no education, on account of their fear of the anger of the ancestral spirits, who might turn against them, and then the child might die or some other evil befall the family. Now, that idea that the child is possessed by a spirit, or that the very essence of the child is an ancestral spirit, corresponds to the fact that the psychology of children does really consist of ancestral spirits, or the collective unconscious. It is a long time before the child develops a psychology of its own, and all our attempts to create a child psychology will be quite fatal as long as we disregard the fact that it is collective psychology. It is impossible to understand children's dreams if one assumes otherwise.[4] They

[3] See above, 27 Mar. 1929, n. 4.

[4] Jung gave seminars or lectures (in German) on children's dreams at the E.T.H., Zurich, in the winter terms of 1936-37, 1938-39, 1939-40, and 1940-41. Transcripts were privately circulated; an English translation was issued for only the 1938-39 lectures. See CW 17, par. 106, editorial n. 3, and *General Bibliography*, CW 19, pp. 214-15.

have dreams which are absolutely adult and more than adult and which come directly from the collective unconscious. That of course is quite understandable, since the child starts in complete unconsciousness. It is the psychology of the collective unconscious, including the ancestors back to remote ages—to the cave-man or the ape-man. Therefore one sees the most amazing symbols in their dreams, and in their behaviour old rites become revivified. And everybody knows the wisdom of little children; they say the most extraordinary things if one cocks one's ears. There is a German proverb that children and fools tell the truth. That is because they speak out of the collective unconscious and therefore reveal things which the ordinary man would never think of revealing.

So the boy, or the boyish element, in an adult man may mean a part of his psychology which reaches back into his remote past and which links up through his instinctive life with the collective unconscious. And inasmuch as our future is brought forth through the collective unconscious, the boy also points to the future. For everything that we are going to be in the future is prepared in the collective unconscious, so it is in a way also the mother of the future. Therefore on the one hand the boy means something exceedingly childish, right back to the monkeys, and on the other hand something that reaches out into the far future. One often sees that a little boy in his games seems to be anticipating the future, as when he is playing with soldiers and arranging battles—he will perhaps do that in reality. The boy is in a way a bridge between the remote past and the remote future. In this case he is a medium, and a medium is a bridge between the conscious and the unconscious, or between this reality and ghost-land. Now, this is all theory, but I should like to know what it means practically, how it feels in reality. How can I bring it home to the dreamer so that he feels it himself?— for that is the main point of dream interpretation, that one brings it right home to the dreamer so that he feels: now it clicks! How would you proceed in that respect? Where does he feel it in himself?

Mrs. Sigg: He might feel it in his physical nature. It seems that the dreamer has sometimes an inclination towards things that are too artificial.

Dr. Jung: It would naturally have the effect that he would get more simple as he becomes a child, but it would have a further effect. You see, the boy is pushed up into the foreground of his dreams, which is simply a graphic demonstration of something which happens to the dreamer himself in reality. How would he feel this in his psychology?

Mr. Schmitz: He was interested in spiritualism before he was occupied with psychology, and since this boy is a medium, it is as if he went back to occult things.

Dr. Jung: Yes, that is an important hint. Obviously this part of the dream is taken from his spiritualistic interests. The boy is a medium, and thus far it is a regression to a former interest; he takes a step out of psychology back into spiritualism. Moreover it is not very mental, it is a piece of infantile psychology—he is becoming partially infantile. But I would like to know if you have any imagination about it, whether you get what that means. You have the hint that the boy is getting into a rigid state of trance, and that would about describe what the dreamer would feel if he could realize the boy.

Dr. Schlegel: Would he not feel somewhat separated from reality?

Dr. Jung: That is true. The trance itself is obviously a means used by the professional medium to cut off the individual from reality, so that the mental process is completely isolated from external influences. It is a sort of sleep, yet not an ordinary sleep; it is a part which is split off from consciousness, isolated from the real surroundings. That is one step, but we must go a bit farther. Why should he get isolated from his surroundings? What is the trance condition?

Mr. Schmitz: Is it a regression to magic—a minor means?

Dr. Jung: Yes, obviously his regression is to a magic mentality, so we must try to find our way through the complications of the primitive mind. This is a piece of primitive life. The situation immediately before, in the dream, is very awkward and could easily become dangerous; the driver has been transformed into a naked ape-man, and he is doing acrobatics. There is a sense of danger in the whole dream which is confirmed by its later development. Of course, it is most uncanny to the dreamer that a quality expressed by a naked ape-man should get loose in himself; that fellow can do God knows what, and immediately following comes his attempt at violence against the great-grandmother, which is a crime. There is an overwhelming, uncontrollable power about, a sort of gorilla, and what can he do against that feeling? And when they begin to shoot, what can he do against cannons? So he is bordering on panic,

676

and in the moment of panic people develop a primitive psychology. This is an inner panic which the man realizes in his dream state. You see, it began originally with the mouse that ran away,[5] and now it is becoming more an avalanche, it is growing on him, he has already to deal with an ape-man. Under such conditions man always regresses to the magic mentality. When you are confronted with a dangerous situation which you don't know how to deal with, what do you do? Did you ever observe yourself at such a moment?

Dr. Howells: People do most absurd things.

Dr. Jung: What would you call absurd? That is a value which comes from our conscious standpoint when we say afterwards: God! have I not been absurd!—or when we see something happen in a panic and call it idiotic, judged from the outside.

Miss Sergeant: Sometimes people pray.

Dr. Jung: Yes, sometimes people who ordinarily never think of praying suddenly begin to pray, or they make corresponding gestures. Or they make quite different gestures—I will tell you something I once saw. A barn was on fire near my house. It was in the night, people came right out of sleep, there were peasant women very scantily dressed and naturally in a state of complete panic. I was one of the first on the spot, and I opened the stables to let out the cattle. Then a woman came running out. She simply walked on the highway in the moon, imploring the gods with tragic gestures, sort of intoning Oh–h–h–! I ran after her and said: "What the devil are you doing here?" Whereupon she fell on my neck and crushed herself against me in the most caressing embrace. Being a psychologist, I knew that it was a moment when sexual cohabitation would be indicated, for here was a great tragedy, the world was going to pieces, and therefore she must propagate on the spot. It was no joke, it was a very serious business. That happened in the streets of Messina at the time of the earthquake,[6] numerous couples were observed. Almost invariably in a family murder, a man has sexual intercourse with his wife before he shoots her; it is the usual thing, a well-known fact, human nature reacts like that. Mind you, that was not the only case on the evening of

[5] See above, dream 24, p. 531.

[6] On Dec. 18, 1908, a violent earthquake destroyed 90 percent of the city of Messina, Sicily. See Jung's comment in a letter to Freud of 19 Jan. 1909 (*The Freud/ Jung Letters*, p. 199).

which I am telling you; there was another woman, a servant, who woke up suddenly and lost her head.

Mr. Schmitz: But also the contrary is true. If sexual intercourse is expected and not fulfilled, then one has a dream of a conflagration.

Dr. Jung: Yes, or a corresponding hallucination that the house is on fire. And in such a moment apotropaic actions, old magic rituals, come about. So our dreamer is obviously in distress about the presence of the ape-man, for one must not think of such a dream as a sort of picture-painting on the wall; it is a drama enacted in him. He is in the throes of the drama and it has got him, a sort of delirium, a fury of emotions, and now in his fear he applies a very peculiar means, a magic ritual: the boy goes into a trance in order to bring up the great-grandmother from Hades. People would have done that a thousand or two thousand years ago when they were in great trouble, or in doubt as to an important decision. We know that from the Bible: they went to the dead, or they went to a witch. Now they go to a doctor, which is the same thing, and he analyses their dreams, calling up the dead, calling the unconscious, all magic ritual from beginning to end. Here the boy is used for the purpose of raising the dead. Boys are very often used for crystal-gazing or for other magic performances.

For instance, I remember the story of a snake-charmer (a true story told me by a Swiss engineer employed in Egypt) who always went about holding a little boy on his arm while he was catching snakes. He was not a professional like the famous man in Cairo,[7] he was a Bedouin who was called in when snakes were really a pest. The country was infested by the horned sand-viper; they are terribly poisonous and they live buried in the sand waiting for their victims, with just the tip of the head sticking out. There had been a number of casualties among the native labourers. They could not catch them, so with some reluctance they called in this snake-charmer, who appeared, whistling, and carrying that little boy. He said the child was absolutely necessary to give him protection. He went from bush to bush, put in his hand, and pulled out the snakes in a completely stiff and charmed condition. You have probably read

[7] When Jung traveled down the Nile in spring 1926, his interest in a snake-charmer was recorded in a film made by H. G. Baynes.

678

such stories, where boys or little girls functioned as mediums in a somnambulistic state. In antiquity it was a sort of profession.

A very interesting example of that was found in an excavation in Egypt. They discovered a list of the servants in the house of a Roman official in imperial times, and among them was a name written in Greek, Walburga Sibylla.[8] Walburga is a German name, and the women of Germany were particularly mediumistic; it is known that many German women slaves were sold to be used as mediums and somnambulists. So that was the name of the house-medium, a German girl who had been sold as a slave up the Nile. She belonged to the household of a distinguished nobleman, and in case of emergency could be his medium; he could ask his Sibylla to prophesy what he should do. And now also we have clairvoyants whom we consult when in doubt. That is an expedient which was used in early civilizations as well as among the primitives, and that is the connection in the dream. The situation becomes awkward, and in his panic this man seizes upon that old means to get advice or help. Because there is no human help, the unconscious is conjured, and in this case it is the great-grandmother.

We still have not gotten down to the concrete fact of how this boy symbolism would function in our patient. It is obviously the childish element; the adult man in him does not know how to solve the problem, and I was incapable of telling him. I told him that there must be some mysterious solution of which I did not know. So he is thrown back upon himself and has most obviously come to the end of all his mental resources. He feels something is creeping upon him, something is increasing in strength and danger, and now it is the ape-man, and under these conditions people become childish. Many neurotics impress themselves upon one through this particular childishness, but if you knew their particular problem, you would understand. When everything is absolutely dark, the only thing to do is to become hysterical or childish. Sometimes it needs very little to reduce a man, no matter how adult, to a whimpering child who simply breaks down and weeps for his mother, and that is what happens to this man. He finds no other way out so he becomes a little boy, and that proves to be the way for the time being. By following that way, which he cannot find by intellectual means, by indulging himself in that regression, he falls down

[8] Greek *sibylla* = "prophetess."

into the archetype of the boy, as millions and millions of people in untold thousands of years have already done. When they were in a bad condition they became childish, utterly absurd. They simply let themselves drop down upon the bedrock of instinct.

Thus is formed the pattern of the boy who doesn't know what to do and in his desperation gets to a state of *ekstasis*. That is the term, for when a panic or a terrible pain reaches the culmination, it ceases and people become ecstatic. Pain cannot be endured in ever-increasing intensity beyond a certain point. Then it turns and becomes *ekstasis*. This symptom is mentioned in the famous book, the *Malleus Maleficarum*,[9] as one of the symptoms of witchcraft; it was called the witches' sleep. When one's mood reaches the deepest blackness, then the light comes. That is the sun myth. One simply falls into the mythical pattern, the archetype; it is the natural way which things take. There are innumerable cases in the Bible: when despair has reached its climax God reveals himself, which is simply a psychological truth. So when this man is reduced to that little boy, perfectly helpless and rigid with fear, after that state of numb-ness and utter exhaustion, then the *ekstasis* comes and the mother appears. Of course, no real mother appears, but the great-grand-mother, which is, as I said, a very high title and honour. It is not as the ordinary mother appears to the little boy; when the adult man becomes like a child, utterly despairing, then the divine mother appears, and she is very old and yet quite young, as the description says in his dream. She has a very young face.

Now before going on, I hope you are sufficiently acquainted with the inner mood of the dreamer. He is rather desperate on account of the coming up of the ape-man. You must realize what it means to a respectable and very rational person when he is suddenly confronted with such a reality. We are naturally inclined to think: Oh, well, dreams are not so real. But in the night these things are terribly real. One may forget oneself for awhile, and then up comes the problem again. He cannot get away from it. He confesses that he knows nothing to do about it, so he simply gives up, and that is the most favourable moment for the manifestation of the un-conscious. When we come to the end of our wits, then the archetype begins to function. For since eternity man has gone through situ-

---

[9] Two Dominican inquisitors, Jakob Sprenger and Heinrich Krämer, published (1489) the *Malleus Maleficarum*, or *Hexenhammer*, "Hammer of Witches," a manual giving rules for discovering and punishing witches.

ations with which he could not cope, where instincts had to step in and solve the situation, either in a cunning way or by a *coup de force*, and that is the situation now. We would expect that the unconscious in such a situation would produce the image that is the most likely to be helpful, and when a man is reduced to a little boy, he is naturally crying for the mother. If an adult man comes to that reduced condition, it is not the ordinary mother, because he knows very well that his own mother would not be very helpful, unless she happened to possess second sight or to be a superior personality. The ordinary mothers are not superior personalities. So it is the great-grandmother, an early mythical mother, the mother of an immense past, who appears.

Mr. Schmitz: I think a man would not do that in his conscious. I know a case where a man met a wild man in a dream and said to himself: Of course, I can do nothing against that man by using force, but there are tricks; people have always been able to kill animals much stronger than themselves in that way. So in the dream he plays a trick and he kills the ape-man. What would you say about that?

Dr. Jung: That was presence of mind. And it was not a case of complete despair. The man kept his rational mind and applied jiu jitsu. The ape-man could obviously be dealt with in such a way. But in this case it is of no use for our dreamer to kill the ape-man.

Mr. Schmitz: The man I am speaking of was satisfied with the dream, but two hours afterwards he had a fit of sickness.

Dr. Jung: That is a very questionable case. You see, in mythology, the hero has to kill a series of monsters and nothing particular happens, but suddenly with a certain monster something does happen. Usually there are quite a series of victories over the ape-man until life is so purified that nothing happens any longer. But then the ape-man comes again, and that time you cannot kill him. The trouble is that no general prescription is possible. In certain cases, one has to say: now kill it, just stamp it out. In another case, quite the contrary. Therefore I give no advice at all.

Mr. Schmitz: That fit of sickness perhaps meant that in his case it would have been better to be a little more masculine; instead of killing it, to go to the grandmother.

Dr. Jung: Well, he could not *choose* to do that, it would be a case of necessity as it is with our dreamer. He has tried practically all means of dealing with his problem, and in such a case there is nothing to do but to go to the mother. Like Faust—he couldn't kill Mephistopheles, and he had to go to the mothers to seek rebirth.[10]

Mr. Schmitz: If he had tried to kill him, it would have been wrong perhaps?

Dr. Jung: If he had been Mr. Smith or Mr. Jones, he might have been allowed to kill the devil. But not Faust. There are many unimportant people who are obliged to kill the devil, but it could have no value at all in such cases. In this case, our dreamer had to deal with the problem of the ape-man. He could not kill him, and the situation was such that the great-grandmother had to come up. Now what is that great-grandmother?

Dr. Schlegel: The whole past of humanity.

Dr. Jung: Yes, in a way, But why not the great-grandfather?— is he not also the whole past?

Miss Bianchi: She is Mother Nature.

Dr. Jung: But why Mother Nature?

Dr. Schlegel: Because man must yield to her. If it were the father, he would not yield.

Dr. Jung: Why not? If I were in such a situation, I would not run to the mother, but if there were a nice old father, I should go to him perhaps.

Mr. Schmitz: He is bound to the paternal principle, and here is a moment where the male principle no longer helps; he must go to the female principle. I believe that is the reason why the man I spoke of was ill. He should not have killed the wild man, he should have gone to the female principle.

Dr. Jung: That is perfectly true. And this is the case of a man who has used up all the masculine means at his disposition. You often find that in mythology. If a man does not know how to solve his problem, he turns to the witch, as Saul in the Old Testament turned to the witch of Endor.[11] In the Wagner legend, it was Wotan and Erda.[12] There are many other examples in mythology where men had to go back to women's advice. A very good case is in *L'île des pingouins,* which I have quoted several times,[13] where all the

---

[10] The theme of the Mothers in *Faust,* Part Two, is dealt with in *Symbols of Transformation* (1952), CW 5, pars. 180ff. and 299 (end). (Also in 1912 edn.)

[11] I Samuel 28:7.

[12] In Richard Wagner's operatic cycle *The Ring of the Nibelungs,* the war god Wotan (or Woden) relies on the counsel of his consort, the earth goddess Erda.

[13] Cf. above, 23 Jan. 1929, at n. 2.

great Fathers in Heaven could not decide about the baptism of the penguins, and finally they had to call in St. Catharine and ask her what she thought about it, and she decided it very nicely. So here, it is obviously a case which cannot be decided by the masculine mind, and therefore Mother Nature, the great-grandmother, as a last resort has to be called in, and she is very old and very young, like eternal nature. She appears to him as a mystical revelation out of the trance of the boy. When childishness appears and *ekstasis* begins, then nature comes in to speak the last word. But now something exceedingly important happens, the ape-man springs upon her to violate her. What does that mean?

Mrs. Baynes: He won't have her compete with his authority. They are naturally two antagonistic forces, and if he possibly can, he will subjugate her.

Dr. Jung: But the ape-man—nature—and the great-grandmother are not antagonistic.

Mrs. Baynes: But I thought, considering the position this man was in, that the great-grandmother would have to cope with the ape-man. I mean, she could not co-operate with him.

Dr. Jung: The unconscious, it is true, reveals the great-grandmother at this moment with the idea of doing something really helpful, but it is not a bit sure whether one's conscious would feel it as that. Sometimes the solution of a problem is something that one would consider far from helpful. Therefore I ask: why should the ape-man not jump on Mother Nature? Is that wrong necessarily?

Mrs. Baynes: In this particular case, I should think it was very wrong.

Mr. Schmitz: He does it, of course, in a very primitive and violent way, but symbolically he must take possession of Nature.

Mrs. Baynes: But the great-grandmother is not going to have it, so that shows that she doesn't think it a good idea.

Dr. Jung: You hold opposite points of view. What are you going to do about it?

Mrs. Baynes: Mr. Schmitz is all theoretical, but I have on my side the great-grandmother who jumped out of the window!

Dr. Draper: Is there an implication of the Osiris myth here, with the figure of the great-grandmother in this case as Isis?

Dr. Jung: You are quite right, it is a complete analogy. The ape-man would fill the role of Set. In contradistinction to all the other

683

Egyptian gods, Osiris was a god-man, he was supposed to have lived on earth like a man, and his fate was the typical fate of the sacrificed god, like Christ, Attis, etc. He was dismembered by Set, the Egyptian devil, who usually appeared in the form of a black pig, utterly despicable and evil, a pig that lived in the mud. The left eye of Osiris was blinded because he had seen Set—that was enough to blind one. The famous motif of the eye of Horus comes in here, which is a very important symbol in Egypt; Horus sacrificed one of his eyes for his father Osiris. Unfortunately the tradition in that respect is quite deficient, we don't know the whole myth.[14] The Catholic Church has justified that cycle of myths as a dogmatic precursor of the Christ myth, because they could not deny the extraordinary analogy. It is the eternal problem of man, the typical situation in which man has found himself millions of times, and therefore it was expressed in a current myth. And the value of the myth in those days was that it was a sort of recipe, a medical prescription what to do in case of trouble. In old Egypt, when someone was in such a typical condition, the medical man, the priest, would read the corresponding chapter from the collection of myths in order to effect a cure, so it had a very practical therapeutic value. For instance, if a man was bitten by a snake, they read the particular legend of Isis, how she prepared a poisonous worm and laid it on the path of Ra—or Osiris—in order to sting him, so he was lamed and very sick. And they had to call in Mother Isis again to cure him, because they had no other means; as she had prepared the poison, she also knew how to heal him; Mother Isis spoke the true word and the god was healed.[15] He was not, however, as strong as he had been, as people are apt to feel rotten after a snake-bite.

That was Egyptian medicine, and we still have something like it. People go to a doctor just to have an opinion. That is very typical of Americans; one must only utter an opinion and they believe. A doctor says: "He is suffering from a catatonic form of schizophrenia," and the Americans believe that something has happened—he has said it! The patient tells all his symptoms, and the doctor says, "Yes, it is so," and gives names to his trouble, and so he

[14] For a summary of the Osiris myth, see *Symbols of Transformation*, pars. 349-357 (as in 1912 edn.). The twins Isis and Osiris were husband and wife; Set, the evil one, was their brother.

[15] See Jung's account, from an Egyptian hymn, ibid., pars. 451-453 (as in 1912 edn.).

assimilates it to the conscious of the patient; he lifts it out of the sphere of pain and anguish and uncertainty into the sphere of contemplation. He reads out a certain chapter of the legend or the hymn, or makes some other incantation about it. Thus he brings up an archetypal image of eternal and universal truth, and that evocation has a peculiar influence upon the unconscious. It is like the effect of music on a company of soldiers after a long march; they may be quite tired and demoralized and don't want to walk any farther, but then the music starts in and the whole thing comes into motion again. Our dreamer is now in despair, as primitive people are when they are ill; if they do not receive a moral kick, they let themselves drop and fade away, and they get such a kick out of certain incantations because that mobilizes the forces of the collective unconscious. Therefore, exactly as it is in the Osiris legend, or the poisoning of the sun-god when the great mother Isis comes in to heal him, here comes in a great-grandmother. And that is simply Nature—Nature as it is, with no moral considerations at all.

You see, that is the position of masculine psychology. I don't know whether women will agree with me, but a man is convinced that the real standpoint of woman is amoral. He is fundamentally convinced of that, no matter what women have attained or to what they aspire. I personally hear a great deal about moral considerations from them, they talk of it because they do not believe in it! So when a man comes to the end, he appeals to that amoral female principle. Having no morality, she is in federation with the devil and knows what to do in such a case. I remember a most respectable lady doctor who was concerned with a typical case and did not know what to do about it. A very distinguished gentleman, quite well known, founded a dairy for poor people during the war. He had appointed two young girls to run it, and became interested in one of them and even fell in love with her. He was a married man, highly respectable, and it dawned upon him that he was up against a conflict, but he had no psychology for the situation. So he went to the lady doctor and asked her advice, and she didn't know what to do in such a delicate case either, so she asked me. I said: "Could his lordship perhaps inform his wife?" "Of course," she said, "but how do you know that? You must be a very wicked man to know that!" Moral considerations right away! But that is exactly what a man thinks; when Isis—Mother Nature—comes in, he fears a hell of a trick, something terribly evil and doubtful.

Now that is the mythological situation. A man would feel exactly as Ra did when Isis was called in, for of course Ra knew who had made that poisonous worm and naturally he mistrusted such a doctor. So one could expect such a reaction here. Obviously the ape-man has not purely friendly intentions. If she understood his action as particularly nice behaviour, she would not jump out of the window, so we must assume that it is not very welcome to her; she finds it somewhat rash perhaps and prefers to withdraw. Therefore we must conclude that the behaviour of the ape-man is not very clever. He obviously frightens Mother Nature very badly so she cannot fulfil the helpful role. Even though it was Nature that got our dreamer into such trouble, she might have known a means, a counterpoison to help the man, but after that interference of the ape-man, she can do nothing, the help she might have brought cannot come off. Now we should understand why the ape-man is jumping on her. It is quite obvious in the dream that he gets sexually excited and that explains his action. But how do you understand that?—a thing that upsets the helpful purposes of the unconscious, the healing properties of the archetype. What if Set had suddenly felt attracted and jumped on Mother Isis, for instance? In *Faust*, the devil is attracted by the nice little angel-boys.

Mr. Holdsworth: You said just now that when a man murders his wife, he first cohabits with her. In this dream do you think the man is ashamed of the unconscious appeal of the great-grandmother and so he wants to kill her?

Dr. Jung: That would be right if we were certain that the ape-man was making a murderous attack upon her, but that is not the case. He is obviously attracted by her sexually, and anger is not mentioned, so we have no evidence for such a conjecture.

Prof. Eaton: Is it not the ape-man himself who has to be regenerated through Isis?—and naturally he would be sexually attracted by her, because he himself is going to be made over.

Dr. Jung: Yes, the ape-man has been generated by just that poisonous worm, and when he sees Mother Isis, he wants to enter her again. It is a sort of incest. It is as if the worm that Isis made wanted to return into her. That is like primitive magic: the primitives hold that when someone with magic influence wants to commit murder, for instance, he sends out a sort of magic projectile which kills the victim; but then it returns, and if the sorcerer is not very careful it will kill him too. The magic effect always returns, according to primitive ideas. And that is a psychological fact; a fascination or magic effect only takes place if the person who causes it is a victim himself. If you are just moderately angry, if you say something rather nasty to the other fellow but in a controlled way, then it has only a surface effect. But if you are overcome by your own anger, made sick by it, then through *contagion mentale* you arouse the same condition in him. The thing that the primitives are most afraid of is arousing the anger of the medicine-man, for that has a most destructive effect on every living thing through unconscious contagion; but it only takes place if the magician himself is under the effects. There is a case of magic influence in a book called *Black Laughter* by Powys,[16] an Englishman, about a sorcerer whose hut had been burnt down. It is based upon the fact that as long as one feels that one's opponent controls his emotion, it is not so dangerous, but if it is really uncontrolled, anything might happen, and one is afraid. Then it reaches you as nothing else does; nothing is so contagious as uncontrolled emotion; it is almost unsurmountable, it just grips one. For instance, if everybody is laughing like mad in an uncontrolled way, one is almost obliged to join in. One sees that very clearly in children and primitives.

Here the magic effect plays a great role. Mother Isis has generated the ape-man and produced that whole conflict, and now the upset reaches a certain culmination, and the mother comes back in order to cure the trouble. She sent out the projectile and to her it returns, and that means terrible danger because it might kill her. Therefore she jumps out of the window. She has to do what the primitive sorcerer does—jump aside when the projectile comes back. He is all the time afraid of ghosts and spells and magic factors, and Mother Nature is working with just such desperate means; she also is the victim of returning projectiles. Of course, that is primitive psychology, that is mythology, but how does it feel in the dreamer himself? You see, he is in a way the primitive man, but when you say to such a person that there is a very natural solution, he says: But one cannot afford to behave like that. The dreamer tries to be very respectable and repress the whole problem, and then nature

[16] Llewelyn Powys, *Black Laughter* (London, 1924), sketches of life in East Africa, where he had lived 1914-1920.

687

works and works so that he cannot deny it any longer. Then the ape-man breaks loose, and in comes Mother Nature and there is the very devil to pay. If he says: "That is *my* nature!—I am the monkey-man!" then nature escapes or nature is destroyed; something happens which should not happen. Now what would be the result if the dreamer were to identify with the ape-man? You see, the dream shows how much he is afraid of it, and yet how great the temptation is to do just that.

Mr. Schmitz: His life would be destroyed.

Dr. Jung: Yes, he would lose all his civilized values, his moral and philosophical values. He would no longer be a conscious rational man, he would fall down into the mud and lose himself entirely. Well, that is exactly what modern nature has produced, that is the eternal paradox. Nature has obviously not only two, but many sides, and it is quite possible that one side destroys another. We might say that she is an equal mixture of construction and destruction; she is not only a kind and generous mother, she is also a beast. She produces not only lovely plants and flowers and animals, but also the hellish parasites which feed upon them. So here is the helpful side of nature which would be destroyed if the other side were allowed to jump on it, and here obviously something must interfere to help the situation. Is there any hint in the dream to show how this problem could be solved? The great-grandmother goes to the police, and then comes the danger of the artillery, and then the photographer appears who saves the whole collection of pictures which he has taken of that scene. That seems to be the solution.

But the main point that we must make clear today is the attack on the great-grandmother. It is by no means easy to formulate, because the psychological concept of nature is as paradoxical as Mother Isis in the myth—almost revoltingly paradoxical. Picture Mother Isis, that treacherous hell of a woman, fixing the poison worm for her husband to step on, and then coming in as saviour, while he is the damned fool in the whole game. That is revolting but that is nature. Nature has produced the problem of our dreamer and nature is meant to cure it. But if nature comes in, he will misunderstand it in the way the ape-man misunderstands it, he will assume: here is complete freedom for the ape-man. That is the eternal mistake.

You have heard of the mistake of the eleven thousand virgins.

There is a little something repressed, perhaps; naturally nature has something to say, so they become neurotic and go to the doctor. And he says: You should live, that is all repressed sex, you should have a friend or you should marry. So if the girl is in the position of having the right kind of parents, they take the thing in hand and put her in the marriage box. But then there is a hell of a trouble, and it does not work at all. People say it is repressed nature and they solve it on the cow-bull level, forgetting that they have to do with a human being. That other is done in stables. A man on that level will think: Oh, well, any woman will do. And then he will wonder afterwards, because he is confronted with all the civilized values he has attained and he has completely lost his self-esteem. Provided he understands this, our dreamer will reflect about what he is doing. He cannot merely live, he has tried it and sees that it did not work.

LECTURE VIII

25 June 1930

Dr. Jung:

Here is a question from Dr. Howells: "Did the dreamer have any feeling of disintegration when he had this dream in which his anima escaped?"

One would assume that he would have a certain feeling about such an agitated dream, that he would feel it in the daytime even, but the fact of such a dream does not necessarily bring about a conscious realization of excitement or nervousness or anything of the sort. We know that dreams are very often compensatory, so the conscious feeling might be quiet. If there is no proper realization of the possible implications, there is no particular excitement. The dream, rather, brings a sort of information about a storm that is beginning to rage in the unconscious. So this man was not particularly restless or nervous. In this phase of his analysis, the dreams were more or less outside of him. In the night he had funny dreams, and in the daytime things were as they usually were. Only commonplace and everyday things happened, and he was not in the least bothered, nor did he feel any direct connection with his dreams. There is an indication in the latter part of this dream that for the first time he gets a sense of his profound relationship to them. Hitherto, they have been quite interesting to him, and naturally he got a lot out of the interpretations, but it was as if they didn't get under his skin. I was for a long time in doubt as to what he would make of it, whether the thing would really grip him or not. He was tremendously objective and scientific in his whole attitude, and I felt that that was the only relationship one had to him, or that the dreamer had to his unconscious; only occasionally was there a glimpse of something more. If he had been deeply agitated in his conscious life, most probably his dreams would have mitigated the conditions, as is often the case.

Last week we were talking about the attack of the ape-man upon the anima, and how she succeeded in getting out of the window and into the world. And when she shouted for help, people instantly came, and the ape-man desisted. Then something quite typical happened, which happened already in the Bible, right in the beginning. It seems to be a basic trouble of mankind, or perhaps one would say of men. What did Adam say when things became awkward?

Mrs. Baynes: He said that Eve tempted him.[1]

Dr. Jung: Yes, there it is. The woman did it. So the ape-man said to her: Why the devil did you break the window? She had to fight for her life and he complained that she had broken the window. That is characteristic of the more or less civilized ape-man. First he raises hell, and then he complains that he has to dust his coat off perhaps. That shows the nature of the ape-man: he is terribly impulsive, he tries to violate her, and when it doesn't work he says: "Oh, excuse me, I just wanted to ask you what time it is." He is a coward. As long as he succeeds it is all right, but when he sees that he has failed, he instantly swings round and complains that she has disturbed the noble household by breaking those windows.

The next thing is that the anima goes away with the people outside, obviously for the police. Now what have the police to do with the situation? That is a very serious turn in the dream.

Mrs. Deady: They are the guardians of the collective situation.

Dr. Jung: Yes, but what is the collective situation?

Mr. Schmitz: The moral situation. The police are the protection of morality.

Dr. Jung: It is not exactly morality but it has to do with it. I told you what the father said to the son when he was twenty-one, but I will repeat it: "You have come of age and I must tell you something that will be important for your later life: For stupid people there is the Bible, but for more intelligent people there is the penal code." That was his concept of morality. Now here the police means a very particular degree of morality. Our dreamer has never been bothered much with the moral problem, yet here it approaches in the form of the police.

[1] Genesis 3:12: ". . . she gave me of the tree, and I did eat."

Mrs. Crowley: It is not the individual standpoint but the collective conventional standpoint.

Dr. Jung: It is the most brutal form of the collective standpoint. When the policeman gets you, it is most convincing, most immediate. It is a stone in at your window. Conflict and trouble. And what is the problem which leads him into collision with the collective powers?

Mr. Schmitz: If one doesn't assimilate the ape-man oneself, the police must interfere, because one gets into opposition to the civilized world.

Dr. Jung: But would you assume that he is played by the ape-man?

Mr. Schmitz: If he is identical with the ape-man, he is in conflict with the police.

Dr. Jung: Have we evidence? It is the ape-man that makes the attack.

Mr. Schmitz: He allows the ape-man to make the attack in the unconscious.

Dr. Jung: But he does not allow it, it just happens. There is a story of three old veterans and an officer who were defending a fortress. The enemy attacks, and suddenly one of the veterans shouts: "I have made a prisoner!" The colonel says: "Bring him here!" and the veteran shouts back: "He won't let me!" That is the story of the ape-man. The complication is that the ape-man seems to be something quite apart, as in reality the dreamer is by no means an ape-man, he is a very nice gentleman. But it happens often that a very nice gentleman has some affiliation with the ape-man though in a very remote degree. And now this ape-man is loose and we don't know how far he will go. In that former dream, the mouse escaped and now it is already the size of a gorilla, and the anima jumps out of the window and calls for help. Nobody knows the ape-man is inside, but from the internal conflict the anima has escaped into the open. Now that is a very special case, and it is not simple. We ought to know what it means in order to understand why the police come in. She is the reason for the police coming, for the mere presence of the ape-man does not call for the police.

Miss Sergeant: She wants protection.

Dr. Jung: That is mythological speech, and we should know how that applies to practical psychology, because I have to make the meaning clear to the dreamer. He naturally would follow one's argument and nod his head as if he understood, but then he goes away completely bewildered, unless something dawns on him on his way home. So we must know what will happen.

Prof. Eaton: The anima is not interested in the ape-man. She wants the other aspect of the man.

Dr. Jung: Yes. Otherwise she would have stayed, she would have had her time. If he had shown some interest in her, she probably would not have run away, but he was indifferent and showed only ape-man activity.

Prof. Eaton: Now she is calling the police because the other side, collective morality, wants the other aspect of his personality.

Dr. Jung: That is exactly true, but how would that work out in human life? I must know in order to show the man how the thing appears on the surface of the world. What does it mean in reality when the anima has escaped? It is as if she were somewhere out in the world.

Dr. Draper: This may be the moment when he meets her as the concrete woman.

Dr. Jung: That is it. When the anima is outside, she is projected into a real woman. When the anima is a psychological spectre, it means just nothing to a matter-of-fact man, it is a theoretical conflict. But when the anima is projected, when she turns up as a real woman, things get really awkward. Now it dawns upon him that she no sooner escapes from his own house than she is incarnated in a woman, and at any moment he may meet her. Then instantly he will be fascinated, caught, for she is reinforced by the whole collective unconscious. And then there will be trouble, because he will be up against conventional morality. It was that which I was trying to make clear to you when we were speaking of the mouse. Of course it was not recognizable there, but most of his libido and his own personality escaped where it could not be reached, and that will probably return to him. For all our split-off parts return, all the people we meet in life who have a fascinating influence upon us are really split-off parts of ourselves, things we have repressed which are brought back by other people, and that is the great value and the great danger and difficulty of human relationship. In this case it is a very serious matter, because when the anima escapes, the whole woman side of this man has a chance to appear anywhere, he doesn't know when or where. Perhaps tomorrow he will step out into the street and along comes a woman who is the anima. He cannot get away from her. He may repress it but it will arouse a hell of sexual fantasies; he will become quite neurotic and be unable to deal with it properly, for the way to deal with such a problem is not generally known. This very complicated situation is what he foresees, and this accounts for the conflict with the police, collective morality.

Now, in this great moment, the moment of the dawn of this insight, another man appears on the scene, the photographer, and he seems to be an extremely indifferent, detached individual, for he assures them that things are all right as far as he is concerned, because he has taken all the pictures and the whole thing will make a most interesting story. Now who is he?

Miss Sergeant: His mirror.

Dr. Jung: Yes, but what would that be literally, in concrete language?

Mr. Schmitz: It is a conflict of the mind. The man has understood everything and now he can go home, but nothing is changed.

Dr. Jung: Yes, that is the observer in him, probably his differentiated function. His mind watches the performance in a more or less detached way, looking down at it, as if he were seeing rather an exciting scene in the movies; his mind takes records, photographs, of the whole performance. As a matter of fact, the dreamer associates this whole series of dreams, all the pictures he has seen in his dreams, with that photographer's film. He has a very personal relationship to his dreams; he values them very highly and has kept all the records and made a book of them. He gave me this copy. It is a most unique collection, very carefully done with associations, and drawings and pictures interspersed. He is quite proud of having the whole collection and he treasures it; he feels that if everything goes to hell, he has at all events rescued this precious material, these precious thoughts. That is a great consolation to him, it is something to stand on. He can open a business, he can sell that film! His mind has achieved something quite positive that is capable of establishing a continuity of experience.

Of course, the undifferentiated function in him has a primitive character. Primitives never take note of experiences and there is no continuity in their minds, everything is like dreams interrupted by conflicting impulses; like children and animals, they cannot concentrate. An animal that has been on the point of death in the next moment begins to play again. That is the inferior function. It makes no history because it is all the time living in the moment that is eternity. But the differentiated function has the quality of the historian, it records things, it gives continuity, and one can always withdraw more or less upon that continuity, upon that sort of historical consciousness; that has been to many people really a refuge, the foundation of an island. For sometimes things move with such rapidity, with such turmoil and chaos, that nobody could keep track of them, and the only thing which holds such people straight and humanly quiet is the continuity of their records. I suppose you have seen that film of the *Titanic*.[2] There is one man, a journalist, who sticks to his records within the turmoil, where everybody becomes unreasonable and goes to pieces. He is the only one who goes under in a complete way, quiet, because he succeeded in withdrawing to the standpoint of the timeless observer. His life is before his eyes, it is moving away, and yet he is peaceful. That is the superiority of the differentiated function.

Prof. Eaton: If feeling were the superior function instead of thinking, would it be the same?

Dr. Jung: Oh yes, because feeling is only in quality a different function, it has the same general principle. So the real religious principle, the idea of God, inner religiousness, is an intellectual as well as a feeling and emotional value. The feeling type is perfectly able to detach his feeling from the turmoil and hold it against external circumstances; it is amazing what he can do, he can hold his feeling in a hypothetical way just by being able to cling, to persevere. The ancients could not do that. For instance, they had all the knowledge of the mechanical processes which would have enabled them to invent machines that worked, but they did not invent them. They only put together a few pieces and a nice toy resulted. Instead of continuing with whatever manifested in that experimental arrangement, they began to play with it and it became a mere curiosity. One still sees that play quality in early machines: they were always decorated with goat's legs and Corinthian columns and all sorts of figures which have nothing whatever to do with the

[2] The film, entitled *Atlantic*, was a British production based on the story of the liner *Titanic*, which on its maiden voyage in April 1912 struck an iceberg and sank, with heavy loss of life. Sound versions of the film were prepared in English, German, and French; the premiere took place in Berlin in November 1929. (The critic of the *New York Times* called the film "puerile.")

meaning of a machine. The real machine is only a very recent discovery, and it has made its own style, but the old machines were covered with flowers and parts of human beings and God knows what, perhaps little angels sitting on the wheels, which simply shows that the artist or inventor was not quite capable of being matter-of-fact.

That playfulness is the reason why children cannot think like adult people; they cannot be entirely concrete and matter-of-fact. And that is the reason why, even in the Middle Ages, men were not able to use all the knowledge they possessed; and, of course, that was still more obvious in antiquity, not to speak of the primitive man who for a hundred thousand years got nowhere at all because he had no power of concentration. That is not merely a point of view, an *aperçu*; it is actually most impressive to see how the mind of the primitive man is easily tired—perfectly strong men, fine male figures of savages. At a palaver,[3] for instance, where one asks them very simple questions, whether they believe in ghosts for instance, after two hours everybody goes to sleep. They say: we are so tired, can't you finish the palaver?—for they cannot go away till the magic word is spoken by the elder, the word meaning: now the business is at an end. But then the same men are able to hunt game for forty-eight hours without eating or sleeping. When they are carrying letters, they walk a hundred and twenty kilometres in one stretch, because in doing that their instinct is roused and they can do things which we cannot do. They can walk in terrible heat sixty-two kilometres, with loads of sixty pounds on their heads. I had all the trouble in the world to keep up with them without carrying such a load—they were almost running. They die at an early age—about fifty—from overwork. They spend themselves utterly, which we are too reasonable to do; we would become doubtful, but they spend themselves to the last breath if they are acting with the instinct. Against the instinct they are very easily tired.

And that is the same with the primitive in us: the primitive undifferentiated functions are not concentrated, they are vague, they are easily interrupted, they have no continuity. These qualities are the virtues of the differentiated function, whatever it is. It doesn't matter which function is differentiated, its main point is that it can

---

[3] Jung is referring to experiences during his sojourn in East Africa in winter 1925-26. See *MDR*, p. 264/248.

hold out against ever-changing nature. It is like the human structure that holds out against every change in environment; or a house,
which is a shelter that does not tumble down or lose its leaves; or
a road, which is not interrupted, which has bridges, for instance.
If one follows an elephant's trail, it is perhaps quite smooth for a
while, one can travel it on one's bicycle, and then suddenly it gets
lost in a swamp and there is an end to it. Civilization is characterized
by the fact that it holds out against the changes of nature; and that
is the virtue of the superior function.

Mr. Schmitz: How would a feeling type behave, as a parallel to
the journalist on the *Titanic?*

Dr. Jung: A loving woman can hold a situation against everything, against death and the devil, and create a duration in chaos
with complete conviction. In thought, Galileo could hold out against
torture—well, he did make denial, but immediately after, he got
up and he said, "E pur si muove."[4] That is holding out against the
disintegrating powers of nature, and it is the same with feeling.
Feeling is a most powerful function.

Mr. Schmitz: We know how the journalist on the *Titanic* behaved.
How would a corresponding feeling type behave?

Dr. Jung: A feeling type would behave like his wife, for instance.
She simply loved him, and she stood death and panic with him. It
was done very beautifully. He was identical with his philosophical
observation of the situation and quite aloof. He was already in a
timeless land. And she too, through love. That is feeling.

Mr. Schmitz: But love is not a capacity of the feeling type only.

Dr. Jung: Naturally, for the feeling of a woman, even the thinking of a woman, can be detached only with the aid of Eros, as the
thought of a man can be detached only with the help of Logos.
Therefore the highest forms of the great helpful powers of the
unconscious correspond to those principles. The highest form of
thinking in a man coincides with Logos, as the highest form of
feeling in a woman coincides with Eros. It was only through the
aid of the gods that man was able to detach himself from the
meaninglessness of nature. Therefore, the greatest redeemer of

---

[4] The astronomer Galileo Galilei (1564-1642), when tried by the inquisition at
Rome for his espousal of the Copernican theory of the solar system—in particular,
the idea that the earth revolved around the sun—abjured his belief but, according
to tradition, murmured "E pur si muove" (nevertheless it does move).

whom we know, Jesus Christ, has been called the Logos. He was the light that rescued us from that darkness.

Mr. Schmitz: But I have the impression that in a feeling type the capacity for loving is greater.

Dr. Jung: No, love is a feeling, yet the principle of Eros is not necessarily loving, it can be hating too. Eros is the principle of relationship, and that is surely the main element in woman's psychology, as Logos is the main element in man's psychology. But the Logos naturally is in relation to feeling as well as to thinking. One can have sensation and intuition more under the influence of Logos or more under the influence of Eros. The functions are interrelated as well as permeated by the two basic principles.

Mr. Schmitz: The fact of being a feeling type does not give one a greater capacity for loving?

Dr. Jung: No, it has nothing to do with loving. A feeling type can be as cold as ice if there is not Eros. He can maintain a feeling of hatred through death and the devil, he can die with hatred all over him, or he may have a feeling of indifference and hold out against anything.

Mr. Schmitz: But also a woman, a feeling type, can be incapable of love?

Dr. Jung: Absolutely. There are women who are feeling types and yet who are entirely cold and without sex. The feeling type is never particularly warm, because the differentiated function is often lacking in human qualities. You must never mix up feeling with love. That is due to a miserable shortcoming of language. For instance, in the war, the political department issued declarations beginning: The President has a feeling about such and such a thing. Perfectly ridiculous. It should be: he has an *opinion* about such and such a thing. That suggests again an entirely different application of the word "feeling." Then there are feelings of duty, of admiration, ten thousand ways of using the word. In the German language it is still worse; even Goethe confuses sensation and sentiment.[5] The French could never do that. The German language is not yet sufficiently developed to make a difference between the most ordinary sensation and the most delicate feelings of love. It is simply a lack of differentiation, for the differentiation there is

[5] According to K. R. Eissler (author of *Goethe: A Psychoanalytic Study 1775-1786*, Detroit, 1963) the terms *Gefühl* (feeling) and *Empfindung* (sensation) were equated in the 18th and 19th centuries. (Personal communication.)

chiefly on the intuitional and intellectual side, and therefore feeling and sensation are all muddled up. Differentiated sensation is the *fonction du réel*, the perception of reality, and it has nothing to do with the functions of the body. People think they are developing sensation when they have sexual experiences, or when they eat and drink well, or when they take a hot bath.

Mr. Schmitz: Yet they are sensations.

Dr. Jung: But in a psychological sense it has nothing to do with sensation. The psychological function of sensation is the perception of reality, and the standpoint of the sensation type is simply the standpoint of facts. When a person practices recognition of facts, he is doing something for his sensation; but taking a hot bath or painting himself with iodine has nothing to do with it. That is an intuitive misconstruction, he is mixing up the sensations of the body with the principle of sensation, which is really the principle of facts. Among the Latin peoples the recognition of sensation, of reality, expresses itself in their language, and sentiment and sensation can never be mixed up. But they are badly mixed up in the German language.

Dr. Schlegel: Is not the so-called feeling of love an emotional element which does not enter into the frame of the functions, as you understand it?

Dr. Jung: The feeling function has to do with the feeling of values, and that has nothing necessarily to do with love. Love is relatedness. One can feel without having relationship. When admiring a beautiful woman, one does not necessarily have a relationship with her or love her. Love has to do with Eros. If love had only to do with feeling, a thinking type couldn't love. We have to use these intuitive concepts, but there are two principles which are beyond functions.

Mr. Schmitz: A thinking type is not necessarily connected with Logos? He can be a blockhead?

Mrs. Baynes: A thinking type cannot be a blockhead surely, for most differentiated functions can do *something*!

Dr. Jung: Only in as much as the type is influenced by other functions.

Mrs. Baynes: He said the thinking type could be a blockhead, and it seems to me that that is contradictory. If he is a blockhead, he becomes some other type.

Dr. Jung: You are quite right in the case of a really differentiated thinking type.

Prof. Eaton: Is Logos constructive planning?

Dr. Jung: It can be constructive planning. Logos is the principle of discrimination, in contrast to Eros, which is the principle of relatedness. Eros brings things together, establishes dynamic relations between things, while the relations which Logos brings about are perhaps analogies or logical conclusions. It is typical that Logos relationships are devoid of emotional dynamics.

Prof. Eaton: More abstract than concrete?

Dr. Jung: You can see these qualities best through practical examples. For instance, the Logos element, being a principle of discrimination, not only allows one but forces one to give equal dignity to any object of thinking or observation. It enables a man to devote himself with almost religious concentration to the classification of lice, or to the different qualities of faeces, to put it quite drastically,[6] as well as to counting the stars. To make a picture of it, suppose there are a series of laboratories. In No. 1 is the observatory of a man who has devoted himself for years to astronomical researches. In the next laboratory is the man who is classifying lice, sixty thousand different specimens, a most interesting enterprise. And in the third is a man tremendously interested in the different qualities of faeces, a very unsavoury undertaking. Yet every man is working with the same concentration, the same spirit. Now what is Eros, represented by a woman, doing in that situation? Let us say she is the charwoman in the place. She finds the astronomer a terribly disagreeable man, hard and cold; he never gives her a tip, and naturally he is a bachelor. Mr. Professor Concerned-with-lice would be quite a nice man if he were not always interested in those ugly things; he occasionally gives her a tip, he is married and has very nice children, he is perfectly respectable and he has a great-uncle somewhere. She knows all that. That is relatedness, you see. It is an entirely different aspect of the world. The man devoted to the stars, who sits there passionately attending to his work, is absolutely unaware of the fact that he can fall in love with a woman. He thinks that falling in love is a kind of illness which happens in early youth and which one combats by marrying—As

---

[6] *Sems.*: "plastically."

a man said to me: "Just in order to get through with the damned thing." That is Logos.

I didn't mean to lose myself in a discussion of these principles, but apparently they still give rise to all sorts of doubts. I find on my desk a question which has just rained down from heaven, apparently, but I am afraid we cannot discuss every item of the theory of psychological functions now. The question is about the perception of the inner reality, in contradistinction to the introverted sensation function. That is a complicated question which I am quite unable to answer now; it would lead us too far away from our dream into the theory of functions. Perhaps for the time being we could leave it with the statement that the functions are vehicles for the forces, or influences, or activities, which emanate from those two principles, those two gods, Logos and Eros. And perhaps you can also understand that if there were no principles whatever outside of the functions, one could never hope to detach anything from the unconscious. There must be something which helps one to detach a function, some principle outside which allows one to tear it away from the original lump of unconsciousness.

One could say that both principles play a tremendous role in the history of the thought of redemption, which is really a psychological affair. For instance, in Christianity it is not only Logos that plays the role of redeemer, it is also Eros in the form of the principle of love. There again one sees the incorporation of the two principles. I may add here that the ideal Logos can only be when it *contains* the Eros; otherwise the Logos is not dynamic at all. A man with only Logos may have a very sharp intellect, but it is nothing but dry rationalism. And Eros without the Logos inside never understands, there is nothing but blind relatedness. Such people can be related to God knows what—like certain women who are dissolved completely in little happy families—cousins, relations—and there is nothing in the whole damned thing, it is all perfectly empty. Exactly like the low sort of Logos people, those classifying fellows with a low understanding.

Mr. Schmitz: But there is a certain affinity between Logos and thinking and between Eros and feeling?

Dr. Jung: As between all other functions. Don't mix up the word "feeling" with love as relationship. As I said, feeling is the function of values. I grant you that in reality nothing is separate, everything is flowing in the same space, so if one talks long enough of psychology, one gets quite mad and confused. As Goethe says: Names, concepts of men, are sound and smoke, feeling is everything.[7] Everything can function in Eros, and everything can function in Logos.

Dr. Draper: I still don't understand what the dreamer's reaction was with that wandering anima. What was his response when he found her outside?

Dr. Jung: Oh, he was afraid of the police, and then comes the discovery with which we are now concerned. Since he is a man with differentiated thinking and differentiated sensation, he has a very accurate observation of reality, and that is expressed by the photographer. And the superior function, as I explained, is exceedingly valuable, it gives that man a standpoint of refuge in the great turmoil, a refuge to which he can return. It gives him a sense of continuity and safety which he would not have in his inferior functions. There the ape-man comes in and there is no discrimination, no reliability; everything is muddled, there is no relatedness. But in this supreme moment when danger appears in all forms, he remembers that he can withdraw, with the recognition: If all else fails, at least I have my inner continuity, I have my records, these images. And when you remember what he has gotten in these dreams, what his vision is, you understand that he has a treasure, something exceedingly valuable. People who have no differentiated function are very badly off indeed in such a turmoil, they are nothing but panic and confusion; but such a man has the chance at least of not necessarily getting into a panic, because he has a basis to stand on.

In many cases of neurosis, it is very important that one builds up first such a differentiated function to which one can retire, and that gives one a chance. When a patient has no such basis, how can one talk to him? There is no place to talk together, the scene shifts and shifts, and the doctor never knows with whom he is talking. While with a man who has a differentiated function, one can always return to some sort of initial statement. One can always say: now we return to our agreement; or now we return to reason; or to actual scientific truth; or to the reliability of a personal relatedness; we return to the fact that you recognize that I am a decent fellow

[7] "Feeling is all; / Name is mere sound and reek / Clouding Heaven's light."— *Goethe's Faust*, tr. Louis MacNeice (1952), p. 113. (Part I: "Martha's Garden.")

and not a humbug, and that you are a human being and not a criminal.

Now, the photographer simply makes the statement that he has those photographs and that he is going to take them to a safe place, and afterwards, in the end, he turns up again and says the whole situation is indifferent to him because his records are safe and that they will be a great success. But just before that is a new scene, and there the danger really begins. On the other side of the river soldiers appear and even artillery, and the dreamer assumes that the bombardment will now take place, that they are going to shoot at his house. This is a very dangerous situation and the symbolism is quite distinct. He makes here a very involved remark in his associations about the external world being hostile to the ego, but I will not translate that again as it is not very important. The important point here is that he understands this attack upon his house as an attack of the external world upon his own safety, and that is on account of the fact that the anima has escaped into that external world. We have already seen that the possible incarnation of the anima in a real woman would constitute a typical danger which would bring him into conflict with conventional morality, so it is a logical conclusion that the police would become interested in the case. But here the thing goes much further. You see, it would be quite enough if two or three policemen came. The dreamer himself would offer no resistance. Neither would the photographer inasmuch as he has rescued his records; the situation is perfectly indifferent to him. So there remains only the ape-man, and perhaps three or four policemen would be quite sufficient to get him down. It seems exaggerated to bring artillery, but the unconscious has probably certain reasons for bringing it into play. How would you explain that?

Mr. Baumann: The photographer has taken the pictures and wants to go off with the films to a safe place.

Dr. Jung: There is no evidence in the dream which would explain why it should be an offence that the photographer gets away with his films. That is no reason for artillery and would not even explain the police, for they are only concerned with public morality. We can allow for the police, but soldiers and artillery—such an upheaval against one single ape-man is going too far.

Dr. Schlegel: It means that the fact must be a very serious one.

Dr. Jung: Yes, it is very serious. If one very determined criminal is defending himself with a gun, the police are needed. And if it is a whole crowd of criminals, soldiers must be called in; they would get one or two cannons into position against such a mob. So here it must be something like that, something very serious which goes quite beyond his individual case.

Mrs. Jaeger: He remarked in the dream that there was a river in between. Perhaps the artillery was needed to shoot across.

Dr. Jung: They could shoot with rifles, they would not need artillery. Moreover, if the anima escaped, we may suppose that there is a bridge. Therefore we may assume that the river is there merely to designate a division, but is not really an obstacle. Make a picture of it in your minds, a house, a river, and the artillery on the opposite side. You see, that is obviously again a story of pairs of op- posites. A river always symbolizes the river of life, the river of energy, the living energy that draws its dynamism from opposition. Without opposition, there is no energy. Where there is opposition, where the opposites clash, energy will result. The river is an eternal image, and fording a river[8] and bridging a river are important symbols for the contact of the opposites that cause energy. It is obvious from the dream that here is such a case. On one side, the ape-man, an impulsive thing with no moral consid- erations, and on the other side the revolt of the collective moral standpoint. That is the clash which is revealed by this picture.

You see, it is not a very individual conflict apparently, because you would not bring big guns into action in that case. It would be terribly exaggerated to turn a battery of big guns on that single ape-man—like shooting sparrows with cannon. Therefore we as- sume that the ape-man stands for more than the personal uncon- scious, he must stand for collectivity, the whole crowd. Only if a whole herd of ape-men attacked the anima would it be reasonable to bring up the artillery. So the tremendous emotion which the dream brings out suggests that this problem of the ape-man is by no means a personal one. Naturally the dreamer would be inclined

---

[8] Jung analysed a dream in which a river and a ford were key symbols in "On the Psychology of the Unconscious" (1943; orig., 1917), CW 7, pars. 123-130, 160, 163. For the earlier version, see *Collected Papers on Analytical Psychology* (2nd edn., 1917), pp. 418f. Jung discussed the ford as archetype in "The Houston Films" (1957), interview with Richard I. Evans, *C. G. Jung Speaking*, pp. 293f.

to assume that it was all his personal shortcoming, for which there was no redemption. People think of their conflicts as subjective only, and therefore they are isolated; they think they are the only ones who have such problems, and that even to a very grotesque degree.

I remember a young man of eighteen who came into my office, saying that he had something terrible to tell me, and requested me to shut the door into my library which I always leave open. I asked if he had committed a murder, and he replied: "If it were only that!" I have a little picture with a curtain over it,[9] and he wanted to know if there was not a window behind where a secretary might sit and listen—that is the usual supposition. Then when everything was absolutely sure and tight he said, "I have to confess something very terrible; if it were known the world would cease to exist." He had discovered masturbation, and he assumed that if it were known, no-one would propagate and the race would die out. People with the neurotic conflict always feel that it is quite subjective in every detail, happening perhaps for the first time in the world; they admit that other people suffer from similar difficulties, but it is not the same. When a person is in love, it seems that there is no love in the world that could be as beautiful. In supreme passions, one always has the feeling of being isolated, and it is true that one is isolated in any kind of extreme emotion; one loses contact with other people, one becomes completely autoerotic. So the dreamer in this conflict labours under the prejudice that he is the only one in such a situation, particularly of course because he cannot talk to his wife. One of the reasons of the success of the analytical treatment is that people can at least confess their secrets, for the more secrets one has the more one is isolated. His feeling is that it is *his* ape-man, but the unconscious says, no, it is *the* ape-man, the ape-man that is in everybody, and it is because it is a public danger that artillery is brought into action.

This naturally reminded him of the war, which we then discussed, with the result that he saw that in the war the ape-man got loose, that people were mutually killing the ape-men in each other. For wherever the ape-man appears there is destruction. Naturally the dreamer cannot realize at once that the conflict is not peculiar to

9 Jung had in his study, behind a curtain, a photograph of the face of Christ on the Holy Shroud in Turin. See his letter to Upton Sinclair, 24 Nov. 1952, in *Letters*, vol. 2, p. 94 (with illustration).

himself, that it is in the entire world, and that it is the coming up of the primitive man in the actual world which has that destructive influence.[10] Therefore we draw up artillery and make wars, seeing the enemy in our neighbours because we are unable to see it in ourselves. The coming up of the ape-man is a release of man's instinctual nature, so we have all sorts of problems; our philosophical and religious feelings go to hell and we are more or less helpless. Formerly we had religious feelings, but now we are disoriented and nobody really knows what we should believe. And our unrest expresses itself in other forms. In art, for instance, the Negro, who we have always thought was a born slave, is now the most admired artist. We admire his dancing; Negro actors play a great role; we find Negro spirituals exceedingly beautiful.[11] We could not possibly tolerate the hypocrisy of other revivalist meetings, but in these Negro spirituals there is living faith, there is something immediate and touching. Don't forget that from the Jews, the most despised people of antiquity, living in the most despicable corner of Palestine or Galilee, came the redeemer of Rome. Why should not our redeemer be a Negro? It would be logical and psychologically correct.

[10] Cf. Jung's remarks on the primitive element in Europeans, in "The Role of the Unconscious" (1918), CW 10, pars. 16ff.

[11] Cf. Jung's praise of the Negro film *The Green Pastures*, in "A Psychological Approach to the Dogma of the Trinity" (1940, 1948), CW 11, par. 266.

INDEX

INDEX

A

abdomen, *see* belly

abnormal, fear of, 463-64

Abraham, 558

Achumawi (Indians), 325n, 332n

acrobatics (dream 30), 660, 662, 663, 670

active/passive, 403-404, 410

Adam, 128, 254, 440

Adam and Eve, 193, 236, 593, 691

Adam Kadmon, 286

Adonis, 174n, 175, 215, 351

aerial trigon, 393, 405

aeroplane (dream 25), 574, 577, 579, 580, 585, 594

Aesculapius/Asklepios, 215-16, 431, 434, 435

Africa/African(s), 5, 133-34, 265-66, 292, 322, 348, 381, 397; dreaming and, 4, 5, 20-21; Islam in, 336; Jung's visits to, 4, 4n, 20, 27, 75, 91, 133-34, 220, 290n, 307, 320-21, 494, 649, 678, 696n; *see also* Egypt; Elgonyi tribe; Negroes, African; Tunis

Agapé, 399

age, 28, 85, 252, 253-54, 411

Aiōn/Deus Leontocephalus, 430f

air, 221, 393

Akbar the Great, 114, 115, 469

Albigenses, 240

alchemy/alchemists, 108, 128, 334-35

Alexander the Great, 57, 542-43

Alleluia, 34

alone/aloneness, 75, 77, 219f, 611-12

Alypius/Aloysius, 12

America(n)/United States of America, 344, 345, 666, 667, 684-85; efficiency in, *see* efficiency; Indians, *see* Indians, North American; Jung's visits to, 4, 4n, 34n, 71, 71n, 216; Negroes, *see* Negroes, American

amulet(s), *see* charm/spell/amulet

analysis, 14, 16, 17-18, 19, 60, 85, 123, 153, 263, 558; acrobatics as, 662; attitude of businessman dreamer toward, 99, 231; climax of the, 468-69; confession and, 22-23, 705; charm/spell and, 135; divine in, 619; effect of wife on, 150; emotions and, 109, 567; experimental aspects of, 150; in dreams: (13), 206ff, (24), 533, (26), 598, 599, 604, 618, (29), 655-56; integration and, 92; length of time of, 148; marriage and, 559-60, 561, 563-64; neuroses and, 454; pain and, 16, 17-18; *participation mystique* and, 564; resistance to, 15, 60, 85, 144, 148-49, 152ff; superior function and, 272, 273; theosophy and, 56; Yoga and, 118

analyst(s), 30, 91, 111f, 496-97; as God, 464-65; importance of/expectations of, 475-76; in a dream, 267-68, 451-52, 458; in dreams: (16), 259, 264, (23) 498, (26), 557, (27), 632, 633-34, 635; patient's relationship with, in dreams, 598-99

analytical code, *see* code, analytical

analytical method, 105, 117-18

anaphylactic/anaplerotic system, 269

ancestors, 24, 320, 321, 399, 674, 675

anchor, 351, 360

Andrew, St., cross of, 348

angel, 104, 285, 513n, 584

Angulo, Jaime de, 325n

anima, 52, 61, 72, 79-80, 180, 222, 253-54, 268, 282-83, 485-87, 537,

—Index by Judith A. Hancock

The Collected Works of C. G. JUNG

The Collected Works of C. G. JUNG

Editors: Sir Herbert Read (d. 1968), Michael Fordham, and Gerhard Adler; executive editor, William McGuire. Translated by R.F.C. Hull (d. 1974), except vol. 2; cf. vol. 6.

(*continued*)

* Published 1957; 2nd edn., 1970.   † Published 1973.

* Published 1960.   † Published 1961.
‡ Published 1956; 2nd edn., 1967.

(*continued*)

* Published 1971.   † Published 1953; 2nd edn., 1966.
‡ Published 1960; 2nd edn., 1969.   ** Published 1959; 2nd edn., 1968.

* Published 1959; 2nd edn., 1968.   † Published 1964; 2nd edn., 1970.
‡ Published 1958; 2nd edn., 1969.

(*continued*)

* Published 1953; 2nd edn., completely revised, 1968.
† Published 1968.   ‡ Published 1963; 2nd edn., 1970.
** Published 1966.
§ Published 1954; 2nd edn., revised and augmented, 1966.

* Published 1954.

C. G. JUNG SPEAKING: Interviews and Encounters
Edited by William McGuire and R.F.C. Hull

C. G. JUNG: Word and Image
Edited by Aniela Jaffé

DREAM ANALYSIS
C. G. Jung Seminars
Edited by William McGuire

THE ESSENTIAL JUNG
Selected and introduced by Anthony Storr

THE ZOFINGIA LECTURES
Supplementary Volume A to The Collected Works
Edited by William McGuire, translated by
Jan van Heurck, introduction by
Marie-Louise von Franz

LIBRARY OF CONGRESS CATALOGING IN PUBLICATION DATA

Jung, C. G. (Carl Gustav), 1875-1961.
  Dream analysis.

  (Bollingen series ; 99. Seminars of C. G. Jung ; v. 1)
  Edited text of the 2nd ed., 1938, privately issued in multigraphed
form by the Psychological Club, Zurich.
  Bibliography: p.
  Includes index.
  1. Dreams.   I. McGuire, William, 1917-   .   II. Title.   III. Series:
Bollingen series ; 99.   IV. Series: Bollingen series. Seminars of C. G.
Jung ; v. 1.
BF1091.J86   1983   154.6′34   82-42787
ISBN 0-691-09896-4